Third Edition

Java™
Illuminated

An Active Learning Approach

Third Edition

BRIEF EDITION

Java™
Illuminated

An Active Learning Approach

Julie Anderson
Loyola University Maryland

Hervé Franceschi
Capitol College

JONES & BARTLETT
LEARNING

World Headquarters
Jones & Bartlett Learning
40 Tall Pine Drive
Sudbury, MA 01776
978-443-5000
info@jblearning.com
www.jblearning.com

Jones & Bartlett Learning
Canada
6339 Ormindale Way
Mississauga, Ontario L5V 1J2
Canada

Jones & Bartlett Learning
International
Barb House, Barb Mews
London W6 7PA
United Kingdom

Jones & Bartlett Learning books and products are available through most bookstores and online booksellers. To contact Jones & Bartlett Learning directly, call 800-832-0034, fax 978-443-8000, or visit our website, www.jblearning.com.

Substantial discounts on bulk quantities of Jones & Bartlett Learning publications are available to corporations, professional associations, and other qualified organizations. For details and specific discount information, contact the special sales department at Jones & Bartlett Learning via the above contact information or send an email to specialsales@jblearning.com.

Production Credits
Chief Executive Officer: Ty Field
President: James Homer
SVP, Chief Operating Officer: Don Jones, Jr.
SVP, Chief Technology Officer: Dean Fossella
SVP, Chief Marketing Officer: Alison M. Pendergast
SVP, Chief Financial Officer: Ruth Siporin
Publisher, Higher Education: Cathleen Sether
Senior Acquisitions Editor: Timothy Anderson
Senior Editorial Assistant: Stephanie Sguigna
Production Director: Amy Rose
Senior Production Editor: Katherine Crighton
Associate Marketing Manager: Lindsay White
V.P., Manufacturing and Inventory Control: Therese Connell
Composition: Northeast Compositors, Inc.
Cover and Title Page Design: Kristin E. Parker
Cover and Title Page Image: © Rob Stark/Dreasmstime.com
Printing and Binding: Courier Kendallville
Cover Printing: Courier Kendallville

To order this product, use ISBN: 978-1-4496-3202-1

Library of Congress Cataloging-in-Publication Data
Anderson, Julie, 1947–
    Java illuminated : an active learning approach / Julie Anderson and Hervé Franceschi. — Brief ed.
        p. cm.
    Includes index.
    ISBN-13: 978-1-4496-0440-0 (pbk.)
    ISBN-10: 1-4496-0440-4 (pbk.)
    1. Java (Computer program language) I. Franceschi, Hervé. II. Title.
    QA76.73.J3A5332 2012
    005.13'3—dc22   2010043041

6048

Printed in the United States of America
15 14 13 12 11   10 9 8 7 6 5 4 3 2 1

Dedications

To the memory of my parents, Glenn and Rosemary Austin, my first teachers. – *Julie Anderson*

A ma mère, trop tôt disparue, et à mon père. – *Hervé Franceschi*

Contents

Preface

The Purpose of This Book and Its Audience

Java Illuminated, Brief Third Edition, covers all of the material required for the successful completion of an introductory course in Java. While the focus is on the material required for the Computer Science I (CS1) curricula, students enrolled in Information Systems, Information Technology, or self-directed study courses will find the book useful as well. It has been written to provide introductory computer science students with a comprehensive overview of the fundamentals of programming using Java as the teaching language.

Throughout the book, we take an "active learning" approach to presenting the material. Instead of merely presenting the concepts to students in a one-sided, rote manner, we ask them to take an active role in their understanding of the language through the use of numerous interactive examples, exercises, and projects.

Coverage and Approach

Our approach is to teach object-oriented programming in a progressive manner. We start in Chapter 1 by presenting an overview of object-oriented programming. In Chapter 3, we delve a little deeper into the concepts of classes and objects and introduce the student to many of the useful classes in the Java class library. Our emphasis at this point is on using classes; we teach the student how to read APIs in order to determine how to instantiate objects and call methods of the classes. In Chapter 7, we move on to designing user-defined classes.

Our philosophy is to emphasize good software engineering practices by focusing on designing and writing correct, maintainable programs. As such, we discuss pseudocode, testing techniques, design trade-offs, and other software engineering tips.

We teach the student basic programming techniques, such as accumulation, counting, calculating an average, finding maximum and minimum values, using flag and toggle variables, and basic searching and sorting algorithms. In doing so, we emphasize the patterns inherent in programming. Concepts are taught first, followed by fully implemented examples with source code. We promote Java standards, conventions, and methodologies.

This book supports the important features of the latest versions of Java (5, 6, and 7). The *Scanner* class is used to simplify user input from the keyboard and in reading from files. In Chapter 5, we demonstrate a new Java 7 feature: performing a *switch* statement with a *String* expression. The *enum* functionality is presented as a user-defined data type in Chapter 7. Autoboxing and unboxing concepts are introduced in Chapter 3 with the Java wrapper classes. We demonstrate generic types and the enhanced *for* loop in the Chapter 9 coverage of *ArrayLists*.

Learning Features

Recognizing today's students' growing interest in animation and visualization, we distribute techniques for producing graphical output and animation throughout the book, starting in Chapter 4 with applets. An example using either animation or graphical output is included in most chapters. Instructors who are not interested in incorporating graphics into their curriculum can simply skip these sections. In addition, some of our examples are small games, which we find motivational for students.

In each chapter, we include one or two Programming Activities, which are designed to provide visual feedback to the students so that they can assess the correctness of their code. In most Programming Activities, we provide a framework, usually with a graphical user interface, to which the student adds code to complete the application. The student should be able to finish the Programming Activity in about 15 to 20 minutes; thus, these activities can be used in the classroom to reinforce the topics just presented. Each Programming Activity also includes several discussion questions that test the student's understanding of the concepts the activity illustrates. The Programming Activities are also appropriate for a closed or open laboratory environment. In short, this book can be used in a traditional lecture environment, a computer-equipped classroom, or a lab environment.

In addition, we supplement each chapter with a browser-based module that animates sample code, visually illustrating the assignment of variable values, evaluation of conditions, and flow of control.

We also provide the instructor and students with an extensive variety of end-of-chapter material: multiple-choice questions, examples that ask the student to predict the output of prewritten code or to fill in missing code, debugging activities, short exercises, programming projects, technical writing assignments, and a higher-difficulty group project.

Chapter-by-Chapter Overview

The chapters are logically organized from simple to more difficult topics, while incorporating object orientation as needed, taking into account the specifics of the Java language. Here is a brief summary of the topics covered in each chapter:

Chapter 1: Introduction to Programming and the Java Language

We introduce the student to the concept of programming, first covering computer hardware and operating systems, and following with a brief evolution of programming languages, including an introduction to object-oriented programming. We explain programming basics and pseudocode as a program design technique. The student writes, compiles, and debugs their first program using an integrated development environment.

Chapter 2: Programming Building Blocks—Java Basics

In this chapter, we concentrate on working with variables and constants of primitive data types and composing arithmetic expressions. We illustrate the differences between integer and floating-point calculations and introduce operator precedence.

Chapter 3: Object-Oriented Programming, Part 1: Using Classes

Chapter 3 introduces classes from the user, or client, standpoint and discusses the benefits of encapsulation and code reuse. The student learns how to instantiate objects and call methods. We also demonstrate useful Java classes for console input and output, dialog boxes, formatting output, performing mathematical calculations, and generating random numbers.

Chapter 4: Introduction to Applets and Graphics

Chapter 4 presents several methods of the *Graphics* class that can be used to create graphical output by drawing shapes and text. The windowing graphics coordinate system is explained and using color is also explored. We demonstrate these graphics methods in applets because an applet window provides an easy-to-use palette for drawing. Instructors wishing to postpone or skip graphics coverage altogether can use as little or as much of this chapter as they desire.

Chapter 5: Flow of Control, Part 1: Selection

Various forms of the *if*, *if/else*, and *if/else if* statements are presented, along with the appropriate situations in which to use each form. We also demonstrate nested *if/else* statements and testing techniques. We begin our coverage of scope by introducing block scope. Later chapters build upon this foundation. As part of our object-oriented programming coverage, we teach the importance of comparing objects using the *equals* method. This chapter also covers the conditional operator and the *switch* statement.

Chapter 6: Flow of Control, Part 2: Looping

This is probably the most important chapter in the book. We have found that looping and repetition are the most difficult basic programming concepts for the average student to grasp. We try to ease the student's understanding of looping techniques by presenting patterns to follow in coding basic algorithms: accumulation, counting, calculating an average, and finding minimum and maximum values. We present a motivational and engaging example of repetition in the animation of a ball rolling across the screen. Looping is further explored as a tool for validation of input values. We continue our coverage of scope by illustrating the scope of variables declared within the *while* loop body and *for* loop header. We concentrate on using the *while* loop for event-controlled and sentinel-controlled repetition and the *for* loop for count-controlled looping. A large section focuses on constructing loop conditions, which is often a challenging task for the student. Sections are also provided on testing techniques for *while* loops and for *for* loops. In this chapter, we also introduce reading data from a text file using the *Scanner* class.

Chapter 7: Object-Oriented Programming, Part 2: User-Defined Classes

In this chapter, we teach the student to write classes, as well as client applications, that use the instantiated objects and call methods of the class. We present class design techniques and standard patterns for writing constructors, mutators and accessors, and the *toString, equals,* and other user-defined methods. We further explain scope in the context of class members and method parameters. We also explain how and when to use the keywords *this* and *static. Enum* is also covered as a user-defined class type. Finally, we teach the student how to use Javadoc and how to create a package.

Chapter 8: Single-Dimensional Arrays

This chapter begins with the declaration, instantiation, and initialization of single-dimensional arrays. From there, the student learns to perform the basic programming techniques (accumulation, counting, calculating an average, and finding maximum and minimum values) on array elements. We also cover arrays as instance variables of a class, and demonstrate maintaining encapsulation while accepting arrays as method parameters and returning arrays from methods. Basic searching and sorting algorithms are also presented, including sequential and binary searches and Selection and Insertion sorts.

Chapter 9: Multidimensional Arrays and the *ArrayList* Class

We focus in this chapter on two-dimensional array processing, including techniques for processing all the elements in the entire array, or the elements in a specific column or row. We also demonstrate the extra processing needed to handle arrays with rows of different lengths. A bar chart of the data in each row of the array is also demonstrated. In addition, we extrapolate the concepts from two-dimensional arrays to discuss multidimensional arrays.

We present the *ArrayList* class as an expandable array and demonstrate using classes with generic types, the enhanced *for* loop, and autoboxing and unboxing.

What's New in *Java Illuminated*

In this edition, we have refined the existing material and incorporated new material as a result of feedback from instructors who have adopted our book.

We revised Chapter 2 to better introduce the concept of programming. We provide a simple, but complete program near the beginning of the chapter so that the student can get a sense of what a simple program looks like and a feel for how a program operates. We have revised both Programming Activities to be more real-world examples: converting inches to centimeters and converting temperatures between Fahrenheit and Celsius. We also introduce arithmetic operators earlier in the chapter so that the student can more quickly write a program that performs calculations. We also help the student to think through the tasks involved with designing a program, such as identifying the data, calculations, and output.

In Chapter 3, we slightly altered Example 3.20 to perform calculations on the values retrieved from the dialog boxes to demonstrate the need for converting the *String* return value to a numeric type.

In Chapter 5, we modified Example 5.14, A Simple Calculator, to use a *String* as the *switch* expression, a new feature supported in Java 7. We also slightly altered Example 5.12, Comparing Strings, so that we also test for inequality using the *equals* method.

Pedagogy

Concepts are always taught first, followed by complete, executable examples illustrating these concepts. Most examples demonstrate real-life applications so that the student can understand the need for the concept at hand. The example code is colored to better illustrate the syntax of the code and to reflect the use of colors in today's IDE tools, as shown in this example from Chapter 3:

```java
 1 /*  A demonstration of reading from the console using Scanner
 2      Anderson, Franceschi
 3 */
 4
 5 import java.util.Scanner;
 6
 7 public class DataInput
 8 {
 9   public static void main( String [ ] args )
10   {
11       Scanner scan = new Scanner( System.in );
12
13       System.out.print( "Enter your first name > " );
14       String firstName = scan.next( );
15       System.out.println( "Your name is " + firstName );
16
17       System.out.print( "\nEnter your age as an integer > " );
```

```
18      int age = scan.nextInt( );
19      System.out.println( "Your age is " + age );
20
21      System.out.print( "\nEnter your GPA > " );
22      float gpa = scan.nextFloat( );
23      System.out.println( "Your GPA is " + gpa );
24   }
25 }
```

EXAMPLE 3.9   Reading from the Console using *Scanner*

Figures and tables are used to illustrate or summarize the concept at hand, such as these from Chapters 6 and 7:

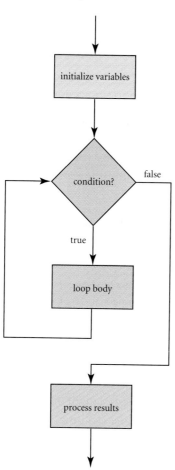

Figure 6.1

Flow of Control of a *while* Loop

TABLE 7.1   Access Modifiers

Access Modifier	Class or member can be referenced by . . .
public	methods of the same class, as well as methods of other classes
private	methods of the same class only
protected	methods in the same class, as well as methods of subclasses and methods in classes in the same package
no modifier (package access)	methods in the same package only

In each chapter, we emphasize good design concepts using "Software Engineering Tips," such as the one to the left from Chapter 7.

We also provide "Common Error Traps," such as the one to the left from Chapter 5, to alert students against common syntax and logic errors.

In each chapter, "active learning" programming activities reinforce concepts with enjoyable, hands-on projects that provide visual feedback to the students. These activities can be done in lab-type classrooms or can be assigned as projects. A header for a Programming Activity looks like this:

SOFTWARE ENGINEERING TIP

Define instance variables of a class as *private* so that only methods of the class will be able to set or change their values.

COMMON ERROR TRAP

Be sure that both operands of the logical AND and logical OR operators are *boolean* expressions. Expressions such as this:
`x < y && z`, with *x*, *y*, and *z* being numeric types, are illegal. Instead, use the expression:
`x < y && x < z`

6.9   Programming Activity 1: Using *while* Loops

In this activity, you will work with a sentinel-controlled *while* loop, performing this activity:

> Write a *while* loop to process the contents of a grocery cart and calculate the total price of the items. It is important to understand that, in this example, we do not know how many items are in the cart.

Supplementing each chapter, we provide a browser-based module implemented as a Flash animation on the CD-ROM, which illustrates the execution of code that implements the concepts taught in the chapter. Each movie animates a brief code sample, one line at a time, and is controlled by the user via a "Next Step" button. These modules can be beneficial for students who learn best with visual aids, graphs, illustrations, and at their own pace outside the classroom. The modules are announced in each chapter using a special icon as in the sample at the top of the next page.

CODE IN ACTION

To see two step-by-step illustrations of do/while loops, look for the Chapter 6 Flash movie on the CD-ROM included with this book. Click on the link for Chapter 6 to start the movie.

Graphics Coverage

Graphics are distributed throughout the book and are used to engage the student and reinforce the chapter concepts. The Graphics coordinate system, methods for drawing shapes and text, and color concepts are presented with simple applets in Chapter 4. Animation using loops is demonstrated in Chapter 6, while drawing a bull's-eye target illustrates both looping and using a toggle variable. Classes for displayable objects are presented in Chapter 7; drawing a bar chart of array data is illustrated in Chapters 8 and 9. The two figures that follow illustrate graphical examples from Chapters 7 and 8.

Figure 7.10
The *AstronautClient2* Window

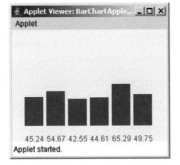

Figure 8.15
The *cellBills* Array as a Bar Chart

End-of-Chapter Exercises and Problems

A large collection of exercises and problems is proposed at the end of each chapter. Short exercises cover programming from a variety of angles: multiple choice concept questions, reading and understanding code segments, filling in some code, correcting errors, and interpreting compiler error messages to diagnose application bugs. Many programming projects are proposed with an emphasis on writing *classes*, not just a *program*. A more challenging group project is proposed in each chapter, allowing students to work as a group and develop communication skills, in accordance with recommendations from accreditation organizations. Small, essay-type questions are also proposed to enable students to acquire proficiency in technical writing and communication.

CD-ROM Accompanying This Book

Included in the CD-ROM accompanying this book are:

- Programming Activity framework code
- Full example code from each chapter
- Browser-based modules with visual step-by-step demonstrations of code execution
- Links to various Integrated Development Environments
- Link to the most recent version of Java™ 2 Standard Edition JDK

Appendices

The appendices include the following:

- Java reserved words and keywords
- Operator precedence
- Unicode character set
- Representing negative numbers
- Representing floating-point numbers
- Java classes and APIs presented in this book
- Answers to selected exercises

Instructor Resources

These materials are available to instructors on the Jones & Bartlett Learning website (http://www.jblearning.com/catalog/9781449604400/), and include

- Programming activity solution code (for instructors only)
- Answers to many end-of-chapter exercises
- PowerPoint® slides for each chapter
- Test items

Contacting the Authors

We have checked and rechecked the many technical details in this book. Despite our best efforts, however, we realize that some errors may have been missed. If you discover a technical error in the book, please contact us at JulieAustinAnderson@gmail.com or hfranceschi@capitol-college.edu. We will post any corrections on the book's website: http://www.jblearning.com/catalog/9781449604400/.

Turing's Craft CodeLab Student Registration Instructions

 turingscraft

CodeLab is the web-based interactive programming exercise service that accompanies this text. It is designed to reduce attrition and raise the overall level of the class. Since 2002, CodeLab has analyzed over twenty-two million exercise submissions from more than 75,000 students.

CodeLab has over 300 short exercises, each focused on a particular programming idea or language construct. The student types in code and the system immediately judges its correctness, offering hints when the submission is incorrect. Through this process, the student gains mastery over the semantics, syntax, and common usage of the language elements.

For the Students

CodeLab offers a tree-based table of content navigation system augmented by prev/next buttons that permit sequential traversal. Exercises are organized within a hierarchy of topics that match the textbook's organization and can be reconfigured as needed by the instructor. The student interface offers three tabs for each exercise: a work-area tab containing the instructions of the exercise and a text area for typing in a submission; a results tab that indicates the correctness of the student's submission and provides an analysis of the submission code in the event of an error; a solutions tab which, by default, is invisible but may be made available at the discretion of the instructor. The solutions tab contains one or more solutions to the exercise; the results tabs contains one or more of the following: correctness indicator, ad hoc hints, marked-up submission indicating possible errors, compiler messages, table of passed and failed test cases. In addition, the usual online amenities of preferences, account management, documentation, and customer support options are provided.

A unique student access code can be found at the beginning of this textbook. Length of student access is 180 days for this brief version of the textbook.

Students can also purchase the access code online at jblearning .turingscraft.com.

Students using an international version of this textbook can also purchase their access code from anywhere online at jblearning.turingscraft.com.

For the Instructors

CodeLab provides the preceding student interface and in addition provides

- a **Course Manager** that permits the instructor to rearrange, rename, and/or omit topics and exercises. It also allows instructors to assign deadlines, specify dates when solutions can be seen by students, dates past which student work will not be "counted," and dates prior to which the exercises will be invisible to students.

- a **Grading Roster** that presents a graphical spreadsheet view of student work, where each row corresponds to a student and each column to an exercise. It is also possible to mail and/or download rosters in CSV format.

- an **Exercise Creation Tool** that permits faculty to create their own exercises.

Custom CodeLab

CodeLab is customized to this textbook as follows:

1. The organization of the CodeLab matches the organization of the textbook.

2. For each chapter that covers an appropriate standard introductory programming topic, the CodeLab offers approximately 50 CodeLab exercises, taken from either the standard set of existing CodeLab exercises or added to fill in any gaps in coverage.

3. Each chapter in the CodeLab implements 5 exercises taken from this text, and, if necessary, the exercises are modified to meet CodeLab requirements.

Demonstration Site for CodeLab

A Jones & Bartlett Learning demonstration site is available online at

jblearning.turingscraft.com

Visitors to this site will be directed to a landing page that provides an overview of the product. By clicking on the selected Jones & Bartlett Learning textbook cover, you will be led to more detailed product description pages. In the detailed product description pages there are further descriptions, examples of or links to examples of specific examples of custom CodeLab tie-ins with this textbook, and a link to a fully functional demo version of the Custom CodeLab. The latter offers full functionality and contains all of the exercise content of the particular Custom CodeLab. To make use of this link, instructors will need a unique Section Creation access code provided by their Jones & Bartlett Learning Computer Science Account Specialist at 1-800-832-0034, or online at www.jblearning.com.

Using this CodeLab Section Creation Code permits instructors to use the online tool to create their own unique CodeLab sections based on the Custom CodeLab. This permits instructors to have instructor accounts that enable access to the Course Manager, roster, and exercise creation tools described above.

Additonally Turing's Craft provides online documentation and support for both prospective adopters and actual faculty users of this text. In creating sections for classroom adopting, instructors will receive CodeLab Section Access Codes that should be provided to their students—enabling their students to associate their accounts (i.e., join their instructor's CodeLab section).

System Requirements: CodeLab runs on recent versions of most browsers (e.g. Internet Explorer, Firefox, Safari) on Windows and MacOS and on many versions of Linux. CodeLab does require the installation of the latest Flash Reader, available from www.adobe.com. (Most systems come with Flash pre-installed.) More details about CodeLab browser compatibility can be found at:

www.turingscraft.com/browsers.html

Acknowledgments

We would like to acknowledge the contributions of many partners, colleagues, and family members to this book.

First and foremost, we would like to thank our publisher, Jones & Bartlett Learning, especially Tim Anderson, Senior Acquisitions Editor; Amy Rose, Production Director; Katherine Crighton, Senior Production Editor; and Stephanie Sguigna, Senior Editorial Assistant. We also want to thank Mike and Sigrid Wile of Northeast Compositors; Mike Boblitt, who proofread the manuscript; and Kristin E. Parker, who designed the text and cover.

Second, we extend our thanks to the reviewers: Katrin Becker, University of Calgary; Yonshik Choi, Illinois Institute of Technology; Raj Gill, Anne Arundel Community College; Mark M. Meysenburg, Doane College; Roberta Evans Sabin and James Glenn, Loyola University Maryland; Aaron Stevens, Boston University; Robert Burton, Brigham Young University; Barbara Guillott, Louisiana State University; James Brzowski, University of Massachusetts, Lowell; Paul Tymann, Rochester Institute of Technology; Daniel Joyce, Villanova University; Paolo Bucci, The Ohio State University; Gian Mario Basani, DePaul University; and Hans Peter Bischof, Rensselaer Polytechnic Institute. We have taken your thoughtful comments to heart and we think the book is better for them.

Julie Anderson would also like to acknowledge the pedagogical insight of Richard Rasala and Viera Proulx of Northeastern University. Thanks also to Jon Dornback, Garth Gerstein, and our former colleagues Pat Smit and Earl Gottsman.

I am extremely grateful for the help extended by many family members: my father, Glenn Austin, sons Brian and Jon Anderson, daughter-in-law Silvia Eckert, sister Kathleen Austin, and mother-in-law Virginia Anderson. And of course, much gratitude goes to my loving husband, Tom, for his support and encouragement.

—Julie Anderson

I also recognize the support of my family. In particular, my brother, Paul, provided feedback on our sample chapter and the movies, and my wife, Kristin, gave her support and provided advice.

—Hervé Franceschi

CHAPTER 1

Introduction to Programming and the Java Language

CHAPTER CONTENTS

Introduction

Computer applications touch almost every aspect of our lives. They run automated teller machines, the grocery store's checkout register, the appointment calendar at your doctor's office, airport kiosks for flight check-in, a restaurant's meal-ordering system, and online auctions, just to name a few applications. On your personal computer, you may run a word processor, virus detection software, a spreadsheet, computer games, and an image processing system.

Someone, usually a team of programmers, wrote those applications. If you're reading this book, you're probably curious about what's involved in writing applications, and you would like to write a few yourself. Perhaps you have an idea for the world's next great application or computer game.

In this book, we'll cover the basics of writing applications. Specifically, we'll use the Java programming language. Keep in mind, however, that becoming a good programmer requires more than mastering the rules, or **syntax**, of a programming language. You also must master basic programming techniques. These are established methods for performing common programming operations, such as calculating a total, finding an average, or arranging a group of items in order.

You also must master good software engineering principles, so that you design code that is readable, easily maintained, and reusable. By readable, we mean that someone else should be able to read your program and figure out what it does and how it does it. Writing readable code is especially important for programmers who want to advance in their careers, because it allows someone else to take over the maintenance of your program while you move on to bigger and better responsibilities. Ease of maintenance is also an important aspect of programming, because the specifications for any program are continually changing. How many programs can you name that have had only one version? Not many. Well-designed code allows you and others to incorporate prewritten and pretested modules into your program, thus reducing the time to develop a program and yielding code that is more robust and has fewer bugs. One useful feature of the Java programming language is the large supply of prewritten code that you are free to use in your programs.

Programming is an exciting activity. It's very satisfying to decompose a complex task into computer instructions and watch your program come alive. It can be frustrating, however, when your program either doesn't run at all or produces the wrong output.

Writing correct programs is critical. Someone's life or life savings may depend on the correctness of your program. Reusing code helps in developing correct programs, but you must also master effective testing techniques to verify that the output of your program is correct.

In this book, we'll concentrate not only on the syntax of the Java language, but also on basic programming techniques, good software engineering principles, and effective testing techniques.

Before you can write programs, however, it's important to understand the platform on which your program will run. A platform refers to the computer hardware and the operating system. Your program will use the hardware for inputting data, for performing calculations, and for outputting results. The operating system will start your program running and will provide your program with essential resources, such as memory, and services, such as reading and writing files.

1.1 Basic Computer Concepts

1.1.1 Hardware

As shown in Figure 1.1, a computer typically includes the following components:

- a CPU, or central processing unit, which executes the instructions of a program

- a memory unit, which holds the instructions and data of a program while it is executing

- a hard disk, used to store programs and data so that they can be loaded into memory and accessed by the CPU

- a keyboard and mouse, used for input of data

- a monitor, used to display output from a program

- an Ethernet port and wireless networking transceiver for connecting to the Internet or a Local Area Network (LAN)

- other components (not shown) such as a graphics card and a DVD drive

Figure 1.1

A Typical Design of a Personal Computer

Motherboard

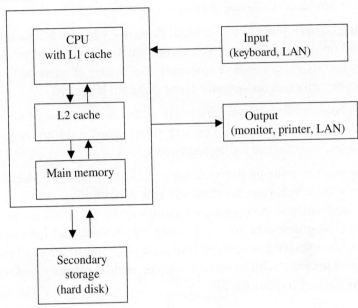

For example, if you were to go to a computer store in search of the latest personal computer, you might be shown a computer with this set of specifications:

- a 2.7-GHz Intel Pentium™ dual-core E5400

- 8 MB of L2 cache memory

- 8 GB of RAM (Random Access Memory)

- a 1 TB (Terabyte) hard disk

In these specifications, the Intel Pentium dual-core E5400 is the CPU. Other processors used as CPUs in desktop computers and servers include the AMD Athlon, the Oracle Sun SPARC, the Hewlett-Packard PA-RISC processor, and the IBM POWER processor.

CPUs consist of an Arithmetic Logic Unit (ALU) [also called an Integer Unit (IU)], which performs basic integer arithmetic and logical operations; a Floating Point Unit (FPU), which performs floating-point arithmetic; a set of hardware registers for holding data and memory addresses; and other supporting hardware, including a control unit to sequence the instructions. Each CPU comes with its own set of instructions, which are the operations that it can perform. The instructions typically perform arithmetic and logic operations, move data from one location to another, and change the flow of the program (that is, determine which instruction is to be executed next).

The first step in executing a program is loading it into memory. The CPU then fetches the program instructions from memory one at a time and executes them. A program consists of many instructions. An Instruction Pointer register (also called a Program Counter) keeps track of the current instruction being executed.

The speed of a CPU is related to its clock cycle, typically rated in GHz (Gigahertz); at the time of this edition, a high-end CPU speed would be rated at 3.4 GHz. It takes one clock cycle for a processor to fetch an instruction from memory, decode an instruction, or execute it. Current RISC processors feature pipelining, which allows the CPU to process several instructions at once, so that while one instruction is executing, the processor can decode the next instruction, and fetch the next instruction after that. This greatly improves performance of applications.

A CPU rated at 2 GHz is capable of executing 2 billion instructions per second. That translates into executing one instruction every 0.5×10^{-9} seconds (or half a nanosecond).

Memory or storage devices, such as L2 cache, memory, or hard disk, are typically rated in terms of their capacity, expressed in bytes. A byte is eight binary digits, or bits. A single bit's value is 0 or 1. Depending on the type of memory or storage device, the capacity will be stated in Kilobytes, Megabytes, Gigabytes, or even Terabytes. The sizes of these units are shown in Table 1.1.

For the CPU to execute at its rated speed, however, instructions and data must be available to the CPU at that speed as well. Instructions and data

TABLE 1.1 Memory Units and Their Sizes

Memory Unit	Size
KB, or Kbytes, or Kilobytes	About 1,000 bytes (exactly 2^{10} or 1,024 bytes)
MB, or Mbytes, or Megabytes	About 1 million bytes (exactly 2^{20} or 1,048,576 bytes)
GB, or Gbytes, or Gigabytes	About 1 billion bytes (exactly 2^{30} or 1,073,741,824 bytes)
TB, or Tbytes, or Terabytes	About 1 trillion bytes (exactly 2^{40} or 1.09951×10^{12} bytes)

come directly from the L1 cache, which is memory directly located on the CPU chip. Since the L1 cache is located on the CPU chip, it runs at the same speed as the CPU. However, the L1 cache typically is small, for example, 32 Kbytes, and eventually the CPU will need to process more instructions and data than can be held in the L1 cache at one time.

At that point, the CPU typically brings data from what is called the L2 cache, which is located on separate memory chips connected to the CPU. A typical speed for the L2 cache would be 10 nanoseconds access time, and this will considerably slow down the rate at which the CPU can execute instructions. L2 cache size today is typically 3 to 8 Mbytes, and again, the CPU will eventually need more space for instructions and data than the L2 cache can hold at one time.

At that point, the CPU will bring data and instructions from main memory, also located outside, but connected to, the CPU chip. This will slow down the CPU even more, because main memory typically has an access time of about 50 nanoseconds. Main memory, though, is significantly larger in size than the L1 and L2 caches, typically anywhere between 3 and 8 Gbytes. When the CPU runs out of space again, it will have to get its data from the hard disk, which is typically between 250 Gbytes and 1 Tbyte, but with an access time in the milliseconds range.

As you can see from these numbers, a considerable amount of speed is lost when the CPU goes from main memory to disk, which is why having sufficient memory is very important for the overall performance of applications.

Another factor that should be taken into consideration is cost per Kilobyte. Typically the cost per Kilobyte decreases significantly stepping down from L1 cache to hard disk, so high performance is often traded for low price.

Main memory (also called RAM) uses DRAM, or Dynamic Random Access Memory technology, which maintains data only when power is applied to the memory and needs to be refreshed regularly in order to retain data. The L1 and L2 caches use SRAM, or Static Random Access Memory technology, which also needs power but does not need to be refreshed in order to retain data. Memory capacities are typically stated in powers of 2. For instance, 256 Kbytes of memory is 2^{18} bytes, or 262,144 bytes.

Memory chips contain cells, each cell containing a bit, which can store either a 0 or a 1. Cells can be accessed individually or as a group of typically

TABLE 1.2   A Comparison of Memory Types

Device	Location	Type	Speed	Capacity (MB)	Cost/KB
L1 cache	On-chip	SRAM	Very fast	Very small	Very high
L2 cache	Off-chip	SRAM	Fast	Small	High
Memory	Off-chip	DRAM	Moderate	Moderate	Moderate
Hard disk	Separate	Disk media	Slow	Large	Small

4, 8, or 16 cells. For instance, a 32-Kbit RAM chip organized as 8K $\times$ 4 is composed of exactly 2^{13}, or 8,192 units, each unit containing four cells. This RAM chip will have four data output pins (or lines) and 13 access pins (or lines), enabling access to all 8,192 cells because each access pin can have a value of 0 or 1. Table 1.2 compares the features of various memory types.

1.1.2 Operating Systems

An operating system (OS) is a software program that

- controls the peripheral devices (for instance, it manages the file system)

- supports multitasking, by scheduling multiple programs to execute during the same interval

- allocates memory to each program, so that there is no conflict among the memory of any programs running at the same time

- prevents the user from damaging the system. For instance, it prevents user programs from overwriting the operating system or another program's memory

The operating system loads, or **boots**, when the computer system is turned on and is intended to run as long as the computer is running.

Examples of operating systems are MacOS for the Macintosh computers, Microsoft Windows, Unix, and Linux. Windows has evolved from a single-user, single-task DOS operating system to the multiuser, multitasking Windows 7. Unix and Linux, on the other hand, were designed from the beginning to be multiuser, multitasking operating systems.

1.1.3   Application Software

Application software consists of the programs written to perform specific tasks. These programs are run by the operating system, or as is typically said, they are run "on top of" the operating system. Examples of applications are word processors, such as Microsoft Word or Corel WordPerfect; spreadsheets, such as Microsoft Excel; database management systems, such as Oracle or Microsoft SQL Server; Internet browsers, such as Mozilla Firefox and Microsoft Internet Explorer; and most of the programs you will write during your study of Computer Science.

1.1.4   Computer Networks and the Internet

Computer Networks

Computer networks connect two or more computers. A common network used by many corporations and universities is a LAN, or Local Area Network. A typical LAN connects several computers that are geographically close to one another, often in the same building, and allows them to share resources, such as a printer, a database, or a file system. In a LAN, most user computers are called **clients**, and one or more computers act as a **server**. The server controls access to resources on the network and can supply services to the clients, such as answering database requests, storing and serving files, or managing email.

The Internet

The Internet is a network of networks, connecting millions of computers around the world. The Internet evolved from ARPANET, a 1969 U.S. military research project whose goal was to design a method for computers to communicate. Most computers on the Internet are clients, typically requesting resources, such as web pages, through an Internet browser. These resources are provided by web servers, which store web pages and respond to these requests.

For example, when you, acting as a client, type *www.yahoo.com/index.html* into your web browser, you are requesting a resource. Here that resource is a web page (*index.html*), from the web server located at *www.yahoo.com*. That request will make its way to the server with the help of routers—special computers that find a path through the Internet networks from your computer to the correct destination.

Every machine on the Internet has a unique ID, called its IP address (IP stands for Internet Protocol). A computer can have a static IP address, which is dedicated to that machine, or a dynamic IP address, which is assigned to the computer when it connects to the Internet. An IP address is made up of four octets, whose values in decimal notation are between 0 and 255. For instance, 58.203.151.103 could represent such an IP address. In binary notation, this IP address is 111010.11001011.10010111.1100111. Later in this chapter, we will learn how to convert a decimal number, such as 103, to its binary equivalent, 1100111.

Most people are familiar with URL (Uniform Resource Locator) addresses that look like *http://java.sun.com/javase/reference/api.jsp.* URLs are actually Internet domain names and the path on that domain to a specific web page. Domain name resolution servers, which implement the Domain Name System (DNS), convert domain names to IP addresses, so that Internet users don't need to know the IP addresses of websites they want to visit. The World Wide Web Consortium (W3C), an international group developing standards for Internet access, prefers the term Uniform Resource Identifier (URI) rather than URL, because URI covers future Internet addressing schemes.

Skill Practice
with these end-of-chapter questions

1.7.1 Multiple Choice Exercises

Questions 1, 2, 3, 4

1.7.3 General Questions

Questions 21, 22, 23

1.7.4 Technical Writing

Questions 31, 32, 33

1.2 Practice Activity: Displaying System Configuration

We have explored hardware and operating systems in general. Now, let's discover some information about the hardware and operating system on your computer. Depending on whether you're using a Windows operating system or a Linux operating system, choose the appropriate directions that follow to display the operating system's name, the CPU type, how much memory the computer has, and your home directory (for Unix/Linux users).

1.2.1   Displaying Windows Configuration Information

To display system configuration information on a Windows computer, run *msinfo32.exe* from the command line. From the *Start* menu, select *Run* and type *msinfo32* into the text box. You will get a display similar to the one in Figure 1.2, although the information displayed varies, depending on your hardware and the version of Windows you are running.

As you can see in Figure 1.2, this computer is running Windows Vista. The CPU is an Intel™ Core™ 2 Duo CPU T6400 processor running at 2.0 GHz, and the computer has 3 GB of memory, 1.5 GB of which is not being used at the time of the display.

1.2.2   Displaying Unix/Linux Configuration Information

1. To retrieve the name of the operating system, at the $ prompt, type echo $OSTYPE.

```
$ echo $OSTYPE
linux-gnu
```

This tells you that the machine is running the GNU version of the Linux operating system.

Figure 1.2
System Information

Item	Value
OS Name	Microsoft® Windows Vista™ Home Basic
Version	6.0.6001 Service Pack 1 Build 6001
Other OS Description	Not Available
OS Manufacturer	Microsoft Corporation
System Name	HERVE-PC
System Manufacturer	Dell Inc.
System Model	Inspiron 1525
System Type	X86-based PC
Processor	Intel(R) Core(TM)2 Duo CPU T6400 @ 2.00GHz, 2000 Mhz, 2 Core(s), 2 Log...
BIOS Version/Date	Dell Inc. A16, 10/16/2008
SMBIOS Version	2.4
Windows Directory	C:\Windows
System Directory	C:\Windows\system32
Boot Device	\Device\HarddiskVolume3
Locale	United States
Hardware Abstraction Layer	Version = "6.0.6001.18104"
User Name	herve-PC\herve
Time Zone	Eastern Daylight Time
Installed Physical Memory (RAM)	3.00 GB
Total Physical Memory	2.99 GB
Available Physical Memory	1.50 GB
Total Virtual Memory	6.19 GB
Available Virtual Memory	4.81 GB
Page File Space	3.28 GB
Page File	C:\pagefile.sys

2. To retrieve the name of your home directory, at the prompt, type `echo $HOME`.

```
$ echo $HOME
/home/username
```

3. To retrieve information about your computer's main memory, at the prompt, type `cat /proc/meminfo`. This will display the contents of the file *meminfo* in the *proc* directory.

```
$ cat /proc/meminfo
MemTotal:      2075540 kB
MemFree:       1255172 kB
Buffers:        164512 kB
Cached:         443788 kB
SwapCached:          0 kB
Active:         459444 kB
Inactive:       260328 kB
HighTotal:     1179584 kB
HighFree:       619484 kB
LowTotal:       895956 kB
LowFree:        635688 kB
SwapTotal:      915664 kB
SwapFree:       915664 kB
```

From this display, we see that the computer has 200 Mbytes of memory, 12 Mbytes of which is not being used at the time of the display. Other types of memory are also shown here, but discussion of these types of memory is beyond the scope of this course.

4. To retrieve information on your computer's CPU, type `cat /proc/cpuinfo`. This will display the contents of the file *cpuinfo* in the *proc* directory.

```
$ cat /proc/cpuinfo
processor       : 0
vendor_id       : GenuineIntel
cpu family      : 15
model           : 2
model name      : Intel(R) Xeon(TM) MP CPU 2.20GHz
stepping        : 8
cpu MHz         : 2189.034
cache size      : 2048 KB
fdiv_bug        : no
```

```
hlt_bug            : no
f00f_bug           : no
coma_bug           : no
fpu                : yes
fpu_exception      : yes
cpuid level        : 2
wp                 : yes
flags              : fpu vme de pse tsc msr pae mce cx8 apic sep mtrr pge
                     mca cmov
                     pat pse36 clflush dts acpi mmx fxsr sse sse2 ss pebs
                     bts
bogomips           : 4395.42
```

From this display, we see that the computer's CPU is an Intel Xeon™ MP, running at 2.2 GHz. Again, discussion of the other information displayed is beyond the scope of this course.

DISCUSSION QUESTIONS **?**

1. Compare the system information on several computers. Is it the same or different from computer to computer? Explain why the information is the same or different.

2. In the sample display for Windows Vista, the computer has 3 GB of memory, but only 1.5 GB of memory is available. Why do you think some memory is not available?

3. Compare your computer to the ones on the previous pages shown here. Which do you think would have better performance? Explain your answer.

1.3 Data Representation

1.3.1 Binary Numbers

As mentioned earlier, a CPU understands only binary numbers, whose digits consist of either 0 or 1. All data is stored in a computer's memory as binary digits. A bit holds one binary digit. A byte holds eight binary digits.

Binary numbers are expressed in the base 2 system, because there are only 2 values in that system, 0 and 1. By contrast, most people are used to the decimal, or base 10, system, which uses the values 0 through 9.

There are other number systems, such as the octal, or base 8, system, which uses the digits from 0 to 7, and the hexadecimal, or base 16, system, which uses the digits 0 to 9 and the letters A to F.

As we know it in the decimal system, the number 359 is composed of the following three digits:

3, representing the hundreds, or 10^2

5, representing the tens, or 10^1

9, representing the ones, or 10^0

Therefore, we can write 359 as

$359 = 3*10^2 + 5*10^1 + 9*10^0$

Thus, the decimal number 359 is written as a linear combination of powers of 10 with coefficients from the base 10 alphabet, that is, the digits from 0 to 9. Similarly, the binary number 11011 is written as a linear combination of powers of 2 with coefficients from the base 2 alphabet, that is, the digits 0 and 1.

For example, the binary number 11011 can be written as

$11011 = 1*2^4 + 1*2^3 + 0*2^2 + 1*2^1 + 1*2^0$

Table 1.3 lists the binary equivalents for the decimal numbers 0 through 8, while Table 1.4 lists the decimal equivalents of the first 15 powers of 2.

TABLE 1.3   Binary Equivalents of Decimal Numbers 0 Through 8

Decimal	Binary
0	0000
1	0001
2	0010
3	0011
4	0100
5	0101
6	0110
7	0111
8	1000

TABLE 1.4   Powers of 2 and Their Decimal Equivalents

2^{14}	2^{13}	2^{12}	2^{11}	2^{10}	2^9	2^8	2^7	2^6	2^5	2^4	2^3	2^2	2^1	2^0
16,384	8,192	4,096	2,048	1,024	512	256	128	64	32	16	8	4	2	1

Note that in Table 1.3, as we count in increments of 1, the last digit alternates between 0 and 1. In fact, we can see that for even numbers, the last digit is always 0 and for odd numbers, the last digit is always 1.

Because computers store numbers as binary, and people recognize numbers as decimal values, conversion between the decimal and binary number systems often takes place inside a computer.

Let's try a few conversions. To convert a binary number to a decimal number, multiply each digit in the binary number by $2^{position-1}$, counting the rightmost position as position 1 and moving left through the binary number. Then add the products together.

Using this method, let's calculate the equivalent of the binary number 11010 in our decimal system.

```
11010 = 1*2⁴ + 1*2³ + 0*2² + 1*2¹ + 0*2⁰
      = 16  +  8  +  0  +  2  +  0
      = 26
```

Now let's examine how to convert a decimal number to a binary number. Let's convert the decimal number 359 into its binary number equivalent. As we can see from the way we rewrote 11011, a binary number can be written as a sum of powers of 2 with coefficients 0 and 1.

The strategy to decompose a decimal number into a sum of powers of 2 is simple: first find the largest power of 2 that is smaller than or equal to the decimal number, subtract that number from the decimal number, then do the same with the remainder, and so on, until you reach 0.

The largest power of 2 that is smaller than 359 is 256, or 2^8 (the next larger power of 2 would be 512, which is larger than 359). Subtracting 256 from 359 gives us 103 ($359 - 256 = 103$), so we now have

```
359 = 2⁸*1 + 103
```

Now we apply the same procedure to 103. The largest power of 2 that is smaller than 103 is 64, or 2^6. That means that there is no factor for 2^7, so that digit's value is 0. Subtracting 64 from 103 gives us 39.

Now we have

```
359 = 2⁸*1 + 2⁷*0 + 2⁶*1 + 39
```

Repeating the procedure for 39, we find that the largest power of 2 smaller than 39 is 32 or 2^5. Subtracting 32 from 39 gives us 7.

So we now have

$359 = 2^8*1 + 2^7*0 + 2^6*1 + 2^5*1 + 7$

Repeating the procedure for 7, the largest power of 2 smaller than 7 is 2^2, or 4. That means that there are no factors for 2^4 or 2^3, so the value for each of those digits is 0. Subtracting 4 from 7 gives us 3, so we have

$359 = 2^8*1 + 2^7*0 + 2^6*1 + 2^5*1 + 2^4*0 + 2^3*0 + 2^2*1 + 3$

Repeating the procedure for 3, the largest power of 2 smaller than 3 is 2, or 2^1, and we have:

$359 = 2^8*1 + 2^7*0 + 2^6*1 + 2^5*1 + 2^4*0 + 2^3*0 + 2^2*1 + 2^1*1 + 1$

1 is a power of 2; it is 2^0, so we finally have

$359 = 2^8*1 + 2^7*0 + 2^6*1 + 2^5*1 + 2^4*0 + 2^3*0 + 2^2*1 + 2^1*1 + 2^0*1$

Removing the power of 2 multipliers, 359 can be represented in the binary system as

$$359 = 2^8*1 + 2^7*0 + 2^6*1 + 2^5*1 + 2^4*0 + 2^3*0 + 2^2*1 + 2^1*1 + 2^0*1$$
$$= 1 \quad 0 \quad 1 \quad 1 \quad 0 \quad 0 \quad 1 \quad 1 \quad 1$$

or

1 0110 0111

CODE IN ACTION

To see a step-by-step demonstration of converting between decimal and binary numbers, look for the Flash movie on the CD-ROM included with this book. Click on the link for Chapter 1 to start the movie.

In a computer program, we will use both positive and negative numbers. Appendix D explains how negative numbers, such as −34, are represented in the binary system. In a computer program, we also use floating-point numbers, such as 3.75. Appendix E explains how floating-point numbers are represented using the binary system.

1.3.2   Using Hexadecimal Numbers to Represent Binary Numbers

As you can see, binary numbers can become rather long. With only two possible values, 0 and 1, it takes 16 binary digits to represent the decimal value +32,768. For that reason, the hexadecimal, or base 16, system is often used as a shorthand representation of binary numbers. The hexadecimal system uses 16 digits: 0 to 9 and A to F. The letters A to F represent the values 10, 11, 12, 13, 14, and 15.

The maximum value that can be represented in four binary digits is $2^4 - 1$, or 15. The maximum value of a hexadecimal digit is also 15, which is represented by the letter F. So you can reduce the size of a binary number by using hexadecimal digits to represent each group of four binary digits.

Table 1.5 displays the hexadecimal digits along with their binary equivalents.

To represent the following binary number in hexadecimal, you simply substitute the appropriate hex digit for each set of four binary digits.

```
0001 1010 1111 1001 1011 0011 1011 1110
  1    A    F    9    B    3    B    E
```

TABLE 1.5   Hexadecimal Digits and Equivalent Binary Values

Hex Digit	Binary Value
0	0000
1	0001
2	0010
3	0011
4	0100
5	0101
6	0110
7	0111
8	1000
9	1001
A	1010
B	1011
C	1100
D	1101
E	1110
F	1111

Here's an interesting sequence of hexadecimal numbers. The first 32 bits of every Java applet are:

```
1100 1010 1111 1110 1011 1010 1011 1110
```

Translated into hexadecimal, that binary number becomes:

```
CAFE BABE
```

1.3.3 Representing Characters with the Unicode Character Set

Java represents characters using the Unicode Worldwide Character Standard, or simply Unicode. Each Unicode character is represented as 16 bits, or two bytes. This means that the Unicode character set can encode 65,536 characters.

The Unicode character set was developed by the Unicode Consortium, which consists of computer manufacturers, software vendors, the governments of several nations, and others. The consortium's goal was to support an international character set, including the printable characters on the standard QWERTY keyboard, as well as international characters such as é or λ.

Many programming languages store characters using the ASCII (American Standard Code for Information Interchange) character set, which uses 7 bits to encode each character, and thus, can represent only 128 characters. For compatibility with the ASCII character set, the first 128 characters in the Unicode character set are the same as the ASCII character set.

Table 1.6 shows a few examples of Unicode characters and their decimal equivalents.

For more information on the Unicode character set, see Appendix C or visit the Unicode Consortium's website at *http://www.Unicode.org*.

Skill Practice
with these end-of-chapter questions

1.7.1 Multiple Choice Exercises

Questions 5, 6, 7, 8

1.7.2 Converting Numbers

Questions 15, 16, 17, 18, 19, 20

1.7.3 General Questions

Questions 24, 25, 26

TABLE 1.6   Selected Unicode Characters and Their Decimal Equivalents

Unicode Character	Decimal Value
NUL, the null character (a nonprintable character)	0
*	42
1	49
2	50
A	65
B	66
a	97
b	98
}	125
delete (a nonprintable character)	127

1.4   Programming Languages

1.4.1   High- and Low-Level Languages

Programming languages can be categorized into three types:

- machine language
- assembly language
- high-level language

In the early days of computing, programmers often used machine language or assembly language. Machine language uses binary codes, or strings of 0s and 1s, to execute the instruction set of the CPU and to refer to memory addresses. This method of programming is extremely challenging and time consuming. Also, the code written in machine language is not portable to other computer architectures. Machine language's early popularity can be attributed largely to the fact that programmers had no other choices. However, programmers rarely use machine language today.

Assembly languages are one step above machine language, using symbolic names for memory addresses and mnemonics for processor instructions—

for example: *BEQ* (branch if equal), *SW* (store), or *LW* (load). An Assembler program converts the code to machine language before it is executed. Like machine language, assembly languages are also CPU-dependent and are not portable among computers with different processors (for instance, between Intel and SPARC). Assembly language is easier to write than machine language, but still requires a significant effort, and thus is usually used only when the program requires features, such as direct hardware access, that are not supported by a high-level language.

High-level languages, such as Fortran, Pascal, Perl, Objective C, PHP, C++, Python, and Java, are closer to the English language than they are to machine language, making them a lot easier to use for software development and more portable among CPU architectures. For this reason, programmers have embraced high-level languages for more and more applications.

Characteristics of high-level languages, such as Java, are

- The languages are highly symbolic. Programmers write instructions using keywords and special characters and use symbolic names for data.

- The languages are somewhat portable (some more portable than others) among different CPUs.

- Programming languages can be specialized; for instance:
  - C++ and Java are used for general-purpose applications.
  - Perl, PHP, and Python are used for Internet applications.
  - Fortran is used for scientific applications.
  - COBOL is used for business applications and reports.
  - Lisp and Prolog are used for artificial intelligence applications.

High-level languages are compiled, interpreted, or a combination of both. A program written in a compiled language, such as C++, is converted by a compiler into machine code, then the machine code is executed.

By contrast, a program written using an interpreted language, such as Perl, is read and converted to machine code, line by line, at execution time. Typically, a program written in an interpreted language will run more slowly than its equivalent written in a compiled language.

Java uses a combination of a compiler and an interpreter. A Java program is first compiled into processor-independent byte codes, then the byte code file is interpreted at run time by software called the Java Virtual Machine (JVM).

1.4.2   An Introduction to Object-Oriented Programming

Initial high-level languages, such as Fortran or Pascal, were procedural. Typically, programmers wrote task-specific code in separate procedures, or functions, and invoked these procedures from other sections of the program in order to perform various tasks. The program's data was generally shared among the procedures.

In the mid-1970s, the first object-oriented programming language, Smalltalk, was introduced, enabling programmers to write code with a different approach. Whereas procedures or functions dealt mainly with basic data types such as integers, real numbers, or single characters, Smalltalk provided the programmer with a new tool: classes and objects of those classes.

A class enables the programmer to encapsulate data and the functions needed to manipulate that data into one package. A class essentially defines a template, or model, from which objects are created. Creating an object is called **instantiation**. Thus, objects are created—instantiated—according to the design of the class.

A class could represent something in real life, such as a person. The class could have various attributes such as, in the example of a "person" class, a first name, a last name, and an age. The class would also provide code, called **methods**, that allow the creator of the object to set and retrieve the values of the attributes.

One big advantage to object-oriented programming is that well-written classes can be reused by new programs, thereby reducing future development time.

Smalltalk was somewhat successful, but had a major deficiency: its syntax was unlike any syntax already known by most programmers. Most programmers who knew C, were attracted by the object-oriented features of Smalltalk, but were reluctant to use it because its syntax was so different from C's syntax. C++ added object-oriented features to C, but also added complexity.

Meanwhile, the Internet was growing by leaps and bounds and gaining popularity daily. Web developers used HTML to develop web pages and soon felt the need to incorporate programming features not only on the server side, but also directly on the client side. Fortunately, Java appeared on the scene.

1.4.3   The Java Language

On May 23, 1995, Sun Microsystems introduced Java, originally named Oak, as a free, object-oriented language targeted at embedded applications for consumer devices. A Java Virtual Machine was incorporated immediately into the Netscape Navigator Internet browser, and as the Internet grew, small Java programs, known as applets, began to appear on web pages in increasing numbers. Java syntax is basically identical (with some minor exceptions) to that of C++, and soon programmers all over the world started to realize the benefits of using Java. Those benefits include

- syntax identical to that of C++, except that Java eliminates some of C++'s more complex features
- object orientation
- Internet-related features, such as applets, which are run by the browser, and servlets, which are run by the web server
- an extensive library of classes that can be reused readily, including Swing classes for providing a Graphical User Interface and Java Database Connectivity (JDBC) for communicating with a database
- portability among every platform that supports a Java Virtual Machine
- built-in networking
- open source availability of the Java Development Kit

As we mentioned earlier, a Java program is first compiled into processor-independent byte codes, then the byte codes are interpreted at run time by the Java Virtual Machine (JVM). As its name implies, the JVM simulates a virtual processor with its own instruction set, registers, and instruction pointer. Thus, to run a Java program, you only need a JVM. Fortunately, JVMs are available on every major computing platform.

Because Java programs are interpreted at run time, they typically run more slowly than their C++ counterparts. However, many platforms provide Java compilers that convert source code directly to machine code. This results in greater execution speed, but with an accompanying loss of portability. Just-in-Time (JIT) compilers are also available. These JITs compile code at run time so that subsequent execution of the same code runs much faster.

Java programs can be written as applets, servlets, or applications.

Java applets are small programs designed to add interactivity to a web page. Applets are launched by an Internet browser; they cannot run standalone. As the user requests a web page that uses an applet, the applet is downloaded to the user's computer and run by the JVM in the browser. Due to browser incompatibilities, limitations imposed by security features, and slow download times, however, applets have fallen out of favor.

Java servlets are invoked by the web server and run on the server, without being downloaded to the client. Typically, servlets dynamically generate web content by reading and writing to a database using JDBC (Java Database Connectivity).

Java applications run standalone on a client computer. In this book, we will write a few applets, but mainly we will write Java applications.

Oracle Corporation, which acquired Sun Microsystems in January 2010, provides a valuable Java website (*www.oracle.com/technetwork/java*), which has information on using the prewritten classes, a tutorial on Java, and many more resources for the Java programmer. We will refer you to that site often in this book.

1.5   An Introduction to Programming

1.5.1   Programming Basics

In many ways, programming is like solving a puzzle. You have a task to perform and you know the operations that a computer can perform (input, calculations, comparisons, rearranging of items, and output). As a programmer, your job is to decompose a task into individual, ordered steps of inputting, calculating, comparing, rearranging, and outputting.

For example, suppose your task is to find the sum of two numbers. First, your program needs to read (input) the numbers into the computer. Next, your program needs to add the two numbers together (calculate). Finally, your program needs to write (output) the sum.

Notice that this program consists of steps, called **instructions**, which are performed in order ("First," "Next," "Finally"). Performing operations in order, one after another, is called **sequential processing**.

The order in which instructions are executed by the computer is critical in programming. You can't calculate the sum of two numbers before you have read the two numbers, and you can't output a sum before you have calculated it. Programming, therefore, requires the programmer to specify the ordering of instructions, which is called the **flow of control** of the program. There are four different ways that the flow of control can progress through a program: sequential execution, method call, selection, and looping. We've just seen sequential execution, and we'll discuss the other types of flow of control in the next section.

Because getting the flow of control correct is essential to getting a program to produce correct output, programmers use a tool called **pseudocode** (pronounced *sue dough code*) to help them design the flow of control before writing the code.

1.5.2 Program Design with Pseudocode

Pseudocode, from *pseudo*, which means "appearing like," is a method for expressing a program's order of instructions in English language, rather than a programming language. In this way, the programmer can concentrate on designing a program without also being bogged down in the syntax of the particular programming language.

The pseudocode for calculating the sum of two numbers would look like Example 1.1.

```
read first number
read second number
set total to (first number + second number)
output total
```

EXAMPLE 1.1   Pseudocode for Summing Two Numbers

Fortunately, the rules for writing pseudocode are not rigid. Essentially, you can use any wording that works for you.

Let's look at another example. Suppose your program needs to calculate the square root of an integer. The instructions for calculating a square root are rather complex; fortunately, Java provides prewritten code that computes the square root of any integer. The prewritten code is called a **method**, and your program can execute that code by **calling the method**. As part of the method call, you tell the method which integer's square root you want to calculate. This is called **passing an argument to the method**. When the method finishes executing its instructions, control is passed back to your program just after the method call. Another way of looking at method calls is to consider what happens when you're reading a book and find a word you don't understand. You mark your place in the book and look up the word in a dictionary. When you're finished looking up the word, you go back to the book and continue reading.

Example 1.2 shows the pseudocode for calculating the square root of an integer.

```
read an integer
call the square root method, passing the integer and receiving the square root
output the square root of the integer
```

EXAMPLE 1.2   Using a Method Call to Calculate a Square Root

The order of operations is still input, calculate, and output, but we're calling a method to perform the calculation for us.

Now suppose your task is to determine whether a number is positive or negative. First, your program should input the number into the computer. Next, you need to determine whether the number is positive or negative. You know that numbers greater than or equal to 0 are positive and numbers less than 0 are negative, so your program should compare the number to 0. Finally, your program should write a message indicating whether the number is positive or negative.

Like Examples 1.1 and 1.2, the operations are input, calculate, and output, in that order. However, depending on whether the number is positive or negative, your program should write a different message. If the number is greater than or equal to 0, the program should write a message that the number is positive, but if the number is less than 0, the program should write a message that the number is negative. Code used to handle this situation is called **selection**; the program selects which code to execute based on the value of the data.

The pseudocode for this program could be written as that shown in Example 1.3.

```
read a number
if the number is greater than or equal to 0
    write "Number is positive."
else
    write "Number is negative."
```

EXAMPLE 1.3   Using Selection

Notice the indentation for the code that will be selected based on the comparison of the number with 0. Programmers use indentation to make it easier to see the flow of control of the program.

Now let's get a little more complicated. Suppose your program needs to find the sum of a group of numbers. This is called **accumulating**. To accomplish this, we can take the same approach as if we were adding a group of numbers using a calculator. We start with a total of 0 and add each number, one at a time, to the running total. When we have no more numbers to add, the running total is the total of all the numbers.

Translating this into pseudocode, we get the code shown in Example 1.4.

```
set total to 0
read a number
while there was a number to read, repeat next two instructions
  add number to total
  read the next number
write total
```

EXAMPLE 1.4 Accumulating a Total

The indented code will be repeated for each number read until there are no more numbers. This repeated execution of the same code is called **looping**, or **iteration**, and is used extensively in programming whenever the same processing needs to be performed on each item in a set.

Accumulating a total and determining whether a number is positive or negative are just two of many commonly performed operations. In programming, you will often perform tasks for which there are standard methods of processing, called **algorithms**. For example, the algorithm for accumulation is to set a total to 0, use looping to add each item to the total, then output the total. More generally, you can think of an algorithm as a strategy to solve a problem. Earlier in the chapter, we used an algorithm to convert a decimal number to its binary representation.

Other common programming tasks are counting items, calculating an average, sorting items into order, and finding the minimum and maximum values. In this book, you will learn the standard algorithms for performing these common operations. Once you learn these algorithms, your programming job will become easier. When you recognize that a program requires these tasks, you can simply plug in the appropriate algorithm with some minor modifications.

Programming, in large part, is simply reducing a complex task to a set of subtasks that can be implemented by combining standard algorithms that use sequential processing, method calls, selection, and looping.

The most difficult part of programming, however, is recognizing which algorithms to apply to the problem at hand. This requires analytical skills and the ability to see patterns. Throughout this book, we will point out common patterns wherever possible.

SOFTWARE ENGINEERING TIP

Looking for patterns will help you determine the appropriate algorithms for your programs.

1.5.3   Developing a Java Application

Writing a Java application consists of several steps: writing the code, compiling the code, and executing the application. Java source code is stored in a text file with the extension *.java*. Compiling the code creates one or more *.class* files, which contain processor-independent byte codes. The Java Virtual Machine (JVM) translates the byte codes into machine-level instructions for the processor on which the Java application is running. Thus, if a Java application is running on an Intel Pentium 4 processor, the JVM translates the byte codes into the Pentium 4's instruction set.

Oracle provides a Java SE Development Toolkit (JDK) on its website (*www.oracle.com/technetwork/java*), which is downloadable free of charge. The JDK contains a compiler, JVM, and an applet viewer, which is a minimal browser. In addition, the JDK contains a broad range of prewritten Java classes that programmers can use in their Java applications.

If you are downloading and installing Java yourself, be sure to follow the directions on the Sun Microsystems website, including the directions for setting the path for *javac,* the Java compiler. You need to set the path correctly so that you can run the Java compiler from any directory on your computer.

To develop an application using the JDK, write the source code using any text editor, such as Notepad, Wordpad, or the vi editor. To compile the code, invoke the compiler from the command line:

```
javac ClassName.java
```

where *ClassName.java* is the name of the source file.

If your program, written in the file *ClassName.java*, compiles correctly, a new file, *ClassName.class*, will be created in your current directory.

To run the application, you invoke the JVM from the command line:

```
java ClassName
```

Typically, programmers use an Integrated Development Environment (IDE) to develop applications. An IDE consists of a program editor, a compiler, and a run-time environment, integrated via a Graphical User Interface. The advantage to using an IDE is that errors in the Java code that are found by the compiler or the JVM can be linked directly to the program editor at the line in the source file that caused the error. Additionally, the Graphical User Interface enables the programmer to switch among the editor, compiler, and execution of the program without launching separate applications.

Some of the many available IDEs include Eclipse from the Eclipse Foundation, Inc.; JGrasp, developed at Auburn University; NetBeans, downloadable from Sun Microsystems; and TextPad from Helios Software Solutions. Some IDEs are freely available, while others require a software license fee. We include several IDEs on the CD-ROM included with this book.

Skill Practice
with these end-of-chapter questions

1.7.1 Multiple Choice Exercises

Questions 9, 10, 11, 12, 13, 14

1.7.3 General Questions

Questions 27, 28, 29, 30

1.7.4 Technical Writing

Question 34

1.5.4 Programming Activity 1: Writing a First Java Application

Let's create our first Java program. This program prints the message, "Programming is not a spectator sport!" on the screen.

Start by launching your IDE and open a new editor window. This is where you will write the code for the program.

Before we type any code, however, let's name the document. We do this by saving the document as *FirstProgram.java*. Be sure to capitalize the F and the P and keep the other letters lowercase. Java is case-sensitive, so Java considers *firstprogram.java* or even *Firstprogram.java* to be a different name.

Keeping case sensitivity in mind, type in the program shown in Example 1.5.

```
1 // First program in Java
2 // Anderson, Franceschi
3
4 public class FirstProgram
5 {
6   public static void main( String [ ] args )
7   {
8       System.out.println( "Programming is not a spectator sport!" );
9
10      System.exit( 0 );
11  }
12 }
```

EXAMPLE 1.5   A First Program in Java

At this point, we ask that you just type the program as you see it here, except for the line numbers, which are not part of the program. Line numbers are displayed in this example to allow easy reference to a particular line in the code. We'll explain a little about the program now; additional details will become clear as the semester progresses.

The first two lines, which start with two forward slashes, are comments. They will not be compiled or executed; they are simply information for the programmer and are used to increase the readability of the program.

Line 4 defines the class name as *FirstProgram*. Notice that the class name must be spelled exactly the same way—including capitalization—as the file name, *FirstProgram.java*.

The curly braces in lines 5 and 12 mark the beginning and ending of the *FirstProgram* class, and the curly braces in lines 7 and 11 mark the beginning and ending of *main*. Every Java application must define a class and

COMMON ERROR TRAP

Java is case-sensitive. The class name and the file name must match exactly, including capitalization.

a *main* method. Execution of a Java application always begins with the code inside *main*. So when this application begins, it will execute line 8, which writes the message "*Programming is not a spectator sport!*" to the system console. Next, it executes line 10, *System.exit(0)*, which exits the program. Including this line is optional; if you omit this line, the application will exit normally.

As you type the program, notice that your IDE automatically colors your text to help you distinguish comments, *String* literals ("*Programming is not a spectator sport!*"), Java class names (*String, System*), and keywords (*public, class, static*), which are reserved for specific uses in Java. Curly braces, brackets, and parentheses, which have syntactical meaning in Java, are usually displayed in color as well. Your IDE may use different colors than those shown in Example 1.5.

When you have completed typing the code in Example 1.5, compile it. If everything is typed correctly, the compiler will create a *FirstProgram.class* file, which contains the byte codes for the program.

If you received any compiler errors, check that you have entered the code exactly as it is written in Example 1.5. We give you tips on finding and fixing the errors in the next section.

If you got a clean compile with no errors, congratulations! You're ready to execute the application. This will invoke the JVM and pass it the *FirstProgram.class* file created by the compiler. If all is well, you will see the message, *Programming is not a spectator sport!*, displayed on the **Java console**, which is the text window that opens automatically. Figure 1.3 shows the correct output of the program.

```
Programming is not a spectator sport!
```

Figure 1.3
Output from Example 1.5

Debugging Techniques

If the compiler found syntax errors in the code, these are called **compiler errors**, not because the compiler caused them, but because the compiler found them. When the compiler detects errors in the code, it writes diagnostic information about the errors.

For example, try typing *println* with a capital P (as *Println*), and recompiling. The compiler displays the following message:

```
FirstProgram.java:8: cannot find symbol
    System.out.Println( "Programming is not a spectator sport!" );
                 ^
  symbol:   method Println(String)
  location: class PrintStream
1 error
```

The first line identifies the file name that contains the Java source code, as well as the line number in the source code where the error occurred. In this case, the error occurred on line 8. The second line identifies the symbol *Println* as being the cause of the error. As further help, the location information in the third and fourth lines display line 8 from the source code, using a caret (^) to point to *Println*. All these messages point you to line 8, especially emphasizing the spelling of *Println*. With most IDEs, double-clicking on the first line in the error message transfers you to the source code window with your cursor positioned on line 8 so you can correct the error.

Many times, the compiler will find more than one error in the source code. When that happens, don't panic. Often, a single problem, such as a missing semicolon or curly brace, can cause multiple compiler errors.

For example, after correcting the preceding error, try deleting the left curly brace in line 7, then recompiling. The compiler reports four errors:

```
FirstProgram.java:6: ';' expected
        public static void main( String [ ] args )
                                                  ^
FirstProgram.java:10: <identifier> expected
        System.exit( 0 );
                   ^
FirstProgram.java:10: illegal start of type
        System.exit( 0 );
                 ^
FirstProgram.java:12: class, interface or enum expected
}
^
4 errors
```

As you can see, the compiler messages do not always report the problem exactly. When you receive a compiler message, looking at the surrounding lines will often help you find the error. Depending on your IDE, you might see messages other than those shown here because some IDEs attempt to interpret the error messages from the compiler to provide more relevant information on the errors.

It is sometimes easier to fix one error at a time and recompile after each fix, because the first fix might eliminate many of the reported errors.

When all the compiler errors are corrected, you're ready to execute the program.

It is possible to get a clean bill of health from the compiler, yet the program still won't run. To demonstrate this, try eliminating the brackets in line 6 after the word *String*. If you then compile the program, no errors are reported. But when you try to run the program, you get a **run-time error**.

Instead of *Programming is not a spectator sport!*, the following message is displayed on the Java console:

Software Engineering Tip

Because one syntax error can cause multiple compiler errors, correct only the obvious errors and recompile after each correction.

```
Error: Main method not found in class FirstProgram, please define the main
method as:
   public static void main(String[] args)
Exception in thread "main" java.lang.RuntimeException: Main method not
found in FirstProgram
        at sun.launcher.LauncherHelper.signatureDiagnostic(
LauncherHelper.java:214)
        at sun.launcher.LauncherHelper.checkAndLoadMain(
LauncherHelper.java:202)
```

This means that the *main* method header (line 6) was not typed correctly.

Thus, we've seen that two types of errors can occur while you are developing a Java program: compiler errors, which are usually caused by language syntax errors or misspellings, and run-time errors, which are often caused by problems using the prewritten classes. Run-time errors can also be caused by exceptions that the JVM detects as it is running, such as an attempt to divide by zero.

Testing Techniques

Once your program compiles cleanly and executes without run-time errors, you may be tempted to conclude that your job is finished. Far from it—you must also verify the results, or output, of the program.

TABLE 1.7   Types of Program Errors and Their Causes

Type of Error	Usual Causes
Compiler errors	Incorrect language syntax or misspellings
Run-time errors	Incorrect use of classes
Logic errors	Incorrect program design or incorrect implementation of the design

In the sample program, it's difficult to get incorrect results—other than misspelling the message or omitting the spaces between the words. But any nontrivial program should be tested thoroughly before declaring it production-ready.

To test a program, consider all the possible inputs and the corresponding correct outputs. It often isn't feasible to test every possible input, so programmers usually test **boundary conditions**, which are the values that sit on the boundaries of producing different output for a program.

For example, to test the code that determines whether an integer is negative or nonnegative, you would feed the program -1 and 0. These are the boundaries of negative and nonnegative integers. In other words, the boundary between negative and nonnegative integers is between -1 and 0.

When a program does not produce the correct output, we say the program contains **logic errors**. By testing your program thoroughly, you can discover and correct most logic errors. Table 1.7 shows types of program errors and their usual causes.

We'll talk more about testing techniques throughout the book.

DISCUSSION QUESTIONS ?

1. In the Debugging Techniques section, we saw that making one typo could generate several compiler errors. Why do you think that happens?

2. Explain why testing boundary conditions is an efficient way to verify a program's correctness.

3. Did any errors occur while you were developing the first application? If so, explain whether they were compiler or run-time errors and what you did to fix them.

1.6 Chapter Summary

- Basic components of a computer include the CPU, memory, a hard disk, keyboard, monitor, and mouse.

- Each type of CPU has its own set of instructions for performing arithmetic and logical operations, moving data, and changing the order of execution of instructions.

- An operating system controls peripheral devices, supports multi-tasking, allocates memory to programs, and prevents the user from damaging the system.

- Computer networks link two or more computers so that they can share resources, such as files or printers.

- The Internet connects millions of computers around the world. Web servers deliver web pages to clients running Internet browsers.

- Binary numbers are composed of 0s and 1s. A bit holds one binary digit. A byte holds eight binary digits.

- To convert a binary number to a decimal number, multiply each digit in the binary number by $2^{position-1}$, counting the rightmost position as position 1 and moving left through the number. Then add the products together.

- To convert a decimal number into a binary number, first find the largest power of 2 that is smaller than or equal to the decimal number, subtract that number from the decimal number, then do the same with the remainder, and so on, until you reach 0.

- Hexadecimal digits can be used to represent groups of four binary digits.

- The Unicode character set, which Java uses, can encode up to 65,536 characters using 16 bits per character.

- Machine language and assembly language are early forms of programming languages that require the programmer to write to the CPU's instruction set. Because this low-level programming is time consuming and difficult, and the programs are not portable to other CPU architectures, machine language and assembly language are rarely used.

- High-level languages are highly symbolic and somewhat portable. They can be compiled, interpreted, or as in the case of Java, converted to byte codes, which are interpreted at run time.

- A good program is readable, easily maintained, and reusable.

- Object-oriented programming uses classes to encapsulate data and the functions needed to manipulate that data. Objects are instantiated according to the class design. An advantage to object-oriented programming is reuse of the classes.

- Programs use a combination of sequential processing, method calls, selection, and iteration to control the order of execution of instructions. Performing operations in order, one after another, is called sequential processing. Temporarily executing other code, then returning, is called a method call. Selecting which code to execute based on the value of data is called selection. Repeating the same code on each item in a group of values is called iteration, or looping.

- Pseudocode allows a programmer to design a program without worrying about the syntax of the language.

- In programming, you will often perform tasks for which there are standard methods of processing, called algorithms. For example, accumulating is a common programming operation that finds the sum of a group of numbers.

- Programming, in large part, is reducing a complex task to a set of subtasks that can be implemented by combining standard algorithms that use sequential processing, selection, and looping.

- Java source code is stored in a text file with an extension of *.java*. Compiling the code produces one or more *.class* files.

- An Integrated Development Environment (IDE) consists of a program editor, a compiler, and a run-time environment, integrated via a Graphical User Interface.

- Compiler errors are detected by the compiler and are usually caused by incorrect Java syntax or misspellings. Run-time errors are detected by the Java Virtual Machine and are usually caused by exceptions or incorrect use of classes. Logic errors occur during program execution and are caused by incorrect program design.

1.7 Exercises, Problems, and Projects

1.7.1 Multiple Choice Exercises

1. Which one of these is not an operating system?

   ❑ Linux

   ❑ Java

   ❑ Windows

   ❑ Unix

2. Which one of these is not an application?

   ❑ Word

   ❑ Internet Explorer

   ❑ Linux

   ❑ Excel

3. How many bits are in three bytes?

   ❑ 3

   ❑ 8

   ❑ 24

   ❑ 0

4. In a network, the computers providing services to the other computers are called

   ❑ clients.

   ❑ servers.

   ❑ laptops.

5. A binary number ending with a 0

   ❏ is even.

   ❏ is odd.

   ❏ cannot tell.

6. A binary number ending with a 1

   ❏ is even.

   ❏ is odd.

   ❏ cannot tell.

7. A binary number ending with two 0s

   ❏ is a multiple of 4.

   ❏ is not a multiple of 4.

   ❏ cannot tell.

8. Using four bits, the largest positive binary number we can represent is 1111.

   ❏ true

   ❏ false

9. Which one of these is not a programming language?

   ❏ C++

   ❏ Java

   ❏ Windows

   ❏ Fortran

10. Which one of these is not an object-oriented programming language?

   ❏ C

   ❏ Java

   ❏ C++

   ❏ Smalltalk

11. What is the file extension for a Java source code file?

   ❏ .java

   ❏ .exe

   ❏ .class

12. What is the file extension of a compiled Java program?

    ❑ .java

    ❑ .exe

    ❑ .class

13. In order to compile a program named *Hello.java*, what do you type at the command line?

    ❑ java Hello

    ❑ java Hello.java

    ❑ javac Hello

    ❑ javac Hello.java

14. You have successfully compiled *Hello.java* into *Hello.class*. What do you type at the command line in order to run the application?

    ❑ java Hello.class

    ❑ java Hello

    ❑ javac Hello

    ❑ javac Hello.class

1.7.2   Converting Numbers

15. Convert the decimal number 67 into binary.

16. Convert the decimal number 1,564 into binary.

17. Convert the binary number 0001 0101 into decimal.

18. Convert the binary number 1101 0101 0101 into decimal.

19. Convert the binary number 0001 0101 into hexadecimal.

20. Convert the hexadecimal number D8F into binary.

1.7.3   General Questions

21. A RAM chip is organized as $\times 8$ memory, i.e., each unit contains 8 bits, or a byte. There are 7 address pins on the chip. How many bytes does that memory chip contain?

22. If a CPU is rated at 1.5 GHz, how many instructions per second can the CPU execute?

23. If a CPU can execute 1.2 billion instructions per second, what is the rating of the CPU in MHz?

24. Suppose we are using binary encoding to represent colors. For example, a black-and-white color system has only two colors and therefore needs only 1 bit to encode the color system as follows:

Bit   Color

0   black

1   white

With 2 bits, we can encode four colors as follows:

Bit pattern   Color

00   black

01   red

10   blue

11   white

With 5 bits, how many colors can we encode?

With n bits (n being a positive integer), how many colors can we encode? (Express your answer as a function of n.)

25. In HTML, a color can be coded in the following hexadecimal notation: *#rrggbb*, where

rr represents the amount of red in the color

gg represents the amount of green in the color

bb represents the amount of blue in the color

rr, *gg*, and *bb* vary between 00 and FF in hexadecimal notation, i.e., 0 and 255 in decimal equivalent notation. Give the decimal values of the red, green, and blue values in the color #33AB12.

26. RGB is a color system representing colors: R stands for red, G for green, and B for blue. A color can be coded as *rgb* where *r* is a number between 0 and 255 representing how much red there is in the color, *g* is a number between 0 and 255 representing how much green there is in the color, and *b* is a number between 0 and 255 representing how

much blue there is in the color. The color gray is created by using the same value for *r*, *g*, and *b*. How many shades of gray are there?

27. List three benefits of the Java programming language.

28. What is the name of the Java compiler?

29. Write the pseudocode for a program that finds the product of two numbers.

30. Write the pseudocode for a program that finds the sums of the numbers input that are greater than or equal to 10 and the numbers input that are less than 10.

1.7.4 Technical Writing

31. List the benefits of having a Local Area Network versus standalone computer systems.

32. For one day, keep a diary of the computer applications that you use. Also note any features of the applications that you think should be improved or any features you'd like to see added.

33. You are looking at two computers with the following specifications, everything else being equal:

PC # 1	PC # 2
2.6-GHz CPU	2.5-GHz CPU
2 GB L2 cache	2 GB L2 cache
1 GB RAM	4 GB RAM
500-GB Hard drive	500-GB Hard drive
$699	$699

    Which PC would you buy? Explain the reasoning behind your selection.

34. Go to Oracle's Java site (*www.oracle.com/technetwork/java*). Explain what resources are available there for someone who wants to learn Java.

1.7.5 Group Project (for a group of 1, 2, or 3 students)

35. In the octal system, numbers are represented using digits from 0 to 7; a 0 is placed in front of the octal number to indicate that the octal

system is being used. For instance, here are some examples of the equivalent of some octal numbers in the decimal system:

Octal	Decimal
000	0
001	1
007	7
010	8
011	9

In the hexadecimal system, numbers are represented using digits from 0 to 9 and letters A to F; 0x is placed in front of the hexadecimal number to indicate that the hexadecimal system is being used. For instance, here are some examples of the decimal equivalents of some hexadecimal numbers:

Hexadecimal	Decimal
0x0	0
0x1	1
0x9	9
0xA	10
0xB	11
0xF	15
0x10	16
0x11	17
0x1C	28

1. Convert 0xC3E (in hexadecimal notation) into an octal number.

2. Convert 0377 (in octal notation) into a hexadecimal number.

3. Discuss how, in general, you would convert a hexadecimal number into an octal number and an octal number into a hexadecimal number.

CHAPTER 2

Programming Building Blocks— Java Basics

CHAPTER CONTENTS

Introduction

If you boil it down to the basics, a program has two elements: instructions and data. The instructions tell the CPU what to do with the data. Typically, a program's structure will consist of the following operations:

1. Input the data.
2. Perform some processing on the data.
3. Output the results.

The data used by a program can come from a variety of sources. The user can enter data from the keyboard, as happens when you type a new document into a word processor. The program can read the data from a file, as happens when you load an existing document into the word processor. Or the program can generate the data randomly, as happens when a computer card game deals hands. Finally, some data is already known; for example, the number of hours in a day is 24, the number of days in December is 31, and the value of pi is 3.14159. This type of data is constant. The Java language provides a syntax for describing a program's data using keywords, symbolic names, and data types.

The data may be different in each execution of the program, but the instructions stay the same. In a word processor, the words (data) are different from document to document, but the operation (instructions) of the word processor remains the same. When a line becomes full, for example, the word processor automatically wraps to the next line. It doesn't matter which words are on the line, only that the line is full. When you select a word and change the font to bold, it doesn't matter which word you select; it will become bold. Thus, a program's instructions (its algorithm) must be written to correctly handle any data it may receive.

In Chapter 1, we discussed the types of operations that the computer can perform: input and output of data and various operations related to processing data, such as arithmetic calculations, comparisons of data and subsequent changes to the flow of control, and movement of data from one location in memory to another. We will write our programs by translating our algorithms into these basic operations.

In this chapter, we'll look at basic Java syntax for defining the data to be used in the program, performing calculations on that data, and outputting program results to the screen.

2.1 Java Application Structure

Every Java program consists of at least one class. It is impossible to write a Java program that doesn't use classes. As we said in Chapter 1, classes

```
 1 /*  An application shell
 2     Anderson, Franceschi
 3 */
 4 public class ShellApplication
 5 {
 6    public static void main( String [ ] args ) //required
 7    {
 8        // write your code here
 9    }
10 }
```

EXAMPLE 2.1   A Shell for a Java Application

describe a logical entity that has data as well as methods (the instructions) to manipulate that data. An object is a physical instantiation of the class that contains specific data. We'll begin to cover classes in detail in the next chapter. For now, we'll just say that your source code should take the form of the shell code in Example 2.1.

In Example 2.1, the numbers to the left of each line are not part of the program code; they are included here for your convenience. IDEs typically allow you to display line numbers.

From application to application, the name of the class, *ShellApplication*, will change, because you will want to name your class something meaningful that reflects its function. Each Java source code file must have the same name as the class name with a *.java* extension. In this case, the source file must be *ShellApplication.java*. Whatever name you select for a class must comply with the Java syntax for identifiers.

Java **identifiers** are symbolic names that you assign to classes, methods, and data. Identifiers must start with a **Java letter** and may contain any combination of letters and digits, but no spaces. A Java letter is any character in the range *a–z* or *A–Z*, the underscore (_), or the dollar sign ($), as well as many Unicode characters that are used as letters in other languages. Digits are any character between 0 and 9. The length of an identifier is essentially unlimited. Identifier names are case-sensitive, so *Number1* and *number1* are considered to be different identifiers.

In addition, none of Java's **reserved words** can be used as identifiers. These reserved words, which are listed in Appendix A, consist of keywords used in Java instructions, as well as three special data values: *true, false,* and *null*. Given that Java identifiers are case-sensitive, note that it is legal to use *True* or *TRUE* as identifiers, but *true* is not a legal variable name. Table 2.1 lists the rules for creating Java identifiers.

TABLE 2.1 Rules for Creating Identifiers
Java Identifiers
▪ Must start with a Java letter (*A–Z, a–z, _, $,* or many Unicode characters)
▪ Can contain an almost unlimited number of letters and/or digits (0–9)
▪ Cannot contain spaces
▪ Are case-sensitive
▪ Cannot be a Java reserved word

The shell code in Example 2.1 uses three identifiers: *ShellApplication, main,* and *args.* The remainder of Example 2.1 consists of comments, Java keywords, and required punctuation.

The basic building block of a Java program is the **statement**. A statement is terminated with a semicolon and can span several lines.

SOFTWARE ENGINEERING TIP

Liberal use of white space makes your program more readable. It is good programming style to surround identifiers, operands, and operators with spaces and to skip lines between logical sections of the program.

Any amount of **white space** is permitted between identifiers, Java keywords, operands, operators, and literals. White space characters are the space, tab, newline, and carriage return. Liberal use of white space makes your program more readable. It is good programming style to surround identifiers, operands, and operators with spaces and to skip lines between logical sections of the program.

A **block**, which consists of 0, 1, or more statements, starts with a left curly brace ({) and ends with a right curly brace (}). Blocks are required for class and method definitions and can be used anywhere else in the program that a statement is legal. Example 2.1 has two blocks: the class definition (lines 5 through 10) and the *main* method definition (lines 7 through 9). As you can see, nesting blocks within blocks is perfectly legal. The *main* block is nested completely within the class definition block.

SOFTWARE ENGINEERING TIP

Include a block comment at the beginning of each source file that identifies the author of the program and briefly describes the function of the program.

Comments document the operation of the program and are notes to yourself and to other programmers who read your code. Comments are not compiled and can be coded in two ways. **Block comments** can span several lines; they begin with a forward slash-asterisk (/*) and end with an asterisk-forward slash (*/). Everything between the /* and */ is ignored by the compiler. Note that there are no spaces between the asterisk and forward slash.

Lines 1–3 in Example 2.1 are block comments and illustrate the good software engineering practice of providing at the beginning of your source code a few comments that identify yourself as the author and briefly describe what the program does.

The second way to include comments in your code is to precede the comment with two forward slashes (//). There are no spaces between the forward slashes. The compiler ignores everything from the two forward slashes to the end of the line. In Example 2.1, the compiler ignores all of line 8, but only the part of line 6 after the two forward slashes.

Let's look at an example to get a sense of what a simple program looks like and to get a feel for how a program operates. Example 2.2 calculates the area of a circle.

```java
 1 /* Calculate the area of a circle
 2    Anderson, Franceschi
 3 */
 4
 5 public class AreaOfCircle
 6 {
 7   public static void main( String [] args )
 8   {
 9     // define the data we know
10     final double PI = 3.14159;
11
12     // define other data we will use
13     double radius;
14     double area;
15
16     // give radius a value
17     radius = 3.5;
18
19     // perform the calculation
20     area = PI * radius * radius;
21
22     // output the results
23     System.out.println( "The area of the circle is " + area );
24   }
25 }
```

Example 2.2   Calculating the Area of a Circle

Figure 2.1a

Output from Example 2.2 with a Radius of 3.5

```
The area of the circle is 38.4844775
```

Figure 2.1b

Output from Example 2.2 with a Radius of 20

```
The area of the circle is 1256.636
```

Figure 2.1a shows the output when the program is run with a radius of 3.5. To calculate the area of a circle with a different radius, replace the value 3.5 in line 17 with the new radius value. For example, to calculate the area of a circle with a radius of 20, change line 17 to

```
radius = 20;
```

Then recompile the program and run it again. Figure 2.1b shows the output for a radius of 20.

You can see that Example 2.2 has the basic elements that we saw in the *ShellApplication* (Example 2.1). We have added some statements in lines 9 to 23 that do the work of the program. First we identify the data we will need. To calculate the area of a circle, we use the formula (πr^2). We know the value of π (3.14159), so we store that value in a memory location we name PI (line 10). We also need places in memory to hold the radius and the area. We name these locations in lines 13 and 14. In line 17 we give the radius a value; here we have chosen 3.5.

Now we're ready to calculate the area. We want this program to output correct results with any radius, so we need to write the algorithm of the program using the formula for calculating a circle's area given above. Java provides arithmetic operators for performing calculations. We use Java's multiplication operator (*) in line 20 to multiply PI times the radius times the radius and store the result into the memory location we named *area*. Now we're ready to output the result. On line 23, we write a message that includes the *area* value we calculated.

2.2 Data Types, Variables, and Constants

In Example 2.2, we used as data the value of PI and the radius, and we calculated the area of the circle. For each of these values, we assigned a name. We also used the Java keyword *double*, which defines the **data type** of the data. The keyword *double* means that the value will be a floating-point number.

Java allows you to refer to the data in a program by defining **variables**, which are named locations in memory where you can store values. A variable can store one data value at a time, but that value might change as the program executes, and it might change from one execution of the program to the next. The real advantage of using variables is that you can name a variable, assign it a value, and subsequently refer to the name of the variable in an expression rather than hard coding the specific value.

When we use a named variable, we need to tell the compiler which kind of data we will store in the variable. We do this by giving a data type for each variable.

Java supports eight primitive data types: *byte*, *short*, *int*, *long*, *float*, *double*, *char*, and *boolean*. They are called primitive data types because they are part of the core Java language.

The data type you specify for a variable tells the compiler how much memory to allocate and the format in which to store the data. For example, if you specify that a data item is an *int*, then the compiler will allocate four bytes of memory for it and store its value as a 32-bit signed binary number. If, however, you specify that a data item is a *double* (a double-precision floating-point number), then the compiler will allocate 8 bytes of memory and store its value as an IEEE 754 floating-point number.

Once you declare a data type for a data item, the compiler will monitor your use of that data item. If you attempt to perform operations that are not allowed for that type or are not compatible with that type, the compiler will generate an error. Because the Java compiler monitors the operations on each data item, Java is called a **strongly typed language**.

Take care in selecting identifiers for your programs. The identifiers should be meaningful and should reflect the data that will be stored in a variable,

SOFTWARE ENGINEERING TIP

When selecting identifiers, choose meaningful names that reflect the use of the identifier in the program; this will make your code self-documented. Use as many characters as necessary to make the identifier clear, but avoid extremely long identifiers. Also, for clarity in your program logic, avoid identifiers that resemble Java keywords.

the concept encapsulated by a class, or the function of a method. For example, the identifier *age* clearly indicates that the variable will hold the age of a person. When you select meaningful variable names, the logic of your program is more easily understood, and you are less likely to introduce errors. Sometimes, it may be necessary to create a long identifier in order to clearly indicate its use, for example, *numberOfStudentsWhoPassedCS1*. Although the length of identifiers is essentially unlimited, avoid creating extremely long identifiers because they are more cumbersome to use. Also, the longer the identifier, the more likely you are to make typos when entering the identifier into your program. Finally, although it is legal to use identifiers, such as *TRUE*, which differ from Java keywords only in case, it isn't a good idea because they easily can be confused with Java keywords, making the program logic less clear.

2.2.1   Declaring Variables

Every variable must be given a name and a data type before it can be used. This is called **declaring a variable**.

The syntax for declaring a variable is:

```
dataType identifier; // this declares one variable
```

or

```
dataType identifier1, identifier2, ...; // this declares multiple
                                        // variables of the same
                                        // data type
```

Note that a comma follows each identifier in the list except the last identifier, which is followed by a semicolon.

SOFTWARE ENGINEERING TIP

Begin variable names with a lowercase letter. If the variable name consists of more than one word, begin each word after the first with a capital letter. Avoid underscores in variable names, and do not begin a variable name with a dollar sign.

By convention, the identifiers for variable names start with a lowercase letter. If the variable name consists of more than one word, then each word after the first should begin with a capital letter. For example, these identifiers are conventional Java variable names: *number1*, *highScore*, *booksToRead*, *ageInYears*, and *xAxis*. Underscores conventionally are not used in variable names; they are reserved for the identifiers of constants, as we shall discuss later in the chapter. Similarly, do not use dollar signs to begin variable names. The dollar sign is reserved for the first letter of programmatically generated variable names—that is, variable names generated by software, not people. Although this may sound arbitrary now, the value of following these conventions will become clearer as you gain more experience in Java and your programs become more complex.

2.2.2 Integer Data Types

An integer data type is one that evaluates to a positive or negative whole number. Java provides four integer data types, *int*, *short*, *long*, and *byte*.

The *int*, *short*, *long*, and *byte* types differ in the number of bytes of memory allocated to store each type and, therefore, the maximum and minimum values that can be stored in a variable of that type. All of Java's integer types are signed, meaning that they can be positive or negative; the high-order, or leftmost, bit is reserved for the sign.

Table 2.2 summarizes the integer data types, their sizes in memory, and their maximum and minimum values.

In most applications, the *int* type will be sufficient for your needs, since it can store positive and negative numbers up into the 2 billion range. The *short* and *byte* data types typically are used only when memory space is critical, and the *long* data type is needed only for data values larger than 2 billion.

Let's look at some examples of integer variable declarations. Note that the variable names clearly indicate the data that the variables will hold.

```
int testGrade;
int numPlayers, highScore, diceRoll;
short xCoordinate, yCoordinate;
long cityPopulation;
byte ageInYears;
```

2.2.3 Floating-Point Data Types

Floating-point data types store numbers with fractional parts. Java supports two floating-point data types: the single-precision *float* and the double-precision *double*.

TABLE 2.2 Integer Data Types

Integer Data Type	Size in Bytes	Minimum Value	Maximum Value
byte	1	−128	127
short	2	−32,768	32,767
int	4	−2,147,483,648	2,147,483,647
long	8	−9,223,372,036,854,775,808	9,223,372,036,854,775,807

REFERENCE POINT

Floating-point numbers are stored using the IEEE 754 standard, which is discussed in Appendix E.

The two types differ in the amount of memory allocated and the size of the number that can be represented. The single-precision type (*float*) is stored in 32 bits, while the double-precision type (*double*) is stored in 64 bits. *Floats* and *doubles* can be positive or negative.

Table 2.3 summarizes Java's floating-point data types, their sizes in memory, and their maximum and minimum positive nonzero values.

Because of its greater precision, the *double* data type is usually preferred over the *float* data type. However, for calculations not requiring such precision, *floats* are often used because they require less memory.

Although integers can be stored as *doubles* or *floats*, it isn't advisable to do so because floating-point numbers require more processing time for calculations.

Let's look at a few examples of floating-point variable declarations:

```
float salesTax;
double interestRate;
double paycheck, sumSalaries;
```

2.2.4 Character Data Type

REFERENCE POINT

The encoding of ASCII and Unicode characters is discussed in Appendix C.

The *char* data type stores one Unicode character. Because Unicode characters are encoded as unsigned numbers using 16 bits, a *char* variable is stored in two bytes of memory.

Table 2.4 shows the size of the *char* data type, as well as the minimum and maximum values. The maximum value is the unsigned hexadecimal number *FFFF*, which is reserved as a special code for "not a character."

TABLE 2.3 Floating-point Data Types

Floating-point Data Type	Size in Bytes	Minimum Positive Nonzero Value	Maximum Value
float	4	1.4E-45	3.4028235E38
double	8	4.9E-324	1.7976931348623157E308

TABLE 2.4 The Character Data Type

Character Data Type	Size in Bytes	Minimum Value	Maximum Value
char	2	The character encoded as *0000*, the *null* character	The value *FFFF*, which is a special code for "not a character"

Obviously, since the *char* data type can store only a single character, such as a *K*, a *char* variable is not useful for storing names, titles, or other text data. For text data, Java provides a *String* class, which we'll discuss later in this chapter.

Here are a few declarations of *char* variables:

```
char finalGrade;
char middleInitial;
char newline, tab, doubleQuotes;
```

2.2.5 Boolean Data Type

The *boolean* data type can store only two values, which are expressed using the Java reserved words *true* and *false*, as shown in Table 2.5.

Booleans are typically used for decision making and for controlling the order of execution of a program.

Here are examples of declarations of *boolean* variables:

```
boolean isEmpty;
boolean passed, failed;
```

2.2.6 The Assignment Operator, Initial Values, and Literals

When you declare a variable, you can also assign an initial value to the data. To do that, use the **assignment operator** (=) with the following syntax:

```
dataType variableName = initialValue;
```

This statement is read as "*variableName* **gets** *initialValue*"

or

```
dataType variable1 = initialValue1, variable2 = initialValue2;
```

Notice that assignment is right to left. The initial value is assigned to the variable.

TABLE 2.5   The *boolean* Data Type

boolean Data Type	Possible Values
boolean	true
	false

COMMON ERROR TRAP

Although Unicode characters occupy two bytes in memory, they still represent a single character. Therefore, the literal must also represent only one character.

One way to specify the initial value is by using a **literal value**. In the following statement, the value *100* is an *int* literal value, which is assigned to the variable *testGrade*.

```
int testGrade = 100;
```

Table 2.6 summarizes the legal characters in literals for all primitive data types.

Notice in Table 2.6 under the literal format for *char*, that *\n* and *\t* can be used to format output. We'll discuss these and other escape sequences in the next section of this chapter.

TABLE 2.6   Literal Formats for Java Data Types

Data Type	Literal Format
int, short, byte	Optional initial sign (+ or −) followed by digits 0–9 in any combination. A literal in this format is an *int* literal; however, an *int* literal may be assigned to a *byte* or *short* variable if the literal is a legal value for the assigned data type. An integer literal that begins with a 0 digit is considered to be an octal number (base 8) and the remaining digits must be 0–7. An integer literal that begins with 0x is considered to be a hexadecimal number (base 16) and the remaining digits must be 0–F.
long	Optional initial sign (+ or −) followed by digits 0–9 in any combination, terminated with an *L* or *l*. It's preferable to use the capital *L*, because the lowercase *l* can be confused with the number *1*. An integer literal that begins with a 0 digit is considered to be an octal number (base 8) and the remaining digits must be 0–7. An integer literal that begins with 0x is considered to be a hexadecimal number (base 16) and the remaining digits must be 0–F.
float	Optional initial sign (+ or −) followed by a floating-point number in fixed or scientific format, terminated by an *F* or *f*.
double	Optional initial sign (+ or −) followed by a floating-point number in fixed or scientific format.
char	▪ Any printable character enclosed in single quotes. ▪ A decimal value from 0 to 65,535. ▪ '\m', where \m is an escape sequence. For example, '\n' represents a newline, and '\t' represents a tab character.
boolean	*true* or *false*

Example 2.3 shows a complete program illustrating variable declarations, specifying a literal for the initial value of each.

```
1  /* Variables Class
2     Anderson, Franceschi
3  */
4
5  public class Variables
6  {
7   public static void main( String [ ] args )
8   {
9     // This example shows how to declare and initialize variables
10
11      int testGrade = 100;
12      long cityPopulation = 425612340L;
13      byte ageInYears = 19;
14
15      float  salesTax = .05F;
16      double interestRate = 0.725;
17      double avogadroNumber = +6.022E23;
18      // avogadroNumber is represented in scientific notation;
19      //     its value is 6.022 x 10 to the power 23
20
21      char finalGrade = 'A';
22      boolean isEmpty = true;
23
24      System.out.println( "testGrade is " + testGrade );
25      System.out.println( "cityPopulation is " + cityPopulation );
26      System.out.println( "ageInYears is " + ageInYears );
27      System.out.println( "salesTax is " + salesTax );
28      System.out.println( "interestRate is " + interestRate );
29      System.out.println( "avogadroNumber is " + avogadroNumber );
30      System.out.println( "finalGrade is " + finalGrade );
31      System.out.println( "isEmpty is " + isEmpty );
32  }
33 }
```

EXAMPLE 2.3   Declaring and Initializing Variables

Line 9 shows a single-line comment. Line 17 declares a *double* variable named *avogadroNumber* and initializes it with its value in scientific notation. The Avogadro number represents the number of elementary particles in one mole of any substance.

Figure 2.2 shows the output of Example 2.3.

Figure 2.2

Output of Example 2.3

```
testGrade is 100
cityPopulation is 425612340
ageInYears is 19
salesTax is 0.05
interestRate is 0.725
avogadroNumber is 6.022E23
finalGrade is A
isEmpty is true
```

Another way to specify an initial value for a variable is to assign the variable the value of another variable, using this syntax:

```
dataType variable2 = variable1;
```

Two things need to be true for this assignment to work:

- *variable1* needs to be declared and assigned a value before this statement appears in the source code.

- *variable1* and *variable2* need to be compatible data types; in other words, the precision of *variable1* must be lower than or equal to that of *variable2*.

For example, in these statements:

```
boolean isPassingGrade = true;
boolean isPromoted = isPassingGrade;
```

isPassingGrade is given an initial value of *true*. Then *isPromoted* is assigned the value already given to *isPassingGrade*. Thus, *isPromoted* is also assigned the initial value *true*. If *isPassingGrade* were assigned the initial value *false*, then *isPromoted* would also be assigned the initial value *false*.

And in these statements:

```
float salesTax = .05f;
double taxRate = salesTax;
```

the initial value of .05 is assigned to *salesTax* and then to *taxRate*. It's legal to assign a *float* value to a *double*, because all values that can be stored as *floats* are also valid *double* values. However, these statements are *not* valid:

```
double taxRate = .05;
float salesTax = taxRate; // invalid; float is lower precision
```

Even though .05 is a valid *float* value, the compiler will generate a "possible loss of precision" error.

Similarly, you can assign a lower-precision integer value to a higher-precision integer variable.

Table 2.7 summarizes compatible data types; a variable or literal of any type in the right column can be assigned to a variable of the data type in the left column.

Variables need to be declared before they can be used in your program, but be careful to declare each variable only once; that is, specify the data type of the variable only the first time that variable is used in the program. If you attempt to declare a variable that has already been declared, as in the following statements:

```
double twoCents;
double twoCents = 2; // incorrect, second declaration of twoCents
```

you will receive a compiler error similar to the following:

```
twoCents is already defined
```

TABLE 2.7 Valid Data Types for Assignment

Data Type	Compatible Data Types
byte	byte
short	byte, short
int	byte, short, int, char
long	byte, short, int, char, long
float	byte, short, int, char, long, float
double	byte, short, int, char, long, float, double
boolean	boolean
char	char

COMMON ERROR TRAP

Declare each variable only once, the first time the variable is used. After the variable has been declared, its data type cannot be changed.

Similarly, once you have declared a variable, you cannot change its data type. Thus, these statements:

```
double cashInHand;
int cashInHand; // incorrect, data type cannot be changed
```

will generate a compiler error similar to the following:

```
cashInHand is already defined
```

CODE IN ACTION

On the CD-ROM included with this book, you will find a Flash movie showing a step-by-step illustration of declaring variables and assigning initial values. Click on the link for Chapter 2 to view the movie.

2.2.7 *String* Literals and Escape Sequences

In addition to literals for all the primitive data types, Java also supports *String* literals. *Strings* are objects in Java, and we will discuss them in greater depth in Chapter 3.

A *String* **literal** is a sequence of characters enclosed by double quotes. One set of quotes "opens" the *String* literal and the second set of quotes "closes" the literal. For example, these are all *String* literals:

```
"Hello"
"Hello world"
"The value of x is "
```

We used a *String* literal in our first program in Chapter 1 in this statement:

```
System.out.println( "Programming is not a spectator sport!" );
```

We also used *String* literals in output statements in Example 2.3 to label the data that we printed:

```
System.out.println( "The area of the circle is " + area );
```

The + operator is the *String* **concatenation operator**. Among other uses, the concatenation operator allows us to print primitive data types along with *Strings*. We'll discuss the concatenation operator in more detail in Chapter 3.

String literals cannot extend over more than one line. If the compiler finds a newline character in the middle of your *String* literal, it will generate a compiler error. For example, the following statement is not valid:

```
System.out.println( "Never pass a water fountain
              without taking a drink." );
```

In fact, that statement will generate several compiler errors:

```
StringTest.java:9: unclosed string literal
     System.out.println( "Never pass a water fountain
                         ^
StringTest.java:9: ';' expected
     System.out.println( "Never pass a water fountain
                                                     ^
StringTest.java:10: ';' expected
            without taking a drink." );
                    ^
StringTest.java:10: unclosed string literal
         without taking a drink." );
                                ^

StringTest.java:10: not a statement
         without taking a drink." );
                              ^
```

`5 errors`

If you have a long *String* to print, break it into several strings and use the concatenation operator. This statement is a correction of the invalid statement above:

```
System.out.println( "Never pass a water fountain,"
                  + " without taking a drink." );
```

Another common programming error is omitting the closing quotes. Be sure that all open quotes have matching closing quotes on the same line.

Now that we know that quotes open and close *String* literals, how can we define a literal that includes quotes? This statement

```
System.out.println( "She said, "Java is fun"" ); // illegal quotes
                                                 // within literal
```

generates this compiler error:

```
StringTest.java:24: ')' expected
     System.out.println( "She said, "Java is fun"" ); // illegal quotes
                                    ^
StringTest.java:24: ';' expected
     System.out.println( "She said, "Java is fun"" ); // illegal quotes
                                                 ^
```

`2 errors`

And since *String* literals can't extend over two lines, how can we create a *String* literal that includes a newline character? Java solves these problems

SOFTWARE ENGINEERING TIP

Add a space to the end of a *String* literal before concatenating a value for more readable output.

COMMON ERROR TRAP

All open quotes for a *String* literal should be matched with a set of closing quotes, and the closing quotes must appear before the line ends.

TABLE 2.8   Java Escape Sequences

Character	Escape Sequence
newline	\n
tab	\t
double quotes	\"
single quote	\'
backslash	\\
backspace	\b
carriage return	\r
form feed	\f

by providing a set of escape sequences that can be used to include a special character within *String* and *char* literals. The escape sequences \n, \t, \b, \r, and \f are nonprintable characters. Table 2.8 lists the Java escape sequences.

In Example 2.4, we see how escape sequences can be used in *Strings*.

```
1  /*  Literals Class
2       Anderson, Franceschi
3  */
4
5  public class Literals
6  {
7    public static void main( String [ ] args )
8    {
9      System.out.println( "One potato\nTwo potatoes\n" );
10     System.out.println( "\tTabs can make the output easier to read" );
11     System.out.println( "She said, \"Java is fun\"" );
12   }
13 }
```

EXAMPLE 2.4   Using Escape Sequences

Figure 2.3 shows the output of Example 2.4. Line 9 shows how \n causes the remainder of the literal to be printed on the next line. The tab character, \t,

Figure 2.3
Output of Example 2.4

```
One potato
Two potatoes

        Tabs can make the output easier to read
She said, "Java is fun"
```

used in line 10, will cause the literal that follows it to be indented one tab stop when output. Line 11 outputs a sentence with embedded double quotes; the embedded double quotes are printed with the escape sequence \ ".

2.2.8   Constants

Sometimes you know the value of a data item, and you know that its value will not (and should not) change during program execution, nor is it likely to change from one execution of the program to another. In this case, it is a good software engineering practice to define that data item as a **constant.**

Defining constants uses the same syntax as declaring variables, except that the data type is preceded by the keyword *final.*

```
final dataType CONSTANT_IDENTIFIER = assignedValue;
```

Assigning a value is optional when the constant is defined, but you must assign a value before the constant is used in the program. Also, once the constant has been assigned a value, its value cannot be changed (reassigned) later in the program. Any attempt by your program to change the value of a constant will generate the following compiler error:

```
cannot assign a value to final variable
```

Think of this as a service of the compiler in preventing your program from unintentionally corrupting its data.

By convention, *CONSTANT_IDENTIFIER* consists of all capital letters, and embedded words are separated by an underscore. This makes constants stand out in the code and easy to identify as constants. Also, constants are usually defined at the top of a program where their values can be seen easily.

Example 2.5 shows how to use constants in a program.

```
1 /* Constants Class
2     Anderson, Franceschi
3 */
4
5 public class Constants
6 {
7   public static void main( String [ ] args )
8   {
9     final char ZORRO = 'Z';
10    final double PI = 3.14159;
11    final int DAYS_IN_LEAP_YEAR = 366, DAYS_IN_NON_LEAP_YEAR = 365;
12
13    System.out.println( "The value of constant ZORRO is " + ZORRO );
14    System.out.println( "The value of constant PI is " + PI );
15    System.out.println( "The number of days in a leap year is "
16                          + DAYS_IN_LEAP_YEAR );
17    System.out.println( "The number of days in a non-leap year is "
18                          + DAYS_IN_NON_LEAP_YEAR );
19
20    // PI = 3.14;
21    // The statement above would generate a compiler error
22    // You cannot change the value of a constant
23  }
24 }
```

EXAMPLE 2.5   Using Constants

SOFTWARE ENGINEERING TIP

Use all capital letters for a constant's identifier; separate words with an underscore (_). Declare constants at the top of the program so their value can be seen easily.

SOFTWARE ENGINEERING TIP

Declare as a constant any data that should not change during program execution. The compiler will then flag any attempts by your program to change the value of the constant, thus preventing any unintentional corruption of the data.

Lines 9, 10, and 11 define four constants. On line 11, note that both *DAYS_IN_LEAP_YEAR* and *DAYS_IN_NON_LEAP_YEAR* are constants. You don't need to repeat the keyword *final* to define two (or more) constants of the same data types. Lines 13 to 18 output the values of the four constants. If line 20 were not commented out, it would generate a compiler error because once a constant is assigned a value, its value cannot be changed. Figure 2.4 shows the output of Example 2.5.

Constants can make your code more readable: PI is more meaningful than 3.14159 when used inside an arithmetic expression. Another advantage of using constants is to keep programmers from making logic errors: Let's say

```
The value of constant ZORRO is Z
The value of constant PI is 3.14159
The number of days in a leap year is 366
The number of days in a non-leap year is 365
```

Figure 2.4
Output of Example 2.5

we set a constant to a particular value and it is used at various places throughout the code (for instance, a constant representing a tax rate); we then discover that the value of that constant needs to be changed. All we have to do is make the change in one place, most likely at the beginning of the code. If we had to change the value at many places throughout the code, that could very well result in logic errors or typos.

Skill Practice
with these end-of-chapter questions

2.6.1   Multiple Choice

Questions 1, 2

2.6.2   Reading and Understanding Code

Questions 4, 5, 6

2.6.3   Fill In the Code

Questions 23, 24, 25, 26

2.6.4   Identifying Errors in Code

Questions 33, 34, 38, 39

2.6.5   Debugging Area

Questions 40, 41

2.6.6   Write a Short Program

Question 46

2.6.8   Technical Writing

Question 52

2.3   Expressions and Arithmetic Operators

2.3.1   The Assignment Operator and Expressions

In a previous section, we mentioned using the assignment operator to assign initial values to variables and constants. Now let's look at the assignment operator in more detail.

The syntax for the assignment operator is:

```
target = expression;
```

An expression consists of operators and operands that evaluate to a single value. The value of the expression is then assigned to *target* (*target* gets *expression*), which must be a variable or constant having a data type compatible with the value of the expression.

If *target* is a variable, the value of the expression replaces any previous value the variable was holding. For example, let's look at these instructions:

```
int numberOfPlayers = 10; // numberOfPlayers value is 10
numberOfPlayers = 8;      // numberOfPlayers value is now 8
```

The first instruction declares an *int* named *numberOfPlayers*. This allocates four bytes in memory to a variable named *numberOfPlayers* and stores the value 10 in that variable. Then, the second statement changes the value stored in the variable *numberOfPlayers* to 8. The previous value, 10, is discarded.

An expression can be a single variable name or a literal of any type, in which case, the value of the expression is simply the value of the variable or the literal. For example, in these statements,

```
int legalAge = 18;
int voterAge = legalAge;
```

the literal *18* is an expression. Its value is *18*, which is assigned to the variable *legalAge*. Then, in the second statement, *legalAge* is an expression, whose value is *18*. Thus the value *18* is assigned to *voterAge*. So after these statements have been executed, both *legalAge* and *voterAge* will have the value *18*.

One restriction, however, is that an assignment expression cannot include another variable unless that variable has been defined previously. The statement defining the *length* variable that follows is **invalid**, because it refers to *width*, which is not defined until the next line.

```
int length = width * 2; // invalid, width is not yet defined
int width;
```

The compiler flags the statement defining *length* as an error

```
cannot find symbol
```

because *width* has not yet been defined.

An expression can be quite complex, consisting of multiple variables, constants, literals, and operators. Before we can look at examples of more complex expressions, however, we need to discuss the *arithmetic operators*.

2.3.2 Arithmetic Operators

Java's arithmetic operators are used for performing calculations on numeric data. Some of these operators are shown in Table 2.9.

All these operators take two operands, which are espressions; thus, they are called **binary operators**.

TABLE 2.9 Arithmetic Operators

Operator	Operation
+	addition
−	subtraction
*	multiplication
/	division
%	modulus (remainder after division)

In Example 2.6, we make a variety of calculations to demonstrate the addition, subtraction, multiplication, and division arithmetic operators. We will discuss integer division and the modulus operator later in the chapter. The output from this program is shown in Figure 2.5.

```java
1 /* Arithmetic Operators
2    Anderson, Franceschi
3 */
4
5 public class ArithmeticOperators
6 {
7   public static void main( String [] args )
8   {
9     // calculate the cost of lunch
10    double salad = 5.95;
11    double water = .89;
12    System.out.println( "The cost of lunch is $"
13                        + ( salad + water ) );
14
15    // calculate your age as of a certain year
16    int targetYear = 2011;
17    int birthYear = 1993;
18    System.out.println( "Your age in " + targetYear + " is "
19                        + ( targetYear - birthYear ) );
20
21    // calculate the total calories of apples
22    int caloriesPerApple = 127;
23    int numberOfApples = 3;
24    System.out.println( "The calories in " +  numberOfApples
25                        + " apples is " +
26                        + ( caloriesPerApple * numberOfApples ) );
27
28    // calculate miles per gallon
29    double miles = 426.8;
30    double gallons = 15.2;
31    double mileage = miles / gallons;
32    System.out.println( "The mileage is "
33                        + mileage + " miles per gallon." );
34  }
35 }
```

Example 2.6   Using Arithmetic Operators

Figure 2.5
Output from Example 2.6

```
The cost of lunch is $6.84
Your age in 2011 is 18
The calories in 3 apples is 381
The mileage is 28.078947368421055 miles per gallon.
```

Figure 2.5
Output from Example 2.6

Example 2.6 demonstrates a number of small operations. To calculate a total price (lines 12 and 13), we add the individual prices. To calculate an age (lines 18 and 19), we subtract the birth year from the target year. To calculate the number of calories in multiple apples (lines 24–26), we multiply the number of calories in one apple by the number of apples. We calculate miles per gallon by dividing the number of miles driven by the number of gallons of gas used (line 31). Note that we can either store the result in another variable, as we did in line 31, and subsequently output the result (lines 32–33), or we can output the result of the calculation directly by writing the expression in the *System.out.println* statement, as we did in the other calculations in this example.

 **SOFTWARE ENGINEERING TIP**

For readable code, insert a space between operators and operands.

 **SOFTWARE ENGINEERING TIP**

Developing and testing your code in steps makes it easier to find and fix errors.

2.3.3   Operator Precedence

The statements in Example 2.6 perform simple calculations, but what if you want to make more complex calculations using several operations, such as calculating how much money you have in coins? Let's say you have two quarters, three dimes, and two nickels. To calculate the value of these coins in pennies, you might use this expression:

```
int pennies = 2 * 25 + 3 * 10 + 2 * 5;
```

In which order should the computer do the calculation? If the value of the expression were calculated left to right, then the result would be

```
= 2 * 25 + 3 * 10 + 2 * 5
=   50   + 3 * 10 + 2 * 5
=       53   * 10 + 2 * 5
=          530   + 2 * 5
=              532 * 5
=                 2660
```

Clearly, 2,660 pennies is not the right answer. To calculate the correct number of pennies, the multiplications should be performed first, then the additions. This, in fact, is the order in which Java will calculate the preceding expression.

The Java compiler follows a set of rules called **operator precedence** to determine the order in which the operations should be performed.

Table 2.10 provides the order of precedence of the operators we've discussed so far. The operators in the first row—parentheses—are evaluated first, then the operators in the second row (*, /, %) are evaluated, and so on with the operators in each row. When two or more operators on the same level appear in the same expression, the order of evaluation is left to right, except for the assignment operator, which is evaluated right to left.

As we introduce more operators, we'll add them to the Order of Precedence chart. The complete chart is provided in Appendix B.

Using Table 2.10 as a guide, let's recalculate the number of pennies:

```
int pennies = 2 * 25 + 3 * 10 + 2 * 5;
            =  50    +   30   +   10
            =  90
```

As you can see, *90* is the correct number of pennies in two quarters, three dimes, and two nickels.

We also could have used parentheses to clearly display the order of calculation. For example,

```
int pennies = (2 * 25) + (3 * 10) + (2 * 5);
            =   50      +    30    +    10
            =   90
```

The result is the same, 90 pennies.

TABLE 2.10   Operator Precedence

Operator Hierarchy	Order of Same-Statement Evaluation	Operation
()	left to right	parentheses for explicit grouping
*, /, %	left to right	multiplication, division, modulus
+, −	left to right	addition, subtraction
=	right to left	assignment

It sometimes helps to use parentheses to clarify the order of calculations, but parentheses are essential when your desired order of evaluation is different from the rules of operator precedence. For example, to calculate the value of this formula:

$$\frac{x}{2y}$$

you could write this code:

```
double result = x / 2 * y;
```

This would generate incorrect results because, according to the rules of precedence, $x/2$ would be calculated first, then the result of that division would be multiplied by y. In algebraic terms, the preceding statement is equivalent to

$$\frac{x}{2} * y$$

To code the original formula correctly, you need to use parentheses to force the multiplication to occur before the division:

```
double result = x / ( 2 * y );
```

2.3.4 Programming Activity 1: Converting Inches to Centimeters

Now that we know how to define variables and constants and make calculations, let's put this all together by writing a program that converts inches into the equivalent centimeters.

Locate the *MetricLength.java* source file found in the Chapter 2, Programming Activity 1 folder on the CD-ROM accompanying this book. Copy the file to your computer.

Open the *MetricLength.java* source file. You'll notice that the class already contains some source code. Your job is to fill in the blanks.

When we write a program, we begin by considering these questions:

1. What data values does the program require?
   a. What data values do we know?
   b. What data values will change from one execution of the program to the next?
2. What processing (algorithm) do we need to implement?
3. What is the output?

The comments in the source file will guide you through the answers to these questions, and by doing so, you will complete the program. Search for five asterisks in a row (*****). This will position you to the places in the source code where you will add your code. The *MetricLength.java* source code is shown in Example 2.7. Sample output for a value of 5.2 inches is shown in Figure 2.6.

```
 1 /* MetricLength - converts inches to centimeters
 2     Anderson, Franceschi
 3 */
 4
 5 public class MetricLength
 6 {
 7     public static void main( String [] args )
 8     {
 9
10         /***** 1. What data values do we know?
11         /* We know that there are 2.54 centimeters in an inch.
12         /* Declare a double constant named CM_PER_INCH.
13         /* Assign CM_PER_INCH the value 2.54.
14         */
15
16
17         /***** 2.    What other data does the program require?
18         /* For this program, we require the number of inches.
19         /* Declare a double variable named inches.
20         /* Assign any desired value to this variable.
21         */
22
23
24         /***** 3. Calculation: convert inches to centimeters
25         /* Declare a double variable named centimeters.
26         /* Multiply inches by CM_PER_INCH
27         /* and store the result in centimeters.
28         */
29
30
31         /***** 4. Output
32         /* Write one or two statements that output
33         /* the original inches and the equivalent centimeters.
34         /* Try to match the sample output in Figure 2.6.
35         */
36
```

Figure 2.6

Sample Output for
Programming Activity 1

```
5.2 inches are equivalent to 13.208 centimeters.
```

```
37
38
39    }
40 }
```

Example 2.7   Converting Feet and Inches to Centimeters

? DISCUSSION QUESTIONS

1. How do you know that your program results are correct?

2. If you change the inches data value, does your program still produce correct results?

2.3.5   Integer Division and Modulus

Division with two integer operands is performed in the Arithmetic Logic Unit (ALU), which can calculate only an integer result. Any fractional part is truncated; no rounding is performed. The remainder after division is available, however, as an integer, by taking the modulus (%) of the two integer operands. Thus, in Java, the integer division (/) operator will calculate the quotient of the division, whereas the modulus (%) operator will calculate the remainder of the division.

```
 1 /* DivisionAndModulus Class
 2    Anderson, Franceschi
 3 */
 4
 5 public class DivisionAndModulus
 6 {
 7   public static void main( String [ ] args )
 8   {
 9     final int PENNIES_PER_QUARTER = 25;
10     int pennies = 113;
11
12     int quarters = pennies / PENNIES_PER_QUARTER;
13     System.out.println( "There are " + quarters + " quarters in "
14             + pennies + " pennies" );
15
```

```
16     int penniesLeftOver = pennies % PENNIES_PER_QUARTER;
17     System.out.println( "There are " + penniesLeftOver
18             + " pennies left over" );
19
20     final double MONTHS_PER_YEAR = 12;
21     double annualSalary = 50000.0;
22
23     double monthlySalary = annualSalary / MONTHS_PER_YEAR;
24     System.out.println( "The monthly salary is " + monthlySalary );
25   }
26 }
```

EXAMPLE 2.8   How Integer Division and Modulus Work

In Example 2.8, we have 113 pennies and we want to convert those pennies into quarters. We can find the number of quarters by dividing 113 by 25. The *int* variable *pennies* is assigned the value 113 at line 10. At line 12, the variable *quarters* is assigned the result of the integer division of *pennies* by the constant *PENNIES_PER_QUARTER*. Since the quotient of the division of 113 by 25 is 4, *quarters* will be assigned 4. At line 16, we use the modulus operator to assign to the variable *penniesLeftOver* the remainder of the division of *pennies* by *PENNIES_PER_QUARTER*. Since the remainder of the division of 113 by 25 is 13, 13 will be assigned to *penniesLeftOver*. Notice that integer division and modulus are independent calculations. You can perform a division without also calculating the modulus, and you can calculate the modulus without performing the division.

At line 23, we divide a *double* by a *double;* therefore, a floating-point division will be performed by the floating-point unit (FPU), and the result will be assigned to the variable *monthlySalary*. Figure 2.7 shows the output of the program.

Figure 2.7

Output of Example 2.8

```
There are 4 quarters in 113 pennies
There are 13 pennies left over
The monthly salary is 4166.666666666667
```

The modulus is actually a useful operator. As you will see later in this book, it can be used to determine whether a number is even or odd, to control the number of data items that are written per line, to determine if one number is a factor of another, and for many other uses.

CODE IN ACTION

To see arithmetic operators used in a program, look for the Chapter 2 Flash movie on the CD-ROM accompanying this book. Click on the link for Chapter 2 to start the movie.

Skill Practice
with these end-of-chapter questions

2.6.2 Reading and Understanding Code

Questions 7, 8, 9, 10, 11, 12, 13

2.6.3 Fill In the Code

Questions 27, 29, 32

2.6.4 Identifying Errors in Code

Question 35

2.6.6 Write a Short Program

Question 44

2.3.6 Division by Zero

As you might expect, Java does not allow integer division by 0. If you include this statement in your program:

```
int result = 4 / 0;
```

the code will compile without errors, but at run time, when this statement is executed, the JVM will generate an exception and print an error message on the Java console:

```
Exception in thread "main" java.lang.ArithmeticException: / by zero
```

In most cases, this stops the program. In Chapter 5, we show you how to avoid dividing by zero by first testing whether the divisor is zero before performing the division.

In contrast, floating-point division by zero does not generate an exception. If the dividend is non-zero, the answer is *Infinity*. If both the dividend and divisor are zero, the answer is *NaN*, which stands for "Not a Number."

Example 2.9 illustrates the three cases of dividing by zero. As we can see on the output shown in Figure 2.8, line 16 of Example 2.9 never executes. The exception is generated at line 15 and the program halts execution.

```java
 1 /* DivisionByZero Class
 2    Anderson, Franceschi
 3 */
 4
 5 public class DivisionByZero
 6 {
 7   public static void main( String [ ] args )
 8   {
 9     double result1 = 4.3 / 0.0;
10     System.out.println( "The value of result1 is " + result1 );
11
12     double result2 = 0.0 / 0.0;
13     System.out.println( "The value of result2 is " + result2 );
14
15     int result3 = 4 / 0;
16     System.out.println( "The value of result3 is " + result3 );
17   }
18 }
```

EXAMPLE 2.9   Results of Division by Zero

Although floating-point division by zero doesn't bring your program to a halt, it doesn't provide useful results either. It's a good practice to avoid dividing by zero in the first place. We'll give you tools to do that in Chapter 5.

Figure 2.8

Output of Example 2.9

```
The value of result1 is Infinity
The value of result2 is NaN
Exception in thread "main" java.lang.ArithmeticException: / by zero
        at DivisionByZero.main(DivisionByZero.java:15)
```

2.3.7 Mixed-Type Arithmetic and Type Casting

So far, we've used a single data type in the expressions we've evaluated. But life isn't always like that. Calculations often involve data of different primitive types.

When calculations of mixed types are performed, lower-precision operands are converted, or **promoted**, to the type of the operand that has the higher precision.

The promotions are performed using the *first* of these rules that fits the situation:

1. If either operand is a *double*, the other operand is converted to a *double*.

2. If either operand is a *float*, the other operand is converted to a *float*.

3. If either operand is a *long*, the other operand is converted to a *long*.

4. If either operand is an *int*, the other operand is promoted to an *int*.

5. If neither operand is a *double*, *float*, *long*, or an *int*, both operands are promoted to *int*.

Table 2.11 summarizes these rules of promotion.

This arithmetic promotion of operands is called **implicit type casting** because the compiler performs the promotions automatically, without our specifying that the conversions should be made. Note that the data type of

TABLE 2.11 Rules of Operand Promotion

Data Type of One Operand	Data Type of Other Operand	Promotion of Other Operand	Data Type of Result
double	*char, byte, short, int, long, float*	*double*	*double*
float	*char, byte, short, int, long*	*float*	*float*
long	*char, byte, short, int*	*long*	*long*
int	*char, byte, short*	*int*	*int*
short	*char, byte*	Both operands are promoted to *int*	*int*
byte	*char*	Both operands are promoted to *int*	*int*

any promoted variable is not permanently changed; its type remains the same after the calculation has been performed.

Table 2.11 shows many rules, but essentially, any arithmetic expression involving integers and floating-point numbers will evaluate to a floating-point number.

Lines 9 to 12 of Example 2.10 illustrate the rules of promotion. At line 11, the expression *PI * radius * radius* is a mixed-type expression. This expression will be evaluated left to right, evaluating the mixed-type expression *PI * radius* first. *PI* is a *double* and *radius* is an *int*. Therefore, *radius* is promoted to a *double* (4.0) and the result of *PI * radius* is a *double* (12.56636). Then, the next calculation (*12.56636 * radius*) also involves a mixed-type expression, so *radius* is again promoted to a *double* (4.0). The final result, 50.26544, is a *double* and is assigned to *area*. Figure 2.9 shows the output of the complete program.

Sometimes, it's useful to instruct the compiler specifically to convert the type of a variable. In this case, you use **explicit type casting**, which uses this syntax:

```
(dataType) ( expression )
```

The expression will be converted, or type cast, to the data type specified. The parentheses around *expression* are needed only when the expression consists of a calculation that you want to be performed before the type casting.

Type casting is useful in calculating an average. Example 2.10 shows how to calculate your average test grade. Your test scores are 94, 86, 88, and 97, making the combined total score 365. We expect the average to be 91.25.

```
 1 /*  MixedDataTypes Class
 2      Anderson, Franceschi
 3 */
 4
 5 public class MixedDataTypes
 6 {
 7    public static void main( String [ ] args )
 8    {
 9       final double PI = 3.14159;
10       int radius = 4;
```

```
11        double area = PI * radius * radius;
12        System.out.println( "The area is " + area );
13
14        int total = 365, count = 4;
15        double average = total / count;
16        System.out.println( "\nPerforming integer division, "
17                               + "then implicit typecasting" );
18        System.out.println( "The average test score is " + average );
19        // 91.0 INCORRECT ANSWER!
20
21        average = ( double ) ( total / count );
22        System.out.println( "\nPerforming integer division, "
23                               +  "then explicit typecasting" );
24        System.out.println( "The average test score is " + average );
25        // 91.0 INCORRECT ANSWER!
26
27        average = ( double ) total / count;
28        System.out.println( "\nTypecast one variable to double, "
29                               +  "then perform division" );
30        System.out.println( "The average test score is " + average );
31        // 91.25 CORRECT ANSWER
32    }
33 }
```

EXAMPLE 2.10   Mixed Data Type Arithmetic

Line 15 first attempts to calculate the average but results in a wrong answer because both *total* and *count* are integers. So integer division is performed, which truncates any remainder. Thus, the result of *total* / *count* is 91. Then 91 is assigned to *average*, which is a *double*, so 91 becomes 91.0.

Line 21 is a second attempt to calculate the average; again, this code does not work correctly because the parentheses force the division to be performed before the type casting. Thus, because *total* and *count* are both integers, integer division is performed again. The quotient, 91, is then cast to a *double*, 91.0, and that *double* value is assigned to *average*.

At line 27, we correct this problem by casting only one of the operands to a *double*. This forces the other operand to be promoted to a *double*. Then floating-point division is performed, which retains the remainder. It doesn't matter whether we cast *total* or *count* to a *double*. Casting either to a *double* forces the division to be a floating-point division.

Figure 2.9
Output of Example 2.10

```
The area is 50.26544

Performing integer division, then implicit typecasting
The average test score is 91.0

Performing integer division, then explicit typecasting
The average test score is 91.0

Typecast one variable to double, then perform division
The average test score is 91.25
```

CODE IN ACTION

To see the calculation of an average using mixed data types, look for the Chapter 2 Flash movie on the CD-ROM accompanying this book. Click on the link for Chapter 2 to view the movie.

2.3.8   Shortcut Operators

A common operation in programming is adding 1 to a number (**incrementing**) or subtracting 1 from a number (**decrementing**). For example, if you were counting how many data items the user entered, every time you read another data item, you would add 1 to a count variable.

Because incrementing or decrementing a value is so common in programming, Java provides shortcut operators to do this: ++ and −−. (Note that there are no spaces between the two plus and minus signs.) The statement

```
count++;
```

adds 1 to the value of *count*, and the statement

```
count−−;
```

subtracts 1 from the value of *count*. Thus,

```
count++;
```

is equivalent to

```
count = count + 1;
```

and

```
count--;
```

is equivalent to

```
count = count - 1;
```

Both of these operators have **prefix** and **postfix** versions. The prefix versions precede the variable name (++a or --a) whereas the postfix versions follow the variable name (a++ or a--). Both increment or decrement the variable. If they are used as a single, atomic statement (as in the preceding statements), there is no difference between the two versions. So

```
a++;
```

is functionally equivalent to

```
++a;
```

and

```
a--;
```

is functionally equivalent to

```
--a;
```

However, if they are used inside a more complex expression, then they differ as follows. The prefix versions increment or decrement the variable first, then the new value of the variable is used in evaluating the expression. The postfix versions increment or decrement the variable after the old value of the variable is used in the expression.

Example 2.11 illustrates this difference.

```
1 /* ShortcutOperators Class
2     Anderson, Franceschi
3 */
4
5 public class ShortcutOperators
6 {
7   public static void main( String [ ] args )
8   {
9     int a = 6;
10    int b = 2;
11
12    System.out.println( "At the beginning, a is " + a );
13    System.out.println( "Increment a with prefix notation: " + ++a );
14    System.out.println( "In the end, a is " + a );
```

```
15
16     System.out.println( "\nAt the beginning, b is " + b );
17     System.out.println( "Increment b with postfix notation: " + b++ );
18     System.out.println( "In the end, b is " + b );
19  }
20 }
```

EXAMPLE 2.11   Prefix and Postfix Increment Operators

Lines 9 and 10 declare and initialize two *int* variables, *a* and *b*, to 6 and 2, respectively. In order to illustrate the effect of both the prefix and postfix increment operators, we output their original values at lines 12 and 16. At line 13, we use the prefix increment operator to increment *a* inside an output statement; *a* is incremented before the output statement is executed, resulting in the output statement using the value 7 for *a*. At line 17, we use the postfix increment operator to increment *b* inside an output statement; *b* is incremented after the output statement is executed, resulting in the output statement using the value 2 for *b*. Lines 14 and 18 simply output the values of *a* and *b* after the prefix and postfix operators were used at lines 13 and 17. Figure 2.10 shows the output of this example.

Another set of shortcut operators simplify common calculations that change a single value. For example, the statement

```
a = a + 2: // add 2 to a
```

can be simplified as

```
a += 2; // add 2 to a
```

The value added to the target variable can be a variable name or a larger expression.

Figure 2.10

Output of Example 2.11

```
At the beginning, a is 6
Increment a with prefix notation: 7
In the end, a is 7

At the beginning, b is 2
Increment b with postfix notation: 2
In the end, b is 3
```

The shortcut addition operator (+=) is a single operator; there are no spaces between the + and the =. Also, be careful not to reverse the order of the operators. For example, in the following statement, the operators are reversed, so the compiler interprets the statement as "assign a positive 2 to a."

```
a =+ 2 ;  // Incorrect! Assigns a positive 2 to a
```

Java provides shortcut operators for each of the basic arithmetic operations: addition, subtraction, multiplication, division, and modulus. These operators are especially useful in performing repetitive calculations and in converting values from one scale to another. For example, to convert feet to inches, we multiply the number of feet by 12. So we can use the *= shortcut operator:

```
int length = 3; // length in feet
length *= 12;    // length converted to inches
```

Converting from one scale to another is a common operation in programming. For example, earlier in the chapter we converted quarters, dimes, and nickels to pennies. You might also need to convert hours to seconds, feet to square feet, or Fahrenheit temperatures to Celsius.

Example 2.12 demonstrates each of the shortcut arithmetic operators. The output is shown in Figure 2.11.

```
 1 /*  Shortcut Arithmetic Operators
 2      Anderson, Franceschi
 3 */
 4
 5 public class ShortcutArithmeticOperators
 6 {
 7    public static void main( String [ ] args )
 8    {
 9       int a = 5;
10       System.out.println( "a is " + a );
11
12       a += 10;     //  a = a + 10;
13       System.out.println( "\nAfter a += 10;  a is " + a );
14
15       a -= 3;      //  a = a - 3;
16       System.out.println( "\nAfter a -= 3; a is " + a );
17
18       a *= 2;      //  a = a * 2;
19       System.out.println( "\nAfter a *= 2; a is " + a );
20
21       a /= 6;      //  a = a / 6;
```

COMMON ERROR TRAP

No spaces are allowed between the arithmetic operator (+) and the equal sign. Note also that the sequence is +=, not =+.

```
22      System.out.println( "\nAfter a /= 6; a is " + a );
23
24      a %= 3;        //  a = a % 3;
25      System.out.println( "\nAfter a %= 3; a is " + a );
26    }
27 }
```

Example 2.12   Shortcut Arithmetic Operators

Figure 2.11

Output of Example 2.12

```
a is 5

After a += 10; a is 15

After a -= 3; a is 12

After a *= 2; a is 24

After a /= 6; a is 4

After a %= 3; a is 1
```

Table 2.12 summarizes the shortcut operators and Table 2.13 shows where the shortcut operators fit into the order of operator precedence.

TABLE 2.12   Shortcut Operators

Shortcut Operator	Example	Equivalent Statement
++	a++; or ++a;	a = a + 1;
−−	a−−; or −−a;	a = a − 1;
+=	a += 3;	a = a + 3;
−=	a −=10;	a = a − 10;
*=	a *= 4;	a = a • 4;
/=	a /= 7;	a = a / 7;
%=	a %= 10;	a = a % 10;

TABLE 2.13 **Order of Operator Precedence**

Operator Hierarchy	Order of Same-Statement Evaluation	Operation
( )	left to right	parentheses for explicit grouping
++, − −	**right to left**	**shortcut postincrement**
++, − −	**right to left**	**shortcut preincrement**
*, /, %	left to right	multiplication, division, modulus
+, −	left to right	addition or *String* concatenation, subtraction
=, +=, −=, *=, /=, %=	right to left	assignment operator and **shortcut assignment operators**

Skill Practice
with these end-of-chapter questions

2.4   Programming Activity 2: Temperature Conversion

For this Programming Activity, you will write a program to convert a temperature in Fahrenheit to Celsius. The conversion formula is the following:

$$T_c = 5/9\ (T_f - 32)$$

where T_c is the temperature in Celsius and T_f is the temperature in Fahrenheit, and 32 is the freezing point of water.

Locate the *TemperatureConversion.java* source file found in the Chapter 2, Programming Activity 2 folder on the CD-ROM accompanying this book. Copy the file to your computer. The source code is shown in Example 2.13.

```
1 /* Temperature Conversion
2    Anderson, Franceschi
3 */
4
5 public class TemperatureConversion
6 {
7    public static void main( String [] args )
8    {
9       //***** 1. declare any constants here
10
11
12       //***** 2.  declare the temperature in Fahrenheit as an int
13
14
15       //***** 3. calculate equivalent Celsius temperature
16
17
18       //***** 4. output the temperature in Celsius
19
20
21       //***** 5. convert Celsius temperature back to Fahrenheit
22
23
24       //***** 6. output Fahrenheit temperature to check correctness
25
26
27    }
28 }
```

Example 2.13   *TemperatureConversion.java*

Open the *TemperatureConversion.java* source file. You'll notice that the class already contains some source code. Your job is to fill in the blanks.

To verify that your code produces the correct output, add code to convert your calculated Celsius temperature back to Fahrenheit and compare that value to the original Fahrenheit temperature. The formula for converting Celsius to Fahrenheit is:

$$T_f = 9/5 * T_c + 32$$

Before writing this program, you need to design a plan of attack. Ask yourself:

- What data do I need to define?
- What calculations should I make?
- What is the output of the program?
- How do I select data values so they will provide good test data for my code?

Choose any input value for the Fahrenheit temperature. After you write the program, try changing the original temperature value, recompiling and rerunning the program to verify that the temperature conversion works for multiple input values.

? DISCUSSION QUESTIONS

1. How did you change the expression 5 / 9 so that the value was not 0?
2. What constant(s) did you define?
3. What data type did you use for the Celsius temperature? Why?

2.5 Chapter Summary

- Java programs consist of at least one class.
- Identifiers are symbolic names for classes, methods, and data. Identifiers should start with a letter and may contain any combination of letters and digits, but no spaces. The length of an identifier is essentially unlimited. Identifier names are case-sensitive.
- Java's reserved words cannot be used as identifiers.
- The basic building block of a Java program is the statement. A statement is terminated with a semicolon and can span several lines.

SUMMARY

- Any amount of white space is permitted between identifiers, Java keywords, operands, operators, and literals. White space characters are the space, tab, newline, and carriage return.

- A block, which consists of 0, 1, or more statements, starts with a left curly brace and ends with a right curly brace. Blocks can be used anywhere in the program that a statement is legal.

- Comments are ignored by the compiler. Block comments are delineated by /* and */. Line comments start with // and continue to the end of the line.

- Java supports eight primitive data types: *double, float, long, int, short, byte, char,* and *boolean.*

- Variables must be declared before they are used. Declaring a variable is specifying the data item's identifier and data type. The syntax for declaring a variable is: `dataType identifier1, identifier2, ...;`

- Begin variable names with a lowercase letter. If the variable name consists of more than one word, begin each word after the first with a capital letter. Do not put spaces between words.

- An integer data type is one that evaluates to a positive or negative whole number. Java recognizes four integer data types: *int, short, long,* and *byte.*

- Floating-point data types store numbers with fractional parts. Java supports two floating-point data types: the single-precision type *float,* and the double-precision type *double.*

- The *char* data type stores one Unicode character. Because Unicode characters are encoded as unsigned numbers using 16 bits, a *char* variable is stored in two bytes of memory.

- The *boolean* data type can store only two values, which are expressed using the Java reserved words *true* and *false.*

- The assignment operator (=) is used to give a value to a variable.

- To assign an initial value to a variable, use this syntax when declaring the variable:

```
dataType variable1 = initialValue1;
```

- Literals can be used to assign initial values or to reassign the value of a variable.

- Constants are data items whose value, once assigned, cannot be changed. Data items that you know should not change throughout the execution of a program should be declared as a constant, using this syntax:

```
final dataType CONSTANT_IDENTIFIER = initialValue;
```

- Constant identifiers, by convention, are composed of all capital letters with underscores separating words.

- An expression consists of operators and operands that evaluate to a single value.

- The value of an expression can be assigned to a variable or constant, which must be a data type compatible with the value of the expression and cannot be a constant that has been assigned a value already.

- Java provides binary operators for addition, subtraction, multiplication, division, and modulus.

- Calculation of the value of expressions follows the rules of operator precedence.

- Integer division truncates any fractional part of the quotient.

- When an arithmetic operator is invoked with operands that are of different primitive types, the compiler temporarily converts, or promotes, one or both of the operands.

- An expression or a variable can be temporarily cast to a different data type using this syntax:

```
(dataType) ( expression )
```

- Shortcut operators ++ and −− simplify incrementing or decrementing a value by 1. The prefix versions precede the variable name and increment or decrement the variable, then use its new value in evaluation of the expression. The postfix versions follow the variable name and increment or decrement the variable after using the old value in the expression.

- Java provides shortcut operators for each of the basic arithmetic operations: addition, subtraction, multiplication, division, and modulus.

EXERCISES, PROBLEMS, AND PROJECTS

2.6   Exercises, Problems, and Projects

2.6.1   Multiple Choice Exercises

1. What is the valid way to declare an integer variable named *a*? (Check all that apply.)

    ❏ `int a;`

    ❏ `a int;`

    ❏ `integer a;`

2. Which of the following identifiers are valid?

    ❏ `a`

    ❏ `sales`

    ❏ `sales&profit`

    ❏ `int`

    ❏ `inter`

    ❏ `doubleSales`

    ❏ `TAX_RATE`

    ❏ `1stLetterChar`

    ❏ `char`

3. Given three declared and initialized *int* variables *a*, *b*, and *c*, which of the following statements are valid?

    ❏ `a = b;`

    ❏ `a = 67;`

    ❏ `b = 8.7;`

    ❏ `a + b = 8;`

    ❏ `a * b = 12;`

    ❏ `c = a − b;`

    ❏ `c = a / 2.3;`

    ❏ `boolean t = a;`

❑ a /= 4;

❑ a += c;

2.6.2 Reading and Understanding Code

4. What is the output of this code sequence?

```
double a = 12.5;
System.out.println( a );
```

5. What is the output of this code sequence?

```
int a = 6;
System.out.println( a );
```

6. What is the output of this code sequence?

```
float a = 13f;
System.out.println( a );
```

7. What is the output of this code sequence?

```
double a = 13 / 5;
System.out.println( a );
```

8. What is the output of this code sequence?

```
int a = 13 / 5;
System.out.println( a );
```

9. What is the output of this code sequence?

```
int a = 13 % 5;
System.out.println( a );
```

10. What is the output of this code sequence?

```
int a = 12 / 6 * 2;
System.out.println( a );
```

11. What is the output of this code sequence?

```
int a = 12 / ( 6 * 2 );
System.out.println( a );
```

12. What is the output of this code sequence?

```
int a = 4 + 6 / 2;
System.out.println( a );
```

13. What is the output of this code sequence?

```
int a = ( 4 + 6 ) / 2;
System.out.println( a );
```

14. What is the output of this code sequence?

```
double a = 12.0 / 5;
System.out.println( a );
```

15. What is the output of this code sequence?

```
int a = (int) 12.0 / 5;
System.out.println( a );
```

16. What is the output of this code sequence?

```
double a = (double) ( 12 ) / 5;
System.out.println( a );
```

17. What is the output of this code sequence?

```
double a = (double) ( 12 / 5 );
System.out.println( a );
```

18. What is the output of this code sequence?

```
int a = 5;
a++;
System.out.println( a );
```

19. What is the output of this code sequence?

```
int a = 5;
System.out.println( a-- );
```

20. What is the output of this code sequence?

```
int a = 5;
System.out.println( --a );
```

21. What is the output of this code sequence?

```
int a = 5;
a += 2;
System.out.println( a );
```

22. What is the output of this code sequence?

```
int a = 5;
a /= 6;
System.out.println( a );
```

2.6.3   Fill In the Code

23. Write the code to declare a *float* variable named *a* and assign *a* the value 34.2.

```
// your code goes here
```

24. Write the code to assign the value 10 to an *int* variable named *a*.

```
int a;
// your code goes here
```

25. Write the code to declare a *boolean* variable named *a* and assign *a* the value *false*.

```
// your code goes here
```

26. Write the code to declare a *char* variable named *a* and assign *a* the character B.

```
// your code goes here
```

27. Write the code to calculate the total of three *int* variables *a*, *b*, and *c* and print the result.

```
int a = 3;
int b = 5;
int c = 8;

// your code goes here
```

28. Write the code to calculate the average of two *int* variables *a* and *b* and print the result. The average should be printed as a floating-point number.

```
int a = 3;
int b = 5;

// your code goes here
```

29. Write the code to calculate and print the remainder of the division of two *int* variables with the values 10 and 3 (the value printed will be 1).

```
int a = 10;
int b = 3;

// your code goes here
```

30. This code increases the value of a variable *a* by 1, using the shortcut increment operator.

```
int a = 7;

// your code goes here
```

31. This code multiplies the value of a variable *a* by 3, using a shortcut operator.

```
int a = 7;

// your code goes here
```

32. Assume that we have already declared and initialized two *int* variables, *a* and *b*. Convert the following sentences to legal Java expressions and statements.

   ❑ b gets a plus 3 minus 7

   ❑ b gets a times 4

   ❑ a gets b times b

   ❑ a gets b times 3 times 5

   ❑ b gets the quotient of the division of a by 2

   ❑ b gets the remainder of the division of a by 3

2.6.4 Identifying Errors in Code

33. Where is the error in this code sequence?

```
int a = 3.3;
```

34. Where is the error in this code sequence?

```
double a = 45.2;
float b = a;
```

35. Where is the error in this code sequence?

```
int a = 7.5 % 3;
```

36. What would happen when this code sequence is compiled and executed?

```
int a = 5 / 0;
```

37. Where is the error in this code sequence?

```
int a = 5;
a - = 4;
```

38. Is there an error in this code sequence? Explain.

```
char c = 67;
```

39. Is there an error in this code sequence? Explain.

```
boolean a = 1;
```

2.6.5 Debugging Area—Using Messages from the Java Compiler and Java JVM

40. You coded the following on line 8 of class *Test.java*:

```
int a = 26.4;
```

When you compile, you get the following message:

```
Test.java:8: possible loss of precision
    int a = 26.4;
            ^
    required: int
    found : double
1 error
```

Explain what the problem is and how to fix it.

41. You coded the following on line 8 of class *Test.java*:

```
int a = 3
```

When you compile, you get the following message:

```
Test.java:8: ';' expected
        int a = 3
                 ^
```

Explain what the problem is and how to fix it.

42. You coded the following in class *Test.java*:

```
int a = 32;
int b = 10;
double c = a / b;
System.out.println( "The value of c is " + c );
```

The code compiles properly and runs, but the result is not what you expected. The output is

```
The value of c is 3.0
```

You expected the value of *c* to be 3.2. Explain what the problem is and how to fix it.

43. You coded the following in class *Test.java*:

```
int a = 5;
a =+ 3;
System.out.println( "The value of a is " + a );
```

The code compiles properly and runs, but the result is not what you expected. The output is

```
The value of a is 3
```

You expected the value of *a* to be 8. Explain what the problem is and how to fix it.

2.6.6   Write a Short Program

44. Write a program that calculates and outputs the square of each integer from 1 to 9.

45. Write a program that calculates and outputs the average of integers 1, 7, 9, and 34.

46. Write a program that outputs the following:

```
****
```

2.6.7   Programming Projects

47. Write a program that prints the letter X composed of asterisks (*). Your output should look like this:

```
*     *
 *   *
   *
 *   *
*     *
```

48. Write a program that converts 10, 50, and 100 kilograms to pounds (1 lb = 0.454 kg).

49. Write a program that converts 2, 5, and 10 inches to millimeters (1 inch = 25.4 mm).

50. Write a program to compute and output the perimeter and the area of a circle having a radius of 3.2 inches.

2.6.8 Technical Writing

51. Some programmers like to write code that is as compact as possible, for instance, using the increment (or decrement) operator in the middle of another statement. Typically, these programmers document their programs with very few comments. Discuss whether this is a good idea, keeping in mind that a program "lives" through a certain period of time.

52. Compare the following data types for integer numbers: *int*, *short*, and *long*. Discuss their representation in binary, how much space they take in memory, and the purpose of having these data types available to programmers.

CHAPTER 3

Object-Oriented Programming, Part 1: Using Classes

CHAPTER CONTENTS

Introduction

Writing computer programs that use classes and objects is called **object-oriented programming**, or **OOP**. Every Java program consists of at least one class.

In this chapter, we'll introduce object-oriented programming as a way to use classes that have already been written. Classes provide services to the program. These services might include writing a message to the program's user, popping up a dialog box, performing some mathematical calculations, formatting numbers, drawing shapes in a window, or many other basic tasks that add a more professional look to even simple programs. The program that uses a class is called the **client** of the class.

One benefit of using a prewritten class is that we don't need to write the code ourselves; it has already been written and tested for us. This means that we can write our programs more quickly. In other words, we shorten the development time of the program. Using prewritten and pretested classes provides other benefits as well, including more reliable programs with fewer errors.

In Chapter 7, we'll show you how to write your own classes. For now, we'll explore how using prewritten classes can add functionality to our programs.

3.1   Class Basics and Benefits

In Java, classes are composed of data and operations—or functions—that operate on the data. Objects of a class are created using the class as a template, or guide. Think of the class as a generic description, and an object as a specific item of that class. Or you can think of a class as a cookie cutter; the objects of that class are the cookies made with the cookie cutter. For example, a *Student* class might have the following data: name, year, and grade point average. All students have these three data items. We can create an object of the *Student* class by specifying an identifier for the object (for example, *student1*) along with a name, year, and grade point average for a particular student (for example, *Maria Gonzales, Sophomore, 3.5*). The identifier of the object is called the **object reference**. Creating an object of a class is called **instantiating an object**, and the object is called an **instance of the class**. Many objects can be instantiated from one class. There can be many instances of the *Student* class, that is, many *Student* objects can be instantiated from the *Student* class. For example, we could create a second object of the *Student* class, *student2*, with its data as *Mike Smith, Junior, 3.0*.

The data associated with an object of a class are called **instance variables**, or **fields**, and can be variables and constants of any primitive data type (*byte, short, int, long, float, double, char,* and *boolean*), or they can be objects of other classes.

The operations for a class, called **methods**, set the values of the data, retrieve the current values of the data, and perform other class-related functions on the data. For example, the *Student* class would provide methods to set the values of the name, year, and grade point average; retrieve the current values of the name, year, and grade point average; and perhaps promote a student to the next year. Invoking a method on an object is called **calling the method**. With a few exceptions, only class methods can directly access or change the instance variables of an object. Other objects must call the methods to set or retrieve the values of the instance variables. Together, the fields and methods of a class are called its **members**.

In essence, a class is a new data type, which is created by combining items of Java primitive data types and objects of other classes. Just as the primitive data types can be manipulated using arithmetic operators (+, −, *, /, and %), objects can be manipulated by calling class methods.

We like to think of classes as similar to M&M™ candies: a protective outer coating around a soft center. Because the methods to operate on the data are included in the class, they provide a protective coating around the data inside. In a well-designed class, only the class methods can change the data. Methods of other classes cannot directly access the data. We say that the data is *private* to the class. In other words, the class **encapsulates** the data and the methods provide the only interface for setting or changing the data values. The benefit from this encapsulation is that the class methods ensure that only valid values are assigned to an object. For example, a method to set a student's grade point average would accept values only between 0.0 and 4.0.

Let's look at another example of a class. The *SimpleDate* class, written by the authors, has the instance variables *month, day,* and *year*. An object of this class, *independenceDay*, could be instantiated with data values of *7, 4,* and *1776*. Another object of that class, *examDay*, might be instantiated with the values *12, 4,* and *2006.* Methods of the *SimpleDate* class ensure that only valid values are set for the month, day, and year. For example, the class methods would not allow us to set a date with a value of January 32. Other class methods increment the date to the next day and provide the date in *mm/dd/yyyy* format.

Notice that the class names we used, *Student* and *SimpleDate,* begin with a capital letter, and the object names, *student1, independenceDay,* and *examDay,* start with a lowercase letter. By convention, class names start with a capital letter. Object names, instance variables, and method names conventionally start with a lowercase letter. Internal words start with a capital letter in class names, object names, variables, and methods.

There are many benefits to using classes in a program. Some of the most important benefits include reusability (not only in the current program but also in other programs), encapsulation, and reliability.

A well-written class can be reused in many programs. For example, a *SimpleDate* class could be used in a calendar program, an appointment-scheduling program, an online shopping program, and many more applications that rely on dates. Reusing code is much faster than writing and testing new code. As an added bonus, reusing a tested and debugged class in another program makes the program more reliable.

Encapsulation of a class's data and methods helps to isolate operations on the data. This makes it easier to track the source of a bug. For example, when a bug is discovered in an object of the *Student* class, then you know to look for the problem in the methods of the *Student* class, because no other code in your program can directly change the data in a *Student* object.

You do not need to know the implementation details of a class in order to use it in your program. Does the *SimpleDate* class store the date in memory as three integers, *month, day,* and *year*? Or is the date stored as the number of milliseconds since 1980? The beauty of object orientation is that we don't need to know the implementation of the class; all we need to know is the class **application programming interface (API)**, that is, how to instantiate objects and how to call the class methods.

The benefits of using classes are clear. We will leave the details of creating our own classes until Chapter 7. In the meantime, let's explore how to use classes that are already written.

3.2   Creating Objects Using Constructors

A class describes a generic template for creating, or instantiating, objects. In fact, an object must be instantiated before it can be used. To understand how to instantiate an object of a class and how to call methods of the class, you must know the API of a class, which the creators of the class make public. Table 3.1 shows the API of the *SimpleDate* class, written by the authors of this textbook.

Instantiating an object consists of defining an object reference—which will hold the address of the object in memory—and calling a special method of the class called a **constructor**, which has the same name as the class. The job of the constructor is to assign initial values to the data of the class.

Example 3.1 illustrates how to instantiate objects of the *SimpleDate* class.

```
 1 /*  A Demonstration of Using Constructors
 2      Anderson, Franceschi
 3 */
 4
 5 public class Constructors
 6 {
 7    public static void main( String [ ] args )
 8    {
 9      SimpleDate independenceDay;
10      independenceDay = new SimpleDate( 7, 4, 1776 );
11
12      SimpleDate graduationDate = new SimpleDate( 5, 15, 2012 );
13
14      SimpleDate defaultDate = new SimpleDate( );
15    }
16 }
```

EXAMPLE 3.1   Demonstrating Constructors

Declaring an object reference is very much like declaring a variable of a primitive type; you specify the data type and an identifier. For example, to declare an integer variable named *number1*, you provide the data type (*int*) and the identifier (*number1*), as follows:

```
int number1;
```

TABLE 3.1   The *SimpleDate* Class API

SimpleDate Class Constructor Summary
SimpleDate( )
creates a *SimpleDate* object with initial default values of 1, 1, 2000.
SimpleDate(int mm, int dd, int yy)
creates a *SimpleDate* object with the initial values of *mm*, *dd*, and *yy*.

SimpleDate Class Method Summary	
Return value	**Method name and argument list**
int	getMonth( ) returns the value of *month*
int	getDay( ) returns the value of *day*
int	getYear( ) returns the value of *year*
void	setMonth(int mm) sets the *month* to *mm*; if *mm* is invalid, sets *month* to 1
void	setDay(int dd) sets the *day* to *dd*; if *dd* is invalid, sets *day* to 1
void	setYear(int yy) sets the *year* to *yy*
void	nextDay( ) increments the date to the next day
String	toString( ) returns the value of the date in the form: *month/day/year*
boolean	equals(Object obj) compares this *SimpleDate* object to another *Simple-Date* object

One notable difference in declaring an object reference is that its data type is a class, not a primitive data type. Here is the syntax for declaring an object reference:

```
ClassName objectReference1, objectReference2, ...;
```

In Example 3.1, lines 9, 12, and 14 declare object references for a *Simple-Date* object. *SimpleDate*, the class name, is the data type, and *independence-Day*, *graduationDate*, and *defaultDate* are the object references.

Object references can refer to **any** object of its class. For example, *Simple-Date* object references can point to any *SimpleDate* object, but a *SimpleDate* object reference cannot point to objects of other classes, such as a *Student* object.

Once an object reference has been declared, you instantiate the object using the following syntax:

```
objectReference = new ClassName( argument list );
```

This calls a constructor of the class to initialize the data. The **argument list** consists of a comma-separated list of initial data values to assign to the object. Classes often provide multiple constructors with different argument lists. Depending on which constructor you call, you can accept default values for the data or specify initial values for the data. When you instantiate an object, your argument list—that is, the number of arguments and their data types—must match one of the constructors' argument lists.

As shown in Table 3.1, the *SimpleDate* class has two constructors. The first constructor, *SimpleDate( )*, is called the **default constructor**, because its **argument list is empty**. This constructor assigns default values to all data in the object. Thus, in line 14 of Example 3.1, which uses the default constructor, the data for the *defaultDate* object is set to the default values for the *SimpleDate* class, which are *1*, *1*, and *2000*.

We see from Table 3.1 that the second constructor for the *SimpleDate* class, *SimpleDate(int mm, int dd, int yy)*, takes three arguments, all of which should evaluate to integer values. The first argument is the value for the month, the second argument is the value for the day, and the third argument is the value for the year.

Lines 10 and 12 of Example 3.1 instantiate *SimpleDate* objects using the second constructor. In line 10, the argument list tells the constructor to give the value *7* to the month, *4* to the day, and *1776* to the year. In line 12, the argument list tells the constructor to give the value *5* to the month, *15* to the day, and *2012* to the year. Note that no data types are given in the argument list, only the initial values for the data. The data types of the arguments are specified in the API so that the client of the class knows what data types the constructor is expecting for its arguments.

Lines 12 and 14 also illustrate that you can combine the declaration of the object reference and instantiation of the object in a single statement.

When an object is instantiated, the JVM allocates memory to the new object and assigns that memory location to its object reference. Figure 3.1 shows the three objects instantiated in Example 3.1.

Figure 3.1

Three *SimpleDate* Objects after Instantiation

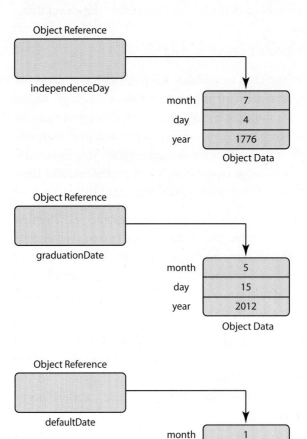

It's important to understand that an object reference and the object data are different: The object reference represents the memory location, and the object data are the data stored at that memory location. Notice in Figure 3.1 that the object references, *independenceDay*, *graduationDate*, and *defaultDate*, point to the locations of the object data.

3.3   Calling Methods

Once an object is instantiated, we can use the object by calling its methods. As we mentioned earlier, the authors of classes publish their API so that their clients know what methods are available and how to call those methods.

Figure 3.2 illustrates how calling a class method alters the flow of control in your program. When this program starts running, the JVM executes instruction 1, then instruction 2, then it encounters a method call. At that

COMMON ERROR TRAP

Do not forget to instantiate all objects that your program needs. Objects must be instantiated before they can be used.

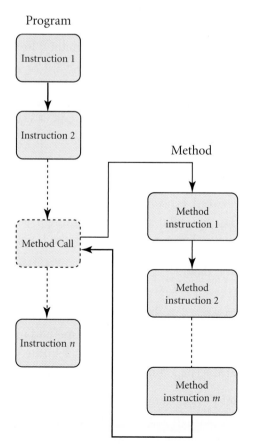

Figure 3.2
Flow of Control of a Method Call

point, the JVM **transfers control to the method** and starts executing instructions in the method. When the method finishes executing, the JVM transfers control back to the program immediately after the point the method was called and continues executing instructions in the program.

A class API consists of the class method names, their return values, and their argument lists. The argument list for a method indicates the order and number of arguments to send to the method, along with the data type of each argument. Each item in the argument list consists of a data type and a name. The arguments can be literals, constants, variables, or any expression that evaluates to the data type specified in the API of the method. For example, the API in Table 3.1 shows that the *setMonth* method takes one argument, which must evaluate to an integer value.

A method may or may not return a value, as indicated by a data type, class type, or the keyword **void** in front of the method name. If the method returns a value, then the data type or class type of its **return value** will precede the method's name. For instance, in Table 3.1, the *getDay* method returns an integer value. The call to a **value-returning method** will be used in an expression. When the method finishes executing, its return value will replace the method call in the expression. If the keyword *void* precedes the method name, the method does not return a value. Because methods with a *void* return type have no value, they cannot be used in an expression; instead, a method call to a method with a *void* return type is a complete statement. In Table 3.1, the *setYear* method is a *void* method.

Another keyword you will see preceding the method call in an API is *public*. This keyword means that any client of the class can call this method. If the keyword *private* precedes the method name, only other methods of that class can call that method. Although we will not formally include the *public* keyword in the API, all the methods we discuss in this chapter are *public*.

To call a method for an object of a class, we use **dot notation**, as follows:

```
objectReference.methodName( arg1, arg2, arg3, . . . )
```

The object reference is followed immediately by a **dot** (a period), which is followed immediately by the method name. (Later in the chapter, when we call *static* methods, we will substitute the class name for the object reference.) The arguments for the method are enclosed in parentheses.

Let's look again at the methods of the *SimpleDate* class. The first three methods in the *SimpleDate* class API take an empty argument list and return an *int*; thus, those methods have a return value of type *int*. You can call these methods in any expression in your program where you could use an *int*. The value of the first method, *getMonth( )*, is the value of the month in the object. Similarly, the value of *getDay( )* is the value of the day in the object, and the value of *getYear( )* is the value of the year. These "get" methods are formally called **accessor methods**; they enable clients to access the value of the instance variables of an object.

The next three methods in the *SimpleDate* class API take one argument of type *int* and do not return a value, which is indicated by the keyword *void*. These methods are called in standalone statements. The first method, *setMonth(int mm)*, changes the value of the month in the object to the value of the method's argument, *mm*. Similarly, *setDay(int dd)* changes the value of the day in the object, and *setYear(int yy)* changes the value of the year in the object to the value of the method's argument. These "set" methods are formally called **mutator methods**; they enable a client to change the value of the instance variables of an object.

Example 3.2 illustrates how to use some of the methods of the *SimpleDate* class. Line 10 calls the *getMonth* method for the *independenceDay* object. When line 10 is executed, control transfers to the *getMonth* method. When the *getMonth* method finishes executing, the value it returns (7) replaces the method call in the statement. The statement then effectively becomes:

```
int independenceMonth = 7;
```

In lines 15–16, we print the value of the day in the *graduationDate* object. Again, control transfers to the *getDay* method, then its return value (15) replaces the method call. So the statement effectively becomes:

```
System.out.println( "The current day for graduation is "
                    + 15 );
```

Line 18 calls the *setDay* method, which is used to change the value of the day for an object. The *setDay* method takes one *int* argument and has a *void* return value. Line 18 is a complete statement, because the method call to a method with a *void* return value is a complete statement. The method changes the value of the day in the *graduationDate* object, which we illustrate in lines 19–20 by printing the new value as shown in Figure 3.3. Then, on line 22, we instantiate another object, *currentDay*, with a day, month, and year of 9, 30, 2008, which we demonstrate by printing the values returned by calls to the *getDay, getMonth,* and *getYear* methods. On line 28, we call the *nextDay* method, which has a *void* return value, and increments the date to the next day, and then we print the new values of the *currentDay* object.

 COMMON ERROR TRAP

When calling a method that takes no arguments, remember to include the empty parentheses after the method's name. The parentheses are required even if there are no arguments.

 COMMON ERROR TRAP

When calling a method, include only values or expressions in your argument list. Including data types in your argument list will cause a compiler error.

```
 1 /*  A demonstration of calling methods
 2     Anderson, Franceschi
 3 */
 4
 5 public class Methods
 6 {
 7   public static void main( String [ ] args )
 8   {
 9     SimpleDate independenceDay = new SimpleDate( 7, 4, 1776 );
10     int independenceMonth = independenceDay.getMonth( );
11     System.out.println( "Independence day is in month "
12                         + independenceMonth );
13
14     SimpleDate graduationDate = new SimpleDate( 5, 15, 2008 );
15     System.out.println( "The current day for graduation is "
16                         + graduationDate.getDay( ) );
17
18     graduationDate.setDay( 12 );
19     System.out.println( "The revised day for graduation is "
20                         + graduationDate.getDay( ) );
21
22     SimpleDate currentDay = new SimpleDate( 9, 30, 2008 );
23     System.out.println( "The current day is "
24                         + currentDay.getMonth( ) + '/'
25                         + currentDay.getDay( ) + '/'
26                         + currentDay.getYear( ) );
27
28     currentDay.nextDay( );
29     System.out.println( "The next day is "
30                         + currentDay.getMonth( ) + '/'
31                         + currentDay.getDay( ) + '/'
32                         + currentDay.getYear( ) );
33   }
34 }
```

EXAMPLE 3.2   Calling Methods

Figure 3.3

Output of Example 3.2

```
Independence day is in month 7
The current day for graduation is 15
The revised day for graduation is 12
The current day is 9/30/2008
The next day is 10/1/2008
```

For now, we'll postpone discussion of the last two methods in the class API, *toString* and *equals*, except to say that their functions, respectively, are to convert the object data to a printable format and to compare the object data to another object's data. All classes provide these methods.

Skill Practice
with these end-of-chapter questions

3.19.1 Multiple Choice Exercises

Questions 2, 3, 4, 5, 9, 10

3.19.8 Technical Writing

Questions 69, 70

3.4 Using Object References

As we have mentioned, an object reference points to the data of an object. The object reference and the object data are distinct entities. Any object can have more than one object reference pointing to it, or an object can have no object references pointing to it.

In Example 3.3, two *SimpleDate* object references, *hireDate* and *promotionDate*, are declared and their objects are instantiated at lines 9 and 14. Lines 10–12 and 15–18 output the respective data member values of *hireDate* and *promotionDate*. Then, line 20 uses the assignment operator to copy the object reference *hireDate* to the object reference *promotionDate*. After line 20, both object references have the same value and therefore point to the location of the same object, as shown in Figure 3.4. The second object, with values (9, 28, 2007), no longer has an object reference pointing to it and is now marked for **garbage collection**. The **garbage collector**, which is part of the JVM, releases the memory allocated to objects that no longer have an

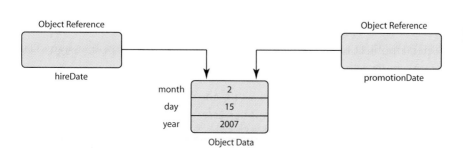

Figure 3.4

Two Object References Pointing to the Same Object

object reference pointing to them. Lines 23–25 and 26–29 output the respective data member values of *hireDate* and *promotionDate* again. These are now identical, as shown in Figure 3.5.

```
1 /*  A demonstration of object reference assignment
2      Anderson, Franceschi
3 */
4
5 public class ObjectReferenceAssignment
6 {
7   public static void main( String [ ] args )
8   {
9       SimpleDate hireDate = new SimpleDate( 2, 15, 2007 );
10      System.out.println( "hireDate is " + hireDate.getMonth( )
11                          + "/" + hireDate.getDay( )
12                          + "/" + hireDate.getYear( ) );
13
14      SimpleDate promotionDate = new SimpleDate( 9, 28, 2007 );
15      System.out.println( "promotionDate is "
16                          + promotionDate.getMonth( )
17                          + "/" + promotionDate.getDay( )
18                          + "/" + promotionDate.getYear( ) );
19
20      promotionDate = hireDate;
21      System.out.println( "\nAfter assigning hireDate "
22                          + "to promotionDate:" );
23      System.out.println( "hireDate is " + hireDate.getMonth( )
24                          + "/" + hireDate.getDay( )
25                          + "/" + hireDate.getYear( ) );
26      System.out.println( "promotionDate is "
27                          + promotionDate.getMonth( )
28                          + "/" + promotionDate.getDay( )
29                          + "/" + promotionDate.getYear( ) );
30  }
31 }
```

EXAMPLE 3.3   Demonstrating Object Reference Assignments

When an object reference is first declared, but has not yet been assigned to an object, its value is a special literal value, **null**.

If you attempt to call a method using an object reference whose value is *null*, Java generates either a compiler error or a run-time error called an

Figure 3.5
Output of Example 3.3

```
hireDate is 2/15/2007
promotionDate is 9/28/2007

After assigning hireDate to promotionDate:
hireDate is 2/15/2007
promotionDate is 2/15/2007
```

exception. The exception is a *NullPointerException* and results in a series of messages printed on the Java console indicating where in the program the *null* object reference was used. Line 10 of Example 3.4 will generate a compiler error, as shown in Figure 3.6, because *aDate* has not been instantiated.

```
1  /*  A demonstration of trying to use a null object reference
2      Anderson, Franceschi
3  */
4
5  public class NullReference
6  {
7    public static void main( String [ ] args )
8    {
9      SimpleDate aDate;
10      aDate.setMonth( 5 );
11    }
12 }
```

EXAMPLE 3.4   Attempting to Use a *null* Object Reference

Figure 3.6
Compiler Error from
Example 3.4

```
NullReference.java:10: variable aDate might not have been initialized
    aDate.setMonth( 5 );
    ^

1 error
```

COMMON ERROR TRAP

Using a *null* object reference to call a method will generate either a compiler error or a *NullPointerException* at run time. Be sure to instantiate an object before attempting to use the object reference.

Java does not provide support for explicitly deleting an object. One way to indicate to the garbage collector that your program is finished with an object is to set its object reference to *null*. Obviously, once an object reference has the value *null*, it can no longer be used to call methods.

```
1  /*  A demonstration of trying to use a null object reference
2      Anderson, Franceschi
3  */
4
5  public class NullReference2
6  {
7    public static void main( String [ ] args )
8    {
9      SimpleDate independenceDay = new SimpleDate( 7, 4, 1776 );
10     System.out.println( "The month of independenceDay is "
11                          + independenceDay.getMonth( ) );
12
13     independenceDay = null;  // set object reference to null
14     // attempt to use object reference
15     System.out.println( "The month of independenceDay is "
16                          + independenceDay.getMonth( ) );
17   }
18 }
```

EXAMPLE 3.5   Another Attempt to Use a *null* Object Reference

Example 3.5 shows a *NullPointerException* being generated at run time. Line 9 instantiates the *independenceDay* object, and lines 10–11 print the month. Line 13 assigns *null* to the object reference, and lines 15–16 attempt to print the month again. As Figure 3.7 shows, a *NullPointerException* is generated. Notice that the console message indicates the name of the application class (*NullReference2*), the method *main*, and the line number *15*, where the exception occurred. The JVM often prints additional lines in the message, depending on where in your program the error occurred.

Figure 3.7

Output of Example 3.5

```
The month of independenceDay is 7
Exception in thread "main" java.lang.NullPointerException
    at NullReference2.main(NullReference2.java:15)
```

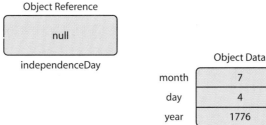

Figure 3.8

The *independenceDay* Object Reference Set to *null*

Figure 3.8 shows the *independenceDay* object reference and object data after setting the object reference to *null*.

3.5   Programming Activity 1: Calling Methods

Let's put this all together with a sample program that uses a *SimpleDate* object. In this Programming Activity, we'll use a program that displays the values of the object data as you instantiate the object and call the methods of the class.

In the Chapter 3 Programming Activity 1 folder on the CD-ROM accompanying this book, you will find three source files: *SimpleDate.java*, *SimpleDateClient.java*, and *Pause.java*. Copy all the *.java* and *.class* files to a directory on your computer. Note that all files should be in the same directory.

Open the *SimpleDateClient.java* source file. You'll notice that the class already contains some source code. Your job is to fill in the blanks. Search for five asterisks in a row (*****). This will position you to the places in the source code where you will add your code. This section of code is shown in Figure 3.9.

Notice that line 15 is a declaration of a *SimpleDate* object reference, *dateObj*. You will use this object reference for instantiating an object and for calling the methods of the *SimpleDate* class.

In the source file, you should see nine commented lines that instruct you to instantiate the object or call a method. You will also notice that there are eight lines that look like this:

```
// animate( "message" );
```

Figure 3.9

Partial Listing of *Simple-DateClient.java*

```
13    private int animationPause = 2; // 2 seconds between animations
14
15    SimpleDate dateObj; // declare Date object reference
16
17    public void workWithDates( )
18    {
19      animate( "dateObj reference declared" );
20
21      /***** Add your code here *****/
22      /**** 1. Instantiate dateObj using an empty argument list  */
23
24
25      //animate( "Instantiated dateObj - empty argument list" );
26
27      /***** 2. Set the month to the month you were born */
28
29
30      //animate( "Set month to birth month" );
31
32
33      /***** 3. Set the day to the day of the month you were born */
34
35
36      //animate( "Set day to birth day" );
37
38
39      /***** 4. Set the year to the year you were born */
40
41
42      //animate( "Set year to birth year" );
43
44
45      /***** 5. Call the nextDay method */
46
47
48      //animate( "Set the date to the next day" );
49
50
51      /***** 6. Set the day to 32, an illegal value */
52
53
54      //animate( "Set day to 32" );
55
56
57      /***** 7. Set the month to 13, an illegal value */
58
59
60      //animate( "Set month to 13" );
61
62
63      /***** 8. Assign the value null to dateObj */
64
65
66      //animate( "Set object reference to null" );
67
68
69      /***** 9. Attempt to set the month to 1 */
70
71    }
```

These lines are calls to an *animate* method in this class that displays the object reference and the object data after you have executed your code. The *message* is a *String* literal that describes what action your code just took. The *animate* method will display the message, as well as the object data. Note that when you call a method in the same class, you don't use an object reference and dot notation.

To complete the Programming Activity, write the requested code on the line between the numbered instruction and the *animate* method call. Then **uncomment** (remove the two slashes from) the *animate* method call.

For example, after you've written the code for the first instruction, lines 22 through 25 should look as follows. The line you write is shown in bold.

```
/* 1. Instantiate a dateObj using empty argument list */

dateObj = new SimpleDate( );
animate( "Instantiated dateObj - empty argument list" );
```

Compile and run the code and you will see a window that looks like the one in Figure 3.10.

As you can see, the *dateObj* reference points to the *SimpleDate* object, and the *month, day,* and *year* instance variables have been assigned default values.

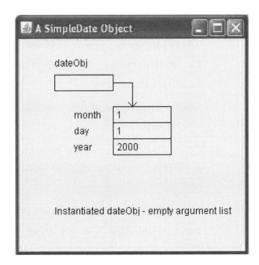

Figure 3.10
Programming Activity 1
Output

Write the code for the remaining instructions, compiling and running the program after completing each task. The program will display the changes you make to the object data.

The pause between animations is set by default to two seconds. To change the pause time, change the value assigned to *animationPause* on line 13 to the number of seconds you would like to pause between animations.

DISCUSSION QUESTIONS ❓

1. After instructions 6 and 7 have executed, why do the day and month values get set to 1?

2. At the end of the execution of the program, a *NullPointerException* is generated. Which statement in the program causes this error? Explain why.

3.6   The Java Class Library

Java provides more than 2,000 predefined classes that you can use to add functionality to your program. In this chapter, we'll discuss a few commonly used Java classes:

- *String,* which provides a data type for character strings, along with methods for searching and manipulating strings

- *Random,* which generates random numbers

- *Scanner,* which provides methods for reading input from the Java console

- *System* and *PrintStream,* which provide data members and methods for printing data on the Java console

- *DecimalFormat* and *NumberFormat,* which allow you to format numbers for output

- *Math,* which provides methods for performing mathematical operations

- Object wrappers, which provide an object equivalent to primitive data types so they can be used in your program as if they were objects

- *JOptionPane,* which allows you to use dialog boxes to display messages to the user or to get input from the user

The Java classes are arranged in **packages**, grouped according to functionality.

TABLE 3.2   Commonly Used Java Packages

Package	Categories of Classes
java.lang	Basic functionality common to many programs, such as the *String* class, *Math* class, and object wrappers for the primitive data types
java.awt	Graphics classes for drawing and using colors, and old-style user interface components
javax.swing	New-style user interface components that have a consistent look and feel across platforms
java.text	Classes for formatting numeric output
java.util	The *Scanner* class, the *Random* class, and other miscellaneous classes
java.io	Classes for reading from and writing to files

Table 3.2 describes some of the Java packages that we will cover in this book. You can find more details on these classes on Oracle's Java website: *www.oracle.com/technetwork/java*.

Many of the commonly used classes, such as *String* and *Math*, reside in the *java.lang* package. Any class in the *java.lang* package is automatically available to your program.

To use a class that is not in the *java.lang* package, you need to tell the compiler in which package the class resides; in other words, you need to tell the compiler where to find the class definition. To do this, you include an **import** statement in your program. The *import* statement is inserted at the top of the program after your introductory comments, but before the *class* statement that begins the program. (Yes, we've defined classes already in the programs we wrote in the previous two chapters.)

For example, if you want to use the *DecimalFormat* class to format a floating-point number for output, you would import the *DecimalFormat* class from the *java.text* package as follows:

```
import java.text.DecimalFormat;
```

If you're using more than one class from a package, you can import the whole package by using an asterisk in place of the class name, as follows:

```
import java.text.*;
```

3.7 The *String* Class

As we've discussed, Java provides the *char* primitive data type, which stores one character. Almost every program, however, needs a data type that stores more than one character. Programs need to process names, addresses, or labels of many kinds. For example, many programs involve a login procedure where the user has to enter a user ID and a password. The program reads the user ID and password, compares them to values stored in a database, and allows the user to continue only if the user ID and password match the database values.

To handle this type of data, Java provides a *String* class. Because the *String* class is part of the *java.lang* package, it is automatically available to any Java program and you do not need to use the *import* statement. The *String* class provides several constructors, as well as a number of methods to manipulate, search, compare, and concatenate *String* objects.

Let's look at two of the *String* class constructors shown in Table 3.3. Example 3.6 shows how to use these two constructors in a program.

```
1 /* Demonstrating the String methods
2     Anderson, Franceschi
3 */
4 public class StringDemo
5 {
6   public static void main ( String [ ] args )
7   {
8     String s1 = new String( "OOP in Java " );
9     System.out.println( "s1 is: " + s1 );
10    String s2 = "is not that difficult. ";
11    System.out.println( "s2 is: " + s2 );
12
13    String s3 = s1 + s2; // new String is s1, followed by s2
14    System.out.println( "s1 + s2 returns: " + s3 );
15
16    System.out.println( "s1 is still: " + s1 ); // s1 is unchanged
```

TABLE 3.3 *String* Class Constructors

String Class Constructor Summary
String(String str)
allocates a *String* object with the value of *str*, which can be a *String* object or a *String* literal
String( )
allocates an empty *String* object

```
17      System.out.println( "s2 is still: " + s2 ); // s2 is unchanged
18
19      String greeting1 = "Hi"; // instantiate greeting1
20      System.out.println( "\nThe length of " + greeting1 + " is "
21                          + greeting1.length( ) );
22
23      String greeting2 = new String( "Hello" ); // instantiate greeting2
24      int len = greeting2.length( );  // len will be assigned 5
25      System.out.println( "The length of " + greeting2 + " is " + len );
26
27      String empty = new String( );
28      System.out.println( "The length of the empty String is "
29                          + empty.length( ) );
30
31      String greeting2Upper = greeting2.toUpperCase( );
32      System.out.println( );
33      System.out.println( greeting2 + " converted to upper case is "
34                          + greeting2Upper );
35
36      String invertedName = "Lincoln, Abraham";
37
38      int comma = invertedName.indexOf( ',' ); // find the comma
39      System.out.println( "\nThe index of " + ',' + " in "
40                          + invertedName + " is " + comma );
41
42      // extract all characters up to comma
43      String lastName = invertedName.substring( 0, comma );
44      System.out.println( "Dear Mr. " + lastName );
45   }
46 }
```

EXAMPLE 3.6   Demonstrating *String* Methods

When this program runs, it will produce the output shown in Figure 3.11.

```
s1 is: OOP in Java
s2 is: is not that difficult.
s1 + s2 returns: OOP in Java is not that difficult.
s1 is still: OOP in Java
s2 is still: is not that difficult.

The length of Hi is 2
The length of Hello is 5
The length of the empty String is 0

Hello converted to upper case is HELLO

The index of , in Lincoln, Abraham is 7
Dear Mr. Lincoln
```

Figure 3.11
Output from Example 3.6

The first constructor

```
String( String str )
```

allocates a *String* object and sets its value to the sequence of characters in the argument *str*, which can be a *String* object or a *String* literal. Line 8 instantiates the *String s1* and sets its value to "OOP in Java". Similarly, line 23 instantiates a *String* named *greeting2*, and assigns it the value "Hello".

The second constructor

```
String( )
```

creates an empty *String*—in other words, a *String* containing no characters. You can add characters to the *String* later. This constructor will come in handy in programs where we build up our output, piece by piece. Line 27 uses the second constructor to instantiate an empty *String* named *empty*.

Additionally, because *Strings* are used so frequently in programs, Java provides special support for instantiating *String* objects without explicitly using the *new* operator. We can simply assign a *String* literal to a *String* object reference. Lines 10 and 19 assign *String* literals to the *s2* and *greeting1* *String* references.

Java also provides special support for appending a *String* to the end of another *String* through the **concatenation operator** (+) and the **shortcut version of the concatenation operator** (+=). This concept is illustrated in Example 3.6. Lines 8–11 declare, instantiate, and print two *String* objects, *s1* and *s2*. Line 13 concatenates *s1* and *s2,* and the resulting *String* is assigned to the *s3 String* reference, which is printed at line 14. Finally, we output *s1* and *s2* again at lines 16 and 17 to illustrate that their values have not changed.

Note that the *String* concatenation operator is the same character as the addition arithmetic operator. In some cases, we need to make clear to the compiler which operator we want to use. For example, this statement uses both the *String* concatenation operator and the addition arithmetic operator:

```
System.out.println( "The sum of 1 and 2 is " + ( 1 + 2 ) );
```

Notice that we put *1 + 2* inside parentheses to let the compiler know that we want to add two *ints* using the addition arithmetic operator (+). The addition will be performed first because of the higher operator precedence of parentheses. Then it will become clear to the compiler that the other +

TABLE 3.4 *String* **Methods**

String **Class Method Summary**	
Return value	**Method name and argument list**
int	length( )
	returns the length of the *String*
String	toUpperCase( )
	converts all letters in the *String* to uppercase
String	toLowerCase( )
	converts all letters in the *String* to lowercase
char	charAt(int index)
	returns the character at the position specified by *index*
int	indexOf(String searchString)
	returns the index of the beginning of the first occurrence of *search-String* or −1 if *searchString* is not found
int	indexOf(char searchChar)
	returns the index of the first occurrence of *searchChar* in the *String* or −1 if *searchChar* is not found
String	substring(int startIndex, int endIndex)
	returns a substring of the *String* object beginning at the character at index *startIndex* and ending at the character at index *endIndex* − 1

operator is intended to be a *String* concatenation operator because its operands are a *String* and an *int*.

Some useful methods of the *String* class are summarized in Table 3.4.

The *length* Method

The *length* method returns the number of characters in a *String*. Sometimes, the number of characters in a user ID is limited, for example, to eight, and this method is useful to ensure that the length of the ID does not exceed the limit.

The *length* method is called using a *String* object reference and the dot operator, as illustrated in lines 21, 24, and 29 of Example 3.6. At lines 21 and 29, the *length* method is called inside an output statement and the respective return values from the *length* method are output. At line 24, we call the *length* method for the *greeting2* object and assign the return value to the *int* variable *len*. Then at line 25, we output the value of the variable *len*. As shown in Figure 3.11, the length of "*Hi*" is 2, the length of "*Hello*" is 5, and the length of the empty *String* is 0.

The *toUpperCase* and *toLowerCase* Methods

The *toUpperCase* method converts all the letters in a *String* to uppercase, while the *toLowerCase* method converts all the letters in a *String* to lowercase. Digits and special characters are unchanged.

At line 31 of Example 3.6, the *toUpperCase* method is called using the object reference *greeting2*, and the return value is assigned to a *String* named *greeting2Upper*, which is then printed at lines 33 and 34.

The *indexOf* Methods

The *indexOf* methods are useful for searching a *String* to see if specific *Strings* or characters are in the *String*. The methods return the location of the first occurrence of a single *char* or the first character of a *String*.

The location, or **index**, of any character in a *String* is counted from the first position in the *String*, which has the index value of 0. Thus in this *String*,

```
String greeting = "Ciao";
```

the *C* is at index 0; the *i* is at index 1; the *a* is at index 2; and the *o* is at index 3. Because indexes begin at 0, the maximum index in a *String* is 1 less than the number of characters in the *String*. So the maximum index for *greeting* is `greeting.length( )`–1, which is 3.

In Example 3.6, line 38 retrieves the index of the first comma in the *String* *invertedName* and assigns it to the *int* variable *comma*; the value of *comma*, here 7, is then output at lines 39 and 40.

The *charAt* and *substring* Methods

The *charAt* and *substring* methods are useful for extracting either a single *char* or a group of characters from a *String*.

The *charAt* method returns the character at a particular index in a *String*. One of the uses of this method is for extracting just the first character of a *String*, which might be advantageous when prompting the user for an answer to a question.

For example, we might ask users if they want to play again. They can answer "y," "yes," or "you bet!" Our only concern is whether the first character is a *y*, so we could use this method to put the first character of their answer into a *char* variable. Assuming the user's answer was previously assigned to a *String* variable named *answerString*, we would use the following statement to extract the first character of *answerString*:

```
char answerChar = answerString.charAt( 0 );
```

In Chapter 5, we'll see how to test whether *answerChar* is a *y*.

The *substring* method returns a group of characters, or **substring**, from a *String*. The original *String* is unchanged. As arguments to the *substring* method, you specify the index at which to start extracting the characters and the index of the first character not to extract. Thus, the *endIndex* argument is one position past the last character to extract. We know this sounds a little awkward, but setting up the arguments this way actually makes the method easier to use, as we will demonstrate.

In Example 3.6, we want to extract the last name in the *String inverted-Name*. Line 38 finds the index of the comma and assigns it to the *int* variable *comma*, then line 43 extracts the substring from the first character (index 0) to the index of the comma (which conveniently won't extract the comma), and assigns it to the *String* variable *lastName*. When the variable *lastName* is output at line 44, its value is *Lincoln*, as shown in Figure 3.11.

When you are calculating indexes and the number of characters to extract, be careful not to specify an index that is not in the *String*, because that will generate a run-time error, *StringIndexOutOfBoundsException*.

 COMMON ERROR TRAP

Specifying a negative start index or a start index past the last character of the *String* will generate a *StringIndexOutOfBounds-Exception*. Specifying a negative end index or an end index greater than the length of the *String* will also generate a *String-IndexOutOfBounds-Exception*.

 REFERENCE POINT

You can read more about the *String* class on Oracle's Java website *www.oracle.com/technetwork/java*.

3.8 Formatting Output with the *DecimalFormat* Class

In a computer program, numbers represent a real-life entity, for instance, a price or a winning percentage. Floating-point numbers, however, are calculated to many decimal places and, as a result of some computations, can end up with more significant digits than our programs need. For example, the price of an item after a discount could look like 3.466666666666666,

TABLE 3.5   A *DecimalFormat* Constructor and the *format* Method

DecimalFormat Class Constructor
DecimalFormat(String pattern)
instantiates a *DecimalFormat* object with the output *pattern* specified in the argument

The *format* Method	
Return value	**Method name and argument list**
String	format(double number)
	returns a *String* representation of *number* formatted according to the *DecimalFormat* object used to call the method

when all we really want to display is $3.47; that is, a leading dollar sign and two significant digits after the decimal point. The *DecimalFormat* class allows you to specify the number of digits to display after the decimal point and to add dollar signs, commas, and percentage signs (%) to your output.

The *DecimalFormat* class is part of the *java.text* package, so to use the *DecimalFormat* class, you should include the following *import* statement in your program:

```
import java.text.DecimalFormat;
```

We can instantiate a *DecimalFormat* object using a simple constructor that takes a *String* object as an argument. This *String* object represents how we want our formatted number to look when it's printed. The API for that constructor is shown in Table 3.5.

The pattern that we use to instantiate the *DecimalFormat* object consists of special characters and symbols and creates a "picture" of how we want the number to look when printed. Some of the more commonly used symbols and their meanings are listed in Table 3.6.

```
1 /* Demonstrating the DecimalFormat class
2     Anderson, Franceschi
3 */
4
5 // import the DecimalFormat class from the java.text package;
6 import java.text.DecimalFormat;
7
```

TABLE 3.6 Special Characters for *DecimalFormat* Patterns

Common Pattern Symbols for a *DecimalFormat* Object	
Symbol	**Meaning**
0	Required digit. Do not suppress 0s in this position.
#	Optional digit. Do not print a leading or terminating digit that is 0.
.	Decimal point.
,	Comma separator.
$	Dollar sign.
%	Multiply by 100 and display a percentage sign.

```
 8 public class DemoDecimalFormat
 9 {
10   public static void main( String [ ] args )
11   {
12     // first, instantiate a DecimalFormat object specifying a
13     // pattern for currency
14     DecimalFormat pricePattern = new DecimalFormat( "$#0.00" );
15
16     double price1 = 78.66666666;
17     double price2 = 34.5;
18     double price3 = .3333333;
19     int price4 = 3;
20     double price5 = 100.23;
21
22     // then print the values using the pattern
23     System.out.println( "The first price is: "
24               + pricePattern.format( price1 ) );
25     System.out.println( "\nThe second price is: "
26               + pricePattern.format( price2 ) );
27     System.out.println( "\nThe third price is: "
28               + pricePattern.format( price3 ) );
29     System.out.println( "\nThe fourth price is: "
30               + pricePattern.format( price4 ) );
31     System.out.println( "\nThe fifth price is: "
32               + pricePattern.format( price5 ) );
33
34     // instantiate another new DecimalFormat object
```

```
35        // for printing percentages
36        DecimalFormat percentPattern = new DecimalFormat( "#0.0%" );
37
38        double average = .980;
39        System.out.println( "\nThe average is: "
40                    + percentPattern.format( average ) );
41        // notice that the average is multiplied by 100
42        // to print a percentage.
43
44
45        // now instantiate another new DecimalFormat object
46        // for printing time as two digits
47        DecimalFormat timePattern = new DecimalFormat( "00" );
48
49        int hours = 5, minutes = 12, seconds = 0;
50        System.out.println( "\nThe time is "
51                    + timePattern.format( hours ) + ":"
52                    + timePattern.format( minutes ) + ":"
53                    + timePattern.format( seconds ) );
54
55        // now instantiate another DecimalFormat object
56        // for printing numbers in the millions.
57        DecimalFormat bigNumber = new DecimalFormat( "#,###" );
58
59        int millions = 1234567;
60        System.out.println( "\nmillions is "
61                    + bigNumber.format( millions ) );
62    }
63 }
```

EXAMPLE 3.7   Demonstrating the *DecimalFormat* Class

Once we have instantiated a *DecimalFormat* object, we format a number by passing it as an argument to the *format* method, shown in Table 3.5. Example 3.7 demonstrates the use of the *DecimalFormat* patterns and calling the *format* method. The output for this program is shown in Figure 3.12.

In Example 3.7, line 14 instantiates the *DecimalFormat* object, *pricePattern*, which will be used to print prices. In the pattern

```
"$#0.00"
```

the first character of this pattern is the dollar sign ($), which we want to precede the price. The # character specifies that leading zeroes should not be printed. The 0 specifies that there should be at least one digit to the left of the decimal point. If there is no value to the left of the decimal point,

Figure 3.12
Output from Example 3.7

```
The first price is: $78.67

The second price is: $34.50

The third price is: $0.33

The fourth price is: $3.00

The fifth price is: $100.23

The average is: 98.0%

The time is 05:12:00

millions is 1,234,567
```

then print a zero. The two 0s that follow the decimal point specify that two digits should be printed to the right of the decimal point; that is, if more than two digits are to the right of the decimal point, round to two digits; if the last digit is a 0, print the zero, and if there is no fractional part to the number, print two zeroes. Using this pattern, we see that in lines 23–24, *price1* is rounded to two decimal places. In lines 25–26, *price2* is printed with a zero in the second decimal place.

In lines 29–30, we print *price4*, which is an integer. The *format* method API calls for a *double* as the argument; however, because all numeric data types can be promoted to a *double*, any numeric data type can be sent as an argument. The result is that two zeroes are added to the right of the decimal point.

Finally, we use the *pricePattern* pattern to print *price5* in lines 31–32, which needs no rounding or padding of extra digits.

Next, line 36 instantiates a *DecimalFormat* object, *percentPattern*, for printing percentages to one decimal point ("#0.0%"). Lines 38–40 define the variable *average*, then print it using the *format* method. Notice that the *format* method automatically multiplies the value of *average* by 100.

REFERENCE POINT

You can read more about the *DecimalFormat* class on Oracle's Java website: *www.oracle.com/ technetwork/java.*

Line 47 defines another pattern, `"00"`, which is useful for printing the time with colons between the hour, minutes, and seconds. When the time is printed on lines 50–53, the hours, minutes, and seconds are padded with a leading zero, if necessary.

Line 57 defines our last pattern, `"#,###"`, which can be used to insert commas into integer values in the thousands and above. Lines 60–61 print the variable *millions* with commas separating the millions and thousands digits. Notice that the pattern is extrapolated for a number that has more digits than the pattern.

3.9   Generating Random Numbers with the *Random* Class

Random numbers come in handy for many operations in a program, such as rolling dice, dealing cards, timing the appearance of a nemesis in a game, or other simulations of seemingly random events.

There's one problem in using random numbers in programs, however: Computers are **deterministic**. In essence, this means that given a specific input to a specific set of instructions, a computer will always produce the same output. The challenge, then, is generating random numbers while using a deterministic system. Many talented computer scientists have worked on this problem, and some innovative and complex solutions have been proposed.

The *Random* class, which is in the *java.util* package, uses a mathematical formula to generate a sequence of numbers, feeding the formula a **seed** value, which determines where in that sequence the set of random numbers will begin. As such, the *Random* class generates numbers that appear to be, but are not truly, random. These numbers are called **pseudorandom** numbers, and they work just fine for our purposes.

Table 3.7 shows a constructor for the *Random* class and a method for retrieving a random integer. The default constructor creates a random number generator using a seed value. Once the random number generator is created, we can ask for a random number by calling the *nextInt* method. Other methods, *nextDouble*, *nextBoolean*, *nextByte*, and *nextLong*, which are not shown in Table 3.7, return a random *double*, *boolean*, *byte*, or *long* value, respectively.

To demonstrate how to use the random number generator, let's take rolling a die as an example. To simulate the roll of a six-sided die, we need to

TABLE 3.7   A *Random* Class Constructor and the *nextInt* Method

Random Class Constructor
Random( )
creates a random number generator

The *nextInt* Method	
Return value	**Method name and argument list**
int	nextInt(int number)
	returns a random integer ranging from 0 up to, but not including, *number* in uniform distribution

simulate random occurrences of the numbers 1 through 6. If we call the *nextInt* method with an argument of 6, it will return an integer between 0 and 5. To get randomly distributed numbers from 1 to 6, we can simply add 1 to the value returned by the *nextInt* method. Thus, if we have instantiated a *Random* object named *random,* we can generate random numbers from 1 to 6, by calling the *nextInt* method in this way:

```
int die = random.nextInt( 6 ) + 1;
```

In general, then, if we want to generate random numbers from n to m, we should call the *nextInt* method with the number of random values we need ($m - n + 1$), and then add the first value of our sequence (n) to the returned value. Thus, this statement generates a random number between 10 and 100 inclusive:

```
int randomNumber =  random.nextInt( 100 - 10 + 1 ) + 10;
```

Line 18 of Example 3.8 will generate a random number between 20 and 200 inclusive.

```
1 /*  A demonstration of the Random class
2      Anderson, Franceschi
3 */
4 import java.util.Random;
5
6 public class RandomNumbers
7 {
8   public static void main( String [ ] args )
```

```
 9  {
10      Random random = new Random( );
11
12      // simulate the roll of a die
13      int die = random.nextInt( 6 ) + 1;
14      System.out.println( "\nThe die roll is " + die );
15
16      // generate a random number between 20 and 200
17      int start = 20, end = 200;
18      int number = random.nextInt( end - start + 1 ) + start;
19      System.out.println( "\nThe random number between " + start
20                          + " and " + end + " is " + number );
21  }
22 }
```

EXAMPLE 3.8   A Demonstration of the *Random* Class

Figure 3.13

Output from Example 3.8

```
The die roll is 2

The random number between 20 and 200 is 117
```

REFERENCE POINT

You can read more about the *Random* class on Oracle's Java website: *www.oracle.com/ technewwork/java*.

When the *RandomNumbers* program executes, it will produce output similar to the window shown in Figure 3.13. The output will vary from one execution of the program to the next because different random numbers will be generated.

3.10   Input from the Console Using the *Scanner* Class

As our programs become more complex, we will need to allow the users of our programs to input data. User input can be read into your program in several ways:

- from the Java console
- from a dialog box
- from a file
- through a Graphical User Interface (GUI)

The Java class library provides classes for all types of data input. In this chapter, we will concentrate on two ways to input data: from the Java console and from a dialog box.

The *Scanner* class provides methods for reading *byte, short, int, long, float, double,* and *String* data types from the Java console. These methods are shown in Table 3.8.

TABLE 3.8   Selected Methods of the *Scanner* Class

A *Scanner* Class Constructor	

```
Scanner( InputStream dataSource )
```

creates a *Scanner* object that will read from the *InputStream dataSource*. To read from the keyboard, we will use the predefined *InputStream System.in*.

Selected Methods of the *Scanner* Class	
Return value	**Method name and argument list**
byte	nextByte( )
	returns the next input as a *byte*
short	nextShort( )
	returns the next input as a *short*
int	nextInt( )
	returns the next input as an *int*
long	nextLong( )
	returns the next input as a *long*
float	nextFloat( )
	returns the next input as a *float*
double	nextDouble( )
	returns the next input as a *double*
boolean	nextBoolean( )
	returns the next input as a *boolean*
String	next( )
	returns the next token in the input line as a *String*
String	nextLine( )
	returns the input line as a *String*

The *Scanner* class is defined in the *java.util* package, so your programs will need to include the following *import* statement:

```
import java.util.Scanner;
```

In order to use the *Scanner* class, you must first instantiate a *Scanner* object and associate it with a data source. We will use the *System.in* input stream, which by default is tied to the keyboard. Thus, our data source for input will be *System.in*. The following statement will instantiate a *Scanner* object named *scan* and associate *System.in* as the data source.

```
Scanner scan = new Scanner( System.in );
```

Once the *Scanner* object has been instantiated, you can use it to call any of the *next.* . . methods to input data from the Java console. The specific *next.* . . method you call depends on the type of input you want from the user. Each of the *next.* . . methods returns a value from the input stream. You will need to assign the return value from the *next.* . . methods to a variable to complete the data input. Obviously, the data type of the variable must match the data type of the value returned by the *next.* . . method.

The *next.* . . methods just perform input. They do not tell the user what data to enter. Before calling any of the *next* methods, therefore, you need to prompt the user for the input you want. You can print a prompt using *System.out.print*, which is similar to using *System.out.println*, except that the cursor remains after the printed text, rather than advancing to the next line.

When writing a prompt for user input, keep several things in mind. First, be specific. If you want the user to enter his or her full name, then your prompt should say just that:

```
Please enter your first and last names.
```

If the input should fall within a range of values, then tell the user which values will be valid:

```
Please enter an integer between 0 and 10.
```

Also keep in mind that users are typically not programmers. It's important to phrase a prompt using language the user understands. Many times, programmers write a prompt from their point of view, as in this bad prompt:

```
Please enter a String:
```

Users don't know, and don't care, about *Strings* or any other data types, for that matter. Users want to know only what they need to enter to get the program to do its job.

When your prompts are clear and specific, the user makes fewer errors and therefore feels more comfortable using your program.

Line 13 of Example 3.9 prompts the user to enter his or her first name. Line 14 captures the user input and assigns the word entered by the user to the *String* variable *firstName*, which is printed in line 15. Similarly, line 17 prompts for the user's age, line 18 captures the integer entered by the user and assigns it to the *int* variable *age*, and line 19 outputs the value of *age*. Reading other primitive data types follows the same pattern. Line 21 prompts for the user's grade point average (a *float* value). Line 22 captures the number entered by the user and assigns it to the *float* variable *gpa*, and line 23 outputs the value of *gpa*.

SOFTWARE ENGINEERING TIP

Provide the user with clear prompts for input. Prompts should be phrased using words the user understands and should describe the data requested and any restrictions on valid input values.

```
1  /*  A demonstration of reading from the console using Scanner
2       Anderson, Franceschi
3  */
4
5  import java.util.Scanner;
6
7  public class DataInput
8  {
9    public static void main( String [ ] args )
10   {
11       Scanner scan = new Scanner( System.in );
12
13       System.out.print( "Enter your first name > " );
14       String firstName = scan.next( );
15       System.out.println( "Your name is " + firstName );
16
17       System.out.print( "\nEnter your age as an integer > " );
18       int age = scan.nextInt( );
19       System.out.println( "Your age is " + age );
20
21       System.out.print( "\nEnter your GPA > " );
22       float gpa = scan.nextFloat( );
23       System.out.println( "Your GPA is " + gpa );
24   }
25 }
```

EXAMPLE 3.9   Reading from the Console Using *Scanner*

Figure 3.14
Data Input with Example 3.9

```
Enter your first name > Syed
Your name is Syed

Enter your age as an integer > 21
Your age is 21

Enter your GPA > 3.875
Your GPA is 3.875
```

When this program executes, the prompt is printed on the console and the cursor remains at the end of the prompt. Figure 3.14 shows the output when these statements are executed and the user enters *Syed*, presses *Enter*, enters 21, presses *Enter*, and enters 3.875, and presses *Enter* again.

The methods *nextByte*, *nextShort*, *nextLong*, *nextDouble*, and *nextBoolean* can be used with the same pattern as *next*, *nextInt*, and *nextFloat*.

> **SOFTWARE ENGINEERING TIP**
>
> End your prompts with some indication that input is expected, and include a trailing space for better readability.

Note that we end our prompt with a space, an angle bracket, and another space. The angle bracket indicates that we are waiting for input, and the spaces separate the prompt from the input. Without the trailing space, the user's input would immediately follow the prompt, which is more difficult to read, as you can see in Figure 3.15.

As you review Table 3.8, you may notice that the *Scanner* class does not provide a method for reading a single character. To do this, we can use the *next* method, which returns a *String*, then extract the first character from the *String* using the *charAt(0)* method call, as shown in Example 3.10. Line 14 inputs a *String* from the user and assigns it to the *String* variable *initialS*, then line 15 assigns the first character of *initialS* to the *char* variable *initial*; *initial* is then output at line 16 as shown in Figure 3.16.

Figure 3.15
Prompt and Input Running Together

```
Enter your age as an integer >21
```

```
1 /*  A demonstration of how to get character input using Scanner
2     Anderson, Franceschi
3 */
4
5 import java.util.Scanner;
6
7 public class CharacterInput
8 {
9   public static void main( String [ ] args )
10  {
11      Scanner scan = new Scanner( System.in );
12
13      System.out.print( "Enter your middle initial > " );
14      String initialS = scan.next( );
15      char initial = initialS.charAt( 0 );
16      System.out.println( "Your middle initial is " + initial );
17  }
18 }
```

EXAMPLE 3.10   Using *Scanner* for Character Input

```
Enter your middle initial > A
Your middle initial is A
```

Figure 3.16
Output of Example 3.10

A *Scanner* object divides its input into sequences of characters called **tokens**, using **delimiters**. The default delimiters are the standard **whitespace** characters, which among others include the space, tab, and newline characters. The complete set of Java whitespace characters is shown in Table 3.9.

By default, when a *Scanner* object tokenizes the input, it skips leading whitespace, then builds a token composed of all subsequent characters until it encounters another delimiter. Thus, if you have this code,

```
System.out.print( "Enter your age as an integer > " );
int age = scan.nextInt( );
```

and the user types, for example, three spaces and a tab, *21*, and a newline:

```
<space><space><space><tab>21<newline>
```

TABLE 3.9   Java Whitespace Characters

Character	Unicode equivalents
space	\u00A0, \u2007, \u202F
tab	\u0009, \u000B
line feed	\u000A
form feed	\u000C
carriage return	\u000D
file, group, unit, and record separators	\u001C, \u001D, \u001E, \u001F

then the *Scanner* object skips the three spaces and the tab, starts building a token with the character *2*, then adds the character *1* to the token, and stops building the token when it encounters the *newline*. Thus, *21* is the resulting token, which the *nextInt* method returns into the *age* variable.

An input line can contain more than one token. For example, if we prompt the user for his or her name and age, and the user enters the following line, then presses *Enter*:

```
<tab>Jon<space>Olsen,<space>21<space>
```

then, the leading whitespace is skipped and the *Scanner* object creates three tokens:

- *Jon*
- *Olsen,*
- *21*

Note that commas are not whitespace, so the comma is actually part of the second token. To input these three tokens, your program would use two calls to the *next* method to retrieve the two *String* tokens and a call to *nextInt* to retrieve the age.

To capture a complete line of input from the user, we use the method *nextLine*. Example 3.11 shows how *nextLine* can be used in a program. Figure 3.17 shows a sample run of the program with the user entering data.

```
1  /*  A demonstration of using Scanner's nextLine method
2      Anderson, Franceschi
3  */
4
5  import java.util.Scanner;
6
7  public class InputALine
8  {
9    public static void main( String [ ] args )
10   {
11     Scanner scan = new Scanner( System.in );
12
13     System.out.print( "Enter a sentence > " );
14     String sentence  = scan.nextLine( );
15     System.out.println( "You said: \"" + sentence + "\"" );
16   }
17 }
```

EXAMPLE 3.11 Using the *nextLine* Method

```
Enter a sentence > Scanner is useful.
You said: "Scanner is useful."
```

Figure 3.17
Output of Example 3.11

REFERENCE POINT

You can read more about the *Scanner* class on Oracle's Java website: *www.oracle.com/ technetwork/java.*

If the user's input (that is, the next token) does not match the data type of the *next...* method call, then an *InputMismatchException* is generated and the program stops. Figure 3.18 demonstrates Example 3.9 when the

```
Enter your first name > Sarah
Your name is Sarah

Enter your age as an integer > a
Exception in thread "main" java.util.InputMismatchException
    at java.util.Scanner.throwFor(Scanner.java:899)
    at java.util.Scanner.next(Scanner.java:1520)
    at java.util.Scanner.nextInt(Scanner.java:2150)
    at java.util.Scanner.nextInt(Scanner.java:2109)
    at DataInput.main(DataInput.java:18)
```

Figure 3.18
An Exception When Input Is Not the Expected Data Type

program calls the *nextInt* method and the user enters a letter, rather than an integer. In Chapter 6, we show you how to avoid this exception.

If the user doesn't type anything when prompted, or if the user types some characters but doesn't press *Enter*, the program will simply wait until the user does press *Enter*.

Skill Practice
with these end-of-chapter questions

3.19.1   Multiple Choice Exercises

Questions 1, 11

3.19.2   Reading and Understanding Code

Questions 14, 15, 16

3.19.3   Fill In the Code

Questions 24, 25, 26, 27

3.19.4   Identifying Errors in Code

Questions 36, 37, 38, 39, 43

3.19.5   Debugging Area

Questions 45, 49

3.19.6   Write a Short Program

Questions 50, 51, 52

3.11   Calling *Static* Methods and Using *Static* Class Variables

Classes can also define **static methods**, which can be called without instantiating an object. These are also called **class methods**. The API of these methods has the keyword *static* before the return type:

```
static dataType methodName( arg1, arg2, . . . )
```

One reason a class may define *static* methods is to provide some quick, one-time functionality without requiring the client to instantiate an object. For example, dialog boxes typically pop up only once in a program. Creating an object for a dialog box, when it is used only once, is a waste of memory and processor time. We'll see later in this chapter how it's possible to create dialog boxes and to perform mathematical calculations without creating an object.

Class, or *static*, methods are invoked using the class name, rather than an object reference, as in the following syntax:

```
ClassName.staticMethodName( argumentList );
```

For example, in this statement:

```
absValue = Math.abs( someNumber );
```

the class name is *Math*, and the *static* method is *abs*, which returns the absolute value of the argument (*someNumber*). We use the class name rather than an object reference, because *static* methods can be called without instantiating an object. Later in this chapter, we will explore some *static* methods of the *Math* class in greater detail.

Because *static* methods can be called without an object being instantiated, *static* methods cannot access the instance variables of the class (because instance variables are object data and exist only after an object has been instantiated). *Static* methods can access **static data**, however, and classes often declare *static* data to be used with *static* methods. *Static* data belong to the class, rather than to a particular object, or instance, of the class.

A common use of *static* class variables is to define constants for commonly used values or for parameters for the *static* class methods. For example, as we'll discuss in Chapter 4, the *Color* class provides *static* constants that can be assigned to a *Color* object reference.

Like *static* methods, *static* constants are also accessed using the class name and dot operator, as in this syntax:

```
ClassName.staticConstant
```

Thus, the *static* constant representing the color blue can be accessed this way:

```
Color.BLUE
```

At first, this may appear to go against our earlier discussion of encapsulation and the restrictions on clients directly accessing object data. Remember we said that the client needed to use accessor ("gets") and mutator ("sets") methods to access object data. The reasoning behind encapsulation is to protect the object data from corruption by the client. However, in this case, the *static* data is constant, so the client is unable to change it. For the client, directly accessing the class constant is easier and faster than calling a method.

3.12   Using *System.in* and *System.out*

In order to print program output to the screen, we have been using statements like

```
System.out.println( "The value of b is " + b );
```

and

```
System.out.print( "Enter your first name > " );
```

And to instantiate a *Scanner* object, we used this statement:

```
Scanner scan = new Scanner( System.in );
```

It is now time to look at these statements in depth and understand them completely.

System is an existing Java class in the *java.lang* package. One of its fields is a *static* constant, *out*, which represents the Java console by default. Another of its fields is a *static* constant, *in*, which represents the keyboard by default. Because *in* and *out* are *static*, we refer to them using the class name, *System*, and the dot notation:

```
System.out
System.in
```

Table 3.10 shows these static constants as well as the *static exit* method, which can be used to terminate a program. Calling *System.exit( )* at the end of a program is optional. After the last instruction is executed, the program will end in any case. However, the *exit* method of the *System* class can be useful if you want to stop execution at a place other than the end of the program.

System.out is an object of the *PrintStream* class, which is also an existing Java class; it can be found in the *java.io* package. The *out* object refers to the **standard output device**, which by default is the Java console.

The methods *print* and *println* belong to the *PrintStream* class and take arguments of any primitive type, a *String*, or an object reference. The only

TABLE 3.10   *Static* **Constants of the** *System* **Class and the** *exit* **Method**

Constant	Value
in	*static* constant that represents the standard input stream, by default the keyboard
out	*static* constant that represents the standard output stream, by default the Java console
A Useful *System* Method	
Return value	**Method name and argument list**
void	exit(int exitStatus)
	static method that terminates the Java Virtual Machine. A value of 0 for *exitStatus* indicates a normal termination. Any other values indicate abnormal termination and are used to signal that the program ended because an error occurred.

difference between *print* and *println* is that *println* will also print a *newline* character after it writes the output. Table 3.11 shows some methods of the *PrintStream* class, which can be used with *System.out.*

TABLE 3.11   *PrintStream* **Methods for Use with** *System.out*

	Useful *PrintStream* Methods
Return value	**Method name and argument list**
void	print(argument)
	prints *argument* to the standard output device. The *argument* can be any primitive data type, a *String* object, or another object reference.
void	println(argument)
	prints *argument* to the standard output device, then prints a *newline* character. The *argument* can be any primitive data type, a *String,* or another object reference.
void	println( )
	prints a *newline* character. This method is useful for skipping a line in the program's output.

Example 3.12 demonstrates various ways to use the *print* and *println* methods:

```
1 /*  Testing the print and println methods
2      Anderson, Franceschi
3 */
4
5 public class PrintDemo
6 {
7   public static void main( String [ ] args )
8   {
9     System.out.println( "Combine the arguments using concatenation" );
10    System.out.println( "A double: " + 23.7 + ", and an int: " + 78 );
11
12    System.out.print( "\nJava is case sensitive: " );
13    System.out.println( 'a' + " is different from " + 'A' );
14
15    System.out.println( "\nCreate a variable and print its value" );
16    String s = new String( "The grade is" );
17    double grade = 3.81;
18    System.out.println( s + " " + grade  );
19
20    System.out.println( );  // skip a line
21    SimpleDate d = new SimpleDate( 4, 5, 2009 );
22    System.out.println( "Explicitly calling toString, d is "
23                           + d.toString( ) );
24    System.out.println( "Implicitly calling toString, d is " + d );
25
26    System.exit( 0 );  // optional
27  }
28 }
```

EXAMPLE 3.12   Demonstrating the *print* and *println* Methods

Lines 10 and 13 show how *print* or *println* can be used with various data types such as *double*, *int*, and *char*. Variables and expressions can also be used instead of literals, as shown in line 18, where the *String s* and the *double* variable *grade* are output.

We can also print objects. All classes have a *toString* method, which converts the object data to a *String* for printing. The *toString* method is called automatically whenever an object is used as a *String*. Notice that our *SimpleDate* class, introduced earlier in the chapter, had a *toString* method that returned the object data as a *String* in the format *mm/dd/yyyy*.

Figure 3.19
The Output from Example 3.12

```
Combine the arguments using concatenation
A double: 23.7, and an int: 78

Java is case sensitive: a is different from A

Create a variable and print its value
The grade is 3.81

Explicitly calling toString, d is 4/5/2009
Implicitly calling toString, d is 4/5/2009
```

The *toString* method's API is

```
String toString( )
```

After the *SimpleDate* object reference *d* is instantiated at line 21, it is printed at lines 22–23 and again at line 24. At lines 22–23, the method *toString* is called explicitly; at line 24, it is called automatically. The output of Example 3.12 is shown in Figure 3.19. Finally, we terminate the program by calling the *exit* method of the *System* class.

3.13 The *Math* Class

The *Math* class is also part of the *java.lang* package. As such, it is automatically available to any Java program; you do not need to use the *import* statement. The *Math* class provides two *static* constants (*E* and *PI*), as well as a number of *static* methods that save the programmer from writing some complex mathematical code.

The two constants, *E* and *PI*, are both *doubles* and represent, respectively, *e* (the base of the natural logarithm, i.e., log e = 1) and *pi*, the ratio of the circumference of a circle to its diameter. Approximate values of *e* and *pi*, as we know them, are 2.78 and 3.14, respectively. These constants are shown in Table 3.12.

Because *E* and *PI* are *static* data members of the *Math* class, they are referenced using the name of the *Math* class and the dot notation as follows:

```
Math.E
Math.PI
```

 REFERENCE POINT

You can read more about the *System* and *PrintStream* classes on Oracle's Java website: *www.oracle.com/technetwork/java*.

TABLE 3.12 *Static* **Constants of the** *Math* **Class**

Constant	Value
E	*e*, the base of the natural logarithm
PI	*pi*, the ratio of the circumference of a circle to its diameter

Useful methods of the *Math* class are shown in Table 3.13. All the methods of the *Math* class are *static*; so they are called using the class name, *Math*, and the dot notation as follows:

```
Math.abs( -5 )
```

TABLE 3.13 **Useful Methods of the** *Math* **Class**

Math Class Method Summary	
Return value	**Method name and argument list**
dataTypeOfArg	abs(arg)
	static method that returns the absolute value of the argument *arg*, which can be a *double, float, int,* or *long*.
double	log(double a)
	static method that returns the natural logarithm (in base e) of its argument, *a*. For example, log(1) returns 0 and log(*Math.E*) returns 1.
dataTypeOfArgs	min(argA, argB)
	static method that returns the smaller of the two arguments. The arguments can be *doubles, floats, ints,* or *longs*.
dataTypeOfArgs	max(argA, argB)
	static method that returns the larger of the two arguments. The arguments can be *doubles, floats, ints,* or *longs*.
double	pow(double base, double exp)
	static method that returns the value of *base* raised to the *exp* power.
long	round(double a)
	static method that returns the closest integer to its argument, *a*.
double	sqrt(double a)
	static method that returns the positive square root of *a*.

Example 3.13 demonstrates how the *Math* constants and the *abs* method can be used in a Java program. In lines 9 and 10, we print the values of *e* and *pi* using the *static* constants of the *Math* class. Then in lines 12 and 15, we call the *abs* method, which returns the absolute value of its argument. We then print the results in lines 13 and 16. The output of Example 3.13 is shown in Figure 3.20.

```
1 /* A demonstration of the Math class methods and constants
2    Anderson, Franceschi
3 */
4
5 public class MathConstants
6 {
7   public static void main( String [ ] args )
8   {
9     System.out.println( "The value of e is " + Math.E );
10    System.out.println( "The value of pi is " + Math.PI );
11
12    double d1 = Math.abs( 6.7 ); // d1 will be assigned 6.7
13    System.out.println( "\nThe absolute value of 6.7 is " + d1 );
14
15    double d2 = Math.abs( -6.7 ); // d2 will be assigned 6.7
16    System.out.println( "\nThe absolute value of -6.7 is " + d2 );
17  }
18 }
```

EXAMPLE 3.13 *Math* **Class Constants and the** *abs* **Method**

```
The value of e is 2.718281828459045
The value of pi is 3.141592653589793

The absolute value of 6.7 is 6.7

The absolute value of -6.7 is 6.7
```

Figure 3.20
Output from Example 3.13

The operation and usefulness of most *Math* class methods are obvious. But several methods—*pow, round,* and *min/max*—require a little explanation.

The *pow* Method

Example 3.14 demonstrates how some of these *Math* methods can be used in a Java program.

```
1  /*  A demonstration of some Math class methods
2      Anderson, Franceschi
3  */
4
5  public class MathMethods
6  {
7    public static void main( String [ ] args )
8    {
9      double d2 = Math.log( 5 );
10     System.out.println( "\nThe log of 5 is " + d2 );
11
12     double d4 = Math.sqrt( 9 );
13     System.out.println( "\nThe square root of 9 is " + d4 );
14
15     double fourCubed = Math.pow( 4, 3 );
16     System.out.println( "\n4 to the power 3 is " + fourCubed );
17
18     double bigNumber = Math.pow( 43.5, 3.4 );
19     System.out.println( "\n43.5 to the power 3.4 is " + bigNumber );
20   }
21 }
```

EXAMPLE 3.14   A Demonstration of Some *Math* Class Methods

The *Math* class provides the *pow* method for raising a number to a power. The *pow* method takes two arguments; the first is the base and the second is the exponent.

Although the argument list for the *pow* method specifies that the base and the exponent are both *doubles*, you can, in fact, send arguments of any numeric type to the *pow* method because all numeric types can be promoted to a *double*. No matter what type the arguments are, however, the return value is always a *double*. Thus, when line 15 calls the *pow* method with two integer arguments, the value of *fourCubed* will be *64.0*. If you prefer that the return value be 64, you can cast the return value to an *int*.

Line 18 shows how to use the *pow* method with arguments of type *double*. The output of Example 3.14 is shown in Figure 3.21.

```
The log of 5 is 1.6094379124341003

The square root of 9 is 3.0

4 to the power 3 is 64.0

43.5 to the power 3.4 is 372274.65827529586
```

Figure 3.21
Output from Example 3.14

The round Method

The *round* method converts a *double* to its nearest integer using these rules:

- Any fractional part .0 to .4 is rounded down.
- Any fractional part .5 and above is rounded up.

Lines 9–13 in Example 3.15 use the *round* method with various numbers. Figure 3.22 shows the output.

```
1  /*  A demonstration of the Math round method
2      Anderson, Franceschi
3  */
4
5  public class MathRounding
6  {
7    public static void main( String [ ] args )
8    {
9      System.out.println( "23.4 rounded is " + Math.round( 23.4 ) );
10     System.out.println( "23.49 rounded is " + Math.round( 23.49 ) );
11     System.out.println( "23.5 rounded is " + Math.round( 23.5 ) );
12     System.out.println( "23.51 rounded is " + Math.round( 23.51 ) );
13     System.out.println( "23.6 rounded is " + Math.round( 23.6 ) );
14   }
15 }
```

EXAMPLE 3.15 A Demonstration of the *Math round* method

```
23.4 rounded is 23
23.49 rounded is 23
23.5 rounded is 24
23.51 rounded is 24
23.6 rounded is 24
```

Figure 3.22
Output from Example 3.15

The min and max Methods

The *min* and *max* methods return the smaller or larger of their two arguments, respectively. Example 3.16 demonstrates how the *min* and *max* methods can be used in a Java program. Figure 3.23 shows the output. Thus the statement on line 9 of Example 3.16

```
int smaller = Math.min( 8, 2 );
```

will assign 2 to the *int* variable *smaller*. At line 12, a similar statement using the *max* method will assign 8 to the *int* variable *larger*.

```
1  /*  A demonstration of min and max Math class methods
2        Anderson, Franceschi
3  */
4
5  public class MathMinMaxMethods
6  {
7    public static void main( String [ ] args )
8    {
9      int smaller = Math.min( 8, 2 );
10     System.out.println( "The smaller of 8 and 2 is " + smaller );
11
12     int larger = Math.max( 8, 2 );
13     System.out.println( "The larger of 8 and 2 is " + larger );
14
15     int a = 8, b = 5, c = 12;
16     int tempSmaller = Math.min( a, b );   // find smaller of a & b
17     int smallest = Math.min( tempSmaller, c ); // compare result to c
18     System.out.println( "The smallest of " + a + ", " + b + ", and "
19                          + c + " is " + smallest );
20   }
21 }
```

EXAMPLE 3.16   A Demonstration of the *min* and *max* Methods

Figure 3.23

Output from Example 3.16

```
The smaller of 8 and 2 is 2
The larger of 8 and 2 is 8
The smallest of 8, 5, and 12 is 5
```

The *min* method can also be used to compute the smallest of three variables. After declaring and initializing the three variables (*a*, *b*, and *c*) at line 15, we assign to a temporary variable named *tempSmaller* the smaller of the first two variables, *a* and *b*, at line 16. Then, at line 17, we compute the smaller of *tempSmaller* and the third variable, *c*, and assign that value to the *int* variable *smallest*, which is output at lines 18 and 19.

The pattern for finding the largest of three numbers is similar, and we leave that as an exercise at the end of the chapter.

 **REFERENCE POINT**

You can read more about the *Math* class on Oracle's Java website: *www.oracle .com/technetwork/java*.

 **Skill Practice**
with these end-of-chapter questions

3.19.1 Multiple Choice Exercises

Questions 6, 7, 8, 13

3.19.2 Reading and Understanding Code

Questions 17, 18, 19, 20, 21, 22, 23

3.19.3 Fill In the Code

Questions 28, 29, 30, 31, 32, 34

3.19.4 Identifying Errors in Code

Questions 40, 41, 42

3.19.5 Debugging Area

Questions 46, 47, 48

3.19.6 Write a Short Program

Questions 53, 54

CODE IN ACTION

To see a step-by-step illustration of how to instantiate an object and call both instance and *static* methods, look for the Chapter 3 Flash movie on the CD-ROM accompanying this book. Click on the link for Chapter 3 to view the movie.

3.14 Formatting Output with the *NumberFormat* Class

Like the *DecimalFormat* class, the *NumberFormat* class can also be used to format numbers for output. The *NumberFormat* class, however, provides specialized *static* methods for creating objects specifically for formatting currency and percentages.

The *NumberFormat* class is part of the *java.text* package, so you need to include the following *import* statement at the top of your program.

```
import java.text.NumberFormat;
```

The static methods of the *NumberFormat* class to format currency and percentages are shown in Table 3.14.

As you can see from the first two method headers, their return type is a *NumberFormat* object. These *static* methods, called **factory methods**, are used instead of constructors to create objects. Thus, instead of using the *new* keyword and a constructor, we will call one of these methods to create our *formatting* object.

The *getCurrencyInstance* method returns a formatting object that reflects the local currency. In the United States, that format is a leading dollar sign and two digits to the right of the decimal place. The *getPercentInstance* method returns a formatting object that prints a fraction as a percentage by multiplying the fraction by 100, rounding to the nearest whole percent, and adding a percent sign (%).

TABLE 3.14   **Useful Methods of the *NumberFormat* Class**

NumberFormat Method Summary	
Return value	**Method name and argument list**
NumberFormat	getCurrencyInstance( )
	static method that creates a format object for money
NumberFormat	getPercentInstance( )
	static method that creates a format object for percentages
String	format(double number)
	returns a *String* representation of *number* formatted according to the object used to call the method

We then use the *format* method from the *NumberFormat* class to display a value either as money or a percentage. The *format* method takes one argument, which is the variable or value that we want to print; it returns the formatted version of the value as a *String* object, which we can then print.

Example 3.17 is a complete program illustrating how to use these three methods.

```
1  /*  Demonstration of currency and percentage formatting
2      using the NumberFormat class.
3      Anderson, Franceschi
4  */
5
6  // we need to import the NumberFormat class from java.text
7  import java.text.NumberFormat;
8
9  public class DemoNumberFormat
10 {
11   public static void main( String [ ] args )
12   {
13       double winningPercentage = .675;
14       double price = 78.9;
15
16       // get a NumberFormat object for printing a percentage
17       NumberFormat percentFormat = NumberFormat.getPercentInstance( );
18
19       // call format method using the NumberFormat object
20       System.out.print( "The winning percentage is " );
21       System.out.println( percentFormat.format( winningPercentage ) );
22
23       // get a NumberFormat object for printing currency
24       NumberFormat priceFormat = NumberFormat.getCurrencyInstance( );
25
26       // call format method using the NumberFormat object
27       System.out.println( "\nThe price is: "
28                           + priceFormat.format( price ) );
29   }
30 }
```

EXAMPLE 3.17 **Demonstrating the *NumberFormat* Class**

The output of this program is shown in Figure 3.24.

Figure 3.24

Output from Example 3.17

```
The winning percentage is 68%

The price is: $78.90
```

3.15   The *Integer, Double,* and Other Wrapper Classes

In Chapter 2, we discussed primitive data types and how they can be used in a program. In this chapter, we've discussed classes and class methods and how useful and convenient classes are in representing and encapsulating data into objects.

Most programs use a combination of primitive data types and objects. Some class methods, however, will accept only objects as arguments, so we need some way to convert a primitive data type into an object. Conversely, there are times when we need to convert an object into a primitive data type. For example, let's say we have a GUI where we ask users to type their age into a text box or a dialog box. We expect the age to be an *int* value; however, text boxes and dialog boxes return their values as *Strings*. To perform any calculations on an age in our program, we will need to convert the value of that *String* object into an *int*.

For these situations, Java provides **wrapper classes**. A wrapper class "wraps" the value of a primitive type, such as *double* or *int*, into an object. These wrapper classes define an instance variable of that primitive data type, and also provide useful constants and methods for converting between the objects and the primitive data types. Table 3.15 lists the wrapper classes for each primitive data type.

All these classes are part of the *java.lang* package. So, the *import* statement is not needed in order to use them in a program.

To convert a primitive *int* variable to an *Integer* wrapper object, we can instantiate the *Integer* object using the *Integer* constructor.

```java
int intPrimitive = 42;
Integer integerObject = new Integer( intPrimitive );
```

However, because this is a common operation, Java provides special support for converting between a primitive numeric type and its wrapper class. Instead of using the *Integer* constructor, we can simply assign the *int* vari-

TABLE 3.15   Wrapper Classes for Primitive Data Types

Primitive Data Type	Wrapper Class
double	Double
float	Float
long	Long
int	Integer
short	Short
byte	Byte
char	Character
boolean	Boolean

able to an *Integer* object reference. Java will automatically provide the conversion for us. This conversion is called **autoboxing**. In Example 3.18, the conversion is illustrated in lines 9 and 10. The *int* variable, *intPrimitive,* and the *Integer* object, *integerObject,* are output at lines 12 and 13 and have the same value (42). The output is shown in Figure 3.25.

Similarly, when an *Integer* object is used as an *int,* Java also provides this conversion, which is called **unboxing**. Thus, when we use an *Integer* object in an arithmetic expression, the *int* value is automatically used. Line 15 of Example 3.18 uses the *Integer* object *integerObject* in an arithmetic expression, adding the *Integer* object to the *int* variable *intPrimitive.* As shown in Figure 3.25, the result is the same as if both operands were *int* variables.

Similar operations are possible using other numeric primitives and their associated wrapper classes.

In addition to automatic conversions between primitive types and wrapper objects, the *Integer* and *Double* classes provide methods, shown in Table 3.16, that allow us to convert between primitive types and objects of the *String* class.

The *parseInt, parseDouble,* and *valueOf* methods are *static* and are called using the *Integer* or *Double* class name and the dot notation. The *parse* methods convert a *String* to a primitive type, and the *valueOf* methods convert a *String* to a wrapper object. For example, line 18 of Example 3.18 converts the *String* "76" to the *int* value 76. Line 19 converts the *String* "76" to an *Integer* object.

```
1 /*  A demonstration of the Wrapper classes and methods
2      Anderson, Franceschi
3 */
4
5 public class DemoWrapper
6 {
7   public static void main( String [ ] args )
8   {
9     int intPrimitive = 42;
10    Integer integerObject = intPrimitive;
11
12    System.out.println( "The int is " + intPrimitive );
13    System.out.println( "The Integer object is " + integerObject );
14
15    int sum = intPrimitive + integerObject;
16    System.out.println( "The sum is " + sum );
17
18    int i1 = Integer.parseInt( "76" );    // convert "76" to an int
19    Integer i2 = Integer.valueOf( "76" ); // convert "76" to Integer
20    System.out.println( "\nThe value of i1 is " + i1 );
21    System.out.println( "The value of i2 is " + i2 );
22
23    double d1 = Double.parseDouble( "58.32" );
24    Double d2 = Double.valueOf( "58.32" );
25    System.out.println( "\nThe value of d1 is " + d1 );
26    System.out.println( "The value of d2 is " + d2 );
27  }
28 }
```

EXAMPLE 3.18   A Demonstration of the Wrapper Classes

Figure 3.25

Output from Example 3.18

```
The int is 42
The Integer object is 42
The sum is 84

The value of i1 is 76
The value of i2 is 76

The value of d1 is 58.32
The value of d2 is 58.32
```

TABLE 3.16 *Methods of the Integer and Double Wrapper Classes*

Useful Methods of the *Integer* Wrapper Class	
Return value	**Method name and argument list**
int	parseInt(String s)
	static method that converts the *String s* to an *int* and returns that value
Integer	valueOf(String s)
	static method that converts the *String s* to an *Integer* object and returns that object

Useful Methods of the *Double* Wrapper Class	
Return value	**Method name and argument list**
double	parseDouble(String s)
	static method that converts the *String s* to a *double* and returns that value
Double	valueOf(String s)
	static method that converts the *String s* to a *Double* object and returns that object

Similarly, line 23 converts the *String* "*58.32*" to a *double*, and line 24 converts the same *String* to a *Double* object.

The usefulness of these wrappers will become clear in the next section of this chapter, where we discuss dialog boxes.

 **REFERENCE POINT**

You can read more about the wrapper classes on Oracle's Java website: *www.oracle.com/ technetwork/java.*

3.16 Input and Output Using *JOptionPane* Dialog Boxes

Java provides the *JOptionPane* class for creating dialog boxes—those familiar pop-up windows that prompt the user to enter a value or notify the user of an error. The *JOptionPane* class is in the *javax.swing* package, so you will need to provide an *import* statement in any program that uses a dialog box.

TABLE 3.17   **Input and Output Methods of the *JOptionPane* Class**

Useful Methods of the *JOptionPane* Class	
Return value	**Method name and argument list**
String	`showInputDialog( Component parent, Object prompt )`
	static method that pops up an input dialog box, where *prompt* asks the user for input. Returns the characters typed by the user as a *String*.
void	`showMessageDialog( Component parent, Object message )`
	static method that pops up an output dialog box with *message* displayed.

Most classes in the *javax.swing* package are designed for GUIs, but *JOption-Pane* dialog boxes can be used in both GUI and non-GUI programs.

Table 3.17 lists some useful *JOptionPane static* methods.

The *showInputDialog* method is used for input—that is, for prompting the user for a value and inputting that value into the program. The *showMessageDialog* method is used for output—that is, for printing a message to the user. Although Java provides several constructors for dialog boxes, it is customary to create dialog boxes that will be used only once using the *static* methods and the *JOptionPane* class name.

Let's look first at the method *showInputDialog*, which gets input from the user. It takes two arguments: a parent component object and a prompt to display. At this point, our applications won't have a parent component object, so we'll always use *null* for that argument.

The second argument, the prompt, is usually a *String*, and lets the user know what kind of input our program needs. Next, notice that the return value of the *showInputDialog* method is a *String*.

Example 3.19 shows how the *showInputDialog* method is used to retrieve user input through a dialog box.

```
1 /* Using dialog boxes for input and output of Strings
2      Anderson, Franceschi
3 */
4
5 import javax.swing.JOptionPane;
6
7 public class DialogBoxDemo1
```

```
 8 {
 9   public static void main( String [ ] args )
10   {
11     String name = JOptionPane.showInputDialog( null,
12                     "Please enter your first and last names" );
13     JOptionPane.showMessageDialog( null, "Hello, " + name );
14   }
15 }
```

EXAMPLE 3.19   Using Dialog Boxes with *Strings*

When lines 11 and 12 are executed, the dialog box in Figure 3.26 appears. The user types his or her name into the white box, then presses either the *Enter* key or clicks the *OK* button. At that time, the *showInputDialog* method returns a *String* representing the characters typed by the user, and that *String* is assigned to the variable *name*.

To output a message to the user, use the *showMessageDialog* method. The *showMessageDialog* method is similar to the *showInputDialog* method in that it takes a parent component object (*null* for now) and a *String* to display. Thus, in Example 3.19, line 13 uses the variable *name* to echo back to the user a greeting.

Notice that because the *showMessageDialog* is a method with a *void* return value, you call it as a standalone statement, rather than using the method call in an expression.

If the user typed "Syed Ali" when prompted for his name, the output dialog box shown in Figure 3.27 would appear.

To input an integer or any data type other than a *String*, however, you need to convert the returned *String* to the desired data type. Fortunately, as we saw in the previous section, you can do this using a wrapper class and its associated *parse* method, as Example 3.20 demonstrates.

Figure 3.26

Dialog Box Prompting for First and Last Names

Figure 3.27

Output Dialog Box from Example 3.19

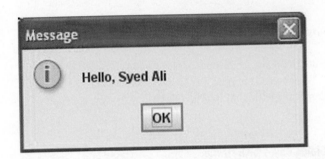

```
1  /* Demonstrating dialog boxes for input and output of numbers
2     Anderson, Franceschi
3  */
4
5  import javax.swing.JOptionPane;
6
7  public class DialogBoxDemo2
8  {
9    public static void main( String [ ] args )
10   {
11     String input = JOptionPane.showInputDialog( null,
12         "Please enter your age in years" );
13     int age = Integer.parseInt( input );
14     JOptionPane.showMessageDialog( null, "Next year your age will be " +
15         ++age );
16
17     double average = Double.parseDouble(
18         JOptionPane.showInputDialog( null,
19         "Enter your grade point average between 0.0 and 4.0" ) );
20     JOptionPane.showMessageDialog( null, "Your average is "
21         + ( 4.0 - average ) + " points from a 4.0" );
22   }
23 }
```

EXAMPLE 3.20   Converting Input *Strings* to Numbers

Lines 11 and 12 pop up an input dialog box and assign the characters entered by the user to the *String input*. Line 13 uses the *parseInt* method of the *Integer* class to convert *input* to an integer, which is assigned to the *int* variable *age*. Line 14 then adds 1 to *age* and displays the age the person will be next year in an output dialog box.

Java programmers often combine multiple related operations into one state-ment in order to type less code and to avoid declaring additional variables. Lines 17–19 illustrate this concept. At first it may look confusing, but if you look at the statement a piece at a time, it becomes clear what is happening.

The *showInputDialog* method is called, returning a *String* representing whatever the user typed into the dialog box. This *String* then becomes the argument passed to *parseDouble*, which converts the *String* to a *double*. Lines 20–21 calculate the difference between 4.0 and the entered grade point average and display the difference in another dialog box.

In this prompt, we included a range of valid values to help the user type valid input. However, including a range of values in your prompt does not prevent the user from entering other values. The *parseDouble* method will accept any *String* that can be converted to a numeric value. After your program receives the input, you will need to verify that the number entered is indeed within the requested range of values. In Chapter 6, we will show you techniques for verifying whether the user has entered valid values.

With either *Double.parseDouble* or *Integer.parseInt*, the value the user types must be convertible to the appropriate data type. If not, an exception is generated. For example, if the user enters *A* for the grade point average, the method generates a *NumberFormatException*.

The various input and output dialog boxes from a sample run of Example 3.20 are shown in Figure 3.28.

REFERENCE POINT

You can read more about the *JOptionPane* class on Oracle's Java website: *www.oracle.com/ technetwork/java.*

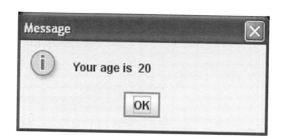

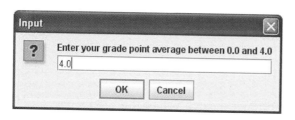

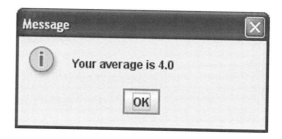

Figure 3.28

Dialog Boxes from Example 3.20

Skill Practice
with these end-of-chapter questions

3.17   Programming Activity 2: Using Predefined Classes

In this Programming Activity, you will write a short program using some of the classes and methods discussed in this chapter. Plus, given the API of a method of an additional class, you will determine how to call the method. Your program will perform the following operations:

1. a. Prompt the user for his or her first name

   b. Print a message saying hello to the user

   c. Tell the user how many characters are in his or her name

2. a. Ask the user for the year of his or her birth

   b. Calculate and print the age the user will be this year

   c. Declare a constant for average life expectancy; set its value to 77.9

   d. Print a message that tells the user the percentage of his or her expected life lived so far

3. a. Generate a random number between 1 and 20

   b. Pop up a dialog box telling the user that the program is thinking of a number between 1 and 20 and ask for a guess

   c. Pop up a dialog box telling the user the number and how far away from the number the user's guess was

To complete this Programming Activity, copy the contents of the Chapter 3 Programming Activity 2 folder on the CD-ROM accompanying this book. Open the *PracticeMethods.java* file and look for four sets of five asterisks (*****), where you will find instructions to write *import* statements and items 1, 2, and 3 for completing the Programming Activity.

Example 3.21 shows the *PracticeMethods.java* file, and Figures 3.29 and 3.30 show the output from a sample run after you have completed the

```
Enter your first name > Esmerelda
Hello Esmerelda
Your name has 9 letters

In what year were you born > 1990
This year, you will be 18
You have lived 23.1% of your life.
```

Figure 3.29
Console Output from a Sample Run of Programming Activity 2

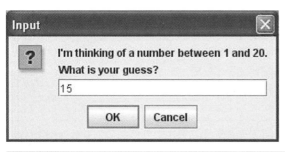

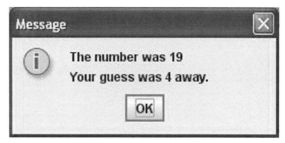

Figure 3.30
Dialog Boxes from a Sample Run of Programming Activity 2

Programming Activity. Because item 3 generates a random number, your output may be different.

```
1 /* Chapter 3 Programming Activity 2
2    Calling class methods
3    Anderson, Franceschi
4 */
5
6 // ***** add your import statements here
7
8 public class PracticeMethods
9 {
10   public static void main( String [ ] args )
11   {
12     //*****
13     // 1.  a. Create a Scanner object to read from the console
14     //     b. Prompt the user for his or her first name
15     //     c. Print a message that says hello to the user
16     //     d. Print a message that says how many letters
17     //              are in the user's name
18     // Your code goes here
19
20     //*****
21     // 2.  a. Skip a line, then prompt the user for the year
22     //            of birth
23     //     b. Calculate and print the age the user will be this year
24     //     c. Declare a constant for average life expectancy,
25     //            set its value to 77.9
26     //     d. Print a message that tells the user the percentage
27     //            of his or her expected life lived
28     //        Use the DecimalFormat class to format the percentage
29
30     //*****
31     // 3.  a. Generate a random integer between 1 and 20
32     //     b. Pop up an input dialog box and ask the user for a guess.
33     //     c. Pop up an output dialog box telling the user the number
34     //          and how far from the number the guess was (hint: use Math.abs)
35
36   }
37 }
```

EXAMPLE 3.21   *PracticeMethods.java*

1. Which methods of the *Scanner* class did you choose for reading the user's name and birth year? Explain your decisions.

2. How would you change your code to generate a random number between 10 and 20?

3.18   Chapter Summary

- Object-oriented programming entails writing programs that use classes and objects. Using prewritten classes shortens development time and creates more reliable programs. Programs that use prewritten classes are called clients of the class.

- Benefits of object-oriented programming include encapsulation, reusability, and reliability.

- Classes consist of data, plus instructions that operate on that data. Objects of a class are created using the class as a template. Creating an object is called instantiating an object, and the object is an instance of the class. The *new* keyword is used to instantiate an object.

- The object reference is the variable name for an object and points to the data of the object.

- The data of a class are called instance variables or fields, and the instructions of the class are called methods. Methods of a class get or set the values of the data or provide other services of the class.

- The name of a method, along with its argument list and return value, is called the Application Programming Interface (API) of that method. Methods that are declared to be *public* can be called by any client of the class.

- By convention, class names in Java start with a capital letter. Method names, instance variables, and object names start with a lowercase letter. In all these names, embedded words begin with a capital letter.

- When your program makes a method call, control transfers to the instructions in the method until the method finishes executing. Then control is transferred back to your program.

CHAPTER SUMMARY

- Instance methods are called using the object reference and the dot notation.

- A constructor is called when an object is instantiated. A constructor has the same name as the class and its job is to initialize the object's data. Classes can have multiple constructors. Constructors have no return values.

- A method's data type is called the method's return type. If the data type is anything other than the keyword *void*, the method returns a value to the program. When a value-returning method finishes executing, its return value replaces the method call in the expression.

- Accessor methods, also called *gets*, allow clients to retrieve the current value of object data. Mutator methods, also called *sets*, allow clients to change the value of object data.

- When an object reference is first declared, its value is *null*. Attempting to use a *null* object reference to call a method generates an error.

- The garbage collector runs occasionally and deletes objects that have no object references pointing to them.

- Java packages are groups of classes arranged according to functionality. Classes in the *java.lang* packages are automatically available to Java programs. Other classes need to be imported.

- The *String* class can be used to create objects consisting of a sequence of characters. *String* constructors accept *String* literals, *String* objects, or no argument, which creates an empty *String*. The *length* method returns the number of characters in the *String* object. The *toUpperCase* and *toLowerCase* methods return a *String* in upper or lower case. The *charAt* method extracts a character from a *String*, while the *substring* method extracts a *String* from a *String*. The *indexOf* method searches a *String* for a character or substring.

- The *DecimalFormat* class, in the *java.text* package, formats numeric output. For example, you can specify the number of digits to display after the decimal point or add dollar signs and percentage signs (%).

- The *Random* class, in the *java.util* package, generates random numbers.

- The *Scanner* class, in the *java.util* package, provides methods for reading input from the Java console. Methods are provided for reading primitive data types and *Strings*.

- When prompting the user for input, phrase the prompt in language the user understands. Describe the data requested and any restrictions on valid input values

- *Static* methods, also called class methods, can be called without instantiating an object. *Static* methods can access only the *static* data of a class.

- *Static* methods are called using the class name and the dot notation.

- *System.out.println* prints primitive data types or a *String* to the Java console and adds a *newline* character. *System.out.println* with no argument skips a line. *System.out.print* prints the same data types to the Java console, but does not add a *newline*. Classes provide a *toString* method to convert objects to a *String* in order to be printed.

- The *Math* class provides *static* constants *PI* and *E* and *static* methods to perform common mathematical calculations, such as finding the maximum or minimum of two numbers, rounding values, and raising a number to a power.

- The *NumberFormat* class, in the *java.text* package, provides *static* methods for formatting numeric output as currency or a percentage.

- Wrapper classes provide an object interface for a primitive data type. The *Integer* and *Double* wrapper classes provide *static* methods for converting between *ints* and *doubles* and *Strings*.

- The *JOptionPane* class, in the *javax.swing* package, provides the *static* methods *showMessageDialog* for popping up an output dialog box and *showInputDialog* for popping up an input dialog box.

3.19 Exercises, Problems, and Projects

3.19.1 Multiple Choice Exercises

1. If you want to use an existing class from the Java class library in your program, what keyword should you use?

   ❏ use

   ❏ import

   ❏ export

   ❏ include

2. A constructor has the same name as the class name.

   ❏ true

   ❏ false

3. A given class can have more than one constructor.

   ❏ true

   ❏ false

4. What is the keyword used to instantiate an object in Java?

   ❏ make

   ❏ construct

   ❏ new

   ❏ static

5. In a given class named *Quiz*, there can be only one method with the name *Quiz*.

   ❏ true

   ❏ false

6. A *static* method is

   ❏ a class method.

   ❏ an instance method.

7. In the *Quiz* class, the *foo* method has the following API:

   ```
   public static double foo( float f )
   ```

   What can you say about *foo*?

❏ It is an instance method.

❏ It is a class field.

❏ It is a class method.

❏ It is an instance variable.

8. In the *Quiz* class, the *foo* method has the following API:

   `public static void foo( )`

   How would you call that method?

   ❏ `Quiz.foo( );`

   ❏ `Quiz.foo( 8 );`

   ❏ `Quiz( foo( ) );`

9. In the *Quiz* class, the *foo* method has the following API:

   `public double foo( int i, String s, char c )`

   How many arguments does *foo* take ?

   ❏ 0

   ❏ 1

   ❏ 2

   ❏ 3

10. In the *Quiz* class, the *foo* method has the following API:

   `public double foo( int i, String s, char c )`

   What is the return type of method *foo*?

   ❏ `double`

   ❏ `int`

   ❏ `char`

   ❏ `String`

11. *String* is a primitive data type in Java.

   ❏ true

   ❏ false

EXERCISES, PROBLEMS, AND PROJECTS

12. Which one of the following is not an existing wrapper class?

   ❑ Integer

   ❑ Char

   ❑ Float

   ❑ Double

13. What is the proper way of accessing the constant *E* of the *Math* class?

   ❑ Math.E( );

   ❑ Math.E;

   ❑ E;

   ❑ Math(E);

3.19.2 Reading and Understanding Code

14. What is the output of this code sequence?

```
String s = new String( "HI" );
System.out.println( s );
```

15. What is the output of this code sequence?

```
String s = "A" + "BC" + "DEF" + "GHIJ";
System.out.println( s );
```

16. What is the output of this code sequence?

```
String s = "Hello";
s = s.toLowerCase( );
System.out.println( s );
```

17. What is the output of this code sequence?

```
int a = Math.min( 5, 8 );
System.out.println( a );
```

18. What is the output of this code sequence?

```
System.out.println( Math.sqrt( 4.0 ) );
```

19. What is the output of this code sequence? (You will need to actually compile this code and run it in order to have the correct output.)

```
System.out.println( Math.PI );
```

20. What is the output of this code sequence?

```
double f = 5.7;
long i = Math.round( f );
System.out.println( i );
```

21. What is the output of this code sequence?

    ```
    System.out.print( Math.round( 3.5 ) );
    ```

22. What is the output of this code sequence?

    ```
    int i = Math.abs( -8 );
    System.out.println( i );
    ```

23. What is the output of this code sequence?

    ```
    double d = Math.pow( 2, 3 );
    System.out.println( d );
    ```

3.19.3   Fill In the Code

24. This code concatenates the three *Strings* "Intro", "to", and "Programming" and outputs the resulting *String*. (Your output should be *Intro to Programming*.)

    ```
    String s1 = "Intro ";
    String s2 = "to";
    String s3 = " Programming";
    // your code goes here
    ```

25. This code prints the number of characters in the *String* "Hello World".

    ```
    String s = "Hello World";
    // your code goes here
    ```

26. This code prompts the user for a *String*, then prints the *String* and the number of characters in it.

    ```
    // your code goes here
    ```

27. This code uses only a single line *System.out.println . . .* statement in order to print

    "Welcome to Java Illuminated"

    on one line using (and only using) the following variables:

    ```
    String s1 = "Welcome ";
    String s2 = "to ";
    String s3 = "Java ";
    String s4 = "Illuminated";
    // your code goes here
    ```

28. This code uses exactly four *System.out.print* statements in order to print

    "Welcome to Java Illuminated"

on the same output line.

```
// your code goes here
```

29. This code assigns the maximum of the values 3 and 5 to the *int* variable *i* and outputs the result.

```
int i;
// your code goes here
```

30. This code calculates the square root of 5 and outputs the result.

```
double d = 5.0;
// your code goes here
```

31. This code asks the user for two integer values, then calculates the minimum of the two values and prints it.

```
// your code goes here
```

32. This code asks the user for three integer values, then calculates the maximum of the three values and prints it.

```
// your code goes here
```

33. This code pops up a dialog box that prompts the user for an integer, converts the *String* to an *int*, adds 1 to the number, and pops up a dialog box that outputs the new value.

```
// your code goes here
```

34. This code asks the user for a *double*, then prints the square of this number.

```
// your code goes here
```

3.19.4 Identifying Errors in Code

35. Where is the error in this statement?

```
import text.NumberFormat;
```

36. Where is the error in this statement?

```
import java.util.DecimalFormat;
```

37. Where is the error in this code sequence?

```
String s = "Hello World";
system.out.println( s );
```

38. Where is the error in this code sequence?

```
String s = String( "Hello" );
System.out.println( s );
```

39. Where is the error in this code sequence?

```
String s1 = "Hello";
String s2 = "ello";
String s = s1 - s2;
```

40. Where is the error in this code sequence?

```
short s = Math.round( 3.2 );
System.out.println( s );
```

41. Where is the error in this code sequence?

```
int a = Math.pow( 3, 4 );
System.out.println( a );
```

42. Where is the error in this code sequence?

```
double pi = Math( PI );
System.out.println( pi );
```

43. Where is the error in this code sequence?

```
String s = 'H';

System.out.println( "s is " + s );
```

3.19.5   Debugging Area—Using Messages from the Java Compiler and Java JVM

44. You coded the following program in the file *Test.java:*

```
public class Test
{
  public static void main( String [ ] args )
  {
    int a = 6;
    NumberFormat nf = NumberFormat.getCurrencyInstance( );
  }
}
```

When you compile, you get the following message:

```
Test.java: 6: cannot find symbol
  NumberFormat nf = NumberFormat.getCurrencyInstance( );
  ^
  symbol : class NumberFormat
  location: class Test
Test.java: 6: cannot find symbol
```

```
NumberFormat nf = NumberFormat.getCurrencyInstance( );
                                 ^
symbol : variable NumberFormat
location: class Test
2 errors
```

Explain what the problem is and how to fix it.

45. You coded the following on lines 10–12 of class *Test.java:*

```
String s;                      // line 10
int l = s.length( );           // line 11
System.out.println( "length is " + l );     // line 12
```

When you compile, you get the following message:

```
Test.java:11: variable s might not have been initialized.
  int l = s.length( );   // line 11
          ^
```

```
1 error
```

Explain what the problem is and how to fix it.

46. You coded the following on lines 10 and 11 of class *Test.java:*

```
double d = math.sqrt( 6 );          // line 10
System.out.println( "d = " + d );   // line 11
```

When you compile, you get the following message:

```
Test.java: 10: cannot find symbol
double d = math.sqrt( 6 ); // line 10
           ^

  symbol : variable math
  location: class Test
  1 error
```

Explain what the problem is and how to fix it.

47. You coded the following on lines 10 and 11 of class *Test.java:*

```
double d = Math.PI( );              // line 10
System.out.println( "d = " + d );  // line 11
```

When you compile, you get the following message:

```
Test.java:10: cannot find symbol
  double d = Math.PI( );   // line 10
                  ^

symbol : method PI ( )
location: class Math
1 error
```

Explain what the problem is and how to fix it.

48. You coded the following on lines 10 and 11 of class *Test.java:*

```
double d = Math.e;                    // line 10
System.out.println( "d = " + d );  // line 11
```

When you compile, you get the following message:

```
Test.java:10: cannot find symbol
        double d = Math.e;                    // line 10
                       ^
    symbol : variable e
    location: class Math
    1 error
```

Explain what the problem is and how to fix it.

49. You imported the *DecimalFormat* class and coded the following in the class *Test.java:*

```
double grade = .895;
DecimalFormat percent =
  new DecimalFormat( "#.0%" );

System.out.println( "Your grade is "
  + grade );
```

The code compiles properly and runs, but the result is not what you expected. You expect this output:

```
Your grade is 89.5%
```

But instead, the output is

```
Your grade is 0.895
```

Explain what the problem is and how to fix it.

3.19.6   Write a Short Program

50. Write a program that reads two words representing passwords from the Java console and outputs the number of characters in the smaller of the two. For example, if the two words are *open* and *sesame*, then the output should be *4*, the length of the shorter word, *open.*

51. Write a program that reads a name that represents a domain name from the Java console. Your program should then concatenate that name with *www.* and *.com* in order to form an Internet domain name and output the result. For instance, if the name entered by the user is *yahoo*, then the output will be *www.yahoo.com.*

52. Write a program that reads a word from the Java console. Your program should then output the same word, output the word in uppercase letters only, output that word in lowercase letters only, and then, at the end, output the original word.

53. Write a program that generates two random numbers between 0 and 100 and prints the smaller of the two numbers.

54. Write a program that takes a *double* as an input from the Java console, then computes and outputs the cube of that number.

55. Write a program that reads a file name from a dialog box. You should expect that the file name has one . (dot) character in it, separating the file name from the file extension. Retrieve the file extension and output it. For instance, if the user inputs *index.html*, you should output *html*; if the user inputs *MyClass.java*, you should output *java*.

56. Write a program that reads a full name (first name and last name) from a dialog box; you should expect the first name and the last name to be separated by a space. Retrieve the first name and output it.

3.19.7   Programming Projects

57. Write a program that reads three integer values from the Java console representing, respectively, a number of quarters, dimes, and nickels. Convert the total coin amount to dollars and output the result with a dollar notation.

58. Write a program that reads from the Java console the radius of a circle. Calculate and output the area and the perimeter of that circle. You can use the following formulas:

area $= \pi * r^2$

perimeter $= 2 * \pi * r$

59. Write a program that generates five random integers between 60 and 100 and calculates the smallest of the five numbers.

60. Write a program that generates three random integers between 0 and 50, calculates the average, and prints the result.

61. Write a program that reads two integers from the Java console: one representing the number of shots taken by a basketball player, the other representing the number of shots made by the same player.

Calculate the shooting percentage and output it with the percent notation.

62. Write a program that takes three *double* numbers from the Java console representing, respectively, the three coefficients a, b, and c of a quadratic equation. Solve the equation using the following formulas:

$x1 = (-b + \text{square root } (b^2 - 4\ ac)) / (2a)$

$x2 = (-b - \text{square root } (b^2 - 4\ ac)) / (2a)$

Run your program on the following sample values:

$a = 1.0, b = 3.0, c = 2.0$

$a = 0.5, b = 0.5, c = 0.125$

$a = 1.0, b = 3.0, c = 10.0$

Discuss the results for each program run, in particular what happens in the last case.

63. Write a program that takes two numbers from the Java console representing, respectively, an investment and an interest rate (you will expect the user to enter a number such as .065 for the interest rate, representing a 6.5% interest rate). Your program should calculate and output (in $ notation) the future value of the investment in 5, 10, and 20 years using the following formula:

future value = investment * (1 + interest rate)^{year}

We will assume that the interest rate is an annual rate and is compounded annually.

64. Write a program that reads from the Java console the (x,y) coordinates for two points in the plane. You can assume that all numbers are integers. Using the *Point* class from Java (you may need to look it up on the Web), instantiate two *Point* objects with your input data, then output the data for both *Point* objects.

65. Write a program that reads a *char* from the Java console. Look up the *Character* class on the Web, in particular the method *getNumericValue*. Using the *getNumericValue* method, find the corresponding Unicode encoding number and output the character along with its corresponding Unicode value. Find all the Unicode values for characters a to z and A to Z.

66. Write a program that reads a telephone number from a dialog box; you should assume that the number is in this format: nnn-nnn-nnnn. You should output this same telephone number but with spaces instead of dashes, that is: nnn nnn nnnn.

67. Write a program that reads a sentence from a dialog box. The sentence has been encrypted as follows: only the first five even-numbered characters should be counted; all other characters should be discarded. Decrypt the sentence and output the result. For example, if the user inputs "Hiejlzl3ow", your output should be *Hello*.

68. Write a program that reads a commercial website URL from a dialog box; you should expect that the URL starts with *www.* and ends with *.com*. Retrieve the name of the site and output it. For instance, if the user inputs *www.yahoo.com*, you should output *yahoo*.

3.19.8   Technical Writing

69. At this point, we have written and debugged many examples of code. When you compile a Java program with the Java compiler, you get a list of all the errors in your code. Do you like the Java compiler? Do the error messages it displays when your code does not compile help you determine what's wrong?

70. Computers, computer languages, and application programs existed before object-oriented programming. However, OOP has become an industry standard. Discuss the advantages of using OOP compared to using only basic data types in a program.

71. Explain and discuss a situation where you would use the method *parseInt* of the class *Integer*.

72. In addition to the basic data types (*int, float, char, boolean,* . . .), Java provides many prewritten classes, such as *Math, NumberFormat,* and *DecimalFormat*. Why is this an advantage? How does this impact the way a programmer approaches a programming problem in general?

3.19.9   Group Project (for a group of 1, 2, or 3 students)

73. Write a program that calculates a monthly mortgage payment; we will assume that the interest rate is compounded monthly.

You will need to do the following:

❑ Prompt the user for a *double* representing the annual interest rate.

❑ Prompt the user for the number of years the mortgage will be held (typical input here is 10, 15, or 30).

❑ Prompt the user for a number representing the mortgage amount borrowed from the bank.

❑ Calculate the monthly payment using the following formulas:

- Monthly payment = $(mIR * M) / (1 - (1 / (1 + mIR)^{(12*nOY)}))$, where:

  - mIR = monthly interest rate = annual interest rate / 12

  - nOY = number of years

  - M = mortgage amount

❑ Output a summary of the mortgage problem, as follows:

- the annual interest rate in percent notation

- the mortgage amount in dollars

- the monthly payment in dollars, with only two significant digits after the decimal point

- the total payment over the years, with only two significant digits after the decimal point

- the overpayment, i.e., the difference between the total payment over the years and the mortgage amount, with only two significant digits after the decimal point

- the overpayment as a percentage (in percent notation) of the mortgage amount

CHAPTER 4

Introduction to Applets and Graphics

CHAPTER CONTENTS

Introduction

To this point, we've written Java applications, which run as standalone programs. Now we'll write a few Java applets, which are run by an Internet browser or an applet viewer.

As we discussed in Chapter 1, applets were originally designed to add interactivity to a web page. For example, a computer chess game on the Web can be run as an applet.

Another advantage to applets is the ease with which you can add graphics to a program. Up to this point, the input and output of our applications have been text—words and numbers. There was one exception, however: Programming Activity 1 in Chapter 3. That application opened a window and drew figures along with the text. How did we do that? We used graphics.

Graphical output is an integral part of many programs today. One compelling reason for using graphics in a program is the ability to present data in a format that is easy to comprehend. For example, our application could output average monthly temperatures as text, like this:

```
Jan    31
Feb    24
Mar    45
Apr    56
May    69
Jun    76
Jul    88
Aug    87
Sep    75
Oct    65
Nov    43
Dec    23
```

Or we could produce the bar chart shown in Figure 4.1.

The bar chart presents the same information as the text output, but it adds a visual component that makes it easier to compare the monthly temperatures—for example, to find the highest or lowest temperature or to spot temperature trends throughout the year. The colors also add information,

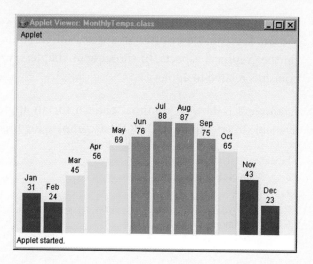

Figure 4.1

Bar Chart of Monthly Temperatures

with the low temperatures shown in blue, the moderate temperatures shown in yellow, and the high temperatures shown in red.

In this chapter, we begin by adding graphical output to applets.

4.1   Applet Structure

The *JApplet* class, an existing Java class of the *javax.swing* package, provides the basic functionality of an applet. An applet class that we write is an extension of the *JApplet* class. In Java, the *extends* keyword specifies that one class is an extension of another and *inherits* the properties of the other class. Inheritance is one of the ways to reuse classes.

An applet automatically opens a window where your program can draw shapes and text. The *main* method is not used in applets. Instead, we will use the *paint* method for our drawing code. The *paint* method is called automatically when the browser or applet viewer launches the applet, as well as any time the applet window needs to redraw itself. An applet might need to redraw itself if the user resizes the applet window or after another window, which was covering all or part of the applet window, is closed or is moved away from the applet window.

There is more to learn about applets than what is covered in this chapter. We will keep our description of applets simple so that you can concentrate on the graphical aspects. In subsequent chapters, we will cover additional concepts related to applets.

Example 4.1 shows a minimal pattern for an applet. This applet shell is available to you on the CD-ROM accompanying this book.

```
1 /* An applet shell
2    Anderson, Franceschi
3 */
4
5 import javax.swing.JApplet;
6 import java.awt.Graphics;
7
8 public class ShellApplet extends JApplet
9 {
10   public void paint( Graphics g )
11   {
12     super.paint( g );
13     // include graphics code here
14   }
15 }
```

EXAMPLE 4.1 The *ShellApplet* Class

Lines 5 and 6 import the two classes that are used in this example: *JApplet*, used at line 8, and *Graphics*, used at line 10. The *Graphics* class is part of the *awt* (Abstract Window Toolkit) package.

Line 8 looks similar to the class header in our Java applications, but it includes two additional words: *extends JApplet*. In this case, we are inheriting from the *JApplet* class. Among other things, our *ShellApplet* class inherits the methods of the *JApplet* class. This means that we don't need to start from scratch to create an applet, so we can write applets that much faster. The *JApplet* class is called the **superclass**, and the *ShellApplet* is called the **subclass**.

The *paint* method, at lines 10–14, is where you put code to display words and graphics that should appear in the applet window. The first statement in the *paint* method is *super.paint(g)*. This statement calls the *paint* method of our superclass, the *JApplet* class, so that it can perform its initialization of the applet window.

The *paint* method's only parameter is a *Graphics* object. This object is automatically generated by the browser or applet viewer, which sends it to the *paint* method. The *Graphics* object represents the graphics context, which, among other things, includes the applet window. The *Graphics* class contains the methods we will need to make text and shapes appear in the applet window.

Skill Practice
with these end-of-chapter questions

4.7.1   Multiple Choice Exercises

Questions 1, 2, 3, 4

4.7.4   Identifying Errors in Code

Questions 26, 27

4.7.5   Debugging Area

Question 28

4.7.8   Technical Writing

Question 38

4.2   Executing an Applet

Like applications, applets need to be compiled before they are run. Once compiled, however, applets are unlike applications in that they do not run standalone. Applets are designed to be run by an Internet browser or an applet viewer. We tell the browser to launch an applet by opening a web page that includes an *APPLET* tag as part of the HTML code. We tell the applet viewer to run the applet by specifying a minimum web page that contains an *APPLET* tag.

If you are not familiar with HTML coding, the language consists of pairs of **tags** that specify formatting for the web page. The opening tag begins the

TABLE 4.1   HTML Tags

HTML Tags	Meaning
<HTML></HTML>	Marks the beginning and end of the web page.
<HEAD></HEAD>	Marks the beginning and end of the header portion of the web page. The header contains general descriptive information about the page.
<TITLE></TITLE>	Marks the beginning and end of the text that will be displayed on the title bar of the browser or applet viewer window.
<BODY></BODY>	Marks the beginning and end of the body of the web page. The body contains the content of the web page.
<APPLET></APPLET>	Identifies the applet to launch in the browser or applet viewer window. The <APPLET> tag supports attributes for specifying the applet name, location of the class file, and size of the applet window. Each attribute consists of the attribute's name followed by an equals sign (=) and the value assigned to that attribute.
	CODE = the class name of the applet
	CODEBASE = the directory in which to search for the class file
	WIDTH = the width of the applet's window in pixels
	HEIGHT = the height of the applet's window in pixels

specific formatting; the closing tag, which is identical to the opening tag except for a leading forward slash (/), ends that formatting. The basic HTML tags used with applets are described in Table 4.1.

Example 4.2 shows a minimal HTML file that you can modify to launch an applet.

```
<HTML>
<HEAD>
    <TITLE>TitleName</TITLE>
</HEAD>
<BODY>
    <APPLET CODE="ClassName.class" CODEBASE="." WIDTH=w
            HEIGHT=h></APPLET>
</BODY>
</HTML>
```

EXAMPLE 4.2   Minimal HTML Page for Launching an Applet

The *CODE* attribute of the *APPLET* tag is the name of the applet class. The *CODEBASE* attribute is the directory in which the JVM should look for the class file. In Example 4.2, the dot (.) for the *CODEBASE* value means that the class file is in the same directory as the HTML page. The *WIDTH* and *HEIGHT* attributes specify in pixels (or picture elements) the width and height of the applet window.

For example, if we had a class called *FirstApplet*, we could use a simple text editor to create the HTML file shown in Example 4.3. In this case, the applet window will be 400 pixels wide and 300 pixels high.

```
<HTML>
<HEAD>
   <TITLE>My First Applet</TITLE>
</HEAD>
<BODY>
   <APPLET CODE="FirstApplet.class" CODEBASE="." WIDTH=400
           HEIGHT=300></APPLET>
</BODY>
</HTML>
```

EXAMPLE 4.3   HTML Page for Launching an Applet Named *FirstApplet*

An applet viewer is provided as part of Sun Microsystems' Java SE Development Kit (JDK). The applet viewer is a minimal browser that enables us to view the applet without needing to open a web browser.

If the name of the web page is *FirstApplet.html*, we can run the applet viewer from the command line as follows:

```
appletviewer FirstApplet.html
```

If you are using an Integrated Development Environment (IDE) such as TextPad, JGrasp, or Eclipse, you can run the applet viewer directly without opening a command line window. In addition, IDEs typically create a minimum web page that contains an *APPLET* tag so that you don't need to create an HTML file for each applet you write.

4.3   Drawing Shapes with *Graphics* Methods

Java's *Graphics* class, in the *java.awt* package, provides methods to draw figures such as rectangles, circles, and lines; to set the colors for drawing; and to write text in a window.

Each drawing method requires you to specify the location in the window to start drawing. Locations are expressed using an (x,y) coordinate system. Each coordinate corresponds to a pixel. The x coordinate specifies the horizontal position, beginning at 0 and increasing as you move across the window to the right. The y coordinate specifies the vertical position, starting at 0 and increasing as you move down the window. Thus for a window that is 400 pixels wide and 300 pixels high, the coordinate (0, 0) corresponds to the upper-left corner; (399, 0) is the upper-right corner; (0, 299) is the lower-left corner, and (399, 299) is the lower-right corner. Figure 4.2 shows a window with a few sample pixels and their (x,y) coordinates.

Table 4.2 shows some useful methods of the *Graphics* class for drawing shapes and displaying text in a window.

As you can see, all these methods have a *void* return type, so they do not return a value. Method calls to these methods should be standalone statements; that is, the method call should be terminated by a semicolon.

The pattern for the method names is simple. The *draw* methods render the outline of the figure, while the *fill* methods render solid figures. The *clearRect* method draws a rectangle in the background color, which effectively erases anything drawn within that rectangle.

Figure 4.3 shows the relationship among the method arguments and the figures drawn.

Figure 4.2

The Graphics Coordinate System

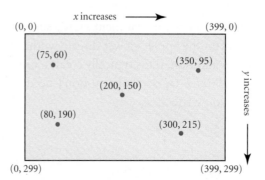

TABLE 4.2   Methods of the *Graphics* Class

Useful Methods of the *Graphics* Class	
Return value	**Method name and argument list**
void	drawLine(int xStart, int yStart, int xEnd, int yEnd)
	draws a line starting at (*xStart, yStart*) and ending at (*xEnd, yEnd*)
void	drawRect(int x, int y, int width, int height)
	draws the outline of a rectangle with its top-left corner at (*x, y*), with the specified *width* and *height* in pixels
void	fillRect(int x, int y, int width, int height)
	draws a solid rectangle with its top-left corner at (*x, y*), with the specified *width* and *height* in pixels
void	clearRect(int x, int y, int width, int height)
	draws a solid rectangle in the current background color with its top-left corner at (*x, y*), with the specified *width* and *height* in pixels
void	drawOval(int x, int y, int width, int height)
	draws the outline of an oval inside an invisible, bounding rectangle with the specified *width* and *height* in pixels. The top-left corner of the rectangle is (*x, y*)
void	fillOval(int x, int y, int width, int height)
	draws a solid oval inside an invisible, bounding rectangle with the specified *width* and *height* in pixels. The top-left corner of the rectangle is (*x, y*)
void	drawString(String s, int x, int y)
	displays the *String s*. If you were to draw an invisible, bounding rectangle around the first letter of the *String*, (*x, y*) would be the lower-left corner of that rectangle
void	drawPolygon(Polygon p)
	draws the outline of *Polygon p*
void	fillPolygon(Polygon p)
	draws the *Polygon p* and fills its area with the current color

Figure 4.3

The Arguments for Drawing Lines, Rectangles, Ovals, and Text

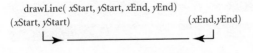

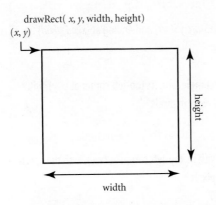

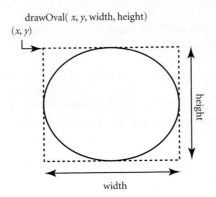

drawString(string, x, y)

Example 4.4 shows how to use the *drawString* method. The coordinate you specify is the lower-left corner of the first character in the *String*. If you want to display more than one line of text in the default font, add 15 to the *y* value for each new line. For example, the statements at lines 13 and 14 print the message "Programming is not a spectator sport!" on two lines.

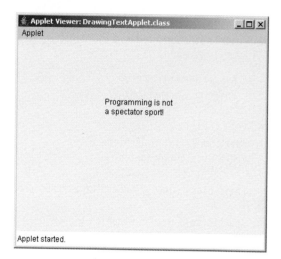

Figure 4.4

**An Applet Displaying
Two Lines of Text**

Figure 4.4 shows the output of the applet.

```
 1 /* Drawing Text
 2    Anderson, Franceschi
 3 */
 4
 5 import javax.swing.JApplet;
 6 import java.awt.Graphics;
 7
 8 public class DrawingTextApplet extends JApplet
 9 {
10   public void paint( Graphics g )
11   {
12     super.paint( g );
13     g.drawString( "Programming is not", 140, 100 );
14     g.drawString( "a spectator sport!", 140, 115 );
15   }
16 }
```

EXAMPLE 4.4   An Applet That Displays Text

To draw a line, you call the *drawLine* method with the coordinates of the beginning of the line and the end of the line. Lines can be vertical, horizontal, or at any angle. In vertical lines, the *startX* and *endX* values are the

same, while in horizontal lines, the *startY* and *endY* values are the same.
Statements at lines 14–16 in Example 4.5 draw a few lines.

```
1 /* A Line Drawing Applet
2    Anderson, Franceschi
3 */
4
5 import javax.swing.JApplet;
6 import java.awt.Graphics;
7
8 public class LineDrawingApplet extends JApplet
9 {
10   public void paint( Graphics g )
11   {
12     super.paint( g );
13
14     g.drawLine( 100, 150, 100, 250 );   // a vertical line
15     g.drawLine( 150, 75, 275, 75 );     // a horizontal line
16     g.drawLine( 0, 0, 399, 299 );       // a diagonal line from
17                                          // the upper-left corner
18                                          // to the lower-right corner
19   }
20 }
```

EXAMPLE 4.5   An Applet That Draws Lines

Figure 4.5 shows these lines drawn in an applet window.

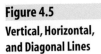

Figure 4.5

Vertical, Horizontal, and Diagonal Lines

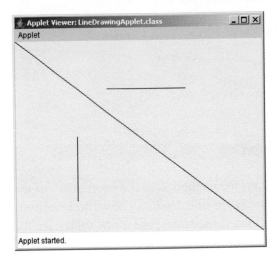

Example 4.6 shows how to use the methods for drawing shapes in an applet. To draw a rectangle, call the *drawRect* or *fillRect* methods with the (*x,y*) coordinate of the upper-left corner, as well as the width in pixels and the height in pixels. Obviously, to draw a square, you specify equal values for the width and height. Line 14 draws a rectangle 40 pixels wide and 100 pixels high; line 15 draws a solid square with sides that are 80 pixels in length.

Drawing an oval or a circle is a little more complex. As you can see in Figure 4.3, you need to imagine a rectangle bounding all sides of the oval or circle. Then the (*x,y*) coordinate you specify in the *drawOval* or *fillOval* method is the location of the upper-left corner of the bounding rectangle. The width and height are the width and height of the bounding rectangle. Line 17 in Example 4.6 draws a filled oval whose upper-left corner is at coordinate (100, 50) and is 40 pixels wide and 100 pixels high; this filled oval is drawn exactly inside the rectangle drawn at line 14. Line 18 draws an oval 100 pixels wide and 40 pixels high, the same dimensions as the oval drawn at line 17, but rotated 90 degrees.

You draw a circle by calling the *drawOval* or *fillOval* methods, specifying equal values for the width and height. If it seems more natural to you to identify circles by giving a center point and a radius, you can convert the center point and radius into the arguments for Java's *drawOval* or *fillOval* methods as done in lines 21–25.

```java
1 /* A Shape Drawing Applet
2    Anderson, Franceschi
3 */
4
5 import javax.swing.JApplet;
6 import java.awt.Graphics;
7
8 public class ShapeDrawingApplet extends JApplet
9 {
10   public void paint( Graphics g )
11   {
12     super.paint( g );
13
14     g.drawRect( 100, 50, 40, 100 );   // rectangle
15     g.fillRect( 200, 70, 80, 80 );    // solid square
16
17     g.fillOval( 100, 50, 40, 100 );   // oval inside the rectangle
18     g.drawOval( 100, 200, 100, 40 );  // same-size oval
19                                       // rotated 90 degrees
```

Figure 4.6

Geometric Shapes and Fills

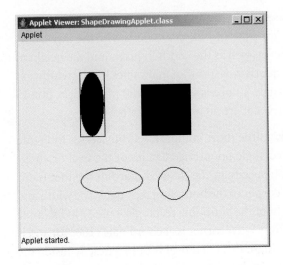

```
20
21    int centerX = 250, centerY = 225;
22    int radius = 25;
23    g.drawOval( centerX - radius, centerY - radius,
24            radius * 2, radius * 2 );  // circle using radius
25                                       // and center
26  }
27 }
```

EXAMPLE 4.6   An Applet That Draws Shapes

Figure 4.6 shows the ovals and rectangles drawn in Example 4.6.

CODE IN ACTION

To see a demonstration of the *Graphics* drawing methods, look for the Chapter 4 Flash movie on the CD-ROM accompanying this book. Click on the link for Chapter 4 to view the movie.

The *Polygon* class, which is in the *java.awt* package, allows us to draw custom shapes. The *Polygon* class represents a polygon as an ordered set of (*x,y*) coordinates; each (*x,y*) coordinate defines a vertex in the polygon. A line, called an edge, connects each (*x,y*) coordinate to the next one in the

TABLE 4.3 A Constructor and Method of the *Polygon* Class

Polygon Constructor		
`Polygon( )`		
creates an empty *Polygon*		
A Useful Method of the *Polygon* Class		
Return value	**Method name and argument list**	
`void`	`addPoint( int x, int y )`	
	appends the coordinate to the polygon	

set. Finally, there is a line connecting the last (x,y) coordinate to the first one. Table 4.3 describes a constructor for the *Polygon* class, as well as a method for adding (x,y) coordinates to the polygon. To draw the polygon, we call the *drawPolygon* or *fillPolygon* methods of the *Graphics* class, shown in Table 4.2.

Example 4.7 demonstrates creating and drawing polygons. On line 7 we import the *Polygon* class from the *java.awt* package. On lines 15–18, we instantiate an empty *Polygon* named *triangle* and add three coordinates to it. Then we draw the triangle as an outlined polygon on line 19. On lines 21–27, we instantiate another *Polygon*, *hexagon*, and add six points to it. We draw this polygon as a solid figure on line 28. The output of this applet is shown in Figure 4.7.

```
1 /* An applet that draws polygons
2    Anderson, Franceschi
3 */
4
5 import javax.swing.JApplet;
6 import java.awt.Graphics;
7 import java.awt.Polygon;
8
9 public class DrawingPolygons extends JApplet
10 {
11   public void paint( Graphics g )
12   {
```

```
13        super.paint( g );
14
15        Polygon triangle = new Polygon( );
16        triangle.addPoint( 75, 50 );
17        triangle.addPoint( 25, 150 );
18        triangle.addPoint( 125, 150 );
19        g.drawPolygon ( triangle );
20
21        Polygon hexagon = new Polygon( );
22        hexagon.addPoint( 150, 100 );
23        hexagon.addPoint( 200, 13 );
24        hexagon.addPoint( 300, 13 );
25        hexagon.addPoint( 350, 100 );
26        hexagon.addPoint( 300, 187 );
27        hexagon.addPoint( 200, 187 );
28        g.fillPolygon ( hexagon );
29    }
30 }
```

EXAMPLE 4.7   Drawing Polygons

Figure 4.7

Output of Example 4.7

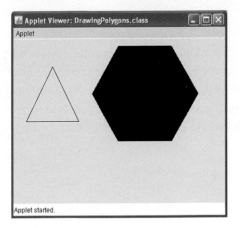

COMMON ERROR TRAP

Do not call the *paint* method. It is called automatically when the applet starts and every time the window contents need to be updated.

What happens if the (x, y) coordinate you specify for a figure isn't inside the window? If a figure's coordinates are outside the bounds of the window, no error will be generated, but the figure won't be visible. If the user resizes the window so that the coordinates are now within the newly sized window, then the figure will become visible.

Now we can write an applet that draws a picture. We've decided to draw an astronaut. Example 4.8 shows the code to do that. Notice that we never call the *paint* method; it is called automatically by the applet viewer or web browser.

```
1  /* An applet with graphics
2       that draws an astronaut
3       Anderson, Franceschi
4  */
5
6  import javax.swing.JApplet;
7  import java.awt.Graphics;
8
9  public class Astronaut extends JApplet
10 {
11
12   public void paint( Graphics g )
13   {
14       super.paint( g );
15
16       int sX = 95, sY = 20; // starting x and y coordinate
17
18       // helmet
19       g.drawOval( sX + 60, sY, 75, 75 );
20       g.drawOval( sX + 70, sY + 10, 55, 55 );
21
22       // face
23       g.drawOval( sX + 83,  sY + 27, 8, 8 );
24       g.drawOval( sX + 103, sY + 27, 8, 8 );
25       g.drawLine( sX + 97, sY + 35, sX + 99, sY + 43 );
26       g.drawLine( sX + 97, sY + 43, sX + 99, sY + 43 );
27       g.drawOval( sX + 90, sY + 48, 15, 6 );
28
29       // neck
30       g.drawRect( sX + 88, sY + 70, 20, 10 );
31
32       // torso
33       g.drawRect( sX + 65, sY + 80, 65, 85 );
34
35       // arms
36       g.drawRect( sX, sY + 80, 65, 20 );
37       g.drawRect( sX + 130, sY + 80, 65, 20 );
38
39       // legs
40       g.drawRect( sX + 75, sY + 165, 20, 80 );
41       g.drawRect( sX + 105, sY + 165, 20, 80 );
```

```
42
43      // flag
44      g.drawLine( sX + 195, sY + 80, sX + 195 , sY );
45      g.drawRect( sX + 195, sY, 75, 45 );
46      g.drawRect( sX + 195, sY, 30, 25 );
47
48      // caption
49      g.drawString( "One small step for man. . .",
50                             sX + 25, sY + 270 );
51   }
52 }
```

EXAMPLE 4.8   An Applet That Draws an Astronaut

When the applet in Example 4.8 runs, our astronaut will look like the one in Figure 4.8.

To draw our astronaut, we used rectangles for the body, arms, legs, and flag; lines for the nose and the flag's stick; circles for the helmet and eyes; and an oval for the mouth. Then we used the *drawString* method to print "One small step for man…"

In line 16, we declare and initialize two variables, *sX* and *sY*. These are the starting *x* and *y* values for the astronaut. The *x* and *y* arguments we send to the *drawRect*, *drawLine*, *drawOval*, and *drawString* methods are specified relative to this starting (*sX*, *sY*) coordinate. By specifying these values, such as *sX* + 60, we are using **offsets**. By using offsets from the starting (*sX*, *sY*) coordinate, we can easily change the position of the astronaut on the screen

SOFTWARE ENGINEERING TIP

When drawing a figure using graphics, specify coordinates as offsets from a starting (*x, y*) coordinate.

Figure 4.8

An Astronaut Made from Rectangles, Ovals, Lines, and Text

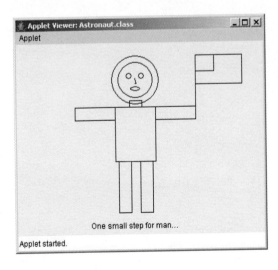

by simply changing the values of *sX* and *sY*. We don't need to change any of the arguments sent to the *Graphics* methods. To demonstrate this, try changing the values of *sX* and *sY* and re-running the applet.

Skill Practice
with these end-of-chapter questions

4.7.1 Multiple Choice Exercises

Questions 6, 7, 8, 9

4.7.2 Reading and Understanding Code

Questions 12, 13, 14, 15

4.7.3 Fill In the Code

Questions 17, 18, 19, 20

4.7.4 Identifying Errors in Code

Questions 21, 22

4.7.6 Write a Short Program

Questions 31, 32, 33

4.7.8 Technical Writing

Question 39

4.4 Using *Color*

All the figures we have drawn were black. That's because when our applet starts, the default drawing color is black. We can add color to the drawing by setting the **current color**, also called the **foreground color**, which is part of the graphics context represented by the *Graphics* object sent to the *paint* method. The *draw* and *fill* methods draw the figures in the current color. The current color remains in effect until it is set to another color. For example, if you set the current color to blue—then call the *drawRect*, *fillOval*, and *drawLine* methods—the rectangle, oval, and line will all be drawn in blue. Then if you set the color to yellow and call the *drawRect* method, that rectangle will be drawn in yellow.

To set the current color, use the *setColor* method of the *Graphics* class as shown in Table 4.4. This method takes a *Color* object as an argument.

TABLE 4.4   The *setColor* Method of the *Graphics* Class

Another Useful Method of the *Graphics* Class	
Return value	**Method name and argument list**
void	setColor(Color c)
	sets the current foreground color to the *Color* specified by *c*

The *Color* class, which is in the *java.awt* package, defines colors using an RGB (Red, Green, Blue) system. Any RGB color is considered to be composed of red, green, and blue components. Each component's value can range from 0 to 255; the higher the value, the higher the concentration of that component in the color. For example, a color with red = 255, green = 0, and blue = 0 is red, and a color with red = 0, green = 0, and blue = 255 is blue.

Gray consists of equal amounts of each component. The higher the value of the components, the lighter the color of gray. This makes sense because white is (255, 255, 255), so the closer a color gets to white, the lighter that color will be. Similarly, the closer the gray value gets to 0, the darker the color, because (0, 0, 0) is black.

The *Color* class provides a set of *static Color* constants representing 13 common colors. Table 4.5 lists the *Color* constants for these common colors and their corresponding red, green, and blue components.

Each color constant is a predefined *Color* object, so you can simply assign the constant to your *Color* object reference. You do not need to instantiate a new *Color* object. *Color* constants can be used wherever a *Color* object is expected. For example, this statement assigns the *Color* constant *Color.RED* to the object reference *red*:

```
Color red = Color.RED;
```

And this statement sets the current color to orange:

```
g.setColor( Color.ORANGE );
```

TABLE 4.5 *Color* Constants and Their Red, Green, and Blue Components

	Color Constant	Red	Green	Blue
	Color.BLACK	0	0	0
	Color.BLUE	0	0	255
	Color.CYAN	0	255	255
	Color.DARK_GRAY	64	64	64
	Color.GRAY	128	128	128
	Color.GREEN	0	255	0
	Color.LIGHT_GRAY	192	192	192
	Color.MAGENTA	255	0	255
	Color.ORANGE	255	200	0
	Color.PINK	255	175	175
	Color.RED	255	0	0
	Color.WHITE	255	255	255
	Color.YELLOW	255	255	0

In addition to using the *Color* constants, you can instantiate your own custom colors using any of the 16 million possible combinations of the component values. The *Color* class has a number of constructors, but for our purposes, we'll need only the constructor shown in Table 4.6.

TABLE 4.6 A *Color* Class Constructor

Color Constructor
`Color( int rr, int gg, int bb )`
allocates a *Color* object with an *rr* red component, *gg* green component, and *bb* blue component

Now let's add color to our astronaut drawing. Example 4.9 shows our modified applet.

```
1 /* An applet with graphics
2    that draws an astronaut in color
3    Anderson, Franceschi
4 */
5
6 import javax.swing.JApplet;
7 import javax.swing.JOptionPane;
8 import java.awt.Graphics;
9 import java.awt.Color;
10
11 public class AstronautWithColor extends JApplet
12 {
13
14   public void paint( Graphics g )
15   {
16     super.paint( g );
17
18     // instantiate a custom color
19     Color spacesuit = new Color( 195, 175, 150 );
20
21     int sX = 100;  // the starting x position
22     int sY = 25;   // the starting y position
23
24     // helmet
25     g.setColor( spacesuit );
26     g.fillOval( sX + 60, sY, 75, 75 );
27     g.setColor( Color.LIGHT_GRAY );
28     g.fillOval( sX + 70, sY + 10, 55, 55 );
29
30     // face
31     g.setColor( Color.DARK_GRAY );
32     g.drawOval( sX + 83,  sY + 27, 8, 8 );
33     g.drawOval( sX + 103, sY + 27, 8, 8 );
34     g.drawLine( sX + 97, sY + 35, sX + 99, sY + 43 );
35     g.drawLine( sX + 97, sY + 43, sX + 99, sY + 43 );
36     g.drawOval( sX + 90, sY + 48, 15, 6 );
37
38     // neck
39     g.setColor( spacesuit );
40     g.fillRect( sX + 88, sY + 70, 20, 10 );
41
42     // torso
```

```
43        g.fillRect( sX + 65, sY + 80, 65, 85 );
44
45        // arms
46        g.fillRect( sX, sY + 80, 65, 20 );
47        g.fillRect( sX + 130, sY + 80, 65, 20 );
48
49        // legs
50        g.fillRect( sX + 75, sY + 165, 20, 80 );
51        g.fillRect( sX + 105, sY + 165, 20, 80 );
52
53        // flag
54        g.setColor( Color.BLACK );
55        g.drawLine( sX + 195, sY + 80, sX + 195 , sY );
56        g.setColor( Color.RED );
57        g.fillRect( sX + 195, sY, 75, 45 );
58        g.setColor( Color.BLUE );
59        g.fillRect( sX + 195, sY, 30, 25 );
60
61        // caption
62        g.setColor( Color.BLACK );
63        g.drawString( "One small step for man...",
64                            sX + 25, sY + 270 );
65    }
66 }
```

EXAMPLE 4.9   An Applet That Draws an Astronaut in Color

Figure 4.9 shows our astronaut in color.

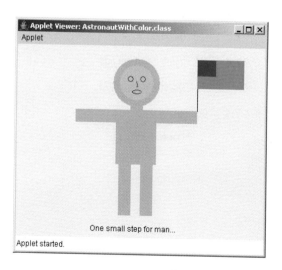

Figure 4.9
Our Astronaut in Color

On line 9, we include an *import* statement for the *Color* class in the *java.awt* package.

For the space suit, we instantiate a custom *Color* object named *spacesuit* on line 19 using the constructor shown in Table 4.6. To draw the astronaut in color, we change the *draw* methods to *fill* methods, and when we draw any figure that is part of the space suit, we make sure the current color is our custom color, *spacesuit.*

It's important to realize that the rendering of the figures occurs in the order in which the *draw* or *fill* methods are executed. Any new figure that occupies the same space as a previously drawn figure will overwrite the previous figure. In this drawing, we intentionally draw the red rectangle of the flag before drawing the blue rectangle. If we drew the rectangles in the opposite order, the blue rectangle would not be visible because the red rectangle, drawn second, would cover the blue rectangle.

Skill Practice
with these end-of-chapter questions

4.7.1   Multiple Choice Exercises

Questions 5, 10

4.7.2   Reading and Understanding Code

Question 11

4.7.3   Fill In the Code

Question 16

4.7.4   Identifying Errors in Code

Questions 23, 24, 25

4.7.5   Debugging Area

Questions 29, 30

4.5 Programming Activity 1: Writing an Applet with Graphics

In this Programming Activity, you will write an applet that uses graphics. You will draw a picture of your own design. The objective of this programming activity is to gain experience with the window coordinate system, the *draw* and *fill* graphics methods, and using colors.

1. Start with the *ShellApplet* class, change the name of the class to represent the figure you will draw, and add an *import* statement for the *Color* class.

2. Create a drawing of your own design. It's helpful to sketch the drawing on graph paper first, then translate the drawing into the coordinates of the applet window. Your drawing should include at least two each of rectangles, ovals, circles, and lines, plus a polygon. Your drawing should also use at least three colors, one of which is a custom color.

3. Label your drawing using the *drawString* method.

Be creative with your drawing!

? DISCUSSION QUESTIONS

1. If you define the starting (x, y) coordinate of the drawing as $(400, 400)$, you might not be able to see the drawing. Explain why and what the user can do to make the drawing visible.

2. What is the advantage to drawing a figure using a starting (x, y) coordinate?

4.6 Chapter Summary

- Applets are Java programs that are run from an applet viewer or an Internet browser. Applets are invoked via the HTML *APPLET* tag.

- When an applet begins executing, the *paint* method is called. The *paint* method is used to display text and graphics on the applet window.

- The *Graphics* class in the *java.awt* package provides methods to draw figures, such as rectangles, circles, polygons, and lines; to set the colors for drawing; and to write text in a window.

SUMMARY

- An (x,y) coordinate system is used to specify locations in the window. Each coordinate corresponds to a pixel (or picture element). The x value specifies the horizontal position, beginning at 0 and increasing as you move right across the window. The y value specifies the vertical position, starting at 0 and increasing as you move down the window.

- All drawing on a graphics window is done in the current color, which is changed using the *setColor* method.

- Objects of the *Color* class, in the *java.awt* package, can be used to set the current color. The *Color* class provides *static* constants for common colors.

- Custom *Color* objects can be instantiated by using a constructor and specifying the red, green, and blue components of the color.

4.7   Exercises, Problems, and Projects

4.7.1   Multiple Choice Exercises

1. What package does the *Graphics* class belong to?
   - ❑ *Graphics*
   - ❑ *java.awt*
   - ❑ *swing*
   - ❑ *Applet*

2. How does a programmer typically get access to a *Graphics* object when coding an applet?
   - ❑ One must be created with the *Graphics* constructor.
   - ❑ It is an instance variable of the class *JApplet*.
   - ❑ It is a parameter of the *paint* method.

3. An applet is a standalone application.
   - ❑ true
   - ❑ false

4. In an applet, the *paint* method is called automatically even if the programmer does not code the method call.
   - ❑ true
   - ❑ false

5. Look at the following code:

```
Color c = Color.BLUE;
```

What is *BLUE*?

❑ a *static* field of the class *Color*

❑ an instance variable of the class *Color*

❑ a *static* method of the class *Color*

❑ an instance method of the class *Color*

6. What can be stated about the line drawn by the following code?

```
g.drawLine( 100, 200, 300, 200 );
```

❑ The line is vertical.

❑ The line is horizontal.

❑ The line is a diagonal.

❑ none of the above.

7. What do the arguments 10, 20 represent in the following statement?

```
g.drawRect( 10, 20, 100, 200 );
```

❑ the (*x,y*) coordinate of the upper-left corner of the rectangle we are drawing

❑ the width and height of the rectangle we are drawing

❑ the (*x,y*) coordinate of the center of the rectangle we are drawing

❑ the (*x,y*) coordinate of the lower-right corner of the rectangle we are drawing

8. What do the arguments 100, 200 represent in the following statement?

```
g.drawRect( 10, 20, 100, 200 );
```

❑ the (*x,y*) coordinate of the upper-left corner of the rectangle we are drawing

❑ the width and height of the rectangle we are drawing

❑ the height and width of the rectangle we are drawing

❑ the (*x,y*) coordinate of the lower-right corner of the rectangle we are drawing

9. How many arguments does the *fillOval* method take?

    ❑ 0

    ❑ 2

    ❑ 4

    ❑ 5

10. In RGB format, a gray color can be coded as *A A A* where the first *A* represents the amount of red in the color, the second *A* the amount of green, and the third *A* the amount of blue. *A* can vary from 0 to 255, including both 0 and 255; how many possible gray colors can we have?

    ❑ 1

    ❑ 2

    ❑ 255

    ❑ 256

    ❑ 257

4.7.2 Reading and Understanding Code

11. In what color will the rectangle be drawn?

```
g.setColor( Color.BLUE );
g.drawRect( 10, 20, 100, 200 );
```

12. What is the length of the line being drawn?

```
g.drawLine( 50, 20, 50, 350 );
```

13. What is the width of the rectangle being drawn?

```
g.fillRect( 10, 20, 250, 350 );
```

14. What is the (*x*,*y*) coordinate of the upper-right corner of the rectangle being drawn?

```
g.fillRect( 10, 20, 250, 350 );
```

15. What is the (*x*,*y*) coordinate of the lower-right corner of the rectangle being drawn?

```
g.drawRect( 10, 20, 250, 350 );
```

4.7.3   Fill In the Code

16. This code sets the current color to red.

```
// assume you have a Graphics object named g
// your code goes here
```

17. This code draws the *String* "Fill in the Code" with the lower-left corner of the first character (the *F*) being at the coordinate (100, 250).

```
// assume you have a Graphics object called g
// your code goes here
```

18. This code draws a filled rectangle with a width of 100 pixels and a height of 300 pixels, starting at the coordinate (50, 30).

```
// assume you have a Graphics object called g
// your code goes here
```

19. This code draws a filled rectangle starting at (50, 30) for its upper-left corner with a lower-right corner at (100, 300).

```
// assume you have a Graphics object called g
// your code goes here
```

20. This code draws a circle of radius 100 with its center located at (200, 200).

```
// assume you have a Graphics object called g
// your code goes here
```

4.7.4   Identifying Errors in Code

21. Where is the error in this code sequence?

```
Graphics g = new Graphics( );
```

22. Where is the error in this code sequence?

```
// we are inside method paint
g.drawString( 'Find the bug', 100, 200 );
```

23. Where is the error in this code sequence?

```
// we are inside method paint
g.setColor( GREEN );
```

24. Where is the error in this code sequence?

```
// we are inside method paint
g.setColor( Color.COBALT );
```

25. Where is the error in this code sequence?

```
// we are inside method paint
g.color = Color.RED;
```

26. Where is the error in this statement?

```
import Graphics;
```

27. Where is the error in this statement?

```
import java.awt.JApplet;
```

4.7.5   Debugging Area—Using Messages from the Java Compiler and Java JVM

28. You coded the following program in the file *MyApplet.java*:

```
import javax.swing.JApplet;
import java.awt.Graphics;

public class MyApplet extends JApplet
{
    public static void paint( Graphics g )    // line 6
    {
        // some code here
    }
}
```

When you compile, you get the following message:

```
MyApplet.java:6: paint(Graphics) in MyApplet cannot
override paint(Graphics) in Container;
 public static void paint( Graphics g )    // line 6
                   ^

 overriding method is static
1 error
```

Explain what the problem is and how to fix it.

29. You imported the *Color* class and coded the following on line 10 of the class *MyApplet.java*:

```
Color c = new Color( 1.4, 234, 23 );    // line 10
```

When you compile, you get the following message:

```
MyApplet.java:10: cannot find symbol

Color c = new Color( 1.4, 234, 23 );    // line 10
                   ^

symbol   : constructor Color (double,int,int)
location : class Color
1 error
```

Explain what the problem is and how to fix it.

30. You coded the following on line 10 of the class *MyApplet.java*:

```
Color c = Color.Blue; // line 10
```

When you compile, you get the following message:

```
MyApplet.java:10: cannot find symbol
        Color c = Color.Blue;    // line 10
                        ^

symbol  : variable Blue
location: class Color
1 error
```

Explain what the problem is and how to fix it.

4.7.6 Write a Short Program

31. Write an applet that displays the five Olympic rings.

32. Write an applet that displays a tic-tac-toe board. Include a few X's and O's.

33. Write an applet that displays a rhombus (i.e., a parallelogram with equal sides). Your rhombus should not be a square.

4.7.7 Programming Projects

34. Write an applet that displays two eyes. An eye can be drawn using an oval, a filled circle, and lines. On the applet, write a word or two about these eyes.

35. Write an applet that displays the following coins: a quarter, a dime, and a nickel. These three coins should be drawn as basic circles (of different diameters) with the currency value inside (for instance, "$.25").

36. Write an applet that displays a basic house, made up of lines (and possibly rectangles). Your house should have multiple colors. On the applet, give a title to the house (for instance, "Java House").

37. Write an applet that displays a black and red bull's eye target, typically made up of several concentric circles.

4.7.8   Technical Writing

38. On the World Wide Web, an applet is a program that executes on the "client side" (a local machine such as your own PC) as opposed to the "server side" (such as a server at *www.yahoo.com*). Do you see any potential problem executing the same program, such as an applet, on possibly millions of different computers worldwide?

39. If the *drawRect* method did not exist, but you still had the *drawLine* method available, explain how you would be able to draw a rectangle.

4.7.9   Group Project (for a group of 1, 2, or 3 students)

40. Write an applet and one HTML file calling the applet.

    The applet should include the following:

    ❏ a drawing of a chessboard piece (it can be in a single color)

    ❏ a description of a particular piece of a chessboard (for instance, a rook) and its main legal moves

    In order to make the description visually appealing, you should use several colors and several fonts. You will need to look up the following on Sun's Java website:

    ❏ the *Font* class

    ❏ how the *Font* class constructors work

    ❏ the method *setFont* of the *Graphics* class

CHAPTER 5

Flow of Control, Part 1: Selection

CHAPTER CONTENTS

Introduction

In Chapter 1, we said that the order of a program's instructions is critical to producing correct results. The order in which the instructions are executed is called the **flow of control** of the program. There are essentially four types of flow of control: sequential execution, method calls, selection, and looping. Most programs use a combination of all types of flow of control.

So far, our programs have used sequential execution and method calls exclusively. In our Java applications, the JVM executed the first instruction in the *main* method, then executed the next instruction in *main*, and continued executing instructions in order until there were no more instructions to execute. Whenever one of the instructions included a method call, the instructions in the method were executed until the method returned and we resumed execution of instructions in order.

Sometimes, however, you don't want to execute every instruction. Some instructions should be executed only for certain input values, but not for others. For example, we may want to count only the odd numbers or perform only the operation that the user selects from a menu. For these applications, we need a way to determine at run time the input values we have and, therefore, which instructions we should execute.

In this chapter, we'll discuss **selection**, which gives us a way to test for certain conditions and to select the instructions to execute based on the results of the test. To perform selection, Java provides a number of alternatives: *if*, *if/else*, *if/else if*, the conditional operator (*?:*), and *switch*.

5.1   Forming Conditions

Often in a program, we need to compare variables or objects. For instance, we could be interested in knowing if a person's age is over 18, or if a student's average test score is above 90. If the age is over 18, that person would be allowed to shop online. If a student has an average of 90 or better, that student will be placed on the honor roll, or if a student's grade is below 60, he or she will be sent a warning.

Java provides equality, relational, and logical operators to evaluate and test whether an expression is true or false. It also provides selection statements to transfer control to a different part of the program depending on the result of that test.

5.1.1 Equality Operators

A common operation is to compare two variables or values of the same data type to determine if their values are equal. For example, we need to compare the user's input to a 'y' to determine whether he or she wants to play again. Or if we want to print a list of students who will continue next year, we need to eliminate the students who are graduating seniors.

To compare values of primitive data types, Java provides the equality operators shown in Table 5.1. Both are binary operators, meaning that they take two operands. The operands may be expressions that evaluate to a primitive numeric or *boolean* type or an object reference. The result of an expression composed of a relational operator and its two operands is a *boolean* value, that is, *true* or *false*.

For instance, if an *int* variable *age* holds the value 32, then

the expression (`age == 32`) will evaluate to *true*, and

the expression (`age != 32`) will evaluate to *false*.

The following expression can be used to eliminate seniors by testing whether the value of the *int* variable *yearInCollege* is not equal to 4:

`yearInCollege != 4`

The following expression can be used in a game program to determine whether the user wants to play again:

`playAgain == 'y'`

TABLE 5.1   Equality Operators

Equality Operator	Type	Meaning
==	binary	is equal to
!=	binary	is not equal to

Assuming the user's input is stored in the *char* variable *playAgain*, then if the user typed 'y', the expression evaluates to *true*; with any other input value, the expression evaluates to *false*.

A common error is to use the assignment operator instead of the equality operator. For example:

```
playAgain = 'y'
```

assigns the value *y* to the variable *playAgain*. Confusing the assignment and equality operators is easy to do—so easy, in fact, that we can almost guarantee that you will make this mistake at least once.

Although the equality operators can be used to compare object references, these operators cannot be used to compare objects. We discuss the comparison of objects later in the chapter.

5.1.2   Relational Operators

To compare values of primitive numeric types, Java provides the relational operators shown in Table 5.2. These operators are binary, meaning that they take two operands, each of which is an expression that evaluates to a primitive numeric type. The relational operators cannot be used with *boolean* expressions or with object references.

Again, if an *int* variable *age* holds the value 32, then

the expression (age < 32) will evaluate to *false*,

the expression (age <= 32) will evaluate to *true*,

the expression (age > 32) will evaluate to *false*, and

the expression (age >= 32) will evaluate to *true*.

COMMON ERROR TRAP

Do not confuse the equality operator == (double equal signs) with the assignment operator = (one equal sign).

TABLE 5.2   Relational Operators

Relational Operator	Type	Meaning
<	binary	is less than
<=	binary	is less than or equal to
>	binary	is greater than
>=	binary	is greater than or equal to

This expression tests whether an *int* variable *testScore* is at least 90:

```
testScore >= 90
```

This code tests whether that test score is less than 60:

```
testScore < 60
```

5.1.3 Logical Operators

A common operation in a program is to test whether a combination of conditions is true or false. For these operations, Java provides the logical operators !, &&, and ||, which correspond to the Boolean logic operators NOT, AND, and OR. These operators, which are shown in Table 5.3, take *boolean* expressions as operands. A *boolean* expression can be any legal combination of *boolean* variables; a condition using relational operators that evaluates to *true* or *false*; or a call to a method that returns a *boolean* value.

The NOT operator (!) takes one *boolean* expression as an operand and inverts the value of that operand. If the operand is *true*, the result will be *false*; and if the operand is *false*, the result will be *true*.

The AND operator (&&) takes two *boolean* expressions as operands; if both operands are *true*, then the result will be *true*; otherwise, it will be *false*.

The OR operator (||) also takes two *boolean* expressions as operands. If both operands are *false*, then the result will be *false*; otherwise, it will be *true*. The OR operator consists of two vertical bars with no intervening space. On the PC keyboard, the vertical bar is the shifted character above the *Enter* key.

The truth table for these logical operators is shown in Table 5.4.

The order of precedence of the relational and logical operators is shown in Table 5.5, along with the arithmetic operators. Note that the Unary NOT

REFERENCE POINT

The complete Operator Precedence Chart is provided in Appendix B.

TABLE 5.3   Logical Operators

Logical Operator	Type	Meaning
!	unary	NOT
&&	binary	AND
||	binary	OR

TABLE 5.4   Truth Table for Logical Operators

Operands		Operations		
a	b	!a	a && b	a || b
true	true	false	true	true
true	false	false	false	true
false	true	true	false	true
false	false	true	false	false

TABLE 5.5   Operator Precedence

Operator Hierarchy	Order of Same-Statement Evaluation	Operation
( )	left to right	parentheses for explicit grouping
++, --	right to left	shortcut postincrement
++, --, !	**right to left**	shortcut preincrement, **logical unary NOT**
*, /, %	left to right	multiplication, division, modulus
+, -	left to right	addition or *String* concatenation, subtraction
<, <=, >, >=	**left to right**	**relational operators: less than, less than or equal to, greater than, greater than or equal to**
==, !=	**left to right**	**equality operators: equal to and not equal to**
&&	**left to right**	**logical AND**
||	**left to right**	**logical OR**
=, +=, -=, *=, /=, %=	right to left	Assignment operator and shortcut assignment operators

operator (!) has the highest precedence of the relational and logical operators, followed by the relational operators, then the equality operators, then AND (&&), then OR (||).

Example 5.1 shows these operators at work.

```
 1 /* Using Logical Operators
 2    Anderson, Franceschi
 3 */
 4
 5 public class LogicalOperators
 6 {
 7  public static void main( String [ ] args )
 8  {
 9    int age = 75;
10    boolean test;
11
12    test = ( age > 18 && age < 65 );
13    System.out.println( age + " > 18 && " + age + " < 65 is " + test );
14
15    // short circuitry with AND
16    test = ( age < 65 && age > 18 );
17    System.out.println( age + " < 65 && " + age + " > 18 is " + test );
18
19    // short circuitry with OR
20    test = ( age > 65 || age < 18 );
21    System.out.println( age + " > 65 || " + age + " < 18 is " + test );
22
23    // AND has higher precedence than OR
24    test = ( age > 65 || age < 18  && false );
25    System.out.println( age + " > 65 || " + age
26                          + " < 18 && false is " + test );
27
28    // use of parentheses to force order of execution
29    test = ( ( age > 65 || age < 18 )  && false );
30    System.out.println( "( " + age + " > 65 || " + age
31                          + " < 18 ) && false is " + test );
32  }
33 }
```

EXAMPLE 5.1   How Logical Operators Work

Line 12 evaluates whether the variable *age* is greater than 18 and less than 65 and assigns the result to the *boolean* variable *test*. Since line 9 set the value of *age* to 75, the first operand (*age* > *18*) evaluates to *true*. The second operand (*age* < *65*) evaluates to *false*; finally,

```
true && false
```

evaluates to *false*, and *false* is assigned to *test*, which is printed at line 13. Line 16 evaluates the same expression as in line 12, but in reverse order. Now the first operand (*age* < *65*) evaluates to *false*, and therefore, since the operator is the logical AND, the overall expression evaluates to *false*, independently of the value of the second operand. Because (*false* && something) always evaluates to *false*, the second operand (*age* > *18*) will never be evaluated by the Java compiler. This is called **short-circuit evaluation**.

Line 20 shows an example of short-circuit evaluation for the logical OR operator. The first operand (*age* > *65*) evaluates to *true*, resulting in the overall expression evaluating to *true*, independently of the value of the second operand. Because (*true* || something) always evaluates to *true*, the second operand will never be evaluated by the Java compiler.

As shown in Table 5.5, the logical AND operator has higher precedence than the logical OR operator. Thus, the expression in line 24 is not evaluated from left to right; rather, the second part of the expression (*age* < *18* && *false*) is evaluated first, which evaluates to *false*. Then (*age* > *65* || *false*) evaluates to *true*, which is assigned to *test*, and then output at lines 25–26. If we want to evaluate the expression from left to right, we have to use parentheses to force this, as in line 29. Then, (*age* > *65* || *age* < *18*) is evaluated first and evaluates to *true*; (*true* && *false*) is evaluated next and evaluates to *false*.

Figure 5.1 shows the output of Example 5.1.

Figure 5.1

Output from Example 5.1

```
75 > 18 && 75 < 65 is false
75 < 65 && 75 > 18 is false
75 > 65 || 75 < 18 is true
75 > 65 || 75 < 18  && false is true
( 75 > 65 || 75 < 18 ) && false is false
```

Suppose we have three *ints*: *x*, *y*, and *z*, and we want to test if *x* is less than both *y* and *z*. A common error is to express the condition this way:

```
x < y && z // incorrect comparison of x to y and z
```

Because *z* is not a *boolean* variable, this statement will generate a compiler error. Both operands of the logical AND and logical OR operators must evaluate to a *boolean* expression. The correct expression is the following:

```
x < y && x < z
```

There are often several ways to express the same condition using the Java logical operators. For instance, suppose we have two *boolean* variables called *flag1* and *flag2* and we want to test if at least one of them is *false*.

In plain English, we would translate it as *flag1 is false OR flag2 is false*.

Table 5.6 provides several equivalent expressions for the preceding test.

Although all the expressions in Table 5.6 are equivalent, the first expression, which is the simplest translation of the condition to test, is the easiest to understand and would be the best selection for readability.

 COMMON ERROR TRAP

Be sure that both operands of the logical AND and logical OR operators are *boolean* expressions. Expressions such as x < y && z, with *x*, *y*, and *z* being numeric types, are illegal. Instead, use the expression x < y && x < z

DeMorgan's Laws

Thanks to the work of the British mathematician Augustus DeMorgan, we have a set of rules to help develop expressions that are equivalent. DeMorgan, who is known for his work in Boolean algebra and set theory, developed what are known as DeMorgan's Laws. They are the following:

1. `NOT( A AND B ) = ( NOT A ) OR ( NOT B )`
2. `NOT( A OR B ) = ( NOT A ) AND ( NOT B )`

TABLE 5.6   Examples of Equivalent Expressions

Equivalent Expressions	English Meaning
`( flag1 == false ) || ( flag2 == false )`	*flag1* is false OR *flag2* is false
`!flag1 || !flag2`	*!flag1* is true OR *!flag2* is true
`! ( flag1 && flag 2 )`	not both *flag1* and *flag2* are true

In Java, therefore, using the first law, we see that

> `!( a && b )` is equivalent to `!a || !b`

Using the second law, we see that

> `!( a || b )` is equivalent to `!a && !b`

These laws can be verified simply by the extended truth table shown in Table 5.7.

Thus, to use DeMorgan's Laws, you need to change the AND operator to OR and change the OR operator to AND, and apply the NOT operator (!) to each operand of a logical operator. When the operands are expressions using relational or equality operators, the negated expressions are shown in Table 5.8.

TABLE 5.7   Truth Table for DeMorgan's Laws

a	b	!a	!b	a && b	a || b	!(a && b)	!a || !b	!(a || b)	!a && !b
true	true	false	false	true	true	false	false	false	false
true	false	false	true	false	true	true	true	false	false
false	true	true	false	false	true	true	true	false	false
false	false	true	true	false	false	true	true	true	true

TABLE 5.8   The Logical NOT Operator Applied to Relational and Equality Operators

Expression	! (Expression)
a == b	a != b
a != b	a == b
a < b	a >= b
a >= b	a < b
a > b	a <= b
a <= b	a > b

TABLE 5.9   More Examples of Equivalent Expressions

Equivalent Expressions	English Meaning
(age <= 18 || age >= 65)	*age* is less than or equal to 18 or *age* is greater than or equal to 65
!(age > 18 && age < 65)	*age* is not between 18 and 65
!(age > 18) || !(age < 65)	*age* is not greater than 18 or *age* is not less than 65

For instance, suppose we have an *int* variable named *age*, representing the age of a person, and we want to assess whether *age* is less than or equal to 18 or greater than or equal to 65.

Table 5.9 provides several equivalent expressions for the preceding test.

Again, although all the expressions in Table 5.9 are equivalent, the first expression, which is the simplest translation of the condition to test, is the easiest to read.

SOFTWARE ENGINEERING TIP

Compose Boolean expressions so that they are easy to read and understand.

Skill Practice
with these end-of-chapter questions

5.14.1   Multiple Choice Exercises

Questions 1, 2, 3, 4, 5, 6, 7

5.14.2   Reading and Understanding Code

Questions 10, 11

5.14.4   Identifying Errors in Code

Questions 31, 32

5.2   Simple Selection with *if*

The simple selection pattern is appropriate when your program needs to perform an operation for one set of data, but not for all other data. For this situation, we use a simple *if* statement, which has this pattern:

```
if ( condition )
{
   true block
}
next statement
```

The true block can contain one or more statements and is executed only if the condition evaluates to *true*. After the true block executes, the instruction following the *if* statement is executed. If the condition is *false*, the true block is skipped and execution picks up at the next instruction after the *if* statement. If the true block contains only one statement, the curly braces are optional. Figure 5.2 illustrates the flow of control of a simple *if* statement.

In Example 5.2, we first prompt the user to enter a grade at lines 12–13. Then we prompt the user for any extra credit points at lines 15–16. At line 18, we test whether the extra credit points are greater than 0. If so, we add the extra credit points to the test grade at line 19. Then, no matter what the extra credit was, lines 21–22 are executed, which print the final grade. Figures 5.3 and 5.4 show two runs of the program, one with extra credit greater than 0, and one with no extra credit.

Figure 5.2

Flow of Control of a Simple *if* Statement

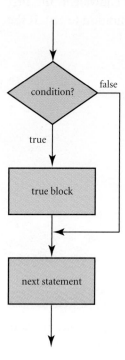

Figure 5.3

Output of Example 5.2 with 10 Extra Credit Points

```
Enter your test grade > 85
Enter your extra credit > 10
Your final test grade is 95
```

Figure 5.4

**Output of Example 5.2
with No Extra Credit**

```
Enter your test grade > 85
Enter your extra credit > 0
Your final test grade is 85
```

```
 1 /* Using if to calculate a final test grade
 2    Anderson, Franceschi
 3 */
 4 import java.util.Scanner;
 5
 6 public class TestGrade
 7 {
 8   public static void main( String [ ] args )
 9   {
10     Scanner scan = new Scanner( System.in );
11
12     System.out.print( "Enter your test grade > " );
13     int grade = scan.nextInt( );
14
15     System.out.print( "Enter your extra credit > " );
16     int extraCredit = scan.nextInt( );
17
18     if ( extraCredit > 0 )
19         grade += extraCredit;
20
21     System.out.println( "Your final test grade is "
22                    + grade ) ;
23   }
24 }
```

EXAMPLE 5.2   Working with *if* Statements

Notice the indentation of the true block (line 19). Indenting clarifies the structure of the program. It's easy to see that we add the extra credit to the test grade only if the condition is true. Notice also that we skipped a line after the end of the *if* statement; this further separates the true block from the instruction that follows the *if* statement, making it easier to see the flow of control.

**SOFTWARE
ENGINEERING TIP**

Indent the true block in an *if* statement for clarity.

Many software engineers believe it's a good practice to include the curly braces even if only one statement is included in the true block, because it increases clarity and ease of maintenance. The curly braces increase clarity because they highlight the section of code to be executed when the condition is *true*. Program maintenance is easier because if the program requirements change and you need to add a second statement to the true block, the curly braces are already in place.

Note that there is no semicolon after the condition. If you place a semicolon after the condition, as in this **incorrect** statement,

```
if ( grade >= 60 );  // incorrect to place semicolon here
      System.out.println( "You passed" );
```

 **COMMON ERROR TRAP**

Adding a semicolon after the condition of an *if* statement indicates that the true block is empty and can cause a logic error at run time.

the compiler will not generate an error. Instead, it will consider the semicolon to indicate that the *if* statement is empty, because a semicolon by itself indicates a statement that does nothing. In this case, the compiler concludes that there is no instruction to execute when the condition is *true*. As a result, when the program runs, the statement

```
System.out.println( "You passed" );
```

is treated as though it follows the *if* statement, and therefore, the message "You passed" will be printed regardless of the value of *grade*.

5.3   Selection Using *if/else*

The second form of an *if* statement is appropriate when the data falls into two mutually exclusive categories and different instructions should be executed for each category. For these situations, we use an *if/else* statement, which has the following pattern:

```
if ( condition )
{
   true block
}
else
{
   false block
}
next statement
```

If the condition evaluates to *true*, the true block is executed and the false block is skipped. If the condition evaluates to *false*, the true block is skipped and the false block is executed. In either situation, the statement following the *if* statement is executed next. Figure 5.5 illustrates the flow of control of an *if/else* statement.

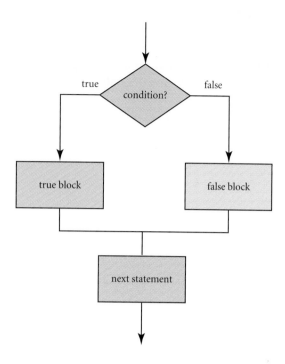

Figure 5.5

Flow of Control of an *if/else* Statement

If the true or false block contains only one statement, the curly braces are optional for that block.

Again, notice the indentation of the true and false blocks and that the *else* and curly braces line up under the *if*. This coding style makes it easy to see which statements belong to the true block and which belong to the false block. If the indentation is incorrect, a reader of your program may misunderstand which statements will be executed. In any event, the compiler ignores the indentation; the indentation is designed only to make it easier for humans to understand the logic of the code.

In Example 5.3, we test a grade to determine whether it is a passing grade (>= 60) or a failing grade (any other value). This is a case where the data is mutually exclusive: either the grade is a passing grade or it is not. We want to print a different message depending on the grade status. After prompting the user for a numeric grade, we declare a *String* to hold the appropriate message (line 16), which will be determined in our *if/else* statement. If the *if* condition, (grade >= 60), is true, then we assign "You passed" to *message*. If the condition is false, we assign "You failed" to *message.* On line 22, after the *if/else* statement completes, we print whatever *String* we have assigned to *message.* Figures 5.6 and 5.7 show two runs of the program, first with a grade greater than or equal to 60, and then with a grade less than 60.

```java
1 /* Using if/else
2    Anderson, Franceschi
3 */
4
5 import java.util.Scanner;
6
7 public class PassingGrade
8 {
9  public static void main( String [ ] args )
10  {
11     Scanner scan = new Scanner( System.in );
12
13     System.out.print( "Enter a grade > " );
14     int grade = scan.nextInt( );
15
16     String message;
17     if ( grade >= 60 )
18      message = "You passed";
19     else
20      message = "You failed ";
21
22     System.out.println( message ) ;
23  }
24 }
```

EXAMPLE 5.3   Working with *if/else* Statements

Figure 5.6

Output from Example 5.3 with *grade* >= 60

```
Enter a grade > 60
You passed
```

Figure 5.7

Output from Example 5.3 with *grade* < 60

```
Enter a grade > 59
You failed
```

Note that we could have used two sequential *if* statements, as in:

```
if ( grade >= 60 )
    message = "You passed";

if ( grade < 60 )
    message = "You failed ";
```

However, if the first condition, (grade >= 60), is false, the second condition, (grade < 60), must be true. So an *if/else* simplifies our processing and avoids unnecessarily testing two conditions when only one of the conditions can be true.

Block Scope

The scope of a variable is the region within a program where the variable can be **referenced**, or used. When we declare a variable, its scope extends from the point at which it is declared until the end of the block in which we declared it. A method, such as *main*, is a block. Thus, in Example 5.3, the scope of the object reference *scan* extends from line 11 through the end of *main*. Thus, we can legally reference *scan* on line 14. Similarly, the scope of *grade* extends from its declaration (line 14) through the end of *main*, and we can legally reference it on line 17 in the *if* condition. Finally, the scope of the *String message* extends from line 16 through the end of *main*, and thus we can legally reference *message* on lines 18, 20, and 22.

The true blocks and false blocks for *if* statements are also blocks. Thus, if instead of declaring the *String message* on line 16, we declare it inside the true block of the *if* statement as in the following,

```
if ( grade >= 60 )
{
    String message = "You passed";
}
else
    message = "You failed ";

System.out.println( message );
```

then the scope of *message* extends from its declaration only until the end of the true block. In this case, the compiler will generate "cannot find symbol" error messages for the references to *message* inside the false block and for the *System.out.println* statement after the *if* statement because *message* is out of scope outside of the true block.

CODE IN ACTION

On the CD-ROM included with this book, you will find a Flash movie illustrating step-by-step how to use an *if/else* statement. Click on the link for Chapter 5 to view the movie.

Skill Practice
with these end-of-chapter questions

5.14.2   Reading and Understanding Code

Questions 12, 13

5.14.3   Fill In the Code

Questions 20, 21, 22, 23, 24, 25, 26, 27, 28, 29, 30

5.14.4   Identifying Errors in Code

Questions 33, 34, 35

5.14.5   Debugging Area

Question 40

5.14.6   Write a Short Program

Questions 42, 43, 46, 48

5.14.8   Technical Writing

Question 54

5.4   Selection Using *if/else if*

The last form of an *if* statement is appropriate when the data falls into more than two mutually exclusive categories and the appropriate instructions to execute are different for each category. For this situation, Java provides the *if/else if* statement.

The *if/else if* statement follows this pattern:

```
if ( condition 1 )
{
    true block for condition 1
}
else if ( condition 2 )
```

```
{
      true block for condition 2
}
. . .
else if ( condition n )
{
      true block for condition n
}
else
{
      false block for all conditions being false
}
next statement
```

The flow of control for this form of the *if* statement is shown in Figure 5.8.

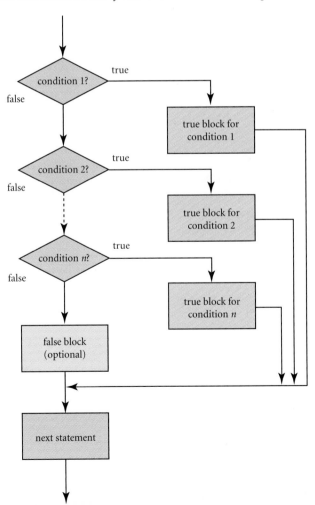

Figure 5.8

Flow of Control of an *if/else if* Statement

There can be any number of conditions in an *if/else if* statement. As you can see, once a condition evaluates to *true* for any value, control moves to the true block for that condition, then skips the remainder of the conditions, continuing execution at any statement that follows the *if/else if* statement. The final false block (along with the final *else*) is optional and is executed only when none of the conditions evaluates to *true*.

We can use the *if/else if* statement to determine a student's letter grade based on his or her numeric grade. Example 5.4 demonstrates a Java application that prompts a student for a test grade and translates that grade into a letter grade.

```
1 /* A program to translate a numeric grade into a letter grade
2     Anderson, Franceschi
3 */
4
5 import java.util.Scanner;
6
7 public class LetterGrade
8 {
9   public static void main( String [ ] args )
10   {
11     Scanner scan = new Scanner( System.in );
12
13     char letterGrade;
14
15     System.out.print( "Enter your test grade: " );
16     int grade = scan.nextInt( );
17
18     if ( grade >= 90 )
19         letterGrade = 'A';
20
21     else if ( grade >= 80 )
22         letterGrade = 'B';
23
24     else if ( grade >= 70 )
25         letterGrade = 'C';
26
27     else if ( grade >= 60 )
28         letterGrade = 'D';
29
```

```
30    else  // grade fits none of the conditions
31        letterGrade = 'F';
32
33    System.out.println( "Your test grade of " + grade
34                    + " is a letter grade of " + letterGrade );
35  }
36 }
```

EXAMPLE 5.4   A Demonstration of *if/else if*

```
Enter your test grade: 83
Your test grade of 83 is a letter grade of B
```

Figure 5.9
Output from Example 5.4

Figure 5.9 shows the output from the program when a student enters a grade of 83.

Notice that each condition is a simple relational expression. Even though we assign a *B* letter grade when the numeric grade is between 80 and 89, the condition for a *B* letter grade (line 21) is simply:

```
if ( grade >= 80 )
```

We don't need to write the condition as

```
if ( grade >= 80 && grade < 90 )
```

because by the time the condition is tested at line 21, all numeric grades greater than or equal to 90 have been eliminated by the test condition at line 18. Any grade greater than or equal to 90 causes the condition at line 18, (grade >= 90), to evaluate to *true*. For those grades, the flow of control is to assign an *A* to *letterGrade* at line 19, then skip the remainder of the conditions, continuing execution at the statement following the *if/else if* statement, which is line 33 in this example. Thus, if the condition at line 21 is evaluated, we know that the *grade* must be less than 90.

CODE IN ACTION

On the CD-ROM included with this book, you will find a Flash movie illustrating step-by-step how to use an *if/else if* statement. Click on the link for Chapter 5 to view the movie.

Skill Practice
with these end-of-chapter questions

5.14.1   Multiple Choice Exercises

Question 8

5.14.2   Reading and Understanding Code

Question 15

5.14.4   Identifying Errors in Code

Questions 36, 37, 38

5.5   Sequential and Nested *if/else* Statements

When you need the results of one *if* statement's processing before you can evaluate the next condition, you can write multiple *if* statements either sequentially or nested within other *if* statements.

5.5.1   Sequential *if/else* Statements

Finding the Minimum or Maximum Values

To illustrate sequential *if* statements, let's look at the problem of finding the smallest of three numbers.

In Chapter 3, we found the smallest of three numbers using the *min* method of the *Math* class. We first found the smaller of two numbers, then found the smaller of that result and the third number. We can use that same logic to find the smallest of three numbers with multiple, sequential *if* statements. First we find the smaller of the first two numbers, then we find the smaller of that result and the third number. The pseudocode for this application is:

```
read number1
read number2
read number3

if number1 is less than number2
    smallest is number1
else
    smallest is number2
```

if number3 is less than smallest

  smallest is number3

Translating the pseudocode into Java, we get the application in Example 5.5, which prompts the user for three integers and outputs the smallest of the three numbers. In this application, we use two *if* statements. The first *if* statement (lines 23–26) uses an *if/else* statement to find the smaller of the first two integers and stores that value into the variable *smallest*. Then, the second *if* statement (lines 28–29) compares the third integer to the value stored in *smallest*. In the second *if* statement, we don't use an *else* clause, because we need to change the value in *smallest* only if the condition is *true,* that is, if the third number is less than *smallest*. Otherwise, the smallest value is already stored in *smallest*.

```java
1   /* Find the smallest of three integers
2       Anderson, Franceschi
3   */
4
5   import java.util.Scanner;
6
7   public class FindSmallest
8   {
9     public static void main( String [ ] args )
10    {
11        int smallest;
12        int num1, num2, num3;
13
14        Scanner scan = new Scanner( System.in );
15
16        System.out.print( "Enter the first integer: " );
17        num1 = scan.nextInt( );
18        System.out.print( "Enter the second integer: " );
19        num2 = scan.nextInt( );
20        System.out.print( "Enter the third integer: " );
21        num3 = scan.nextInt( );
22
23        if ( num1 < num2 )
24            smallest = num1;
25        else
26            smallest = num2;
27
```

```
28          if ( num3 < smallest )
29              smallest = num3;
30
31          System.out.println( "The smallest is " + smallest );
32      }
33  }
```

EXAMPLE 5.5   An Application with Sequential *if* Statements

When the program in Example 5.5 is run using 6, 7, and 5 for the three integers, the output is as shown in Figure 5.10.

One more point. The code only checks that one number is less than another. What happens if two or more of the numbers are equal? The code still works! We only need to find the smallest value; we don't care which of the variables holds that smallest value.

5.5.2   Nested *if/else* Statements

If statements can be written as part of the true or false block of another *if* statement. These are called nested *if* statements. Typically, you nest *if* statements when more information is required beyond the results of the first *if* statement.

One difficulty that arises with nested *if* statements is specifying which *else* clause pairs with which *if* statement, especially if some *if* statements have *else* clauses and others do not. The compiler matches any *else* clause with the most previous *if* statement that doesn't already have an *else* clause. If this matching is not what you want, you can use curly braces to specify the desired *if/else* pairing.

In this code, we have one *if* statement nested within another *if* statement.

```
if ( x == 2 )
        if ( y == x )
            System.out.println( "x and y equal 2" );
        else
            System.out.println( "x equals 2, but y does not" );
```

Figure 5.10

Output from Example 5.5

```
Enter the first integer: 6
Enter the second integer: 7
Enter the third integer: 5
The smallest is 5
```

Without curly braces, the entire second *if* statement comprises the true block of the first condition (x == 2), and the *else* is paired with the second condition (y == x), because this is the most previous *if* condition that doesn't have an *else*.

However, we can force the *else* clause to be paired with the first condition by using curly braces, as follows:

```
if ( x == 2 )
{
   if ( y == x )
      System.out.println( "x and y equal 2" );
}
else
   System.out.println( "x does not equal 2" );
```

With the curly braces added, the *if* condition (y == x), along with its true block, becomes the complete true block for the condition (x == 2), and the *else* clause now belongs to the first *if* condition (x == 2).

Why can't we just alter the indentation to indicate our meaning? Remember that indentation increases the readability of the code for humans. The compiler ignores indentation and instead follows Java's syntactic rules.

Dangling else

A common error is writing *else* clauses that don't match any *if* conditions. This is called a **dangling else**. For example, the following code, which includes three *else* clauses and only two *if* conditions, will generate this compiler error:

```
   'else' without 'if'
```

```
if ( x == 2 )

   if ( y == x )
      System.out.println( "x and y equal 2" );

   else // matches y==x
      System.out.println( "y does not equal 2" );

else // matches x==2
   System.out.println( "x does not equal 2" );

else // no matching if!
   System.out.println( "x and y are not equal" );
```

COMMON ERROR TRAP

Be sure that all *else* clauses match an *if* condition. Writing *else* clauses that don't match *if* conditions will generate an `'else'` `without 'if'` compiler error.

For a more complex and real-world example of nested *if* statements, let's generate a random number between 1 and 10. After we generate the random number, we'll prompt the user for a guess. First we'll verify that the guess is between 1 and 10. If it isn't, we'll print a message. Otherwise, we'll check whether the user has guessed the number. If so, we'll print a congratulatory message. If the user has not guessed the number, we'll display the number, then determine whether the guess was close. We'll define "close" as within three numbers. We'll print a message informing the user whether the guess was close, then we'll wish the user better luck next time. The pseudocode for this program looks like this:

```
generate a secret random number between 1 and 10
prompt the user for a guess

if guess is not between 1 and 10
      print message
else
   if guess equals the secret number
      print congratulations
   else
      print the secret number
      if  guess is not within 3 numbers
         print "You missed it by a mile!"
      else
         print "You were close."

      print "Better luck next time."
```

This pseudocode uses three nested *if* statements; the first determines if the guess is within the requested range of numbers. If it isn't, we print a message. Otherwise, the second *if* statement tests whether the user has guessed the secret number. If so, we print a congratulatory message. If not, we print the secret number, and our last nested *if* statement determines whether the guess was not within 3 numbers of the secret number. If not, we print "You missed it by a mile!"; otherwise, we print "You were close." In either case, we print "Better luck next time."

Example 5.6 is the result of translating this pseudocode into a Java application.

```
1   /* Guess a number between 1 and 10
2      Anderson, Franceschi
3   */
4
5   import java.util.Random;
6   import java.util.Scanner;
7
8   public class GuessANumber
9   {
10    public static void main( String [ ] args )
11    {
12      Random random = new Random( );
13      int secretNumber = random.nextInt( 10 ) + 1;
14
15      Scanner scan = new Scanner( System.in );
16
17      System.out.print( "I'm thinking of a number"
18                  + " between 1 and 10. What is your guess? " );
19      int guess = scan.nextInt( );
20
21      if ( guess < 1 || guess > 10 )
22      {
23         System.out.println( "Well, if you're not going to try,"
24                             + " I'm not playing." );
25      }
26      else
27      {
28         if ( guess == secretNumber )
29             System.out.println( "Hoorah. You win!" );
30         else
31         {
32             System.out.println( "The number was " + secretNumber );
33
34             if ( Math.abs( guess - secretNumber ) > 3 )
35                 System.out.println( "You missed it by a mile!" );
36             else
37                 System.out.println( "You were close." );
38
39             System.out.println( "Better luck next time." );
40         }
41      }
42    }
43  }
```

EXAMPLE 5.6   Nested *if* Statements

Figure 5.11

Output from the
***GuessANumber* Program**
in Example 5.6

```
I'm thinking of a number between 1 and 10. What is your guess? 2
The number was 10
You missed it by a mile!
Better luck next time.
```

On line 34, we used the *abs* method of the *Math* class to determine whether the guess was within three integers of the secret number. By taking the absolute value of the difference between the guess and the secret number, we don't need to worry about which number is higher than the other; we will always receive a positive difference from the *abs* method.

Figure 5.11 shows the output of a sample run of this program.

5.6   Testing Techniques for *if/else* Statements

When an application uses *if/else* statements, the application's flow of control depends on the user's input or other data values. For one input value, the application may execute the true block, while for another input value, the application may execute the false block. Obviously, running an application only once is no guarantee that the program is correct, because if the true block was executed, then the false block was not executed, and therefore, was not tested. Similarly, if the false block was executed, then the true block was not executed, and therefore was not tested.

To test an application for correctness, we could attempt to test all execution paths. To do this, we devise a **test plan** that includes running the application with different data values designed to execute all the statements in the application.

For example, an application that determines whether an integer is positive or negative might have this code:

```
System.out.print( "Enter an integer > " );
int x = scan.nextInt( );
if  ( x > 0 )
   System.out.println( x + " is positive" );
else
   System.out.println( x + " is negative" );
```

We could test this code by running the application twice, the first time entering the value 1, and the second time entering the value −1. We see that the results for those two values are correct: 1 is positive and −1 is negative. We have executed all the statements successfully, but can we say for certain that the program is correct? What if we entered the value 0, which is considered neither a positive nor a negative integer? As written, our program determines that 0 is negative, which is incorrect.

We see, then, that testing the true and false blocks is not sufficient; we need to test the condition of the *if/else* statement as well. There are three possibilities: *x* is less than 0, *x* is equal to 0, or *x* is greater than 0. To test the condition, we should run the application with input values that meet these three criteria. So we should run the application one more time with the input value of 0. This will show us that the program is incorrect, because our code identifies 0 as a negative number.

To correct the program, we should add another condition (x < 0) so we can separate 0 from the negative numbers. The code would then become:

```java
System.out.print( "Enter an integer > " );
int x = scan.nextInt( );
if  ( x > 0 )
   System.out.println( x + " is positive" );
else if ( x < 0 )
   System.out.println( x + " is negative" );
else
   System.out.println( "The integer is 0" );
```

Now if we retest the program with input values −1, 1, and 0, we get correct results for each of these values.

Another testing method is to treat the program like a black box, that is, as if the program's inner workings are unknown and unknowable to us. We devise our test plan based solely on the specifications of the program and develop input values that test the program logically. Thus, if our specifications are that we should determine whether an integer is positive or negative, we deduce that we should run the program with inputs that are a negative number, a positive number, and the special case, 0.

Both testing methods work together to ensure that a program is correct.

**SOFTWARE
ENGINEERING TIP**

When testing your program, develop input values that test all execution paths and confirm that the logic implements the program specifications.

5.7   Programming Activity 1: Working with *if/else*

In this activity, you will write an *if/else* selection statement to decide how a golfer's score compares to par.

Copy to a directory on your computer all the files in the Chapter 5 Programming Activity 1 folder on the CD-ROM accompanying this book.

Open the *PathClient.java* source file. You will add your code to the *workWithIfElse* method. Part of the method has been coded for you. Search for ***** in the source file.

You should be positioned at the code shown in Example 5.7.

```
public void workWithIfElse( int score )
{
     String result = "???";
     // ***** Student code starts here
     // If score is greater than 72, assign "over par" to result
     // If score is equal to 72, assign "par" to result
     // If score is less than 72, assign "below par" to result



     //
     // Student code ends here
     //

     firstTime = false;
     animate( score, result );
}
```

EXAMPLE 5.7   The Student Code Portion of Programming Activity 1

Where indicated in the code, you should write an *if/else* statement to perform the following function:

- In the method header of the method *workWithIfElse*, you see (int score). The *int* variable *score* represents a golf score. This variable will be an input from the user; the dialog box that prompts the user for the score has already been coded for you and stores the user's input in the variable *score*, which is available to your code as a parameter of the *workWithIfElse* method. Do not declare the variable *score* inside the method; just use it.

Figure 5.12
The Beginning of the Application

- We want to know if the golf score is "over par," "par," or "below par." Par is 72.

- Inside the *if/else* statement, you need to assign a value to the *String* variable named *result*, as follows:

   If *score* is higher than 72, then assign "over par" to *result*; if score is exactly 72, assign "par" to *result*; and if score is lower than 72, assign "below par" to *result*.

- You do not need to write the code to call the method *animate*; that part of the code has already been written for you.

Animation: The application window will display the correct path of the *if/else* statement (in green), which may or may not be the same as your path, depending on how you coded the *if/else* statement. The animation will also assess your result, that is, the value of the variable *result*, and give you feedback on the correctness of your result.

To test your code, compile and run the application and enter an integer in the dialog box. Try the following input values for *score*: 45, 71, 72, 73, and 89. Be sure your code produces the correct result for all input values.

When the program begins, you will see an empty graphics window and the dialog box of Figure 5.12, prompting you for an integer value.

Figure 5.13 demonstrates the correct code path when the input value is 82 and assesses that the student's code is correct.

Figure 5.14 again demonstrates the correct code path when the input value is 82, but in this case, the student's code is incorrect.

? DISCUSSION QUESTIONS

1. How many conditions did you use in the complete *if/else* statement?

2. Your code should be correct if the application gets correct results for the input values 71, 72, and 73. Explain why.

Figure 5.13

A Correct *if/else*
Statement

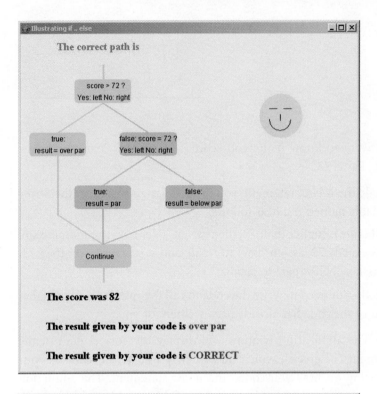

Figure 5.14

An Incorrect *if/else*
Statement

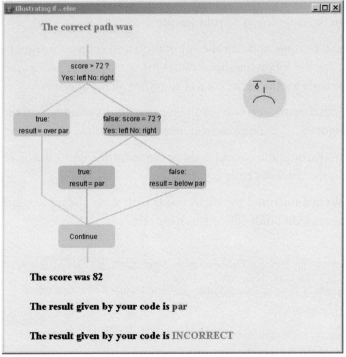

5.8 Comparing Floating-Point Numbers

As we explain in Appendix E, *floats* and *doubles* are stored using IEEE 754 standard format, which can introduce minor rounding errors when arithmetic is performed. That said, it is not advisable to simply rely on the equality operators to compare floating-point numbers.

Let's take a look at Example 5.8, which computes 11 * .1 two ways. First, at line 11, we assign .0 to a *double* variable, *d1*, and at lines 12–22 we add .1 to *d1* eleven times. Then, at line 24, we declare a second *double* variable, *d2*, and assign it the result of multiplying .1 times 11. You would expect, then, that *d1* and *d2* would have the same value. Not so, as the output of the program shows in Figure 5.15.

You can also see the effects of rounding when comparing a *float* to a *double*. For example, at lines 35 and 36 of Example 5.8, we assign the same floating-point number (PI) to a double variable *piD* and to a float variable *piF*, then compare the two values at line 40. As you can see from the output in Figure 5.15, they do not compare as equal. The reason is that double-precision floating-point numbers are able to store a larger number of significant digits than single-precision floating-point numbers.

REFERENCE POINT

Binary representation of floating-point numbers is discussed in Appendix E.

```
1 /* Using equality operators on floating-point numbers
2    Anderson, Franceschi
3 */
4
5 public class EqualityFloatingPoint
6 {
7   public static void main( String [ ] args )
8   {
9     // Part 1: Compute 11 * .1 two ways
10
11    double d1 = .0; // add .1 to 0 eleven times
12    d1 += .1;  // 1
13    d1 += .1;  // 2
14    d1 += .1;  // 3
15    d1 += .1;  // 4
16    d1 += .1;  // 5
17    d1 += .1;  // 6
18    d1 += .1;  // 7
19    d1 += .1;  // 8
20    d1 += .1;  // 9
21    d1 += .1;  // 10
```

```
22   d1 += .1;  // 11
23
24   double d2 = .1 * 11; // compute 11 * .1
25
26   System.out.println( "d1 = " + d1 );
27   System.out.println( "d2 = " + d2 );
28   if ( d1 == d2 )
29       System.out.println( "d1 and d2 are equal" );
30   else
31       System.out.println( "d1 and d2 are not equal" );
32
33   // Part 2: Compare float and double with same value
34
35   float  piF = 3.141592653589793f;
36   double piD = 3.141592653589793;
37
38   System.out.println( "\npiF = " + piF );
39   System.out.println( "pid = " + piD );
40   if ( piF == piD )
41       System.out.println( "piF and piD are equal" );
42   else
43       System.out.println( "piF and piD are not equal" );
44 }
45 }
```

EXAMPLE 5.8   Using the Equality Operator to Compare Floating-Point Numbers

Figure 5.15
Output from Example 5.8

```
d1 = 1.0999999999999999
d2 = 1.1
d1 and d2 are not equal

piF = 3.1415927
pid = 3.141592653589793
piF and piD are not equal
```

Instead of using the equality operator to compare floating-point numbers, it's better to compare the absolute value of the difference to a small value, called a **threshold**. The value of the threshold should be the difference we can tolerate and still consider the numbers equal. Let's redo Example 5.8. Instead of using the equality operator, we'll use the *Math.abs* method to compute a difference between the two numbers and compare the difference to a threshold value. We'll set the threshold at .0001, meaning that if the numbers differ by less than .0001, we'll consider them equal. The results of this approach are shown in Example 5.9 and the output is given in Figure 5.16.

```
1 /* Using a threshold to compare floating-point numbers
2    Anderson, Franceschi
3 */
4
5 public class ComparingFloatingPoint
6 {
7  public static void main( String [ ] args )
8  {
9     final double THRESHOLD = .0001;
10
11    // Part 1: Compute 11 * .1 two ways
12    double d1 = .0; // add .1 to 0 eleven times
13    d1 += .1;  // 1
14    d1 += .1;  // 2
15    d1 += .1;  // 3
16    d1 += .1;  // 4
17    d1 += .1;  // 5
18    d1 += .1;  // 6
19    d1 += .1;  // 7
20    d1 += .1;  // 8
21    d1 += .1;  // 9
22    d1 += .1;  // 10
23    d1 += .1;  // 11
24
25    double d2 = .1 * 11; // compute 11 * .1
26
27    System.out.println( "d1 = " + d1 );
28    System.out.println( "d2 = " + d2 );
29    if ( Math.abs( d1 - d2 ) < THRESHOLD )
30        System.out.println( "d1 and d2 are considered equal" );
31    else
32        System.out.println( "d1 and d2 are not equal" );
33
34    // Part 2: Compare float and double with same value
35    float  piF = 3.141592653589793f;
36    double piD = 3.141592653589793;
```

```
37
38    System.out.println( "\npiF = " + piF );
39    System.out.println( "piD = " + piD );
40    if ( Math.abs( piF - piD ) < THRESHOLD )
41        System.out.println( "piF and piD are considered equal" );
42    else
43        System.out.println( "piF and piD are not equal" );
44  }
45 }
```

Example 5.9   Comparing Floating-Point Numbers Using a Threshold

When you need exact precision in calculations with decimal numbers, you can use the *BigDecimal* class in the Java Class Library. The *BigDecimal* class, which is in the *java.math* package, provides methods that perform addition, subtraction, multiplication, and division of *BigDecimal* objects so that the results are exact, without the rounding errors caused by floating-point operations. Table 5.10 shows a constructor of the *BigDecimal* class and several useful methods for performing calculations and comparing *BigDecimal* objects.

 REFERENCE POINT

You can read more about the *BigDecimal* class on Oracle's Java website *www.oracle.com/ technetwork/java.*

In Example 5.10, we perform the same calculations as in Example 5.9, but we use *BigDecimal* objects instead of *doubles*. On lines 11 and 12, we instantiate two *BigDecimal* objects, *d1* and *pointOne*, to represent 0.0 and 0.1, respectively. Then on lines 16–26, we call the *add* method to add 0.1 to *d1* 11 times. We instantiate two more *BigDecimal* objects on lines 29 and 30, then call the *multiply* method to multiply 0.1 * 11. On line 35, we compare the resulting *BigDecimal* objects by calling the *compareTo* method, and find

Figure 5.16

Output of Example 5.9

```
d1 = 1.0999999999999999
d2 = 1.1
d1 and d2 are considered equal

piF = 3.1415927
piD = 3.141592653589793
piF and piD are considered equal
```

TABLE 5.10 The *BigDecimal* Class API

BigDecimal Class Constructor Summary	
BigDecimal(String ddd)	
creates a *BigDecimal* object equivalent to the decimal number expressed as a *String*	

BigDecimal Class Method Summary	
Return value	**Method name and argument list**
BigDecimal	add(BigDecimal num) returns a *BigDecimal* object equal to the current *BigDecimal* object plus *num*
BigDecimal	subtract(BigDecimal num) returns a *BigDecimal* object equal to the current *BigDecimal* object minus *num*
BigDecimal	multiply(BigDecimal num) returns a *BigDecimal* object equal to the current *BigDecimal* object times *num*
BigDecimal	divide(BigDecimal num) returns a *BigDecimal* object equal to the current *BigDecimal* object divided by *num*
int	compareTo(BigDecimal num) returns 0 if the current *BigDecimal* object is equal to *num*; -1 if the current *BigDecimal* object is less than *num*; and 1 if the current *BigDecimal* object is greater than *num*

that the two results are in fact equal. The output of Example 5.10 is shown in Figure 5.17.

```
1 /* Using BigDecimal to compute precise decimal numbers
2    Anderson, Franceschi
3 */
4
5 import java.math.BigDecimal;
6
```

```
 7 public class UsingBigDecimal
 8 {
 9  public static void main( String [ ] args )
10  {
11    BigDecimal  d1 = new BigDecimal( "0.0" );
12    BigDecimal  pointOne = new BigDecimal( "0.1" );
13
14    // Compute 11 * .1 two ways
15    // add .1 to 0 eleven times
16    d1 = d1.add( pointOne ); // 1
17    d1 = d1.add( pointOne ); // 2
18    d1 = d1.add( pointOne ); // 3
19    d1 = d1.add( pointOne ); // 4
20    d1 = d1.add( pointOne ); // 5
21    d1 = d1.add( pointOne ); // 6
22    d1 = d1.add( pointOne ); // 7
23    d1 = d1.add( pointOne ); // 8
24    d1 = d1.add( pointOne ); // 9
25    d1 = d1.add( pointOne ); // 10
26    d1 = d1.add( pointOne ); // 11
27
28    // multiply .1 * 11
29    BigDecimal  d2 = new BigDecimal( "0.1" );
30    BigDecimal  eleven = new BigDecimal( "11" );
31    d2 = d2.multiply( eleven );
32
33    System.out.println( "d1 = " + d1 );
34    System.out.println( "d2 = " + d2 );
35    if ( d1.compareTo( d2 ) == 0 )
36        System.out.println( "d1 and d2 are equal" );
37    else
38        System.out.println( "d1 and d2 are not equal" );
39  }
40 }
```

EXAMPLE 5.10   Comparing Floating-Point Numbers Using *BigDecimal*

Figure 5.17

Output of Example 5.10

```
d1 = 1.1
d2 = 1.1
d1 and d2 are equal
```

5.9   Comparing Objects

5.9.1   The *equals* Method

Often, you'll want to compare whether two objects are equal; typically, we will say that two objects are equal if they have the same data. If you use the equality operator (==) to compare object references, however, you are comparing the value of the object references. In other words, you are comparing whether the object references point to the same object, that is, the same memory location. To compare object data, you need to use the *equals* method, which all classes inherit from the *Object* class. Many classes provide a custom version of the *equals* method. The API of the *equals* method, which is an instance method, is the following:

```
public boolean equals( Object ob )
```

Typically, the *equals* method returns *true* if the data in the parameter object matches the data in the object for which the method was called.

The program in Example 5.11 creates the *SimpleDate* object references and objects shown in Figure 5.18. The program compares the object references using the equality operator and then compares the object data using the *equals* method. The output from this program is shown in Figure 5.19.

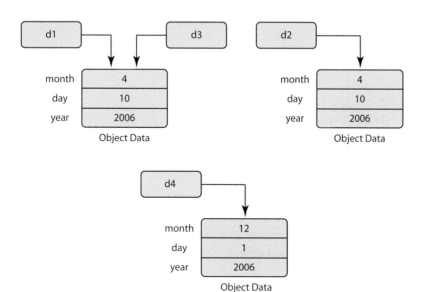

Figure 5.18
SimpleDate **Objects and References**

```
1 /* Comparing object references and data
2     Anderson, Franceschi
3 */
4
5 public class ComparingObjects
6 {
7   public static void main( String [ ] args )
8   {
9     // instantiate two SimpleDate objects with identical data
10    SimpleDate d1 = new SimpleDate( 4, 10, 2006 );
11    SimpleDate d2 = new SimpleDate( 4, 10, 2006 );
12
13    // assign object reference d1 to d3
14    SimpleDate d3 = d1;  // d3 now points to d1
15
16    // instantiate another object with different data
17    SimpleDate d4 = new SimpleDate( 12, 1, 2006 );
18
19    // compare references using the equality operator
20    if ( d1 == d2 )
21       System.out.println( "d1 and d2 are equal\n" );
22    else
23       System.out.println( "d1 and d2 are not equal\n" );
24
25    if ( d1 == d3 )
26       System.out.println( "d1 and d3 are equal\n" );
27    else
28       System.out.println( "d1 and d3 are not equal\n" );
29
30    // compare object data using the equals method
31    if ( d1.equals( d2 ) )
32       System.out.println( "d1 data and d2 data are equal\n" );
33    else
34       System.out.println( "d1 data and d2 data are not equal\n" );
35
36    if ( ! d1.equals( d4 ) )
37       System.out.println( "d1 data and d4 data are not equal" );
38    else
39       System.out.println( "d1 data and d4 data are equal" );
40   }
41 }
```

EXAMPLE 5.11   Comparing Object Data

Figure 5.19
Output from Example 5.11

```
d1 and d2 are not equal

d1 and d3 are equal

d1 data and d2 data are equal

d1 data and d4 data are not equal
```

Lines 10 and 11 instantiate two *SimpleDate* objects with the same data. Line 14 sets the *d3* object reference to point to the *d1* object. Line 17 instantiates the *d4* object with different data.

In line 20, when we compare *d1* and *d2* using the equality operator, the result is *false*, because the object references *d1* and *d2* point to two different objects. However, when we compare *d1* and *d3* (line 25), the result is *true*, because *d1* and *d3* point to the same object. Thus, object references are equal only when they point to the same object.

COMMON ERROR TRAP

Do not use the equality operators to compare object data; instead, use the *equals* method.

We get different results using the *equals* method. When line 31 compares *d1* and *d2* using the *equals* method, the result is *true*, because *d1* and *d2* have identical data. As you would expect, *d1* and *d4* are not equal (line 36) because the objects have different data. Line 36 demonstrates that we can test for inequality by using the NOT operator (!) to negate the return value from the *equals* method.

5.9.2   *String* Comparison Methods

Because *Strings* are objects, you can also compare *Strings* using the *equals* method. In addition, the *String* class provides two other methods, *equalsIgnoreCase* and *compareTo*, for comparing the values of *Strings*. These methods, along with the *equals* method are summarized in Table 5.11.

The *equalsIgnoreCase* method is similar to the *equals* method, except that it is insensitive to case. Thus, the *equalsIgnoreCase* method returns *true* if the two *String* objects have the same sequence of characters, regardless of capitalization. For example, the *equalsIgnoreCase* method considers *ABC, AbC,* and *abc* to be equal.

The *compareTo* method returns an integer value, rather than a *boolean* value. The *compareTo* method's return value represents whether the *String* object is less than, equal to, or greater than the *String* argument passed to

TABLE 5.11   Comparison Methods of the *String* Class

String Methods for Comparing *String* Values	
Return value	**Method name and argument list**
boolean	equals(String str)
	compares the value of two *Strings*. Returns *true* if the *Strings* are equal; *false* otherwise.
boolean	equalsIgnoreCase(String str)
	compares the value of two *Strings*, treating upper and lowercase characters as equal. Returns *true* if the *Strings* are equal; *false* otherwise.
int	compareTo(String str)
	compares the value of the two *Strings* in lexicographic order. If the *String* object is less than the *String* argument, *str,* a negative integer is returned. If the *String* object is greater than the *String* argument, a positive number is returned; if the two *Strings* are equal, 0 is returned.

REFERENCE POINT

The first 128 Unicode values are given in Appendix C.

the *compareTo* method. The *compareTo* method uses lexicographic order—the Unicode collating sequence—to compare the *Strings*. Using the Unicode collating sequence means that a character with a lower Unicode numeric value is considered less than a character with a higher Unicode numeric value. Thus, an *a* is lower than a *b*; an *A* is lower than a *B*; and *0* is lower than *1*.

The *compareTo* method scans the two *Strings* from left to right. If it finds different characters in the same position in the two *Strings*, it immediately returns an integer value representing the difference between the Unicode values of those characters. For example, the distance between *a* and *c* is −2; the distance between *K* and *F* is 5.

If the *Strings* differ in length, but the characters they have in common are identical, then the *compareTo* method returns the difference in the length of the *Strings*.

In most cases, however, the exact return value is not important; it is sufficient to know whether the *String* object is less than, greater than, or equal to the *String* argument. In other words, all that we usually need to know is whether the return value is positive, negative, or 0.

Example 5.12 demonstrates how these methods can be used in a Java application to compare *String*s. The output of the program is shown in Figure 5.20.

```
1 /* Demonstration of the String comparison methods
2    Anderson, Franceschi
3 */
4
5 public class ComparingStrings
6 {
7   public static void main( String [ ] args )
8   {
9     String title1 = "Green Pastures";
10    String title2 = "Green Pastures II";
11    String title3 = "green pastures";
12
13    System.out.print( "Using equals: " );
14    if ( title1.equals( title3 ) )
15      System.out.println( title1 + " equals " + title3 );
16    else
17      System.out.println( title1 + " is not equal to " + title3 );
18
19    System.out.print( "Using equalsIgnoreCase: " );
20    if ( title1.equalsIgnoreCase( title3 ) )
21      System.out.println( title1 + " equals " + title3 );
22    else
23      System.out.println( title1 + " is not equal to " + title3 );
24
25    System.out.print( "Using compareTo: " );
26    if ( title1.compareTo( title3 ) > 0 )
27      System.out.println( title1 + " is greater than " + title3 );
28    else if ( title1.compareTo ( title3 ) < 0 )
29      System.out.println( title1 + " is less than " + title3 );
30    else
31      System.out.println( title1 + " is equal to " + title3 );
32
33    System.out.print( "Using compareTo: " );
34    if ( title1.compareTo( title2 ) > 0 )
35      System.out.println( title1 + " is greater than " + title2 );
36    else if ( title1.compareTo( title2 ) < 0 )
37      System.out.println( title1 + " is less than " + title2 );
38    else
39      System.out.println( title1 + " is equal to " + title2 );
40  }
41 }
```

EXAMPLE 5.12   Comparing *Strings*

Figure 5.20

Output from Example 5.12

```
Using equals: Green Pastures is not equal to green pastures
Using equalsIgnoreCase: Green Pastures equals green pastures
Using compareTo: Green Pastures is less than green pastures
Using compareTo: Green Pastures is less than Green Pastures II
```

In Example 5.12, we define three similar *Strings: title1 (Green Pastures),* *title2 (Green Pastures II),* and *title3 (green pastures).* When we compare *title1, Green Pastures,* to *title3, green pastures,* using the *equals* method (line 14), the result is *false,* because the *Strings* do not match in case. When we perform the same comparison using the *equalsIgnoreCase* method (line 20), however, the result is *true,* because except for capitalization, these two *Strings* are identical in character sequence and length.

Using the *compareTo* method (line 34), *Green Pastures* evaluates to less than *Green Pastures II.* Although all the characters of the first *String* are found in the second *String* in the same order, the first *String* has fewer characters than the second *String.* The reason that *Green Pastures* evaluates to less than *green pastures* (line 26) is not so obvious—until you look at the Unicode character chart. The capital letters have lower numeric values than the lowercase letters, so a capital *G* is less than a lowercase *g.*

5.10   The Conditional Operator (?:)

The conditional operator (?:), while not a statement in itself, can be used in expressions. It evaluates a condition and contributes one of two values to the expression based on the value of the condition. The conditional operator is especially useful for handling invalid input and for outputting similar messages. The syntax of the conditional operator is shown here:

```
( condition ?  expression1 : expression2 )
```

The value of an expression containing a conditional operator is determined by evaluating the condition, which is any expression that evaluates to *true* or *false.* If the condition evaluates to *true, expression1* becomes the value of the expression; if the condition evaluates to *false, expression2* becomes the value of the expression.

When assigning the result of that expression to a variable, the statement:

```
variable = ( condition ? expression1 : expression2 );
```

is equivalent to

```
if ( condition )
      variable = expression1;
else
      variable = expression2;
```

Some programmers like to use the conditional operator because it enables them to write compact code; other programmers feel that an *if/else* sequence is more readable.

Suppose that we want to write a simple game where we ask the user to pick between two doors. Behind one door is a prize and behind the other door is nothing. Example 5.13 shows some code to do this. We first use the conditional operator on line 17 to validate the user input. If the user enters anything other than a 2, we assign the value 1 to the variable *door*. The statement at line 17 is equivalent to this code:

```
int door;
if ( inputNum == 2 )
   door = inputNum;
else
   door = 1;
```

So, instead of using five lines to declare the variable *door* and perform the *if* statement, the conditional operator performs the same function in only one line.

We then print a message about whether the chosen door was correct (Figure 5.21). If the user has selected door number 1, we print:

```
You have chosen the wrong door
```

Otherwise, we print:

```
You have chosen the correct door
```

as shown in Figure 5.22. As you can see, depending on the value of *door*, the messages we want to print differ only in one word (*correct* or *wrong*). So on lines 19–20, we use the conditional operator in the argument of the *println* method to determine which word to insert into the message.

```
1 /* Using the conditional operator
2    Anderson, Franceschi
3 */
4
```

```
5 import java.util.Scanner;
6
7 public class DoorPrize
8 {
9   public static void main( String [ ] args )
10  {
11    Scanner scan = new Scanner( System.in );
12
13    System.out.print( "Enter 1 or 2 to pick a door: " );
14    int inputNum = scan.nextInt( );
15    System.out.println( "You entered " + inputNum + "\n" );
16
17    int door = ( inputNum == 2 ? inputNum : 1 );
18
19    System.out.println( "You have chosen the "
20            + ( door == 1 ? "wrong" : "correct" ) + " door" );
21  }
22 }
```

EXAMPLE 5.13   Using the Conditional Operator

Table 5.12, Operator Precedence, shows that the conditional operator is low in precedence, being just above the assignment operators.

Figure 5.21

A Run of Example 5.13

```
Enter 1 or 2 to pick a door: 8
You entered 8


You have chosen the wrong door
```

Figure 5.22

Another Run of Example 5.13

```
Enter 1 or 2 to pick a door: 2
You entered 2

You have chosen the correct door
```

TABLE 5.12   Operator Precedence

Operator Hierarchy	Order of Same-Statement Evaluation	Operation
( )	left to right	parentheses for explicit grouping
++, ––	right to left	shortcut postincrement
++, ––, !	right to left	shortcut preincrement, logical unary NOT
*, /, %	left to right	multiplication, division, modulus
+, –	left to right	addition or *String* concatenation, subtraction
<, <=, >, >=	left to right	relational operators: less than, less than or equal to, greater than, greater than or equal to
==, !=	left to right	equality operators: equal to and not equal to
&&	left to right	logical AND
||	left to right	logical OR
?:	**left to right**	**conditional operator**
=, +=, –=, *=, /=, %=	right to left	assignment operator and shortcut assignment operators

5.11   The *switch* Statement

The *switch* statement can be used instead of an *if/else if* statement for selection when the condition consists of comparing the value of an expression to constant integers (*byte, short,* or *int*), characters (*char*), or *Strings*. The capability to *switch* on a *String* is a new feature in Java version 7. The syntax of the *switch* statement is the following:

```
switch ( expression )
{
   case constant1:
        statement1;
        . . .
        break; // optional
   case constant2:
```

```
          statement1;
              . . .
          break; // optional
      . . .
   default:  // optional
          statement1;
              . . .

}
```

The expression is first evaluated, then its value is compared to the *case* constants in order. When a match is found, the statements under that *case* constant are executed in sequence. The execution of statements continues until either a *break* statement is encountered or the end of the *switch* block is reached. If other *case* statements are encountered before a *break* statement, then their statements are also executed. This allows you to execute the same code for multiple values of the expression.

As you can see in the preceding syntax, the *break* statements are optional. Their job is to terminate execution of the *switch* statement. The *default* label and its statements, which are also optional, are executed when the value of the expression does not match any of the *case* constants. The statements under a *case* constant are also optional, so multiple *case* constants can be written in sequence if identical operations will be performed for those values. We'll use this feature in our examples of the *switch* statement.

Let's look at how a *switch* statement can be used to implement a simple calculator. We first prompt the user for two numbers on which they want to perform a calculation, and then the operation they want to perform. We let them enter either the words ADD, SUBTRACT, MULTIPLY, or DIVIDE, or the symbol for the operation (+, -, *, or /). We can use a *switch* statement to determine the selected operation and *case* constants for each possible operation. Example 5.14 shows the code for our simple calculator.

```
 1 /* A simple calculator
 2    Anderson, Franceschi
 3 */
 4
 5 import java.text.DecimalFormat;
 6 import java.util.Scanner;
 7
 8 public class Calculator
 9 {
10   public static void main( String [] args )
```

```
11   {
12     double fp1, fp2;
13     String operation;
14
15     Scanner scan = new Scanner( System.in );
16
17     // set up the output format of the result
18     DecimalFormat twoDecimals = new DecimalFormat( "#,###,###.##" );
19
20     // print a welcome message
21     System.out.println( "Welcome to the Calculator" );
22
23     // read the two operands
24     System.out.print( "Enter the first operand: " );
25     fp1 = scan.nextDouble( );
26     System.out.print( "Enter the second operand: " );
27     fp2 = scan.nextDouble( );
28
29     //  print a menu, then prompt for the operation
30     System.out.println( "\nOperations are: "
31                          + "\n\t ADD or + for addition"
32                          + "\n\t SUBTRACT or - for subtraction"
33                          + "\n\t MULTIPLY or * for multiplication"
34                          + "\n\t DIVIDE or / for division" );
35     System.out.print( "Enter your selection: " );
36     operation = scan.next( );
37     operation = operation.toUpperCase( );
38
39     //perform the operation and print the result
40     switch ( operation )
41     {
42      case "ADD":
43      case "+":
44          System.out.println( "The sum is "
45                  + twoDecimals.format( fp1 + fp2 ) );
46          break;
47      case "SUBTRACT":
48      case "-":
49          System.out.println( "The difference is "
50                  + twoDecimals.format( fp1 - fp2 ) );
51          break;
52      case "MULTIPLY":
53      case "*":
54          System.out.println( "The product is "
55                  + twoDecimals.format( fp1 * fp2 ) );
56          break;
```

```
57    case "DIVIDE":
58    case "/":
59        if ( fp2 == 0.0 )
60          System.out.println( "Dividing by 0 is not allowed" );
61        else
62          System.out.println( "The quotient is "
63                  + twoDecimals.format( fp1 / fp2 ) );
64        break;
65      default:
66        System.out.println( operation + " is not valid." );
67    }
68  }
69 }
```

Example 5.14   A Simple Calculator

We declared the two numbers on which to perform the operation as *doubles* (line 12) and prompt the user using the *nextDouble* method of the *Scanner* class (lines 23–27). Because a *double* variable can hold any numeric value equal to or lower in precision than a *double*, using *doubles* for our calculator allows the user to enter either *ints* or *doubles*. Conversely, if we used *int* variables and the *nextInt* method of the *Scanner* class, the user would be restricted to entering integers only.

When the calculator begins, we set up a *DecimalFormat* object for outputting the result to a maximum of two decimal places (line 18).

We print a menu to let the user know what options are available, using the newline (\n) and tab (\t) escape characters to format the menu message (lines 29–35). To read the user's selection (lines 36–37), we use the *next* method of the *Scanner* class, which returns a *String*. We convert the input to uppercase using the *toUpperCase* method of the *String* class.

We are now ready to determine which operation the user has chosen, by using a *switch* statement with the user's input as the *switch expression*. We determine which operation the user has selected by providing two *case* statements for each possible operation. We can use uppercase words as the *case* constants, because we have converted the input to uppercase. This allows the user to enter the desired operation in any combination of uppercase or lowercase letters. We handle the situation where the user has entered a mathematical symbol instead of a word by adding a second *case* constant to each operation. For example, if the user enters ADD (in any combination of uppercase and lowercase letters) or a plus sign (+), the input will match one of our *case* constants on lines 42 and 43. We will then execute the addition and output the result on lines 44 and 45. When we encounter the *break* statement on line 46, the execution of the *switch* statement ends. The *break* statement is important. If we had omitted the *break* statement, execution would have continued onto lines 49 and 50, and we would have performed the subtraction as well. Then the *break* statement on line 51 would have ended the execution of the *switch* statement.

What if the user doesn't enter any of the valid words or mathematical symbols? This is where the *default* case comes in handy, allowing us to write an error message to the user (lines 65–66).

Figure 5.23 shows the output from Example 5.14 when the user selects multiplication, and Figure 5.24 shows the output when the user enters an unsupported operation.

One more note on the calculator: We need to check whether the divisor is 0 before performing division (line 59). Although we discussed earlier in the chapter that we should compare floating-point numbers by comparing the difference between the two numbers with a threshold value, in this case, we care only if the second operand is exactly 0, so we can safely compare its

Figure 5.23

The Calculator Performing Multiplication

```
Welcome to the Calculator
Enter the first operand: 23.4
Enter the second operand: 3

Operations are:
    ADD or + for addition
    SUBTRACT or - for subtraction
    MULTIPLY or * for multiplication
    DIVIDE or / for division
Enter your selection: multiply
The product is 70.2
```

Figure 5.24

The Calculator with an Invalid Entry for the Operation

```
Welcome to the Calculator
Enter the first operand: 52
Enter the second operand: 34.5

Operations are:
    ADD or + for addition
    SUBTRACT or - for subtraction
    MULTIPLY or * for multiplication
    DIVIDE or / for division
Enter your selection: f
f is not valid
```

value to 0.0. If the second operand is 0.0, we print an error message; otherwise, we perform the division.

Let's look at an example that performs a *switch* on an integer. We'll create an applet that simulates rolling a die and drawing the die corresponding to the roll. Example 5.15 shows the code to do this.

```java
 1 /*  An applet that rolls and draws a die
 2       Anderson, Franceschi
 3 */
 4
 5 import javax.swing.JApplet;
 6 import java.awt.Graphics;
 7 import java.awt.Color;
 8 import java.util.Random;
 9
10 public class RollDie extends JApplet
11 {
12   public void paint( Graphics g )
13   {
14       super.paint( g );
15
16       Random random = new Random( );
17       int roll = random.nextInt( 6 ) + 1;
```

```
18
19        int startX = 150, startY = 100;
20
21        g.setColor( Color.PINK ); // die will be pink
22        g.fillRect( startX, startY, 60, 60 ); // draw the die
23
24        g.setColor( Color.BLACK ); // dots will be black
25        switch ( roll )
26        {
27           case  1:   // draw the center dot
28              g.fillRect( startX + 25, startY + 25, 10, 10 );
29              break;
30
31           case  3:   // draw center dot, continue through 2
32              g.fillRect( startX + 25, startY + 25, 10, 10 );
33           case  2:   // draw diagonal corner dots
34              g.fillRect( startX + 5, startY + 5, 10, 10 );
35              g.fillRect( startX + 45, startY + 45, 10, 10 );
36              break;
37
38           case  5:   // draw center dot, continue through 4
39              g.fillRect( startX + 25, startY + 25, 10, 10 );
40           case  4:   // draw four corner dots
41              g.fillRect( startX + 5, startY + 5, 10, 10 );
42              g.fillRect( startX + 45, startY + 45, 10, 10 );
43              g.fillRect( startX + 5, startY + 45, 10, 10 );
44              g.fillRect( startX + 45, startY + 5, 10, 10 );
45              break;
46
47           case  6:   // draw all six dots
48              g.fillRect( startX + 5, startY + 5, 10, 10 );
49              g.fillRect( startX + 45, startY + 45, 10, 10 );
50              g.fillRect( startX + 5, startY + 45, 10, 10 );
51              g.fillRect( startX + 45, startY + 5, 10, 10 );
52              g.fillRect( startX + 5, startY + 25, 10, 10 );
53              g.fillRect( startX + 45, startY + 25, 10, 10 );
54        }
55     }
56 }
```

EXAMPLE 5.15   Using *switch* to Draw a Die

In Example 5.15, we first generate a random number between 1 and 6 to simulate the roll of a die (lines 16–17). We set *startX* and *startY* values that we will use as the upper-left corner of the die (line 19), and then draw the die itself as a 60-by-60 pink square (lines 21–22). We set the color to black for drawing the dots (line 24) and we will use a *switch* statement on *roll* (lines 25–54) to determine which dots we should draw.

If we look at a die, we see that many of the rolls cause one or more of the same dots to be drawn. For example, a 3 consists of the center dot and the two diagonal dots, whereas the 2 consists of just the two diagonal dots. One advantage to the *switch* statement is that once a match is found between the *switch* variable and a *case* constant, all following statements are executed until a *break* is encountered. Using this feature, we can set up *case* 3 to draw just the center dot without using a *break* statement, then follow immediately with *case* 2, which draws the two diagonal dots and *breaks* (lines 31–36). When a roll of 3 is generated, the *switch* statement will match the *case* for 3, draw the center dot, and then fall through to the *case* 2 statements, which draws the two diagonal dots and *breaks*. When a roll of 2 is generated, we draw only the two diagonal dots and *break*. We do similar processing for rolls of 5 and 4 (lines 38–45). For *case* 5, we draw the center dot, then fall through to *case* 4, which draws the four corner dots and *breaks*. Many other combinations are possible. Note that we don't need a *default* case because the random generator will only generate values from 1 to 6, and we have provided *case* statements to handle each of those values. The output from one roll of the die is shown in Figure 5.25.

Figure 5.25

Output of Example 5.15

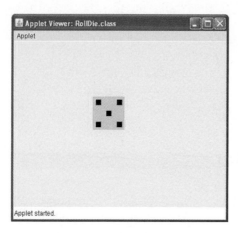

CODE IN ACTION

To see a step-by-step illustration of using a *switch* statement, look for the Chapter 5 Flash movie on the CD-ROM included with this book. Click on the link for Chapter 5 to start the movie.

Skill Practice
with these end-of-chapter questions

5.14.1   Multiple Choice Exercises

Question 9

5.14.2   Reading and Understanding Code

Questions 14,16,17,18,19

5.14.5   Debugging Area

Questions 39, 41

5.14.6   Write a Short Program

Questions 44, 45, 47

5.14.8   Technical Writing

Question 53

5.12   Programming Activity 2: Using the *switch* Statement

In this activity, you will write a *switch* statement that selects a path depending on an input value. The framework will animate your code so that you can watch the path that the code takes in the *switch* block.

Copy to a directory on your computer all the files in the Chapter 5 Programming Activity 2 directory on the CD-ROM accompanying this book.

Search for five stars (*****) in the *MultiPathClient.java* source code to find where to add your code. The five stars are inside the method *workWithSwitch* (the method header has already been coded for you).

You should be positioned at the code shown in Example 5.16.

```
// ***** 1 student writes this method
public void workWithSwitch( int value )
{
```

```
//
// Student code starts here
//




//
// Student code ends here
//

mp.setControl( false );
mp.resetPath( );
mp.setCount( 0 );
mp.setCurrent( -1 );


}
// end of workWithSwitch
```

EXAMPLE 5.16	The Student Code Portion of Programming Activity 2

Where indicated in the code, write a *switch* statement, as follows:

- In the method header of the method *workWithSwitch*, you see (`int value`). The *int* variable *value* represents the input from the user; the dialog box that prompts the user and reads the score has already been coded for you. This variable, *value*, is the input value for the *switch* statement; it is available to your code as a parameter of the *workWithSwitch* method. Do not declare the variable *value* inside the method; just use it.

- Write *case* statements for the following integer constants: *0, 1, 2, 3, 4*, as well as a *default* statement.

- Within each *case* statement, you should do two things:

  - Print a message to the screen indicating which value was input. The message for the *default* case should indicate that the input value is not one of the valid values.
  - Call the *animate* method. The API for the *animate* method is

    `void animate( int caseConstant, int value )`

    The first argument is the *case* constant; the second argument is the input variable, *value*. For instance, for the statement `case 2:`, your *animate* method call is

    `animate( 2, value );`

For the default case, the method call should be

```
animate( -1, value );
```

To test your code, compile and run the *MultiPathClient* application. When the program begins, you will see an empty graphics window and the dialog box of Figure 5.26, prompting you for an integer value.

To execute your *switch* statement, enter an integer in the dialog box. Depending on how you coded the *case* statements, the *break* statements, and the input value, the window will display (in green) the path of execution of your code. For example, Figure 5.27 demonstrates the code path when the input value is 3. If the path is not what you expected, you will need to correct your code.

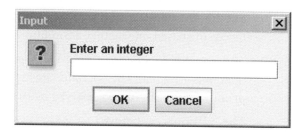

Figure 5.26

The Input Box of the *MultiPathClient* Application

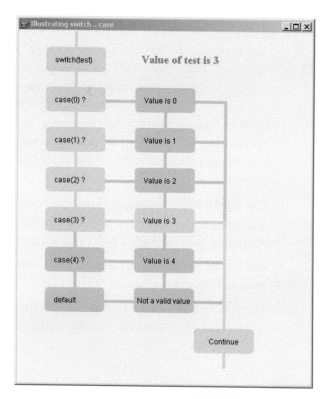

Figure 5.27

A Sample Run of the *MultiPathClient* Application

After each execution of the *switch* statement, the dialog box will reappear, prompting you for another integer. To test your code, enter each integer from 0 to 4 into the dialog box, plus some other integer value. To exit the application, click the *Cancel* button on the dialog box.

DISCUSSION QUESTIONS **?**

1. Explain the purpose of the *default* case in a *switch* statement.

2. Explain what happens when you omit a *break* statement in a *case* statement.

5.13   Chapter Summary

- Java provides equality, relational, and logical operators to evaluate a condition, and selection statements to choose which instructions to execute based on whether a condition evaluates to *true* or *false*.

- The equality operators (==, !=) are used to test whether two operands are equal. The operands are expressions that evaluate to a primitive numeric or *boolean* type or an object reference.

- The relational operators (<, <=, >, >=) compare the values of two operands that are expressions that evaluate to a primitive numeric type.

- The logical operators (!, &&, and ||) take *boolean* expressions as operands. The logical NOT (!) takes one operand, and inverts its value, changing *true* to *false* and *false* to *true*. The AND operator (&&) takes two *boolean* expressions as operands; if both operands are *true*, then the result is *true*; otherwise, the result is *false*. The OR operator (||) also takes two *boolean* expressions as operands. If both operands are *false*, then the result is *false*; otherwise, the result is *true*.

- The logical NOT operator (!) has the highest precedence of these operators, followed by the relational operators, then the equality operators, then the logical AND (&&), then the logical OR(||).

- DeMorgan's Laws can be used to form equivalent logical expressions to improve readability of the code.

- The *if* statement is used to perform certain operations for one set of data and do nothing for all other data.

CHAPTER SUMMARY

- Curly braces are required when the true or false block of an *if* statement consists of more than one statement.

- The *if/else* statement is used to perform certain operations for one set of data and other operations for all other data.

- The *if/else if* statement is appropriate when the data falls into more than two mutually exclusive categories and the appropriate instructions to execute are different for each category.

- *if/else* statements can be coded sequentially and can be nested inside other *if/else* statements.

- When *if* statements are nested, the compiler matches any *else* clause with the most previous *if* condition that doesn't already have an *else* clause.

- Because rounding errors can be introduced in floating-point calculations, do not use the equality operators to compare two floating-point numbers. Instead, compare the absolute value of the difference between the numbers to some threshold value.

- When you need exact precision in calculations with decimal numbers, you can use the *BigDecimal* class in the Java Class Library.

- Using the equality operator on object references compares the values of the references, not the object data. Two object references will be equal only if they point to the same object.

- Use the *equals* method to determine whether the data in two objects is equal.

- In addition to the *equals* method, two *Strings* can also be compared using the *equalsIgnoreCase* method and the *compareTo* method of the *String* class.

- The conditional operator (?:) is used in expressions where one of two values should be used depending on the evaluation of a condition. The conditional operator is useful for validating input and for outputting similar messages.

- The *switch* statement evaluates an integer or character expression or a *String*, then compares the expression's value to *case* constants. When a match is found, it executes the statements until either a *break* statement or the end of the *switch* block is encountered.

5.14   Exercises, Problems, and Projects

5.14.1   Multiple Choice Exercises

1. Given the following code declaring and initializing two *int* variables *a* and *b* with respective values 3 and 5, indicate whether the value of each expression is *true* or *false*.

```
int a = 3;
int b = 5;
```

Expression	true	false
❑ a < b	——	——
❑ a != b	——	——
❑ a == 4	——	——
❑ (b - a) <= 1	——	——
❑ Math.abs(a - b) >= 2	——	——
❑ (b % 2 == 1)	——	——
❑ b <= 5	——	——

2. Given the following code declaring and initializing three *boolean* variables *a*, *b*, and *c*, with respective values *true*, *true*, and *false*, indicate whether the value of each expression is *true* or *false*.

```
boolean a = true;
boolean b = true;
boolean c = false;
```

Expression	true	false
❑ !a	——	——
❑ a && b	——	——
❑ a && c	——	——
❑ a || c	——	——
❑ !(a || b)	——	——
❑ !a || b	——	——
❑ !(!(a && c))	——	——
❑ a && !(b || c)	——	——

3. Given two *boolean* variables *a* and *b*, are the following expressions equivalent?

    ❑ !(!a)

    ❑ a

4. Given two *boolean* variables *a* and *b*, are the following expressions equivalent?

    ❑ !(a && b)

    ❑ !a || !b

5. Given two *boolean* variables *a* and *b*, are the following expressions equivalent?

    ❑ !(!a && !b)

    ❑ a && b

6. Given two *boolean* variables *a* and *b*, are the following expressions equivalent?

    ❑ !(!a && !b)

    ❑ a || b

7. Given the following code declaring and initializing two *int* variables *a* and *b* with respective values 3 and 5, indicate whether the operand (b < 10) will be evaluated.

    ```
    int a = 3;
    int b = 5;
    ```

Expression	yes	no
❑ a < b || b < 10	____	____
❑ a != b && b < 10	____	____
❑ a == 4 || b < 10	____	____
❑ a > b && b < 10	____	____

8. Mark all the valid Java selection keywords.

    ❑ if

    ❑ else if

    ❑ else

    ❑ elsif

9. How do we compare the value of two *String* objects in Java? (Mark all that apply.)

    ❑ using the = operator

    ❑ using the == operator

    ❑ using the *equals* method

5.14.2   Reading and Understanding Code

10. What is the output of this code sequence?

```
boolean a = true;
System.out.println( a );
```

11. What is the output of this code sequence?

```
boolean a = ( true && false );
System.out.println( a );
```

12. What is the output of this code sequence?

```
if ( ( true || false ) && ( false || true ) )
    System.out.println( "Inside true block" );
System.out.println( "End of sequence" );
```

13. What is the output of this code sequence?

```
if ( 27 % 3 == 0 )
    System.out.println( "27 is divisible by 3" );
else
    System.out.println( "27 is not divisible by 3" );
System.out.println( "End of sequence" );
```

14. What is the output of this code sequence?

```
String s = "Hello";
if ( s.equals( "hello" ) )
    System.out.println( "String is hello" );
else
    System.out.println( "String is not hello" );
System.out.println( "End of sequence" );
```

15. What is the output of this code sequence?

```
int grade = 77;
if ( grade >= 90 )
    System.out.println( "A" );
else if ( grade >= 80 )
    System.out.println( "B" );
```

```
else if ( grade >= 70 )
   System.out.println( "C" );
else
   System.out.println( "D or lower" );
System.out.println( "Done" );
```

16. What is the output of this code sequence?

```
int a = 65;
boolean b = false;

if ( a >= 70 )
{
   System.out.println( "Hello 1" );
   if ( b == true )
      System.out.println( "Hello 2" );
}
else
{
   System.out.println( "Hello 3" );
   if ( b == false )
      System.out.println( "Hello 4" );
}
System.out.println( "Done" );
```

17. What is the output of this code sequence?

```
int season = 3;
switch ( season )
{
   case  1:
         System.out.println( "Season is Winter" );
         break;
   case  2:
         System.out.println( "Season is Spring" );
         break;
   case  3:
         System.out.println( "Season is Summer" );
         break;
   case  4:
         System.out.println( "Season is Fall" );
         break;
   default:
         System.out.println( "Invalid Season" );
}
```

18. What is the output of this code sequence?

```java
char c = 'e';
switch ( c )
{
    case 'H':
        System.out.println( "letter 1" );
        break;
    case 'e':
        System.out.println( "letter 2" );
        break;
    case 'l':
        System.out.println( "letters 3 and 4" );
        break;
    case 'o':
        System.out.println( "letter 5" );
        break;
    default:
        System.out.println( "letter is not in Hello" );
}
```

19. What is the output of this code sequence?

```java
int n = 3;
switch ( n )
{
    case 1:
      System.out.println( "Number 1" );
    case 2:
      System.out.println( "Number 2" );
    case 3:
      System.out.println( "Number 3" );
    case 4:
      System.out.println( "Number 4" );
    default:
      System.out.println( "Other number" );
}
```

5.14.3   Fill In the Code

For Exercises 20 through 30, assume that a *boolean* variable named *a* has been declared and assigned the value *true* or *false*. You should also assume that two *int* variables named *b* and *c* have been declared and assigned some integer values.

20. If *a* is *true*, increment *b* by 1.

    ```
    // your code goes here
    ```

21. If *a* is *true*, increment *b* by 2; if *a* is *false*, decrement *b* by 1.

    ```
    // your code goes here
    ```

22. If *a* is *true*, change *a* to *false*; if *a* is *false*, change *a* to *true*.

    ```
    // your code goes here
    ```

23. If *b* is equal to *c*, then assign *true* to *a*.

    ```
    // your code goes here
    ```

24. If *b* is less than *c*, increment *b* by 1; otherwise, leave *b* unchanged.

    ```
    // your code goes here
    ```

25. If *b* is a multiple of *c*, set *a* to *true*; otherwise, set *a* to *false*.

    ```
    // your code goes here
    ```

26. If *c* is not equal to 0, assign to *b* the value of *b* divided by *c*.

    ```
    // your code goes here
    ```

27. If the product *b* times *c* is greater than or equal to 100, then invert *a* (if *a* is *true*, *a* becomes *false*; if *a* is *false*, *a* becomes *true*); otherwise, assign *true* to *a*.

    ```
    // your code goes here
    ```

28. If *a* is *true* and *b* is greater than 10, increment *c* by 1.

    ```
    // your code goes here
    ```

29. If both *b* and *c* are less than 10, then assign *true* to *a*; otherwise, assign *false* to *a*.

    ```
    // your code goes here
    ```

30. If *b* or *c* is greater than 5, then assign *true* to *a*; otherwise, assign *false* to *a*.

    ```
    // your code goes here
    ```

5.14.4 Identifying Errors in Code

For Exercises 31 through 38, assume that two *boolean* variables named *b1* and *b2* have been declared and assigned the value *true* or *false* earlier in the program. You should also assume that two *int* variables named *a1* and *a2* have been declared and assigned some integer values earlier in the program.

31. Where is the error in this code sequence?

```
b1 = a1 && a2;
```

32. Where is the error in this expression?

```
( b2 == b1 ) AND ( a1 <= a2 )
```

33. Where is the logical error in this code sequence?

```
if ( a1 == 4 );
    System.out.println( "a1 equals 4" );
```

34. Where is the error in this code sequence?

```
boolean b1 = true;
if b1
    System.out.println( "b1 is true" );
```

35. Where is the error in this code sequence?

```
if { b2 == true }
    System.out.println( "b2 is true" );
```

36. Where is the error in this code sequence?

```
if ( b1 == true )
    System.out.println( "b1 is true" );
else
    System.out.println( "b1 is false" );
else if ( a1 < 100 )
    System.out.println( "a1 is <= 100" );
```

37. Is there an error in this code sequence? Explain.

```
if ( b2 == b1 )
        System.out.println( "b2 and b1 have the same value" );
else if ( a1 == a2 )
        System.out.println( "a1 and a2 have the same value" );
else
        System.out.println( "All variables are different" );
```

38. Is there an error in this code sequence? Explain.

```
if ( b2 )
        System.out.println( "b2 is true" );
else if ( a1 <= 10 || a2 > 50 )
{
        System.out.print( "a1 <= 10 or " );
        System.out.println( "a2 > 50" );
}
else
        System.out.println( "none of the above" );
```

5.14.5 Debugging Area—Using Messages from the Java Compiler and Java JVM

39. You coded the following in class *Test.java*:

```java
boolean b = true;
if ( b )
      System.out.println( "Inside true block" );
      System.out.println( "b was true" );
else          // line 12
      System.out.println( "Inside false block" );
```

At compile time, you get the following error:

```
Test.java:12: 'else' without 'if'

   else       // line 12
   ^
      1 error
```

Explain what the problem is and how to fix it.

40. You coded the following in the class *Test.java*:

```java
int a = 32;
if ( a = 31 )     // line 9
      System.out.println( "The value of a is 31" );
else
      System.out.println( "The value of a is not 31" );
```

At compile time, you get the following error:

```
Test.java:9: incompatible types
   if ( a = 31 )     // line 9
           ^
required: boolean
found   : int
1 error
```

Explain what the problem is and how to fix it.

41. You coded the following in the class *Test.java*:

```java
boolean b = true;
if ( b )
{
      System.out.println( "Inside true block" );
      System.out.println( "b was true" );
else          // line 13
      System.out.println( "Inside false block" );
}
System.out.println( "Done" );
```

At compile time, you get the following error:

```
Test.java:13: 'else' without 'if'.
else         // line 13
^

1 error
```

Explain what the problem is and how to fix it.

5.14.6   Write a Short Program

42. Write a program that takes two *ints* as input from the keyboard, representing the number of hits and the number of at-bats for a batter. Then calculate the batter's hitting percentage and check if the hitting percentage is above .300. If it is, output that the player is eligible for the All Stars Game; otherwise, output that the player is not eligible.

43. Write a program that reads a *char* as an input from the keyboard and outputs whether it comes before or after the letter *b* in Unicode order.

44. Write a program that calculates the area of the following figures:

    ❏ a square of side 0.666666667

    ❏ a rectangle of sides ⅑ and 4

    Test the two calculated areas for equality; discuss your result.

45. Write a program that reads a sentence using a dialog box. Depending on the last character of the sentence, output another dialog box identifying the sentence as declarative (ends with a period), interrogative (ends with a question mark), exclamatory (ends with an exclamation point), or other.

46. An email address contains the @ character. Write a program that takes a word from the keyboard and outputs whether it is an email address based on the presence of the @ character. Do not worry about what else is in the word.

47. Write a program that takes two words as input from the keyboard, representing a password and the same password again. (Often, websites ask users to type their password twice when they register to make sure there was no typo the first time around.) Your program should do the following:

    ❏ if both passwords match, then output "You are now registered as a new user"

    ❏ otherwise, output "Sorry, there is a typo in your password"

48. Write a program that takes a word as input from the keyboard, representing a user ID. (Often, websites place constraints on user IDs.) Your program should do the following:

    ❏ if the user ID contains between 6 and 10 characters inclusive, then output "Welcome barbara" (assuming *barbara* is the user ID entered)

    ❏ otherwise, output "Sorry, user ID invalid"

5.14.7 Programming Projects

49. Write a program that reads a web address (for instance, *www.yahoo.com*) from the keyboard and outputs whether this web address is for a government, a university, a business, an organization, or another entity.

    ❏ If the web address contains *gov*, it is a government web address.

    ❏ If the web address contains *edu*, it is a university web address.

    ❏ If the web address contains *com*, it is a business web address.

    ❏ If the web address contains *org*, it is an organization web address.

    ❏ Otherwise, it is a web address for another entity.

50. Write a program that reads a temperature as a whole number from the keyboard and outputs a "probable" season (winter, spring, summer, or fall) depending on the temperature.

    ❏ If the temperature is greater than or equal to 90, it is probably summer.

    ❏ If the temperature is greater than or equal to 70 and less than 90, it is probably spring.

    ❏ If the temperature is greater than or equal to 50 and less than 70, it is probably fall.

    ❏ If the temperature is less than 50, it is probably winter.

    ❏ If the temperature is greater than 110 or less than -5, then you should output that the temperature entered is outside the valid range.

51. Write a program that takes a *String* as input from the keyboard, representing a year. Your program should do the following:

    ❏ If the year entered has two characters, convert it to an *int*, add 2000 to it, and output it.

❑ If the year entered has four characters, just convert it to an *int* and output it.

❑ If the year entered has neither two nor four characters, output that the year is not valid.

52. Write a program that takes two words as input from the keyboard, representing a user ID and a password. Your program should do the following:

❑ If the user ID and the password match "admin" and "open," respectively, then output "Welcome."

❑ If the user ID matches "admin" and the password does not match "open," output "Wrong password."

❑ If the password matches "open" and the user ID does not match "admin," output "Wrong user ID."

❑ Otherwise, output "Sorry, wrong ID and password."

5.14.8   Technical Writing

53. When comparing two *doubles* or *floats* for equality, programmers calculate the difference between the two numbers and check if that difference is sufficiently small. Explain why and give a real-life example.

54. Look at the following code segment:

```
int b = 44;
if ( b = 23 )
      System.out.println( "Inside true block" );
```

In Java, this code will generate the following compiler error:

```
Test.java:9: Incompatible types
found   : int
required: boolean
if ( b = 23 )
       ^
1 error
```

In the C++ programming language, the equivalent code will compile and run and will give you the following output:

```
Inside true block
```

Discuss whether Java handles this situation better than C++ and why.

5.14.9 Group Project (for a group of 1, 2, or 3 students)

55. We want to build a simple "English language" calculator that does the following:

   ❏ takes three inputs from the keyboard, two of them single digits (0 to 9)

   ❏ takes a *char* from the keyboard, representing one of five operations from the keyboard: + (addition), – (subtraction), * (multiplication), / (division), and ^ (exponentiation)

   ❏ outputs the description of the operation in plain English, as well as the numeric result

For instance, if the two numbers are 5 and 3, and the operation is *, then the output should be

```
five multiplied by three is 15
```

Note that the result is given as a number, not a word.

If the two numbers are 2 and 9, and the operation is –, then the output should be

```
two minus nine is -7
```

Hint: to perform the exponentiation, use the *pow* method of the *Math* class.

If the two numbers are 5 and 2, and the operation is ^, then the output should be

```
five to the power two is 25
```

Hint: to perform the exponentiation, use the *pow* method of the *Math* class.

If the two numbers are 5 and 0, and the operation is /, then the output should be

```
Division by zero is not allowed
```

Here the operation will not be performed.

If the two numbers are 25 and 3, and the operation is +, then the output should be

```
Invalid number
```

As for the operators, they should be translated into English as follows:

+   plus

−   minus

*   multiplied by

/   divided by

∧   to the power

You should use the *switch … case* selection statement to translate the input values into words.

You need to consider these special situations:

❑ For division, there is a special constraint: you cannot divide by 0, and you should therefore test whether the second number is 0. If it is 0, then you should output a message saying that you are not allowed to divide by 0.

❑ The "operator" is not one of the preceding five operators; in that case, output a message saying that the operator is not a valid one.

❑ One or two of the numbers is not a valid digit; again, you should output a message to that effect.

Hint: You can deal with these special situations in the *default* statement of the *switch* block and possibly use some *boolean* variables to keep track of this information, as you may need it later in your program.

EXERCISES, PROBLEMS, AND PROJECTS

CHAPTER 6

Flow of Control, Part 2: Looping

CHAPTER CONTENTS

Introduction

Have you ever watched the cashier at the grocery store? Let's call the cashier Jane. Jane's job is to determine the total cost of a grocery purchase. To begin, Jane starts with a total cost of $0.00. She then reaches for the first item and scans it to record its price, which is added to the total. Then she reaches for the second item, scans that item to record its price, which is added to the total, and so on. Jane continues scanning each item, one at a time, until there are no more items to scan. Usually, the end of an order is signaled by a divider bar lying across the conveyor belt. When Jane sees the divider bar, she knows she is finished. At that point, she tells us the total cost of the order, collects the money, and gives us a receipt.

So we see that Jane's job consists of performing some preliminary work, processing each item one at a time, and reporting the result at the end.

In computing, we often perform tasks that follow this same pattern:

1: initialize values

2: process items one at a time

3: report results

The flow of control that programmers use to complete jobs with this pattern is called **looping**, or **repetition**.

6.1   Event-Controlled Loops Using *while*

If we attempt to write pseudocode for the grocery store cashier, we may start with something like this:

```
set total to $0.00
reach for first item
if item is not the divider bar
    add price to total
reach for next item
if item is not the divider bar
    add price to total
reach for next item
if item is not the divider bar
    add price to total
... (finally)
reach for next item
item is the divider bar,
    tell the customer the total price
```

We can see a pattern here. We start with an order total of $0.00. Then we repeat a set of operations for each item. We reach for the item and check whether it's the divider bar. If the item is not the divider bar, we add the item's price to the order total. We reach for the next item and check whether it's the divider bar, and so on. When we reach for the item and find that it is the divider bar, we know there are no more items to process, so the total we have at that time is the total for the whole order. In other words, we don't know the number of items that will be placed on the conveyor belt. We just process the order, item by item, until we see the divider bar, which we do not process.

In Java, the *while* loop is designed for repeating a set of instructions for each input value when we don't know at the beginning how many input values there will be. We simply process each input value, one at a time, until a signal—an event—tells us that there is no more input. This is called **event-controlled looping**. In the cashier's case, the signal for the end of input was the divider bar. In other tasks, the signal for the end of the input may be a special value that the user enters, called a **sentinel value**, or it may be that we've reached the end of an input file.

6.2   General Form for *while* Loops

The *while* loop has this syntax:

```
// initialize variables
while ( condition )
{
    // process data; loop body
}
// process the results
```

The condition is a *boolean* expression, that is, any expression that evaluates to *true* or *false*. When the *while* loop statement is encountered, the condition is evaluated; if the value is *true*, the statements in the **loop body** are executed. The condition is then reevaluated and, if *true*, the loop body is executed again. This repetition continues until the loop condition evaluates to *false*, at which time, the loop body is skipped and execution continues at the instruction following the loop body.

The curly braces are needed only if the loop body has more than one statement—that is, if more than one statement should be executed if the condition evaluates to *true*.

The scope of any variable defined within the *while* loop body extends from its declaration to the end of the *while* loop. Thus, any variable that is declared within a *while* loop body cannot be referenced after the *while* loop ends.

The flow of control of a *while* loop is shown in Figure 6.1.

Each execution of the loop body is called an **iteration** of the loop. Thus, if the loop body executes five times before the condition evaluates to *false*, we say there were five iterations of the *while* loop.

What happens if the loop condition is *false* the first time it is evaluated? Because the loop condition is evaluated before executing the *while* loop body, and the loop body is executed only if the condition is *true*, it is possible that the *while* loop body is never executed. In that case, there would be **zero iterations** of the loop.

Figure 6.1

Flow of Control of a *while* Loop

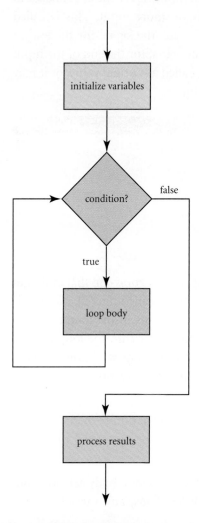

Using a *while* loop construct, the pseudocode for the cashier would look like this:

```
set total to $0.00
reach for first item
while item is not the divider bar
{
    add price to total
    reach for next item
}
// if we get here, the item is the divider bar
output the total price
```

It is also possible to construct a *while* loop whose condition *never* evaluates to *false*. That results in an **endless loop**, also known as an **infinite loop**. Because the condition always evaluates to *true*, the loop body is executed repeatedly, without end. This might happen if items other than the divider bar were placed continuously on the conveyor belt. One symptom of an endless loop is that the program doesn't terminate; it appears to "hang." However, if the program writes some output in the loop body, you will see that output spewing out on the Java console. Normally, the only recourse is for the user to abort the program.

The way to ensure that the condition will eventually evaluate to *false* is to include code, called a **loop update statement**, within the loop body that appropriately changes the variable that is being tested by the loop condition. If, for example, the loop condition tests for reading the sentinel value, the loop update statement should read the next input value.

One common logic error that causes an endless loop is putting a semicolon after the condition, as in the following:

```
while ( condition );  // semicolon causes endless loop if condition is true
```

A semicolon immediately following the condition indicates an empty loop body. Although some advanced programming techniques call for the use of an empty loop body, we will not be using those techniques in this book.

COMMON ERROR TRAP

Avoid putting a semicolon after the condition of a *while* loop. Doing so creates an empty loop body and could result in an endless loop.

6.3   Event-Controlled Looping

The *while* loop is used when we don't know how many times the loop will execute; that is, when the loop begins, we don't know how many iterations of the loop will be required. We rely on a signal, or **event**, to tell us that we have processed all the data. For example, when the cashier begins checking out an order, she doesn't (necessarily) know how many items are in the grocery cart; she only knows to stop when she sees the divider bar on the conveyor belt. We call this an event-controlled loop because we continue processing data until an event occurs, which signals the end of the data.

When we're prompting the user to enter data from the console, and we don't know at the beginning of the loop how much data the user has to be processed, we can define a special value, called the sentinel value. The sentinel value can vary from task to task and is typically a value that is outside the normal range of data for that task.

Sometimes the data our program needs is in a text file. For example, a file could store a company's monthly sales for the last five years. We may want to calculate average monthly sales or perform other statistical computations on that data. In this case, we need to read our data from the file, instead of asking the user to enter the data from the keyboard. Typically, we use a file when a large amount of data is involved because it would be impractical for a user to enter the data manually.

Reading from a file is also an event-controlled loop because we don't know at the beginning of the program how much data is in the file. Thus, we need some way to determine when we have finished processing all the data in the file. Java, and other languages, provides some indicator that we have reached the end of the file. Thus, for input from a file, sensing the end-of-file indication is the event that signals that there is no more data to read.

6.3.1   Reading Data from the User

Let's look at the general form for using a *while* loop to process data entered from the user.

```
initialize variables
read the first data item  // priming read
while data item is not the sentinel value
{
    process the data

    read the next data item  // update read
}
report the results
```

After performing any initialization, we attempt to read the first item. We call this the **priming read** because, like priming a pump, we use that value to feed the condition of the *while* loop for the first iteration. If the first item is not the sentinel value, we process it. Processing may consist of calculating a total, counting the number of data items, comparing the data to previously read values, or any number of operations. Then we read the next data item. This is called the **update read** because we update the data item in preparation for feeding its value into the condition of the *while* loop for the next iteration. This processing, followed by an update read, continues until we do read the sentinel value, at which time we do not execute the *while* loop body. Instead, we skip to the first instruction following the *while* loop. Note that the sentinel value is not meant to be processed. Like the divider bar for the cashier, it is simply a signal to stop processing.

We illustrate this pattern in Example 6.1, which prompts the user for integers and echoes to the console whatever the user enters. We chose the sentinel value to be –1; that is, when the user enters a –1, we stop processing.

```
 1 /*  Working with a sentinel value
 2      Anderson, Franceschi
 3 */
 4 import java.util.Scanner;
 5
 6 public class EchoUserInput
 7 {
 8    public static void main( String [ ] args )
 9    {
10       final int SENTINEL = -1;
11       int number;
12
13       Scanner scan = new Scanner( System.in );
14
15       // priming read
16       System.out.print( "Enter an integer, or -1 to stop > " );
17       number = scan.nextInt( );
18
19       while ( number != SENTINEL )
20       {
21          // processing
22          System.out.println( number );
23
24          // update read
25          System.out.print( "Enter an integer, or -1 to stop > " );
```

```
26            number = scan.nextInt( );
27        }
28
29        System.out.println( "Sentinel value detected. Goodbye" );
30    }
31 }
```

EXAMPLE 6.1   Echoing Input from the User

Figure 6.2 shows the output from this program when the user enters 23, 47, 100, and –1.

On line 10, we declare the sentinel value, –1, as a constant because the value of the sentinel will not change during the execution of the program, and it lets us clearly state via the *while* loop condition (line 19) that we want to execute the loop body only if the input is not the sentinel value.

Then on lines 16–17, we perform the priming read. The *while* loop condition on line 19 checks for the sentinel value. If the user enters the sentinel value first, we skip the *while* loop altogether and execute line 29, which prints a message that the sentinel value was entered, and we exit the program. If the user enters a number other than the sentinel value, we execute the body of the *while* loop (lines 21–26). In the *while* loop, we simply echo the user's input to the console, then perform the update read. Control then skips to the *while* loop condition, where the value the user entered in the update read is compared to the sentinel value. If this entry is the sentinel value, the loop is skipped; otherwise, the body of the loop is executed: The value is echoed, then a new value is read. This same processing continues until the user does enter the sentinel value.

Figure 6.2

Output from Example 6.1, Using a Sentinel Value

```
Enter an integer, or -1 to stop > 23
23
Enter an integer, or -1 to stop > 47
47
Enter an integer, or -1 to stop > 100
100
Enter an integer, or -1 to stop > -1
Sentinel value detected. Goodbye
```

A common error in constructing *while* loops is forgetting the update read. Without the update read, the *while* loop continually processes the same data item, leading to an endless loop.

Another common error is omitting the priming read and, instead, reading data inside the *while* loop before the processing, as in the following pseudocode:

```
initialize variables
while data item is not the sentinel value
{
    read the next data
    process the data
}
report the results
```

This structure has several problems. The first time we evaluate the *while* loop condition, we haven't read any data, so the result of that evaluation is unpredictable. Second, when we do read the sentinel value, we will process it, leading to incorrect results.

COMMON ERROR TRAP

Omitting the update read may result in an endless loop.

COMMON ERROR TRAP

Omitting the priming read leads to incorrect results.

6.3.2   Reading Data from a Text File

The *Scanner* class enables us to read data easily from a text file. Java also provides a whole set of classes in the *java.io* package to enable programmers to perform user input and output from a file.

For the *Scanner* class, the general form for reading data from a text file is a little different from reading the data from the user. First, instead of reading a value and checking whether it is the sentinel value, we check whether there is more data in the file, then read a value. Second, we don't need to print a prompt because the user doesn't enter the data; we just read the next value from the file. For the *Scanner* class, the pseudocode for reading from a text file is shown here:

```
initialize variables
while we have not reached end of file
```

```
{
    read the next data item
    process the data
}
report the results
```

Scanner class methods, including a constructor for reading from a text file, are shown in Table 6.1. Another class we will use is the *File* class, which associates a file name with a file. The constructor for the *File* class is shown in Table 6.2.

The constructor shown in Table 6.1 can be used to associate a *Scanner* object with a file. The *Scanner* object will tokenize the contents of the file and return the tokens as we call the *next* methods. The *hasNext* method in the *Scanner* class returns *true* if the input has another token, and *false* otherwise. Thus, when the *hasNext* method returns *false*, we know we have reached the end of the file.

Example 6.2 reads integers from a file named *input.txt* and echoes the integers to the console. The contents of *input.txt* are shown in Figure 6.3 and the output from the program is shown in Figure 6.4.

On line 14 of Example 6.2, we use the constructor of the *File* class to convert the file name, *input.txt*, to a platform-independent file name. Because we are specifying the simple file name, the JVM will look for the file in the same directory as our source file. If the file is located in another directory, we need to specify the path as well as the file name. For example, if the file were located on a flash drive in a Windows system, we would pass the *String* "*e:\\input.txt*" to the constructor. Notice that we need to use an escape sequence of two backslashes in order to specify the pathname, *e:\input.txt*.

The *File* class belongs to the *java.io* package, so we include an *import* statement for that class in line 5.

In line 15, we construct a *Scanner* object associated with the *inputFile* object. If the file is not found, the constructor generates a *FileNotFoundException*. It is also possible that an *IOException* may be generated if we encounter problems reading the file. Java requires us to acknowledge that these exceptions may be generated. One way to do that is to include the phrase *throws IOException* in the header for *main* (line 10). We also import the *IOException* class on line 6.

Figure 6.3

Contents of *input.txt*

 REFERENCE POINT

The *String* escape sequences are discussed in Chapter 2.

TABLE 6.1 Selected Methods of the *Scanner* Class

Selected Methods of the *Scanner* Class	
Constructor	
`Scanner( File file )`	
creates a *Scanner* object and associates it with a file	

Return value	**Method name and argument list**
`boolean`	`hasNext( )`
	returns *true* if there is another token in the input stream; *false,* otherwise
`byte`	`nextByte( )`
	returns the next input as a *byte*
`short`	`nextShort( )`
	returns the next input as a *short*
`int`	`nextInt( )`
	returns the next input as an *int*
`long`	`nextLong( )`
	returns the next input as a *long*
`float`	`nextFloat( )`
	returns the next input as a *float*
`double`	`nextDouble( )`
	returns the next input as a *double*
`boolean`	`nextBoolean( )`
	returns the next input as a *boolean*
`String`	`next( )`
	returns the next token in the input line as a *String*

TABLE 6.2 *File* Class Constructor

A Constructor for the *File* Class
`File( String pathname )`
constructs a *File* object with the *pathname* file name so that the file name is platform-independent

REFERENCE POINT

You can read more about the *Scanner* class on Oracle's Java website: *www.oracle.com/ technetwork/java.*

On line 17, the first time our *while* loop condition is evaluated, we check whether there is any data in the file. If the file is empty, the *hasNext* method will return *false*, and we will skip execution of the loop body, continuing at line 25, where we print a message and exit the program.

The body of the *while* loop (lines 19–22) calls the *nextInt* method to read the next integer in the file and echoes that integer to the console. We then reevaluate the *while* loop condition (line 17) to determine if more data is in the file. When no more integers remain to be read, the *hasNext* method returns *false*, and we skip to line 25, where we print a message and exit the program.

Notice that we do not use a priming read because the *hasNext* method essentially peeks ahead into the file to see if there is more data. If the *hasNext* method returns *true*, we know that there is another integer to read, so we perform the read in the first line of the *while* loop body (line 20).

```
1 /* Reading a Text File
2    Anderson, Franceschi
3 */
4 import java.util.Scanner;
5 import java.io.File;
6 import java.io.IOException;
7
8 public class EchoFileData
9 {
10    public static void main( String [ ] args ) throws IOException
11    {
12       int number;
13
14       File inputFile = new File( "input.txt" );
15       Scanner scan = new Scanner( inputFile );
16
17       while ( scan.hasNext( ) )
18       {
19          // read next integer
20          number = scan.nextInt( );
21          // process the value read
22          System.out.println( number );
23       }
24
25       System.out.println( "End of file detected. Goodbye" );
26    }
27 }
```

EXAMPLE 6.2   Echoing Input from a File

```
23
47
100
End of file detected. Goodbye
```

Figure 6.4
**Output from Example 6.2,
Reading from a File**

6.4   Looping Techniques

You will find that the *while* loop is an important tool for performing many common programming operations on a set of input values. For example, the *while* loop can be used to calculate the sum of values, count the number of values, find the average value, find the minimum and maximum values, animate an image, and perform other operations.

6.4.1   Accumulation

Let's look at a common programming operation for which a *while* loop is useful: calculating the sum of a set of values. To do this, we will build a simple calculator that performs one function: addition. We will prompt the user for numbers one at a time. We'll make the sentinel value a 0; that is, when the user wants to stop, the user will enter a 0. At that point, we will print the total.

The calculator can be developed using an event-controlled *while* loop and a standard computing technique: **accumulation**. In the accumulation operation, we initialize a *total* variable to 0. Each time we input a new value, we add that value to the *total*. When we reach the end of the input, the current value of *total* is the total for all the input.

Here is the pseudocode for the addition calculator:

set total to 0
read a number   // priming read
while the number is not the sentinel value
{
    add the number to total
    read the next number   // update read
}
output the total

Notice that this operation is almost identical to the grocery cashier's job in that we perform a priming read before the *while* loop. Inside the *while* loop, we process each number one at a time—adding each number to the total, then we read the next value, until we see the sentinel value, which is the signal to stop.

Example 6.3 provides the code for the addition calculator and Figure 6.5 shows the output for a sample execution of the calculator.

```
 1 /*  Addition Calculator
 2     Anderson, Franceschi
 3 */
 4
 5 import java.util.Scanner;
 6
 7 public class Calculator
 8 {
 9    public static void main( String [ ] args )
10    {
11       final int SENTINEL = 0;
12       int number;
13       int total = 0;
14
15       Scanner scan = new Scanner( System.in );
16
17       System.out.println( "Welcome to the addition calculator.\n" );
18
19       System.out.print( "Enter the first number"
20                         + " or 0 for the total > " );
21       number = scan.nextInt( );
22
23       while ( number != SENTINEL )
24       {
25          total += number;
26
27          System.out.print( "Enter the next number"
28                            + " or 0 for the total > " );
29          number = scan.nextInt( );
30       }
31
32       System.out.println( "The total is " + total );
33    }
34 }
```

EXAMPLE 6.3   An Addition Calculator

```
Welcome to the addition calculator.

Enter the first number or 0 for the total > 34
Enter the next number or 0 for the total > -10
Enter the next number or 0 for the total > 2
Enter the next number or 0 for the total > 5
Enter the next number or 0 for the total > 8
Enter the next number or 0 for the total > 0
The total is 39
```

Figure 6.5
Output from a Sample Run of the Addition Calculator

Line 13 declares and initializes the *total* to *0*. This is an important step because the loop body will add each input value to the total. If the total is not set to 0 before the first input, we will get incorrect results. Furthermore, if *total* is declared but not initialized, our program will not compile.

Lines 19–21 read the first input value (the priming read). The *while* loop begins at line 23, and its condition checks for the sentinel value. The first time the *while* loop is encountered, this condition will check the value of the input from the priming read.

The loop body processes the input (line 25), which consists of adding the input value to the *total*. The final step in the loop body (lines 27–29) is to read the next input (the update read).

When the end of the loop body is reached, control is transferred back to line 23, where the loop condition is again tested with the input value read on line 29. If the condition is *true*, that is, if the input just read is not the sentinel value, then the loop body is reexecuted and the condition is retested, continuing until the input *is* the sentinel value, which causes the condition to evaluate to *false*. At that time, the loop body is skipped and line 32 is executed, which reports the results by printing the *total*.

Notice that the body of the *while* loop is indented and that the opening and closing curly braces are aligned in the same column as the *w* in the *while*. This style lets you easily see which statements belong to the *while* loop body.

 **COMMON ERROR TRAP**

Forgetting to initialize the total to 0 will produce incorrect results.

 **SOFTWARE ENGINEERING TIP**

Indent the body of a *while* loop to clearly illustrate the logic of the program.

COMMON ERROR TRAP

Choosing the wrong sentinel value may result in logic errors.

It is important to choose the sentinel value carefully. Obviously, the sentinel value cannot be a value that the user might want to be processed. In the addition calculator, we want to allow the user to enter positive or negative integers. We chose 0 as the sentinel value for two reasons. First, adding 0 to a total has no effect, so it is unlikely that the user will want to enter that value to be processed. Second, to the user, it is logical to enter a 0 to signal that there are no more integers to be added.

CODE IN ACTION

To see a step-by-step illustration of a *while* loop with a sentinel value, look for the Flash movie in the Chapter 6 folder on the CD-ROM included with this book. Click on the link for Chapter 6 to start the movie.

6.4.2   Counting Items

Counting is used when we need to know how many items are input or how many input values fit some criterion, for example, how many items are positive numbers or how many items are odd numbers. Counting is similar to accumulation in that we start with a count of 0 and increment (add 1 to) the count every time we read a value that meets the criterion. When there are no more values to read, the count variable contains the number of items that meet our criterion.

For example, let's count the number of students who passed a test. The pseudocode for this operation is as follows:

```
set countPassed to 0
read a test score
while the test score is not the sentinel value
{
  if the test score >= 60
  {
    add 1 to countPassed
  }
  read the next test score
}
output countPassed
```

The application in Example 6.4 counts the number of students that passed a test. We also calculate the percentage of the class that passed the test. To do this, we maintain a second count: the number of scores entered. This value will be incremented each time we read a score, whereas the *countPassed* value will be incremented only if the score is greater than or equal to 60. The sentinel value is –1. A sample run of this program is shown in Figure 6.6.

```
1 /* Counting passing test scores
2    Anderson, Franceschi
3 */
4
5 import java.util.Scanner;
6 import java.text.DecimalFormat;
7
8 public class CountTestScores
9 {
10    public static void main( String [ ] args )
11    {
12       int countPassed = 0;
13       int countScores = 0;
14       int score;
15       final int SENTINEL = -1;
16
17       Scanner scan = new Scanner( System.in );
18
19       System.out.println( "This program counts "
20                   + "the number of passing test scores." );
21       System.out.println( "Enter a -1 to stop." );
22
23       System.out.print( "Enter the first score > " );
24       score = scan.nextInt( );
25
26       while ( score != SENTINEL )
27       {
28          if ( score >= 60 )
29          {
30                countPassed++;
31          }
32
33          countScores++;
34
35          System.out.print( "Enter the next score > " );
36          score = scan.nextInt( );
37       }
38
```

```
39        System.out.println( "You entered " + countScores + " scores" );
40        System.out.println( "The number of passing test scores is "
41                              + countPassed );
42        if ( countScores != 0 )
43        {
44           DecimalFormat percent = new DecimalFormat( "#0.0%" );
45           System.out.println(
46             percent.format( (double) ( countPassed ) / countScores )
47             + " of the class passed the test." );
48        }
49     }
50 }
```

EXAMPLE 6.4   Counting Passing Test Scores

Figure 6.6

Counting Passing Test Scores

```
This program counts the number of passing test scores.
Enter a -1 to stop.
Enter the first score > 98
Enter the next score > 75
Enter the next score > 60
Enter the next score > 59
Enter the next score > 45
Enter the next score > 88
Enter the next score > 94
Enter the next score > 96
Enter the next score > 56
Enter the next score > 77
Enter the next score > 82
Enter the next score > 89
Enter the next score > 100
Enter the next score > 78
Enter the next score > 95
Enter the next score > -1
You entered 15 scores
The number of passing test scores is 12
80.0% of the class passed the test.
```

COMMON ERROR TRAP

Forgetting to initialize the count variables will produce a compiler error.

Lines 12 and 13 declare the variables *countPassed* and *countScores* and initialize both to 0. Initializing these values to 0 is critical; otherwise, we will get the wrong results or a compiler error. We initialize these values to 0 because at that point, we have not yet processed any test scores.

Our *while* loop framework follows the familiar pattern. We perform the priming read for the first input (lines 23–24); our *while* loop condition checks for the sentinel value (line 26); and the last statements of the *while* loop (lines 35–36) read the next value.

In the processing portion of the *while* loop, line 28 checks if the score just read is a passing score, and if so, line 30 adds 1 to *countPassed*. For each score entered, regardless of whether the student passed, we increment *countScores* (line 33).

When the sentinel value is entered, the *while* loop condition evaluates to *false* and control skips to line 39, where we output the number of scores entered and the number of passing scores. So that we avoid dividing by 0, note that line 42 checks whether no scores were entered. Note also that in line 46 we type cast *countPassed* to a *double* to force floating-point division, rather than integer division, so that the fractional part of the quotient will be maintained.

6.4.3 Calculating an Average

Calculating an average is a combination of accumulation and counting. We use accumulation to calculate the total and we use counting to count the number of items to average.

Here's the pseudocode for calculating an average:

```
set total to 0
set count to 0
read a number
while the number is not the sentinel value
{
    add the number to total
    add 1 to the count

    read the next number
}
set the average to total / count
output the average
```

Thus, to calculate an average test score for the class, we need to calculate the total of all the test scores, then divide by the number of students who took the test.

```
average = total / count;
```

It's important to remember that if we declare *total* and *count* as integers, then the *average* will be calculated using integer division, which truncates the remainder. To get a floating-point average, we need to type cast one of the variables (either *total* or *count*) to a *double* or a *float* to force the division to be performed as floating-point.

```java
double average = (double) ( total ) / count;
```

The application in Example 6.5 calculates an average test score for a class of students. The output is shown in Figure 6.7.

```java
1  /* Calculate the average test score
2       Anderson, Franceschi
3  */
4
5  import java.util.Scanner;
6  import java.text.DecimalFormat;
7
8  public class AverageTestScore
9  {
10   public static void main( String [ ] args )
11   {
12     int count = 0;
13     int total = 0;
14     final int SENTINEL = -1;
15     int score;
16
17     Scanner scan = new Scanner( System.in );
18
19     System.out.println( "To calculate a class average," );
20     System.out.println( "enter each test score." );
21     System.out.println( "When you are finished, enter a -1" );
22
23     System.out.print( "Enter the first test score > " );
24     score = scan.nextInt( );
25
26     while ( score != SENTINEL )
27     {
28       total += score;   // add score to total
29       count++;          // add 1 to count of test scores
30
31       System.out.print( "Enter the next test score > " );
32       score = scan.nextInt( );
33     }
34
35     if ( count != 0 )
36     {
37       DecimalFormat oneDecimalPlace = new DecimalFormat( "##.0" );
38       System.out.println( "\nThe class average is "
39         + oneDecimalPlace.format( (double) ( total ) / count ) );
40     }
```

```
41     else
42         System.out.println( "\nNo grades were entered" );
44     }
45 }
```

EXAMPLE 6.5 Calculating an Average Test Score

```
To calculate a class average,
enter each test score.
When you are finished, enter a -1
Enter the first test score > 88
Enter the next test score > 78
Enter the next test score > 96
Enter the next test score > 75
Enter the next test score > 99
Enter the next test score > 56
Enter the next test score > 78
Enter the next test score > 84
Enter the next test score > 93
Enter the next test score > 79
Enter the next test score > 90
Enter the next test score > 85
Enter the next test score > 79
Enter the next test score > 92
Enter the next test score > 99
Enter the next test score > 94
Enter the next test score > -1

The class average is 85.3
```

Figure 6.7

Calculating the Average Test Score

In Example 6.5, lines 12 and 13 declare both *count* and *total* variables as *ints* and initialize each to 0. Again, our *while* loop structure follows the same pattern. Lines 23–24 read the first input value; the *while* loop condition (line 26) checks for the sentinel value; and the last statements in the *while* loop (lines 31–32) read the next score. For the processing portion of the *while* loop, we add the score to the total and increment the count of scores (lines 28–29). When the sentinel value is entered, we stop executing the *while* loop and skip to line 35.

In line 35, we avoid dividing by 0 by checking whether *count* is 0 (that is, if no scores were entered) before performing the division. If *count* is 0, we

COMMON ERROR TRAP

Forgetting to check whether the denominator is 0 before performing division is a logic error.

   **REFERENCE POINT**

The difference between floating-point division and integer division is explained in Chapter 2.

simply print a message saying that no grades were entered. If *count* is not 0, we calculate and print the average. We first instantiate a *DecimalFormat* object (line 37) so that we can output the average to one decimal place. Remember that we need to type cast the *total* to a *double* (lines 38–39) to force floating-point division, rather than integer division.

6.4.4   Finding Maximum or Minimum Values

In Chapter 5, we illustrated a method for finding the maximum or minimum of three numbers. But that method won't work when we don't know how many numbers will be input. To find the maximum or minimum of an unknown number of input values, we need another approach.

In previous examples, we calculated a total for a group of numbers by keeping a running total. We started with a total of 0, then added each new input value to the running total. Similarly, we counted the number of input items by keeping a running count. We started with a count of 0 and incremented the count each time we read a new value. We can apply that same logic to calculating a maximum or minimum. For example, to find the maximum of a group of values, we can keep a "running," or current, maximum. We start by assuming that the first value we read is the maximum. In fact, it is the largest value we have seen so far. Then as we read each new value, we compare it to our current maximum. If the new value is greater, we make the new value our current maximum. When we come to the end of the input values, the current maximum is the maximum for all the input values.

Finding the minimum value, of course, uses the same approach, except that we replace the current minimum only if the new value is less than the current minimum.

Here's the pseudocode for finding a maximum value in a file:

```
read a first number and make it the maximum
while there is another number to read
{
    read the next number
    if number > maximum
```

```
    {
        set maximum to number
    }
}
output the maximum
```

Example 6.6 shows the code to find a maximum test grade in a file. As shown in Figure 6.8, the grades are stored as integers, one per line, in the file *grades.txt*. When this program runs, its output is shown in Figure 6.9.

```
1  /* Find the maximum test grade
2     Anderson, Franceschi
3  */
4
5  import java.util.Scanner;
6  import java.io.*;
7
8  public class FindMaximumGrade
9  {
10     public static void main( String [ ] args ) throws IOException
11     {
12         int maxGrade;
13         int grade;
14
15         Scanner scan = new Scanner( new File( "grades.txt" ) );
16
17         System.out.println( "This program finds the maximum grade "
18                             + "for a class" );
19
20         if ( ! scan.hasNext( ) )
21         {
22             System.out.println( "No test grades are in the file" );
23         }
24         else
25         {
26             maxGrade = scan.nextInt( );  // make first grade the max
27
28             while ( scan.hasNext( ) )
29             {
30                 grade = scan.nextInt( );  // read next grade
```

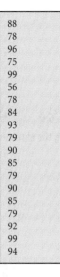

```
88
78
96
75
99
56
78
84
93
79
90
85
79
90
85
79
92
99
94
```

Figure 6.8
The Contents of *grades.txt*

```
31
32              if ( grade > maxGrade )
33                  maxGrade = grade;     // save as current max
34          }
35
36          System.out.println( "The maximum grade is " + maxGrade );
37      }
38  }
39 }
```

EXAMPLE 6.6   Finding the Maximum Value

Figure 6.9

Finding the Maximum Value

```
This program finds the maximum grade for a class
The maximum grade is 99
```

In line 20, we call the *hasNext* method to test whether the file is empty. If so, we print a message (line 22) and the program ends. If, however, the file is not empty, we read the first value and automatically make it our maximum by storing the grade in *maxGrade* (line 26). In line 28, our *while* loop condition tests whether we have reached end of file. If not, we execute the body of the *while* loop (lines 30–33). We read the next grade and check whether that grade is greater than the current maximum. If so, we assign that grade to *maxGrade*; otherwise, we leave *maxGrade* unchanged. Then control is transferred to line 28 to retest the *while* loop condition.

When we do reach end of file, the *while* loop condition becomes *false*; control is transferred to line 36, and we output *maxGrade* as the maximum value.

 **COMMON ERROR TRAP**

Initializing a maximum or a minimum to an arbitrary value, such as 0 or 100, is a logic error and could result in incorrect results.

A common error is to initialize the maximum or minimum to an arbitrary value, such as 0 or 100. This will not work for all conditions, however. For example, let's say we are finding the maximum number and we initialize the maximum to 0. If the user enters all negative numbers, then when the end of data is encountered, the maximum will still be 0, which is clearly an error. The same principle is true when finding a minimum value. If we initialize the minimum to 0, and the user enters all positive numbers greater than 0, then at the end of our loop, our minimum value will still be 0, which is also incorrect.

Skill Practice
with these end-of-chapter questions

6.14.1 Multiple Choice Exercises

Question 1

6.14.2 Reading and Understanding Code

Questions 5, 6, 7, 8, 20

6.14.3 Fill In the Code

Questions 21, 22, 23, 24, 25, 26

6.14.4 Identifying Errors in Code

Questions 30, 31

6.14.5 Debugging Area

Question 37

6.14.6 Write a Short Program

Questions 44, 45

6.14.8 Technical Writing

Questions 70, 71

6.4.5 Animation

Animation is another operation that can be performed using *while* loops. For example, to move an object across a graphics window, we change the x or y values and draw the object in a new position in each iteration of the loop. We stop moving the object when we reach the edges of the window. Therefore, the sentinel value for the loop is that the x or y coordinate has reached the edge of the window.

If we want to roll a ball from left to right along an imaginary line, we can represent the ball by a filled circle. We start with an *x* value of 0 and some *y* value; our *while* loop draws the object at the current *x, y* position, then increments the *x* value.

Thus, to test for the sentinel value—that is, whether the ball has reached the right edge of the window—we add the diameter of the ball to the current *x* position of the ball and compare that result to the *x* coordinate of the right edge of the window.

For this animation, we'll use a *Circle* class written by the authors. Table 6.3 shows the constructors and methods of the *Circle* class.

Example 6.7 shows a *while* loop that simulates rolling a ball from the left edge of the window to the right edge.

```
1 /* RollABall, Version 1
2    Anderson, Franceschi
3 */
4
5 import java.awt.Graphics;
6 import java.awt.Color;
7 import javax.swing.JApplet;
8
9 public class RollABall1 extends JApplet
10 {
11    public void paint( Graphics g )
12    {
13        super.paint( g );
14
15        final int X = 0;          // the x value of the ball
16        final int Y = 50;         // the y value of the ball
17        final int DIAMETER = 15;  // the diameter of the ball
18        final Color COLOR = Color.BLUE; // the color of the ball
19        final int SPACER = 5;     // space between balls
20
21        // instantiate the ball as a Circle object
22        Circle ball = new Circle( X, Y, DIAMETER, COLOR );
23
24        // get ball diameter
25        int ballDiameter = ball.getDiameter( );
26        int sentinel = getWidth( ); // edge of the window is sentinel
27
```

TABLE 6.3 The *Circle* Class API

The *Circle* Class API

Constructors

`Circle( )`

constructs a *Circle* object with default values; *x* and *y* are set to 0, diameter to 10, and color to black

`Circle( int startX, int startY, int sDiameter,`
`        Color circleColor )`

constructs a *Circle* object; sets *x* and *y* to *startX* and *startY*, respectively; diameter to *sDiameter*; and color to *circleColor*

Return value	Method name and argument list
`int`	`getX( )` returns the ball's current *x* value
`int`	`getY( )` returns the ball's current *y* value
`int`	`getDiameter( )` returns the current diameter of the circle
`Color`	`getColor( )` returns the current color of the circle
`void`	`setX( int newX )` sets the *x* value to *newX*
`void`	`setY( int newY )` sets the *y* value to *newY*
`void`	`setDiameter( int newDiameter )` sets the diameter to *newDiameter*
`void`	`setColor( Color newColor )` sets the circle color to *newColor*
`void`	`draw( Graphics g )` draws a filled circle with *x* and *y* being the upper-left corner of a bounding rectangle, with the diameter and color set in the object

```
28          while ( ball.getX( ) + ballDiameter < sentinel )
29          {
30            ball.draw( g );   // draw the ball
31
32            // set x to next drawing location
33            ball.setX( ball.getX( ) + ballDiameter + SPACER );
34          }
35      }
36 }
```

EXAMPLE 6.7   Roll a Ball, Version 1

In the *paint* method, we instantiate the ball (line 22). It will start with an *x* value of 0 (the left edge of the screen), *y* value of 50, diameter of 15, and a blue color. We use a *while* loop (lines 28–34) to repeatedly draw a ball and increment the *x* value. The sentinel value occurs when the *x* value of the next ball (*x* + *ballDiameter*) reaches the right edge of the applet window. We determine the value of the right edge of the window by calling the *getWidth* method of the *JApplet* class (line 26), which returns the width of the applet window.

We chose to increment the *x* value by the width of the ball (the diameter) plus 5 pixels so that each ball is 5 pixels apart (line 33). Let's take a closer look at that statement:

```
ball.setX( ball.getX( ) + ballDiameter + SPACER );
```

We call the *setX* method of the *Circle* class to set the *x* value of the next ball. In order to set the *x* value to a new value, we need to get the current *x* value of the *ball* object and the current diameter. We do that by calling the *getX* method and adding the *ballDiameter* value we got earlier from the *getDiameter* method (line 25). Thus, by adding the diameter of the ball to the current *x* value, we calculate the *x* value of the right side of the ball. Adding the constant *SPACER* to that result puts a space of 5 pixels between the last ball drawn and the next.

Figure 6.10 shows the output when the applet is run.

This is fine for a first effort, but it isn't the effect we want. The result is just a series of balls drawn from left to right. There's another problem with *RollABall1*, which you can appreciate only if you run the applet: all

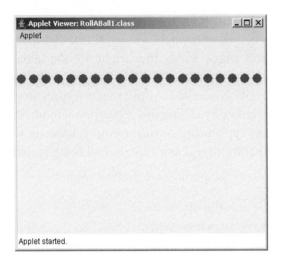

Figure 6.10
Roll a Ball, Version 1

the balls appear at once. There's no visual effect of the ball moving from left to right.

To get a rolling movement, we need to slow down the execution of the applet. To do that, we can use the *Pause* class provided by the authors and available in the directory on the CD-ROM containing this code. The *wait* method of the *Pause* class has the following API:

```
static void wait( double seconds )
```

Because the *wait* method is *static*, we invoke it using the *Pause* class name. For example, the following statement will pause the applet for approximately 3/100th of a second:

```
Pause.wait( .03 );
```

Also, we want to see only one ball at any time, and that should be the ball at the current (x, y) coordinate. To get this effect, we need to "erase" the previous ball before we draw the next ball in the new location. To erase the ball, we have two options: we can redraw the ball in the background color or we can clear the whole window by calling the *clearRect* method, which draws a rectangle in the background color. The default background color for the *JApplet* class is not one of the *Color* constants (*Color.BLUE*, etc.), so it's a difficult color to match. That being the case, we opt for the *clearRect* method, which has the following API:

```
void clearRect( int x, int y, int width, int height )
```

Using the *clearRect* method, we can erase the whole applet window by treating it as a rectangle whose (*x, y*) coordinate is the upper-left corner (0, 0) and whose width and height are the same as the applet window. We've already seen that we can get the width of the window by calling the *getWidth* method. As you might suspect, we can get the height of the applet window by calling the *getHeight* method. Note that after we call *clearRect*, the applet window will be empty; however, we draw the next ball so quickly that the user doesn't see the ball being erased.

Here's the pseudocode for the animation:

```
set starting (x, y) coordinate
instantiate the ball object
while the x value is not the edge of the window
{
  draw the ball
  pause
  erase the ball
  set (x, y) coordinate to next drawing position
}
```

Example 6.8 shows the revised version of the rolling ball.

```
 1 /* RollABall, version 2
 2    Anderson, Franceschi
 3 */
 4
 5 import java.awt.Graphics;
 6 import java.awt.Color;
 7 import javax.swing.JApplet;
 8 import javax.swing.JOptionPane;
 9
10 public class RollABall2 extends JApplet
11 {
12   public void paint( Graphics g )
13   {
14     super.paint( g );
15
16     final int X = 0;        // the x value of the ball
17     final int Y = 50;       // the y value of the ball
```

```
18      final int DIAMETER = 15;   // the diameter of the ball
19      final Color COLOR = Color.BLUE; // the color of the ball
20      final int SPACER = 5;       // space between balls
21
22      // instantiate the ball as a Circle object
23      Circle ball = new Circle( X, Y, DIAMETER, COLOR );
24
25      // get ball diameter and width & height of the applet window
26      int ballDiameter = ball.getDiameter( );
27      int windowWidth = getWidth( );
28      int windowHeight = getHeight( );
29
30      // rolling horizontally
31      // check whether ball is at right edge of window
32      while ( ball.getX( ) + ballDiameter < windowWidth )
33      {
34          ball.draw( g );  // draw the ball
35
36          Pause.wait( 0.03 ); // wait 3/100th of a second
37
38          // clear the window
39          g.clearRect( 0, 0, windowWidth, windowHeight );
40
41          // position to next location for drawing ball
42          ball.setX( ball.getX( ) + SPACER ); // increment x by 5
43      }
44
45      ball.draw( g );  // draw the ball in the current position
46   }
47 }
```

EXAMPLE 6.8   Roll a Ball, Version 2

In the *paint* method, we now draw a ball (line 34), pause for approximately
3/100ths of a second (line 36), then use the *clearRect* method to erase the
window (line 39) before positioning *x* to the next location for drawing the
ball (line 42). Now, only one ball is visible at any time, and the ball appears
to roll across the screen, as shown in Figure 6.11. After the *while* loop completes, we draw the ball one more time (line 45) because when the *while*
loop ends, the last ball drawn will have been erased.

Figure 6.11

Roll a Ball, Version 2

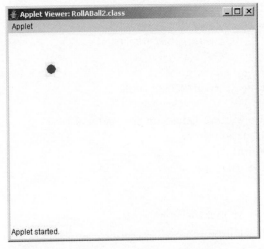

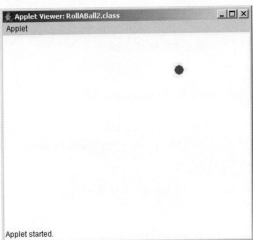

6.5   Type-Safe Input Using *Scanner*

One problem with reading input using *Scanner* is that if the next token does not match the data type we expect, an *InputMismatchException* is generated, which stops execution of the program. This could be caused by a simple typo on the user's part; for example, the user may type a letter or other nonnumeric character when our program prompts for an integer. To illustrate this problem, Example 6.9 shows a small program that prompts the user for an integer and calls the *nextInt* method of the *Scanner* class to read the integer, and Figure 6.12 shows the *InputMismatchException* generated when the user enters an *a* instead of an integer. Notice that the program ends when the exception is generated; we never execute line 15, which echoes the age to the console.

```
1  /* Reading an integer from the user
2     Anderson, Franceschi
3  */
4  import java.util.Scanner;
5
6  public class ReadInteger
7  {
8    public static void main( String [ ] args )
9    {
10         Scanner scan = new Scanner( System.in );
11
12         System.out.print( "Enter your age as an integer > " );
13         int age = scan.nextInt( );
14
15         System.out.println( "Your age is " + age );
16   }
17 }
```

EXAMPLE 6.9   Reading an Integer

```
Enter your age as an integer > a
Exception in thread "main" java.util.InputMismatchException
        at java.util.Scanner.throwFor(Scanner.java:899)
        at java.util.Scanner.next(Scanner.java:1520)
        at java.util.Scanner.nextInt(Scanner.java:2150)
        at java.util.Scanner.nextInt(Scanner.java:2109)
        at ReadInteger.main(ReadInteger.java:13)
```

Figure 6.12
Input Failure

We can make our program more robust by checking, before we read, that the next token matches our expected input. The *Scanner* class provides *hasNext* methods for doing this, which are shown in Table 6.4. The *hasNext* methods return *true* if the next token can be read as the data type specified. For example, if we expect an integer, we can test whether the user has typed characters that can be interpreted as an integer by calling the *hasNextInt* method. If that method returns *true*, it is safe to read the value using the *nextInt* method. If the next token is not what we need, that is, if the *hasNextInt* method returns *false*, then reading that value as an *int* will

TABLE 6.4   *Scanner* Methods for Testing Tokens

Selected Input Stream Testing Methods of the *Scanner* Class	
Return value	**Method name and argument list**

boolean	hasNext( )
	    returns *true* if there is another token in the input stream;
	    false, otherwise

boolean	hasNextByte( )
	    returns *true* if the token in the input stream can be read as
	    a *byte*; *false*, otherwise

boolean	hasNextShort( )
	    returns *true* if the token in the input stream can be read as
	    a *short*; *false*, otherwise

boolean	hasNextInt( )
	    returns *true* if the token in the input stream can be read as
	    an *int*; *false*, otherwise

boolean	hasNextLong( )
	    returns *true* if the token in the input stream can be read as
	    a *long*; *false*, otherwise

boolean	hasNextFloat( )
	    returns *true* if the token in the input stream can be read as
	    a *float*; *false*, otherwise

boolean	hasNextDouble( )
	    returns *true* if the token in the input stream can be read as
	    a *double*; *false*, otherwise

boolean	hasNextBoolean( )
	    returns *true* if the token in the input stream can be read as
	    a *boolean*; *false*, otherwise

String	nextLine( ) returns the remainder of the input line as a *String*

generate the *InputMismatchException*. In that case, we need to notify the user that the value typed is not valid and reprompt for new input. But first we need to clear the invalid input. We can flush the invalid input by calling the *nextLine* method of the *Scanner* class, which returns any remaining tokens on the input line as a *String*. Then we just ignore that *String*. Example 6.10 shows a revised version of Example 6.9 that is type-safe, meaning we guarantee we have an integer to read before reading it.

On line 14 of Example 6.10, we prompt for the integer. Then on line 15, the *while* loop condition checks whether the user has, indeed, typed an integer value. If not, we ignore whatever the user did type by calling the *nextLine* method (line 17). On line 18, we reprompt the user. The *while* loop continues executing until the user does enter an integer and the *hasNextInt* method returns *true*. At that point, we execute line 20, which reads the integer into the *age* variable. Figure 6.13 shows the output of this program when the user enters data other than integers, then finally enters an integer.

```
 1   /* Type-Safe Input Using Scanner
 2      Anderson, Franceschi
 3   */
 4
 5   import java.util.Scanner;
 6
 7   public class TypeSafeReadInteger
 8   {
 9     public static void main( String [ ] args )
10     {
11         Scanner scan = new Scanner( System.in );
12         String garbage;
13
14         System.out.print( "Enter your age as an integer > " );
15         while ( ! scan.hasNextInt( ) )
16         {
17             garbage = scan.nextLine( );
18             System.out.print( "\nPlease enter an integer > " );
19         }
20         int age = scan.nextInt( );
21         System.out.println( "Your age is " + age );
22     }
23   }
```

EXAMPLE 6.10   Type-Safe Input

Figure 6.13

Reprompting Until the User Enters an Integer

```
Enter your age as an integer > asd

Please enter an integer > 12wg

Please enter an integer > 12.4

Please enter an integer > 23
Your age is 23
```

6.6   Constructing Loop Conditions

Constructing the correct loop condition may seem a little counterintuitive. The loop executes as long as the loop condition evaluates to *true*. Thus, if we want our loop to terminate when we read the sentinel value, then the loop condition should check that the input value is *not* the sentinel value. In other words, the loop continuation condition is the inverse of the loop termination condition. For a simple sentinel-controlled loop, the condition normally follows this pattern:

```
while ( inputValue != sentinel )
```

In fact, you can see that the loop conditions in many of the examples in this chapter use this form of *while* loop condition. Examples 6.7 and 6.8 use a similar pattern. We want to roll the ball as long as the ball is completely within the window. The loop termination condition is that the starting *x* value plus the diameter of the ball is greater than or equal to the *x* value of the right side of the window. The loop continuation condition, therefore, is that the *x* value of the ball plus the diameter is less than the *x* value of the right side of the window.

```
while ( ball.getX( ) + ballDiameter < windowWidth )
```

For some applications, there may be multiple sentinel values. For example, suppose we provide a menu for a user with each menu option being a single character. The user can repeatedly select options from the menu, with the sentinel value being *S* for stop. To allow case-insensitive input, we want to recognize the sentinel value as either *S* or *s*. To do this, we need a compound loop condition, that is, a loop condition that uses a logical AND (`&&`) or logical OR (`||`) operator.

Our first inclination might be to form the condition this way, which is **incorrect**:

```
while ( option != 'S' || option != 's' )   // INCORRECT
```

With this condition, the loop will execute forever. Regardless of what the user enters, the loop condition will be *true*. If the user types *S*, the first expression (`option != 'S'`) is *false*, but the second expression (`option != 's'`) is *true*. Thus, the loop condition evaluates to *true* and the *while* loop body is executed. Similarly, if the user types *s*, the first expression (`option != 'S'`) is *true*, so the loop condition evaluates to *true* and the *while* loop body is executed.

An easy method for constructing a correct *while* loop condition consists of three steps:

1. Define the loop termination condition; that is, define the condition that will make the loop stop executing.

2. Create the loop continuation condition—the condition that will keep the loop executing—by applying the logical NOT operator (!) to the loop termination condition.

3. Simplify the loop continuation condition by applying DeMorgan's Laws, where possible.

Let's use these three steps to construct the correct loop condition for the menu program.

REFERENCE POINT

DeMorgan's Laws are explained in Chapter 5.

1. Define the loop termination condition:

   The loop will stop executing when the user enters an *S* or the user enters an *s*. Translating that into Java, we get

   ```
   ( option == 'S' || option == 's' )
   ```

2. Create the loop continuation condition by applying the ! operator:

   ```
   ! ( option == 'S' || option == 's' )
   ```

3. Simplify by applying DeMorgan's Laws:

   To apply DeMorgan's Laws, we change the == equality operators to !=

and change the logical OR operator (||) to the logical AND operator (&&), producing an equivalent, but simpler expression:

```
( option != 'S' && option != 's' )
```

We now have our loop condition.

To illustrate, let's write an application that calculates the cost of cell phone service. We'll provide a list of options, and the user will select options one at a time until the user enters *S* or *s* to stop. This is an accumulation operation because we are accumulating the total cost of the cell phone service. Example 6.11 shows the code for this application and Figure 6.14 shows the output of a sample run.

```
 1 /* Calculate price for cell phone service
 2    Anderson, Franceschi
 3 */
 4
 5 import java.util.Scanner;
 6 import java.text.DecimalFormat;
 7
 8 public class CellService
 9 {
10    public static void main( String [ ] args )
11    {
12      String menu = "\nAvailable Options";
13      menu += "\n\tA  1,000 anytime minutes: $25.49";
14      menu += "\n\tU  Unlimited weekend minutes: $6.99";
15      menu += "\n\tN  Nationwide long distance: $12.99";
16      menu += "\n\tT  Text messaging: $5.99";
17
18      String optionS;
19      char option;
20      double cost = 10.99; // base cost
21
22      DecimalFormat money = new DecimalFormat( "$###.00" );
23      Scanner scan = new Scanner( System.in );
24
25      System.out.println( "Select the options "
26                           + "for your cell phone service: " );
27      System.out.println( "Base cost: " + money.format( cost ) );
28
29      System.out.println( menu ); // print the menu
30      System.out.print( "Enter an option, "
31                           + "or \"S\" to stop > " );
32      option = scan.next( ).charAt( 0 );
33
```

```
34        while ( option != 'S' && option != 's' )
35        {
36          switch ( option )
37          {
38            case 'a':
39            case 'A':
40               System.out.println( "1,000 anytime minutes: "
41                                      + "$25.49" );
42               cost += 25.49;
43               break;
44            case 'u':
45            case 'U':
46               System.out.println( "Unlimited weekend minutes: "
47                                      + "$6.99" );
48               cost += 6.99;
49               break;
50            case 'n':
51            case 'N':
52               System.out.println( "Nationwide long distance: "
53                                      + "$12.99" );
54               cost += 12.99;
55               break;
56            case 't':
57            case 'T':
58               System.out.println( "Text messaging: "
59                                      + "$5.99" );
60               cost += 5.99;
61               break;
62            default:
63               System.out.println( "Unrecognized option" );
64          }
65
66          System.out.println( "Current cost: "
67                                   + money.format( cost ) );
68
69          System.out.println( menu ); // print the menu
70          System.out.print( "Enter an option, "
71                                   + "or \"S\" to stop > " );
72          option = scan.next( ).charAt( 0 );
73        }
74
75        System.out.println( "\nTotal cost of cell service is "
76                                 + money.format( cost ) );
77    }
78 }
```

EXAMPLE 6.11   A Compound Loop Condition

Figure 6.14

Calculating Cell Phone Service

```
Select the options for your cell phone service:
Base cost: $10.99

Available Options
        A  1,000 anytime minutes; $25.49
        U  Unlimited weekend minutes: $6.99
        N  Nationwide long distance; $12.99
        T  Text messaging: $5.99
Enter an option, or "S" to stop > a
1,000 anytime minutes: $25.49
Current cost: $36.48

Available Options
        A  1,000 anytime minutes: $25.49
        U  Unlimited weekend minutes: $6.99
        N  Nationwide long distance: $12.99
        T  Text messaging: $5.99
Enter an option, or "S" to stop > U
Unlimited weekend minutes: $6.99
Current cost: $43.47

Available Options
        A  1,000 anytime minutes: $25.49
        U  Unlimited weekend minutes: $6.99
        N  Nationwide long distance: $12.99
        T  Text messaging: $5.99
Enter an option, or "S" to stop > s

Total cost of cell service is $43.47
```

In Example 6.11, we use the compound condition in the *while* loop (line 34). Then within the *while* loop, we use a *switch* statement (lines 36–64) to determine which menu option the user has chosen. We handle case-insensitive input of menu options by including *case* constants for both the lowercase and uppercase versions of each letter option.

Note that we don't provide *case* statements for the sentinel values. Instead, we use the *while* loop condition to detect when the user enters the sentinel values.

Animation is another operation that may require a *while* loop with a compound condition. For example, suppose that instead of rolling our ball horizontally, we roll it diagonally down and to the right. To roll the ball diagonally down and to the right, we need to change both the *x* and the *y* values in the

COMMON ERROR TRAP

Do not check for the sentinel value inside a *while* loop. Let the *while* loop condition detect the sentinel value.

while loop body. Thus, within the while loop, we increment both x and y. We continue as long as the ball has not rolled beyond the right edge of the window and the ball has also not rolled beyond the bottom of the window.

Let's develop the condition by applying our three steps:

1. The loop termination condition is that the ball has rolled beyond either the right edge of the window or the bottom edge of the window.

```
// the ball is out of bounds
( ball.getX( ) + ballDiameter > windowWidth
      || ball.getY( ) + ballDiameter > windowHeight )
```

2. The loop continuation condition is created by applying the logical NOT operator (!) to the loop termination condition:

```
// the ball is not out of bounds
!  ( ball.getX( ) + ballDiameter > windowWidth
          || ball.getY( ) + ballDiameter > windowHeight )
```

3. Simplifying the condition by applying DeMorgan's Law, we get:

```
// the ball is in bounds
( ball.getX( ) + ballDiameter <= windowWidth
      && ball.getY( ) + ballDiameter <= windowHeight )
```

Example 6.12 shows the *RollABall3* class, which uses four *while* loops to roll the ball diagonally down to the right (x is incremented, y is incremented), then diagonally down to the left (x is decremented, y is incremented), then diagonally up to the left (x is decremented, y is decremented), and finally diagonally up to the right (x is incremented, y is decremented). We set the starting y value to 10 and the starting x value two-thirds of the way across the window. When the program runs, the ball appears to bounce off the walls of the window, as shown in Figure 6.15.

```
1  /* RollABall, Version 3
2       Rolls the ball diagonally
3       Anderson, Franceschi
4  */
5
6  import java.awt.Graphics;
7  import java.awt.Color;
8  import javax.swing.JApplet;
9
10 public class RollABall3 extends JApplet
```

```
11 {
12    public void paint( Graphics g )
13    {
14        super.paint( g );
15
16        final int Y = 10;            // the y value of the ball
17        final int DIAMETER = 15;   // the diameter of the ball
18        final Color COLOR = Color.BLUE; // the color of the ball
19        final int SPACER = 2;       // space between balls
20
21        // get width & height of the applet window
22        int windowWidth = getWidth( );
23        int windowHeight = getHeight( );
24
25        // start x 2/3 across the window
26        int x =  windowWidth * 2 / 3;
27
28        // instantiate the ball as a Circle object
29        Circle ball = new Circle( x, Y, DIAMETER, COLOR );
30
31        // get ball diameter
32        int ballDiameter = ball.getDiameter( );
33
34        // rolling diagonally down to the right
35        while ( ball.getX( ) + ballDiameter <= windowWidth
36                && ball.getY( ) + ballDiameter <= windowHeight )
37        {
38
39            ball.draw( g );  // draw the ball
40
41            Pause.wait( 0.03 ); // pause for 3/100 of a second
42            // erase the ball
43            g.clearRect( 0, 0, windowWidth, windowHeight );
44
45            ball.setX( ball.getX( ) + SPACER ); // move right
46            ball.setY( ball.getY( ) + SPACER ); // and down
47        }
48
49        // rolling diagonally down to the left
50        while ( ball.getY( )  + ballDiameter < windowHeight
51                && ball.getX( ) > 0 )
52        {
53            ball.draw( g );  // draw the ball
54
```

```
55          Pause.wait( 0.03 ); // pause for 3/100 of a second
56          // erase the ball
57          g.clearRect( 0, 0, windowWidth, windowHeight );
58
59          ball.setX( ball.getX( ) - SPACER ); // move left
60          ball.setY( ball.getY( ) + SPACER ); // and down
61       }
62
63       // rolling diagonally up to the left
64       while ( ball.getY( ) > 0 && ball.getX( ) > 0 )
65       {
66          ball.draw( g );  // draw the ball
67
68          Pause.wait( 0.03 ); // pause for 3/100 of a second
69          // erase the ball
70          g.clearRect( 0, 0, windowWidth, windowHeight );
71
72          ball.setX( ball.getX( ) - SPACER ); // move left
73          ball.setY( ball.getY( ) - SPACER ); // and up
74       }
75
76       // rolling diagonally up to the right
77       while ( ball.getY( )  > 0
78              && ball.getX( ) + ballDiameter < windowWidth )
79       {
80          ball.draw( g );  // draw the ball
81
82          Pause.wait( 0.03 ); // pause for 3/100 of a second
83          // erase the ball
84          g.clearRect( 0, 0, windowWidth, windowHeight );
85
86          ball.setX( ball.getX( ) + SPACER ); // move right
87          ball.setY( ball.getY( ) - SPACER ); // and up
88       }
89
90       ball.draw( g ); // draw the ball
91    }
92 }
```

EXAMPLE 6.12   The *RollABall3* Class

Figure 6.15

Output from *RollABall3*

6.7   Testing Techniques for *while* Loops

It's a good feeling when your code compiles without errors. Getting a clean compile, however, is only part of the job for the programmer. The other part of the job is verifying that the code is correct; that is, that the program produces accurate results.

It usually isn't feasible to test a program with all possible input values, but we can get a reasonable level of confidence in the accuracy of the program by concentrating our testing in three areas:

1. Does the program produce correct results with a set of known input?

2. Does the program produce correct results if the sentinel value is the first and only input?

3. Does the program deal appropriately with invalid input?

Let's take a look at these three areas in more detail:

1. Does the program produce correct results with known input?

To test the program with known input, we select valid input values and determine what the results should be by performing the program's operation either by hand or by using a calculator. For example, to test whether a total or average is computed correctly, enter some values and compare the program's output to a total or average you calculate by entering those same values into a calculator.

It's especially important to select input values that represent boundary conditions, that is, values that are the lowest or highest expected values. For example, to test a program that determines whether a person is old enough to vote in a presidential election (that is, the person is 18 or older), we should select test values of 17, 18, and 19. These values are the boundary conditions for age >= 18; the test values are one integer less, the same value, and one integer greater than the legal voting age. We then run the program with the three input values and verify that the program correctly identifies 17 as an illegal voting age and 18 and 19 as legal voting ages.

   2. Does the program produce correct results if the sentinel value is the first and only input?

In our *while* loops, when we find the sentinel value, the flow of control skips the *while* loop body and picks up at the statement following the *while* loop. When the sentinel value is the first input value, our *while* loop body does not execute at all. We simply skip to the statement following the *while* loop. In cases like this, the highly respected computer scientist Donald Knuth recommends that we "do exactly nothing, gracefully."

In many programs that calculate a total or an average for the input values, when no value is input, your program should either report the total or average as 0 or output a message that no values were entered. Thus, it's important to write your program so that it tolerates no input except the sentinel value; therefore, we need to test our programs by entering the sentinel value first.

Let's revisit the earlier examples in this chapter to see how they handle the case when only the sentinel value is entered.

In the addition calculator (Example 6.3), we set the total to 0 before the *while* loop and simply report the value of total after the *while* loop. So we get the correct result (0) with only the sentinel value.

SOFTWARE ENGINEERING TIP

Expect that the user might enter the sentinel value first. Your program needs to handle this special case.

In Example 6.4 where we count the percentage of passing test scores, we handle the sole sentinel value by performing some additional checking after the *while* loop. If only the sentinel value is entered, the count will be 0. We check for this case and if we find a count of 0, we skip reporting the percentage so that we avoid dividing by 0. We use similar code in Example 6.5, where we calculate the average test score. If we detect a count of 0, we also skip the calculation of the average to avoid dividing by 0 and simply report the class average as 0.

   3. Does the program deal appropriately with invalid input?

If the program expects a range of values or certain discrete values, then it should notify the user when the input doesn't fit the expected values.

In Example 6.11, we implemented a menu for calculating the cost of cell phone service. The user could enter s, a, u, n, or t (or the corresponding capital letters) representing their desired service options. If the user enters a letter other than those expected values, we use the *default* clause of the *switch* statement to issue an error message, "*Unrecognized option.*"

In the next section, we explain how to validate that user input is within a range of values using a *do/while* loop.

6.8   Event-Controlled Loops Using *do/while*

Another form of loop that is especially useful for validating user input is the *do/while* loop. In the *do/while* loop, the loop condition is tested at the end of the loop (instead of at the beginning, as in the *while* loop). Thus the body of the *do/while* loop is executed at least once.

The syntax of the *do/while* loop is the following:

```
// initialize variables
do
{
   // body of loop
} while ( condition );
// process the results
```

Figure 6.16 shows the flow of control of a *do/while* loop.

To use the *do/while* loop to validate user input, we insert the prompt for the input inside the body of the loop, then use the loop condition to test the value of the input. Like the *while* loop, the body of the loop will be reexecuted if the condition is *true*. Thus, we need to form the condition so that it's *true* when the user enters invalid values.

Example 6.13 implements a *do/while* loop (lines 14–18) that prompts the user for an integer between 1 and 10. Figure 6.17 shows the output of the program. If the user enters a number outside the valid range, we reprompt the user until the input is between 1 and 10. Thus the condition for the *do/while* loop (line 18) is

```
while ( number < 1 || number > 10 )
```

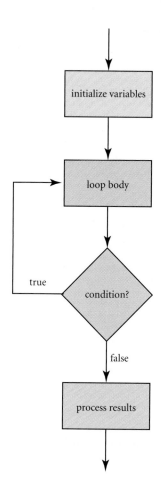

Figure 6.16
The Flow of Control of a
***do/while* Statement**

```
Enter a number between 1 and 10 > 20
Enter a number between 1 and 10 > -1
Enter a number between 1 and 10 > 0
Enter a number between 1 and 10 > 11
Enter a number between 1 and 10 > 5
Thank you!
```

Figure 6.17
Validating Input

```
1 /* Validate input is between 1 and 10
2    Anderson, Franceschi
3 */
4
5 import java.util.Scanner;
6
7 public class ValidateInput
8 {
9   public static void main( String [ ] args )
10  {
11    int number;  // input value
12    Scanner scan = new Scanner( System.in );
13
14    do
15    {
16       System.out.print( "Enter a number between 1 and 10 > " );
17       number = scan.nextInt( );
18    } while ( number < 1 || number > 10 );
19
20    System.out.println( "Thank you!" );
21  }
22 }
```

EXAMPLE 6.13   Validating User Input

For validating input, you may be tempted to use an *if* statement rather than a *do/while* loop. For example, to perform the same validation as Example 6.13, you may try this **incorrect** code:

```
System.out.print( "Enter a number between 1 and 10 > " );
number = scan.nextInt( );

if ( number < 1 || number > 10 ) // INCORRECT!
{
    System.out.print( "Enter a number between 1 and 10 > " );
    number = scan.nextInt( );
}
```

COMMON ERROR TRAP

Do not use an *if* statement to validate input because it will catch invalid values entered the first time only. Use a *do/while* loop to reprompt the user until the user enters a valid value.

The problem with this approach is that the *if* statement will reprompt the user only once. If the user enters an invalid value a second time, the program will not catch it. A *do/while* loop, however, will continue to reprompt the user as many times as needed until the user enters a valid value.

Skill Practice
with these end-of-chapter questions

CODE IN ACTION

To see two step-by-step illustrations of *do/while* loops, look for the Flash movie in the Chapter 6 folder on the CD-ROM included with this book. Click on the link for Chapter 6 to start the movie.

6.9 Programming Activity 1: Using *while* Loops

In this activity, you will work with a sentinel-controlled *while* loop, performing this activity:

Write a *while* loop to process the contents of a grocery cart and calculate the total price of the items. It is important to understand that, in this example, we do not know how many items are in the cart.

The framework will animate your code and display the current subtotal so that you can check the correctness of your code. The window will display the various *Item* objects moving down a conveyor belt toward a grocery bag. It will also display the unit price of the item and your current subtotal, as well as the correct subtotal.

For example, Figure 6.18 demonstrates the animation: We are currently scanning the first item, a milk carton, with a unit price of $2.00; thus, the correct subtotal is $2.00.

As the animation will show, *Item* objects could be milk, cereal, orange juice, or the divider bar. The number of *Item* objects in the cart is determined

Figure 6.18
**Animation of the *Cashier*
Application**

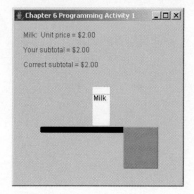

randomly; as you watch the animation, sometimes you will find that there are two items in the cart, sometimes six, sometimes three, and so forth. Scanning the divider bar signals the end of the items in the cart.

Task Instructions

Copy the files in the Chapter 6 Programming Activity 1 directory on the CD-ROM accompanying this book to a directory on your computer. Searching for five stars (*****) in the *Cashier.java* source code will show you where to add your code. You will add your code inside the *checkout* method of the *Cashier* class (the method header for the *checkout* method has already been coded for you). Example 6.14 shows a fragment of the *Cashier* class, where you will add your code:

```java
public void checkout( )
{
  /* ***** Student writes the body of this method ***** */
  //
  //   Using a while loop, calculate the total price
  //   of the groceries.
  //
  // The getNext method (in this Cashier class) returns the
  // next item on the conveyor belt, which is an Item object
  // (we do not know which item and we do not know how many items
  // are in the cart - this is randomly generated).
  // getNext does not take any arguments. Its API is:
  //       Item getNext( )
  //
  // Right after you update the current subtotal,
  // you should call the animate method.
  // The animate method takes one parameter: a double,
  // which is your current subtotal.
  // For example, if the name of your variable representing
```

```
//  the current subtotal is total, your call to the animate
//  method should be:
//      animate( total );
//
//  The instance method getPrice of the Item class
//  returns the price of the Item object.
//  The method getPrice does not take any arguments.
//  Its API is:
//          double getPrice( )
//
//  The cart is empty when the getNext method returns
//  the divider Item.
//  You detect the divider Item because its price
//  is -0.99. So an Item with a price of -0.99
//  is the sentinel value for the loop.
//
//  After you scan the divider, display the total
//  for the cart in a dialog box.

//  End of student code
}
```

EXAMPLE 6.14   The *checkout* Method in *Cashier.java*

- You can access items in the cart by calling the *getNext* method of the *Cashier* class, which has the following API:

```
Item getNext( )
```

The *getNext* method returns an *Item* object, which represents an *Item* in the cart. As you can see, the *getNext* method does not take any arguments. Since we call the method *getNext* from inside the *Cashier* class, we call the method without an object reference. For example, a call to *getNext* could look like the following:

```
Item newItem;

newItem = getNext( );
```

The *getNext* method is already written and contains code to generate the animation; it is written in such a way that the first *Item* object on the conveyor belt may or may not be the divider. (If the first *Item* is the divider, the cart is empty.)

- After you get a new *Item*, you can "scan" the item to get its price by calling the *getPrice* method of the *Item* class. The *getPrice* method has this API:

```
double getPrice( )
```

Thus, you would get an item, then get its price using code like the following:

```
Item newItem;
double price;

newItem = getNext( );
price = newItem.getPrice( );
```

- After adding the price of an item to your subtotal, call the *animate* method of the *Cashier* class. This method will display both your subtotal and the correct subtotal so that you can verify that your code is correct.

  The animate method has the following API:

  ```
  void animate( double subtotal )
  ```

  Thus, if your variable representing the current total is *total*, you would call the animate method using the following code:

  ```
  animate( total );
  ```

- We want to exit the loop when the next *Item* is the divider. You will know that the *Item* is the divider because its price will be –0.99 (negative 0.99); thus, scanning an *Item* whose price is –0.99 should be your condition to exit the *while* loop.

- After you scan the divider, display the total for the cart in a dialog box. Verify that your total matches the correct subtotal displayed.

- To test your code, compile and run the application from the *Cashier* class.

Troubleshooting

If your method implementation does not animate or animates incorrectly, check these items:

- Verify that you have correctly coded the priming read.
- Verify that you have correctly coded the condition for exiting the loop.
- Verify that you have correctly coded the body of the loop.

DISCUSSION QUESTIONS   **?**

1. What is the sentinel value of your *while* loop?

2. Explain the purpose of the priming read.

6.10 Count-Controlled Loops Using *for*

Before the loop begins, if you know the number of times the loop body should execute, you can use a *count-controlled loop*. The *for* loop is designed for count-controlled loops, that is, when the number of iterations is determined before the loop begins.

6.10.1 Basic Structure of *for* Loops

The *for* loop has this syntax:

```
for ( initialization; loop condition; loop update )
{
      // loop body
}
```

Notice that the initialization, loop condition, and loop update in the *for* loop header are separated by semicolons (not commas). Notice also that there is no semicolon after the closing parenthesis in the *for* loop header. A semicolon here would indicate an empty *for* loop body. Although some advanced programs might correctly write a *for* loop with an empty loop body, the programs we write in this book will have at least one statement in the *for* loop body.

The scope of any variable declared within the *for* loop header or body extends from the point of declaration to the end of the *for* loop body.

The flow of control of the *for* loop is shown in Figure 6.19. When the *for* loop is encountered, the initialization statement is executed. Then the loop condition is evaluated. If the condition is true, the loop body is executed, then the loop update statement is executed, and the loop condition is reevaluated. Again, if the condition is true, the loop body is executed, followed by the loop update, then the reevaluation of the condition, and so on, until the condition is false.

The *for* loop is equivalent to the following *while* loop:

```
// initialization
while ( loop condition )
{
    // loop body
    // loop update
}
```

As you can see, *while* loops can be used for either event-driven or count-controlled loops. A *for* loop is especially useful for count-controlled loops,

COMMON ERROR TRAP

Use semicolons, rather than commas, to separate the statements in a *for* loop header.

COMMON ERROR TRAP

Adding a semicolon after the closing parenthesis in the *for* loop header indicates an empty loop body and will likely cause a logic error.

Figure 6.19

Flow of Control of the *for* Loop

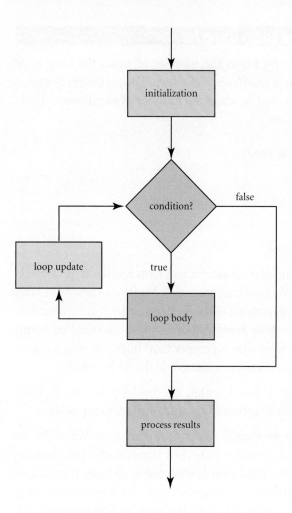

however. Because all the loop control is contained in the *for* loop header, you can easily see what condition will stop the loop and how the condition will be updated after each iteration.

6.10.2   Constructing *for* Loops

Typically, we use a **loop control variable** in a *for* loop; that control variable is usually used for counting. We set its initial value in the initialization statement, increment or decrement its value in the loop update statement, and check its value in the loop condition.

For example, if we want to find the sum of five integers, we know the loop body should execute five times—once for each integer. We set our loop control variable to 1 in the initialization statement, increment the loop control variable by 1 in the loop update statement, and check if its value is less than or equal to 5 in the loop condition. When the loop update statement increments the control variable's value to 6, we will have executed the loop body five times. The pseudocode for this program is the following:

set total to 0
for i = 1 to 5 by 1
{
   read integer
   add integer to total
}
print the total

With a *for* loop, we do not need to perform a priming read because the condition for exiting the loop is controlled by a counter, not by an input value.

Example 6.15 shows the *for* loop for calculating the sum of five integers.

```java
1 /* Find the total of 5 numbers
2      Anderson, Franceschi
3 */
4
5 import java.util.Scanner;
6
7 public class Sum5Numbers
8 {
9   public static void main( String [ ] args )
10   {
11      int total = 0;  // stores the sum of the 5 numbers
12      int number;     // stores the current input
13
14      Scanner scan = new Scanner( System.in );
15
16      for ( int i = 1; i <= 5; i++ )
17      {
18        System.out.print( "Enter an integer > " );
19        number = scan.nextInt( );
20
21        total += number;  // add input to total
22      }
23
24      // process results by printing the total
```

```
25      System.out.println( "The total is " + total );
26   }
27 }
```

EXAMPLE 6.15   Finding the Sum of Five Numbers

In this example, which is a standard accumulation operation, the *for* loop initialization statement declares *i*, which will be our loop control variable. We start *i* at 1, and after each execution of the loop body, we increment *i* by 1 in the loop update statement. The loop condition checks if the value of *i* is less than or equal to 5; when *i* reaches 6, we have executed the loop body five times. Figure 6.20 shows the execution of this *for* loop.

Note that because we declare our loop counter variable *i* in the *for* loop header, we cannot reference *i* after the *for* loop ends. Thus, this code would generate a compiler error, because *i* is out of scope on line 24:

```
16      for ( int i = 1; i <= 5; i++ )
17      {
18        System.out.print( "Enter an integer > " );
19        number = scan.nextInt( );
20
21        total += number;  // add input to total
22      }
23
24      System.out.println( "The total for " + ( i - 1 )
25                            + " number is " + total );
```

Defining a new variable using the same name as a variable already in scope is invalid and generates a compiler error. However, a variable name can be reused when a previously defined variable with the same name is no longer in scope. In the code above, the scope of the variable *i* defined in line 16 is

Figure 6.20

Finding the Sum of Five Integers

```
Enter an integer > 12
Enter an integer > 10
Enter an integer > 5
Enter an integer > 7
Enter an integer > 3
The total is 37
```

limited to the *for* loop on lines 16–22. We cannot define another variable named *i* in that *for* loop; however, as shown here, we could reuse the name *i* in a subsequent *for* loop (lines 24–29), because the first *i* is no longer in scope. In fact, programmers often reuse the variable name *i* for the counter variable in their *for* loops.

```
16      for ( int i = 1; i <= 5; i++ )
17      {
18        System.out.print( "Enter an integer > " );
19        number = scan.nextInt( );
20
21        total += number;  // add input to total
22      }
23
24      for ( int i = 1; i <= 10; i++ )
25      {
26        System.out.print( "Enter integer " + i + " > " );
27        number = scan.nextInt( );
28      }
```

If you do want to refer to the loop variable after the loop ends, you can define the variable before the *for* loop, as shown in the following code:

```
15      int i;
16      for ( i = 1; i <= 5; i++ )
17      {
18        System.out.print( "Enter an integer > " );
19        number = scan.nextInt( );
20
21        total += number;  // add input to total
22      }
23
24      System.out.println( "The total for " + ( i - 1 )  // i is 6
25                           + " numbers is " + total );
```

We can also increment the loop control variable by values other than 1. Example 6.16 shows a *for* loop that increments the control variable by 2 to print the even numbers from 0 to 20.

The pseudocode for this program is the following:

set output to an empty *String*
for i = 0 to 20 by 2
{
    append i and a space to the output *String*
}
print the output *String*

We start with an empty *String* variable, *toPrint*, and with each iteration of the loop we append the next even number and a space. When the loop completes, we output *toPrint*, which prints all numbers on one line, as shown in Figure 6.21.

```
1 /* Print the even numbers from zero to twenty
2    Anderson, Franceschi
3 */
4
5 public class PrintEven
6 {
7   public static void main( String [ ] args )
8   {
9     String toPrint = "";  // initialize output String
10
11    for ( int i = 0; i <= 20; i += 2 )
12    {
13      toPrint += i + " "; // append current number and a space
14    }
15
16    System.out.println( toPrint ); // print results
17  }
18 }
```

EXAMPLE 6.16   Printing Even Numbers

Figure 6.21
Printing Even Numbers from 0 to 20

```
0 2 4 6 8 10 12 14 16 18 20
```

In this example, we initialize the loop control variable to 0, then increment *i* by 2 in the loop update statement (i += 2) to skip the odd numbers. Notice that we used the value of the loop control variable *i* inside the loop. The loop control variable can perform double duty such as this because the loop control variable is available to our code in the loop body.

The loop control variable also can be used in our prompt to the user. For example, in Example 6.15, we could have prompted the user for each integer using this statement:

```
System.out.print( "Enter integer " + i  + " > " );
```

```
Enter integer 1 > 23
Enter integer 2 > 12
Enter integer 3 > 10
Enter integer 4 > 11
Enter integer 5 > 15
The total is 71
```

Figure 6.22
Adding the Loop Control Variable to the Prompt

Then the user's prompt would look like that shown in Figure 6.22.

CODE IN ACTION

To see a step-by-step illustration of a *for* loop, look for the Flash movie in the Chapter 6 folder on the CD-ROM included with this book. Click on the link for Chapter 6 to start the movie.

We can also decrement the loop control variable. Example 6.17 shows an application that reads a sentence entered by the user and prints the sentence backward.

The pseudocode for this program is the following:

```
set backwards to an empty String
read a sentence

for i = ( length of sentence − 1 ) to 0  by −1
{
   get character at position i in sentence
   append character to backwards
}
print backwards
```

To print a sentence backward, we treat the sentence, a *String*, like a stream of characters; each iteration of the loop extracts and processes one character from the *String*, using the *charAt* method of the *String* class. Line 10 declares two *Strings*: *original*, to hold the sentence the user enters, and *backwards* (initialized as an empty *String*), to hold the reverse of the user's sentence. Lines

Figure 6.23

Printing a Sentence Backward

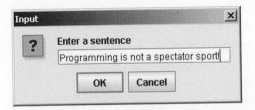

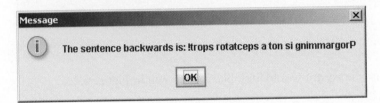

12–13 prompt the user for a sentence. Lines 15 through 18 make up the *for* loop, whose purpose is to copy the original sentence backward into the *String backwards*. We do this by starting the copying at the last character in the original *String* and moving backward in the *String* one character at a time until we have copied the first character in *original*. Thus, we initialize our loop variable to the position of the last character in *original* (`original.length( ) - 1`) and extract one character at a time, appending it to *backwards*. The loop update statement (`i--`) moves the loop variable backward by one position, and our loop condition (`i >= 0`) checks whether we have reached the beginning of the *String original*. Figure 6.23 shows the execution of the program with the user entering the sentence, "*Programming is not a spectator sport!*"

```
1 /* Print a sentence backward
2    Anderson, Franceschi
3 */
4 import javax.swing.JOptionPane;
5
6 public class Backwards
7 {
8   public static void main( String [ ] args )
9   {
10    String original, backwards = "";
11
12    original = JOptionPane.showInputDialog( null,
13                        "Enter a sentence" );
14
15    for ( int i = original.length( ) - 1; i >= 0; i-- )
16    {
17        backwards += original.charAt( i );
```

```
18      }
19
20      JOptionPane.showMessageDialog( null,
21                "The sentence backwards is: " + backwards );
22   }
23 }
```

EXAMPLE 6.17   Printing a Sentence Backward

We can display some interesting graphics using *for* loops. The applet in Example 6.18 draws the bull's-eye target shown in Figure 6.24. To make the bull's-eye target, we draw 10 concentric circles (circles that have the same center point), beginning with the largest circle and successively drawing a smaller circle on top of the circles already drawn. Thus, the bull's-eye target circles have the same center point, but different diameters. The pseudocode for this program is

```
for diameter = 200 to 20 by –20
{
    instantiate a circle
    draw the circle
    if color is black
        set color to red
    else
        set color to black
}
```

Figure 6.24

Drawing a Bull's-Eye Target

REFERENCE POINT

The API for the *Circle* class
is given in Section 6.4.5

We can again use the *Circle* class introduced in Section 6.4.5, when we rolled a ball.

Translating the pseudocode into Java, we get the code shown in Example 6.18.

```java
1  /* Bull's-eye target
2     Anderson, Franceschi
3  */
4
5  import javax.swing.JApplet;
6  import java.awt.Color;
7  import java.awt.Graphics;
8
9  public class Bullseye extends JApplet
10 {
11    // center of bullseye
12    private int centerX = 200, centerY = 150;
13    // color of first circle
14    private Color toggleColor = Color.BLACK;
15    // each circle will be a Circle object
16    private Circle circle;
17
18    public void paint( Graphics g )
19    {
20      super.paint( g );
21
22      for ( int diameter = 200; diameter >= 20; diameter -= 20 )
23      {
24        // instantiate circle with current diameter and color
25        circle = new Circle( centerX - diameter / 2,
26                             centerY - diameter / 2,
27                             diameter, toggleColor );
28
29        circle.draw( g ); // draw the circle
30
31        if ( toggleColor.equals( Color.BLACK ) )
32          toggleColor = Color.RED;   // if black, change to red
33        else
34          toggleColor = Color.BLACK; // if red, change to black
35      }
36    }
37 }
```

EXAMPLE 6.18   Drawing a Bull's-Eye Target

Our *for* loop initialization statement in line 22 sets up the diameter of the largest circle as 200 pixels and the loop update statement decreases the diameter of each circle by 20 pixels. The smallest circle we want to draw should have a diameter of 20 pixels, so we set the loop condition to check that the diameter is greater than or equal to 20. We need to start with the largest circle rather than the smallest circle so that new circles we draw don't hide the previously drawn circles.

Drawing the bull's-eye target circles illustrates two common programming techniques: conversion between units and a toggle variable.

We need to convert between units because the *Circle* class constructor takes as its arguments the upper-left (x, y) coordinate and the width and height of the circle's bounding rectangle (this is consistent with the *fillOval* method of the *Graphics* class). However, all our circles have the same center point, but not the same upper-left x and y coordinates. Given the diameter and the center point of the circle, however, we can calculate the (x, y) coordinate of the upper-left corner. Figure 6.25 shows how we make the conversion.

The difference between the center point and the upper-left corner of the bounding rectangle is the radius of the circle, which is half of the diameter

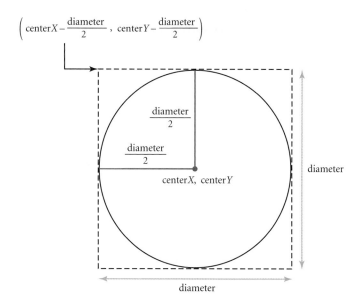

Figure 6.25
Converting Circle Coordinates

(`diameter` / 2). So, the upper-left *x* value is the *x* value of the center point minus half the diameter (`centerX` − `diameter` / 2). Similarly, the upper-left *y* value is the *y* value of the center point minus half the diameter (`centerY` − `diameter` / 2).

Thus, we instantiate each circle using the following statement:

```
circle = new Circle( centerX - diameter / 2,
                     centerY - diameter / 2,
                     diameter, toggleColor );
```

SOFTWARE
ENGINEERING TIP

Use a toggle variable when
you need to alternate
between two values.

To alternate between red and black circles, we use a **toggle variable**, which is a variable whose value alternates between two values. We use a *Color* object for our toggle variable, *toggleColor*, and initialize it to *Color.BLACK*. After drawing each circle, we switch the color (lines 31–34). If the current color is black, we set it to red; otherwise, the color must be red, so we set the color to black.

Skill Practice
with these end-of-chapter questions

6.14.1 Multiple Choice Exercises

Questions 2, 3, 4

6.14.2 Reading and Understanding Code

Questions 11, 12, 13, 14, 15, 16, 17, 18, 19

6.14.3 Fill In the Code

Questions 27, 29

6.14.5 Identifying Errors in Code

Questions 32, 33, 35

6.14.5 Debugging Area

Questions 38, 39, 40, 41, 42

6.14.6 Write a Short Program

Questions 43, 46, 47, 48, 49, 50, 51, 52

6.10.3   Testing Techniques for *for* Loops

One of the most important tests for *for* loops is that the starting and ending values of the loop variable are set correctly. For example, to execute a *for* loop five times, we could set the initial value of the loop variable to 0 and use the condition (i < 5), or we could set the initial value of the loop variable to 1 and use the condition (i <= 5). Either of these *for* loop headers will cause the loop to execute five times.

```
for ( int i = 0; i < 5; i++ ) // executes 5 times
```

or

```
for ( int i = 1; i <= 5; i++ ) // executes 5 times
```

However, the following *for* loop header is incorrect; the loop will execute only four times.

```
for ( int i = 1; i < 5; i++ ) // INCORRECT! executes only 4 times
```

Thus to test the *for* loop in Example 6.15 that prompts for five integers, we need to verify that the program outputs exactly five prompts. To test that we are prompting the user five times, we can enter the integers 1, 2, 3, 4, and 5 at the prompts. Another option, shown in Figure 6.26, is to append a number to the prompt, which does double duty. Besides keeping the user informed of the number of integers entered so far, it also helps to verify that we have the correct number of prompts.

Like *while* loops, the body of a *for* loop may not be executed at all. If the loop condition is *false* the first time it is tested, the body of the *for* loop is skipped. Thus, when testing, we want to simulate input that would cause the loop condition to be *false* when the *for* loop statement is first encountered. For example, in the *Backwards* class in Example 6.17, we need to test

Figure 6.26
Counting Five Prompts

```
Enter integer 1 > 23
Enter integer 2 > 12
Enter integer 3 > 10
Enter integer 4 > 11
Enter integer 5 > 15
The total is 71
```

Figure 6.27

The Backwards Class with an Empty Sentence

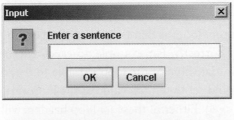

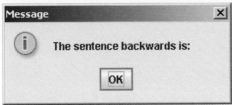

the *for* loop with an empty sentence. In other words, when the prompt appears to enter a sentence, we simply press the *OK* button. If you try this, you will find that the application still works, as Figure 6.27 shows.

The program works correctly with an empty sentence because the *for* loop initialization statement is

```
int i = original.length( ) - 1;
```

Because the length of an empty *String* is 0, this statement sets *i* to –1. The loop condition (i >= 0) is *false*, so the loop body is never executed. The flow of control skips to the statement following the loop,

```
JOptionPane.showMessageDialog( null,
          "The sentence backwards is: " + backwards );
```

which prints an empty *String*. Although it would be more user-friendly to check whether the sentence is empty and print a message to that effect, the program does indeed do exactly nothing, gracefully.

6.11   Nested Loops

Loops can be nested inside other loops; that is, the body of one loop can contain another loop. For example, a *while* loop can be nested inside another *while* loop or a *for* loop can be nested inside another *for* loop. In fact, the nested loops do not need to be the same loop type; that is, a *for* loop can be nested inside a *while* loop, and a *while* loop can be nested inside a *for* loop.

Nested loops may be useful if you are performing multiple operations, each of which has its own count or sentinel value. For example, we may be interested in processing data in a statistics table containing rows and columns. In order to process all the data, we could loop from the first row to the last row; inside that loop, we would process each row by looping from the first column to the last column of that row. A statistics table can be stored in what is called a two-dimensional array, a subject we discuss in Chapter 9.

Going back to Jane, our grocery cashier, her workday can be modeled using nested loops. In Programming Activity 1, we wrote the code for our cashier to calculate the total cost of the contents of one customer's grocery cart. But cashiers check out multiple customers, one after another. While the line of people in front of the cashier is not empty, she will help the next customer. For each customer, she will set the total order to $0.00 and start scanning items and add the prices to the total. While the current customer still has items in the cart, Jane will scan the next item. When Jane finishes processing a customer's cart, she will check to see if there is a customer waiting in line. If there is one, she will set the total to $0.00 and start scanning the next customer's items.

Thus, the cashier's job can be described using a *while* loop nested inside another *while* loop. The pseudocode for these nested loops is shown here:

 REFERENCE POINT

Nested *for* loops are useful for processing data stored in two-dimensional arrays, which are discussed in Chapter 9. Simple *for* loops are useful to process data stored in standard arrays; standard arrays are discussed in Chapter 8.

```
look for a customer
while there is a customer in line
{
  set total to $0.00
  reach for first item
  while item is not the divider bar
  {
      add price to total
      reach for next item
  }
  // if we get here, the item is the divider bar
  output the total price

  look for another customer
}
```

The important point to understand with nested loops is that the inner (or nested) loop executes completely (executes all its iterations) for each single iteration of the outer loop.

Let's look at a simple example that uses nested *for* loops. Suppose we want to print five rows of numbers as shown here:

```
1
1 2
1 2 3
1 2 3 4
1 2 3 4 5
```

We can see a pattern here. In the first line, we print one number; in the second line, we print two numbers, and so on. In other words, the quantity of numbers we print and the line number are the same. The pseudocode for this pattern is the following:

```
for line = 1 to 5 by 1
{
    for number = 1 to line by 1
    {
      print number and a space
    }
    print a new line
}
```

Translating this pseudocode into nested *for* loops, we get the code shown in Example 6.19.

```
1 /*  Printing numbers using nested for loops
2      Anderson, Franceschi
3 */
4
5 public class NestedForLoops
6 {
7    public static void main( String [ ] args )
8    {
9      // outer for loop prints 5 lines
10     for ( int line = 1; line <= 5; line++ )
11     {
12       // inner for loop prints one line
13       for ( int number = 1; number <= line; number++ )
```

```
14        {
15          // print the number and a space
16          System.out.print( number + " " );
17        }
18
19        System.out.println( );    // print a newline
20      }
21    }
22 }
```

EXAMPLE 6.19   Nested *for* Loops

Notice that the inner *for* loop (lines 12–17) uses the value of *line*, which is set by the outer *for* loop (lines 9–20). Thus, for the first iteration of the outer loop, *line* equals 1, so the inner loop executes once, printing the number 1 and a space. Then we print a newline character because line 19 is part of the outer *for* loop. The outer loop then sets the value of *line* to 2, and the inner loop starts again at 1 and executes two times (until *number* equals the line number in the outer loop). Then we again print a newline. This operation continues until the *line* exceeds 5, when the outer loop terminates. The output from Example 6.19 is shown in Figure 6.28.

Note that we needed to use different names for our *for* loop control variables. The loop control variable *line* is in scope from lines 10 to 20, which includes the inner *for* loop.

Let's look at another example of a nested loop. We'll let the user enter positive integers, with a 0 being the sentinel value. For each number, we'll find all its factors; that is, we will find all the integers that are evenly divisible into the number, except 1 and the number itself.

If a number is evenly divisible by another, the remainder after division will be 0. The modulus operator (%) will be useful here, because it calculates the remainder after integer division. Thus, to find all the factors of a number,

```
1
1 2
1 2 3
1 2 3 4
1 2 3 4 5
```

Figure 6.28
Output from Example 6.19

we can test all integers from 1 up to the number to see if the remainder after division is 0. But let's think about whether that's a good approach. The number 1 will be a factor for every number, because every number is evenly divisible by 1. So we can test integers beginning at 2. Then, because 2 is the smallest factor, there's no need to test integers higher than *number / 2.* Thus, our range of integers to test will be from 2 to *number / 2.*

For this example, we'll use a *for* loop nested inside a *while* loop. The pseudocode for this example is

```
read first number  // priming read
while number is not 0
{
    print "The factors for number are "
    for factor = 2 to ( number / 2 ) by 1
    {
      if number % factor is 0
          print factor and a space
    }
    print a new line

    read next number  // update read
}
```

But what happens if we don't find any factors for a number? In that case, the number is a prime number. We can detect this condition by using a *boolean* variable called a **flag**. We set the flag to *false* before starting the *for* loop that checks for factors. Inside the *for* loop, we set the flag to *true* when we find a factor. In other words, we signal (or flag) the fact that we found a factor. Then after the *for* loop terminates, we check the value of the flag. If it is still *false*, we did not find any factors and the number is prime. Our pseudocode for this program now becomes

```
read first number   // priming read
while number is not 0
{
    print "The factors for number are "
    set flag to false
```

```
for factor = 2 to ( number / 2 ) by 1
{
    if number % factor is 0
    {
        print factor and a space
        set flag to true
    }
}

if flag is false
    print "number is prime"

print a new line

read next number   // update read
}
```

Since we want to read positive numbers only, the lines "read first number" and "read next number" in the preceding pseudocode will actually be more complex than a simple statement. Indeed, we will prompt the user to enter a positive number until the user does so. In order to do that, we will use a *do/while* loop to validate the input from the user. Therefore, inside the *while* loop, we nest not only a *for* loop, but also a *do/while* loop. In the interest of keeping the pseudocode simple, we did not show that *do/while* loop. However, it is included in the code in Example 6.20 at lines 17–23 and 45–51.

Translating this pseudocode into Java, we get the code shown in Example 6.20; the output of a sample run of the program is shown in Figure 6.29.

```java
1  /* Factors of integers
2       with checks for primes
3       Anderson, Franceschi
4  */
5  import java.util.Scanner;
6
7  public class Factors
8  {
9      public static void main( String [ ] args )
10     {
```

```
11    int number;          // positive integer entered by user
12    final int SENTINEL = 0;
13    boolean factorsFound; // flag signals whether factors are found
14
15    Scanner scan = new Scanner( System.in );
16
17    // priming read
18    do
19    {
20      System.out.print( "Enter a positive integer "
21                        + "or 0 to exit > " );
22      number = scan.nextInt( );
23    } while ( number < 0 );
24
25    while ( number != SENTINEL )
26    {
27      System.out.print( "Factors of " + number + ":  " );
28      factorsFound = false;  // reset flag to no factors
29
30      for ( int factor = 2; factor <= number / 2; factor++ )
31      {
32        if ( number % factor == 0 )
33        {
34            System.out.print( factor + " " );
35            factorsFound = true;
36        }
37      } // end of for loop
38
39      if ( ! factorsFound )
40          System.out.print( "none, " + number + " is prime" );
41
42      System.out.println( );  // print a newline
43      System.out.println( );  // print a second newline
44
45      // read next number
46      do
47      {
48          System.out.print( "Enter a positive integer "
49                            + "or 0 to exit > " );
50          number = scan.nextInt( );
51      } while ( number < 0 );
52    } // end of while loop
53  }
54 }
```

EXAMPLE 6.20   Finding Factors

Figure 6.29
Output of Finding Factors

```
Enter a positive integer or 0 to exit > 100
Factors of 100:  2 4 5 10 20 25 50

Enter a positive integer or 0 to exit > 25
Factors of 25:  5

Enter a positive integer or 0 to exit > 21
Factors of 21:  3 7

Enter a positive integer or 0 to exit > 13
Factors of 13:  none, 13 is prime

Enter a positive integer or 0 to exit > 0
```

6.12   Programming Activity 2: Using *for* Loops

In this activity, you will write a *for* loop:

> For this Programming Activity, we will again calculate the total cost of the items in a grocery cart. This time, however, we will write the program for the Express Lane. In this lane, the customer is allowed up to 10 items. The user will be asked for the number of items in the grocery cart. Your job is to write a *for* loop to calculate the total cost of the items in the cart.

Like Programming Activity 1, the framework will animate your *for* loop, displaying the items in the cart moving down a conveyor belt toward a cashier station (a grocery bag). It will also display the unit price of the item, the correct subtotal, and your current subtotal. By comparing the correct subtotal to your subtotal, you will be able to check whether your code is calculating the correct value.

Figure 6.30 demonstrates the animation. The cart contains five items. The third item, a carton of orange juice, is being scanned at a unit price of $3.00, bringing the correct subtotal for the cart to $8.50.

Figure 6.30

Sample Animation

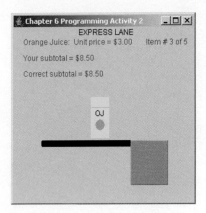

Copy the files in the Chapter 6 Programming Activity 2 directory on the CD-ROM accompanying this book to a directory on your computer. Searching for five stars (*****) in the _Cashier.java_ code will show you where to add your code. You will add your code inside the _checkout_ method of the _Cashier_ class (the method header for the _checkout_ method has already been coded for you). Example 6.21 shows a fragment of the _Cashier_ class, where you will add your code:

```
public void checkout( int numberOfItems )
{
    /* ***** Student writes the body of this method ***** */
    //
    //  The parameter of this method, numberOfItems,
    //  represents the number of items in the cart. The
    //  user will be prompted for this number.
    //
    //  Using a for loop, calculate the total price
    //  of the groceries for the cart.
    //
    //  The getNext method (in this Cashier class) returns the next
    //  item in the cart, which is an Item object (we do not
    //  know which item will be returned; this is randomly generated).
    //  getNext does not take any arguments. Its API is
    //      Item getNext( )
    //
```

```
//  As the last statement of the body of your for loop,
//  you should call the animate method.
//  The animate method takes one parameter:  a double,
//  which is your current subtotal.
//  For example, if the name of your variable representing
//  the current subtotal is total, your call to the animate
//  method should be:
//      animate( total );
//
//  The getPrice method of the Item class
//  returns the price of the Item object as a double.
//  The getPrice method does not take any arguments. Its API is
//      double getPrice( )
//
//  After you have processed all the items, display the total
//  for the cart in a dialog box.



//
//  End of student code
//
}
```

EXAMPLE 6.21 **The *checkout* Method in the *Cashier* Class**

To write the body of your *for* loop, you can use the following methods:

- You can access items in the cart using the *getNext* method of the *Cashier* class, which has the following API:

```
Item getNext( )
```

The *getNext* method returns an *Item* object, which represents an *Item* in the cart. As you can see, the *getNext* method does not take any arguments. Since we call the method *getNext* from inside the *Cashier* class, we can simply call the method without an object reference. For example, a call to *getNext* could look like the following:

```
Item newItem;

newItem = getNext( );
```

- After you get a new *Item*, you can "scan" the item to get its price by calling the *getPrice* method of the *Item* class. The *getPrice* method has this API:

```
double getPrice( )
```

Thus, you would get the next item, then get its price using code like the following:

```
Item newItem;
double price;

newItem = getNext( );
price = newItem.getPrice( );
```

When you have finished writing the code for the *checkout* method, compile and run the application from the *Cashier* class. When the application finishes executing, verify that your code is correct by:

- checking that your subtotal matches the correct subtotal displayed
- checking that you have processed all the items in the cart by verifying that the current item number matches the total number of items. For example, if the cart has five items, check that the message in the upper-right corner of the screen displays: `Item # 5 of 5`.

Troubleshooting

If your method implementation does not animate or animates incorrectly, check these items:

- Verify that you have correctly coded the header of your *for* loop.
- Verify that you have correctly coded the body of the loop.

DISCUSSION QUESTIONS **?**

1. Explain why a *for* loop is appropriate for this activity.

2. Explain how you set up your *for* loop; that is, what initialization statement did you use, what was your condition, and what was the loop update statement?

6.13   Chapter Summary

- Looping repeats a set of operations for each input item while a condition is *true*.

- The *while* loop is especially useful for event-controlled looping. The *while* loop executes a set of operations in the loop body as long as the loop condition is *true*. Each execution of the loop body is an iteration of the loop.

- If the loop condition evaluates to *false* the first time it is evaluated, the body of the *while* loop is never executed.

- If the loop condition never evaluates to *false*, the result is an infinite loop.

- In event-controlled looping, processing of items continues until the end of input is signaled either by a sentinel value or by reaching the end of the file.

- A sentinel value is a special input value that signals the end of the items to be processed. With a sentinel value, we perform a priming read before the *while* loop. The body of the loop processes the input, then performs an update read of the next data item.

- When reading data from an input file, we can test whether we have reached the end of the file by calling a *hasNext* method of the *Scanner* class.

- In the accumulation programming technique, we initialize a total variable to 0 before starting the loop. In the loop body, we add each input value to the total. When the loop completes, the current total is the total for all processed input values.

- In the counting programming technique, we initialize a count variable to 0 before starting the loop. In the loop body, we increment the count variable for each input value that meets our criteria. When the loop completes, the count variable contains the number of items that met our criteria.

- To find an average, we combine accumulation and counting. We add input values to the total and increment the count. When the loop completes, we calculate the average by dividing the total by the count. Before computing the average, however, we should verify that the divisor (that is, the count) is not 0.

- To find the maximum or minimum values in a set of input, we assign the first input to a running maximum or minimum. In the loop body, we compare each input value to our running maximum or minimum. If the input value is less than the running minimum, we assign the input value to the running minimum. Similarly, if the input value is greater than the running maximum, we assign the input value to the running maximum. When the loop completes, the running value is the maximum or minimum value of all the input values.

- To animate an image, the loop body draws the image, pauses for a short interval, erases the image, and changes the starting *x* or *y* values to the next location for drawing the image.

- To avoid generating exceptions when the user types characters other than the data type expected, use the *hasNext* methods of the *Scanner* class.

- To construct a loop condition, construct the inverse of the loop termination condition.

- When testing a program that contains a loop, test that the program produces correct results by inputting values and comparing the results with manual calculations. Also test that the results are correct if the *while* loop body never executes. Finally, test the results with input that is invalid.

- The *do/while* loop checks the loop condition after executing the loop body. Thus, the body of a *do/while* loop always executes at least once. This type of loop is useful for validating input.

- The *for* loop is useful for count-controlled loops, that is, loops for which the number of iterations is known when the loop begins.

- When the *for* loop is encountered, the initialization statement is executed. Then the loop condition is evaluated. If the condition is *true*, the loop body is executed. The loop update statement is then executed and the loop condition is reevaluated. Again, if the condition is *true*, the loop body is executed, followed by the loop update, then the reevaluation of the condition, and so on, until the condition evaluates to *false*.

- Typically, we use a loop counting variable in a *for* loop. We set its initial value in the initialization statement, increment or decrement its value in the loop update statement, and check its value in the loop condition.

- The loop update statement can increment or decrement the loop variable by any value.

- In a *for* loop, it is important to test that the starting and ending values of the loop variable are correct. Also test with input for which the *for* loop body does not execute at all.

6.14 Exercises, Problems, and Projects

6.14.1 Multiple Choice Exercises

1. How do you discover that you have an infinite loop in your code?
   - ❏ The code does not compile.
   - ❏ The code compiles and runs but gives the wrong result.
   - ❏ The code runs forever.
   - ❏ The code compiles, but there is a runtime error.

2. If you want to execute a loop body at least once, what type of loop would you use?
   - ❏ *for* loop
   - ❏ *while* loop
   - ❏ *do/while* loop
   - ❏ none of the above

3. What best describes a *for* loop?
   - ❏ It is a count-controlled loop.
   - ❏ It is an event-controlled loop.
   - ❏ It is a sentinel-controlled loop.

4. You can simulate a *for* loop with a *while* loop.
   - ❏ true
   - ❏ false

6.14.2   Reading and Understanding Code

5. What is the output of this code sequence? (The user successively enters 3, 5, and −1.)

```
System.out.print( "Enter an int > " );
int i = scan.nextInt( );
while ( i != -1 )
{
    System.out.println( "Hello" );

    System.out.print( "Enter an int > " );
    i = scan.nextInt( );
}
```

6. What is the output of this code sequence? (The user successively enters 3, 5, and −1.)

```
int i = 0;
while ( i != -1 )
{
    System.out.println( "Hello" );
    System.out.print( "Enter an int > " );
    i = scan.nextInt( );
}
```

7. What is the output of this code sequence? (The user successively enters 3, 5, and −1.)

```
System.out.print( "Enter an int > " );
int i = scan.nextInt( );
while ( i != -1 )
{
    System.out.print( "Enter an int > " );
    i = scan.nextInt( );

    System.out.println( "Hello" );
}
```

8. What are the values of *i* and *sum* after this code sequence is executed?

```
int sum  = 0;
int i = 17;
while ( i % 10 != 0 )
{
  sum += i;
  i++;
}
```

9. What are the values of *i* and *product* after this code sequence is executed?

```
int i = 6;
int product = 1;
do
{
    product *= i;
    i++;
} while ( i < 9 );
```

10. What are the values of *i* and *product* after this code sequence is executed?

```
int i = 6;
int product = 1;
do
{
    product *= i;
    i++;
} while ( product < 9 );
```

11. What is the output of this code sequence?

```
for ( int i = 0; i < 3; i++ )
    System.out.println( "Hello" );
System.out.println( "Done" );
```

12. What is the output of this code sequence?

```
for ( int i = 0; i <= 2; i++ )
    System.out.println( "Hello" );
System.out.println( "Done" );
```

13. What is the value of *i* after this code sequence is executed?

```
int i = 0;
for ( i = 0; i <= 2; i++ )
    System.out.println( "Hello" );
```

14. What is the value of *i* after this code sequence is executed?

```
int i = 0;
for ( i = 0; i < 2034; i++ )
    System.out.println( "Hello" );
```

15. What are the values of *i* and *sum* after this code sequence is executed?

```
int i = 0;
int sum = 0;
for ( i = 0; i < 5; i++ )
{
    sum += i;
}
```

16. What are the values of *i* and *sum* after this code sequence is executed?

```
int i = 0;
int sum  = 0;
for ( i = 0; i < 40; i++ )
{
    if ( i % 10 == 0 )
        sum += i;
}
```

17. What is the value of *sum* after this code sequence is executed?

```
int sum  = 0;
for ( int i = 1; i < 10; i++ )
{
    i++;
    sum += i;
}
```

18. What is the value of *sum* after this code sequence is executed?

```
int sum  = 0;
for ( int i = 10; i > 5; i-- )
{
    sum += i;
}
```

19. What is printed when this code sequence is executed?

```
for ( int i = 0; i < 5; i++ )
{
    System.out.println( Math.max( i, 3 ) );
}
```

20. What are the values of *i* and *sum* after this code sequence is executed?

```
int i = 0;
int sum  = 0;
while ( i != 7 )
{
    sum += i;
    i++;
}
```

6.14.3   Fill In the Code

21. This *while* loop generates random integers between 3 and 7 until a 5 is generated and prints them all out, excluding 5.

```
Random random = new Random( );
int i = random.nextInt( 5 ) + 3;
```

22. This *while* loop takes an integer input from the user, then prompts for additional integers and prints all integers that are greater than or equal to the original input until the user enters 20, which is not printed.

```
System.out.print( "Enter a starting integer > " );

int start = scan.nextInt( );

// your code goes here
```

23. This *while* loop takes integer values as input from the user and finds the sum of those integers until the user types in the value −1 (which is not added).

```
System.out.print( "Enter an integer value, "
                    + "enter -1 to stop > " );
int value = scan.nextInt( );
// your code goes here
```

24. This loop calculates the sum of the first four positive multiples of 7 using a *while* loop (the sum will be equal to 7 + 14 + 21 + 28 = 70).

```
int sum = 0;
int countMultiplesOf7 = 0;
int count = 1;
// your code goes here
```

25. This loop takes words as input from the user and concatenates them until the user types in the word "end" (which is not concatenated). The code then outputs the concatenated *String*.

```
String sentence = "";
String word;
// your code goes here

while ( ! word.equals( "end" ) )
{
    '// and your code goes here

}
System.out.println( "The sentence is " + sentence );
```

26. This loop reads integers from a file (already associated with the *Scanner* object reference *scan*) and computes the sum. We don't know how many integers are in the file.

```
int sum = 0;
// your code goes here
```

27. Here is a *while* loop; write the equivalent *for* loop.

```
int i = 0;
while ( i < 5 )
{
    System.out.println( "Hi there" );
    i++;
}


// your code goes here
```

28. This loop reads integers from the user until the user enters either 0 or 100. Then it prints the sum of the numbers entered (excluding the 0 or 100).

```
// your code goes here
```

29. This loop calculates the sum of the integers from 1 to 5 using a *for* loop.

```
int sum = 0;
// your code goes here
```

6.14.4   Identifying Errors in Code

30. Where is the problem with this code sequence (although this code sequence does compile)?

```
int i = 0;
while ( i < 3 )
    System.out.println( "Hello" );
```

31. Where is the error in this code sequence that is supposed to read and echo integers until the user enters −1?

```
int num;
while ( num != -1 )
{
    System.out.print( "Enter an integer > " );
    num = scan.nextInt( );
    System.out.println( num );
}
```

32. The following code sequence intends to print *Hello* three times; however, it does not. Where is the problem in this code sequence?

```java
for ( int i = 0; i < 3; i++ );
   System.out.println( "Hello" );
```

33. Where is the error in this code sequence, which is intended to print *Hello* 10 times?

```java
for ( int i = 10; i > 0; i++ )
   System.out.println( "Hello" );
```

34. Where is the problem with this code sequence? The code is intended to generate random numbers between 1 and 10 until the number is either a 7 or a 5.

```java
Random random = new Random( );
int number   =  1 + random.nextInt( 10 );
while ( number != 5 || number != 7 )
{
    number  =  1 + random.nextInt( 10 );
}
System.out.println( "The number is " + number );
```

35. Where is the error with this code sequence?

```java
int sum = 0;
for ( int i = 1; i < 6; i++ )
    sum += i;

System.out.println( "The value of i is " + i );
```

6.14.5   Debugging Area—Using Messages from the Java Compiler and Java JVM

36. You coded the following in the class *Test.java*:

```java
int i = 0;
int sum = 0;
do
{
    sum += i;
    i++;
} while ( i < 3 )    // line 11
```

At compile time, you get the following error:

```
Test.java:11: ';' expected
while( i < 3 )   // line 10
              ^
1 error
```

Explain what the problem is and how to fix it.

37. You coded the following in the class *Test.java*:

```
int i = 0;
while ( i < 3 )
{
    System.out.println( "Hello" );
    i--;
}
```

The code compiles but never terminates.

Explain what the problem is and how to fix it.

38. You coded the following in the class *Test.java*:

```
for ( int i = 0; i++; i < 3 )      // line 5
    System.out.println( "Hello" );
```

At compile time, you get the following error:

```
Test.java:5: not a statement
for ( int i = 0; i++; i < 3 )      // line 5
                 ^
1 error
```

Explain what the problem is and how to fix it.

39. You coded the following in the class *Test.java*:

```
for ( int i = 1; i < 3; i++ )        // line 5
    System.out.println( "Hello" );
```

The code compiles and runs, but only prints *Hello* twice, whereas we expected to print *Hello* three times.

Explain what the problem is and how to fix it.

40. You coded the following in the class *Test.java*:

```
int product = 1;
for ( int i = 1, i < 5, i++ )            // line 8
    product *= i;
System.out.println( "Product is " + product ); // line 10
```

At compile time, you get the following errors:

```
Test.java:8: ';' expected
    for ( int i = 1, i < 5, i++ )          // line 8
                   ^

Test.java:8: illegal start of type
    for ( int i = 1, i < 5, i++ )          // line 8
                   ^

Test.java:8: illegal start of expression
      for( int i = 1, i < 5, i++ )         // line 8
                   ^

Test.java:8: ';' expected
      for( int i = 1, i < 5, i++ )         // line 8
                   ^

Test.java:8: illegal start of expression
        for( int i = 1, i < 5, i++ )       // line 8
                   ^

5 errors
```

Explain what the problem is and how to fix it.

41. You coded the following in the class *Test.java*:

```
for ( int i = 0; i < 3; i++ )
    System.out.println( "Hello" );
System.out.println( "i = " + i );   // line 8
```

At compile time, you get the following error:

```
Test.java:8: cannot find symbol
        System.out.println( "i = " + i ); // line 8
                                    ^

symbol  : variable i
location: class Test
1 error
```

Explain what the problem is and how to fix it.

42. You coded the following in the class *Test.java*:

```
int i = 0;
for ( int i = 0; i < 3; i++ ) // line 6
    System.out.println( "Hello" );
```

At compile time, you get the following error:

```
Test.java:6: i is already defined in main( java.lang.String[] )
  for( int i = 0; i < 3; i++ )       // line 6
           ^

1 error
```

Explain what the problem is and how to fix it.

EXERCISES, PROBLEMS, AND PROJECTS

6.14.6   Write a Short Program

43. Write a program that prompts the user for a value greater than 10 as an input (you should loop until the user enters a valid value) and finds the square root of that number and the square root of the result, and continues to find the square root of the result until we reach a number that is smaller than 1.01. The program should output how many times the square root operation was performed.

44. Write a program that expects a word containing the @ character as an input. If the word does not contain an @ character, then your program should keep prompting the user for a word. When the user types in a word containing an @ character, the program should simply print the word and terminate.

45. Write a program that reads *double* values from a file named *input.txt* and outputs the average.

46. Write a program that uses a *for* loop to output the sum of all the integers between 10 and 20, inclusive, that is, $10 + 11 + 12 + \ldots + 19 + 20$.

47. Write a program that uses a *for* loop to output the product of all the integers between 3 and 7, inclusive, that is, $3 * 4 * 5 * 6 * 7$.

48. Write a program that uses a *for* loop to count how many multiples of 7 are between 33 and 97, inclusive.

49. Write a program that reads a value (say *n*) from the user and outputs *Hello World n* times. Verify that the user has entered an integer. If the input is 3, the output will be *Hello World* printed three times.

50. Write a program that takes a word as an input from the keyboard and outputs each character in the word, separated by a space.

51. Write a program that takes a value as an input from the keyboard and outputs the factorial of that number; the factorial of an integer n is $n * (n-1) * (n-2) * \ldots * 3 * 2 * 1$. For instance, the factorial of 4 is $4 * 3 * 2 * 1$, or 24.

52. Using a loop, write a program that takes 10 integer values from the keyboard and outputs the minimum value of all the values entered.

53. Write an applet that displays a rectangle moving horizontally from the right side of the window to the left side of the window.

6.14.7 Programming Projects

54. Write a program that inputs a word representing a binary number (0s and 1s). First, your program should verify that it is indeed a binary number, that is, the number contains only 0s and 1s. If that is not the case, your program should print a message that the number is not a valid binary number. Then, your program should count how many 1s are in that word and output the count.

55. Perform the same operations as Question 54, with the following modification: If the word does not represent a valid binary number, the program should keep prompting the user for a new word until a word representing a valid binary number is input by the user.

56. Write a program that inputs a word representing a binary number (0s and 1s). First, your program should check that it is indeed a binary number, that is, the number contains only 0s and 1s. If that is not the case, your program should output that the number is not a valid binary number. If that word contains exactly two 1s, your program should output that that word is "accepted," otherwise that it is "rejected."

57. Perform the same operations as Question 56, with the following modification: If the word does not represent a valid binary number, the program should keep prompting the user for a new word until a word representing a valid binary number is input by the user.

58. Write a program that inputs a word representing a binary number (0s and 1s). First, your program should check that it is indeed a binary number, that is, that it contains only 0s and 1s. If that is not the case, your program should output that the number is not a valid binary number. If that word contains at least three consecutive 1s, your program should output that that word is "accepted," otherwise that it is "rejected."

59. Perform the same operations as Question 58 with the following modification: If the word does not represent a valid binary number, the program should keep prompting the user for a new word until a word representing a valid binary number is input by the user.

60. Write a program that takes website names as keyboard input until the user types the word *stop* and counts how many of the website names

are commercial website names (i.e., end with .*com*), then outputs that count.

61. Using a loop, write a program that takes 10 values representing exam grades (between 0 and 100) from the keyboard and outputs the minimum value, maximum value, and average value of all the values entered. Your program should not accept values less than 0 or greater than 100.

62. Write a program that takes an email address as an input from the keyboard and, using a loop, steps through every character looking for an @ sign. If the email address has exactly one @ character, then print a message that the email address is valid; otherwise, print a message that it is invalid.

63. Write a program that takes a user ID as an input from the keyboard and steps through every character, counting how many digits are in the user ID; if there are exactly two digits, output that the user ID is valid, otherwise that it is invalid.

64. Write a program that takes an integer value as an input and converts that value to its binary representation; for instance, if the user inputs 17, then the output will be 10001.

65. Write a program that takes a word representing a binary number (0s and 1s) as an input and converts it to its decimal representation; for instance, if the user inputs 101, then the output will be 5; you can assume that the *String* is guaranteed to contain only 0s and 1s.

66. Write a program that simulates an XOR operation. The input should be a word representing a binary number (0s and 1s). Your program should XOR all the digits from left to right and output the results as "True" or "False." In an XOR operation, *a* XOR *b* is *true* if *a* or *b* is *true* but not both; otherwise, it is *false*. In this program, we will consider the character "1" to represent true and a "0" to represent false. For instance, if the input is 1011, then the output will be 1 (1 XOR 0 is 1, then 1 XOR 1 is 0, then 0 XOR 1 is 1, which causes the output to be "True"). You can assume that the input word is guaranteed to contain only 0s and 1s.

67. Write a program that takes a sentence as an input (using a dialog box) and checks whether that sentence is a palindrome. A palindrome is a

word, phrase, or sentence that is symmetrical; that is, it is spelled the same forward and backward. Examples are "otto," "mom," and "Able was I ere I saw Elba." Your program should be case-insensitive; that is, "Otto" should also be counted as a palindrome.

68. Write a program that takes an HTML-like sequence as an input (using a dialog box) and checks whether that sequence has the same number of opening brackets (<) and closing brackets (>).

69. Write an applet that shows a small circle getting bigger and bigger. Your applet should allow the user to input the starting radius and the ending radius (and also verify that the starting radius is smaller than the ending radius).

6.14.8   Technical Writing

70. In programming, a programmer can make syntax errors that lead to a compiler error; these errors can then be corrected. Other errors can lead to a runtime error; these errors can also be corrected. Logic errors, however, can lead to an incorrect result or no result at all. Discuss examples of logic errors that can be made when coding loops and the consequences of these logic errors.

71. Discuss how you would detect whether you have an infinite loop in your code.

6.14.9   Group Project (for a group of 1, 2, or 3 students)

72. Often on a web page, the user is asked to supply personal information, such as a telephone number. Your program should take an input from the keyboard representing a telephone number. We will consider that the input is a valid telephone number if it contains exactly 10 digits and any number of dash (-) and whitespace characters. Keep prompting the user for a telephone number until the user gives you a valid one. Once you have a valid telephone number, you should assume that the digits (only the digits, not the hyphen[s] nor the whitespace) in the telephone number may have been encrypted by shifting each number by a constant value. For instance, if the shift is 2, a 0 becomes a 2, a 1 becomes a 3, a 2 becomes a 4, . . . , an 8 becomes a 0, and a 9 becomes a 1. However, we know that the user is from New York where the decrypted area code (after the shift is applied), represented by the first three digits of the input, is 212. Your

program needs to decrypt the telephone number and output the decrypted telephone number with the format 212-xxx-xxxx, as well as the shift value of the encryption. If there was an error in the input and the area code cannot be decrypted to 212, you should output that information.

CHAPTER 7

Object-Oriented Programming, Part 2: User-Defined Classes

CHAPTER CONTENTS

Introduction

When you see the title of this chapter, you might say, "Finally, we get to write our own classes." Actually, we've been writing classes all along. All Java source code belongs to a class. The classes we've been writing are application and applet classes. Now it's time to write some service classes—classes that encapsulate data and methods for use by applications, applets, or even other service classes. These are called **user-defined classes** because we, rather than the Java authors, create them.

First, let's take a moment to examine why we want to create user-defined classes.

We have written a lot of programs using Java's primitive data types (*boolean, char, int, double*, etc.), but the real world requires manipulation of more complex data than just individual *booleans* or *ints*. For example, if you are the programmer for an online bookstore, you will need to manipulate data associated with books. Books typically have an ISBN, a title, an author, a price, an in-stock quantity, and perhaps other pieces of data. We can create a *Book* class so that each object will hold the data for one book. For example, the ISBN, the title, and the author can be represented by *Strings*, the price by a *double*, and the in-stock quantity by an *int*. If we create this *Book* class, our program will be able to store and manipulate all the data of a book as a whole. This is one of the concepts of object-oriented programming.

By incorporating into the class the methods that work with the book data, we also are able to hide the details involved with handling that data. An application can simply call the methods as needed. Thus, creating your own classes can simplify your program.

Finally, a well-written class can be reused in other programs. Thus, user-defined classes speed up development.

7.1   Defining a Class

Classes encapsulate the data and functionality for a person, place, or thing, or more generally, an object. For example, a class might be defined to represent a student, a college, or a course.

To define a class, we use the following syntax:

```
accessModifier class ClassName
{
    // class definition goes here
}
```

This syntax should look familiar as the first line in our applications and applets. You may also notice that our class names have been nouns and have started with a capital letter: *Astronaut, Calculator, CellService*, and so forth. These names follow the conventions encouraged by the Java developers.

Inside the curly braces we define the data of the class, called its **fields**, and the methods. An important function performed by the class methods is maintaining the values of the class data for the **client programs**, which are the users of the class, in that the clients create objects and call the methods of the class. Our applications and applets have been clients of many Java classes, such as *String, DecimalFormat*, and *Math*. The fields and methods of a class are called the **members** of the class.

For each class and for each member of a class, we need to provide an **access modifier** that specifies where the class or member can be used (see Table 7.1). The possible access modifiers are *public, private*, and *protected*, or no modifier at all, which results in package access. The *public* access modifier allows the class or member to be used, or **referenced**, by methods of the same or other classes. The *private* access modifier specifies that the class or member can be referenced only by methods of the same class. Package access specifies that the

SOFTWARE ENGINEERING TIP

Use a noun for the class name and start the class name with a capital letter.

TABLE 7.1   Access Modifiers

Access Modifier	Class or member can be referenced by ...
public	methods of the same class, as well as methods of other classes
private	methods of the same class only
protected	methods in the same class, as well as methods of subclasses and methods in classes in the same package
no modifier (package access)	methods in the same package only

class or member can be accessed by methods in classes that are in the same package. Later in the chapter, we will learn how to create our own package.

Typically, the *accessModifier* for a class will be *public*, and we know that a *public* class must be stored in a file named *ClassName.java* where *ClassName* is the name of the class.

Let's start to define a class that represents an automobile, which we can use to calculate miles per gallon. We'll name the class *Auto*, and we'll use the *public* access modifier so that any application can use this class. The class header will look like the following:

```
public class Auto
{

}
```

When we write a class, we will make known the *public* method names and their APIs so that a client program will know how to instantiate objects and call the methods of the class. We will not publish the implementation (or code) of the class, however. In other words, we will publish the APIs of the methods, but not the method bodies. This is called **data hiding**. A client program can use the class without knowing how the class is implemented, and we, as class authors, can change the implementation of the methods as long as we don't change the interface, or APIs.

7.2   Defining Instance Variables

The instance variables of a class hold the data for each object of that class. Thus, we also say that the instance variables represent the properties of the object. Each object, or instance of a class, gets its own copy of the instance variables, each of which can be given a value appropriate to that object. The values of the instance variables, therefore, can represent the state of the object.

SOFTWARE ENGINEERING TIP

Define instance variables of a class as *private* so that only methods of the class will be able to set or change their values.

Instance variables are defined using the following syntax:

```
accessModifier dataType identifierList;
```

The *private* modifier is typically used for the nonconstant instance variables of the class. This permits only methods of the same class to set or change the values of the instance variables. In this way, we achieve encapsulation; the class provides a protective shell around the data.

The data type of an instance variable can be any of Java's primitive types or a class type.

The *identifierList* consists of one or more names for instance variables of the same data type and can optionally assign initial values to the instance variables. If more than one instance variable name is given, a comma is used as a separator. By convention, identifier names for instance variables are nouns and begin with a lowercase letter; internal words begin with a capital letter. Each instance variable and class variable must be given a name that is unique to the class. It is legal to use the same names for instance variables in different classes, but within a class, the same name cannot be used for more than one instance variable or class variable. Thus, we say that the fields of a class have **class scope**.

Optionally, you can declare an instance variable to be a constant (*final*).

The following statements are examples of instance variable definitions:

```
private String name = "";    // an empty String
private final int PERFECT_SCORE = 100, PASSING_SCORE = 60;
private int startX, startY, width, height;
```

What criteria should you use to select the instance variables of the class? The answer is to select the data that all objects will have in common. For example, for a *Student* class, you might select the student name, grade point average, and projected graduation date. For a *Calculator* class, you might select two operands, an operator, and a result.

Thus, for our *Auto* class, we will define instance variables to hold the model of the automobile, the number of miles the auto has been driven, and the gallons of gas used. Thus, our *Auto* class definition now becomes the following:

```
public class Auto
{
    private String model;
    private int milesDriven;
    private double gallonsOfGas;
}
```

SOFTWARE ENGINEERING TIP

Use nouns for identifier names for instance variables. Begin the identifier with a lowercase letter and capitalize internal words.

SOFTWARE ENGINEERING TIP

Define instance variables for the data that all objects will have in common.

7.3 Writing Class Methods

We declared the instance variables of the *Auto* class as *private* so that only the methods of the *Auto* class will be able to access or change the values of the instance variables directly. Clients of the *Auto* class will need to use the methods of the class to access or change any of the instance variables. So we'll need to write some methods.

Methods have this syntax:

```
accessModifier returnType methodName( parameter list ) // method header
{
     // method body
}
```

where *parameter list* is a comma-separated list of data types and variable names.

The method header syntax should be familiar because we've seen the API for many class methods. One difference is just a matter of semantics. The method caller sends **arguments**, or **actual parameters**, to the method; the method refers to these arguments as its **formal parameters**.

Because methods provide a function for the class, typically method names are verbs. Like instance variables, the method name should begin with a lowercase letter, with internal words beginning with a capital letter.

The access modifier for methods that provide services to the client will be *public*. Methods that provide services only to other methods of the class are typically declared to be *private*.

The return type of a method is the data type of the value that the method returns to the caller. The return type can be any of Java's primitive data types, any class type, or *void*. Methods with a return type of *void* do not return a value to the caller.

The body of each method, which consists of the code that performs the method's function, is written between the beginning and ending curly braces. Unlike *if* statements and loops, however, these curly braces are not optional; the curly braces are required, regardless of the number of statements in the method body.

Several compiler errors can result from forgetting one or both of the curly braces. You might receive either of these messages:

```
illegal start of expression
```

or

```
';' expected
```

In the method body, a method can declare variables, call other methods, and use any of the program structures we've discussed: *if/else* statements, *while* loops, *for* loops, *switch* statements, and *do/while* loops.

All objects of a class share one copy of the class methods.

We have actually written methods already. For example, we've written the method *main*. Its definition looks like this:

```java
public static void main( String [ ] args )
{
    // application code
}
```

We know that the *static* keyword means that the Java Virtual Machine (JVM) can call *main* to start the application running without first instantiating an object. The return type is *void* because *main* does not return a value. The parameter list expects one argument, a *String* array. We discuss arrays in the next chapter.

We have not previously written a value-returning method. A value-returning method sends back its results to the caller using a *return* statement in the method body. The syntax for the *return* statement is

```java
return expression;
```

As you would expect, the data type of the expression must match the return type of the method. Recall that a value-returning method is called from an expression, and when the method completes its operation, its return value replaces the method call in the expression.

If the data type of the method is *void*, as in *main*, we have a choice of using the *return* statement without an expression, as in this statement:

```java
return;
```

or omitting the *return* statement altogether. Given that control automatically returns to the caller when the end of the method is reached, most programmers omit the *return* statement in *void* methods.

7.4 Writing Constructors

A constructor is a special method that is called when an object is instantiated using the *new* keyword. A class can have several constructors. The job of the class constructors is to initialize the fields of the new object.

The syntax for a constructor follows:

```
accessModifier ClassName( parameter list )
{
    // constructor body
}
```

Notice that a constructor has the same name as the class and has no return type—not even *void*.

It's important to use the *public* access modifier for the constructors so that applications can instantiate objects of the class.

The constructor can either assign default values to the instance variables or the constructor can accept initial values from the client through parameters when the object is instantiated.

Providing a constructor for a class is optional. If you don't write a constructor, the compiler provides a **default constructor**, which is a constructor that takes no arguments. This default constructor assigns default initial values to all instance variables; this is called **autoinitialization**. Numeric variables are given the value of 0, characters are given the Unicode null character, *boolean* variables are given the value *false*, and object references are given the value *null*. Table 7.2 shows the values the default constructor assigns to instance variables.

If we do provide a constructor, any instance variables our constructor does not initialize will still be given the predefined default value.

TABLE 7.2   Default Initial Values of Instance Variables

Data Type	Initial Value
byte	0
short	0
int	0
long	0
float	0.0
double	0.0
char	null character ('\u0000')
boolean	*false*
object reference	*null*

Example 7.1 shows Version 1 of our *Auto* class with two constructors.

```
1  /* Auto class, Version 1
2     Anderson, Franceschi
3  */
4
5  public class Auto
6  {
7      // instance variables
8      private String model;        //  model of auto
9      private int milesDriven;     //  number of miles driven
10     private double gallonsOfGas; //  number of gallons of gas
11
12     // Default constructor:
13     //   initializes model to "unknown";
14     //   milesDriven is autoinitialized to 0
15     //        and gallonsOfGas to 0.0
16     public Auto( )
17     {
18        model = "unknown";
19     }
20
21     // Overloaded constructor:
22     // allows client to set beginning values for
23     //   model, milesDriven, and gallonsOfGas.
24     public Auto( String startModel,
25                  int startMilesDriven,
26                  double startGallonsOfGas )
27     {
28        model = startModel;
29
30        // validate startMilesDriven parameter
31        if ( startMilesDriven >= 0 )
32           milesDriven = startMilesDriven;
33        else
34        {
35           System.err.println( "Miles driven is negative." );
36           System.err.println( "Value set to 0." );
37        }
38
39        // validate startGallonsOfGas parameter
40        if ( startGallonsOfGas >= 0.0 )
41           gallonsOfGas = startGallonsOfGas;
42        else
```

```
43        {
44             System.err.println( "Gallons of gas is negative" );
45             System.err.println( "Value set to 0.0." );
46        }
47    }
48 }
```

EXAMPLE 7.1   The *Auto* Class, Version 1

Our default constructor (lines 12–19) does not set values for the *miles-Driven* and *gallonsOfGas* instance variables. Because *ints* and *doubles* are autoinitialized to 0 and 0.0, respectively, we just accept those default values.

However, it is necessary for our constructor to set the *model* instance variable to a valid *String* value. Because *Strings* are object references, they are autoinitialized to *null*. Any attempt to call a method using the *model* instance variable with a *null* value would generate a *NullPointerException*.

As mentioned earlier, you can provide multiple constructors for a class. We provide a second constructor (lines 21–47) that lets the client set initial values for all the instance variables. Because the class is the caretaker of its fields, it is the class's responsibility to ensure that the data for each object is valid. Thus, when the constructor sets initial values for the instance variables, it should first check whether its parameters are, indeed, valid values. What constitutes a valid value for any instance variable depends in part on the data type of the variable and in part on the class and is a design decision. For our *Auto* class, we have decided that *milesDriven* and *gallonsOfGas* cannot be negative. If the constructor finds that the *startMilesDriven* or *startGallonsOfGas* parameters are negative, it prints an error message to *System.err*—which by default is the Java console—and sets the instance variables to default values. Some methods in the Java class library generate an exception when a parameter value is invalid; others substitute a default value for the invalid parameter. Again, how your classes handle invalid argument values is a design decision.

When we provide multiple constructors, we are **overloading** a method. To overload a method, we provide a method with the same name but with a different number of parameters, or with the same number of parameters but with at least one parameter having a different data type. The name of the method, along with the number, data types, and order of its parameters, is called the method's **signature**. Thus, to overload a method, the new method must have a different signature. Notice that the return type is not part of the signature.

When a client calls a method that is overloaded, Java determines which version of the method to execute by looking at the number, data types, and order of the arguments in the method call. Example 7.2 shows a client program that instantiates three *Auto* objects.

```
 1 /* Auto Client, Version 1
 2    Anderson, Franceschi
 3 */
 4
 5 public class AutoClient
 6 {
 7   public static void main( String [ ] args )
 8   {
 9      System.out.println( "Instantiate sedan" );
10      Auto sedan = new Auto( );
11
12      System.out.println( "\nInstantiate suv" );
13      Auto suv = new Auto( "Trailblazer", 7000, 437.5 );
14
15      System.out.println( "\nInstantiate mini" );
16      // attempt to set invalid value for gallons of gas
17      Auto mini = new Auto( "Mini Cooper", 200, -1.0 );
18   }
19 }
```

EXAMPLE 7.2   The *Auto* Client, Version 1

Line 10 causes the default constructor to be called because no arguments are passed to the constructor. Line 13 causes the overloaded constructor to be called because it passes three arguments to the constructor. If the client attempted to instantiate a new object with a number of parameters other than 0 or 3, the compiler would generate an error because there is no constructor that matches those arguments. In general, the arguments sent to an overloaded method must match the formal parameters of some version of that method.

The number of constructors you provide is a design decision and depends on the class. Providing multiple constructors gives the client a choice of ways to create an object. It is good practice to provide, at minimum, a default constructor. The reason for this will become clear as we explore

 **SOFTWARE ENGINEERING TIP**

Provide, at the minimum, a default constructor and a constructor that accepts initial values for all instance variables.

Figure 7.1

Output from *Auto* Client, Version 1

```
Instantiate sedan

Instantiate suv

Instantiate mini
Gallons of gas is negative
Value set to 0.0.
```

classes in more depth. It is also good practice to provide another constructor that accepts values for all the instance variables.

On line 17, we instantiate an *Auto* object with an invalid argument for gallons of gas. As Figure 7.1 shows, the constructor prints an error message. The object is still created, but the value of its *gallonsOfGas* instance variable is 0.0.

Beware of this common error: declaring a *void* return type for a constructor. Remember that constructors have no return type at all. For example, the following invalid constructor definition declares a return type of *void:*

```
// Error! void return value specified
public void Auto( String model,
                  int startMilesDriven,
                  double startGallonsOfGas )
{
    // body of constructor
}
```

This is a difficult error to find. The class file will compile without an error because the compiler doesn't recognize this method as a constructor. Instead, the client program will get a compiler error when it attempts to instantiate an *Auto* object. For example, this statement in a client program

```
Auto gm = new Auto( "Prius", 350, 15.5 );
```

would generate this compiler error:

```
AutoClient.java:15: constructor Auto in class Auto cannot be applied to
given types
      Auto gm = new Auto( "Prius", 350, 15.5 );
                ^
  required: no arguments
  found: String,int,double
1 error
```

COMMON ERROR TRAP

Specifying a return value for a constructor will cause a compiler error in the client program when the client attempts to instantiate an object of that class.

Notice that both constructors access the instance variables directly. Remember that instance variables have class scope, which means that they can be accessed anywhere in the class. Thus, any method of the class can access any of the instance variables directly. In our *Auto* class, any method can access the instance variables *model*, *milesDriven*, and *gallonsOfGas*.

Methods have class scope as well. Any method can call any of the methods in the class, regardless of whether the methods have been declared *private*, *public*, or *protected*.

In addition to accessing the instance variables, a method can also access its own parameters. When a method begins executing, its parameters have been declared and have been given the values of the arguments sent by the caller of the method.

The parameters have **local scope** in that a method can access its parameters directly. We call this local scope because the parameters are local to a method; that is, a method can access its own parameters, but attempting to access another method's parameters generates a compiler error.

Table 7.3 summarizes the rules of scope.

Attempting to use an identifier that is not in scope will generate the following compiler error:

```
cannot find symbol
```

TABLE 7.3   Rules of Scope

A method in a class can access
• the instance variables of its class
• any parameters sent to the method
• any variable the method declares within its body from the point of declaration until the end of the method or until the end of the block in which the variable was declared, whichever comes first
• any methods in the class

You may wonder why the compiler calls an identifier a **symbol**. The Java compiler generates a **symbol table** as it reads your code. Each identifier you declare is put into the symbol table, along with the identifier's data type and where in the program it was defined. This symbol table allows the compiler to track the identifiers that are in scope at any given time. Thus, if an identifier is not in scope, the compiler will not be able to find that symbol in its table for that section of code.

When the client in Example 7.2 runs, it instantiates three objects, but there is nothing more our application can do with them. To allow our client to manipulate the *Auto* objects further, we need to provide more methods.

Skill Practice
with these end-of-chapter questions

    7.18.1   Multiple Choice Exercises

                Questions 1, 2, 3, 4, 5, 6, 7

    7.18.3   Fill In the Code

                Questions 28, 30, 31

    7.18.5   Debugging Area

                Questions 47, 48, 49

    7.18.8   Technical Writing

                Question 73

7.5   Writing Accessor Methods

Because clients cannot directly access *private* instance variables of a class, classes usually provide *public* accessor methods for the instance variables. These methods have a simple, almost trivial, standard form:

```
public returnType getInstanceVariable( )
{
    return instanceVariable;
}
```

The standard name of the method is *get*, followed by the instance variable's name with an initial capital letter. The method takes no arguments and simply returns the current value of the instance variable. Thus, the return type is the same data type as the instance variable.

You can see this simple pattern in the accessor methods for Version 2 of our *Auto* class, shown in Example 7.3 (lines 49–68).

```
1 /* Auto class, Version 2
2    Anderson, Franceschi
3 */
4
5 public class Auto
6 {
7      // instance variables
8      private String model;          //  model of auto
9      private int milesDriven;       //  number of miles driven
10     private double gallonsOfGas;   //  number of gallons of gas
11
12     // Default constructor:
13     //   initializes model to "unknown";
14     //   milesDriven is autoinitialized to 0
15     //        and gallonsOfGas to 0.0
16     public Auto( )
17     {
18        model = "unknown";
19     }
20
21     // Overloaded constructor:
22     // allows client to set beginning values for
23     //    model, milesDriven, and gallonsOfGas.
24     public Auto( String startModel,
25                  int startMilesDriven,
26                  double startGallonsOfGas )
27     {
28        model = startModel;
29
30        // validate startMilesDriven parameter
31        if ( startMilesDriven >= 0 )
32           milesDriven = startMilesDriven;
33        else
34        {
35           System.err.println( "Miles driven is negative." );
36           System.err.println( "Value set to 0." );
37        }
```

```
38
39        // validate startGallonsOfGas parameter
40        if ( startGallonsOfGas >= 0.0 )
41           gallonsOfGas = startGallonsOfGas;
42        else
43        {
44           System.err.println( "Gallons of gas is negative" );
45           System.err.println( "Value set to 0.0." );
46        }
47     }
48
49     // Accessor method:
50     // returns current value of model
51     public String getModel( )
52     {
53        return model;
54     }
55
56     // Accessor method:
57     // returns current value of milesDriven
58     public int getMilesDriven( )
59     {
60        return milesDriven;
61     }
62
63     // Accessor method:
64     //  returns current value of gallonsOfGas
65     public double getGallonsOfGas( )
66     {
67        return gallonsOfGas;
68     }
69 }
```

EXAMPLE 7.3   *Auto* Class, Version 2

In the client code in Example 7.4, we've added a few statements to call the accessor methods for the two *Auto* objects we've instantiated. Then we print the values, as shown in Figure 7.2.

```
1 /* Auto Client, Version 2
2    Anderson, Franceschi
3 */
4
5 public class AutoClient
```

```
 6 {
 7     public static void main( String [ ] args )
 8     {
 9         Auto sedan = new Auto( );
10         String sedanModel = sedan.getModel( );
11         int sedanMiles = sedan.getMilesDriven( );
12         double sedanGallons = sedan.getGallonsOfGas( );
13         System.out.println( "sedan: model is " + sedanModel
14                     + "\n miles driven is " + sedanMiles
15                     + "\n gallons of gas is " + sedanGallons );
16
17         Auto suv = new Auto( "Trailblazer", 7000, 437.5 );
18         String suvModel = suv.getModel( );
19         int suvMiles = suv.getMilesDriven( );
20         double suvGallons = suv.getGallonsOfGas( );
21         System.out.println( "suv: model is " + suvModel
22                     + "\n miles driven is " + suvMiles
23                     + "\n gallons of gas is " + suvGallons );
24     }
25 }
```

EXAMPLE 7.4   *Auto* Client, Version 2

```
sedan: model is unknown
 miles driven is 0
 gallons of gas is 0.0
suv: model is Trailblazer
 miles driven is 7000
 gallons of gas is 437.5
```

Figure 7.2

Output from *Auto* Client, Version 2

SOFTWARE ENGINEERING TIP

Provide *public* accessor methods for any instance variable for which the client should be able to retrieve the value. Each accessor method returns the current value of the corresponding instance variable.

Because the *sedan* object was instantiated by calling the default constructor, its model is *unknown* and the miles driven and gallons of gas are set to default values. On the other hand, the *suv* object data reflects the values sent to the overloaded constructor when the *suv* object was instantiated.

Thus, Version 2 of our *Auto* class lets our clients instantiate objects and get the values of the instance variables. But we still need to give the client a way to change the instance variables. In order to do this, we provide mutator methods.

7.6   Writing Mutator Methods

As we have discussed, we declare the instance variables as *private* to encapsulate the data of the class: We allow only the class methods to directly set the values of the instance variables. Thus, it is customary to provide a *public* **mutator** method for any instance variable that the client will be able to change.

The general form of a mutator method is the following:

```
public void setInstanceVariable( dataType newValue )
{
    // validate newValue, then assign to the instance variable
}
```

SOFTWARE ENGINEERING TIP

Provide a mutator method for any instance variable that you want to allow the client to change. If the argument sent to the method is not a valid value for the instance variable, one option is for the mutator method to print a message to *System.err* and leave the value of the instance variable unchanged.

We declare mutator methods as *public* so that client programs can use the methods to change the values of the instance variables. We do not return a value, so we declare the return type as *void*. By convention, the name of each mutator method starts with the lowercase word, *set*, followed by the instance variable name with an initial capital letter. For obvious reasons, the data type of the method's parameter should match the data type of the instance variable being set.

Whenever possible, the body of your mutator method should validate the parameter value passed by the client. If the parameter value is valid, the mutator assigns that value to the instance variable; otherwise, one option is for the mutator to print a message on the system error device (*System.err*), which, by default, is the Java console.

Example 7.5 shows Version 3 of our *Auto* class.

```
 1 /* Auto class, Version 3
 2    Anderson, Franceschi
 3 */
 4
 5 public class Auto
 6 {
 7     // instance variables
 8     private String model;          // model of auto
 9     private int milesDriven;       // number of miles driven
10     private double gallonsOfGas;   // number of gallons of gas
11
12     // Default constructor:
13     //  initializes model to "unknown";
```

```
14      //  milesDriven is autoinitialized to 0
15      //        and gallonsOfGas to 0.0
16      public Auto( )
17      {
18        model = "unknown";
19      }
20
21      // Overloaded constructor:
22      // allows client to set beginning values for
23      //   model, milesDriven, and gallonsOfGas.
24      public Auto( String startModel,
25                   int startMilesDriven,
26                   double startGallonsOfGas )
27      {
28        model = startModel;
29        setMilesDriven( startMilesDriven );
30        setGallonsOfGas( startGallonsOfGas );
31      }
32
33      // Accessor method:
34      // returns current value of model
35      public String getModel( )
36      {
37        return model;
38      }
39
40      // Accessor method:
41      // returns current value of milesDriven
42      public int getMilesDriven( )
43      {
44        return milesDriven;
45      }
46
47      // Accessor method:
48      //   returns current value of gallonsOfGas
49      public double getGallonsOfGas( )
50      {
51        return gallonsOfGas;
52      }
53
54      // Mutator method:
55      // allows client to set model
56      public void setModel( String newModel )
57      {
```

```
58        model = newModel;
59      }
60
61      // Mutator method:
62      // allows client to set value of milesDriven;
63      // prints an error message if new value is less than 0
64      public void setMilesDriven( int newMilesDriven )
65      {
66        if ( newMilesDriven >= 0 )
67          milesDriven = newMilesDriven;
68        else
69        {
70          System.err.println( "Miles driven cannot be negative." );
71          System.err.println( "Value not changed." );
72        }
73      }
74
75      // Mutator method:
76      // allows client to set value of gallonsOfGas;
77      // prints an error message if new value is less than 0.0
78      public void setGallonsOfGas( double newGallonsOfGas )
79      {
80        if ( newGallonsOfGas >= 0.0 )
81          gallonsOfGas = newGallonsOfGas;
82        else
83        {
84          System.err.println( "Gallons of gas cannot be negative." );
85          System.err.println( "Value not changed." );
86        }
87      }
88 }
```

EXAMPLE 7.5   *Auto* Class, Version 3

SOFTWARE ENGINEERING TIP

Write the validation code for instance variables in mutator methods and have the constructor call the mutator methods to set initial values.

The mutator methods for the *milesDriven* (lines 61–73) and *gallonsOfGas* (lines 75–87) instance variables validate that the parameter value is greater than 0. If not, the methods print a message to *System.err* and do not change the value of the instance variable. In previous versions of our *Auto* class, the constructor performed the same validation. Now that the mutator methods perform this validation, the constructor can call the mutator methods. In this way, we eliminate duplicate code; the validation of each parameter's value is performed in one place. If later we decide to impose other restrictions on any instance variable's value, we will need to change the code in only one place. In this way, a client cannot set invalid values for *milesDriven* or *gallonsOfGas*, either when the object is instantiated or by calling a mutator method.

```
1 /* Auto Client, Version 3
2    Anderson, Franceschi
3 */
4
5 public class AutoClient
6 {
7   public static void main( String [ ] args )
8   {
9     Auto suv = new Auto( "Trailblazer", 7000, 437.5 );
10
11    // print initial values of instance variables
12    System.out.println( "suv: model is " + suv.getModel( )
13          + "\n miles driven is " + suv.getMilesDriven( )
14          + "\n gallons of gas is " + suv.getGallonsOfGas( ) );
15
16    // call mutator method for each instance variable
17    suv.setModel( "Sportage" );
18    suv.setMilesDriven( 200 );
19    suv.setGallonsOfGas( 10.5 );
20
21    // print new values of instance variables
22    System.out.println( "\nsuv: model is " + suv.getModel( )
23          + "\n miles driven is " + suv.getMilesDriven( )
24          + "\n gallons of gas is " + suv.getGallonsOfGas( ) );
25
26    // attempt to set invalid value for milesDriven
27    suv.setMilesDriven( -1 );
28    // print current values of instance variables
29    System.out.println( "\nsuv: model is " + suv.getModel( )
30          + "\n miles driven is " + suv.getMilesDriven( )
31          + "\n gallons of gas is " + suv.getGallonsOfGas( ) );
32  }
33 }
```

EXAMPLE 7.6   *Auto* Client, Version 3

In Example 7.6, our client instantiates one *Auto* object, *suv* (line 9), and prints the values of its instance variables (lines 11–14). Then we call each mutator method, setting new values for each instance variable (lines 16–19). We again print the values of the instance variables (lines 21–24) to show that the values have been changed. Then, in line 27, we attempt to set an invalid value for *milesDriven*. As Figure 7.3 shows, the mutator method prints an error message and does not change the value, which we verify by again printing the values of the instance variables (lines 28–31).

When a method begins executing, the parameters have been defined and have been assigned the values sent by the client. When the client calls the *setModel* method at line 17, the *newModel* parameter has the value *Sportage* when the method starts executing.

A common error in writing mutator methods is using the instance variable name for the parameter name. When a method parameter has the same name as an instance variable, the parameter "hides" the instance variable. In other words, the parameter has **name precedence**, so any reference to that name refers to the parameter, not to the instance variable.

For example, the intention in this incorrectly coded method is to set a new value for the *model* instance variable:

```
// Incorrect!  parameter hides instance variable
public void setModel( String model )
{
    model = model;
}
```

Because the parameter, *model*, has the same identifier as the *model* instance variable, the result of this method is to assign the value of the parameter to the parameter! This is called a ***No-op***, which stands for "No operation," because the statement has no effect. To avoid this logic error, choose a different name

Figure 7.3

Output from *Auto* Client, Version 3

```
suv: model is Trailblazer
 miles driven is 7000
 gallons of gas is 437.5

suv: model is Sportage
 miles driven is 200
 gallons of gas is 10.5
Miles driven cannot be negative.
Value not changed.

suv: model is Sportage
 miles driven is 200
 gallons of gas is 10.5
```

for the parameter. To avoid name conflicts, we name each parameter using the pattern *newInstanceVariable.*

A similar common error is to declare a local variable with the same name as the instance variable, as shown in the following incorrectly coded method:

```
// Incorrect! declared local variable hides instance variable
public void setModel( String newModel )
{
      String model; // declared variable hides instance variable
      model = newModel;
}
```

Any variable that a method declares is a local variable because its scope is local to the method. Thus, the declared variable, *model,* is a local variable to the *setModel* method.

With the preceding code, the *model* local variable hides the instance variable with the same name, so the method assigns the parameter value to the local variable, not to the instance variable. The result is that the value of the *model* instance variable is unchanged.

The instance variable, *model,* is defined already in the class. Thus, the method should simply assign the parameter value to the instance variable without attempting to declare the instance variable (again) in the method.

Finally, another common error is declaring the parameter, as shown below:

```
// Incorrect! Declaring the parameter; parameters are declared already
public void setModel( String newModel )
{
      String newModel; // local variable has same name as parameter
      model = newModel;
}
```

This code generates this compiler error:

```
newModel is already defined in setModel(String)
```

COMMON ERROR TRAP

Be aware that a method parameter or local variable that has the same name as an instance variable hides the instance variable.

COMMON ERROR TRAP

Do not declare the parameters of a method inside the method body. When the method begins executing, the parameters exist and have been assigned the values set by the client in the method call.

7.7   Writing Data Manipulation Methods

Now we finally get down to the business of the class. Usually you will define a class not only to encapsulate the data, but also to provide some service. Thus, you would provide one or more methods that perform the functionality of the class. These methods might calculate a value based on the instance variables or manipulate the instance variables in some way. The

API of these methods depends on the function being performed. If a method merely manipulates the instance variables, it requires no parameters because instance variables are accessible from any method and, therefore, are in scope.

For example, in our *Auto* class, part of the functionality of our class is to calculate miles per gallon, so we provide a *calculateMilesPerGallon* method in our *Auto* class, Version 4, shown in Example 7.7.

```
1   /* Auto class, Version 4
2      Anderson, Franceschi
3   */
4
5   public class Auto
6   {
7       // instance variables
8       private String model;          //  model of auto
9       private int milesDriven;       //  number of miles driven
10      private double gallonsOfGas;   //  number of gallons of gas
11
12      // Default constructor:
13      //   initializes model to "unknown";
14      //   milesDriven is autoinitialized to 0
15      //          and gallonsOfGas to 0.0
16      public Auto( )
17      {
18         model = "unknown";
19      }
20
21      // Overloaded constructor:
22      // allows client to set beginning values for
23      //    model, milesDriven, and gallonsOfGas.
24      public Auto( String startModel,
25                   int startMilesDriven,
26                   double startGallonsOfGas )
27      {
28         model = startModel;
29         setMilesDriven( startMilesDriven );
30         setGallonsOfGas( startGallonsOfGas );
31      }
32
33      // Accessor method:
34      // returns current value of model
35      public String getModel( )
```

```
36      {
37          return model;
38      }
39
40      // Accessor method:
41      // returns current value of milesDriven
42      public int getMilesDriven( )
43      {
44          return milesDriven;
45      }
46
47      // Accessor method:
48      // returns current value of gallonsOfGas
49      public double getGallonsOfGas( )
50      {
51          return gallonsOfGas;
52      }
53
54       // Mutator method:
55       // allows client to set model
56       public void setModel( String newModel )
57       {
58          model = newModel;
59       }
60
61       // Mutator method:
62       // allows client to set value of milesDriven;
63       // prints an error message if new value is less than 0
64       public void setMilesDriven( int newMilesDriven )
65       {
66         if ( newMilesDriven >= 0 )
67            milesDriven = newMilesDriven;
68         else
69         {
70           System.err.println( "Miles driven cannot be negative." );
71           System.err.println( "Value not changed." );
72         }
73       }
74
75       // Mutator method:
76       // allows client to set value of gallonsOfGas;
77       // prints an error message if new value is less than 0.0
78       public void setGallonsOfGas( double newGallonsOfGas )
79       {
80         if ( newGallonsOfGas >= 0.0 )
```

```
81          gallonsOfGas = newGallonsOfGas;
82        else
83        {
84          System.err.println( "Gallons of gas cannot be negative." );
85          System.err.println( "Value not changed." );
86        }
87      }
88
89      // Calculates miles per gallon.
90      //   if no gallons of gas have been used, returns 0.0;
91      //   otherwise, returns miles per gallon
92      //        as milesDriven / gallonsOfGas
93      public double calculateMilesPerGallon( )
94      {
95        if ( gallonsOfGas != 0.0 )
96          return milesDriven / gallonsOfGas;
97        else
98          return 0.0;
99      }
100   }
```

EXAMPLE 7.7   *Auto* Class, Version 4

Our class now provides the method to calculate mileage for an *Auto* object. The *calculateMilesPerGallon* method (lines 89–99) needs no parameters since it accesses only instance variables of the class, which are in scope. As you can see from the code, we guard against dividing by 0 by checking the value of *gallonsOfGas* before using it as the divisor. If *gallonsOfGas* is not equal to zero, we divide *milesDriven* by *gallonsOfGas* and return the result as a *double*. Otherwise, we return 0.0.

Example 7.8 shows a client program that instantiates an *Auto* object, calls the *calculateMilesPerGallon* method, and prints the return value, as shown in Figure 7.4.

Figure 7.4

Output from *Auto* Client, Version 4

```
Mileage for suv is 16.0
```

```
1 /* Auto Client, Version 4
2    Anderson, Franceschi
3 */
4
5 public class AutoClient
6 {
7    public static void main( String [ ] args )
8    {
9      Auto suv = new Auto( "Trailblazer", 7000, 437.5 );
10
11     double mileage = suv.calculateMilesPerGallon( );
12     System.out.println( "Mileage for suv is "
13                        + mileage );
14   }
15 }
```

EXAMPLE 7.8   *Auto* Client, Version 4

Skill Practice
with these end-of-chapter questions

7.18.1   Multiple Choice Exercises

Questions 8, 9, 10, 11, 12, 13

7.18.2   Reading and Understanding Code

Questions 17, 18, 19, 20, 24, 26

7.18.3   Fill In the Code

Questions 32, 33, 36, 37

7.18.4   Identifying Errors in Code

Questions 38, 39, 43, 45

7.18.5   Debugging Area

Question 52

7.8   Programming Activity 1: Writing a Class Definition, Part 1

In this programming activity, you will write the methods for an *Airport* class. Then you will run a prewritten client program that instantiates several *Airport* objects, calls the methods that you have written, and displays the values of the objects' data.

The *Airport* class has two instance variables: the airport code and the number of gates.

In the Chapter 7 Programming Activity 1 folder on the CD-ROM accompanying this book, you will find three source files: *Airport.java*, *Airport-Client.java*, and *Pause.java*, as well as the *.class* files for *AirportClient* and *Pause*. Copy these files to a directory on your computer. Note that all files should be in the same directory.

Load the *Airport.java* source file; you'll notice that the class already contains some source code. The method names and APIs are described in comments. Your job is to define the instance variables and write the methods. It is important that you define the method headers exactly as described, including method name, return value, and parameters, because our *AirportClient* class will call each method to test it. Search for five asterisks in a row (*****). This will position you at the seven places in the class definition where you will add your code. The *Airport.java* code is shown here in Example 7.9.

```
 1 /* Airport class
 2     Anderson, Franceschi
 3 */
 4
 5 public class Airport
 6 {
 7    // 1. ***** Define the instance variables  *****
 8    //  airportCode is a String
 9    //  gates is an integer
10
11
12
13    // 2. ***** Write this method *****
14    // Default constructor:
15    // method name: Airport
```

```
16    // return value:  none
17    // parameters: none
18    // function: sets the airportCode to an empty String
19
20
21
22    // 3. ***** Write this method *****
23    // Overloaded constructor:
24    // method name: Airport
25    // return value: none
26    // parameters:  a String startAirportCode and an int startGates
27    // function:
28    //      calls the setAirportCode method,
29    //      passing startAirportCode parameter;
30    //      calls the setGates method, passing startGates parameter
31
32
33
34
35    // 4. ***** Write this method *****
36    // Accessor method for the airportCode instance variable
37    // method name: getAirportCode
38    // return value: String
39    // parameters: none
40    // function: returns airportCode
41
42
43
44    // 5. ***** Write this method *****
45    // Accessor method for the gates instance variable
46    // method name: getGates
47    // return value: int
48    // parameters: none
49    // function: returns gates
50
51
52
53    // 6. ***** Write this method *****
54    // Mutator method for the airportCode instance variable
55    // method name: setAirportCode
56    // return value: void
57    // parameters: String newAirportCode
```

```
58    // function: assigns airportCode the value of the
59    //        newAirportCode parameter
60
61
62
63    // 7. ***** Write this method *****
64    // Mutator method for the gates instance variable
65    // method name: setGates
66    // return value:  void
67    // parameters: int newGates
68    // function: validates the newGates parameter.
69    //    if newGates is greater than or equal to 0,
70    //        sets gates to newGates;
71    //        otherwise, prints an error message to System.err
72    //        and does not change value of gates
73
74
75
76
77    }  // end of Airport class definition
```

EXAMPLE 7.9   *Airport.java*

When you finish writing the methods for the *Airport* class, compile the source file. When *Airport.java* compiles without errors, load the *Airport-Client.java* file. This source file contains *main*, so you will execute the application from this file. When the application begins, you should see the window shown in Figure 7.5.

Figure 7.5

Programming Activity 1 Opening Window

```
Using the Airport Class          _ □ ×

    airport1
    ┌─────────────┐
    │ null        │
    └─────────────┘




    airport2
    ┌─────────────┐
    │ null        │
    └─────────────┘




Two airport object references declared:
    Airport airport1, airport2;
```

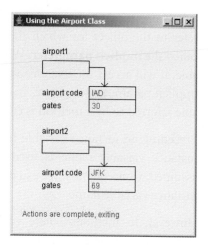

Figure 7.6

AirportClient **When Complete**

As you can see, the *AirportClient* has declared two *Airport* object references, *airport1* and *airport2*. The references are *null* because no *Airport* objects have been instantiated.

The client application, *AirportClient*, will instantiate the *Airport* objects and call the methods you have written for the *Airport* class. As the application does its work, it displays a status message at the bottom of the window that indicates which method it has called. It also displays the current values of both *Airport* objects. You can check your work by comparing the values in the objects with the status message. Figure 7.6 shows the *AirportClient* application when it has finished instantiating *Airport* objects and calling *Airport* methods.

? DISCUSSION QUESTIONS

1. Why is *main* in a different source file from the *Airport* class definition?

2. Explain the importance of using standard naming conventions for accessor and mutator methods.

7.9   The Object Reference *this*

When an object is instantiated, a copy of each of the instance variables is created. However, all objects of a class share one copy of the methods. How, then, does a method know for which object the method was called? In other words, how does a method know which instance variables it should get, set, or use to calculate a value? The answer is the special object reference named *this*.

When a method begins executing, the JVM sets the object reference, *this*, to refer to the object for which the method has been called. That object is called the **implicit parameter**. When a method references an instance variable, it will access the instance variable that belongs to the object that the implicit parameter references. In other words, by default, any instance variable referred to by a method is considered to be *this.instanceVariable*.

Preceding an instance variable name with *this* is optional; when just the instance variable name is used (without any object reference), *this* is assumed. Consequently, we usually omit the *this* reference and use just the instance variable name.

However, in methods where you need to avoid ambiguity in variable names, you can precede an instance variable name with *this*. That approach comes in handy as a way to avoid one of the common errors we discussed earlier in the chapter: A parameter to a mutator method with the same name as the instance variable being changed hides the instance variable. We can eliminate this problem by using the *this* reference with the instance variable, which effectively "uncovers" the instance variable name.

For instance, some programmers would code the *setModel* mutator as follows:

```
public void setModel( String model )
{
   this.model = model;
}
```

Here we give the parameter, *model*, the same name as the instance variable it represents. Then in the assignment statement, we use the *this* reference to distinguish the instance variable from the parameter. Now it is clear that the parameter value, *model*, should be assigned to the instance variable, *this.model*.

7.10   The *toString* and *equals* Methods

In addition to constructors, mutator methods, and accessor methods, a well-designed class usually implements the *toString* and *equals* methods.

The *toString* method is called automatically when an object reference is used as a *String*. For example, the *toString* method for an object is called when the object reference is used with, or as, a parameter to *System.out.println*. The function of the *toString* method is to return a printable representation of the object data.

The *equals* method is designed to compare two objects for equality; that is, it typically returns *true* if the corresponding instance variables in both objects are equal in value. The *equals* method takes an *Object* reference parameter that is expected to be an *Auto* reference and returns *true* if the values of its fields are equal to the values of the fields of this *Auto* object, *false* otherwise.

All classes inherit a version of the *toString* and the *equals* methods from the *Object* class, but these versions do not provide the functionality we describe earlier. Thus, it is good practice to provide new versions of these methods. To do that, we use the same header as the methods in the *Object* class, but provide a new method body. This is called **overriding a method**.

The APIs of the *toString* and *equals* methods are the following:

```
public String toString( )
public boolean equals( Object o )
```

Example 7.10 shows Version 5 of the *Auto* class with implementations of the *toString* method (lines 98–106) and the *equals* method (lines 108–125).

```
 1 /* Auto class, Version 5
 2    Anderson, Franceschi
 3 */
 4
 5 import java.text.DecimalFormat;
 6
 7 public class Auto
 8 {
 9     // instance variables
10     private String model;        //  model of auto
11     private int milesDriven;     //  number of miles driven
12     private double gallonsOfGas; //  number of gallons of gas
13
14     // Constructors:
15     //   initializes model to "unknown";
16     //   milesDriven is autoinitialized to 0
17     //          and gallonsOfGas to 0.0
18     public Auto( )
19     {
20         model = "unknown";
21     }
22
23     // allows client to set beginning values for
```

```
24     //   model, milesDriven, and gallonsOfGas.
25     public Auto( String startModel,
26                     int startMilesDriven,
27                     double startGallonsOfGas )
28     {
29        model = startModel;
30        setMilesDriven( startMilesDriven );
31        setGallonsOfGas( startGallonsOfGas );
32     }
33
34     // Accessor methods:
35     // returns current value of model
36     public String getModel( )
37     {
38        return model;
39     }
40
41     // returns current value of milesDriven
42     public int getMilesDriven( )
43     {
44        return milesDriven;
45     }
46
47     // returns current value of gallonsOfGas
48     public double getGallonsOfGas( )
49     {
50        return gallonsOfGas;
51     }
52
53     // Mutator methods:
54     // allows client to set model
55     public void setModel( String newModel )
56     {
57        model = newModel;
58     }
59
60     // allows client to set value of milesDriven
61     // prints an error message if new value is less than 0
62     public void setMilesDriven( int newMilesDriven )
63     {
64        if ( newMilesDriven >= 0 )
65           milesDriven = newMilesDriven;
66        else
67        {
68           System.err.println( "Miles driven cannot be negative." );
69           System.err.println( "Value not changed." );
70        }
```

```
71      }
72
73      // allows client to set value of gallonsOfGas;
74      // prints an error message if new value is less than 0.0
75      public void setGallonsOfGas( double newGallonsOfGas )
76      {
77        if ( newGallonsOfGas >= 0.0 )
78          gallonsOfGas = newGallonsOfGas;
79        else
80        {
81          System.err.println( "Gallons of gas cannot be negative." );
82          System.err.println( "Value not changed." );
83        }
84      }
85
86      // Calculates miles per gallon.
87      //   If no gallons of gas have been used, returns 0.0;
88      //   otherwise, returns miles per gallon
89      //         as milesDriven / gallonsOfGas
90      public double calculateMilesPerGallon( )
91      {
92        if ( gallonsOfGas != 0.0 )
93          return milesDriven / gallonsOfGas;
94        else
95          return 0.0;
96      }
97
98      // toString: returns a String of instance variable values
99      public String toString( )
100     {
101       DecimalFormat gallonsFormat = new DecimalFormat( "#0.0" );
102       return "Model: " + model
103              + "; miles driven: " + milesDriven
104              + "; gallons of gas: "
105              + gallonsFormat.format( gallonsOfGas );
106     }
107
108     // equals: returns true if fields of parameter object
109     //         are equal to fields in this object
110     public boolean equals( Object o )
111     {
112         if ( ! ( o instanceof Auto ) )
113             return false;
114         else
115         {
116             Auto objAuto = ( Auto ) o;
117             if ( model.equals( objAuto.model )
```

```
118                           && milesDriven == objAuto.milesDriven
119                           && Math.abs( gallonsOfGas - objAuto.gallonsOfGas )
120                                                 < 0.0001 )
121                       return true;
122               else
123                       return false;
124           }
125       }
126   }
```

EXAMPLE 7.10   *Auto* Class, Version 5

In the *toString* method (lines 98–106), we begin by instantiating a *Decimal-Format* object for formatting the gallons of gas as a floating-point number with one decimal place. Note that *gallonsFormat* is a local variable for the *toString* method; that is, only the *toString* method can use the *gallonsFormat* object. To use the *DecimalFormat* class, we import the class on line 5. We then build the *String* to return by concatenating labels for each instance variable with the values of the instance variables. The *toString* method can be used in a client class containing the *main* method, for instance, to print *Auto* objects using a single statement instead of calling all the class accessor methods.

To implement our *equals* method (lines 108–125), we first need to check that the parameter's type is *Auto*. The *instanceof* binary operator, whose left operand is an object reference and right operand is a class, returns *true* if the object reference can be cast to an instance of the class (for example, if it is an object reference of that class) and *false* otherwise. (See Table 7.4.) We use the *instanceof* operator at line 112 to determine if the parameter *o* can be cast to an *Auto* object reference (most likely, when sent by a client, *o* will be an *Auto* reference). If it cannot, we return *false*; otherwise, we can pro-

TABLE 7.4   The *instanceof* Operator

Operator	Syntax	Operation
instanceof	*objectReference* instanceof *ClassName*	evaluates to *true* if *objectReference* is of *ClassName* type; *false* otherwise.

ceed with comparing *o*'s fields and this *Auto* object's fields. Before performing the comparison, we must cast the *Object* reference *o* to an *Auto* (line 116). Otherwise, there would be a compiler error when trying to access the instance variable *model* with the *Object o*, because *model* is an instance variable of class *Auto* and not of class *Object*.

We compare each instance variable in the parameter object, *objAuto*, with the same instance variable in this object. We return *true* if the corresponding instance variables in each object have the same values; otherwise, we return *false*.

Notice that line 117 calls the *equals* method of the *String* class to compare the values of *model* in the objects because *model* is a *String* object reference. Notice also that because instance variables are in scope for methods, our *equals* method is able to directly access the instance variables of both this object and the *Auto* object, *objAuto*.

Example 7.11 puts Version 5 of the *Auto* class to work. We instantiate two objects that differ only in the model. On line 10, we explicitly call *toString* to print the fields of the *sporty* object. On line 14, we implicitly call the *toString* method; *toString* is called automatically because the *compact* object is the argument sent to the *println* method, which converts the object to a *String*. On lines 16–19, we compare the two objects using the *equals* method and print the results. The output is shown in Figure 7.7.

REFERENCE POINT

Type casting is discussed in Chapter 2.

```
1   /* Auto Client, version 5
2      Anderson, Franceschi
3   */
4
5   public class AutoClient
6   {
7     public static void main( String [ ] args )
8     {
9        Auto sporty = new Auto( "Spyder", 0, 0.0 );
10       System.out.println( sporty.toString( ) );
11
12       Auto compact = new Auto( "Accent", 0, 0.0 );
13       System.out.println( );
14       System.out.println( compact );
15
```

```
16        if ( compact.equals( sporty ) )
17          System.out.println( "\nsporty and compact are equal" );
18        else
19          System.out.println( "\nsporty and compact are not equal" );
20    }
21 }
```

EXAMPLE 7.11   *Auto* Client, Version 5

Figure 7.7
Output from Example 7.11

```
Model: Spyder; miles driven: 0; gallons of gas: 0.0

Model: Accent; miles driven: 0; gallons of gas: 0.0


sporty and compact are not equal
```

CODE IN ACTION

On the CD-ROM included with this book, you will find a Flash movie with step-by-step illustrations on how to define a class. Click on the link for Chapter 7 to view the movie.

7.11   *Static* Class Members

As we have mentioned, a separate set of instance variables is created for each object that is instantiated. In addition to instance variables, classes can define **class variables**, which are created only once, when the JVM initializes the class. Thus, class variables exist before any objects are instantiated, and each class has only one copy of its class variables.

You can designate a class variable by using the keyword *static* in its definition. Also, *static* variables that are constants are usually declared to be *public* because they typically are provided to allow the client to set preferences for the operations of a class. For example, we can directly use the *INFORMATION_MESSAGE static* constant in the *JOptionPane* class to specify the type of icon to display in a dialog box.

Another purpose for *static* variables is to make it easier to use the class. For example, the *PI* and *E static* constants in the *Math* class are provided so that our applications do not need to define those commonly used values. Also, as we saw in the programming activity in Chapter 2, the maximum and minimum values for data types are made available as the *MAX_VALUE* and *MIN_VALUE public static* constants of the *Integer, Double,* and *Character* wrapper classes.

If, however, you define a *static* variable for your class that is not a constant, it is best to define it as *private* and provide accessor and mutator methods, as appropriate, for client access to the *static* variable.

We finish our *Auto* class, with Version 6 shown in Example 7.12, by defining a *private static* variable to count the number of objects that have been instantiated during the application. We call this class variable *countAutos* and initialize it to 0 (line 14). Because a constructor is called whenever an object is instantiated, we can update the count by incrementing the value of *countAutos* in the class constructors (lines 24 and 37).

When you define a *static* variable for your class, its accessor and mutator methods must be defined as ***static* methods**, also called **class methods**. To do this, insert the keyword *static* in the method headers after the access modifier. We provide a *static* accessor method for the client to get the count of *Auto* objects (lines 59–63). We do not provide a mutator method, however, because clients of the class should not be able to update the value of *countAutos* except via the constructors, which update the count automatically.

Methods that are defined to be *static* are subject to the following important restrictions, which are summarized in Table 7.5:

- *static* methods can reference only *static* variables.

- *static* methods can call only *static* methods.

- *static* methods cannot use the object reference *this.*

TABLE 7.5   Access Restrictions for *static* and Non-*static* Methods

	static Method	Non-*static* Method
Access instance variables?	no	yes
Access *static* class variables?	yes	yes
Call *static* class methods?	yes	yes
Call non-*static* instance methods?	no	yes
Use the reference *this*?	no	yes

Again, it makes sense that *static* methods cannot access instance variables because *static* methods are associated with the class, not with any object. Further, a *static* method can be called before any objects are instantiated, so there will be no instance variables to access. Attempting to access an instance variable *xxx* from a *static* method will generate this compiler error:

```
non-static variable xxx cannot be referenced from a static context
```

Notice that the *getCountAutos* method (lines 59–63) is declared to be *static* and references only the *static countAutos* variable.

A non-*static*, or **instance**, method, on the other hand, can reference both class variables and instance variables, as well as class methods and instance methods.

At this point, we can explain a little more about the *main* method. Its header is

```
public static void main( String [ ] args )
```

Because *main* is defined as *static*, the JVM can execute *main* without first creating an object.

```
1  /* Auto class, Version 6
2     Anderson, Franceschi
3  */
4
5  import java.text.DecimalFormat;
6
7  public class Auto
8  {
9     // instance variables
10    private String model;        //  model of auto
11    private int milesDriven;     //  number of miles driven
12    private double gallonsOfGas; //  number of gallons of gas
13
14    private static int countAutos = 0;  // static class variable
15
16    // Constructors:
17    //  initializes model to "unknown";
18    //  milesDriven is autoinitialized to 0
19    //        and gallonsOfGas to 0.0;
20    // increments countAutos
21    public Auto( )
22    {
23       model = "unknown";
24       countAutos++;    // increment static count of Auto objects
25    }
26
```

```
27      // allows client to set beginning values for
28      // model, milesDriven, and gallonsOfGas;
29      // increments countAutos
30      public Auto( String startModel,
31                   int startMilesDriven,
32                   double startGallonsOfGas )
33      {
34        model = startModel;
35        setMilesDriven( startMilesDriven );
36        setGallonsOfGas( startGallonsOfGas );
37        countAutos++;    // increment static count of Auto objects
38      }
39
40      // Accessor methods
41      // returns current value of model
42      public String getModel( )
43      {
44        return model;
45      }
46
47      // returns current value of milesDriven
48      public int getMilesDriven( )
49      {
50        return milesDriven;
51      }
52
53      // returns current value of gallonsOfGas
54      public double getGallonsOfGas( )
55      {
56        return gallonsOfGas;
57      }
58
59      // returns countAutos
60      public static int getCountAutos( )
61      {
62        return countAutos;
63      }
64
65      // Mutator methods:
66      // allows client to set model
67      public void setModel( String newModel )
68      {
69          model = newModel;
70      }
71
```

```
72     // allows client to set value of milesDriven;
73     // prints an error message if new value is less than 0
74     public void setMilesDriven( int newMilesDriven )
75     {
76        if ( newMilesDriven >= 0 )
77           milesDriven = newMilesDriven;
78        else
79        {
80           System.err.println( "Miles driven cannot be negative." );
81           System.err.println( "Value not changed." );
82        }
83     }
84
85     // allows client to set value of gallonsOfGas;
86     // prints an error message if new value is less than 0.0
87     public void setGallonsOfGas( double newGallonsOfGas )
88     {
89        if ( newGallonsOfGas >= 0.0 )
90           gallonsOfGas = newGallonsOfGas;
91        else
92        {
93           System.err.println( "Gallons of gas cannot be negative." );
94           System.err.println( "Value not changed." );
95        }
96     }
97
98     // Calculates miles per gallon.
99     // If no gallons of gas have been used, returns 0.0;
100    // otherwise, returns miles per gallon
101    //    as milesDriven / gallonsOfGas
102    public double calculateMilesPerGallon( )
103    {
104       if ( gallonsOfGas != 0.0 )
105           return milesDriven / gallonsOfGas;
106       else
107           return 0.0;
108    }
109
110    // toString: returns a String with values of instance variable
111    public String toString( )
112    {
113       DecimalFormat gallonsFormat = new DecimalFormat( "#0.0" );
114       return "Model: " + model
115            + "; miles driven: " + milesDriven
116            + "; gallons of gas: "
```

```
117                   + gallonsFormat.format( gallonsOfGas );
118       }
119
120     // equals: returns true if fields of parameter object
121     //          are equal to fields in this object
122     public boolean equals( Object o )
123     {
124         if ( ! ( o instanceof Auto ) )
125             return false;
126         else
127         {
128             Auto objAuto = ( Auto ) o;
129             if ( model.equals( objAuto.model )
130                 && milesDriven == objAuto.milesDriven
131                 && Math.abs( gallonsOfGas - objAuto.gallonsOfGas )
132                             < 0.0001 )
133                 return true;
134             else
135                 return false;
136         }
137     }
138 }
```

EXAMPLE 7.12 *Auto* **Class, Version 6**

Example 7.13 shows Version 6 of our *AutoClient* class. In line 11, we call the *getCountAutos* method before instantiating any objects, then in line 17, we call the *getCountAutos* method again after instantiating one object. As Figure 7.8 shows, the *getCountAutos* method first returns 0, then 1. Notice that in both calls to the *static* method, we use the dot operator with the class name rather than an object reference.

```
1  /* Auto Client, Version 6
2     Anderson, Franceschi
3  */
4
5  public class AutoClient
6  {
7    public static void main( String [ ] args )
8    {
9      System.out.println( "Before instantiating an Auto object:"
10                        + "\nthe count of Auto objects is "
11                        + Auto.getCountAutos( ) );
12
```

```
13      Auto sporty = new Auto( "Spyder", 0, 0.0 );
14
15      System.out.println( "\nAfter instantiating an Auto object:"
16                        + "\nthe count of Auto objects is "
17                        + Auto.getCountAutos( ) );
18  }
19 }
```

EXAMPLE 7.13   *Auto* **Client, Version 6**

Figure 7.8

Output from Example 7.13

```
Before instantiating an Auto object:
the count of Auto objects is 0

After instantiating an Auto object:
the count of Auto objects is 1
```

Well, there it is. We've finished defining our *Auto* class. Although it's a large class, we were able to build the *Auto* class incrementally using stepwise refinement.

7.12   Graphical Objects

Let's revisit the astronaut from Chapter 4. We drew the astronaut in the *paint* method. The code for the astronaut and the applet was intertwined, or tightly coupled. We couldn't run the applet without drawing the astronaut, and we couldn't draw the astronaut without running the applet.

Now that we know how to design our own classes, we can separate the astronaut from the applet. We can define the astronaut as its own *Astronaut* class and make the applet the client of the *Astronaut* class. This will allow us to encapsulate the astronaut's data and the code for drawing the astronaut within the *Astronaut* class. It also promotes reuse of the *Astronaut* class by other programmers, who might want to create *Astronaut* objects for different applications.

The *Astronaut* class is shown in Example 7.14. We started by identifying the instance variables of the *Astronaut* class. Obviously, we need the starting (x, y) coordinate to draw the astronaut, so we define two *int* instance variables to hold those values (lines 11–12).

In addition, we added one more instance variable, *scale* (line 13), to allow the client to draw astronauts of different sizes. For example, a scaling factor of 1.0 will draw the astronaut at full size, 0.5 will draw the astronaut at half size, and 2.0 will draw a double-sized astronaut.

Our default constructor (lines 15–23) sets the starting *x* and *y* values to 0 and the scaling factor to 1.0 so that by default the astronaut is drawn in the upper-left corner of the window at full size. The overloaded constructor (lines 25–33) accepts values for these instance variables.

We provide one mutator method to change both *x* and *y* values (lines 36–40), as well as another mutator to change the scaling factor (lines 42–48).

We moved the code that draws the astronaut from the applet's *paint* method into its own method, which we named *draw* (lines 50–131). Because the astronaut is drawn using methods of the *Graphics* class, the applet client will need to pass its *Graphics* object as an argument to the *draw* method. Also, because the space suit color is used only in the *draw* method, we made it a local variable (line 59). If we wanted to let the client choose the space suit color, we could define another instance variable for it and add a corresponding parameter to the overloaded constructor.

Inside the *draw* method, we made a few changes to make the astronaut easier to scale. First, we converted the starting *x* and *y* coordinates to the center of the astronaut's head. In this way, the calculations for scaling the astronaut are simplified because we can capitalize on the astronaut's symmetry. Next we drew each part of the astronaut by multiplying any length measurement by the scaling factor. Finally, because the scaling factor is a *double* and the *Graphics* methods expect integer arguments, we type cast our calculated measurement to an *int* when needed.

We did not provide accessor methods or write a *toString* or an *equals* method for the *Astronaut* class. For a graphical object, these methods are less useful, given that the major purpose of graphical objects is to be drawn.

```
1   /* An Astronaut Class
2       Anderson, Franceschi
3   */
4
5   import java.awt.Graphics;
6   import java.awt.Color;
7
8   public class Astronaut
9   {
```

```
10     // the starting x and y coordinates for the astronaut
11     private int sX;
12     private int sY;
13     private double scale; // scaling factor, 1.0 is full size
14
15     // Default constructor:
16     // sets starting x and y coordinates to 0
17     // sets scaling factor to 1.0
18     public Astronaut( )
19     {
20       sX = 0;  // draw in upper-left corner
21       sY = 0;
22       scale = 1.0;  // draw full size
23     }
24
25     // Overloaded constructor:
26     // sets starting x and y coordinates
27     //  and scaling factor to values set by client
28     public Astronaut( int startX, int startY, double startScale )
29     {
30       sX = startX;
31       sY = startY;
32       setScale ( startScale );
33     }
34
35     // Mutator methods:
36     public void setCoordinates( int newX, int newY )
37     {
38       sX = newX;
39       sY = newY;
40     }
41
42     public void setScale( double newScale )
43     {
44       if ( newScale > 0 )
45         scale = newScale;
46       else
47         scale = 1.0;
48     }
49
50     // draw method:
51     // draws astronaut using starting (x,y) coordinate
52     //  and scaling factor
53     public void draw( Graphics g )
54     {
```

```
55        // convert between starting x, y coordinates and center of head
56        int oX = sX + (int) (65 * 2 * scale);
57        int oY = sY + (int) (75 * scale);
58
59        Color spacesuit = new Color( 195, 175, 150 );
60        // helmet
61        g.setColor( spacesuit );
62        g.fillOval( oX - (int) (75 * scale / 2),
63                       oY - (int) (75 * scale / 2),
64                       (int) (75 * scale), (int) (75 * scale) );
65        g.setColor( Color.LIGHT_GRAY );
66        g.fillOval( oX - (int) (55 * scale / 2),
67                       oY - (int) (55 * scale / 2),
68                       (int) (55 * scale), (int) (55 * scale) );
69
70        // face
71        g.setColor( Color.DARK_GRAY );
72        g.drawOval( oX - (int) ( (55 * scale / 4 )
73                          + (8 * scale / 2) ),
74                       oY - (int) (55 * scale / 4), (int) (8 * scale),
75                       (int) (8 * scale) );
76        g.drawOval( oX + (int) ( (55 * scale / 4)
77                          - (8 * scale / 2) ),
78                       oY - (int) (55 * scale / 4), (int) (8 * scale),
79                       (int) (8 * scale) );
80        g.drawLine( oX,  oY - (int) (6 * scale),
81                       oX + (int) (2  *  scale),
82                       oY + (int) (6 * scale) );
83        g.drawLine( oX, oY + (int) (6 * scale),
84                       oX + (int) (2  *  scale),
85                       oY + (int) (6 * scale) );
86        g.drawOval( oX - (int) (15 * scale / 2),
87                       oY + (int) (55 * scale / 4),
88                       (int) (15 * scale), (int) (6 * scale) );
89
90        // neck
91        g.setColor( spacesuit );
92        g.fillRect( oX - (int) (20 * scale / 2),
93                       oY + (int) (-1 + 75 * scale / 2),
94                       (int) (20 * scale), (int) (1 + 10 * scale) );
95
96        // torso
97        g.fillRect( oX - (int) (65 * scale / 2),
98                       oY +(int) (-1 + 75 * scale / 2 + 10 * scale),
99                       (int) (65 * scale), (int) (1 + 85 * scale) );
```

```
100
101    // arms
102    g.fillRect( oX - (int) (65 * 3 * scale / 2),
103                      oY + (int) (75 * scale / 2 + 10 * scale),
104                      (int) (1 + 65 * scale), (int) (20 * scale) );
105    g.fillRect( oX + (int) (-1 + 65 * scale / 2),
106                      oY + (int) (75 * scale / 2 + 10 * scale),
107                      (int) (1 + 65 * scale), (int) (20 * scale) );
108
109    // legs
110    g.fillRect( oX - (int) (55 * scale / 2),
111                      oY + (int) (-1 + 75 * scale / 2 + 95 * scale),
112                      (int) (20 * scale), (int) (80 * scale) );
113    g.fillRect( oX + (int) (55 * scale / 2 - 20 * scale),
114                      oY + (int) (- 1 + 75 * scale / 2 + 95 * scale ),
115                      (int) (20 * scale), (int) (80 * scale) );
116
117    // flag
118    g.setColor( Color.BLACK );
119    g.drawLine( oX + (int) (65 * scale / 2 + 65 * scale),
120                       oY + (int) (75 * scale / 2 + 10 * scale),
121                       oX + (int) (65 * scale / 2 + 65 * scale),
122                       oY );
123    g.setColor( Color.RED );
124    g.fillRect( oX + (int) (65 * scale / 2 + 65 * scale),
125                      oY - (int) (75 * scale / 2),
126                      (int) (75 * scale), (int) (45 * scale) );
127    g.setColor( Color.BLUE );
128    g.fillRect( oX + (int) (65 * scale / 2 + 65 * scale ),
129                      oY - (int) (75 * scale / 2),
130                      (int) (30 * scale), (int) (25 * scale) );
131  }
132 }
```

EXAMPLE 7.14   The *Astronaut* Class

Now, we can create the applet class, which will be the client of the *Astronaut* class. Our simplified *AstronautClient* applet is shown in Example 7.15. The applet has one instance variable, which is an *Astronaut* object reference, *astro*. We instantiate the *Astronaut* object in the *init* method (lines 13–17). The *init* method, which is part of the *JApplet* class and therefore is inherited by the *Astronaut* class, is a place to put initialization code, such as assigning initial values to instance variables. Similar to a constructor, the *init* method is called automatically when an applet begins running. We did not use the *init* method in applet examples in previous chapters; in fact, if your applet does not have any instance variables and so doesn't need to perform any initialization, then the *init* method is optional.

We call the *Astronaut*'s *draw* method in the applet's *paint* method (line 23), passing to *draw* the *Graphics* object reference *g* that was passed to *paint*. The applet window is shown in Figure 7.9.

```
1   /* Astronaut client
2      Anderson, Franceschi
3   */
4
5   import javax.swing.JApplet;
6   import java.awt.Graphics;
7
8   public class AstronautClient extends JApplet
9   {
10    // instance variable is an Astronaut
11    private Astronaut astro;
12
13    public void init( )
14    {
15      // instantiate the Astronaut object
16      astro = new Astronaut( 50, 12, 1 );
17    }
18
19    public void paint( Graphics g )
20    {
21      super.paint( g );
22
23      astro.draw( g ); // draw the astronaut
24    }
25  }
```

EXAMPLE 7.15   The *AstronautClient* Applet

Figure 7.9
The *AstronautClient* Window

An advantage to separating the *Astronaut* class from the *AppletClient* class is that it is now easy to draw two or more astronauts. Example 7.16 shows the code for the *AstronautClient2* class, which draws two astronauts, one full size and one half size. To add a second astronaut, all we needed to do was declare a second *Astronaut* object reference (line 11), instantiate it in *init* (line 17), and call the *draw* method for the second astronaut in the applet's *paint* method (line 26).

There is one other small change we needed to make. With two astronauts, we need a larger window, so we call the *setSize* method (line 18), passing it the new width and height of the applet window. The *setSize* method is inherited from the *JApplet* class. As such, it is a method of our *Astronaut-Client2* class, so we call *setSize* without an object reference. Figure 7.10 shows the output from the applet.

```
1   /* Astronaut client with two astronauts
2      Anderson, Franceschi
3   */
4
5   import javax.swing.JApplet;
6   import java.awt.Graphics;
7
8   public class AstronautClient2 extends JApplet
9   {
10    // instance variables
11    private Astronaut astro1, astro2;
12
13    public void init( )
14    {
15      // instantiate the Astronaut objects
16      astro1 = new Astronaut( 25, 10, 1.0 );  // full size
17      astro2 = new Astronaut( 225, 155, 0.5 ); // half size
18      setSize( 500, 300 ); // set the window size
19    }
20
21    public void paint( Graphics g )
22    {
23        super.paint( g );
```

```
24
25        astro1.draw( g ); // draw first Astronaut
26        astro2.draw( g ); // draw second Astronaut
27    }
28 }
```

EXAMPLE 7.16   The *AstronautClient2* Class with Two Astronauts

Figure 7.10
**The *AstronautClient2*
Window**

7.13   Enumeration Types

Enumeration types are designed to increase the readability of programs. The enumeration type, *enum*, is a special kind of class declaration. It allows us to define a set of named constant objects that can be used instead of numbers in a program.

Enum types are useful for managing ordered sets where each member of the set has a name. Examples are the days of the week, months of the year, and playing cards. To represent these sets in a program, we often use numbers, such as 1 through 7 for the days of the week or 1 through 12 for the months of the year. The problem is that to input or output these values, we need to convert between our internal numeric representation (for example, 1–7) and the words that users recognize (Sunday, Monday, Tueday, etc.). The *enum* type allows us to instantiate a constant object for each value in a set. The set of objects will be ordered so that we can refer to the objects by name, without the need for using numbers.

The *enum* functionality is built into *java.lang*, so we can define *enum* types without using an *import* statement.

The syntax for creating a set of *enum* objects is

```
enum EnumName { obj1, obj2, . . . };
```

where obj1, obj2, etc. are names for the constant objects.

For example, the following statement defines an *enum* type to represent the days of the week:

```
enum Days { Sun, Mon, Tue, Wed, Thur, Fri, Sat };
```

When that statement is executed, an object is instantiated for each name in the list. Each name in the list, therefore, is a reference to an object of the *enum* type *Days*.

COMMON ERROR TRAP

Do not use *String* literals in the initialization list for *enum* types.

Note that the values in the initialization list are object references (*Sun*), not *String* literals ("*Sun*").

Each object has an instance variable that holds a numeric value, which is determined by its position in the list of *enum* objects. By default, the first object has the value 0, the second object has the value 1, and so on. Because the objects are an ordered set, for example, the object *Thur* is higher in value than *Wed*. We can use the *enum* objects, however, without relying on the specific value of each object.

The *enum* objects are instantiated as constant objects, meaning that their values cannot be changed.

To refer to any of the constant objects in an *enum* type, we use the following dot syntax:

```
enumType.enumObject
```

Thus, to refer to the *Wed* object in our *Days enum* type, we use this syntax:

```
Days.Wed
```

Once we have defined an *enum* type, we can declare an object reference of that type. For example, the following statement defines a *Days* object reference *d*:

```
Days d;
```

Like any other object reference, the value of *d* will be *null* initially. To assign a value to the reference *d*—for example, *Thur*—we use the following statement:

```
d = Days.Thur;
```

Table 7.6 lists some useful methods that can be called with *enum* objects, and Example 7.17 demonstrates the use of these methods.

TABLE 7.6   Useful Methods for *enum* Objects

Useful Methods for *enum* Objects	
Return type	**Method name and argument list**
int	compareTo (Enum eObj)
	compares two *enum* objects and returns a negative number if *this* object is less than the argument, a positive number if *this* object is greater than the argument, and 0 if the two objects are the same
boolean	equals(Object eObj)
	returns *true* if this object is equal to the argument *eObj*; returns *false* otherwise
int	ordinal( )
	returns the numeric value of the *enum* object. By default, the value of the first object in the list is 0, the value of the second object is 1, and so on
String	toString( )
	returns the name of the *enum* constant
enum	valueOf(String enumName)
	static method that returns the *enum* object whose name is the same as the String argument *enumName*

```
1 /* Demonstration of enum
2    Anderson, Franceschi
3 */
4
5 public class EnumDemo
6 {
7   public enum Days { Sun, Mon, Tue, Wed, Thur, Fri, Sat };
8
9   public static void main( String [ ] args )
10  {
11     Days d1, d2;  // declare two Days object references
12
13     d1 = Days.Wed;
14     d2 = Days.Fri;
15
16     System.out.println( "Comparing objects using equals" );
17     if ( d1.equals( d2 ) )
18       System.out.println( d1 + " equals " + d2 );
19     else
20       System.out.println( d1 + " does not equal " + d2 );
21
22     System.out.println( "\nComparing objects using compareTo" );
23     if ( d1.compareTo( d2 ) > 0 )
24       System.out.println( d1 + " is greater than " + d2 );
25     else if ( d1.compareTo( d2 ) < 0 )
26       System.out.println( d1 + " is less than " + d2 );
27     else
28       System.out.println( d1 + " is equal to " + d2 );
29
30     System.out.println( "\nGetting the  ordinal value" );
31     System.out.println( "The value of " + d1 + " is "
32                          + d1.ordinal( ) );
33
34     System.out.println( "\nConverting a String to an object" );
35     Days day = Days.valueOf( "Mon" );
36     System.out.println( "The value of day is " + day );
37   }
38 }
```

EXAMPLE 7.17   A Demonstration of *enum* Methods

Line 7 defines the *enum* type *Days*; this instantiates the seven constant objects representing the days of the week. On line 11, we declare two object references of the *Days enum* type. Then on lines 13 and 14, we assign *d1* a reference to the *Wed* object, and we assign *d2* a reference to the *Fri* object.

Figure 7.11

Output from Example 7.17

```
Comparing objects using equals
Wed does not equal Fri

Comparing objects using compareTo
Wed is less than Fri

Getting the ordinal value
The value of Wed is 3

Converting a String to an object
The value of day is Mon
```

Line 17 compares *d1* and *d2* using the *equals* method. Because *Wed* and *Fri* are different objects, the *equals* method returns *false*. Lines 18 and 20 implicitly call the *toString* method, which prints the name of the objects.

Lines 23 and 25 call the *compareTo* method, which returns a negative number, indicating that *Wed* is lower in value than *Fri*.

We then retrieve the value of the *d1* object by calling the *ordinal* method (lines 31–32), which returns 3 because *Wed* is the fourth object in the *enum* list.

Finally, line 35 converts from a *String* to an *enum* object using the *valueOf* method. Notice that the *valueOf* method is *static*, so we call it using our *enum* type, *Days*.

If the *String* passed to the *valueOf* method is not a name in our set of defined *enum* objects, the *valueOf* method generates an *IllegalArgument-Exception*.

The output from Example 7.17 is shown in Figure 7.11.

We can use *enum* objects in *switch* statements to make the *case* constants more meaningful, which in turn makes the code more readable. Example 7.18 uses our *Days enum* class to display the daily specials offered in the cafeteria.

```
 1 /** Specials of the Day
 2     Anderson, Franceschi
 3 */
 4
 5 import java.util.Scanner;
 6
 7 public class DailySpecials
```

```java
 8 {
 9   public enum Days { Sun, Mon, Tue, Wed, Thur, Fri, Sat };
10
11   public static void main( String [ ] args )
12   {
13     Scanner scan = new Scanner( System.in );
14
15     System.out.print( "Enter a day\n"
16                       + "(Sun, Mon, Tue, Wed, Thur, Fri, Sat) > " );
17     String inputDay = scan.next( );
18     Days day = Days.valueOf( inputDay );
19
20     switch ( day )
21     {
22       case Mon:
23           System.out.println( "The special for "
24                               + day + " is barbeque chicken." );
25           break;
26
27       case Tue:
28           System.out.println( "The special for "
29                               + day + " is tacos" );
30           break;
31
32       case Wed:
33           System.out.println( "The special for "
34                               + day + " is chef's salad" );
35           break;
36
37       case Thur:
38           System.out.println( "The special for "
39                               + day + " is a cheeseburger" );
40           break;
41
42        case Fri:
43           System.out.println( "The special for "
44                               + day + " is fish fillet" );
45           break;
46
47       default: // if day is Sat or Sun
48           System.out.println( "Sorry, we're closed on "
49                               + day );
50     }
51   }
52 }
```

EXAMPLE 7.18   *DailySpecials* Class

```
Enter a day
(Sun, Mon, Tue, Wed, Thur, Fri, Sat) > Fri
The special for Fri is fish fillet
```

Figure 7.12
Output from *DailySpecials*

Figure 7.12 shows the output from Example 7.18 when the user enters *Fri*.

In the *DailySpecials* program, we prompt the user for a day (lines 15–17), then read the *String* entered by the user and convert it to an *enum* object by calling the *valueOf* method at line 18.

Once we have a valid *enum* value, we can use it as a *switch* variable (line 20).

Notice that we use each *enum* object name in a *case* label without qualifying it with the *Days* type. Including the *enum* type in a *switch* statement generates the following compiler error:

```
an enum switch case label must be the unqualified name of an
enumeration constant
```

Skill Practice
with these end-of-chapter questions

7.18.1   Multiple Choice Exercises

Questions 14, 15, 16

7.18.2   Reading and Understanding Code

Questions 21, 22, 23, 25, 27

7.18.3   Fill In the Code

Questions 29, 34, 35

7.18.4   Identifying Errors in Code

Questions 40, 41, 42, 44, 46

7.18.5   Debugging Area

Questions 50, 51, 53, 54

7.18.6   Write a Short Program

Questions 55, 56, 57, 58, 59, 60, 61, 62

7.18.8   Technical Writing

Question 72

7.14   Programming Activity 2: Writing a Class Definition, Part 2

In this programming activity, you will complete the definition of the *Airport* class. Then you will run a prewritten client program that instantiates several *Airport* objects, calls the methods that you have written, and displays the values of the objects' data.

Copy into a directory on your computer all the files from the Chapter 7 Programming Activity 2 folder on the CD-ROM accompanying this book. Note that all files should be in the same directory.

Load the *Airport.java* source file; you'll notice that the class already contains the class definition from Programming Activity 1. Your job is to complete the class definition by adding a *static* class variable (and its supporting code) and writing the *toString* and *equals* methods. It is important to define the *static* class variable and the methods exactly as described in the comments because the *AirportClient* class will call each method to test its implementation. Searching for five asterisks in a row (*****) will position you at the six places in the class definition where you will add your code. The *Airport.java* code is shown here in Example 7.19:

```
1 /* Airport class
2     Anderson, Franceschi
3 */
4
5 public class Airport
6 {
7
8    // instance variables
9    private String airportCode;
10    private int gates;
11
12    // 1. ***** Add a static class variable *****
13    //   countAirports is an int
14    //   assign an initial value of 0
15
16
17    // 2. ***** Modify this method *****
18    // Default constructor:
19    // method name: Airport
20    // return value:  none
21    // parameters: none
22    // function: sets the airportCode to a blank String
23    //     ***** add 1 to countAirports class variable
```

```
24   public Airport( )
25   {
26      airportCode = "";
27
28   }
29
30   // 3. ***** Modify this method *****
31   // Overloaded constructor:
32   // method name: Airport
33   // return value: none
34   // parameters:  a String airport code and an int startGates
35   // function: assigns airportCode the value of the
36   //      startAirportCode parameter;
37   //      calls the setGates method,
38   //      passing the startGates parameter
39   //   ***** add 1 to countAirports class variable
40   public Airport( String startAirportCode, int startGates )
41   {
42      airportCode = startAirportCode;
43      setGates( startGates );
44
45   }
46
47   // Accessor method for the airportCode instance variable
48   // method name: getAirportCode
49   // return value: String
50   // parameters: none
51   // function: returns airportCode
52   public String getAirportCode( )
53   {
54      return airportCode;
55   }
56
57   // Accessor method for the gates instance variable
58   // method name: getGates
59   // return value: int
60   // parameters: none
61   // function: returns gates
62   public int getGates( )
63   {
64      return gates;
65   }
66
67   // 4. ***** Write this method *****
68   // Accessor method for the countAirports class variable
```

```
69    // method name: getCountAirports
70    // return value: int
71    // parameters: none
72    // function: returns countAirports
73
74
75
76
77    // Mutator method for the airportCode instance variable
78    // method name: setAirportCode
79    // return value: void
80    // parameters: String newAirportCode
81    // function: assigns airportCode the value of the
82    //                     newAirportCode parameter
83    public void setAirportCode( String newAirportCode )
84    {
85       airportCode = newAirportCode;
86    }
87
88    // Mutator method for the gates instance variable
89    // method name: setGates
90    // return value:  void
91    // parameters: int newGates
92    // function: validates the newGates parameter.
93    //   if newGates is greater than 0, sets gates to newGates;
94    //   otherwise, prints an error message to System.err
95    //   and does not change value of gates
96    public void setGates( int newGates )
97    {
98       if ( newGates  >=  0 )
99          gates = newGates;
100      else
101      {
102         System.err.println( "Gates must be at least 0" );
103         System.err.println( "Value of gates unchanged." );
104      }
105   }
106
107   // 5. ***** Write this method *****
108   // method name:  toString
109   // return value: String
110   // parameters: none
111   // function:  returns a String that contains the airportCode
```

```
112  //    and gates
113
114
115
116
117
118
119  // 6. ***** Write this method *****
120  // method name: equals
121  // return value: boolean
122  // parameter:  Airport object
123  // function:  returns true if airportCode
124  //     and gates in this object
125  //     are equal to those in the parameter object;
126  //     returns false otherwise
127
128
129
130
131
132
133
134  }  // end of Airport class definition
```

EXAMPLE 7.19   The *Airport.java* File

When you finish modifying the *Airport* class, compile the source file. When *Airport.java* compiles without any errors, load and compile the *Airport-Client.java* file. This source file contains *main*, so you will execute the application from this file. When the application begins, you should see the window shown in Figure 7.13.

As you can see, the *AirportClient* has declared two *Airport* object references, *airport1* and *airport2*. The references are *null* because no *Airport* objects have been instantiated. Note also that the value of the *countAirports* class variable is displayed.

The *AirportClient* application will call methods of the *Airport* class to instantiate the two *Airport* objects, call the *toString* and *equals* methods, and get the value of the *static* class variable, *countAirports*. As the application does its work, it displays a status message at the bottom of the window indicating which method has been called and it also displays the current

Figure 7.13

AirportClient **Opening Window**

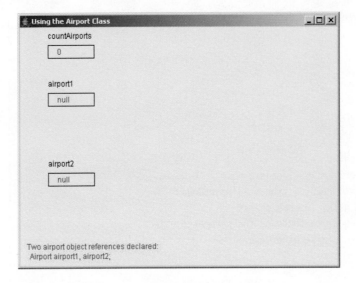

state of the *Airport* objects. You can check your work by comparing the state of the objects with the status message.

DISCUSSION QUESTIONS ?

1. Explain why the *countAirports* class variable has a value of 0 before any *Airport* objects have been instantiated.

2. How does a client call the *getCountAirports* method?

3. Explain why the client calls the *equals* method rather than directly comparing the object references *airport1* and *airport2* using the following *if* statement:

   ```
   if ( airport1 == airport2 )
   ```

7.15   Creating Packages

As we have mentioned, one of the advantages of a well-written class is that it can be reused. Ideally, as you write programs, you will look for functionality that is common to many programs. It is a good practice to encapsulate this functionality into a class so that you can reuse that code in future programs. Java provides the concept of a package for easily reusing classes.

 **SOFTWARE ENGINEERING TIP**

Put classes that provide reusable functionality into a package.

A **package** is a collection of related classes that can be imported into programs. We have imported classes from multiple Java packages: *java.awt*, *java.util*, *java.text*, and others. We can also create our own packages, which allows us to reuse a class without needing to physically store that class in the same directory as our other source files. Instead, we create the package and *import* the class from that package into our source file.

Let's look at an example of a class that can provide reusable functionality to our programs. In Chapter 6, we demonstrated how to detect and recover from an error when the user enters data that is a different type from what we expect. For example, if we prompt the user for an integer and the user enters a letter instead, the default behavior of the *Scanner* class is to generate an *InputMismatchException*. Our solution in Chapter 6 was to check whether the user's input matched our expected data type before attempting to read the value. For example, we inserted the following code to read an *int*:

```
System.out.print( "Enter . . . as an integer > " );
while ( ! scan.hasNextInt( ) )
{
    String garbage = scan.nextLine( );
    System.out.print( "\nPlease enter an integer > " );
}
int x = scan.nextInt( );
```

Although looping until the user enters a valid value solves the input mismatch problem, that's a lot of code to include in our program every time we need to read data that is a primitive data type.

Instead, we can create a class that provides the functionality we need, but that hides the complexity of the validation code. When we need input from the user, we'll call the methods of that class instead of coding the *while* loop. Example 7.20 shows the code for a *ConsoleIn* class that provides methods for type-safe reading of integers. That class can easily be expanded to include methods for type-safe reading of other primitive types.

```
1 /** Type-Safe Input Using Scanner
2  *    Anderson, Franceschi
3  */
4 package com.jbpub.af;
5
6 import java.util.Scanner;
7
8 public class ConsoleIn
9 {
10     private Scanner scan;
11
12     public ConsoleIn( )
13     {
```

```
14        scan = new Scanner( System.in );
15    }
16
17    public int readInt( String prompt )
18    {
19      System.out.print( prompt + " > " );
20      while ( ! scan.hasNextInt( ) )
21      {
22        String garbage = scan.nextLine( );
23        System.out.println( "Input is not an integer" );
24        System.out.print( prompt + " > " );
25      }
26      return scan.nextInt( );
27    }
28 }
```

EXAMPLE 7.20   *ConsoleIn* Class

We provide a constructor for the class (lines 12–15) that instantiates an object of the *Scanner* class and associates it with the console (*System.in*).

Although we only provide a method to read *ints*, we could easily provide *read* methods for each primitive data type; the general API would be the following:

```
public dataType readDataType( String prompt )
```

Let's look at the *readInt* method (lines 17–27). Its API is

```
public int readInt( String prompt )
```

Line 19 displays the prompt and appends a space, the > character, and another space. Lines 20 through 25 consist of a *while* loop that tests whether the input the user entered is an integer. The *hasNextInt* method of the *Scanner* class returns *true* if the input is an integer. So if the *hasNextInt* method returns *false*, we flush the bad input by calling the *nextLine* method of the *Scanner* class to ignore the returned data. We then print an error message and reprompt the user. This process repeats until the user types an integer, at which time, the *hasNextInt* method returns *true*. We then skip to line 26, which reads and returns the integer the user entered. The methods for reading the other primitive data types follow the same pattern.

Now that we have the *ConsoleIn* class, we can put the class into a package to make it available for use in other programs.

To create a package, you insert a *package* statement into the source file as the first line after the header comments. The *package* statement has the following syntax:

```
package packageName;
```

In the *ConsoleIn* class, we define our package as *com.jbpub.af* (line 4). Because many programmers create packages, we need to avoid a situation, called **name collision**, where multiple programmers choose the same name for their packages. The convention, therefore, is to name your package using your domain name. Specifically, the package name should use the reverse of the domain name (without the *www*). Thus, because our domain name is *www.jbpub.com*, we begin all our package names with *com.jbpub*. For this package, we append a dot and *af*. Each part of the package name represents a directory. So our package will be stored in the directory structure *com\jbpub\af* or *com/jbpub/af*, depending on the operating system. In an *import* statement, the dots in the package name separate the directory names in a platform-independent way.

The next step in creating a package is to create the directory where you want to place the package. Later on, as you create more classes you can put these classes in that same package or create a new package in the same or a different directory.

For our package, we created the *com* directory, then created a subdirectory, *jbpub*, and an *af* subdirectory in the *jbpub* directory.

The next step is to copy the source file into the package directory and compile it. We copied the *ConsoleIn.java* source file into the *af* directory and compiled it.

So that the compiler can find the package you just created, the final step is to modify your *CLASSPATH* environment variable, which tells the Java compiler where to look for packages. This step is system-dependent. We've included instructions for Windows 2000 and Linux systems. For other operating systems, consult your system documentation or Sun Microsystems' Java website.

For a Windows 2000 machine, we suggest the following steps:

Let's assume that you have decided to put the packages you create into the *My Documents* folder. For the package *com.jbpub.af*, you would create the directories in such a way that *af* will be a subdirectory of *jbpub*, itself a subdirectory of *com*, itself a subdirectory of *My Documents*.

Open the *Control Panel* and select the *System* icon. (On Windows XP, in the *Control Panel*, you will need to select the *Performance and Maintenance* icon before you can select the *System* icon.) From the *Advanced* tab, select the *Environment Variables* button. You will see two windows. In the top window, labeled *User variables*, look for *classpath* under the *variable* column.

If you see *classpath*, click the *edit* button. Append a semicolon and the pathname to the *My Documents* folder to the value that *classpath* currently has.

If *classpath* does not appear under the *variable* column, click the *new* button. Type *classpath* into the *Variable name* text box and type the pathname to the *My Documents* folder into the *Variable value* text box. You will probably need to add the current directory, designated by a dot (.), to the value.

When you finish, the *classpath* variable value might look like this:

```
.;c:\documents and settings\yourusername\my documents\
```

The initial dot (.) indicates that the compiler should look first in the current directory for classes.

On a typical Linux machine, we suggest using the following steps:

Let's assume that you have decided to put the packages that you create in the following directory, where *studentName* would be your user ID:

```
/home/studentName/myOwnClasses
```

At the Unix prompt, type the following command. (We use the # sign below to represent the Unix prompt.)

```
# export CLASSPATH=$CLASSPATH:/home/studentName/myOwnClasses
```

This statement appends */home/studentName/myOwnClasses* to the *CLASSPATH* environment variable. To check that this command was successful, at the Unix prompt type:

```
# echo $CLASSPATH
```

Your result should look something like this:

```
/usr/local/java/jre/lib:.:/home/studentName/myOwnClasses
```

You can see three directory paths separated by a colon (:):

- `/usr/local/java/jre/lib` is the directory (depending on your machine and your versions of Unix and Java, it could very well be another one) where the Java Class Library is located.

- `.` (dot) is the current directory.

- /home/studentName/myOwnClasses is the directory where you are planning to place the packages that you create.

Once the package is created, you can import the class to use its functionality. Example 7.21 shows client code that uses the *ConsoleIn* class to read an integer.

```
1 /*  ConsoleIn Client
2      Anderson, Franceschi
3 */
4 import com.jbpub.af.ConsoleIn; // import ConsoleIn from package
5
6 public class ConsoleInClient
7 {
8     public static void main( String [ ] args )
9     {
10        ConsoleIn console = new ConsoleIn( );
11
12        int age = console.readInt( "Enter your age" );
13        System.out.println( "Your age is " + age );
14    }
15 }
```

EXAMPLE 7.21   *ConsoleInClient* Class

In Example 7.21, we import the *ConsoleIn* class on line 4. Line 10 instantiates a *ConsoleIn* object, then line 12 uses that object reference to call the *readInt* method. Figure 7.14 shows the output of the *ConsoleInClient* class when the user enters invalid input, then valid input.

```
Enter your age > abc
Input is not an integer
Enter your age > 23.4
Input is not an integer
Enter your age > 23
Your age is 23
```

Figure 7.14

Output from the *ConsoleInClient* Class

7.16   Generating Web-Style Documentation with Javadoc

In most corporations and organizations, programmers share code and frequently use classes developed by another programmer. If the class is well designed and well documented, it will be easy for others to use that class. After all, that is essentially what we have been doing by using existing Java classes. It has been easy to understand what functions these existing classes perform, what they encapsulate, how the constructors work, what the methods do, and how to use the classes. The reason that these classes are easy to understand and use is not only that they are well designed and written, but also that the available documentation, particularly on Sun Microsystems' Java website, is clear, easy to understand, complete, and represents these classes well.

We, too, will learn how to produce HTML-based documentation similar to the documentation available on Sun Microsystems' Java website.

Indeed, there is a tool, called **Javadoc**, provided in the Java Development Kit (JDK), to do just that. Javadoc is an executable program (actually *javadoc.exe*) located in the *bin* directory. It is invoked much the same way as the *javac* compiler, except that instead of creating *.class* files, it creates *.html* files that document the class.

For instance, to generate documentation for our *Auto* class, we would type the following at the command line:

```
javadoc Auto.java
```

If we want to generate documentation for all the source files in the directory, we would type:

```
javadoc *.java
```

Table 7.7 shows the files generated for the *Auto* class.

If you double-click on *index.html*, you will open a web page with the same look as the ones on Sun's Java website.

REFERENCE POINT

The full documentation for using Javadoc can be found at *www.oracle.com/ technetwork/java.*

We will review a few basic Javadoc features here. Full documentation on Javadoc is available on Sun's website.

To write comments that will be included in the Javadoc documentation, we use a special form of block comment ahead of any class, field, constructor, or method. The syntax for including Javadoc comments follows.

TABLE 7.7 HTML Files Generated by Javadoc	
File Name	**Short Description**
Auto.html	*Auto* class documentation (without frames)
allclasses-frame.html	List of the classes with links (with frames)
allclasses-noframe.html	List of the classes with links (without frames)
constant-values.html	Constants of the class with links
deprecated-list.html	List of deprecated methods
help-doc.html	How these files are organized
index-all.html	Links to class, constructors, methods
index.html	*Auto* class documentation (with frames)
overview-tree.html	Class hierarchy
package-frame.html	Frame for this package
package-tree.html	Class hierarchy
resources	Directory containing one or more GIFs
stylesheet.css	Style sheet
package-list	List of packages

```
/**
Javadoc comment here
*/
```

As we already know, the syntax for a Java block comment is

```
/*
Java block comment here
*/
```

So a Javadoc comment is just a special Java block comment. The *javac* compiler will simply ignore it, but the Javadoc executable will look for it and generate the appropriate documentation. Javadoc discards all whitespace characters and the * at the beginning of each line until a non–whitespace

TABLE 7.8   Selected Javadoc Tags

Tag	Most common syntax	Explanation
@param	`@param variableName description`	Adds a parameter to the parameter section
@return	`@return text`	Adds a description for the return type

character and non * character is encountered. The industry convention is to start every line of a Javadoc comment with a *. Therefore, we recommend the following syntax:

```
/**
 *  A Javadoc comment here
 *  A second Javadoc comment here
 *  . . . .
 */
```

SOFTWARE ENGINEERING TIP

When coding a documentation block, use an * at the beginning of each line to indicate that this is a documentation comment.

Class documentation comprises two parts:

- A description section

- A tag section

Javadoc recognizes two types of tags: block tags and inline tags. We will discuss block tags only.

Block tags start with the character @. Table 7.8 lists two block tags, *@param* and *@return*, along with an explanation of each.

In the description section and inside the tag section, the text should be written in HTML; therefore, HTML tags such as
 (break) or <B> (bold) can be used. The tag <BR> inserts a new line; the tag <B> will change the text style to bold until the end tag </B> is encountered.

Example 7.22 shows a simplified version of our *Auto* class incorporating some documentation comments:

```
1 /*  Simplified Auto Class with Javadoc comments
2      Anderson, Franceschi
3 */
4
5 public class SimplifiedAuto
6 {
7  private String model;
```

```
 8   private int milesDriven;
 9   private double gallonsOfGas;
10
11
12
13   /**
14    * Default constructor:<BR>
15    * initializes model to "unknown"<BR>
16    * milesDriven are autoinitialized to 0, and gallonsOfGas to 0.0
17    */
18   public SimplifiedAuto( )
19   {
20      model = "unknown";
21   }
22
23   /**
24    * Overloaded constructor:<BR>
25    * Allows client to set beginning values for model,
26    *    milesDriven, and gallonsOfGas<BR>
27    * This constructor takes three parameters<BR>
28    * Calls mutator methods to validate new values
29    * @param startModel the model of the car
30    * @param startMilesDriven the number of miles driven
31    * @param startGallonsOfGas the number of gallons of gas used
32    */
33   public SimplifiedAuto( String startModel, int startMilesDriven,
34                          double startGallonsOfGas )
35   {
36      model = startModel;
37      setMilesDriven( startMilesDriven );
38      setGallonsOfGas( startGallonsOfGas );
39   }
40
41   /**
42    * Mutator method:<BR>
43    * Allows client to set value of milesDriven<BR>
44    * Prints an error message if new value is less than 0<BR>
45    * <B>setMilesDriven</B> does not change the value
46    * of <B>milesDriven</B> if newMilesDriven has negative value
47    * @param newMilesDriven the new number of miles driven
48    */
49   public void setMilesDriven( int newMilesDriven )
50   {
51      if ( newMilesDriven > 0 )
52          milesDriven = newMilesDriven;
53      else
```

```
54      {
55          System.err.println( "Miles driven cannot be negative." );
56          System.err.println( "Value not changed." );
57      }
58  }
59
60  /**
61   * Mutator method:<BR>
62   * Allows client to set value of gallonsOfGas<BR>
63   * If new value is less than 0, prints an error message<BR>
64   *     and does not change the value of <B>gallonsOfGas</B>
65   * @param newGallonsOfGas the new number of gallons of gas used
66   */
67  public void setGallonsOfGas( double newGallonsOfGas )
68  {
69      if ( newGallonsOfGas >= 0 )
70          gallonsOfGas = newGallonsOfGas;
71      else
72      {
73          System.err.println( "Gallons of gas cannot be negative." );
74          System.err.println( "Value not changed." );
75      }
76  }
77
78  /**
79   * equals method:<BR>
80   * Compares two SimplifiedAuto objects for the same field values
81   * @param a1 another SimplifiedAuto object
82   * @return a boolean, true if this object
83   * has the same field values as the parameter a1
84   */
85  public boolean equals( Object a1 )
86  {
87      if ( ! ( a1 instanceof SimplifiedAuto ) )
88        return false;
89      else
90      {
91         SimplifiedAuto objAuto = ( SimplifiedAuto ) a1;
92         return ( model.equals( objAuto.model )
93               && milesDriven == objAuto.milesDriven
94               && Math.abs( gallonsOfGas - objAuto.gallonsOfGas )
95                                 < 0.0001 );
96      }
97  }
98  }
```

EXAMPLE 7.22   The *SimplifiedAuto* **Class**

Class SimplifiedAuto

```
java.lang.Object
  └ SimplifiedAuto
```

```
public class SimplifiedAuto
extends java.lang.Object
```

Constructor Summary

SimplifiedAuto()
> Default constructor:
initializes model to "unknown"
milesDriven are autoinitialized to 0, and gallonsOfGas to 0.0

SimplifiedAuto(java.lang.String startModel, int startMilesDriven, double startGallonsOfGas)
> Overloaded constructor:
Allows client to set beginning values for model, milesDriven, and gallonsOfGas
This constructor takes three parameters
Calls mutator methods to validate new values

Figure 7.15

SimplifiedAuto Class Web-Style Documentation

> startMilesDriven - the number of miles driven
> startGallonsOfGas - the number of gallons of gas used

Method Detail

setMilesDriven

```
public void setMilesDriven(int newMilesDriven)
```

> Mutator method:
> Allows client to set value of milesDriven
> Prints an error message if new value is less than 0
> **setMilesDriven** does not change the value of **milesDriven** if newMilesDriven has negative value

> **Parameters:**
> > newMilesDriven - the new number of miles driven

---

setGallonsOfGas

```
public void setGallonsOfGas(double newGallonsOfGas)
```

> Mutator method:
> Allows client to set value of gallonsOfGas
> If new value is less than 0, prints an error message
> and does not change the value of **gallonsOfGas**

> **Parameters:**
> > newGallonsOfGas - the new number of gallons of gas used

Figure 7.16

Web-Style Documentation for the *Mutator* Methods

Figure 7.15 shows part of the generated *index.html* file, and Figure 7.16 shows the generated documentation for the *setMilesDriven* and *setGallonsOfGas* methods.

7.17   Chapter Summary

- The members of a Java class include its instance variables, class variables, and methods.

- One copy of each instance variable is created for every object instantiated from the class. One copy of each class variable and method is shared by all objects of the class.

- By convention, class names are nouns and begin with a capital letter; all internal words begin with a capital letter, and other letters are lowercase. Method names are verbs and begin with a lowercase letter; internal words begin with a capital letter, and all other letters are lowercase. Nonconstant instance variables are nouns and follow the same capitalization rules as methods. Constant fields have all capital letters with internal words separated by an underscore.

- The *public* access modifier allows the class or member to be accessed by other classes. The *private* access modifier specifies that the class or member can be accessed only by other members of the same class. Package access allows other classes in the same package to access the class or class members.

- Classes, constructors, *final* class variables, and class methods typically are declared as *public*, and instance variables typically are declared as *private*.

- Instance variables reflect the properties that all objects will have in common. Instance variables are defined by specifying an access modifier, data type, and identifier, and optionally, an initial value. Instance variables can be declared to be *final*.

- A method is defined by providing a method header, which specifies the access modifier, a return type, method name, and parameter list. The method body is enclosed in curly braces. Value-returning methods return the result of the method using one or more *return* statements. A method with a *void* return type does not return a value.

- The scope of an identifier is the range of code in which that identifier can be accessed. Instance variables and methods have class scope in that they can be accessed anywhere in the class.

- A method can reference the instance variables of its class, the parameters sent to the method, and local variables declared by the method and can call other methods of its class.

- A method can be overloaded by defining another method with the same name but a different signature, that is, with a different number of parameters or with parameters of different data types.

- Constructors are responsible for initializing the instance variables of the class.

- If you don't provide a constructor, the compiler provides a default constructor, which is a constructor that takes no arguments. This default constructor assigns default initial values to all the instance variables. Numeric variables are given the value of 0, characters are given the value *space*, *boolean* variables are given the value of *false*, and object references are given the value of *null*. Local variables declared in methods are not given initial values automatically.

- Accessor methods are named *getIV*, where *IV* is an instance variable name; the return data type is the same as the instance variable and the body of the method simply returns the value of the instance variable.

- Mutator methods are named *setIV*, where *IV* is an instance variable name; the return data type is *void*, and the method takes one argument, which is the same data type as the instance variable and contains the new value for the instance variable. The body of the method should validate the new value and, if the new value is valid, assign the new value to the instance variable.

- When a method begins executing, the JVM sets the object reference *this* to refer to the object for which the method has been called.

- The *toString* method is called automatically when an object reference is used as a *String* and its job is to provide a printable representation of the object data.

- The *equals* method compares two objects for equality; that is, it should return *true* only if the corresponding instance variables in both objects are equal in value, and *false* otherwise.

- *Static* class variables are created when the class is initialized. Thus, class variables exist before any objects are instantiated, and each class has only one copy of the class variables. *Static* variables that are constants are usually declared to be *public* because they typically are provided to allow the client to set preferences for the operations of a class.

- *Static* class methods can reference only *static* variables, can call only *static* methods, and cannot use the object reference *this*.

- A non-*static*, or instance, method can reference both class and instance variables, as well as class and instance methods, and the reference *this*.

- A graphical object usually has instance variables for the starting (*x, y*) coordinate. It also provides a *draw* method that takes a *Graphics* object as a parameter and includes the code to draw the graphical object.

- Enumeration types can be defined to give meaning to ordered sets that are represented in a program by numbers. For each name in an *enum* type initialization list, a constant object is created with an instance variable having a sequential numeric value. References can be defined of the *enum* type. Objects of the *enum* type can be compared, printed, and requested to return their numeric value.

- Javadoc, which is part of the Java JDK, generates documentation for classes. To use Javadoc, you enclose a description of each class, method, and field in a block comment beginning with /** and ending with */. In addition, you can describe each parameter using the *@param* tag and return value using the *@return* tag.

7.18 Exercises, Problems, and Projects

7.18.1 Multiple Choice Exercises

1. What can you say about the name of a class?

❏ It must start with an uppercase letter.

❏ The convention is to start with an uppercase letter.

2. What can you say about the name of constructors?

❏ They must be the same name as the class name.

❏ They can be any name, just like other methods.

3. What is a constructor's return type?

❏ *void*

❏ *Object*

❏ The class name

❏ A constructor does not have a return type.

4. It is legal to have more than one constructor in a given class.

❏ true

❏ false

5. In a class, if a field is *private,*

❏ it can be accessed directly from any class.

❏ it can be accessed directly only from inside its class.

6. In a typical class, what is the general recommendation for access modifiers?

❏ Instance variables are *private* and methods are *private.*

❏ Instance variables are *private* and methods are *public.*

❏ Instance variables are *public* and methods are *private.*

❏ Instance variables are *public* and methods are *public.*

7. In a class, fields

❏ can only be basic data types.

❏ can only be basic data types or existing Java types (from existing classes).

❏ can be basic data types, existing Java types, or user-defined types (from user-defined classes).

8. Accessors and mutators are

   ❏ instance variables of a class.

   ❏ used to access and modify field variables of a class from outside the class.

   ❏ constructor methods.

9. Accessor methods typically take

   ❏ no parameter.

   ❏ one parameter, of the same type as the corresponding field.

10. Mutator methods typically take

    ❏ no parameter.

    ❏ one parameter, of the same type as the corresponding field.

11. Accessor methods typically

    ❏ are *void* methods.

    ❏ return the same type as the corresponding field.

12. Mutator methods typically

    ❏ are *void* methods.

    ❏ return the same type as the corresponding field.

13. When coding a method that performs calculations on fields of that class,

    ❏ these fields must be passed as parameters to the method.

    ❏ these fields do not need to be passed as parameters to the methods because the class methods have direct access to them.

14. What is the keyword used for declaring a constant?

    ❏ *static*

    ❏ *final*

    ❏ *constant*

15. What is the keyword used for declaring a class variable or method?

    ❏ *static*

    ❏ *final*

    ❏ *class*

16. What can you say about *enum*?

    ❏ It is part of the package *java.lang.*

    ❏ It can be used for self-documentation, improving the readability of your code.

    ❏ An *enum* object is a constant object.

    ❏ All of the above.

7.18.2 Reading and Understanding Code

For Questions 17 and 18, consider that inside the class *Sky*, we have already coded the following:

```
public class Sky
{
    private Color color;
    public Sky( Color c )
    {
        color = c;
    }
}
```

17. Consider the following method header:

```
public Color getColor( )
```

Is this method a constructor, mutator, or accessor?

18. Consider the following method header:

```
public void setColor( Color c )
```

Is this method a constructor, mutator, or accessor?

For Questions 19 to 24, consider that the class *Airplane* has two methods with the following method headers; we also have a default constructor already coded.

```
public static double foo1( String s )
public String foo2( char c )
```

19. What is the return type of method *foo1*?

20. What is the return type of method *foo2*?

21. Is method *foo1* a class or instance method? Explain.

22. Is method *foo2* a class or instance method? Explain.

23. Write a line or two of code to call method *foo1* from a client class.

24. Write a line or two of code to call method *foo2* from a client class. Assume we have instantiated an object named *a1*.

25. Inside method *main*, we see code like

    ```
    Airplane.foo3( 34.6 );
    ```

    From this, reconstruct the header of method *foo3* (which belongs to the class *Airplane*); make appropriate assumptions if necessary.

26. Inside method *main*, we see code like

    ```
    Airplane a = new Airplane( );
    int n = a.foo4( "Hello" );
    ```

    From this, reconstruct the header of method *foo4* (which belongs to class *Airplane*).

27. If you have defined the following *enum* constants:

    ```
    enum Seasons { Winter, Spring, Summer, Fall };
    ```

    What is the output of the following code sequence?

    ```
    System.out.println( Seasons.Spring.ordinal( ) );
    ```

7.18.3   Fill In the Code

28. Declare two instance variables *grade*, which is an integer, and *letterGrade*, which is a *char*.

    ```
    // declare grade here

    // declare letterGrade here
    ```

29. Declare a class field for a federal tax rate, a constant, with value .07.

    ```
    // declare federal tax rate constant; value is 0.07
    ```

For Questions 30 to 37, we will assume that class *TelevisionChannel* has three fields: *name*, a *String*; *number*, an integer; and *cable*, a *boolean*, which represents whether the channel is a cable channel.

30. Code a default constructor for that class: initialize the fields to an empty string, 0, and *false*, respectively.

    ```
    // your default constructor code goes here
    ```

31. Code a constructor for that class that takes three parameters.

    ```
    // your constructor code goes here
    ```

32. Code the three accessors for that class.

    ```
    // your code goes here
    ```

33. Code the three mutators for that class.

    ```
    // your code goes here
    ```

34. Code the *toString* method.

    ```
    // your code goes here
    ```

35. Code the *equals* method.

    ```
    // your code goes here
    ```

36. Code a method returning the number of digits in the channel number. For instance, if the channel number is 21, the method returns 2; if the channel number is 412, the method returns 3.

    ```
    // your code goes here
    ```

37. Code a method returning the word *cable* if the current object represents a cable channel and returning the word *network* if the current object does not represent a cable channel.

    ```
    // your code goes here
    ```

7.18.4 Identifying Errors in Code

For Questions 38 to 45, consider that inside the class *Gift*, we have already coded the following:

```java
public class Gift
{
    private String description;
    private double price;
    private String occasion;
    private boolean taxable;

    public static final double TAX_RATE = 0.05;

    public Gift( String d, double p, String o, boolean t )
    {
        description = d;
        price = p;
        occasion = o;
        taxable = t;
    }
```

```java
public void setPrice( double p )
{
    price = p;
}

public void setTaxable( boolean t )
{
    taxable = t;
}
}
```

38. We are coding the following inside the class *Gift*; where is the error?

```java
public void getPrice( )
{
    return price;
}
```

39. We are coding the following inside the class *Gift*; where is the error?

```java
public void setOccasion( String occasion )
{
    occasion = occasion;
}
```

40. We are coding the following inside the class *Gift*; where is the error?

```java
public String toString( )
{
  System.out.println( "description = " + description );
  System.out.println( "price = " + price );
  System.out.println( "occasion = " + occasion );
  System.out.println( "taxable = " + taxable );
}
```

41. We are coding the following inside the class *Gift*; where is the error?

```java
public boolean equals( Object g )
{
  return ( this == g );
}
```

42. We are coding the following inside the class *Gift*; where is the error?

```java
public void setTaxRate( double newTaxRate )
{
    TAX_RATE = newTaxRate;
}
```

43. We are coding the following inside the class *Gift*; where is the error?

```
public double calcTax( TAX_RATE )
{
  return ( TAX_RATE * price );
}
```

44. We are coding the following in the *main* method inside the class *GiftClient*; where is the error?

```
Gift g = new Gift( "radio", 59.99, "Birthday", false );
Gift.setPrice( 99.99 );
```

45. We are coding the following in the *main* method inside the class *GiftClient*; where is the error?

```
Gift g = new Gift( "radio", 59.99, "Birthday", false );
g.setTaxable( ) = true;
```

46. Where are the errors in the following statement?

```
enum Months = { "January", "February", "March" };
```

7.18.5   Debugging Area—Using Messages from the Java Compiler and Java JVM

For Questions 47 and 48, consider the following class *Grade*:

```
public class Grade
{
  private char letterGrade;

  public Grade( char lg )
  {
    letterGrade = lg;
  }
  public char getLetterGrade( )
  {
    return  letterGrade;
  }
  public void setLetterGrade( char lg )
  {
    letterGrade = lg;
  }
}
```

47. In the *main* method of the class *GradeClient*, you have coded

```
Grade g = new Grade( 'B' );
g.letterGrade = 'A';          // line 10
```

When you compile, you get the following message:

```
GradeClient.java:10: letterGrade has private access in Grade
g.letterGrade = 'A';
              ^
1 error
```

Explain what the problem is and how to fix it.

48. In the *main* method of the class *GradeClient*, you have coded

```
Grade g = new Grade( "A" );  // line 10
```

When you compile, you get the following message:

```
GradeClient.java:10: constructor Grade in class Grade cannot be applied
to given types
    Grade g = new Grade ( "A" ); // line 10
                  ^
  required: char
  found: String
1 error
```

Explain what the problem is and how to fix it.

49. You coded the following definition for the class *Grade*:

```
public class Grade
{
    private char letterGrade;

    public char Grade( char startLetter )
    {
        letterGrade = startLetter;
    } // line 10
}
```

When you compile, you get the following message:

```
Grade.java:10: missing return statement
  } // line 10
  ^
1 error
```

Explain what the problem is and how to fix it.

50. You coded the following definition for the class *Grade*:

```
public class Grade
{
  private char letterGrade;
  public Grade( char lg )
```

```
  {
    letterGrade = lg;
  }
  public String toString( )      // line 10
  {                              // line 11
    return letterGrade;          // line 12
  }                              // line 13
}
```

When you compile, you get the following message:

```
Grade.java:12: incompatible types
 return letterGrade;
         ^

found   : char
required: String
1 error
```

Explain what the problem is and how to fix it.

51. You coded the following definition for the class *Grade*:

```
public class Grade
{
  private char letterGrade;
  public Grade( char lg )
  {
    letterGrade = lg;
  }
  public String toString( )    // line 10
  {                            // line 11
    return lg;                 // line 12
  }                            // line 13
}
```

When you compile, you get the following message:

```
Grade.java:12: cannot find symbol
 return lg; // line 12
         ^
symbol  : variable lg
location: class Grade
1 error
```

Explain what the problem is and how to fix it.

52. You coded the following definition for the class *Grade*:

```
public class Grade
{
    private char letterGrade;
    public Grade( char letterGrade )
    {
        letterGrade = letterGrade;
    }
    public char getLetterGrade( )
    {
        return letterGrade;
    }
}
```

In the *main* method of the class *GradeClient*, you have coded:

```
Grade g1 = new Grade( 'A' );
System.out.println( g1.getLetterGrade( ) );
```

The code compiles properly and runs, but the result is not what you expected.

The client's output is a space, not an *A*.

Explain what the problem is and how to fix it.

53. You have defined the following *enum* constants:

```
enum Seasons { Winter, Spring, Summer, Fall };
```

In the *main* method of the class *Test*, you have coded:

```
Seasons s = Seasons.Spring;
if ( s.equals( Winter ) )    // line 10
        System.out.println( "It is cold" );
else
        System.out.println( "The weather is fine" );
```

When you compile, you get the following message:

```
Test.java:10: cannot find symbol
  if ( s.equals( Winter ) )  // line 10
                 ^
symbol  : variable Winter
location: class Test
1 error
```

Explain what the problem is and how to fix it.

54. You have defined the following *enum* constants:

```
enum Seasons { Winter, Spring, Summer, Fall };
```

In the *main* method of the class *Test*, you have coded

```
Seasons.Fall = Autumn;  // line 10
```

When you compile, you get the following message:

```
Test.java:10: cannot assign a value to final variable Fall
   Seasons.Fall = Autumn;  // line 10
        ^
Test.java:10: cannot find symbol
   Seasons.Fall = Autumn;  // line 10
        ^
symbol  : variable Autumn
location: class Test
2 errors
```

Explain what the problem is and how to fix it.

7.18.6   Write a Short Program

55. Write a class encapsulating the concept of a team (for example, "Orioles"), assuming a team has only one attribute: the team name. Include a constructor, the accessor and mutator, and methods *toString* and *equals*. Write a client class to test all the methods in your class.

56. Write a class encapsulating the concept of a television set, assuming a television set has the following attributes: a brand and a price. Include a constructor, the accessors and mutators, and methods *toString* and *equals*. Write a client class to test all the methods in your class.

57. Write a class encapsulating the concept of a course grade, assuming a course grade has the following attributes: a course name and a letter grade. Include a constructor, the accessors and mutators, and methods *toString* and *equals*. Write a client class to test all the methods in your class.

58. Write a class encapsulating the concept of a course, assuming a course has the following attributes: a code (for instance, CS1), a description, and a number of credits (for instance, 3). Include a constructor, the accessors and mutators, and methods *toString* and *equals*. Write a client class to test all the methods in your class.

59. Write a class encapsulating the concept of a student, assuming a student has the following attributes: a name, a social security number, and a GPA (for instance, 3.5). Include a constructor, the accessors and mutators, and methods *toString* and *equals*. Write a client class to test all the methods in your class.

60. Write a class encapsulating the concept of website statistics, assuming website statistics have the following attributes: number of visitors and type of site (commercial, government, etc.). Include a constructor, the accessors and mutators, and methods *toString* and *equals*. Write a client class to test all the methods in your class.

61. Write a class encapsulating the concept of a corporate name (for example, "IBM"), assuming a corporate name has only one attribute: the corporate name itself. Include a constructor, the accessors and mutators, and methods *toString* and *equals*. Also include a method returning a potential domain name by adding *www.* at the beginning and *.com* at the end of the corporate name (for instance, if the corporate name is IBM, that method should return *www.ibm.com*). Write a client class to test all the methods in your class.

62. Write a class encapsulating the concept of a file, assuming a file has only a single attribute: the name of the file. Include a constructor, the accessors and mutators, and methods *toString* and *equals*. Also, code a method returning the extension of the file, that is, the letters after the last dot in the file (for instance, if the file name is *Test.java*, then the method should return *java*); if there is no dot in the file name, then the method should return "*unknown extension.*" Write a client class to test all the methods in your class.

7.18.7   Programming Projects

63. Write a class encapsulating the concept of the weather forecast, assuming that it has the following attributes: the temperature and the sky conditions, which could be sunny, snowy, cloudy, or rainy. Include a constructor, the accessors and mutators, and methods *toString* and *equals*. Temperature, in Fahrenheit, should be between -50 and $+150$; the default value is 70, if needed. The default sky condition is sunny. Include a method that converts Fahrenheit to Celsius. Celsius temperature = (Fahrenheit temperature $- 32$) * 5 / 9. Also include a method that checks whether the weather attributes are consistent

(there are two cases where they are not consistent: when the temperature is below 32 and it is not snowy, and when the temperature is above 100 and it is not sunny). Write a client class to test all the methods in your class.

64. Write a class encapsulating the concept of a domain name, assuming a domain name has a single attribute: the domain name itself (for instance, *www.yahoo.com*). Include a constructor, the accessors and mutators, and methods *toString* and *equals*. Also include the following methods: one returning whether or not the domain name starts with *www*; another returning the extension of the domain name (i.e., the letters after the last dot, for instance *com*, *gov*, or *edu*; if there is no dot in the domain name, then you should return "*unknown*"); and another returning the name itself (which will be the characters between *www* and the extension; for instance, *yahoo* if the domain is *www.yahoo.com*—if there are fewer than two dots in the domain name, then your method should return "*unknown*"). Write a client class to test all the methods in your class.

65. Write a class encapsulating the concept of an HTML page, assuming an HTML statement has only a single attribute: the HTML code for the page. Include a constructor, the accessors and mutators, and methods *toString* and *equals*. Include the following methods: one checking that there is a > character following each < character, one counting how many images are on the page (i.e., the number of IMG tags), and one counting how many links are on the page (i.e., the number of times we have "A HREF"). Write a client class to test all the methods in your class.

66. Write a class encapsulating the concept of coins, assuming that coins have the following attributes: a number of quarters, a number of dimes, a number of nickels, and a number of pennies. Include a constructor, the accessors and mutators, and methods *toString* and *equals*. Also code the following methods: one returning the total amount of money in dollar notation with two significant digits after the decimal point, and others returning the money in quarters (for instance, 0.75 if there are three quarters), in dimes, in nickels, and in pennies. Write a client class to test all the methods in your class.

67. Write a class encapsulating the concept of a user-defined *double*, assuming a user-defined *double* has only a single attribute: a *double*.

Include a constructor, the accessor and mutator, and methods *toString* and *equals*. Add a method, taking one parameter specifying how many significant digits we want to have, and returning a *double* representing the original *double* truncated so that it includes the specified number of significant digits after the decimal point (for instance, if the original *double* is 6.9872 and the argument of the method is 2, this method will return 6.98). Write a client class to test all the methods in your class.

68. Write a class encapsulating the concept of a circle, assuming a circle has the following attributes: a *Point* representing the center of the circle, and the radius of the circle, an integer. Include a constructor, the accessors and mutators, and methods *toString* and *equals*. Also include methods returning the perimeter (2 * π * radius) and area (π * radius^2) of the circle. Write a client class to test all the methods in your class.

69. Write a class encapsulating the concept of a rational number, assuming a rational number has the following attributes: an integer representing the numerator of the rational number, and another integer representing the denominator of the rational number. Include a constructor, the accessors and mutators, and methods *toString* and *equals*. You should not allow the denominator to be equal to 0; you should give it the default value 1 in case the corresponding argument of the constructor or a method is 0. Also include methods performing multiplication of a rational number by another and addition of a rational number to another, returning the resulting rational number in both cases. Write a client class to test all the methods in your class.

70. Write a class encapsulating the concept of an investment, assuming the investment has the following attributes: the amount of the investment, and the interest rate at which the investment will be compounded. Include a constructor, the accessors and mutators, and methods *toString* and *equals*. Also include a method returning the future value of the investment depending on how many years we hold it before selling it, which can be calculated using the formula:

```
future value = investment ( 1 + interest rate )^numberOfYears
```

We will assume that the interest rate is compounded annually. Write a client class to test all the methods in your class.

71. Write a class encapsulating the concept of a telephone number, assuming a telephone number has only a single attribute: a *String* representing the telephone number. Include a constructor, the accessor and mutator, and methods *toString* and *equals*. Also include methods returning the area code (the first three digits/characters of the phone number; if there are fewer than three characters in the phone number or if the first three characters are not digits, then this method should return "*unknown area code*"). Write a client class to test all the methods in your class.

7.18.8   Technical Writing

72. An advantage of object-oriented programming is code reuse, not just by the programmer who wrote the class, but by other programmers. Describe the importance of proper documentation and how you would document a class so that other programmers can use it easily.

73. Java has a number of naming conventions for classes, methods, and field variables. Is this important? Why is it good to respect these conventions?

7.18.9   Group Project (for a group of 1, 2, or 3 students)

74. Write a program that solves a quadratic equation in all cases, including when both roots are complex numbers. For this, you need to set up the following classes:

   Complex, which encapsulates a complex number

   ComplexPair, which encapsulates a pair of complex numbers

   Quadratic, which encapsulates a quadratic equation

   SolveEquation, which contains the *main* method

Along with the usual constructors, accessors, and mutators, you will need to code additional methods:

   In the *Complex* class, a method that determines whether a complex object is real

   In the *ComplexPair* class, a method that determines whether both complex numbers are identical

   In the *Quadratic* class, a method to solve the quadratic equation and return a *ComplexPair* object

Additionally, you need to include code in the *main* method to solve several examples of quadratic equations input from the keyboard. Your output should make comments as to what type of roots we get (double real root, distinct real roots, distinct complex roots). You should check that your code works in all four basic cases:

❑ The quadratic equation is actually a linear equation.

❑ Both roots are complex.

❑ There is a double real root.

❑ There are two distinct real roots.

CHAPTER 8

Single-Dimensional Arrays

CHAPTER CONTENTS

Introduction

Up to this point, we have been working with individual, or scalar, variables; that is, each variable has held one value at a time. To process a group of variables of the same type—for example, counting the number of odd integers entered by the user—we used a *while* loop or a *for* loop.

Thus, to find the average high temperature for the last year, we would use a *for* loop:

```java
double dailyTemp;
double total = 0.0;
for ( int i = 1; i <= 365; i++ )
{
    System.out.print( "Enter a temperature" );
    dailyTemp = scan.nextDouble( );
    total += dailyTemp;
}
double average = total / 365;
```

We defined one variable, *dailyTemp*, to hold the data. We read each temperature into our *dailyTemp* variable, added the temperature to our total, then read the next value into the *dailyTemp* variable, added that temperature to the total, and so on, until we finished reading and processing all the temperatures. Each time we read a new temperature, it overwrote the previous temperature, so that at the end of the loop, we had access to the last temperature only.

But suppose we want to perform multiple operations on those temperatures. Perhaps we want to find the highest or lowest temperature or find the median. Or suppose we don't know what operations we will perform, or in what order, until the user chooses them from a menu. In those cases, one scalar variable, *dailyTemp*, won't work; we want to store all the temperatures in memory at the same time. An array allows us to do just that without declaring several variables individually.

An **array** is a sequence of variables of the same data type. The data type could be any Java primitive data type, such as *int, float, double, byte, boolean, char, short,* or *long,* or it could be a class. Each variable in the array, called an **element**, is accessed using the array name and a subscript, called an **index**, which refers to the element's position in the array.

Arrays are useful for many applications: for example, calculating statistics on a group of data values or processing data stored in tables, such as matrices or game boards.

8.1   Declaring and Instantiating Arrays

In Java, arrays are implemented as objects, so creating an array takes two steps:

1. Declaring the object reference for the array.

2. Instantiating the array.

In arrays of primitive types, each element in the array contains a value of that type. For example, in an array of *doubles*, each element contains a *double* value. In arrays of objects, each element is an object reference, which stores the location of an object.

8.1.1   Declaring Arrays

To declare an array, you specify the name of the array and the data type, as you would for any other variable. Adding an empty set of brackets ([ ]) indicates that the variable is an array.

Here is the syntax for declaring an array:

```
datatype [ ] arrayName;
```

For example, the following statement creates a reference to an array that will hold daily high temperatures:

```
double [ ] dailyTemps; // each element is a double
```

The brackets can be placed before or after the array name. So the following syntax is also valid:

```
datatype arrayName [ ];
```

Thus, we could have declared the preceding array using the following statement:

```
double dailyTemps [ ];
```

Although you will see Java code written using either syntax, we prefer the first format with the brackets right after the data type, because it's easier to read as "a *double* array."

To declare an array to hold the titles of all tracks on a CD, you might declare it this way:

```
String [ ] cdTracks; // each element is a String object reference
```

SOFTWARE ENGINEERING TIP

An array's data type can be any primitive type or any predefined or user-defined class. The important thing to remember is that each element of an array with a class data type is a reference to the object; it is not the object itself.

Similarly, this statement declares an array to hold the answers to a true/false test:

```
boolean [ ] answers; // each element is a boolean value
```

Using our *Auto* class from Chapter 7, this statement declares an array to hold *Auto* objects:

```
Auto [ ] cars; // each element is an Auto object reference
```

You can declare multiple arrays of the same data type in one statement by inserting a comma after each array name, using this syntax:

```
datatype [ ] arrayName1, arrayName2;
```

For example, the following statement will declare three integer arrays to hold quiz scores for current courses:

```
int [ ] cs101, bio201, hist102;  // all elements are int values
```

 **COMMON ERROR TRAP**

Putting the size of the array inside the brackets in the array declaration will generate a compiler error.

Note that an array declaration does not specify how many elements the arrays will have. The declaration simply specifies an object reference for the array and the data type of the elements. Thus, **declaring an array does not allocate memory for the array**.

8.1.2   Instantiating Arrays

As we mentioned earlier, Java arrays are objects, so to allocate memory for an array, you need to instantiate the array using the *new* keyword. Here is the syntax for instantiating an array:

```
arrayName = new datatype [size];
```

> where size is an expression that evaluates to an integer and
> specifies the number of elements in the array.

The following statements will instantiate the arrays declared earlier:

```
dailyTemps = new double [365]; // dailyTemps has 365 elements

cdTracks = new String [15];    // cdTracks has 15 elements

int numberOfQuestions = 30;
answers = new boolean [numberOfQuestions]; // answers has 30 elements

cars = new Auto [3];           // cars has 3 elements

cs101 = new int [5];           // cs101 has 5 elements

bio201 = new int [4];          // bio201 has 4 elements

hist102 = new int [6];         // hist102 has 6 elements
```

TABLE 8.1   Default Initial Values of Array Elements

Element Data Type	Initial Value
double	0.0
float	0.0
int, long, short, byte	0
char	null character ('\u0000')
boolean	*false*
object reference	*null*

When an array is instantiated, the elements are given initial values automatically.

Numeric elements are set to 0, *boolean* elements are set to *false, char* elements are set to the Unicode null character, and object references are set to *null,* as shown in Table 8.1.

Thus, all the elements in the *dailyTemps* array are given an initial value of 0.0; the elements in the *cs101, bio201,* and *hist102* arrays are given an initial value of 0; the elements of the *answers* array are given an initial value of *false*; and the elements of the *cdTracks* and *cars* arrays are given an initial value of *null.*

8.1.3   Combining the Declaration and Instantiation of Arrays

Arrays also can be instantiated when they are declared. To combine the declaration and instantiation of an array, use this syntax:

```
datatype [ ] arrayName = new datatype [size];

    where size is an expression that evaluates to an integer and
    specifies the number of elements in the array.
```

Thus, this statement:

```
double [ ] dailyTemps = new double [365];
```

is equivalent to:

```
double [ ] dailyTemps;
dailyTemps = new double [365];
```

Similarly, this statement:

```
String [ ] cdTracks = new String [15];
```

is equivalent to:

```
String [ ] cdTracks;
cdTracks = new String [15];
```

8.1.4   Assigning Initial Values to Arrays

Java allows you to instantiate an array by assigning initial values when the array is declared. To do this, you specify the initial values using a comma-separated list within curly braces:

```
datatype [ ] arrayName = { value0, value1, value2, ... };
```

> where *valueN* is an expression that evaluates to the data type
> of the array and is the value to assign to the element at index *N*.

Note that we do not use the *new* keyword and we do not specify a size for the array. The number of elements in the array is determined by the number of values in the initialization list.

For example, this statement declares and instantiates an array of odd numbers:

```
int nine = 9;
int [ ] oddNumbers = { 1, 3, 5, 7, nine, nine + 2, 13, 15, 17, 19 };
```

Because 10 values are given in the initialization list, this array has 10 elements. Notice that the values can be an expression, for example, *nine* and *nine + 2.*

Similarly, we can declare and instantiate an array of objects by providing objects in the list, as shown next. The *cars* array of *Auto* objects has three elements.

```
Auto sportsCar = new Auto( "Ferrari", 0, 0.0 );
Auto [ ] cars = { new Auto( "BMW", 100, 15.0 ), sportsCar, new Auto( ) };
```

8.2   Accessing Array Elements

Elements of an array are accessed using this syntax:

```
arrayName[exp]
```

> where exp is an expression that evaluates to an integer.

Exp is the element's position, or **index**, within the array. The index of the first element in the array is always 0; the index of the last element is always 1 less than the number of elements.

COMMON ERROR TRAP

An initialization list can be given only when the array is declared. Attempting to assign values to an array using an initialization list after the array is instantiated will generate a compiler error.

COMMON ERROR TRAP

The *new* keyword is not used when an array is instantiated using an initialization list. No size is given; the number of values in the list specifies the size of the array.

TABLE 8.2 Accessing Array Elements	
Element	**Syntax**
Element 0	`arrayName[0]`
Element *i*	`arrayName[i]`
Last element	`arrayName[arrayName.length - 1]`

Arrays have a read-only, integer instance variable, **length**, which holds the number of elements in the array. To access the number of elements in an array named *arrayName*, use this syntax:

`arrayName.length`

Thus, to access the last element of an array, use this syntax:

`arrayName[arrayName.length - 1]`

Note that regardless of the data type of the elements in an array, the *length* of an array is always an integer, because *length* represents the number of elements in the array.

Table 8.2 summarizes the syntax for accessing elements of an array.

For example, suppose we want to analyze our monthly cell phone bills for the past six months. We want to calculate the average bill, the total payments for the six months, and the lowest and highest bills. We can use an array of *double*s with six elements, as shown in Example 8.1.

 COMMON ERROR TRAP

Note that for an array, *length*—with no parentheses—is an instance variable, whereas for *Strings*, *length( )*—with parentheses—is a method. Note also that the instance variable is named *length*, rather than *size*.

```
1  /* Array of Cell Phone Bills
2     Anderson, Franceschi
3  */
4
5  public class CellBills
6  {
7    public static void main( String [ ] args )
8    {
9      // declare and instantiate the array
10     double [ ] cellBills = new double [6];
11
12     // assign values to array elements
13     cellBills[0] = 45.24;
14     cellBills[1] = 54.67;
15     cellBills[2] = 42.55;
```

```
16      cellBills[3] = 44.61;
17      cellBills[4] = 65.29;
18      cellBills[5] = 49.75;
19
20      System.out.println( "The first monthly cell bill is "
21                          + cellBills[0] );
22      System.out.println( "The last monthly cell bill is "
23                          + cellBills[cellBills.length - 1] );
24   }
25 }
```

EXAMPLE 8.1   The *cellBills* Array

In lines 9–10, we declare and instantiate the *cellBills* array. Because the elements of *cellBills* are *doubles*, instantiating the array also initializes each element to 0.0 and sets the value of *cellBills.length* to 6. Thus, Figure 8.1 represents the *cellBills* array after line 10 is executed.

Lines 12–18 store values into each element of the array. The element at index *i* of the array is *cellBills[i]*. Remember that the first element of an array is always at index 0. Thus, the last element is *cellBills[5]*, or equivalently, *cellBills[cellBills.length – 1]*. Figure 8.2 shows how the *cellBills* array looks after lines 13–18 are executed.

Lines 20–21 print the value of the first element, and lines 22–23 print the value of the last element. The output of Example 8.1 is shown in Figure 8.3.

Array indexes *must* be between 0 and *arrayName.length – 1*. Attempting to access an element of an array using an index less than 0 or greater than *arrayName.length – 1* will compile without errors, but will generate an *ArrayIndexOutOfBoundsException* at run time. By default, this exception halts execution of the program.

Figure 8.1

The *cellBills* Array After Instantiation

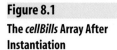
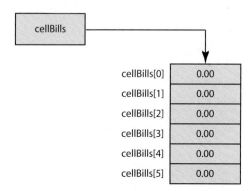

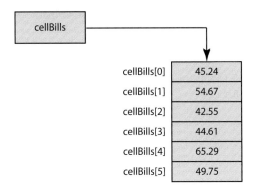

Figure 8.2
The *cellBills* Array After Assigning Values

```
cellBills[0]    45.24
cellBills[1]    54.67
cellBills[2]    42.55
cellBills[3]    44.61
cellBills[4]    65.29
cellBills[5]    49.75
```

Figure 8.3
Output of Example 8.1

```
The first monthly cell bill is 45.24
The last monthly cell bill is 49.75
```

For example, all the following expressions are invalid:

```
// invalid indexes for the cellBills array!!

cellBills[-1]                 // the lowest valid index is 0

cellBills[cellBills.length]   // the highest valid index is
                              // cellBills.length - 1

cellBills[150]                // the highest valid index is 5
```

COMMON ERROR TRAP

Attempting to access an element of an array using an index less than 0 or an index greater than *arrayName.length - 1* will generate an *ArrayIndexOutOfBoundsException* at run time.

Instantiating an array with a class data type involves two steps:

1. Instantiate the array.

2. Instantiate the objects.

Remember that the elements of an array with a class data type are object references. When the array is instantiated, all elements are set to *null.* Thus, the second step needs to be instantiating each object and assigning its reference to an array element.

Example 8.2 illustrates how to work with an array of objects. In this example, we reuse the *Auto* class from Chapter 7.

```
1 /* Working with an Array of Objects
2    Anderson, Franceschi
3 */
4
5 public class AutoArray
6 {
7   public static void main( String [ ] args )
8   {
9     // 1. instantiate cars array
10    Auto [ ] cars = new Auto [3];
11
12    // 2. instantiate Auto objects
13    Auto sportsCar = new Auto( "Ferrari", 100, 15.0 );
14    cars[0] = sportsCar;    // assign sportsCar to element 1
15    cars[1] = new Auto( );  // default Auto object
16    // cars[2] has not been instantiated and is null
17
18    // call Auto methods
19    System.out.println( "cars[0] is a " + cars[0].getModel( ) );
20
21    Auto myCar = cars[1];
22    System.out.println( "myCar has used " + myCar.getGallonsOfGas( )
23                        + " gallons of gas" );
24
25    // attempt to call method when Auto object is not instantiated
26    System.out.println( "cars[2] is a " + cars[2].getModel( ) );
27  }
28 }
```

EXAMPLE 8.2   Working with an Array of Objects

At lines 9–10, we declare and instantiate *cars*, an array of three *Auto* objects. At this point, each element has the value of *null*. Thus, our second step is to instantiate objects of the *Auto* class and assign their references to the array elements.

COMMON ERROR TRAP

With an array of objects, be sure that an array element points to an instantiated object before attempting to use that element to call a method of the class. Otherwise, a *NullPointer-Exception* will be generated.

At lines 13–14, we instantiate the *Auto* object *sportsCar* and assign the *sportsCar* reference to element 0. At line 15, we instantiate a default *Auto* object and assign its reference to element 1. We do not instantiate an object for element 2, which remains *null*.

We then call methods of the *Auto* class. Because the array elements are object references, to call a method for an object in an array, we use the array name and index, along with the dot notation. This is illustrated in line 19, where we print the model of element 0 by calling the *getModel* method. In

```
cars[0] is a Ferrari
myCar has used 0.0 gallons of gas
Exception in thread "main" java.lang.NullPointerException
        at AutoArray.main(AutoArray.java:26)
```

Figure 8.4
Output of Example 8.2

lines 21–23, we assign element 1 to the *Auto* reference *myCar*, then call the *getGallonsOfGas* method using the *myCar* reference.

Finally, line 26 attempts to retrieve the model of element 2; however, because *cars[2]* is *null*, a *NullPointerException* is generated. Figure 8.4 shows the output of this program.

Skill Practice
with these end-of-chapter questions

8.10.1 Multiple Choice Exercises

Questions 1, 2, 3, 4, 5, 7, 8

8.10.2 Reading and Understanding Code

Questions 13, 14, 15

8.10.4 Identifying Errors in Code

Questions 36, 37, 38, 40, 42, 44

8.10.5 Debugging Area

Question 45

8.10.8 Technical Writing

Questions 73, 75

8.3 Aggregate Array Operations

Once the array is declared and instantiated, it would be convenient if we could just use the array name to perform operations on the whole array, such as printing the array, copying the array to another array, inputting values to the array, and so on. Unfortunately, Java does not support these aggregate operations on arrays.

For example, attempting to print the array using the array name will *not* print all the elements of the array. Instead, this statement:

```
System.out.println( cellBills ); // incorrect attempt to print array!
```

calls the *toString* method of the *Array* class, which simply prints the name of the object's class and the hash code of the array name, for example, `[D@310d42`.

8.3.1 Printing Array Elements

To print all elements of an array, we need to use a loop that prints each element individually. A *for* loop is custom-made for processing all elements of an array in order. In fact, the following *for* loop header is a standard way to process all elements in an array:

```
for ( int i = 0; i < arrayName.length; i++ )
```

Note that the initialization statement:

```
int i = 0;
```

sets *i* to the index of the first element of the array.

The loop update statement:

```
i++;
```

increments *i* to the next index so that we process each element in order.

The loop condition:

```
i < arrayName.length
```

continues execution of the loop as long as the index is less than the *length* of the array.

Note that we use the *less than* operator ($<$) in the condition. Using the *less than or equal to* operator ($<=$) would cause us to attempt to reference an element with an index of *arrayName.length*, which is beyond the end of the array.

Inside the *for* loop, we refer to the current element being processed as

```
arrayName[i]
```

Example 8.3, whose output is shown in Figure 8.5, demonstrates how to print each element in an array.

 COMMON ERROR TRAP

In a *for* loop, using the condition:

```
i <= arrayName.length
```

will generate an *ArrayIndexOutOfBoundsException* because the index of the last element of an array is *arrayName.length – 1*.

```
1 /* Printing Array Elements
2      Anderson, Franceschi
3 */
```

```
 4
 5 public class PrintingArrayElements
 6 {
 7   public static void main( String [ ] args )
 8   {
 9     double [ ] cellBills = new double [6];
10     cellBills[0] = 45.24;
11     cellBills[1] = 54.67;
12     cellBills[2] = 42.55;
13     cellBills[3] = 44.61;
14     cellBills[4] = 65.29;
15     cellBills[5] = 49.75;
16
17     System.out.println( "Element\tValue" );
18     for ( int i = 0; i < cellBills.length; i++ )
19     {
20       System.out.println( i + "\t" + cellBills[i] );
21     }
22   }
23 }
```

EXAMPLE 8.3   Printing All Elements of an Array

In lines 9–15, we instantiate the *cellBills* array and assign values to its six elements. In line 18, we use the standard *for* loop header. Inside the *for* loop (line 20), we print each element's index and value.

8.3.2   Reading Data into an Array

Similarly, we can use the standard *for* loop to input data into an array. In Example 8.4, we use a *for* loop to prompt the user for each monthly cell phone bill and to assign the input value to the appropriate array elements.

```
Element Value
0       45.24
1       54.67
2       42.55
3       44.61
4       65.29
5       49.75
```

Figure 8.5

Output of Example 8.3

```
1 /* Reading data into an array
2    Anderson, Franceschi
3 */
4
5 import java.util.Scanner;
6
7 public class ReadingDataIntoAnArray
8 {
9   public static void main( String [ ] args )
10  {
11    Scanner scan = new Scanner( System.in );
12
13    double [ ] cellBills = new double[6];
14    for ( int i = 0; i < cellBills.length; i++ )
15    {
16      System.out.print( "Enter bill amount for month "
17                          + ( i + 1 ) + "\t" );
18      cellBills[i] = scan.nextDouble( ); // read current bill
19    }
20  }
21 }
```

EXAMPLE 8.4   Reading Data from the Console into an Array

At lines 14–19, our *for* loop prompts the user for a value for each element in the *cellBills* array. Note that our prompt uses the expression $(i + 1)$ for the month number. Although array indexes start at 0, people start counting at 1. If we used the array index in the prompt, we would ask the user for the bills for months 0 to 5. By adding 1 to the array index, we are able to prompt the user for months 1 through 6, which are the month numbers that the user expects.

SOFTWARE ENGINEERING TIP

Prompt for data in terms the user understands.

The output of Example 8.4 is shown in Figure 8.6.

Figure 8.6

Reading Data into an Array

```
Enter bill amount for month 1    63.33
Enter bill amount for month 2    54.27
Enter bill amount for month 3    71.19
Enter bill amount for month 4    59.03
Enter bill amount for month 5    62.65
Enter bill amount for month 6    65.08
```

8.3.3   Summing the Elements of an Array

To sum the elements of the array, we again use the standard *for* loop, as shown in Example 8.5.

```java
1 /* Summing Array Elements
2    Anderson, Franceschi
3 */
4
5 import java.text.NumberFormat;
6
7 public class SummingArrayElements
8 {
9  public static void main( String [ ] args )
10  {
11     double [ ] cellBills = new double [6];
12     cellBills[0] = 45.24;
13     cellBills[1] = 54.67;
14     cellBills[2] = 42.55;
15     cellBills[3] = 44.61;
16     cellBills[4] = 65.29;
17     cellBills[5] = 49.75;
18
19     double totalBills = 0.0;  // initialize total
20     for ( int i = 0; i < cellBills.length; i++ )
21     {
22       totalBills += cellBills[i];
23     }
24
25     NumberFormat priceFormat = NumberFormat.getCurrencyInstance( );
26     System.out.println( "Total for the bills: "
27                       + priceFormat.format( totalBills ) );
28  }
29 }
```

EXAMPLE 8.5   Summing the Elements of an Array

We fill the *cellBills* array with values at lines 12–17. We declare the *double* variable *totalBills* and initialize it to 0.0 at line 19. The *for* loop, at lines 20–23, adds each element of the array to *totalBills*. We use the *NumberFormat* class to format the value of *totalBills* as currency for output (lines 25–27). The output of Example 8.5 is shown in Figure 8.7.

Figure 8.7

Calculating the Total of All Elements

```
Total for the bills: $302.11
```

8.3.4   Finding Maximum or Minimum Values

Suppose we want to find the month that has the lowest bill. That would require finding a minimum value in the array and noting its index. Similarly, to find a month with the highest bill, we would need to find a maximum value in the array and note its index.

To find a maximum or minimum value in an array, we use a variation of the standard *for* loop. Example 8.6 finds the highest array value and its array index for our *cellBills* array of monthly cell bills.

```
1 /* Finding the maximum array value
2    Anderson, Franceschi
3 */
4
5 import java.text.NumberFormat;
6
7 public class MaxArrayValue
8 {
9  public static void main( String [ ] args )
10  {
11    double [ ] cellBills = new double [6];
12    cellBills[0] = 45.24;
13    cellBills[1] = 54.67;
14    cellBills[2] = 42.55;
15    cellBills[3] = 44.61;
16    cellBills[4] = 65.29;
17    cellBills[5] = 49.75;
18
19    int maxIndex = 0;    // initialize to index of first element
20    for ( int i = 1; i < cellBills.length; i++ )
21    {
22     if ( cellBills[i] > cellBills[maxIndex] )
23       maxIndex = i;  // save index of maximum value
24    }
25
26    NumberFormat priceFormat = NumberFormat.getCurrencyInstance( );
27    System.out.println ( "The highest bill, "
```

```
28                      + priceFormat.format( cellBills[maxIndex] )
29                      + ", was found at index " + maxIndex );
30   }
31 }
```

EXAMPLE 8.6   Finding a Maximum Value in an Array

We start by assuming that the first element is a maximum value. So we initialize an integer variable, *maxIndex*, to 0, at line 19. Then, at lines 20–24, starting at element 1, we step through the array, comparing the value of each element with the element at *maxIndex*. Whenever we find a value higher than the current maximum, we assign its index to *maxIndex* (line 23). When the *for* loop completes, *maxIndex* holds the index of the array element with a highest value. We then print both that index and the corresponding array value at lines 26–29. The output is shown in Figure 8.8.

What happens if the array has only one value? Will we still get the correct result? The answer is yes, because the single element will be at index 0. We start by assigning 0 to *maxIndex*. Then the *for* loop body will not execute because the condition will evaluate to *false*. So *maxIndex* will not be changed and remains set to 0.

What happens if more than one element holds the highest value? We find the index of the first element only, because our condition requires that the element value must be greater than the current maximum to change *maxIndex*.

8.3.5   Copying Arrays

Suppose we create a second array to hold a copy of our cell phone bills, as shown in the following statement:

```
double [ ] billsBackup = new double [6];
```

At this point, all elements of the *billsBackup* array are initialized automatically to 0.0. Figure 8.9 shows the current state of the *cellBills* and *billsBackup* arrays.

```
The highest bill, $65.29, was found at index 4
```

Figure 8.8
Output of Example 8.6

Figure 8.9

The *cellBills* and *billsBackup* Arrays

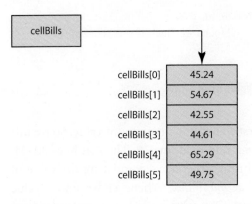

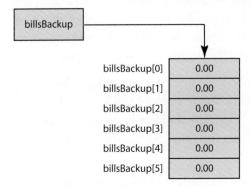

Then, if we want to copy the elements of the *cellBills* array to the corresponding elements of the *billsBackup* array, we might be tempted to use the assignment operator:

```
billsBackup = cellBills; // incorrect attempt to copy array elements!
```

This won't work. Because arrays are objects, the assignment operator copies the *cellBills* object reference to the *billsBackup* object reference. Both *cellBills* and *billsBackup* now point to the same object. The array data was not copied. In fact, we just lost the original *billsBackup* array. With no object reference pointing to it, the array is a candidate for garbage collection, as shown in Figure 8.10.

If we were to assign a new value to an element in the *billsBackup* array, we would change the element in the *cellBills* array also, because they are now the same array.

This statement:

```
billsBackup[4] = 38.00;
```

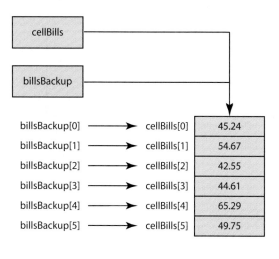

Figure 8.10
Assigning *cellBills* to *billsBackup*

has the effect shown in Figure 8.11.

Example 8.7 shows how to copy the elements in one array to another array.

```
1 /* Copying Array Elements to Another Array
2    Anderson, Franceschi
3 */
4
5 public class CopyingArrayElements
6 {
7  public static void main( String [ ] args )
8  {
9    double [ ] cellBills = { 45.24, 54.67, 42.55, 44.61, 65.29, 49.75 };
10
11    double billsBackup [ ] = new double [cellBills.length];
12    for ( int i = 0; i < cellBills.length; i++ )
13    {
14      billsBackup[i] = cellBills[i]; // copy each element
15    }
16
```

Figure 8.11

**Altering *billsBackup*
Alters *cellBills* Array**

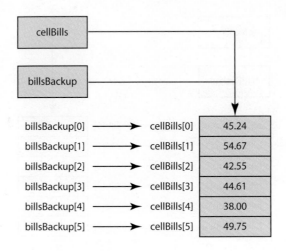

```
17    billsBackup[4] = 38.00;  // change value in billsBackup
18
19    System.out.println( "cellBills\nElement\tValue " );
20    for ( int i = 0; i < cellBills.length; i++ )
21    {
22      System.out.println ( i + "\t" + cellBills[i] );
23    }
24
25    System.out.println( "\nbillsBackup\nElement\tValue " );
26    for ( int i = 0; i < billsBackup.length; i++ )
27    {
28      System.out.println ( i + "\t" + billsBackup[i] );
29    }
30  }
31 }
```

EXAMPLE 8.7   Copying Array Elements into Another Array

At line 9, we instantiate the array *cellBills* using an initialization list. At line 11, we declare and instantiate the array *billsBackup* to have the same size as the original array *cellBills*. At lines 12–15, we use a standard *for* loop to copy one element at a time from the *cellBills* array to the *billsBackup* array.

Now the *billsBackup* array and the *cellBills* array are separate arrays with their own copies of the element values, as shown in Figure 8.12. Changing an element in one array will have no effect on the value of the corresponding element in the other array.

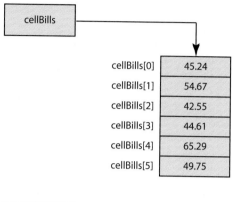

Figure 8.12

Arrays After Copying Each Element

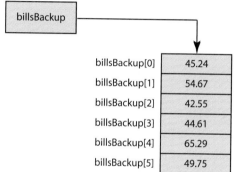

We illustrate this by assigning a new value to an element in the array *billsBackup* (line 17). Finally, we use two *for* loops to print the contents of both arrays. As Figure 8.13 shows, the value is changed only in the array *billsBackup*.

Be aware, however, that when you copy an array whose elements are objects, even using the *for* loop structure, you are copying object references. The result is that the corresponding elements of each array will point to the same object. If an object in one array is changed, that change will be reflected in the other array as well.

8.3.6   Changing the Size of an Array

Arrays are assigned a length when they are instantiated, and the *length* of an array becomes a constant value. But what if we want to change the number of elements in an array after it has been instantiated?

For example, our *cellBills* array contains six elements, holding six months' worth of cell phone bills. If we decide to collect a year's worth of cell phone

Figure 8.13

Output of Example 8.7

```
cellBills
Element Value
0       45.24
1       54.67
2       42.55
3       44.61
4       65.29
5       49.75

billsBackup
Element Value
0       45.24
1       54.67
2       42.55
3       44.61
4       38.0
5       49.75
```

bills, we would need an array with 12 elements. We could instantiate a new version of the *cellBills* array with 12 elements, using this statement:

```
cellBills = new double [12];
```

That statement instantiates a new array of *doubles* all initialized to 0.0. But what happened to the original array of six elements? Since the *cellBills* reference now refers to the new, 12-element array, the 6-element array has no object reference pointing to it, so there is no way we can access the array's values. That is not the result we intended!

To expand the size of an array while maintaining the values of the original array, we can use the following technique:

1. Instantiate an array with the new size, giving the new array a temporary reference.

2. Copy the elements from the original array to the new array.

3. Point the original array reference to the new array.

4. Assign a *null* value to the temporary array reference.

Thus, instead of immediately pointing *cellBills* to the new array, we should instantiate a 12-element array using a temporary array name, copy the six elements from the *cellBills* array into the 12-element array, assign the *cellBills* reference to the new array, and assign *null* to the temporary array reference. The following code will do that:

```
double [ ] temp = new double [12];   //instantiate new array

// copy all elements from cellBills to temp
for ( int i = 0; i < cellBills.length; i++ )
{
     temp[i] = cellBills[i]; // copy each element
}

cellBills = temp; // assign temp to cellBills
temp = null;      // temp no longer points to cellBills
```

The last statement sets *temp* to *null* so that we don't have two references to the *cellBills* array.

This is a tedious operation. And what if after having increased the size of an array, we find later in our program that we need to increase the size again? Clearly, arrays are not meant to be expanded via this artificial process. In Chapter 9, we introduce the *ArrayList* class, which allows for automatic expansion.

 **REFERENCE POINT**

The *ArrayList* class is discussed in Chapter 9; it offers array functionality with automatic expansion as needed.

8.3.7   Comparing Arrays for Equality

To compare whether two arrays are equal, first determine if they are equal in length, and then use a *for* loop to compare the corresponding elements in each array. That is, compare element 0 in the first array to element 0 in the second array; compare element 1 in the first array to element 1 in the second array; and so on. If all elements in the first array are equal to the corresponding elements in the second array, then the arrays are equal. Example 8.8 compares two arrays of *doubles*, a primitive data type.

```
1 /* Comparing Arrays of basic data types
2    Anderson, Franceschi
3 */
4
5 public class ComparingArrays
6 {
```

```
 7  public static void main( String [ ] args )
 8  {
 9    double [ ] cellBills1 = { 45.24, 54.67, 42.55, 44.61, 65.29, 49.75 };
10    double [ ] cellBills2 = { 45.24, 54.67, 41.99, 44.61, 65.29, 49.75 };
11
12    boolean isEqual = true;
13    if ( cellBills1.length != cellBills2.length )
14    {
15      isEqual = false; // arrays are not the same size
16    }
17    else
18    {
19      for ( int i = 0; i < cellBills1.length && isEqual; i++ )
20      {
21        if ( Math.abs( cellBills1[i] - cellBills2[i] ) > 0.001 )
22        {
23          isEqual = false; // elements are not equal
24        }
25      }
26    }
27
28    if ( isEqual )
29      System.out.println( "cellBills1 and cellBills2 are equal" );
30    else
31      System.out.println( "cellBills1 and cellBills2 are not equal" );
32  }
33 }
```

EXAMPLE 8.8   Comparing Arrays of Primitive Data Types

Before we begin the *for* loop, we declare at line 12 a *boolean* variable, *isEqual*, and set it to *true*. In this way, we assume the arrays are equal. Then, our first step is to compare whether the two arrays have the same length (line 13). If they are not the same size, the arrays cannot be equal, so we set *isEqual* to *false* and execution skips to line 28. If the two arrays are the same size, we use a *for* loop at lines 19–25 to test whether the corresponding elements in each array are equal. Note that we have added a second test to the *for* loop condition (*isEqual*). If any corresponding elements are not equal, we set *isEqual* to *false* at line 23. This will cause the condition of the *for* loop to evaluate to *false*, and we exit the *for* loop. Thus, when the *for* loop finishes executing, if any corresponding elements did not match, *isEqual* will be

```
cellBills1 and cellBills2 are not equal
```

Figure 8.14
Output of Example 8.8

false. If both arrays are the same size and all corresponding elements are equal, we never change the value of *isEqual*, so it remains *true*. The output from this example is shown in Figure 8.14.

Naturally, if the elements of the arrays are *ints*, *booleans*, or *chars*, we would use the equality operator (!=) at line 21 as in:

```
if ( intArray1[i] != intArray2[i] )
```

assuming the two arrays we are comparing have names *intArray1* and *intArray2*.

If the elements of the arrays are objects, your *for* loop should call the *equals* method of the objects' class. Thus, to compare two arrays of *Auto* objects, named *cars1* and *cars2*, we would use the following code instead of the condition at line 21:

```
if ( ! cars1[i].equals( cars2[i] ) )
```

A pitfall to avoid is attempting to test whether two arrays are equal using the equality operator (==). This code:

```
if ( cellBills == billsBackup )
```

will not compare the data of the two arrays. It will compare whether the *cellBills* and *billsBackup* object references are equal; that is, whether they point to the same array.

Similarly, the *equals* method inherited from *Object* also returns the wrong results.

This code:

```
if ( cellBills.equals( billsBackup ) )
```

will return *true* only if both object references point to the same array.

COMMON ERROR TRAP

Because arrays are objects, attempting to compare two arrays using the equality operator (==) will compare whether the two array references point to the same array in memory, not whether the data in the two arrays are equal. Calling the *equals* method inherited from the *Object* class yields similar results.

8.3.8   Displaying Array Data as a Bar Chart

One way to display array data is graphically, by drawing a bar chart. For example, the bar chart in Figure 8.15 displays the data in the *cellBills* array.

Each bar is simply a rectangle. Example 8.9 shows the code to generate Figure 8.15.

```
1  /* BarChart Applet
2     Anderson, Franceschi
3  */
4
5  import javax.swing.JApplet;
6  import java.awt.Graphics;
7  import java.awt.Color;
8
9  public class BarChartApplet extends JApplet
10 {
11   final int LEFT_MARGIN = 20;         // starting x coordinate
12   final int BASE_Y_BAR  = 150;        // bottom of the bars
13   final int BASE_Y_VALUE = 175;       // bottom of the values
14   final int BAR_WIDTH = 30;           // width of each bar
15   final int SPACE_BETWEEN_BARS = 5;   // pixels between bars
16   double [ ] cellBills = { 45.24, 54.67, 42.55, 44.61, 65.29, 49.75 };
17
18   public void paint( Graphics g )
19   {
20     super.paint( g );
21
```

Figure 8.15

The *cellBills* Array as a Bar Chart

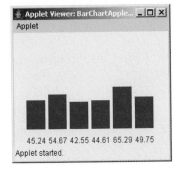

```
22   g.setColor( Color.BLUE );          // bars will be blue
23   int xStart = LEFT_MARGIN;           // x value for first bar
24
25   for ( int i = 0; i < cellBills.length; i++ )
26   {
27     g.fillRect( xStart, BASE_Y_BAR - ( int )( cellBills[i] ),
28                 BAR_WIDTH, ( int )( cellBills[i] ) );
29
30     g.drawString( Double.toString( cellBills[i] ),
31                   xStart, BASE_Y_VALUE );
32
33     // move to starting x value for next bar
34     xStart += BAR_WIDTH + SPACE_BETWEEN_BARS;
35   }
36 }
37 }
```

EXAMPLE 8.9   Displaying Array Values as a Bar Chart

To create the bar chart, we use our standard *for* loop at lines 25–35 in the *paint* method and call the *fillRect* method of the *Graphics* class to draw a rectangle for each element (lines 27–28). We use the *drawString* method at lines 30–31 to print the value of each element.

REFERENCE POINT

The *fillRect* and *drawString* methods of the *Graphics* class are discussed in Chapter 4.

As you recall, the *fillRect* method takes four arguments: the upper-left *x* value, the upper-left *y* value, the rectangle's width, and the rectangle's height.

We can determine the argument values for the *fillRect* method for each element using the following approach, as illustrated in Figure 8.16:

- Width: The width of the bar is a constant value. For our bar chart, we chose a width of 30 pixels; the constant *BAR_WIDTH* stores that value (line 14).

- Height: The height for each bar is the value of the array element being charted. Because the *fillRect* method expects an integer value for the height, however, we will need to type cast each *cellBills* element to an *int*. Thus, in the *fillRect* method call (lines 27–28), we represent the height of a bar as:

  ```
  ( int )( cellBills[i] )
  ```

- Upper-left *y* value: Similarly, the upper-left *y* value will be the height of the bar subtracted from the base *y* value for all the bars; the base *y* value for all the bars is the constant *BASE_Y_BAR* defined in line 12. We subtract the value of the element from the base of the bar because *y* values increase from the top of the window to the bottom. Thus, in our *fillRect* method call, we represent the upper-left *y* value of a bar as:

```
BASE_Y_BAR - ( int )( cellBills[i] )
```

- Upper-left *x* value: We'll start the first bar at the left side of the window, plus a left margin value, represented by the constant *LEFT_MARGIN* (line 11). After we draw each bar, our *for* loop needs to move the starting *x* value to the position of the next bar. To do this, at line 34, we increment the starting *x* value by the width of the bar, *BAR_WIDTH* (defined on line 14), plus the space between bars, *SPACE_BETWEEN_BARS* (defined on line 15).

The arguments to the *drawString* method of the *Graphics* class are the *String* to display and the base *x* and *y* values. At lines 30–31, we convert the *cellBills* element to a *String* using the *toString* method of the *Double* wrapper class. The base *x* value is the same as the starting *x* value for the

Figure 8.16

Arguments for Drawing Each Bar

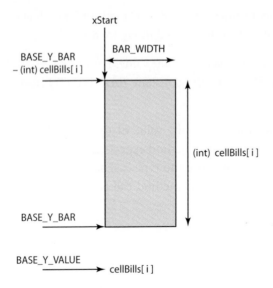

element's bar, and the base y coordinate, *BASE_Y_VALUE*, is the base position for printing the array values (defined on line 13).

CODE IN ACTION

On the CD-ROM included with this book, you will find a Flash movie with step-by-step illustrations of working with arrays. Click on the link for Chapter 8 to start the movie.

Skill Practice
with these end-of-chapter questions

8.10.1   Multiple Choice Exercises

Questions 6, 9, 10

8.10.2   Reading and Understanding Code

Questions 16, 17, 18, 19, 20, 21

8.10.3   Fill In the Code

Questions 27, 28, 29, 30, 31

8.10.4   Identifying Errors in Code

Questions 39, 41, 43

8.10.5   Debugging Area

Questions 46, 47, 48

8.10.8   Technical Writing

Question 76

8.4   Programming Activity 1: Working with Arrays

In this activity, you will work with a 15-element integer array. Specifically, you will write the code to perform the following operations:

1. fill the array with random numbers between 50 and 80

2. print the array

3. set every array element to a specified value

4. count the number of elements with a specified value

5. find the minimum value in the array

The framework for this Programming Activity will animate your algorithm so that you can check the accuracy of your code. For example, Figure 8.17 shows the application counting the elements having the value 73.

Figure 8.17

Animation of the Programming Activity

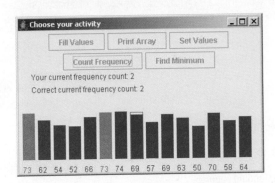

At this point, the application has found the value 73 in elements 0 and 5 and is comparing the value 73 with the value 69 in element 7.

Instructions

In the Chapter 8 Programming Activity 1 directory on the CD-ROM accompanying this book, you will find the source files needed to complete this activity. Copy all the files to a directory on your computer. Note that all files should be in the same directory.

Open the *ArrayPractice1.java* source file. Searching for five asterisks (*****) in the source code will position you at the sample method and the four other locations where you will add your code. We have provided the sample code for task number 1, which you can use as a model for completing the other tasks. In every task, you will fill in the code for a method that will manipulate an existing array of 15 integers. You should not instantiate the array; we have done that for you. Example 8.10 shows the section of the *ArrayPractice1* source code where you will add your code.

Note that for the *countFrequency* and *findMinimum* methods, we provide a dummy *return* statement (*return 0;*) We do this so that the source code will compile. In this way, you can write and test each method separately, using stepwise refinement. When you are ready to write the *countFrequency* and *findMinimum* methods, just replace the dummy *return* statements with the appropriate *return* statement for that method.

```
// ***** 1. The first method has been coded as an example
/**  Fills the array with random numbers between 50 and 80.
 *    The instance variable arr is the integer array
 *    to be filled with values
 */
public void fillValues( )
{
    Random rand = new Random( );
    for ( int i = 0; i < arr.length; i++ )
    {
        arr[i] = rand.nextInt( 31 ) + 50;
        animate( -1 );  // needed to create visual feedback
    }
}
// end of fillValues method


// ***** 2. student writes this method
/** Prints the array to the console with elements separated
 *    by a space
 *    The instance variable arr is the integer array to be printed
 */
public void printArray(  )
{
 // Note:  to animate the algorithm, put this method call as the
 // last statement in your for loop:
 //                  animate( i );
 //     where i is the index of the current array element
 // Write your code here:


} // end of printArray method


// ***** 3. student writes this method
/** Sets all the elements in the array to parameter value
 *    The instance variable arr is the integer array to be processed
 *    @param  value    the value to which to set the array elements
 */
public void setValues( int value )
{
 // Note:  to animate the algorithm, put this method call as the
 // last statement in your for loop
 //            animate( i );
 //      where i is the index of the current array element
```

```java
 // Write your code here:


} // end of setValues method

// ***** 4. student writes this method
/** Counts number of elements equal to parameter value
 *     The instance variable arr is the integer array to be processed
 *       @param  value     the value to count
 *       @return   the number of elements equal to value
 */
public int countFrequency( int value )
{
 // Note:  to animate the algorithm, put this method call as the
 // last statement in your for loop
 //          animate( i, count );
 //          where i is the index of the current array element
 //                 count is the variable holding the frequency
 // Write your code here:


    return 0; // replace this line with your return statement

} // end of countFrequency method

// ***** 5. student writes this method
/** Finds and returns the minimum value in arr
 *     The instance variable arr is the integer array to be processed
 *       @return the minimum value found in arr
 */
public int findMinimum(  )
{
 // Note:  to animate the algorithm, put this method call as the
 // last statement in your for loop
 //        animate( i, minimum );
 //             where i is the index of the current array element
 //                 minimum is the variable holding the minimum
 // Write your code here:



    return 0; // replace this line with your return statement

} // end of findMinimum method

// End of student code
```

EXAMPLE 8.10   Location of Student Code in *ArrayPractice1*

Our framework will animate your algorithm so that you can watch your code work. For this to happen, be sure that your *for* loop calls the *animate* method. The arguments that you send to *animate* will differ depending on the task you are coding. Detailed instructions for each task are included in the code.

To test your code, compile and run the *ArrayPractice1* source code. Figure 8.18 shows the graphics window when the program begins. Because the values of the array are randomly generated, the values will be different each time the program runs. To test any method, click the appropriate button.

Troubleshooting

If your method implementation does not animate, follow these tips:

- Verify that the last statement in your *for* loop is a call to the *animate* method and that you passed the appropriate arguments to the *animate* method.

- Verify that your *for* loop has curly braces. For example, the *animate* method call is outside the body of this *for* loop:

```
for ( int i = 0; i< arr.length; i++ )
    System.out.println ( arr [i] );
    animate( i );  // this statement is outside the for loop
```

Remember that without curly braces, the *for* loop body consists of only the first statement following the *for* loop header. Enclosing both statements within curly braces will make the *animate* method call part of the *for* loop body.

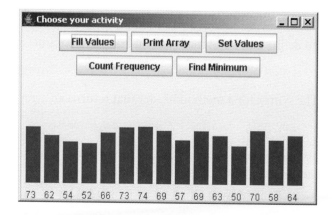

Figure 8.18

The Graphics Window When the Application Begins

```
for ( int i = 0; i < arr.length; i++ )
{
        System.out.println ( arr [i] );
        animate( i );
}
```

- Verify that you did not instantiate a new array. Perform all operations on the array passed to the method as a parameter.

DISCUSSION QUESTIONS ?

1. Could you use the following *for* loop header in every method? Explain why or why not.

   ```
   for ( int i = 0; i < arr.length; i++ )
   ```

2. How would you modify the *findMinimum* method to return the index of the minimum value?

8.5   Using Arrays in Classes

8.5.1   Using Arrays in User-Defined Classes

An array can be used inside a user-defined class just like any other variable. In particular,

- an array can be an instance variable.

- an array can be a parameter to a method.

- a method can return an array.

- an array can be a local variable inside a method.

> **COMMON ERROR TRAP**
>
> If you think of the brackets as being part of the data type of the array, then it's easy to remember that the brackets are included in the method header—where the data types of parameters are given—but that brackets are not included in method calls, where the data itself is given.

To define a method that takes an array as a parameter, use this syntax:

```
accessModifier returnType methodName( dataType [ ] arrayName )
```

The syntax for a method header that returns an array is

```
accessModifier dataType [ ] methodName( parameterList )
```

To pass an array as an argument to a method, just use the array name without brackets as the argument value:

```
methodName( arrayName )
```

In Example 8.11, we define a class named *CellPhone* that illustrates the use of arrays in a class.

```
1  /** CellPhone class
2  *    Anderson, Franceschi
3  */
4
5  import java.text.DecimalFormat;
6
7  public class CellPhone
8  {
9    public final int MONTHS = 6;  // default number of months
10   private String phoneNumber;
11   private double [ ] cellBills;
12
13   /** Default constructor
14   *    creates cellBills with MONTHS elements
15   */
16   public CellPhone( )
17   {
18      phoneNumber = "";
19      cellBills = new double [MONTHS];
20   }
21
22   /** Constructor
23   *  @param  number  cell phone number
24   *  @param  bills   array of monthly bills
25   */
26   public CellPhone( String number, double [ ] bills )
27   {
28     phoneNumber = number;
29
30     // instantiate array with same length as parameter
31     cellBills = new double [bills.length];
32
33     // copy parameter array to cellBills array
34     for ( int i = 0; i < cellBills.length; i++ )
35     {
36       cellBills[i] = bills[i];
37     }
38   }
39
40   /** Returns the phone number
41   *    @return the phone number
42   */
43   public String getPhoneNumber( )
44   {
```

```
45      return phoneNumber;
46    }
47
48    /** Returns an array of cell phone bills
49     *   @return   copy of cellBills array
50     */
51    public double [ ] getCellBills( )
52    {
53      double [ ] temp = new double [cellBills.length];
54      for ( int i = 0; i < cellBills.length; i ++ )
55      {
56        temp[i] = cellBills[i];
57      }
58      return temp;
59    }
60
61    /**  Calculates total of all cell phone bills
62     *    @return  total of all elements in cellBills array
63     */
64    public double calcTotalBills( )
65    {
66      double total = 0.0;  // initialize total to 0.0
67
68      for ( int i = 0; i < cellBills.length; i++ )
69      {
70        total += cellBills[i];  // add current element to total
71      }
72      return total;
73    }
74
75    /** Finds a maximum bill
76     * @return largest value in cellBills array
77     */
78    public double findMaximumBill( )
79    {
80      double max = cellBills[0]; // assume first element is max
81
82      for ( int i = 1; i < cellBills.length; i++ )
83      {
84        if ( cellBills[i] > max )
85          max = cellBills[i];  // save new maximum
86      }
87      return max;
88    }
89
90    /** Returns printable version of CellPhone object
91     *   @return phone number plus each month's bill
```

```
92     */
93     public String toString( )
94     {
95       String returnValue = phoneNumber + "\n";
96       DecimalFormat money = new DecimalFormat( "$##0.00" );
97       for ( int i = 0; i < cellBills.length; i++ )
98       {
99           returnValue += money.format( cellBills[i] ) + "\t";
100      }
101      returnValue += "\n";
102
103      return returnValue;
104    }
105
106    /**  Compares two CellPhone objects for equality
107     *    @param c CellPhone object
108     *    @return  true if objects are equal; false, otherwise
109     */
110    public boolean equals( Object c )
111    {
112      if ( !( c instanceof CellPhone ) )
113          return false;
114      else
115      {
116          CellPhone objCP = ( CellPhone ) c;
117          if ( !( phoneNumber.equals( objCP.phoneNumber ) ) )
118            return false;
119
120          if ( cellBills.length != objCP.cellBills.length )
121            return false; // arrays are not the same length
122
123          for ( int i = 0; i < cellBills.length; i++ )
124          {
125             if ( cellBills[i] != objCP.cellBills[i] )
126               return false;
127          }
128          return true;
129      }
130    }
131 }
```

EXAMPLE 8.11   The *CellPhone* Class

Our *CellPhone* class defines three instance variables in lines 9–11: the phone number (a *String* named *phoneNumber*), monthly bills (an array of *doubles* named *cellBills*), and a constant named *MONTHS*, whose value, 6, represents the number of monthly cell bills, and therefore the length of the *cellBills* array if a *CellPhone* object is instantiated using the default constructor. Note that since *MONTHS* is a constant, we made it *public.*

When your class has instance variables that are arrays, you will need to take a little extra care to ensure that encapsulation is not violated.

Let's start with initialization of the array. The overloaded constructor of the *CellPhone* class, whose method header is at line 26, includes an array parameter. With parameters of primitive types, the constructor can simply assign the value of the parameter to the instance variable. As we have seen, however, the name of an array is an object reference, which contains the location of the array in memory. If the constructor merely assigns the array parameter, *bills*, to our array instance variable, *cellBills*, as in the following code:

```
cellBills = bills;  // incorrect! Client still has reference!
```

then *bills* and *cellBills* would point to the same array. That means that the client still has a reference to the array, and the client can change the array values without going through the mutator methods of the class. For example, if the client executes this statement:

```
bills[2] = 75.00;
```

then *cellBills[2]* also gets the value 75.00, because they are the same array. This is clearly a violation of encapsulation, which means that a client should be able to change the *private* fields of a class only by calling the mutator methods of the class.

To avoid this problem, our constructor instantiates a new *cellBills* array that is the same size as the array passed as a parameter, and then copies the elements of the parameter array into the new *cellBills* array (lines 30–37).

SOFTWARE ENGINEERING TIP

Sharing array references with the client violates encapsulation. To return an array from a method, copy the elements of the instance variable array to a temporary array and return a reference to the temporary array. Similarly, to accept an array as a parameter to a method, instantiate a new array and copy the elements of the parameter array to the new array.

There are similar considerations in implementing the accessor method of an array instance variable. With instance variables of primitive types, the accessor methods simply return the value of the instance variable. Our accessor for *cellBills* (lines 48–59) has an array as a return value. If we return the *cellBills* reference, however, we run into the same problem with encapsulation; that is, if our accessor for the *cellBills* instance variable uses this statement:

```
return cellBills; // incorrect! Client has reference to instance variable
```

we give the client a reference to the *cellBills* array, and the client can directly change the values of the array without calling the mutator methods of the class. Just as the constructor instantiated a new array and copied the parameter array's value to the new array, the accessor method should instantiate a new array, copy the *cellBills* array to it, and return a reference to the new array. Thus, at line 53, we declare and instantiate a local array variable named *temp*. At lines 54–57, we copy the contents of *cellBills* into *temp*, and return *temp* at line 58.

We also provide a method *calcTotalBills* (lines 61–73) that calculates the total of the monthly bills using the accumulation technique discussed earlier in the chapter and a *findMaximumBill* method (lines 75–88), which finds a maximum value in the *cellBills* array, also using techniques discussed earlier in the chapter.

Our *toString* method (lines 90–104) builds up a *String* named *returnValue* by first including *phoneNumber*, then formatting each bill using a *DecimalFormat* pattern for money and concatenating that value, plus a tab, to *returnValue*.

The *equals* method (lines 106–130) compares the phone number and each element of the *cellBills* array in the object with the phone number and corresponding element in the *cellBills* array in the parameter object.

We can test our *CellPhone* class with the client class shown in Example 8.12. The output is shown in Figure 8.19 on page 505.

```
 1 /**  Client to exercise the CellPhone class
 2 *  Anderson, Franceschi
 3 */
 4
 5 import java.text.DecimalFormat;
 6
 7 public class CellPhoneClient
 8 {
 9    public static void main( String [ ] args )
10    {
11       double [ ] bills = new double[3]; // array of cell phone bills
12       bills[0] = 24.60; // assign values
13       bills[1] = 48.75;
14       bills[2] = 62.50;
15
16       // instantiate CellPhone object using default constructor
17       CellPhone c1 = new CellPhone( );
18
19       // instantiate two identical CellPhone objects
20       CellPhone c2 = new CellPhone( "555-555-5555", bills );
21       CellPhone c3 = new CellPhone( "555-555-5555", bills );
22
23       // print data from c1 and c2
24       System.out.println( "c1 = " + c1.toString( ) );
25       System.out.println( "c2 = " + c2.toString( ) );
26
27       // find and print maximum bill
```

```
28      DecimalFormat money = new DecimalFormat( "$##0.00" );
29      System.out.println( "\nThe highest bill is "
30                      + money.format( c2.findMaximumBill( ) ) );
31
32      // find and print total of all bills
33      System.out.println( "\nThe total of all bills is "
34                      + money.format( c2.calcTotalBills( ) ) );
35
36      System.out.println( ); // print blank line
37      // call equals method
38      if ( c2.equals( c3 ) )
39          System.out.println( "c2 and c3 are equal" );
40      else
41          System.out.println( "c2 and c3 are not equal" );
42
43      // test encapsulation
44      // set new value in original array
45      bills[2] = 100.00;
46      // print c2 to show value in object not changed
47      System.out.println( "\nafter client changes original array\n"
48                          + "c2 = "  + c2.toString( ) );
49
50      // test encapsulation further
51      // get array of cell bills and store in new array
52      double [ ] billsCopy = c2.getCellBills( );
53
54      billsCopy[1] = 50.00;  // change value of one element
55      // print c2 to show value in object not changed
56      System.out.println( "\nafter client changes returned array\n"
57                          + "c2 = "  + c2.toString( ) );
58   }
59 }
```

EXAMPLE 8.12 **The *CellPhoneClient* Class**

In the *CellPhoneClient*, we instantiate three *CellPhone* objects. We instantiate *c1* using the default constructor (line 17), giving it an empty phone number and six months of bills initialized to 0.00, as shown in line 24, when we use the *toString* method to print *c1*'s data. We set up a *bills* array with three values (lines 11–14) and pass *bills* to the overloaded constructor (lines 20–21) to instantiate *c2* and *c3* with identical data. We then use *toString* to print *c2*'s data (line 25).

We then call the *findMaximumBill* method and print its return value (lines 27–30). Next, we call the *calcTotalBills* method and print its return value (lines 32–34).

Figure 8.19
Output from the
CellPhoneClient Class

```
c1 =
$0.00    $0.00    $0.00    $0.00    $0.00    $0.00

c2 = 555-555-5555
$24.60   $48.75   $62.50

The highest bill is $62.50

The total of all bills is $135.85

c2 and c3 are equal

after client changes original array
c2 = 555-555-5555
$24.60   $48.75   $62.50

after client changes returned array
c2 = 555-555-5555
$24.60   $48.75   $62.50
```

A call to the *equals* method to compare *c2* and *c3* (lines 37–41) returns a value of *true*, because the two objects have the same data.

Finally, we test encapsulation two ways. First, we change a value in the *bills* array, then print *c2* again to verify that its data has not changed (lines 43–48). Second, we call the accessor method for the *cellBills* array and change a value in the array returned from the method call. We again print *c2* to verify that its data is unchanged (lines 50–57). Testing the *CellPhone* class with such an example is helpful in checking that we have correctly implemented the class.

8.5.2   Retrieving Command Line Arguments

The syntax of an array parameter for a method might look familiar to you. We've seen it repeatedly in Java applications in the header for the *main* method:

```
public static void main( String [ ] args )
```

As you can see, *main* receives a *String* array as a parameter. That array of *Strings* holds the arguments, if any, that the user sends to the program from the command line. An argument might be the name of a file for the program to read or some configuration parameters that specify preferences in how the application should perform its function.

The sample program in Example 8.13 demonstrates how to retrieve the parameters sent to a Java application. Because *args* is a *String* array, we can use the *length* field to get the number of parameters (lines 8–9), and we use our standard *for* loop format (lines 10–13) to retrieve and print each parameter, as shown in Figure 8.20.

```
1  /** Print Command Line arguments
2   *    Anderson, Franceschi
3   */
4  public class CommandLineArguments
5  {
6    public static void main( String [ ] args )
7    {
8      System.out.println( "The number of parameters is "
9                            + args.length );
10     for ( int i = 0; i < args.length; i ++ )
11     {
12         System.out.println( "args[" + i + "]: "  + args[i] );
13     }
14   }
15 }
```

EXAMPLE 8.13   Retrieving Command Line Arguments

Figure 8.20 shows the output produced when we invoke the program as

```
java CommandLineArguments input.txt output.txt
```

Skill Practice
with these end-of-chapter questions

8.10.1 Multiple Choice Exercises

Question 11

8.10.2 Reading and Understanding Code

Questions 22, 23, 24, 25, 26

8.10.3 Fill In the Code

Questions 32, 33, 34, 35

8.10.6 Write a Short Program

Questions 49, 50, 51, 52, 53, 54, 55, 56, 58, 59, 60, 61

```
The number of parameters is 2
args[0]: input.txt
args[1]: output.txt
```

Figure 8.20
**Output from Example
8.13**

8.6 Searching and Sorting Arrays

Arrays are great instruments for storing a large number of related values. As seen earlier in this chapter, we can use arrays to store daily temperatures, CD titles, telephone bills, quiz grades, and other sets of related values. Once the data is stored in an array, we will want to manipulate that data. A very common operation is searching an array for a specific value.

8.6.1 Sequential Search of an Unsorted Array

Let's assume you are the manager of a DVD rental store. Each member customer gets a card with a unique member ID. You have decided to pick five member IDs at random and give those members a free gift the next time they visit the store. So you set up a *DVDWinners* class with two array instance variables:

- An array of *ints* that holds the member IDs of the winners

- An array of *Strings* that holds the corresponding prizes

Note that both arrays have five elements and that there is a one-to-one correspondence between the two arrays. Winner #1 will receive prize #1, winner #2 will receive prize #2, and so on. This programming technique is called **parallel arrays**.

You fill the *winners* array with member IDs chosen randomly from entry cards members have filled out. You fill the *prizes* array with *Strings* representing prize descriptions. When a member rents a DVD, you can look through the *winners* array for the member's ID. If the member's ID is in the *winners* array, you use its array index in the *prizes* array to retrieve the prize that the member won. If the member ID is not found in the array, you know the member is not a winner.

The *DVDWinners* class is shown in Example 8.14.

```
1 /** Winners of Free DVD Rentals
2  *   Anderson, Franceschi
3  */
```

```
4
5  import java.util.Random;
6
7  public class DVDWinners
8  {
9     // array to hold winning member numbers chosen at random
10    private int [ ] winners;
11    // parallel array that holds prizes
12    private String [ ] prizes = { "3 free rentals!",
13                                  "2 free rentals!",
14                                  "1 free rental!",
15                                  "free popcorn!",
16                                  "a free box of candy!" };
17    /** Default constructor instantiates winners array
18     *    and randomly generates winning member IDs
19     */
20    public DVDWinners( )
21    {
22      winners  = new int [prizes.length];
23      fillWinners( ); // generate winner member IDs
24    }
25
26    /** Utility method generates winner member IDs
27     *    and stores them in the winners array
28     */
29    private void fillWinners( )
30    {
31      Random rand = new Random( );
32      for ( int i = 0; i < winners.length; i++ )
33      {
34        winners[i] = rand.nextInt( 5000 ) + 1;
35      }
36    }
37
38    /** Calls indexOfWinner with the member number
39     *    then translates return value into the prize won
40     *    @param memberNumber value to find
41     *    @return prize
42     */
43    public String getPrize( int memberNumber )
44    {
45      int prizeIndex = indexOfWinner( memberNumber );
```

```
46     if ( prizeIndex == -1 )
47         return "Sorry, member is not a winner.";
48     else
49         return "You win " + prizes[prizeIndex];
50   }
51
52   /** Performs sequential search of winners array
53    *   @param key member ID to find in winners array
54    *   @return index of key if found, -1 if not found
55    */
56   private int indexOfWinner( int key )
57   {
58     for ( int i = 0; i < winners.length; i++ )
59     {
60       if ( winners[i] == key )
61           return i;
62     }
63     return -1;
64   }
65
66   /** Returns printable version of DVDWinners object
67    *   @return winning numbers separated by a tab
68    */
69   public String toString( )
70   {
71     String returnValue = "";
72     for ( int i = 0; i < winners.length; i++ )
73     {
74       returnValue += winners[i] + "\t";
75     }
76     return returnValue;
77   }
78 }
```

EXAMPLE 8.14   The *DVDWinners* Class

The constructor randomly generates values to fill the array by calling the utility method, *fillWinners* (lines 26–36). In the interest of keeping things simple, we have coded the *fillWinners* method in such a way that it does not necessarily generate different numbers; however, the likelihood of two winning numbers being equal is very small. We declare the *fillWinners* method as *private* because it is designed to be called only by the methods of this class.

Our *indexOfWinner* method (lines 52–64) performs a **Sequential Search,** which compares the member ID to each element in the array one by one. The *indexOfWinner* method accepts a parameter, *key,* which is the member ID to search for in the array. If *key* is found, *indexOfWinner* returns the index of that array element. If *key* is not found, that is, if none of the elements in the array matches the value of *key, indexOfWinner* returns –1. Since –1 is not a valid array index, it's a good value to use to indicate that the search was unsuccessful.

Notice that if the current array element matches the *key,* the *indexOfWinner* method returns immediately to the caller (line 61); that is, the method stops executing. The return value is the index of the element that matched the *key.* If, however, the method finishes executing all iterations of the *for* loop, then the method has looked at every element in the array without finding a match. In that case, the method returns –1 (line 63), indicating that the *key* was not found.

Our *getPrize* method (lines 38–50) calls *indexOfWinner* to check if its *memberNumber* parameter is a winning number; if it is, it uses the array index returned by *indexOfWinner* in order to return the corresponding element of the array *prizes* (line 49).

Example 8.15 shows a client application that uses our *DVDWinners* class.

```
 1 /** Client for the DVDWinners class
 2     Anderson, Franceschi
 3 */
 4 import java.util.Scanner;
 5
 6 public class DVDWinnersClient
 7 {
 8   public static void main( String [ ] args )
 9   {
10     // instantiate the winningIDs array
11     DVDWinners winningIDs = new DVDWinners( );
12
13     // prompt for the member ID
```

```
14      Scanner scan = new Scanner( System.in );
15      System.out.print( "Enter the member's ID "
16                               + "or 0 to stop > " );
17      int searchID = scan.nextInt( );
18
19      while ( searchID != 0 )
20      {
21        // determine whether member is a winner
22        System.out.println( winningIDs.getPrize( searchID ) );
23
24        System.out.print( "\nEnter the next member's ID "
25                               + "or 0 to stop > " );
26        searchID = scan.nextInt( );
27      }
28
29      System.out.println( "\nThe winners were "
30                               + winningIDs.toString( ) );
31    }
32 }
```

EXAMPLE 8.15   Client Application for the *DVDWinners* Class

We instantiate a *DVDWinners* object reference named *winningIDs* (lines 10–11). We then prompt for a member ID (lines 15–17) and call the *get-Prize* method (line 22) in order to output any prize that may have been won by the current member. Figure 8.21 shows a possible output of running the *DVDWinnersClient* application.

SOFTWARE ENGINEERING TIP

When you write a class that uses corresponding lists of items with different data types, consider using parallel arrays.

```
Enter the member's ID or 0 to stop > 1234
Sorry, member is not a winner.

Enter the next member's ID or 0 to stop > 3980
You win free popcorn!

Enter the next member's ID or 0 to stop > 0

The winners were 619 4510 2272 3980 4004
```

Figure 8.21
Output of Example 8.15

8.6.2   Selection Sort

The member IDs in the preceding *winners* array were in random order, so when a member was not a winner, our *findWinners* method needed to look at every element in the array before discovering that the ID we were looking for was not in the array. This is not efficient, since most members are not winners. The larger the array, the more inefficient a sequential search becomes. We could simplify the search by arranging the elements in numeric order, which is called **sorting the array**. Once the array is sorted, we can use various algorithms to speed up a search. Later in this chapter, we discuss how to search a sorted array.

In this chapter, we present two basic sorting algorithms, **Selection Sort** and **Insertion Sort**.

Selection Sort derives its name from the algorithm used to sort the array. We select a largest element in the array and place it at the end of the array. Then we select a next-largest element and put it in the next-to-last position in the array. To do this, we consider the unsorted portion of the array as a **subarray**. We repeatedly select a largest value in the current subarray and move it to the end of the subarray, then consider a new subarray by eliminating the elements that are in their sorted locations, until the subarray has only one element. At that time, the array is sorted.

In more formal terms, we can state the Selection Sort algorithm, presented here in pseudocode, in this way:

To sort an array with *n* elements in ascending order:

1. Consider *m* elements as a subarray with *m* = *n* elements.
2. Find the index of a largest value in this subarray.
3. Swap the values of the element with the largest value and the element in the last position in the subarray.
4. Consider a new subarray of *m* = *m* − 1 elements by eliminating the last element in the previous subarray.
5. Repeat steps 2 through 4 until *m* = 1.

For example, let's walk through a Selection Sort on the following array. At the beginning, the entire array is the subarray (shown here with shading).

We begin by considering the entire array as an unsorted subarray. We find that the largest element is 26 at index 1.

Unsorted subarray

Value	17	26	5	2
Index	0	1	2	3

Next we move element 1 to the last element by swapping the values of the elements at indexes 1 and 3.

The value 26 is now in the right place, and we consider elements 0 through 2 as the unsorted subarray.

Unsorted subarray   Sorted element

Value	17	2	5	26
Index	0	1	2	3

The largest element in the new subarray is 17 at index 0. So we move element 0 to the last index of the subarray (index 2) by swapping the elements at indexes 0 and 2.

The value 17 is now in the right place, and we consider elements 0 and 1 as the new unsorted subarray.

Unsorted subarray   Sorted elements

Value	5	2	17	26
Index	0	1	2	3

The largest element in the new subarray is 5 at index 0. We move element 0 to the last index of the subarray (index 1) by swapping the elements at indexes 0 and 1.

The value 5 is now in the right place, and we consider element 0 as the new subarray. But because there is only one element in the subarray, the subarray is sorted. Thus the whole array is sorted, and our job is done.

	Sorted elements			

Value	2	5	17	26
Index	0	1	2	3

A critical operation in a Selection Sort is swapping two array elements. Before going further, let's examine the algorithm for swapping two array elements.

To swap two values, we need to define a temporary variable that is of the same data type as the values being swapped. This variable will temporarily hold the value of one of the elements, so that we don't lose the value during the swap.

The algorithm, presented here in pseudocode, involves three steps:

To swap elements *a* and *b*:

1. Assign the value of element *a* to the temporary variable.
2. Assign the value of element *b* to element *a*.
3. Assign the value in the temporary variable to element *b*.

For instance, if an array named *array* has *int* elements, and we want to swap the element at index 3 with the element at index 6, we will use the following code:

```
int temp = array[3];     // line 1
array[3] = array[6];     // line 2
array[6] = temp;         // line 3
```

The order of these operations is critical; changing the order might result in loss of data and erroneous data stored in the array.

The following illustrates line by line what happens during the swap:

Before line 1 is executed, our array looks like this:

Value	23	45	7	33	78	90	82	80	90	66
Index	0	1	2	3	4	5	6	7	8	9

Line 1 assigns the value of element 3 to *temp*. After line 1 is executed, the value of *temp* is 33. The array is unchanged.

Value	23	45	7	33	78	90	82	80	90	66		33
Index	0	1	2	3	4	5	6	7	8	9		temp

Line 2 assigns the value of element 6 (82) to element 3. After line 2 is executed, both element 6 and element 3 have the same value. But that's OK, because we saved the value of element 3 in *temp*.

Value	23	45	7	82	78	90	82	80	90	66		33
Index	0	1	2	3	4	5	6	7	8	9		temp

Line 3 assigns the value we saved in *temp* to element 6. After line 3 is executed, the values of elements 3 and 6 have been successfully swapped.

Value	23	45	7	82	78	90	33	80	90	66		33
Index	0	1	2	3	4	5	6	7	8	9		temp

 COMMON ERROR TRAP

When swapping elements, be sure to save a value before replacing it with another value to avoid losing data.

Example 8.16 shows the *Sorter* class, which provides a *static selectionSort* method for an integer array.

```
1 /* Sort Utility Class
2 *  Anderson, Franceschi
3 */
4
5 public class Sorter
6 {
7    /** Uses Selection Sort to sort
8     *      an integer array in ascending order
9     *      @param array the array to sort
10    */
11   public static void selectionSort( int [ ] array )
12   {
13     int temp; // temporary location for swap
14     int max;  // index of maximum value in subarray
15
16     for ( int i = 0; i < array.length; i++ )
17     {
```

```
18         // find index of largest value in subarray
19         max = indexOfLargestElement( array, array.length - i );
20
21         // swap array[max] and array[array.length - i - 1]
22         temp = array[max];
23         array[max] = array[array.length - i - 1];
24         array[array.length - i - 1] = temp;
25      }
26   }
27
28   /**  Finds index of largest element
29    *     @param    size   the size of the subarray
30    *     @param    array the array to search
31    *     @return   the index of the largest element in the subarray
32    */
33   private static int indexOfLargestElement( int [ ] array, int size )
34   {
35      int index = 0;
36      for( int i = 1; i < size; i++ )
37      {
38         if ( array[i] > array[index] )
39             index = i;
40      }
41      return index;
42   }
43 }
```

EXAMPLE 8.16   The *Sorter* Class

Part of the Selection Sort algorithm is finding the index of the largest element in a subarray, so we implement the Selection Sort with two methods. At lines 7–26 is the *selectionSort* method, which implements the Selection Sort algorithm. To perform its work, the *selectionSort* method calls the utility method, *indexOfLargestElement* (lines 28–42), which returns the index of the largest element in a subarray. This method uses the algorithm discussed earlier in the chapter for finding a maximum value in an array. We declare this method *private* because its only function is to provide a service to the *selectionSort* method. The *indexOfLargestElement* method must also be declared as *static* because the *selectionSort* method is *static*, and thus can call only *static* methods.

In Example 8.17, the client code instantiates an integer array and prints the array before and after the Selection Sort is performed. Because *selectionSort* is a *static* method, we call it using the *Sorter* class name. The output of a sample run is shown in Figure 8.22.

```
1 /** Client for Selection Sort
2 *   Anderson, Franceschi
3 */
4 import java.util.Random;
5
6 public class SelectionSortClient
7 {
8   public static void main( String [ ] args )
9   {
10    // instantiate an array and fill with random values
11    int [ ] numbers = new int [6];
12    Random rand = new Random( );
13    for ( int i = 0; i < numbers.length; i++ )
14    {
15      numbers[i] = rand.nextInt( 5000 ) + 1;
16    }
17
18    System.out.println( "Before Selection Sort, the array is" );
19    for ( int i = 0; i < numbers.length; i++ )
20      System.out.print( numbers[i] + "\t" );
21    System.out.println( );
22
23    Sorter.selectionSort( numbers ); // sort the array
24
25    System.out.println( "\nAfter Selection Sort, the array is" );
26    for ( int i = 0; i < numbers.length; i++ )
27      System.out.print( numbers[i] + "\t" );
28    System.out.println( );
29  }
30 }
```

EXAMPLE 8.17   Using Selection Sort

```
Before Selection Sort, the array is
3394     279     1181     2471     3660     221

After Selection Sort, the array is
221      279     1181     2471     3394     3660
```

Figure 8.22
Using Selection Sort

8.6.3   Insertion Sort

Like Selection Sort, Insertion Sort also derives its name from the algorithm used to sort the array. The basic approach to an Insertion Sort is to sort elements much like a card player arranges the cards in sorted order in his or her hand. The player inserts cards one at a time in such a way that the cards on the left side of his or her hand are sorted at all times; the cards on the right side of his or her hand have not yet been inserted into the sorted part of the hand. As Figure 8.23a shows, the three yellow cards on the left (3, 5, and 9) are already arranged in sorted order, and the white cards on the right (4, 2, and 8) have yet to be inserted into their correct location. Note that the "sorted" yellow cards on the left side are not necessarily in their final position yet. We will now insert the 4. We first compare it to the 9; since 4 is smaller than 9, we shift the 9 to the right (Figure 8.23b). We then compare the 4 to the 5; since 4 is smaller than 5, we shift the 5 to the right

Figure 8.23a
The next card to insert is a 4

Figure 8.23b
9 is shifted to the right

Figure 8.23c
5 is shifted to the right

Figure 8.23d
4 is inserted

(Figure 8.23c). We then compare the 4 to the 3; since 4 is larger than 3, the 3 stays in place and we insert the 4 in the empty slot (Figure 8.23d). We are now ready to insert the next card, the 2.

To sort an array of n elements in ascending order, Insertion Sort implements a double loop:

- The outer loop executes $n - 1$ times and iterates through the array elements from indexes 1 through $n - 1$. If the variable i represents the counter of the outer loop, the array can be thought of as made of three parts:

  - a sorted subarray (although the elements may not be in their final position yet) from index 0 to $i - 1$,
  - the array element (at index i) that we are currently inserting, and

- a subarray (from index $i + 1$ to $n - 1$) of elements that have not yet been inserted.
  - At each iteration of the outer loop, we insert the current array element at its proper place within the sorted subarray. The inner loop compares the current array element to the elements of the sorted array from right to left and shifts these elements to the right until it finds the proper insert location.
  - After all elements have been inserted, the array is sorted.

The pseudocode for the Insertion Sort is

```
for i = 1 to last array index by 1
    j = i
    temp = element at index i
    while ( j != 0 and value of current element is less than value of element at index j − 1 )
        shift element at index j − 1 to the right
        decrement j by 1
    assign current element value (stored in temp) to element at index j
```

For example, let's walk through an Insertion Sort on the following array. At the beginning, the unsorted array is

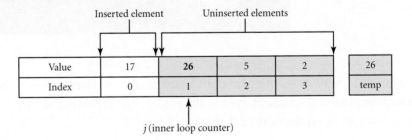

The first element of the array, 17, is automatically in the correct position when we consider the subarray as consisting of that element only. The value of the outer loop counter (i) is 1, and we will now insert the second array element, 26, into the left subarray. First, we save the value of the element to be inserted by storing it in *temp*. We need to save the value because it is possible that we will shift other values, in which case we would overwrite that element. The value of the inner loop counter (j) is set to the value of the outer loop counter (i), i.e., 1. We compare elements 26 (index $j = 1$) and 17 (index $j - 1 = 0$). Since 26 is larger than 17, we exit the inner loop (and therefore we do not shift 17 to the right). We then assign the value of the current element, 26, stored in *temp*, to the element at index $j = 1$; in this case, there is no change to the array. The value 26 has been inserted.

The outer loop counter (i) is incremented, and its value is 2. We will now insert the third array element, 5, into the left subarray (at this point comprised of the two inserted elements, 17 and 26).

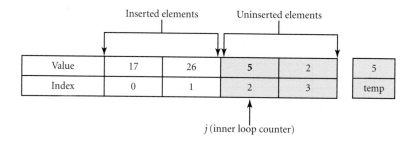

The value of the inner loop counter (j) is set to the value of the outer loop counter (i), i.e., 2. We compare the current element, 5, stored in *temp*, and 26 (index $j - 1 = 1$). Since 5 is smaller than 26, we shift 26 to the right and decrement j by 1; j now has the value 1.

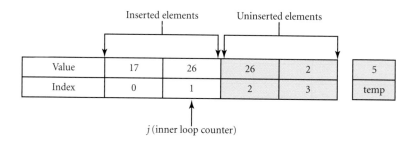

We then compare the current element, 5, stored in *temp*, and 17 (index $j - 1 = 0$). Since 5 is smaller than 17, we shift 17 to the right and decrement j by 1; j now has the value 0.

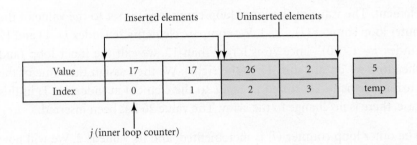

Since j is 0, we exit the inner loop and assign the value of the current element, 5, stored in *temp*, to the array element at index $j = 0$. The value 5 has now been inserted.

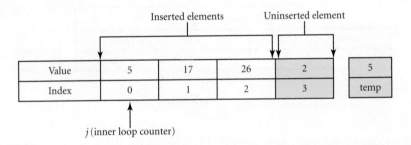

The outer loop counter (i) is incremented, and its value is 3. We will now insert the fourth array element, 2, into the left subarray (at this point comprised of the three inserted elements, 5, 17, and 26).

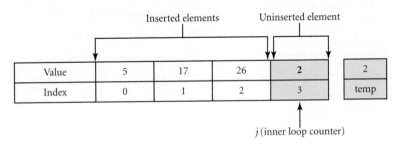

The value of the inner loop counter (j) is set to the value of the outer loop counter (i), i.e., 3. We compare the current element, 2, stored in *temp*, and 26 (index $j - 1 = 2$). Since 2 is smaller than 26, we shift 26 to the right and decrement j by 1; j now has the value 2.

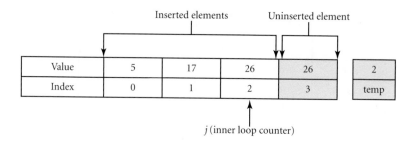

We then compare the current element, 2, stored in *temp*, and 17 (index $j - 1 = 1$). Since 2 is smaller than 17, we shift 17 to the right and decrement j by 1; j now has the value 1.

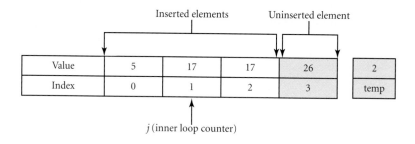

We then compare the current element, 2, stored in *temp*, and 5 (index $j - 1 = 0$). Since 2 is smaller than 5, we shift 5 to the right and decrement j by 1; j now has the value 0.

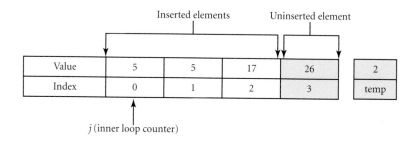

Since j is 0, we exit the inner loop and assign the value of the current element, 2, stored in *temp*, to the array element at index j. The value 2 has now been inserted.

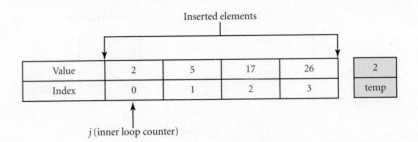

Inserted elements

Value	2	5	17	26		2
Index	0	1	2	3		temp

j (inner loop counter)

COMMON ERROR TRAP

When looping through an array, be careful not to access an element outside the bounds of the array. Your code will compile, but will generate an *Array-IndexOutOfBounds-Exception* at run time.

The outer loop counter (i) is incremented, and its value is 4, which causes the outer loop to terminate. All the elements have been inserted; the array is now sorted.

Example 8.18 shows our *Sorter* class with the Insertion Sort algorithm implemented in lines 43–63.

```
1  /* Sort Utility Class
2     Anderson, Franceschi
3  */
4
5  public class Sorter
6  {
7    /**  Performs a Selection Sort on
8     *       an integer array
9     *    @param the array to sort
10    */
11   public static void selectionSort( int [ ] array )
12   {
13     int temp; // temporary location for swap
14     int max;  // index of maximum value in subarray
15
16     for ( int i = 0; i < array.length; i++ )
17     {
18       // find index of largest value in subarray
19       max = indexOfLargestElement( array, array.length - i );
20
21       // swap array[max] and array[array.length - i - 1]
22       temp = array[max];
23       array[max] = array[array.length - i - 1];
24       array[array.length - i - 1] = temp;
25     }
26   }
27
```

```
28    /**  Finds index of largest element
29     *      @param     size  the size of the subarray
30     *      @return    the index of the largest element in the subarray
31     */
32    private static int indexOfLargestElement( int [ ] array, int size )
33    {
34       int index = 0;
35       for( int i = 1; i < size; i++ )
36       {
37           if ( array[i] > array[index] )
38               index = i;
39       }
40       return index;
41    }
42
43    /**  Performs an Insertion Sort on an integer array
44     *      @param array   array to sort
45     */
46    public static void insertionSort( int [ ] array )
47    {
48      int j, temp;
49
50      for ( int i = 1; i < array.length; i++ )
51      {
52         j = i;
53         temp = array[i];
54
55         while ( j != 0 && array[j - 1] > temp )
56         {
57            array[j] = array[j - 1];
58            j--;
59         }
60
61         array[j] = temp;
62      }
63    }
64 }
```

EXAMPLE 8.18   Sorter Class with Insertion Sort

Example 8.19 shows a client program that instantiates an integer array, fills it with random values, and then prints the array before and after performing the Insertion Sort. Figure 8.24 shows a sample run, using the Insertion Sort algorithm to sort an array of integers.

```
1 /** Client for Insertion Sort
2 *   Anderson, Franceschi
3 */
4 import java.util.Random;
5
6 public class InsertionSortClient
7 {
8   public static void main( String [ ] args )
9   {
10    // instantiate an array and fill with random values
11    int [ ] numbers = new int [6];
12    Random rand = new Random( );
13    for ( int i = 0; i < numbers.length; i++ )
14    {
15      numbers[i] = rand.nextInt( 5000 ) + 1;
16    }
17
18    System.out.println( "Before Insertion Sort, the array is" );
19    for ( int i = 0; i < numbers.length; i++ )
20      System.out.print( numbers[i] + "\t" );
21    System.out.println( );
22
23    Sorter.insertionSort( numbers ); // sort the array
24
25    System.out.println( "\nAfter Insertion Sort, the array is"  );
26    for ( int i = 0; i < numbers.length; i++ )
27        System.out.print( numbers[i] + "\t" );
28    System.out.println( );
29  }
30 }
```

EXAMPLE 8.19   Using Insertion Sort

Figure 8.24

Using Insertion Sort

```
Before Insertion Sort, the array is
2856     2384     3979     3088     1176     284

After Insertion Sort, the array is
284     1176     2384     2856     3088     3979
```

8.6.4 Sorting Arrays of Objects

We saw earlier in the chapter that data items to be sorted can be primitive data types, such as integers or *doubles*. But they can also be objects. With an array of objects, it is important to understand that we need to sort the objects themselves, not the array elements, which are merely the object references, or memory locations of the objects.

Arrays of objects are sorted using a sort key, which is one or more of the instance variables of the objects. For instance, if we have email objects, they can be sorted by date received, by author, by subject, and so on. It is important to note that when we sort objects, the integrity of the objects must be respected; for instance, when we sort a collection of email objects by sender, we sort a collection of email objects, not a collection of senders.

Thus, to perform the Insertion Sort on the *cars* array of *Auto* objects, we need to decide which field (or fields) of the *Auto* object determines the order of the objects. If we say that the *model* is the sort field, then the comparison statement would compare the models in two objects, that is, two *Strings*. As you recall from Chapter 5, the *compareTo* method of the *String* class compares the values of two *Strings*. It returns a positive number if the *String* for which the method is invoked is greater than the *String* passed as an argument.

To sort the *cars* array using an Insertion Sort, we would need to make several revisions to the *InsertionSort* method. First, the data type of the array must be declared as an *Auto* in the parameter list. Second, *temp* needs to be defined as an *Auto* reference, and finally, we need to substitute the *compareTo* method in the condition that compares array elements.

 **REFERENCE POINT**

The *compareTo* method of the *String* class is discussed in detail in Chapter 5.

The revised Insertion Sort code becomes:

```
/* * Insertion sorts an array of Autos
*       @param arr an array of Autos
*/
public static void insertionSort( Auto [ ] arr )
{
  Auto temp;
  int j;

  for ( int i = 1; i < arr.length; i++ )
```

```
        {
            j = i;
            temp = arr[i];

            while ( j != 0 && ( temp.getModel( ) ).compareTo(
                    arr[j - 1].getModel( ) ) < 0 )
            {
                arr[j] = arr[j - 1];
                j--;
            } // end while loop

            arr[j] = temp;

        } // end for loop
    } // end InsertionSort method
```

8.6.5   Sequential Search of a Sorted Array

Earlier in the chapter, the *DVDWinners* class sequentially searched an array. The algorithm assumed the elements were not in order. If we sort the array, a Sequential Search can be implemented more efficiently for the case when the search key is not present in the array. Instead of searching the entire array before discovering that the search key is not in the array, we can stop as soon as we pass the location where that element would be if it were in the array. In other words, if the array is sorted in ascending order, we can recognize an unsuccessful search when we find an element in the array that is greater than the search key. Because the array is sorted in ascending order, all the elements after that array element are larger than that element, and therefore are also larger than the search key.

To implement this algorithm, we can add another test to the *for* loop condition, so that we exit the loop as soon as we find an element that is greater than the search key. The improved algorithm shown next could be used to replace the *indexOfWinner* method shown in Example 8.14 for Sequential Search of a sorted *winners* array:

```
public int indexOfWinner( int key )
{
    for ( int i = 0; i < winners.length && winners[i] <= key; i++ )
    {
        if ( winners[i] == key )
```

```
        return i;
    }

    return -1; // end of array reached without finding key
               // or an element larger than the key was found
}
```

In fact, if the array is sorted, it can be searched even more efficiently using an algorithm called Binary Search, which we explain in the next section.

8.6.6 Binary Search of a Sorted Array

If you've played the "Guess a Number" game, you probably have used the concept of a **Binary Search**. In this game, someone asks you to guess a secret number between 1 and 100. For each number you guess, they tell you whether the secret number is larger or smaller than your guess. A good strategy is to guess the number in the middle, which in this example is 50. Whether the secret number is larger or smaller than 50, you will have eliminated half of the possible values. If the secret number is greater than 50, then you know your next guess should be 75 (halfway between 50 and 100). If the secret number is less than 50, your next guess should be 25 (halfway between 1 and 50). If you continue eliminating half the possible numbers with each guess, you will quickly guess the secret number. This approach works because we are "searching" a sorted set of numbers (1 to 100).

Similarly, a Binary Search of a sorted array works by eliminating half the remaining elements with each comparison. First, we look at the middle element of the array. If the value of that element is the search key, we return its index. If, however, the value of the middle element is greater than the search key, then the search key cannot be found in elements with array indexes higher than that element. Therefore, we will search the left half of the array only. Similarly, if the value of the middle element is lower than the search key, then the search key cannot be found in elements with array indexes lower than the middle element. Therefore, we will search in the right half of the array only. As we keep searching, the subarray we search keeps shrinking in size. In fact, the size of the subarray we search is cut in half at every iteration.

If the search key is not in the array, the subarray we search will eventually become empty. At that point, we know that we will not find our search key, and we return −1.

Example 8.20 shows our Binary Search algorithm.

```
1  /** Binary Search
2  *    Anderson, Franceschi
3  */
4
5  import java.util.Scanner;
6
7  public class BinarySearcher
8  {
9    public static void main( String [ ] args )
10   {
11     // define an array sorted in ascending order
12     int [ ] numbers = { 3, 6, 7, 8, 12, 15, 22, 36, 45,
13                         48, 51, 53, 64, 69, 72, 89, 95 };
14
15     Scanner scan  = new Scanner( System.in );
16     System.out.print( "Enter a value to search for > " );
17     int key = scan.nextInt( );
18
19     int index = binarySearch( numbers, key );
20     if ( index != -1 )
21         System.out.println( key + " found at index " + index );
22     else
23         System.out.println( key + " not found" );
24   }
25
26   public static int binarySearch( int [ ] arr, int key )
27   {
28     int start = 0;
29     int end = arr.length - 1;
30     int middle;
31
32     while ( end >= start )
33     {
34       middle = ( start + end ) / 2; // element in middle of array
35
36       if ( arr[middle] == key )
37       {
38         return middle;        // key found at middle
39       }
40       else if ( arr[middle] > key )
41       {
42         end = middle - 1;   // search left side of array
```

```
43          }
44        else
45        {
46            start = middle + 1; // search right side of array
47        }
48      }
49    return -1;
50  }
51 }
```

EXAMPLE 8.20   Binary Search of a Sorted Array

We start by declaring and initializing an integer array with 17 sorted elements (lines 12–13). We then prompt the user for a search key and call the *binarySearch* method (lines 16–19).

The *binarySearch* method is coded at lines 26–50. The local variables *start* and *end* store the first and last index of the subarray to search. Because we begin by searching the entire array, we initialize these to the indexes of the first and last element of the array that was passed as a parameter. The local variable *middle*, declared at line 30, will store the index of the middle element in the subarray to search.

The search is performed in a *while* loop (lines 32–48), whose condition determines whether the subarray is empty. If the subarray is not empty, we calculate the value for *middle* by adding the indexes of the first and last elements and dividing by 2 (line 34). Next we test whether the value at the *middle* index is equal to the key. If so, we have found the key and we return its index, which is *middle* (lines 36–39). If not, we test whether the value in the middle of the subarray is greater than the key. If so, we reduce the subarray to the elements with indexes less than *middle* (lines 40–43) and greater than or equal to *start*. If the value in the middle of the subarray is less than the key, we reduce the subarray to the elements with indexes greater than *middle* (lines 44–47) and smaller than or equal to *end*.

When the *while* loop continues, we reevaluate the condition to determine whether the subarray is empty, and if not, continue making our comparisons and either returning the index of the search key or reducing the size of the subarray. If the search key is not in the array, the subarray eventually becomes empty, and we exit the *while* loop and return –1 (line 49). Figure 8.25 shows the output when the search key is found.

Figure 8.25

Output from Example 8.20

```
Enter a value to search for > 64
64 found at index 12
```

Let's run through the Binary Search algorithm on the key 7 to illustrate how the algorithm works when the key is found in the array. Here is the array *numbers*:

Value	3	6	7	8	12	15	22	36	45	48	51	53	64	69	72	89	95
Index	0	1	2	3	4	5	6	7	8	9	10	11	12	13	14	15	16

When the *binarySearch* method is called, it sets *start* to 0 and *end* to *arr.length – 1*, which is 16. Thus, the value of *middle* is 8.

The element at index 8 (45) is greater than 7, so we set *end* to 7 (*middle – 1*), and we will now search the left subarray, highlighted next. The value of *middle* is now 3 ((0 + 7) / 2).

Value	3	6	7	8	12	15	22	36	45	48	51	53	64	69	72	89	95
Index	0	1	2	3	4	5	6	7	8	9	10	11	12	13	14	15	16

The element at index 3 (8) is greater than 7, so we set *end* to 2 (*middle – 1*) and keep searching in the left subarray, highlighted next. The value of *middle* is now 1 ((0 + 2) / 2).

Value	3	6	7	8	12	15	22	36	45	48	51	53	64	69	72	89	95
Index	0	1	2	3	4	5	6	7	8	9	10	11	12	13	14	15	16

The element at index 1 (6) is smaller than 7, so we set *start* to 2 (*middle + 1*) and search in the right subarray, highlighted next. The value of *middle* is now 2 ((2 + 2) / 2).

Value	3	6	7	8	12	15	22	36	45	48	51	53	64	69	72	89	95
Index	0	1	2	3	4	5	6	7	8	9	10	11	12	13	14	15	16

The element at index 2 (7) is equal to 7. We have found the value and return its index, 2.

Let's now run the preceding example on the key 34 to illustrate how the algorithm works when the key is not found in the array.

Here is the array *numbers* again:

Value	3	6	7	8	12	15	22	36	45	48	51	53	64	69	72	89	95
Index	0	1	2	3	4	5	6	7	8	9	10	11	12	13	14	15	16

Again, when the *binarySearch* method is called, it sets *start* to 0 and *end* to *arr.length − 1*, which is 16. Thus, *middle* is assigned the value 8 for the first comparison.

The element at index 8 (45) is greater than 34, so we set *end* to 7 (*middle − 1*), and keep searching in the left subarray. The value of *middle* becomes 3 for the next comparison.

Value	3	6	7	8	12	15	22	36	45	48	51	53	64	69	72	89	95
Index	0	1	2	3	4	5	6	7	8	9	10	11	12	13	14	15	16

The element at index 3 (8) is smaller than 34, so we search in the right subarray highlighted below. The value of *middle* is now 5.

Value	3	6	7	8	12	15	22	36	45	48	51	53	64	69	72	89	95
Index	0	1	2	3	4	5	6	7	8	9	10	11	12	13	14	15	16

The element at index 5 (15) is smaller than 34, so we search in the right subarray. The value of *middle* is now 6.

Value	3	6	7	8	12	15	22	36	45	48	51	53	64	69	72	89	95
Index	0	1	2	3	4	5	6	7	8	9	10	11	12	13	14	15	16

The element at index 6 (22) is smaller than 34, so we search in the right subarray. The value of *middle* is now 7.

Value	3	6	7	8	12	15	22	36	45	48	51	53	64	69	72	89	95
Index	0	1	2	3	4	5	6	7	8	9	10	11	12	13	14	15	16

At this point, *start*, *end*, and *middle* all have the value 7. The element at index 7 (36) is larger than 34, so we assign *end* the value *middle – 1*, which is 6. This makes *end* less than *start* and consequently makes the *while* loop condition evaluate to *false*. We have not found 34, so we return −1.

8.7 Programming Activity 2: Searching and Sorting Arrays

In this activity, you will work again with a 15-element integer array, performing these activities:

1. Write a method to perform a Sequential Search of an array.

2. Write a method to implement the Bubble Sort algorithm to sort an array.

The basic approach to a Bubble Sort is to make multiple passes through the array. In each pass, we compare adjacent elements. If any two adjacent elements are out of order, we put them in order by swapping their values.

To sort an array of n elements in ascending order, Bubble Sort implements a double loop:

- The outer loop executes $n - 1$ times.
- For each iteration of the outer loop, the inner loop steps through all the unsorted elements of the array and does the following:
  - Compares the current element with the next element in the array.
  - If the next element is smaller, it swaps the two elements.

Outer loop counter	Indexes of element(s) at the sorted position
0	$n - 1$
1	$n - 2, n - 1$
2	$n - 3, n - 2, n - 1$
...	...
$n - 3$	$2, 3, 4, ..., n - 3, n - 2, n - 1$
$n - 2$	$1, 2, 3, 4, ..., n - 3, n - 2, n - 1$

At this point, $n - 1$ elements have been moved to their correct positions. That leaves only the element at index 0, which is therefore automatically at the correct position within the array. The array is now sorted.

As the outer loop counter goes from 0 to $n - 2$, it iterates $n - 1$ times.

The pseudocode for the Bubble Sort is

```
for i = 0 to last array index – 1 by 1
   for j = 0 to ( last array index – i –1 ) by 1
      if (2 consecutive elements are in the wrong order)
         swap them
```

For example, let's walk through a Bubble Sort on the following array. At the beginning, the unsorted array is

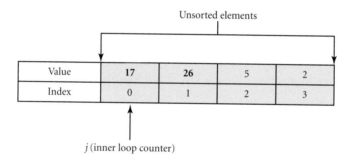

The value of the outer loop counter (i) is 0, and the value of the inner loop counter (j) is also 0. We compare elements 17 (index $j = 0$) and 26 (index $j + 1 = 1$). Since 17 is smaller than 26, we do not swap them.

The inner loop counter (j) is incremented, and its value is now 1.

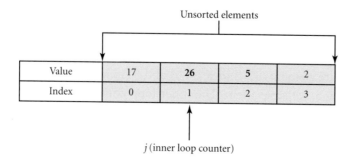

We compare elements 26 (index $j = 1$) and 5 (index $j + 1 = 2$). Since 26 is larger than 5, we swap them. The inner loop counter (j) is incremented, and its value is now 2.

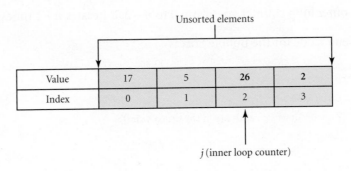

We compare elements 26 (index $j = 2$) and 2 (index $j + 1 = 3$). Since 26 is larger than 2, we swap them.

The inner loop counter (j) is incremented, and its value is now 3; therefore, we exit the inner loop. (We have reached the end of the unsorted subarray, which at this point is the whole array.) At the end of one execution of the inner loop, the value 26 has "bubbled up" to its correct position within the array.

We now go back to the outer loop, and the outer loop counter (i) is incremented; its value is now 1. We reenter the inner loop, and the value of the inner loop counter (j) is reinitialized to 0.

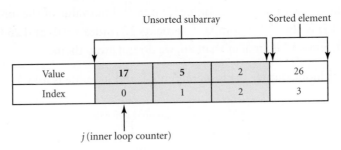

We compare elements 17 (index $j = 0$) and 5 (index $j + 1 = 1$). Since 17 is larger than 5, we swap them. The inner loop counter (j) is incremented, and its value is now 1.

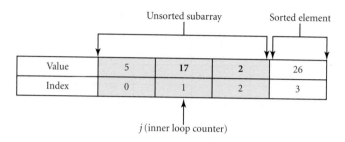

We compare elements 17 (index $j = 1$) and 2 (index $j + 1 = 2$). Since 17 is larger than 2, we swap them.

The inner loop counter (j) is incremented, and its value is now 2; therefore, we exit the inner loop. (We have reached the end of the unsorted subarray.) At this point, the element 17 has "bubbled up" to its correct position within the array.

We go back to the outer loop, and the outer loop counter (i) is incremented; its value is now 2, and this will be the last iteration of the outer loop. We reenter the inner loop, and the value of the inner loop counter (j) is reinitialized to 0.

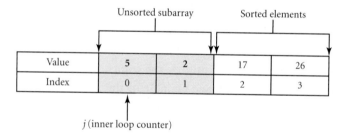

We compare elements 5 (index $j = 0$) and 2 (index $j + 1 = 1$). Since 2 is smaller than 5, we swap them.

The inner loop counter (j) is incremented, and its value is now 1; therefore, we exit the inner loop. (We have reached the end of the unsorted subarray.) At this point, the element 5 has "bubbled up" to its correct position within the array.

We go back to the outer loop, and the outer loop counter (i) is incremented; its value is now 3, and therefore, we exit the outer loop. For the four elements in the array, we executed the outer loop three times.

The array is now sorted.

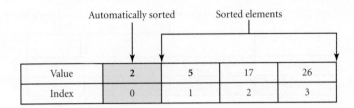

The framework for this Programming Activity will animate your algorithm so that you can watch your algorithm work and check the accuracy of your code. For example, Figure 8.26 demonstrates the Bubble Sort at work. At this point, the program has completed three passes through the array and is comparing the values of elements 5 and 6.

Instructions

In the Chapter 8 Programming Activity 2 directory on the CD-ROM accompanying this book, you will find the source files needed to complete this activity. Copy all the files to a directory on your computer. Note that all files should be in the same directory.

Open the *ArrayPractice2.java* source file. Searching for five asterisks (*****) in the source code will position you at the two locations where you will add your code. Your first task is to complete the *sequentialSearch* method, which searches the *arr* array, an instance variable of the *ArrayPractice2* class. The array *arr* has already been instantiated for you and filled with random values. The second task is to complete the *bubbleSort* method. Example 8.21 shows the section of the *ArrayPractice2* source code where you will add your code. Note that in each method, you are asked to call the *animate* method so that your method code can be animated as it works. Note also

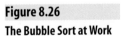

Figure 8.26
The Bubble Sort at Work

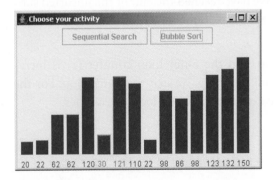

that for the *sequentialSearch* method, we provide a dummy *return* statement (*return 0;*). We do this so that the source code will compile. In this way, you can write and test each method separately, using stepwise refinement. When you are ready to write the *sequentialSearch* method, just replace the dummy *return* statement with the appropriate *return* statement for that method.

```java
// 1. ***** student writes this method
/** Searches for key in integer array named arr
//    arr is an instance variable of the class and has been
//    instantiated and filled with random values.
// @param key value to search for
// @return  if key is found, the  index of the first element
//    in array whose value is key; if key is not found,
//     the method returns -1
*/
public int sequentialSearch( int key )
{
// Note:  To animate the algorithm, put this method call as the
// first statement in your for loop
//  animate( i, 0 );
//         where i is the index of the current array element


   return 0; // replace this statement with your return statement

} // end of sequentialSearch

// 2. *****  student writes this method
/** Sorts arr in ascending order using the bubble sort algorithm
*/
public void bubbleSort( )
{
// Note:  To animate the algorithm, put this method call as the
// last statement in your innermost for loop
//  animate( i, j );
//           where i is the value of the outer loop counter
//            and j is the value of the inner loop counter,
//             or the index of the current array element


} // end of bubbleSort
```

EXAMPLE 8.21   Student Section of *ArrayPractice2*

Figure 8.27
Opening Window of
ArrayPractice2

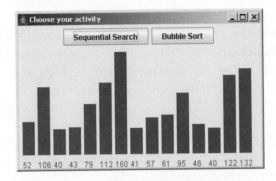

When you have finished writing your code, compile and run the application. Figure 8.27 shows the graphics window when the application begins. To test any method, click on the appropriate button.

Troubleshooting

If your method implementation does not animate, consider these tips:

- Verify that your *for* loop calls the *animate* method as instructed in the method comments.

- Verify that you did not instantiate a new array. Perform all operations on the instance variable array named *arr*.

DISCUSSION QUESTIONS ?

1. The sequential search finds only the first occurrence of the parameter *key*. How would you modify the *sequentialSearch* method to count the occurrences of *key*?

2. It is possible that the array might be completely sorted before all the passes have been completed. How would you modify your code so that you exit the *bubbleSort* method as soon as possible?

8.8   Using Arrays as Counters

In some circumstances, it is useful to use an array of integers as an ordered group of accumulators, or counters. For example, suppose you are analyzing a survey that has four possible answers, 0 through 3. You want to count how many people selected each answer. You could set up four counters and use an *if/else* statement to increment the appropriate counter. The pseudocode would be:

```
read first survey
while ( not end of surveys )
{
  if answer is 0
    increment counter0
  else if answer is 1
    increment counter1
  else if answer is 2
    increment counter2
  else if answer is 3
    increment counter3

  read next survey
}
```

That would work if you have only a few possible answers, but what if you had 100 or more answers? You would end up writing a very long *if/else* statement.

Instead, you could set up an array of counters and let the counter for answer 0 be *array[0]*, the counter for answer 1 be *array[1]*, and so on. This approach—using an array of counters—is simpler to code and saves processing time.

As another example, suppose we want to throw a die 500 times and count the number of times each outcome occurs; that is, we want to count the number of ones, twos, threes, fours, fives, and sixes that are rolled. To do this, we set up a simple *Die* class shown in Example 8.22, with a method for rolling a value. Then we set up the client class, *DieCount*, shown in Example 8.23, that has an array with six integer elements; each element will hold the number of times a particular roll occurs.

```
 1 /** Die class
 2  *    Anderson, Franceschi
 3  */
 4 import java.util.Random;
 5
 6 public class Die
 7 {
 8      public final int SIDES = 6;
 9      private Random rand;
10
11      /** default constructor
12       *    instantiates the Random object
13       */
14      public Die( )
15      {
```

```
16        rand = new Random( );
17    }
18
19    /** rolls the die
20     *  @return   the value of the roll
21     */
22    public int roll( )
23    {
24        return rand.nextInt( SIDES ) + 1;
25    }
26 }
```

EXAMPLE 8.22   The *Die* Class

```
1 /** DieCount Class
2 *    Anderson, Franceschi
3 */
4
5 public class DieCount
6 {
7   public static void main( String [ ] args )
8   {
9       final int FACES = 6, NUMBER_OF_ROLLS = 500;
10
11      // instantiate the counter array
12      // which sets initial values to 0
13      int [ ] rollCount = new int [FACES];
14
15      // instantiate the Die
16      Die d1 = new Die( );
17
18      // roll the die 500 times
19      for ( int i = 1; i <= NUMBER_OF_ROLLS; i++ )
20      {
21         int myRoll = d1.roll( );
22         rollCount[myRoll - 1]++;  // increment the counter for roll
23      }
24
25      // print count for each roll
26      System.out.println( "Roll\tCount" );
27      for ( int i = 0; i < rollCount.length; i++ )
28      {
29         System.out.println( ( i + 1 ) + "\t" + rollCount[i] );
30      }
31   }
32 }
```

EXAMPLE 8.23   The *DieCount* Class

In the *Die* class constructor, we instantiate the *Random* object *rand*, which will be used by the *roll* method (lines 19–25), which in turn generates a random number between 1 and 6 to simulate the roll of a die.

In the *DieCount* class, we instantiate our array of six counters, *rollCount*, on line 13, which autoinitializes each element to 0—exactly what we want for counters.

To count the number of times each roll occurs, we use a *for* loop that iterates 500 times, with each iteration calling the *roll* method of the *Die* class. We then need to count each roll. That's where our array of counters, *rollCount*, comes in.

Since the *rollCount* array has six elements, the index of the first element is 0, and the index of the last element is 5. We will use *rollCount[0]* to hold the number of times we rolled a 1, *rollCount[1]* to hold the number of times we rolled a 2, and continue that way until we use *rollCount[5]* to hold the number of times we rolled a 6. Thus, to get the index of the appropriate counter, we need to decrement the roll by 1. So our statement to increment the count for a roll (line 22) becomes

```
rollCount[myRoll - 1]++;
```

After rolling the die 500 times and counting each roll, we print the total times each roll occurred (lines 25–30). Note that we increment the loop variable to convert between our counter index and the roll number. The output from a sample run of this program is shown in Figure 8.28. Because the program generates the rolls randomly, your output may be slightly different.

```
Roll    Count
1       81
2       82
3       89
4       78
5       87
6       83
```

Figure 8.28
Output from *DieCount*

Our algorithm is not ideal, however. We need to subtract 1 from the index in order to increment the counter, and we need to add 1 to the index to print the outcome.

A better approach would be to create the array with seven elements. Then we can use elements 1 through 6 as the counters for the rolls 1 through 6. The index and the roll number will be the same. What happens to element 0? Nothing. We just ignore it.

The revised *DieCount2* class is shown in Example 8.24.

```
1 /** DieCount2 Class
2 *    Anderson, Franceschi
3 */
4
5 public class DieCount2
6 {
7   public static void main( String [ ] args )
8   {
9     final int FACES = 7, NUMBER_OF_ROLLS = 500;
10
11    // instantiate the counter array
12    // which sets initial values to 0
13    int [ ] rollCount = new int [FACES];
14
15    // instantiate the Die
16    Die d1 = new Die( );
17
18    // roll the die 500 times
19    for ( int i = 1; i <= NUMBER_OF_ROLLS; i++ )
20    {
21      int myRoll = d1.roll( );
22      rollCount[myRoll]++;  // increment the counter for roll
23    }
24
25    // print count for each roll
26    System.out.println( "Roll\tCount" );
27    for ( int i = 1; i < rollCount.length; i++ )
28    {
29      System.out.println(  i  + "\t" + rollCount[i] );
30    }
31  }
32 }
```

EXAMPLE 8.24   The *DieCount2* Class

Notice the changes to the code in this example. First, we set *FACES* to 7 (line 9), so we will instantiate an array with seven elements. Then we can use the roll of the die as the index into the counter array to increment the appropriate count (line 22). One last change is that when we loop through the *rollCount* array to print the counters, we initialize our loop counter to 1 (line 27), since we are not using element 0 as a counter and we simply use *i* as the roll number.

It's true that we're allocating an extra integer (four bytes of memory) that is never used, but we're eliminating 500 subtract operations and 6 addition operations! The program is more efficient, easier to write, and easier to read.

Skill Practice
with these end-of-chapter questions

8.10.1   Multiple Choice Exercises

Question 12

8.10.4   Identifying Errors in Code

Question 44

8.10.6   Write a Short Program

Question 57

8.10.8   Technical Writing

Question 74

8.9   Chapter Summary

- An array is a sequence of variables of the same data type. The data type can be any Java primitive data type, such as *int, float, double, byte, boolean,* or *char,* or it can be a class.

- Each element in the array is accessed using the array name and an index, which refers to the element's position in the array.

- Arrays are implemented as objects. Creating an array consists of declaring an object reference for the array and instantiating the array. The size of the array is given when the array is instantiated.

- In arrays of primitive types, each element of the array contains a value of that type. In arrays of objects, each element is an object reference.

SUMMARY

- When an array is instantiated, the elements are given initial values automatically, depending on the data type. Numeric types are set to 0; *boolean* types are set to *false*; *char* types are set to a space; and object references are set to *null*.

- Instantiating an array of object references involves two steps: instantiating the array and instantiating the objects.

- Arrays can be instantiated when they are declared by assigning initial values in a comma-separated list within curly braces. The number of values in the initialization list determines the number of elements in the array.

- Array elements are accessed using the array name and an index. The first element's index is 0 and the last element's index is the size of the array −1.

- Arrays have an integer instance variable, *length*, which holds the number of elements in the array.

- Attempting to access an element of an array using an index less than 0 or greater than *arrayName.length − 1* will generate an *ArrayIndexOutOfBoundsException* at run time.

- Aggregate array operations, such as printing and copying arrays, are not supported for arrays. Using a *for* loop, you can process each array element individually.

- To change the size of an array, instantiate an array of the desired size with a temporary name, copy the appropriate elements from the original array to the new array, and assign the new array reference to the original array. Assign *null* to the temporary array name.

- Arrays can be passed as arguments to methods and can also be the return type of methods.

- When an array is an instance variable of a class, the constructor should instantiate a new array and copy the elements of the parameter array into the new array.

- A Sequential Search determines whether a particular value, the search key, is in an array by comparing the search key to each element in the array.

- A Selection Sort arranges elements in the array in order by value by reducing the array into successively smaller subarrays and placing the largest element in each subarray into the last position of the subarray.

- An Insertion Sort arranges elements of an array much like a card player arranges cards in sorted order in his or her hand. The elements are inserted one at a time in ascending order into the left side of the array.

- To sort an array of objects, you can use the class method provided to compare objects' values.

- A sorted array can be searched more efficiently using a Binary Search, which successively reduces the number of elements to search by half.

- Arrays of integers can be used as an ordered group of counters.

8.10   Exercises, Problems, and Projects

8.10.1   Multiple Choice Exercises

1. What are the valid ways to declare an integer array named *a*? (Check all that apply.)

   ❏ `int [ ] a;`

   ❏ `int a[ ];`

   ❏ `array int a;`

   ❏ `int array a;`

2. What is the index of the first element of an array?

   ❏ −1

   ❏ 0

   ❏ 1

3. An array *a* has 30 elements; what is the index of its last element?

   ❏ 29

   ❏ 30

   ❏ 31

4. What is the default value of the elements in an array of *ints* after declaration and instantiation of the array?

   ❑ 0

   ❑ *null*

   ❑ undefined

5. How do you access the element of array *a* located at index 6?

   ❑ `a{6}`

   ❑ `a( 6 )`

   ❑ `a[6]`

6. Which of the following assertions is true?

   ❑ An array cannot be sized dynamically.

   ❑ An array can be sized dynamically, but cannot be resized without instantiating it again.

   ❑ An array can be sized dynamically and can also be resized without instantiating it again.

7. How do you retrieve the number of elements in an array *a*?

   ❑ `a.length( )`

   ❑ `a.length`

   ❑ `a.size( )`

   ❑ `a.size`

8. All the elements of an array must be of the same type.

   ❑ true

   ❑ false

9. Array aggregate assignment is possible in Java.

   ❑ true

   ❑ false

10. Aggregate comparison of arrays is possible in Java.

    ❑ true

    ❑ false

11. An array can be returned by a method.

    ❏ true

    ❏ false

12. A Sequential Search on a sorted array is typically faster than a Sequential Search on an unsorted array.

    ❏ true

    ❏ false

8.10.2   Reading and Understanding Code

13. What is the output of this code sequence?

```
double [ ] a = { 12.5, 48.3, 65.0 };
System.out.println( a[1] );
```

14. What is the output of this code sequence?

```
int [ ] a = new int [6];
System.out.println( a[4] );
```

15. What is the output of this code sequence?

```
double [ ] a = { 12.5, 48.3, 65.0 };
System.out.println( a.length );
```

16. What is the output of this code sequence?

```
int [ ] a = { 12, 48, 65 };

for ( int i = 0; i < a.length; i++ )
   System.out.println( a[i] );
```

17. What is the output of this code sequence?

```
int [ ] a = { 12, 48, 65 };

for ( int i = 0; i < a.length; i++ )
   System.out.println( "a[" + i + "] = " + a[i] );
```

18. What is the output of this code sequence?

```
int s = 0;
int [ ] a = { 12, 48, 65 };

for ( int i = 0; i < a.length; i++ )
   s += a[i];

System.out.println( "s = " + s );
```

19. What is the output of this code sequence?

```
int [ ] a = new int[10];

for ( int i = 0; i < a.length; i++ )
  a[i] = i + 10;

System.out.println( a[4] );
```

20. What is the output of this code sequence?

```
double [ ] a = { 12.3, 99.6, 48.2, 65.8 };
double temp = a[0];

for ( int i = 1; i < a.length; i++ )
{
    if ( a[i] > temp )
       temp = a[i];
}
System.out.println( temp );
```

21. What is the output of this code sequence?

```
int [ ] a = { 12, 48, 65, 23 };
int temp = a[1];
a[1] = a[3];
a[3] = temp;

for ( int i = 0; i < a.length; i++ )
   System.out.print( a[i] + " " );
```

22. What does this method do?

```
public int foo( int [ ] a )
{
   int temp = 0;

   for ( int i = 0; i < a.length; i++ )
   {
       if ( a[i] == 5 )
           temp++;
   }
   return temp;
}
```

23. What does this method do?

```java
public int foo( int [ ] a )
{
    for ( int i = 0; i < a.length; i++ )
    {
        if ( a[i] == 10 )
            return i;
    }
    return -1;
}
```

24. What does this method do?

```java
public boolean foo( int [ ] a )
{
    for ( int i = 0; i < a.length; i++ )
    {
        if ( a[i] < 0 )
            return false;
    }
    return true;
}
```

25. What does this method do?

```java
public String [ ] foo( String [ ] a )
{
    String [ ] temp = new String[a.length];
    for ( int i = 0; i < a.length; i++ )
    {
        temp[i] = a[i].toLowerCase( );
    }
    return temp;
}
```

26. What does this method do?

```java
public boolean [ ] foo( String [ ] a )
{
    boolean [ ] temp = new boolean[a.length];

    for ( int i = 0; i < a.length; i++ )
    {
        if ( a[i].contains( "@" ) )
            temp[i] = true;
```

```
            else
                    temp[i] = false;
        }
        return temp;
    }
```

8.10.3   Fill In the Code

27. This code assigns the value 10 to all the elements of an array *a*.

```
int [ ] a = new int[25];
for ( int i = 0; i < a.length; i++ )
{
        // your code goes here

}
```

28. This code prints all the elements of array *a* that have a value greater than 20.

```
double [ ] a = { 45.2, 13.1, 12.8, 87.4, 99.0, 100.1, 43.8, 2.4 };

for ( int i = 0; i < a.length; i++ )
{
        // your code goes here

}
```

29. This code prints the average of the elements of array *a*.

```
int [ ] a = { 45, 13, 12, 87, 99, 100, 43, 2 };
double average = 0.0;

for ( int i = 0; i < a.length; i++ )
{
        // your code goes here

}

// ... and your code continues here
```

30. This code calculates and prints the dot product of two arrays ($\Sigma\ a[i] * b[i]$).

```
int [ ] a = { 3, 7, 9 };
int [ ] b = { 2, 9, 4 };
```

```
int dotProduct = 0;

for ( int i = 0; i < a.length; i++ )
{
      // your code goes here

}
```

31. This code prints the following three lines:

```
a[0] = 3
a[1] = 6
a[2] = 10
```

```
int [ ] a = { 3, 6, 10 };

for ( int i = 0; i < a.length; i++ )
{
      // your code goes here

}
```

32. This method returns *true* if an element in an array of *Strings* passed as a parameter contains the substring *IBM*; otherwise, it returns *false*.

```
public boolean foo( String [ ] a )
{
    // your code goes here
}
```

33. This method returns the number of elements in an array passed as a parameter that are multiples of 7.

```
public int foo( int [ ] a )
{
    // your code goes here
}
```

34. This method returns *true* if the first two elements of the array passed as a parameter have the same value; otherwise, it returns *false*.

```
public boolean foo( String [ ] a )
{
      // your code goes here
}
```

35. This method takes an array of *ints* as a parameter and returns an array of *booleans*. For each element in the parameter array whose value is 0, the corresponding element of the array returned will be assigned *false*; otherwise, the element will be assigned *true*.

```
public boolean [ ] foo( int [ ] a )
{
  // your code goes here
}
```

8.10.4 Identifying Errors in Code

36. Where is the error in this code sequence?

```
double [ ] a = { 3.3, 26.0, 48.4 };
a[4] = 2.5;
```

37. Where is the error in this code sequence?

```
double [ ] a = { 3.3, 26.0, 48.4 };
System.out.println( a[-1] );
```

38. Where is the error in this code sequence?

```
double [ ] a = { 3.3, 26.0, 48.4 };
System.out.println( a{1} );
```

39. Where is the error in this code sequence?

```
double [ ] a = { 3.3, 26.0, 48.4 };
for ( int i = 0; i <= a.length; i++ )
        System.out.println( a[i] );
```

40. Where is the error in this code sequence?

```
double a[3] = { 3.3, 26.0, 48.4 };
```

41. Where is the error (although this code will compile and run) in this code sequence?

```
int a[ ] = { 3, 26, 48, 5 };
int b[ ] = { 3, 26, 48, 5 };

if ( a != b )
        System.out.println( "Array elements are NOT identical" );
```

42. Where is the error in this code sequence?

```
int [ ] a = { 3, 26, 48, 5 };
a.length = 10;
```

43. Where is the logic error in this code sequence?

```
int [ ] a = { 3, 26, 48, 5 };
System.out.println( "The array elements are " + a );
```

44. Where is the error in this code sequence?

```
Integer i1 = new Integer( 10 );
Integer i2 = new Integer( 15 );
Double d1 = new Double( 3.4 );
String s = new String( "Hello" );
Integer [ ] a = { i1, i2, d1, s };
```

8.10.5 Debugging Area—Using Messages from the Java Compiler and Java JVM

45. You coded the following on line 26 of the class *Test.java*:

```
int a[6] = { 2, 7, 8, 9, 11, 16 };   // line 26
```

When you compile, you get the following messages:

```
Test.java:26: ']' expected
        int a[6] = { 2, 7, 8, 9, 11, 16}; // line 26
            ^
Test.java:26: illegal start of expression
        int a[6] = { 2, 7, 8, 9, 11, 16}; // line 26
            ^
Test.java:26: illegal start of expression
        int a[6] = { 2, 7, 8, 9, 11, 16}; // line 26
                ^
Test.java:26: not a statement
        int a[6] = { 2, 7, 8, 9, 11, 16}; // line 26
                ^
Test.java:26: ';' expected
        int a[6] = { 2, 7, 8, 9, 11, 16}; // line 26
                  ^
Test.java:29: class, interface, or enum expected
}
^
6 errors
```

Explain what the problem is and how to fix it.

46. You coded the following on lines 26, 27, and 28 of the class *Test.java*:

```
int [ ] a = { 2, 7, 8, 9, 11, 16 };   // line 26 of class Test.java
for ( int i = 0; i <= a.length; i++ ) // line 27 of class Test.java
    System.out.println( a[i] );       // line 28 of class Test.java
```

The code compiles properly, but when you run, you get the following output:

```
2
7
8
9
11
16
Exception in thread "main" java.lang.ArrayIndexOutOfBoundsException: 6
at Test.main(Test46.java:28)
```

Explain what the problem is and how to fix it.

47. You coded the following in the class *Test.java*:

```
int [ ] a = { 1, 2, 3 };
int [ ] b = { 1, 2, 3 };
if ( a == b )
      System.out.println( "Arrays are equal" );
else
      System.out.println( "Arrays are NOT equal" );
```

The code compiles properly and runs, but the result is not what you expected; the output is

```
Arrays are NOT equal
```

Explain what the problem is and how to fix it.

48. You coded the following in the class *Test.java*:

```
int [ ] a = { 1, 2, 3 };
System.out.println( a );
```

The code compiles properly and runs, but the result is not what you expected; the output is similar to the following:

```
[I@f0326267
```

Explain what the problem is and how to fix it.

8.10.6   Write a Short Program

49. Write a value-returning method that returns the number of elements in an integer array.

50. Write a value-returning method that returns the product of all the elements in an integer array.

51. Write a *void* method that sets to 0 all the elements of an integer array.

52. Write a *void* method that multiplies by 2 all the elements of an array of *floats*.

53. Write a method that returns the percentage of elements greater than or equal to 90 in an array of *ints*.

54. Write a method that returns the difference between the largest and smallest elements in an array of *doubles*.

55. Write a method that returns the sum of all the elements of an array of *ints* that have an odd index.

56. Write a method that returns the percentage of the number of elements that have the value *true* in an array of *booleans*.

57. Write a method that returns *true* if an array of *Strings* contains the String "*Hello*"; *false* otherwise.

58. Write a method that prints all the elements of an array of *chars* in reverse order.

59. Write a method that returns an array composed of all the elements in an array of *chars* in reverse order.

60. Write an array-returning method that takes a *String* as a parameter and returns the corresponding array of *chars*.

61. Code an array-returning method that takes an array of *ints* as a parameter and returns an array of *booleans*, assigning *true* for any element of the parameter array greater than or equal to 100; and *false* otherwise.

8.10.7   Programming Projects

62. Write a class encapsulating the concept of statistics for a baseball team, which has the following attributes: a number of players, a list of number of hits for each player, a list of number of at-bats for each player.

Write the following methods:

❑ A constuctor with two equal-length arrays as parameters, the number of hits per player, and the number of at-bats per player.

❑ Accessors, mutators, *toString*, and *equals* methods.

❑ Generate and return an array of batting averages based on the attributes given.

❏ Calculate and return the total number of hits for the team.

❏ Calculate and return the number of players with a batting average greater than .300.

❏ A method returning an array holding the number of hits, sorted in ascending order.

Write a client class to test all the methods in your class.

63. Write a class encapsulating the concept of student grades on a test, assuming student grades are composed of a list of integers between 0 and 100.

Write the following methods:

❏ A constructor with just one parameter, the number of students; all grades can be randomly generated

❏ Accessor, mutator, *toString*, and *equals* methods

❏ A method returning an array of the grades sorted in ascending order

❏ A method returning the highest grade

❏ A method returning the average grade

❏ A method returning the median grade (*Hint:* The median grade will be located in the middle of the sorted array of grades.)

❏ A method returning the mode (the grade that occurs most often) (*Hint:* Create an array of counters; count how many times each grade occurs; then pick the maximum in the array of counters; the array index is the mode.)

Write a client class to test all the methods in your class.

64. Write a class encapsulating the concept of daily temperatures for a week.

Write the following methods:

❏ A constructor accepting an array of seven temperatures as a parameter

❏ Accessor, mutator, *toString*, and *equals* methods

❏ A method returning how many temperatures were below freezing

❏ A method returning an array of temperatures above 100 degrees

❑ A method returning the largest change in temperature between any two consecutive days

❑ A method returning an array of daily temperatures, sorted in descending order

Write a client class to test all the methods in your class.

65. Write a class encapsulating the concept of a tic-tac-toe game as follows:

Two players will be playing, player 1 and player 2.

The board is represented by an array of 9 integer elements: elements at indexes 0, 1, and 2 represent the first row; elements at indexes 3, 4, and 5 represent the second row; elements at indexes 6, 7, and 8 represent the third row.

The value 0 in the array indicates that this space is available; the value 1 indicates the space is occupied by player 1; and the value 2 indicates that this space is occupied by player 2.

In the *main* method of your client class, your program will simulate a tic-tac-toe game from the command line (or a *JOptionPane* dialog box), doing the following:

❑ Create a *TicTacToe* object and instantiate it.

❑ In a loop, prompt for plays, as *ints*, from the user. At each iteration of the loop, you will need to call methods of the *TicTacToe* class to update the *TicTacToe* object. You need to keep track of who is playing (player 1 or 2), enforce the rules, check if either player has won the game. It is clear that if anyone has won the game, it is the last player who played.

❑ If a player wins, you will need to exit the loop and present the result of the game. If the game ends in a tie, you should output that result.

In your *TicTacToe* class, you will need to code the following methods:

❑ A default constructor instantiating the array representing the board.

❑ A method that allows a player to make a move; it takes two arguments: the player number and the position played on the board.

❏ A method checking if a play is legal.

❏ A method checking if a player has won the game; you can break up that method into several methods if you like (for instance, check if a player has won the game by claiming an entire horizontal row).

❏ A method that checks whether the game is a tie (if no player has won and all squares have been played, the game is tied).

❏ A method that displays the results of the game ("Player 1 won," "Player 2 won," or "Tie game").

Write a client class, where the *main* method is located, to test all the methods in your class and enable the user to play.

66. When a new user logs in for the first time on a website, the user has to submit personal information, such as user_id, password, name, email address, telephone number, and so forth. Typically, there are two fields for passwords, requiring the user to enter the password twice, to ensure that the user did not make a typo in the first password field.

Write a class encapsulating the concept of processing a form with the following elements:

User_id

Password

Reenter password

Email address

Name

Street address

City

State

Zip

Telephone

In your class, write the following methods:

❏ A constructor with one parameter, a sequence of 10 words in an array of *Strings*, your only instance variable.

❏ Accessor, mutator, *toString*, and *equals* methods.

❏ A method checking that no *Strings* in the array are empty. (All fields are mandatory.) If at least one is empty, it returns *false*; otherwise, it returns *true*.

❏ A method returning the number of characters in the user_id.

❏ A method checking if the two *Strings* representing the passwords (representing the password typed in twice) are identical. If they are, it returns *true*; if not, it returns *false*.

❏ A method checking if the *String* representing the email address actually "looks like" an email address; to simplify, we can assume that an email address contains one and only one @ character and contains one or more periods after the @ character. If it does "look like" an email address, then the method returns *true*; otherwise, it returns *false*.

❏ A method checking if the *String* representing the state has exactly two characters. If it does, it returns *true*; otherwise, it returns *false*.

Write a client class to test all the methods in your class.

67. We want to write a program that performs some syntax checking on HTML code; for simplicity reasons, we will assume that the HTML code is syntactically correct if the number of < characters in any word is the same as the number of > characters in that word. We will also assume that the syntax is correct if the first word is *<HTML>* and the last word is *</HTML>*.

Write a class encapsulating that concept, including the following methods:

❏ A constructor with one parameter, an array of the words in the HTML sentence, your only instance variable. Your constructor should then get user input from the console for that same number of words and store them in an array of *Strings*, your only data member.

❏ Accessor, mutator, *toString*, and *equals* methods.

❏ A method returning how many words are in the array.

❏ A method returning *true* if the first word is *<HTML>* and the last word is *</HTML>*; *false* otherwise.

❑ A method checking if each array element contains the same number of < characters as > characters. If that is the case, the method returns *true*; otherwise, it returns *false*. For this, we suggest the following method to help you:

■ Write an *int*-returning method that takes a *String* and a *char* as parameters and returns how many times that *char* appears in the *String*; you can convert the *String* to an array of *chars* and loop through it, or use another strategy of your choice.

❑ A method counting and returning the number of IMG tags overall.

Write a client class to test all the methods in your class.

68. Write a class encapsulating the concept of converting integer grades to letter grades (A, B, C, D, or F), assuming grades are composed of a list of integers between 0 and 100.

Write the following methods:

❑ A constructor with just one parameter, the number of students; all grades can be randomly generated.

❑ Accessor, mutator, *toString*, and *equals* methods.

❑ A method returning an array of *chars* corresponding to the integer grades (90 or above should be converted to A, 80 or above to B, 70 or above to C, 60 or above to D, and 59 or less to F).

❑ A method returning the number of A's.

❑ A method returning an array of *ints* counting how many A's, B's, C's, D's, and F's were received.

Write a client class to test all the methods in your class.

69. Write a class encapsulating the concept of printing a letter as a 7 × 5 grid of either spaces or asterisks (*). That letter is made up of a list of thirty-five 1's and 0's, which will be stored in an array representing the letter, the only instance variable of the class.

For instance, the following is what the input file would look like for the letter I. A 1 will print as an *, and a 0 as a space.

After every five elements have been printed, you will need to print a new line.

If the input is

0 1 1 1 0 0 0 1 0 0 0 0 1 0 0 0 0 1 0 0 0 0 1 0 0 0 0 1 0 0 0 1 1 1 0

when printed, that letter would look like this:

```
***
  *
  *
  *
  *
  *
***
```

Write the following methods:

- ❑ A constructor with one parameter, an array of thirty-five 0's or 1's, your only instance variable. Be sure to enforce the constraint of having only 1's and 0's.

- ❑ Accessor, mutator, *toString*, and *equals* methods.

- ❑ A method printing out the letter as in the output example above.

- ❑ A method returning the number of 1's.

- ❑ A method returning the percentage of 0's.

Write a client class to test all the methods in your class.

70. Write a class encapsulating the concept of a team of baseball players, assuming a baseball player has the following attributes: a name, a position, and a batting percentage. In addition to that class, you will need to design and code a *Player* class to encapsulate the concept of a baseball player.

In your class encapsulating the team, you should write the following methods:

- ❑ A constructor taking an array of *Player* objects as its only parameter and assigning that array to the array data member of the class, its only instance variable. In your client class, when you test all your methods, you can hard-code nine baseball *Player* objects.

- ❑ Accessor, mutator, *toString*, and *equals* methods.

- ❑ A method checking that all positions are different, returning *true* if they are, *false* if they are not.

❏ A method returning the batting percentage of the team.

❏ A method checking that we have a pitcher (that is, the name of the position) on the team. If we do not have any, it returns *false*; otherwise, it returns *true*.

❏ A method returning the array of *Player* objects sorted in ascending order using the batting percentage as the sorting key.

❏ A method checking if a certain person (a parameter of the method) is on the team, based on the name of that person. If the person is on the team, the method returns *true*; otherwise, it returns *false*.

❏ A method returning an array of *Player* objects, sorted in ascending order based on batting percentages.

Write a client class to test all the methods in your class.

71. Write a class encapsulating a similar concept to the one used in the die counting problem of Section 8.8. Here, we want to roll two dice; the total of the numbers rolled will be between 2 and 12. We want to keep track of how many times each possible roll was rolled.

Write the following methods:

❏ A constructor with no parameter; it randomly generates two numbers between 1 and 6, representing the dice.

❏ Accessor, mutator, *toString*, and *equals* methods.

❏ A method returning the total of the two dice.

❏ A method checking if the two dice have identical values. If they do, it returns *true*; otherwise, it returns *false*.

The number of times we roll the dice should be an input from the user at the command line (not inside the program). Your program should output the total for each possible roll (from 2 to 12), as well as the number of times the two dice had identical values.

Write a client class to test all the methods in your class.

72. Write an applet that creates two *Die* objects and rolls the two dice 5,000 times. Display the results showing the frequency of each possible total in a bar chart. Pick a scale that is appropriate for the maximum height of your bar chart.

8.10.8 Technical Writing

73. What do you think are advantages and disadvantages of arrays?

74. Write the pseudocode to perform a Selection Sort on an array of *Auto* objects based on the instance variable *model*.

75. When you try to use an array index that is out of bounds, your code will compile, but you will generate a run-time exception. Discuss whether this is an advantage or a disadvantage, and why.

76. When instantiating an array, you can assign the number of elements in the array dynamically, using a variable (as opposed to using a constant). Discuss a situation where that would be useful.

8.10.9 Group Project (for a group of 1, 2, or 3 students)

77. Security is an important feature of information systems. Often, text is encrypted before being sent, and then decrypted upon receipt. We want to build a class (or several classes) encapsulating the concept of encryption. You will need to test that class with a client program where the *main* method is located.

    For this project, encrypting consists of translating each character into another character. For instance, if we consider the English alphabet, including characters *a* through *z*, each character is randomly encrypted into another, which could be the same character. (If you like, you can design your program so that no character is encrypted into itself.) To represent this concept, we can have an array of characters for the original alphabet, and another array of characters for the encrypted alphabet. For example, we could have

Original alphabet	Encrypted alphabet
a	u
b	p
c	h
d	a
e	s
f	x
g	z
h	b
i	j
. . .	. . .

To encrypt a word, each letter in the word is replaced by the corresponding letter in the encryted alphabet. For example, the word *caged* would be encrypted into *huzsa*. To decrypt a word, the letters in the encrypted word are replaced by the corresponding letter in the original alphabet. For example, the encrypted word *xssa* would be decrypted as *feed*.

If we have 26 different characters in the original alphabet, then we will have 26 different characters in the encrypted alphabet. Furthermore, the encrypted alphabet should be randomly generated.

In your *main* method, you should prompt the user for a sentence. Your program should encrypt the sentence, output the encrypted sentence, then decrypt it, and output the decrypted sentence, which should be identical to the original sentence that was input by the user.

For extra credit, use an array to keep track of the number of occurrences of each character. Convert these occurrences to percentages, and then use these percentages to attempt to decrypt a large, encrypted message.

CHAPTER 9

Multidimensional Arrays and the *ArrayList* Class

CHAPTER CONTENTS

Introduction

In Chapter 8, we learned that arrays could be useful when we have a lot of data to store in memory. If we write a program to perform statistics on last year's temperatures, it is convenient to set up an array of *double*s of size 365 to store the daily temperature data.

But what if in addition to analyzing daily temperatures, we want to analyze temperatures by the week, or by a particular day of the week? For instance, if we sail on weekends, we could want to know how many times the temperature was above 65 degrees on Saturdays and Sundays. If we are considering investing in air conditioning at home, we might be interested in knowing how many weeks had temperatures above 90 degrees. If we are avid skiers, we could be interested in the number of weeks with temperatures lower than 32 degrees.

In this situation, we would want to organize our data along two dimensions: weeks and days of the week. If we were to visualize the data as a table, we could imagine a table made up of 52 rows, each row representing a week. Each row would have seven columns, representing the days of the week. This table is shown in Figure 9.1. Or we could imagine a table of seven rows, each row representing a day of the week, and 52 columns, each column representing a week of the year. In either case, we can represent the rows and columns of our temperature table using a two-dimensional array. More generally, **multidimensional** arrays allow us to represent data organized along *n* dimensions with a single array.

Figure 9.1

Temperature Data for the Previous 52 Weeks

	Sunday	Monday	Tuesday	Wednesday	Thursday	Friday	Saturday
Week 1	35	28.6	29.3	38	43.1	45.6	49
Week 2	51.9	37.9	34.1	37.1	39	40.5	43.2
...							
...							
...							
...							
...							
Week 51	56.2	51.9	45.3	48.7	42.9	35.5	38.2
Week 52	33.2	27.1	24.9	29.8	37.7	39.9	38.8

9.1 Declaring and Instantiating Multidimensional Arrays

Just like single-dimensional arrays, multidimensional arrays are implemented as objects, so creating a multidimensional array takes the same two steps as creating a single-dimensional array:

1. declaring the object reference for the array
2. instantiating the array

In arrays with elements of primitive types, each element of the array contains a value of that type. For example, in an array of *doubles*, each element contains a *double* value. In arrays with a class data type, each element is an object reference, which points to the location of an object of that class.

9.1.1 Declaring Multidimensional Arrays

To declare a multidimensional array, we use the same syntax as for a single-dimensional array, except that we include an empty set of brackets for each dimension.

Here is the syntax for declaring a two-dimensional array:

```
datatype [ ][ ] arrayName;
```

Here is the syntax for declaring a three-dimensional array:

```
datatype [ ][ ][ ] arrayName;
```

In order to keep things simple, we will concentrate on two-dimensional arrays at this point. We will discuss three- and four-dimensional arrays later in the chapter.

The following statement declares an array to hold the daily high temperatures for the last 52 weeks:

```
double [ ][ ] dailyTemps;
```

The brackets can be placed before or after the array name. So the following syntax for declaring a two-dimensional array is also valid:

```
datatype arrayName [ ][ ];
```

We prefer to put the brackets right after the data type, because it's easier to read.

To store quiz grades for students, we could declare a two-dimensional array, where each row will store the quiz grades for a particular student and each column will store the grades for a particular quiz:

```
char [ ][ ] quizzes;    // each element is a char
```

The syntax is the same whether we declare arrays with basic data types or class types.

Imagine that we are interested in keeping track of a fleet of cars within a multinational corporation. The corporation operates in various countries, and in each of these countries, some employees have a company car. For this situation, we can declare a two-dimensional array where the first dimension will represent the country and the second dimension will represent the employee. Using our *Auto* class from Chapter 7, the following statement declares this two-dimensional array to hold *Auto* objects:

```
Auto [ ][ ] cars;
```

You can also declare multiple multidimensional arrays of the same data type in one statement by inserting a comma after each array name, using this syntax:

```
datatype [ ][ ] arrayName1, arrayName2;
```

For example, the following statement will declare two integer arrays to hold the number of stolen bases for two baseball players for each game in their career:

```
int [ ][ ] brian, jon;
```

The first dimension represents the games (per season), and the second dimension represents the season.

Notice that when we declare a multidimensional array, we do not specify how many elements the array will have. Declaring a multidimensional array does not allocate memory for the array; this is done in step 2, when we instantiate the array.

For example, this code from the file *Test.java*:

```
double [7][52] dailyTemps;
```

will generate the following compiler errors:

```
Test.java:5: ']' expected
  double [7][52] dailyTemps;
         ^
Test.java:5: not a statement
  double [7][52] dailyTemps;
         ^
Test.java:5: illegal start of expression
    int [7][52] dailyTemps;
        ^
Test.java:5: ';' expected
    int [7][52] dailyTemps;
        ^
```

COMMON ERROR TRAP

Specifying the size of any of the dimensions of a multidimensional array in the declaration will generate a compiler error.

```
Test.java:5: not a statement
    int [7][52] dailyTemps;
         ^

Test.java:5: ';' expected
    int [7][52] dailyTemps;
         ^

Test.java:5: not a statement
  double [7][52] dailyTemps;
          ^

7 errors
```

9.1.2   Instantiating Multidimensional Arrays

Just like instantiating single-dimensional arrays, you instantiate a multidimensional array using the *new* keyword. Here is the syntax for instantiating a two-dimensional array:

```
arrayName = new datatype [exp1][exp2];

   where exp1 and exp2 are expressions that evaluate to integers and
   specify, respectively, the number of rows and the number of columns in
   the array.
```

This statement allocates memory for the array. The number of elements in a two-dimensional array is equal to the sum of the number of elements in each row. When all the rows have the same number of columns, the number of elements in the array is equal to the number of rows multiplied by the number of columns.

For example, if we instantiate the following *dailyTemps* array with 52 rows and 7 columns, the array will have 52 * 7, or 364, elements:

```
dailyTemps = new double [52][7]; // dailyTemps has 52 rows
                                 // and 7 columns,
                                 // for a total of 364 elements
```

These statements will instantiate the other arrays declared above:

```
int numberOfStudents = 25;
int numberOfQuizzes = 10;
quizzes = new char [numberOfStudents][numberOfQuizzes];
// quizzes has 25 rows and 10 columns
// for a total of 250 elements

cars = new Auto [5][50];
// cars has 5 rows and 50 columns
// cars will store 250 Auto objects

brian = new int [80][20];
```

```
// brian has 80 rows and 20 columns
// there are 80 games per season
// brian played baseball for 20 seasons

jon = new int [80][10];
// jon has 80 rows and 10 columns
// jon played baseball for 10 seasons
```

REFERENCE POINT

The initial values automatically given to array elements depend on the data type of the array and are discussed in Chapter 8.

When a multidimensional array is instantiated, the elements are given initial values automatically. Elements of arrays with numeric types are initialized to 0, elements of *char* type are initialized to the Unicode null character, elements of *boolean* type are initialized to *false*, and elements of class types are initialized to *null*.

9.1.3 Combining the Declaration and Instantiation of Multidimensional Arrays

Multidimensional arrays, like single-dimensional arrays, can also be instantiated when they are declared. To combine the declaration and instantiation of a two-dimensional array, use this syntax:

```
datatype [ ][ ] arrayName = new datatype [exp1][exp2];

   where exp1 and exp2 are expressions that evaluate to integers and
   specify, respectively, the number of rows and columns in the array.
```

Thus, this statement:

```
double [ ][ ] dailyTemps = new double [52][7];
```

is equivalent to:

```
double [ ][ ] dailyTemps;
dailyTemps = new double [52][7];
```

Similarly, this statement:

```
char [ ][ ] quizzes = new char [25][10];
```

is equivalent to:

```
char [ ][ ] quizzes;
quizzes = new char [25][10];
```

Furthermore, this statement:

```
Auto [ ][ ] cars = new Auto [5][50];
```

is equivalent to:

```
Auto [ ][ ] cars;
cars = new Auto [5][50];
```

9.1.4   Assigning Initial Values to Multidimensional Arrays

We can instantiate a two-dimensional array by assigning initial values when the array is declared. To do this, we specify the initial values using comma-separated lists of initial values, enclosed in an outer set of curly braces:

```
datatype [ ][ ] arrayName =
      { { value00, value01, ... }, { value10, value11, }, ... };
```

where *valueMN* is an expression that evaluates to the data type of the array and is the value to assign to the element at row M and column N.

The list contains a number of sublists, separated by commas. The number of these sublists determines the number of rows in the array. For each row, the number of values in the corresponding sublist determines the number of columns in the row. Thus, Java allows a two-dimensional array to have a different number of columns in each row. For example, in our *Auto* array, each country (row) could have a different number of employees (columns) with company cars.

Indeed, a two-dimensional array is an array of arrays. The first dimension of a two-dimensional array consists of an array of array references, with each reference pointing to a single-dimensional array. Thus, a two-dimensional array is composed of an array of rows, where each row is a single-dimensional array. Therefore, each row can have a different number of elements, or columns.

For example, this statement declares and instantiates a two-dimensional array of integers:

```
int [ ][ ] numbersList1 = { { 0, 5, 10 },
                            { 0, 3, 6, 9 } };
```

Because two sublists are given, this two-dimensional array has two rows. The first sublist specifies three values, and therefore, the first row will have three columns; the second sublist specifies four values, and therefore, the second row will have four columns.

Figure 9.2 shows the *numbersList1* array after the preceding statement is executed.

An initialization list can be given only when the array is declared. If a two-dimensional array has already been instantiated, attempting to assign values

Figure 9.2

The *numbersList1* **Array After Instantiation**

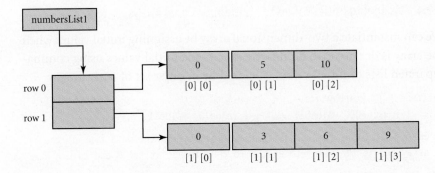

to an array using an initialization list will generate a compiler error. For example, this code from the file *Test.java:*

```
int [ ][ ] grades = new int [2][3];
grades = { { 89, 73, 98 },
          { 88, 65, 92 } };
```

will generate the following compiler errors:

```
Test.java:6: illegal start of expression
  grades = { { 89, 73, 98 },
           ^
Test.java:6: not a statement
      grades = { { 89, 73, 98 },
               ^
Test.java:6: ';' expected
      grades = { { 89, 73, 98 },
                 ^
Test.java:6: illegal start of expression
      grades = { { 89, 73, 98 },
                              ^
Test.java:7: not a statement
              { 88, 65, 92 } };
              ^
Test.java:7: ';' expected
              { 88, 65, 92 } };
                ^
Test.java:9: class, interface, or enum expected
}
^

7 errors
```

We can declare and instantiate an array of objects by providing object references in the list:

```
Auto sportsCar = new Auto( "Ferrari", 0, 0.0 );
Auto sedan1 = new Auto( "BMW", 0, 0.0 );
Auto sedan2 = new Auto( "BMW", 100, 15.0 );
Auto sedan3 = new Auto( "Toyota", 0, 0.0 );
```

```
Auto rv1 = new Auto( "Jeep", 0, 0.0 );

Auto [ ][ ] cars = { { sportsCar, sedan1 },
                     { rv1, new Auto( ) },
                     { sedan2, sedan3 } };
```

This array of *Auto* objects has three rows with two columns in each row. The elements of the array *cars* are object references to *Auto* objects.

In most situations, the number of columns will be the same for each row. However, there are situations where it is useful to have a different number of columns for each row. For instance, Dr. Smith, a college professor, keeps track of grades using a two-dimensional array. The rows represent the courses she teaches and the columns represent the grades for the students in those sections. Grades are A, B, C, D, or F, so she declares the array with *char* elements. Dr. Smith teaches four courses: CS1, CS2, Database Management, and Operating Systems. Thus, she has four rows in the array. But in each course, Dr. Smith has a different number of students: There are 23 students in CS1, 16 in CS2, 12 in Database Management, and 28 in Operating Systems. So the first row will have 23 columns, the second row 16 columns, the third row 12 columns, and the fourth and last row will have 28 columns.

Using an initialization list, it is easy to instantiate a two-dimensional array with a different number of columns for every row. But sometimes the data is retrieved dynamically—read from a file, for example—and it is not possible to use an initialization list.

To instantiate a two-dimensional array with a different number of columns for each row, you can do the following:

- First, instantiate the two-dimensional array.

- Second, instantiate each row, as a single-dimensional array.

For the preceding example, we can use the following code:

```
char [ ][ ] grades;           // declare the array
grades = new char [4][ ];     // instantiate the array
                              // grades has 4 null array elements

grades[0] = new char [23];    // instantiate row 0; 23 char elements
grades[1] = new char [16];    // instantiate row 1; 16 char elements
grades[2] = new char [12];    // instantiate row 2; 12 char elements
grades[3] = new char [28];    // instantiate row 3; 28 char elements
```

COMMON ERROR TRAP

An initialization list can be given only when the two-dimensional array is declared. Attempting to assign values to an array using an initialization list after the array is instantiated will generate a compiler error.

The second statement:

```
grades = new char [4][ ];
```

instantiates the two-dimensional array *grades* as an array having four rows, none of which has been instantiated yet. Because a two-dimensional array is an array of arrays, each element of the first dimension of the *grades* array is an array reference. Thus, before being instantiated, each element of the first dimension of the *grades* array has the value *null*.

As explained earlier, in a two-dimensional array, each row is a single-dimensional array. The last four statements instantiate each row, *grades[0]*, *grades[1]*, *grades[2]*, and *grades[3]*, each row having a different number of elements, or columns. The elements in these arrays are *char*s, initialized to a space.

Later in this chapter, we will define a general pattern for processing two-dimensional array elements so that it applies to all situations: an identical number of columns for each row, or a different number of columns for each row.

9.2   Accessing Multidimensional Array Elements

Elements of a two-dimensional array are accessed using this syntax:

```
arrayName[exp1][exp2]
```

> where *exp1* and *exp2* are expressions that evaluate to integers.

Exp1 is the element's row position, or **row index**, within the two-dimensional array. *Exp2* is the element's column position, or **column index**, within the two-dimensional array. The row index of the first row is always 0; the row index of the last row is always 1 less than the number of rows. The column index of the first column is always 0. The column index of the last column is always 1 less than the number of columns in that row.

Because a two-dimensional array is an array of arrays, the length of a two-dimensional array is its number of arrays, or rows. We access the number of rows in a two-dimensional array using the following syntax:

```
arrayName.length
```

Similarly, the length of each row is the number of columns (or elements) in that row's array. To access the number of columns in row *i* of a two-dimensional array named *arrayName*, use this syntax:

```
arrayName[i].length
```

Table 9.1 summarizes the syntax for accessing elements of a two-dimensional array.

TABLE 9.1   Accessing Two-Dimensional Array Elements

Array Element	Syntax
Row 0, column *j*	`arrayName[0][j]`
Row *i*, column *j*	`arrayName[i][j]`
Last row, column *j*	`arrayName[arrayName.length - 1][j]`
Last row, last column	`arrayName[arrayName.length - 1]` `    [arrayName[arrayName.length - 1].length - 1]`
Number of rows in the array	`arrayName.length`
Number of columns in row *i*	`arrayName[i].length`

Suppose we want to analyze the monthly cell phone bills for the past three months for a family of four persons. The parents, Joe and Jane, each have a cell phone, and so do the children, Mike and Sarah. We want to calculate the average monthly bill for each person, the total payments for the three months, and determine which family member had the lowest and highest bills. We could use a two-dimensional array of *doubles* with three rows and four columns. The rows will represent the months and the columns will represent the family members. For example, we could have the following mapping for the row and column indexes:

> row 0 : July
> row 1 : August
> row 2 : September

> column 0 : Joe
> column 1 : Jane
> column 2 : Mike
> column 3 : Sarah

We could visualize our two-dimensional array as the table shown in Table 9.2.

TABLE 9.2   Visualizing a Two-Dimensional Array

	Joe	Jane	Mike	Sarah
July	45.24	54.67	32.55	25.61
August	65.29	49.75	32.08	26.11
September	75.24	54.53	34.55	28.16

We'll name the array *familyCellBills*. Each element in the array will be referenced as *familyCellBills[i][j]*, where *i* is the index of the row (the month), and *j* is the index of the column (the person). Remember that the first element in a row or column is at index 0, so the first element in the first row is at index [0][0].

In lines 13–15 of Example 9.1, we declare and instantiate the *familyCellBills* array. Because the elements of *familyCellBills* are *doubles*, instantiating the array also initializes each element to 0.0. Lines 18–31 store values into each element of the array. Figure 9.3 shows how the *familyCellBills* array looks after lines 18–31 are executed.

```
1  /* Two-Dimensional Array of Cell Phone Bills
2     Anderson, Franceschi
3  */
4
5  public class FamilyCellBills
6  {
7    public static void main( String [ ] args )
8    {
9      // declare constants for the number of rows and columns
10     final int NUMBER_OF_MONTHS = 3;
11     final int NUMBER_OF_PERSONS = 4;
12
13     // declare and instantiate the array
14     double [ ][ ] familyCellBills =
15        new double [NUMBER_OF_MONTHS][NUMBER_OF_PERSONS];
16
17     // assign values to array elements
18     familyCellBills[0][0] = 45.24;  // row 0
19     familyCellBills[0][1] = 54.67;
20     familyCellBills[0][2] = 32.55;
21     familyCellBills[0][3] = 25.61;
22
23     familyCellBills[1][0] = 65.29;  // row 1
24     familyCellBills[1][1] = 49.75;
25     familyCellBills[1][2] = 32.08;
26     familyCellBills[1][3] = 26.11;
27
28     familyCellBills[2][0] = 75.24;  // row 2
29     familyCellBills[2][1] = 54.53;
30     familyCellBills[2][2] = 34.55;
31     familyCellBills[2][3] = 28.16;
32
33     System.out.println( "The first monthly cell bill for the first "
34        + "family member is\n"
35        + familyCellBills[0][0] );
```

```
36    System.out.println( "The last monthly cell bill for the last "
37       + "family member is\n"
38       + familyCellBills[NUMBER_OF_MONTHS - 1][NUMBER_OF_PERSONS - 1] );
39
40    int numRows = familyCellBills.length;
41    System.out.println( "\nThe number of rows is " + numRows );
42
43    for ( int i = 0; i < numRows; i++ )
44    {
45      System.out.print( "The number of columns in row " + i + " is " );
46      System.out.println( familyCellBills[i].length );
47    }
48  }
49 }
```

EXAMPLE 9.1   The *familyCellBills* Array

Note that the last element is *familyCellBills[2][3]*, with a row index that is 1 less than *familyCellBills.length*, and a column index that is 1 less than *familyCellBills[2].length*, which is the number of columns in the last row. More generally, for a two-dimensional array named *arr*, the last element is:

```
arr[arr.length - 1][arr[arr.length - 1].length - 1]
```

Lines 33–38 output the first and last element of the array *familyCellBills*.

Line 40 assigns the number of rows in the *familyCellBills* array to the *int* variable *numRows*. The variable *numRows* now has the value 3 and is output at line 41.

At lines 43–47, a *for* loop outputs the number of columns in each row of *familyCellBills*. Figure 9.4 shows the output of this example.

Row indexes of a two-dimensional array *must* be between 0 and *arrayName.length − 1*. Attempting to access an element of an array using a row

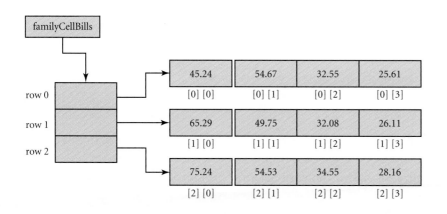

Figure 9.3
The *familyCellBills* Array After Assigning Values

Figure 9.4
Output of Example 9.1

```
The first monthly cell bill for the first family member is
45.24
The last monthly cell bill for the last family member is
28.16

The number of rows is 3
The number of columns in row 0 is 4
The number of columns in row 1 is 4
The number of columns in row 2 is 4
```

index less than 0 or greater than *arrayName.length – 1* will compile without errors, but will generate an *ArrayIndexOutOfBoundsException* at run time. By default, this exception halts execution of the program.

For example, all the following expressions are invalid:

```
// invalid row indexes for the familyCellBills array!!

familyCellBills[-1][2]
// the lowest valid row index is 0

familyCellBills[cellBills.length][2]
// the highest valid row index is familyCellBills.length - 1
```

> **COMMON ERROR TRAP**
>
> Attempting to access an element of a two-dimensional array using a row index less than 0 or greater than *arrayName.length – 1* will generate an *ArrayIndexOutOfBoundsException* at run time. Similarly, attempting to access an element of row *i* of a two-dimensional array using a column index less than 0 or greater than *arrayName[i].length – 1* also will generate an *ArrayIndexOutOfBounds-Exception*.

Similarly, column indexes of a two-dimensional array *must* be between 0 and *arrayName[i].length – 1*, where *i* is the row index. Attempting to access an element of row *i* in a two-dimensional array using a column index less than 0 or greater than *arrayName[i].length – 1* will compile without errors, but will generate an *ArrayIndexOutOfBoundsException* at run time.

For example, all the following expressions are invalid:

```
// invalid column indexes for the familyCellBills array!!

familyCellBills[1][-1]
// the lowest valid column index is 0

familyCellBills[1][familyCellBills[1].length]
// the highest valid column index of row i is
// familyCellBills[i].length - 1
```

Example 9.2 illustrates how to work with an array of objects. In this example, we reuse the *Auto* class from Chapter 7. At lines 17–20, we declare and initialize *cars*, a two-dimensional array of *Auto* objects. Before using an ele-

Figure 9.5

Output of Example 9.2

```
cars[1][0]'s description is:
Model: Ferrari; miles driven: 0; gallons of gas: 0.0
```

ment of *cars*, that *Auto* element has to be instantiated; failure to do so could generate a *NullPointerException* at run time.

There are three rows in *cars*: the first row has three columns, and the second and third rows have two columns each. Line 22 retrieves the array element at row 1 and column 0—here *sportsCar*—and assigns it to the *Auto* object reference *retrievedCar*, which is then printed at lines 25–26, where *toString* is called implicitly. Figure 9.5 shows the output of this example.

```
 1 /* Working with a Two-Dimensional Array of Objects
 2    Anderson, Franceschi
 3 */
 4
 5 public class TwoDimAutoArray
 6 {
 7  public static void main( String [ ] args )
 8  {
 9   // instantiate several Auto object references
10   Auto sedan1 = new Auto( "BMW", 0, 0.0 );
11   Auto sedan2 = new Auto( "BMW", 100, 15.0 );
12   Auto sedan3 = new Auto( "Toyota", 0, 0.0 );
13   Auto sportsCar = new Auto( "Ferrari", 0, 0.0 );
14   Auto rv1 = new Auto( "Jeep", 0, 0.0 );
15   Auto rv2 = new Auto( "Ford", 200, 30.0 );
16
17   // declare and initialize two-dimensional array of Autos
18   Auto [ ][ ] cars = { { sedan1, sedan2, sedan3 },
19                        { sportsCar, new Auto( ) },
20                        { rv1, rv2 } };
21
22   Auto retrievedCar = cars[1][0];
23   // retrievedCar gets the sportsCar object reference
24
25   System.out.println( "cars[1][0]'s description is:\n"
26                       + retrievedCar );
27  }
28 }
```

EXAMPLE 9.2   Two-Dimensional Array of *Auto* Objects

Skill Practice
with these end-of-chapter questions

9.10.1   Multiple Choice Exercises

Questions 1,2,3,4,5,6,7,8

9.10.2   Reading and Understanding Code

Questions 14,15,16,17,18

9.10.3   Fill In the Code

Questions 33,34

9.10.4   Identifying Errors in Code

Questions 50,51,52,53

9.10.5   Debugging Area

Question 59

9.10.6   Write a Short Program

Question 65

9.10.8   Technical Writing

Question 97

9.3   Aggregate Two-Dimensional Array Operations

As with single-dimensional arrays, Java does not support aggregate operations on multidimensional arrays. For example, you cannot print the contents of an array using only the array name. Instead, you need to process each element individually.

9.3.1   Processing All the Elements of a Two-Dimensional Array

To process all the elements of a two-dimensional array, we use nested *for* loops that access and process each element individually. Often, the most logical way to process all elements is in row order, and within each row, in column order. We could also process elements one column at a time if that is more logical for the problem at hand.

In our nested *for* loops, the outer *for* loop will process the rows and the inner *for* loop will process the columns within each row. We will use *i* for the row index and *j* for the column index.

For the outer *for* loop, we can use the same header as we use to process single-dimensional arrays:

```
for ( int i = 0; i < arrayName.length; i++ )
```

Note that the initialization statement of the outer loop:

```
int i = 0;
```

sets *i* to the index of the first row of the two-dimensional array. Then the outer loop update statement increments *i*, so that we process each row in order.

The outer loop condition:

```
i < arrayName.length
```

continues execution of the outer loop as long as the row index is less than the *length* of the two-dimensional array, which represents the number of rows. Note that we use the *less than* operator (<) instead of the *less than or equal to* operator (<=). Using the less than or equal to operator would cause us to illegally attempt to reference an element with a row index of *arrayName.length*.

The *for* loop header for the inner loop, which processes the columns of the current row, is as follows:

```
for ( int j = 0; j < arrayName[i].length; j++ )
```

The initialization statement of the inner loop:

```
int j = 0;
```

sets *j* to the index of the first column of the current row. Then the inner loop update statement increments *j* to the next column index, so that we process each column of the current row in order.

The inner loop condition:

```
j < arrayName[i].length
```

continues execution of the inner loop as long as the column index is less than the *length* of the current row (row *i*). Given that each row can have a different number of columns, this will ensure that we do not attempt to access an element beyond the last column index of the current row.

Note, again, that we use the *less than* operator (<), not the *less than or equal to* operator (<=), which would cause us to illegally attempt to reference an element with a column index of *arrayName[i].length*.

Inside the inner *for* loop, we refer to the current element being processed as:

```
arrayName[i][j]
```

Thus, the general pattern for processing the elements of a two-dimensional array called *arrayName* in row-first, column-second order using nested *for* loops is:

```
for ( int i = 0; i < arrayName.length; i++ )
{
   for ( int j = 0; j < arrayName[i].length; j++ )
   {
      // process element arrayName[i][j]
   }
}
```

Example 9.3 illustrates how to print all the elements of the two-dimensional array *familyCellBills* in row order. The array is declared and initialized at lines 10–12. At lines 16–23, the nested *for* loops, using the standard pattern described earlier, print all the elements of the array. Figure 9.6 shows the output of the program.

```
1  /* Processing a Two-Dimensional Array of Cell Phone Bills
2     Anderson, Franceschi
3  */
4
5  public class OutputFamilyCellBills
6  {
7   public static void main( String [ ] args )
8   {
9    // declare and initialize the array
10   double [ ][ ] familyCellBills = { {45.24, 54.67, 32.55, 25.61},
11                                     {65.29, 49.75, 32.08, 26.11},
12                                     {75.24, 54.53, 34.55, 28.16} };
13
14   System.out.println( "\tData for family cell bills" );
15
16   for ( int i = 0; i < familyCellBills.length; i++ )
17   {
18    System.out.print( "\nrow " + i + ":\t" );
19    for ( int j = 0; j < familyCellBills[i].length; j++ )
20    {
```

COMMON ERROR TRAP

In the outer *for* loop, using the following condition:

```
i <= arrayName.length
```

will generate an *ArrayIndexOutOfBoundsException* because the last row of a two-dimensional array is *arrayName.length* – 1. Similarly, in the inner *for* loop, using the condition:

```
j <=
arrayName[i].length
```

will generate an *ArrayIndexOutOfBoundsException* because the last column of row *i* in a two-dimensional array is

```
arrayName[i].length –
1.
```

```
21        System.out.print( familyCellBills[i][j] + "\t" );
22      }
23    }
24    System.out.println( );
25  }
26 }
```

EXAMPLE 9.3   Two-Dimensional Array Processing

```
   Data for family cell bills

 row 0:    45.24     54.67     32.55     25.61
 row 1:    65.29     49.75     32.08     26.11
 row 2:    75.24     54.53     34.55     28.16
```

Figure 9.6
Output of Example 9.3

9.3.2   Processing a Given Row of a Two-Dimensional Array

What if we want to process just one row of a two-dimensional array? For instance, we could be interested in calculating the sum of the cell bills for the whole family for a particular month, or identifying who had the highest cell bill in a particular month.

The general pattern for processing the elements of row i of a two-dimensional array called *arrayName* uses a single *for* loop:

```
for ( int j = 0; j < arrayName[i].length; j++ )
{
    // process element arrayName[i][j]
}
```

Example 9.4 shows how to sum all the elements of a particular row of the two-dimensional array *familyCellBills*.

```
1 /* Processing One Row of a Two-Dimensional Array
2    Anderson, Franceschi
3 */
4
5 import java.util.Scanner;
6 import java.text.NumberFormat;
7
8 public class SumARowFamilyCellBills
9 {
```

```
10  public static void main( String [ ] args )
11  {
12   // declare and initialize the array
13   double [ ][ ] familyCellBills = { {45.24, 54.67, 32.55, 25.61},
14                                     {65.29, 49.75, 32.08, 26.11},
15                                     {75.24, 54.53, 34.55, 28.16} };
16
17   String [ ] months = { "July", "August", "September" };
18   for ( int i = 0; i < months.length; i++ )
19     System.out.println( "Month " + i + " : " + months[i] );
20
21   Scanner scan = new Scanner( System.in );
22   int currentMonth;
23   do
24   {
25     System.out.print( "Enter a month number between 0 and 2 > " );
26     currentMonth = scan.nextInt( );
27   } while ( currentMonth < 0 || currentMonth > 2 );
28
29   double monthlyFamilyBills = 0.0;
30   for ( int j = 0; j < familyCellBills[currentMonth].length; j++ )
31   {
32     // add current family member bill to total
33     monthlyFamilyBills += familyCellBills[currentMonth][j];
34   }
35
36   NumberFormat priceFormat = NumberFormat.getCurrencyInstance( );
37   System.out.println( "\nThe total family cell bills during "
38                       + months[currentMonth] + " is "
39                       + priceFormat.format( monthlyFamilyBills ) );
40  }
41 }
```

EXAMPLE 9.4   Processing One Row in a Two-Dimensional Array

Since the rows correspond to the months, we declare and initialize at line 17 a single-dimensional *String* array named *months* in order to make our prompt more user-friendly. At lines 18–19, we print a menu for the user, providing month names and the corresponding indexes. At lines 23–27, we use a *do/while* loop to prompt the user for a month index until the user enters a valid value between 0 and 2.

To calculate the total of the family cell bills for the month index that the user inputs, we first initialize the variable *monthlyFamilyBills* to 0.0 at line 29. We then use a single *for* loop at lines 30–34, following the pattern

```
Month 0 : July
Month 1 : August
Month 2 : September
Enter a month number between 0 and 2 > 1

The total family cell bills during August is $173.23
```

Figure 9.7
Output of Example 9.4

described earlier, to sum all the family member bills for the month chosen by the user. We then format and output the total at lines 36–39. Figure 9.7 shows the output of the program when the user chooses 1 for the month.

9.3.3 Processing a Given Column of a Two-Dimensional Array

If we want to determine the highest cell bill for Mike or calculate the average cell bill for Sarah, we will need to process just one column of the two-dimensional array.

The general pattern for processing the elements of column j of a two-dimensional array called *arrayName* uses a single *for* loop:

```
for ( int i = 0; i < arrayName.length; i++ )
{
   if ( j < arrayName[i].length )
      // process element arrayName[i][j]
}
```

Because rows may have a different number of columns, a given row i may not have a column j. Thus, we need to check that the current column number is less than *arrayName[i].length* before we attempt to access *arrayName[i][j]*.

Because our two-dimensional array *familyCellBills* has the same number of columns (4) in every row, no extra precaution is necessary here. It is a good software engineering practice, however, to verify that the column index is valid before attempting to process the array element.

Example 9.5 shows how to find the maximum value of all the elements of a particular column.

SOFTWARE ENGINEERING TIP

Before processing an element in a column, check whether the current row contains an element in that column. Doing so will avoid an *ArrayIndexOutOf-BoundsException*.

```
1 /* Processing One Column of a Two-Dimensional Array
2     Anderson, Franceschi
3 */
4
5 import java.util.Scanner;
```

```
6 import java.text.NumberFormat;
7
8 public class MaxMemberBill
9 {
10  public static void main( String [ ] args )
11  {
12   // declare and initialize the array
13   double [ ][ ] familyCellBills = { {45.24, 54.67, 32.55, 25.61},
14                                     {65.29, 49.75, 32.08, 26.11},
15                                     {75.24, 54.53, 34.55, 28.16} };
16
17   String [ ] familyMembers = { "Joe", "Jane", "Mike", "Sarah" };
18   for ( int i = 0; i < familyMembers.length; i++ )
19       System.out.println( "Family member " + i + " : "
20                               + familyMembers[i] );
21
22   Scanner scan = new Scanner( System.in );
23   int currentMember;
24   do
25   {
26    System.out.print( "Enter a family member between 0 and 3 > " );
27    currentMember = scan.nextInt( );
28   } while ( currentMember < 0 || currentMember > 3 );
29
30   double memberMaxBill = familyCellBills[0][currentMember];
31   for ( int i = 1; i < familyCellBills.length; i++ )
32   {
33    if ( currentMember < familyCellBills[i].length )
34    {
35      // update memberMaxBill if necessary
36      if ( familyCellBills[i][currentMember] > memberMaxBill )
37        memberMaxBill = familyCellBills[i][currentMember];
38    }
39   }
40
41   NumberFormat priceFormat = NumberFormat.getCurrencyInstance( );
42   System.out.println ( "\nThe max cell bill for "
43                           + familyMembers[currentMember] + " is "
44                           + priceFormat.format( memberMaxBill ) );
45  }
46 }
```

EXAMPLE 9.5   Processing a Column in a Two-Dimensional Array

At line 17, we declare and initialize a single-dimensional *String* array named *familyMembers* to make our prompt more user-friendly. At lines

24–28, we again use a *do/while* loop to prompt the user for a valid family member index.

To calculate the maximum value of the family member cell bills, we first initialize the variable *memberMaxBill* to the first element in the column (*familyCellBills[0][currentMember]*) at line 30. We then use a standard *for* loop at lines 31–39, following the pattern described earlier to update the value of *memberMaxBill* as necessary. There is one minor difference; we do not need to start the row at index 0 because we initialized *memberMaxBill* to the value of the element in row 0 of the column *currentMember*. Note that we assume that there is an element at column 0 of each row; that is, each row has been instantiated. The value of the variable *memberMaxBill* is then formatted and printed at lines 41–44. Figure 9.8 shows the output of the program.

9.3.4   Processing a Two-Dimensional Array One Row at a Time

Earlier, we calculated the sum of the elements of a given row of a two-dimensional array. But what if we are interested in calculating that sum for each row? In this case, we need to initialize our total variable before we process each row and print the results after we process each row.

The general pattern for processing each row of a two-dimensional array called *arrayName* using nested *for* loops is

```
for ( int i = 0; i < arrayName.length; i++ )
{
   // initialize processing variables for row i
   for ( int j = 0; j < arrayName[i].length; j++ )
   {
      // process element arrayName[i][j]
   }
   // finish the processing of row i
}
```

```
Family member 0 : Joe
Family member 1 : Jane
Family member 2 : Mike
Family member 3 : Sarah
Enter a family member between 0 and 3 > 2

The max cell bill for Mike is $34.55
```

Figure 9.8

Output of Example 9.5

There are two important additions to the general pattern for processing all elements of the array:

- Before processing each row, that is, before the inner loop, we need to initialize the processing variables for the current row. If we are summing elements, we initialize the total variable to 0. If we are calculating a minimum or maximum value, we initialize the current minimum or maximum to the value of the first element of the current row.

- When we reach the end of each row, that is, after each completion of the inner loop, we finish processing the current row. For instance, we may want to print the sum or maximum value for that row.

Example 9.6 shows how to sum the elements of each row of the two-dimensional array *familyCellBills*.

```
1 /* Processing Each Row of a Two-Dimensional Array
2    Anderson, Franceschi
3 */
4
5 import java.util.Scanner;
6 import java.text.NumberFormat;
7
8 public class SumEachRowFamilyCellBills
9 {
10  public static void main( String [ ] args )
11  {
12    // declare and initialize the array
13    double [ ][ ] familyCellBills = { {45.24, 54.67, 32.55, 25.61},
14                                      {65.29, 49.75, 32.08, 26.11},
15                                      {75.24, 54.53, 34.55, 28.16} };
16
17    String [ ] months = { "July", "August", "September" };
18
19    NumberFormat priceFormat = NumberFormat.getCurrencyInstance( );
20    double currentMonthTotal;
21    for ( int i = 0; i < familyCellBills.length; i++ )
22    {
23      currentMonthTotal = 0.0;  // initialize total for row
24      for ( int j = 0; j < familyCellBills[i].length; j++ )
25      {
26        // add current family member bill to current monthly total
27        currentMonthTotal += familyCellBills[i][j];
```

```
28    }
29    // print total for row
30    System.out.println( "The total for " + months[i] + " is "
31                          + priceFormat.format( currentMonthTotal ) );
32    }
33  }
34 }
```

EXAMPLE 9.6   Processing Each Row in a Two-Dimensional Array

Again, the rows correspond to the months, and we declare and initialize at line 17 a *String* array named *months* in order to make the output user-friendly.

To calculate the total of the family cell bills for each month, we use nested *for* loops at lines 21–32, following the pattern described earlier.

Inside the outer *for* loop, we initialize the *currentMonthTotal* at line 23 before processing each row. Without this statement, the variable *current-MonthTotal* would continue to accumulate, as if we were summing all the elements of the array instead of calculating a separate sum for each row.

After the inner loop finishes, we complete the processing of row *i* by printing the value of *currentMonthTotal* at lines 29–31. Figure 9.9 shows the output of the program.

COMMON ERROR TRAP

Failing to initialize the row processing variables before each row is a logic error and will generate incorrect results.

9.3.5   Processing a Two-Dimensional Array One Column at a Time

Processing each column of a two-dimensional array requires a little extra checking. If the number of columns in each row differs, we must be careful not to attempt to access an element with an out-of-bounds column index. Generally, we will need to determine the number of columns in the largest row in the array before coding the outer loop header.

For example, suppose you are keeping track of your test grades in three classes: Intro to Java, Database Management, and English Composition. You have two test grades in Intro to Java, four in Database Management,

```
The total for July is $158.07
The total for August is $173.23
The total for September is $192.48
```

Figure 9.9
Output of Example 9.6

and three in English Composition. We can use a two-dimensional array to store these test grades as follows:

```
int [ ][ ] grades = { { 89, 75 },
                      { 84, 76, 92, 96 },
                      { 80, 88, 95 } };
```

There are three rows in the array *grades.* The maximum number of columns in any row is four; therefore, in order to process all the columns, our outer loop should loop from column index 0 to column index 3. Our inner loop should check that the current column number exists in the row before attempting to process the element.

Let's assume, at this point, that we stored the maximum number of columns in an *int* variable called *maxNumberOfColumns.* The general pattern for processing elements of a two-dimensional array, *arrayName,* one column at a time is:

```
// maxNumberOfColumns holds the number of columns
// in the largest row of familyCellBills
for ( int j = 0; j < maxNumberOfColumns; j++ )
{
   for ( int i = 0; i < arrayName.length; i++ )
   {
      if ( j < arrayName[i].length )
      {
         // process element arrayName[i][j]
      }
   }
}
```

The outer loop condition:

```
j < maxNumberOfColumns
```

continues execution of the outer loop as long as the column index is less than the maximum number of columns of the two-dimensional array, which has been computed and assigned to the variable *maxNumberOfColumns.*

The inner loop condition:

```
i < arrayName.length
```

continues execution of the inner loop as long as the row index is less than the number of rows.

Again, because each row may have a different number of columns, a given row *i* may not have a column *j*. Thus, using the following *if* condition, we check that an element in column *j* exists—*j* is less than *array-Name[i].length*—before we attempt to access *arrayName[i][j]*:

```
if ( j < arrayName[i].length )
```

Example 9.7 shows how this pattern can be implemented in a program.

```
1 /* Processing Each Column in a Two-Dimensional Array
2    Anderson, Franceschi
3 */
4
5 public class GradesProcessing
6 {
7  public static void main( String [ ] args )
8  {
9    int [ ][ ] grades = { { 89, 75 },
10                        { 84, 76, 92, 96 },
11                        { 80, 88, 95 } };
12
13   // compute the maximum number of columns
14   int maxNumberOfColumns = grades[0].length;
15   for ( int i = 1; i < grades.length; i++ )
16   {
17    if ( grades[i].length > maxNumberOfColumns )
18        maxNumberOfColumns = grades[i].length;
19   }
20   System.out.println( "The maximum number of columns in grades is "
21                       + maxNumberOfColumns );
22
23   for ( int j = 0; j < maxNumberOfColumns; j++ )
24   {
25    System.out.print( "\nColumn " + j + ": " );
26    for ( int i = 0; i < grades.length; i++ )
27    {
28     if ( j < grades[i].length )
29         System.out.print( grades[i][j] );
30     System.out.print( "\t" );
31    }
32   }
33   System.out.println( );
34  }
35 }
```

EXAMPLE 9.7   Processing a Two-Dimensional Array in Column Order

Figure 9.10
The Output of Example 9.7

```
The maximum number of columns in grades is 4

Column 0: 89    84      80
Column 1: 75    76      88
Column 2:       92      95
Column 3:       96
```

The array *grades* is declared and initialized at lines 9–11. Lines 13–19 compute the maximum number of columns in a row and store the value in the *int* variable *maxNumberOfColumns*. First, we initialize *maxNumberOfColumns* to the number of columns of row 0 at line 14. At lines 15 to 19, we loop through each remaining row in *grades* and update *maxNumberOfColumns* if we find that the current row has more columns than *maxNumberOfColumns*.

At lines 23–32, we use nested loops to print all the elements of *grades* in column order, following the general pattern described earlier. The output of the program is shown in Figure 9.10.

9.3.6   Displaying Two-Dimensional Array Data as a Bar Chart

Another way to display two-dimensional array data is graphically, by drawing a bar chart. For example, the bar chart in Figure 9.11 displays the data in the *familyCellBills* array.

REFERENCE POINT

Chapter 8 provides instructions on drawing a bar chart from the data in a single-dimensional array.

Each bar is a rectangle. So to create a bar chart, we use our standard nested *for* loops, and call the *fillRect* method of the *Graphics* class to draw a rectangle for each element. We use the *drawString* method to print the value of each element. To change colors for each row, we set up an array of *Color* objects, and loop through the array to set the current color for each row iteration. Furthermore, each time we process a row, we must reset the (x, y) coordinate of the first bar of the current row.

Example 9.8 shows the applet code that displays the bar chart shown in Figure 9.11.

```
1 /* Displaying a Two-Dimensional Array as a Bar Chart
2    Anderson, Franceschi
3 */
4
```

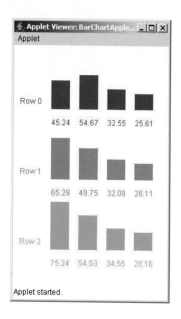

Figure 9.11
The *familyCellBills* Array as a Bar Chart

```
 5 import javax.swing.JApplet;
 6 import java.awt.Graphics;
 7 import java.awt.Color;
 8
 9 public class BarChartApplet extends JApplet
10 {
11  final int LEFT_MARGIN = 60;          // starting x value
12  final int BASE_Y_BAR  = 100;         // bottom of the bars
13  final int BASE_Y_VALUE = 125;        // bottom of the values
14  final int BAR_WIDTH = 30;            // width of each bar
15  final int SPACE_BETWEEN_BARS = 15;   // pixels between bars
16  final int ROW_HEIGHT = 110;          // pixels between rows
17  double [ ][ ] familyCellBills = { { 45.24, 54.67, 32.55, 25.61 },
18                                    { 65.29, 49.75, 32.08, 26.11 },
19                                    { 75.24, 54.53, 34.55, 28.16 } };
20  Color [ ] colors = { Color.BLUE, Color.RED, Color.GREEN };
21
22  public void init( )
23  {
24    setSize( 250, 375 );
25  }
26
27  public void paint( Graphics g )
```

```
28  {
29    int xStart = LEFT_MARGIN;     // x value for 1st column (bars)
30    int yStart = BASE_Y_VALUE;    // y value for 1st row (data)
31    int yStartBar = BASE_Y_BAR;   // y value for 1st row (bars)
32
33    for ( int i = 0; i < familyCellBills.length; i++ )
34    {
35      g.setColor( colors[i] );    // set color for current row
36      g.drawString( "Row " + i, xStart - LEFT_MARGIN + 10,
37                    (int) ( yStart - .3 * ROW_HEIGHT ) );
38
39      for ( int j = 0; j < familyCellBills[i].length; j++ )
40      {
41        g.fillRect( xStart, yStartBar - (int) ( familyCellBills[i][j] ),
42                    BAR_WIDTH, (int) ( familyCellBills[i][j] ) );
43
44        g.drawString( Double.toString( familyCellBills[i][j] ),
45                      xStart, yStart );
46
47        // move to starting x value for next bar
48        xStart += BAR_WIDTH + SPACE_BETWEEN_BARS;
49      }
50
51      // new row:  increase yStart and yStartBar
52      yStart += ROW_HEIGHT;        // increment yStart for next row
53      yStartBar += ROW_HEIGHT;     // increment yStartBar for next row
54      xStart = LEFT_MARGIN;        // reset xStart for next row
55    }
56  }
57 }
```

EXAMPLE 9.8   Applet Displaying a Two-Dimensional Array as a Bar Chart

The *Color* single-dimensional array *colors* that we use to determine the color of each row of bars is declared and initialized at line 20. It has the same number of rows as *familyCellBills*. The first row of bars will be displayed in blue, the second row in red, and the third row in green.

In the *paint* method, at the beginning of the outer loop and before the inner loop, we set the color for the current row (line 35) by using the row number as an index into the *colors* array. At lines 36–37, we display the row number.

In the body of the inner loop (lines 39–49), we draw the rectangle for the element value at row *i* and column *j* of *familyCellBills*, then display a *String* representing the same value. We then increment *xStart* to the location of the next bar to draw.

After the inner loop and before restarting the outer loop, we update the values of *yStart*, *yStartBar*, and *xStart* (lines 51–54) so that they are properly set for processing the next row. Earlier, we said that initializing variable values for the next row is usually done at the beginning of the outer loop body before entering the inner loop, but it also can be done after the inner loop and before re-entering the outer loop, as shown here.

CODE IN ACTION

To see a step-by-step illustration showing how to use two-dimensional arrays, look for the Flash movie on the CD-ROM included with this book. Click on the link for Chapter 9 to start the movie.

Skill Practice
with these end-of-chapter questions

9.10.2 Reading and Understanding Code

Questions 19, 20, 21, 22, 23, 24, 25, 26, 27, 28

9.10.3 Fill In the Code

Questions 35, 36, 37, 38, 39, 40, 41, 42, 43, 44, 45

9.10.4 Identifying Errors in Code

Question 54

9.10.5 Debugging Area

Questions 60, 61, 62

9.10.6 Write a Short Program

Questions 66, 67, 68, 69, 70, 71, 72, 73, 74, 75, 76, 77, 78, 79

9.4 Two-Dimensional Arrays Passed to and Returned from Methods

Writing methods that take two-dimensional arrays as parameters and/or return two-dimensional arrays is similar to working with single-dimensional arrays.

The syntax for a method that accepts a two-dimensional array as a parameter is the following:

```
returnType methodName( arrayType [ ][ ] arrayParameterName )
```

The syntax for a method that returns a two-dimensional array is the following:

```
returnArrayType [ ][ ]  methodName( parameterList )
```

The caller of the method passes the argument list and assigns the return value to a reference to a two-dimensional array of the appropriate data type.

Combining both possibilities, the syntax for a method that accepts a two-dimensional array as a parameter and whose return value is a two-dimensional array is the following:

```
returnArrayType [ ][ ]  methodName( arrayType [ ][ ] arrayParameterName )
```

The caller of the method simply passes the name of the array without any brackets and assigns the return value to a reference to a two-dimensional array of the appropriate data type.

For example, suppose we want to tally votes in an election. We have four candidates running in six districts. We want to know how many votes each candidate received and how many votes were cast in each district. Thus, we can set up a two-dimensional array with each row representing a district and each column representing a candidate, with the values in each element representing the votes a candidate received in that district. We need to compute the sum of each row to find the number of votes per district and the sum of each column to find the number of votes per candidate.

To do this, we create a class, *Tally*, that has a two-dimensional array instance variable, *voteData*, storing the votes. The *Tally* class also has a method, *arrayTally*, that will compute the sums for each column and row of *voteData*. The sums will be returned from the method as a two-dimensional array with two rows. The first row will hold the totals for each column of *voteData*, and the second row will hold the totals for each row of *voteData*.

Example 9.9 shows the *Tally* class.

```
1 /** Two-Dimensional Arrays as Method Parameters
2  *   and Return Values: the Tally class
3  *   Anderson, Franceschi
4 */
5
6 public class Tally
7 {
8   int [ ][ ] voteData;
9
10  /** overloaded constructor
11   *   @param    newVoteData   an array of vote counts
12   */
13  public Tally( int [ ][ ] newVoteData )
14  {
15    voteData = new int [newVoteData.length][ ];
16    for ( int i = 0; i < newVoteData.length; i++ )
17        voteData[i] = new int [newVoteData[i].length];
18
19    for ( int i = 0; i < newVoteData.length; i++ )
20    {
21      for ( int j = 0; j < newVoteData[i].length; j++ )
22      {
23        voteData[i][j] = newVoteData[i][j];
24      }
25    }
26  }
27
28  /** arrayTally method
29   *   @return    a two-dimensional array of votes
30   */
31  public int [ ][ ] arrayTally( )
32  {
33    // create array of tallies, all elements are 0
34    int [ ][ ] returnTally = new int [2][ ];
35    returnTally[0] = new int [voteData[0].length];
36    returnTally[1] = new int [voteData.length];
37
38    for ( int i = 0; i < voteData.length; i++ )
39    {
40      for ( int j = 0; j < voteData[i].length; j++ )
41        {
```

```
42          returnTally[0][j] += voteData[i][j];  // add to column sum
43          returnTally[1][i] += voteData[i][j];  // add to row sum
44        }
45      }
46    return returnTally;
47  }
48 }
```

EXAMPLE 9.9   The *Tally* Class

The overloaded constructor, coded at lines 10–26, receives the two-dimensional array argument *newVoteData*. After instantiating *voteData* at line 15, we copy *newVoteData* into *voteData* one element at a time at lines 19–25.

We coded the *arrayTally* method at lines 28–47. Our first job is to instantiate the *returnArray*, which is the array the method will return to the caller. We know that the array will have two rows, one holding the sums of the columns and one holding the sums of the rows. Because each row in the *returnArray* will have a different number of columns, we instantiate the array with two rows, but do not give a value for the number of columns (line 34). We then instantiate each row with the appropriate number of columns (lines 35–36). Row 0, the sums of the columns, will have the same number of columns as the *voteData* array. In the interest of keeping this example simple, we have assumed that *voteData* has the same number of columns in every row, that is, each candidate was on the ballot in each district. Thus, that number is therefore equal to the number of columns in the first row, *voteData[0].length* (line 35). Row 1, the sum of the rows, will have the same number of columns as the number of rows in the *voteData* array.

In lines 38–45, we loop through the parameter array, computing the sums. We add each element's value to the sum for its column (line 42) and the sum for its row (line 43). When we finish, we return the *returnTally* array to the caller (line 46).

Example 9.10 shows a client program that instantiates a *Tally* object reference and calls the *arrayTally* method.

```
1 /** Tally votes: the VoteTally class
2 *    Anderson, Franceschi
3 */
4
5 public class VoteTally
6 {
```

```
 7   public static void main( String [ ] args )
 8   {
 9     // votes are for 4 candidates in 6 districts.
10     int [ ][ ] votes = { { 150, 253, 125, 345 },
11                          { 250, 750, 234, 721 },
12                          { 243, 600, 212, 101 },
13                          { 234, 243, 143, 276 },
14                          { 555, 343, 297, 990 },
15                          { 111, 426, 834, 101 } };
16     // candidate names
17     String [ ] candidates = { "Smith", "Jones",
18                               "Berry", "Chase" };
19
20     // instantiate a Tally object reference
21     Tally tally = new Tally( votes );
22
23     // call arrayTally method to count the votes
24     int [ ][ ] voteCounts = tally.arrayTally( );
25
26     // print totals for candidates
27     System.out.println( "Total votes per candidate" );
28     for ( int i = 0; i < candidates.length; i++ )
29       System.out.print( candidates[i] + "\t" );
30     System.out.println( );
31     for ( int j = 0; j < voteCounts[0].length; j++ )
32       System.out.print( voteCounts[0][j] + "\t" );
33     System.out.println( );
34
35     // print totals for districts
36     System.out.println("\nTotal votes per district" );
37     for ( int i = 0; i < voteCounts[1].length; i++ )
38       System.out.print( ( i + 1 ) + "\t" );
39     System.out.println( );
40     for ( int i = 0; i < voteCounts[1].length; i++ )
41       System.out.print( voteCounts[1][i] + "\t" );
42     System.out.println( );
43   }
44 }
```

EXAMPLE 9.10   The *VoteTally* Class

We start by defining our two-dimensional array, *votes*, which holds the votes for each candidate for each district (lines 9–15). Most likely, we would read these values from a file, but for simplicity, we hard-coded the values in

Figure 9.12

Output from Example 9.10

```
Total votes per candidate
Smith     Jones     Berry     Chase
1543      2615      1845      2534


Total votes per district
1      2      3      4      5      6
873    1955   1156   896    2185   1472
```

the initialization list. We also define a single-dimensional array of *Strings*, *candidates*, which holds the candidates' names (lines 16–18). Each name in the *candidates* array corresponds to the column in the *votes* array that holds that candidate's votes.

On lines 20–21, we instantiate the *Tally* object *tally*, passing the two-dimensional array *votes* to the *Tally* overloaded constructor. Notice that for the argument, we use only the array name, *votes*, without brackets.

On line 24, we call the *arrayTally* method, assigning the return value to a two-dimensional array reference named *voteCounts*.

Lines 26–33 print the totals per candidate by printing the elements in row 0 of the returned array, and lines 35–42 print the totals per district by printing the elements in row 1 of the returned array. The output is shown in Figure 9.12.

9.5   Programming Activity 1: Working with Two-Dimensional Arrays

In this activity, you will work with a 4-row, 20-column, two-dimensional array of integers. Specifically, you will write methods to perform the following operations:

1. Fill the array with random numbers between 50 and 80.

2. Print the array.

3. Set every array element of a given row to a specified value. The value is a parameter of a method.

4. Find the minimum value in a given column of the array. The column is a parameter of a method.

5. Count the number of elements of the array having a specified value. The value is a parameter of a method.

The framework for this Programming Activity will animate your algorithm so that you can check the accuracy of your code. For example, Figure 9.13 shows the application counting the elements having the value 56:

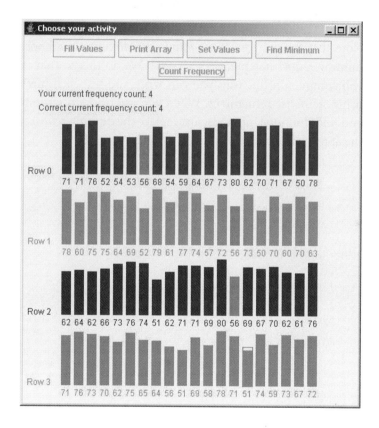

Figure 9.13

Animation of the Programming Activity

At this point, the application has found the value 56 in four array elements: one in each row.

Instructions

In the Chapter 9 Programming Activity 1 directory on the CD-ROM accompanying this book, you will find the source files needed to complete this activity. Copy all the files to a directory on your computer. Note that all files should be in the same directory.

Open the *TwoDimArrayPractice1.java* source file. Searching for five asterisks (*****) in the source code will position you at the sample method and the four other locations where you will add your code. We have provided the sample code for task number 1, which you can use as a model for completing the other tasks. In every task, you will fill in the code for a method that will manipulate an existing array of 4 rows and 20 columns. You should not instantiate the array; we have done that for you. Example 9.11 shows the section of the *TwoDimArrayPractice1* source code where you will add your code.

Note that for the *countFound* and *findMinimum* methods, we provide a dummy *return* statement: (*return 0;*). We do this so that the source code will compile. In this way, you can write and test each method separately, using step-wise refinement. When you are ready to write the *countFound* and *findMinimum* methods, just replace the dummy *return* statements with the appropriate *return* statement for that method.

```java
// ***** 1.  This method has been coded as an example
/** Fills the array with random numbers between 50 and 80
 *  The instance variable named intArray is the integer array to be
 *  filled with values
 */
public void fillValues( )
{
 for ( int row = 0; row < intArray.length; row++ )
 {
     System.out.print( row + "\t" );
     for ( int column = 0; j < intArray[row].length; column++ )
     {
      intArray[row][column] = ( int ) ( Math.random( ) * 31 ) + 50;
      animate( row, column );  // needed for visual feedback
      }
     System.out.println( );
 }
}  // end of fillValues method

// ***** 2.  Student writes this method
/** Prints array to the console, elements are separated by a space
 *  The instance variable named intArray is the integer array to be
 *  printed
 */
public void printArray( )
```

```
{
  // Note:  To animate the algorithm, put this method call as the
  // last element in your inner for loop
  //              animate( row, column );
  //      where row is the index of the array's current row
  //   and column is the index of the array's current column
  // Write your code here:

}  // end of printArray method


// ***** 3.  Student writes this method
/** Sets all the elements in the specified row to the specified value
 * The instance variable named intArray is the integer array
 *  @param value     the value to assign to the element of the row
 *  @param row       the row in which to set the elements to value
 */
public void setValues( int value, int row )
{
  // Note:  To animate the algorithm, put this method call as the
  // last element in your for loop
  //              animate( row, column );
  //      where row is the index of the array's current row
  //      where column is the index of the array's current column
  // Write your code here:

}  // end of setValues method


// ***** 4.  Student writes this method
/** Finds minimum value in the specified column
 *  The instance variable named intArray is the integer array
 *  @param column    the column to search
 *  @return          the minimum value found in the column
 */
public int findMinimum( int column )
{
  // Note:  To animate the algorithm, put this method call as the
  // last element in your for loop
  //              animate( row, column, minimum );
  //   where row is the index of the array's current row
  //       column is the index of the array's current column
  //       minimum is the variable storing the current minimum
  // Write your code here:
```

```
  return 0; // replace this line with your return statement


} // end of findMinimumn method


// ***** 5.  Student writes this method
/** Finds the number of times value is found in the array
 *  The instance variable named intArray is the integer array
 *  @param value      the value to count
 *  @return           the number of times value was found
 */
public int countFound( int value )
{
 // Note:  To animate the algorithm, put this method call as the
 // last element in your inner for loop
 //            animate( row, column, num );
 // where row is the index of the array's current row
 //       column is the index of the array's current column
 //       num is the local variable storing the current frequency
 //        count
 // Write your code here:


  return 0;  // replace this line with your return statement


}
// end of countFound method
```

EXAMPLE 9.11   **Location of Student Code in _TwoDimArrayPractice1_**

The framework will animate your algorithm so that you can watch your code work. For this to happen, be sure that your single or nested _for_ loops call the method _animate_. The arguments that you send to _animate_ are not always the same and the location of the call to _animate_ will differ depending on the task you are coding. Detailed instructions for each task are included in the code.

To test your code, compile and run the _TwoDimArrayPractice1_ source code. Figure 9.14 shows the graphics window when the program begins. Because the values of the array are randomly generated, the values will be different each time the program runs. To test any method, click on the appropriate button.

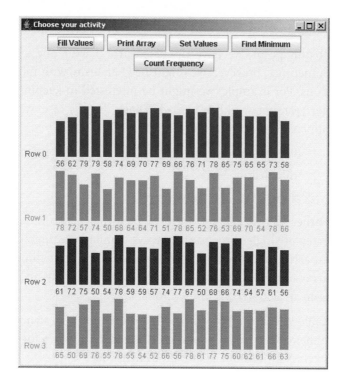

Figure 9.14

The Graphics Window When the Application Begins

Troubleshooting

If your method implementation does not animate, check these tips:

- Verify that the last statement in your single *for* loop or inner *for* loop is a call to the *animate* method and that you passed the appropriate arguments. For example:

```
animate( row, column );
```

- Verify that your exit conditions for your *for* loops are correct. Sometimes the exit condition depends on the length of the array (i.e., the number of rows in the array), and sometimes it depends on the number of columns in the current row of the array.

? DISCUSSION QUESTIONS

1. With a two-dimensional array, for which operations would you use nested *for* loops and for which operations would you use a single *for* loop?

2. When performing an operation on a given row, which index is fixed and which index is used as the looping variable? When performing an operation on a given column, which index is fixed and which index is used as the looping variable?

9.6   Other Multidimensional Arrays

To this point, we have discussed arrays with one and two dimensions. Sometimes, however, we might need an array with more than two dimensions. For example, we might be interested in keeping track of sales on a per-year, per-week, and per-day basis. In this case, we would use a three-dimensional array as follows:

1st dimension: year

2nd dimension: week

3rd dimension: day of the week

Earlier in this chapter, we explained that a two-dimensional array is an array of single-dimensional arrays. Similarly, a three-dimensional array is an array of two-dimensional arrays. And a four-dimensional array is an array of three-dimensional arrays. More generally, an n-dimensional array is an array of $(n-1)$-dimensional arrays.

Table 9.3 shows how an n-dimensional array is structured dimension by dimension; $i_1, i_2, \ldots, i_n$ are used as generic indexes for the first dimension, second dimension, ..., and n^{th} dimensions.

If we keep track of sales over a period of 10 years, then we would have a 10-by-52-by-7 array. The principles discussed for a two-dimensional array still

TABLE 9.3   Structure of an *n*-Dimensional Array

Dimension	Array Element
first	`arrayName[i`$_1$`]` is an `(n — 1)`-dimensional array
second	`arrayName[i`$_1$`][i`$_2$`]` is an `(n — 2)`-dimensional array
k^{th}	`arrayName[i`$_1$`][i`$_2$`][i`$_3$`][..][i`$_k$`]` is an `(n — k)` multi-dimensional array
$(n-2)^{th}$	`arrayName[i`$_1$`][i`$_2$`][i`$_3$`][..][i`$_{n-2}$`]` is a two-dimensional array
$(n-1)^{th}$	`arrayName[i`$_1$`][i`$_2$`][i`$_3$`][..][i`$_{n-1}$`]` is a single-dimensional array
n^{th}	`arrayName[i`$_1$`][i`$_2$`][i`$_3$`][..][i`$_{n-1}$`][i`$_n$`]` is an array element

apply; we just have three dimensions instead of two. The following code sequence illustrates how to declare, instantiate, and access elements of this three-dimensional array:

```
double [ ][ ][ ] sales;              // declare a three-dimensional array

sales = new double [10][52][7];      // instantiate the array

sales[0][0][0] = 638.50;             // access the first element

sales[4][22][3] = 928.20;            // access another element

sales[9][51][6] = 1234.90;           // access the last element
```

To process elements of a single-dimensional array, we use a simple *for* loop; for a two-dimensional array, we use a double *for* loop. For a three-dimensional array, we use a triple *for* loop.

The general pattern for processing elements in a three-dimensional array is

```
for ( int i = 0; i < arrayName.length; i++ )
{
   for ( int j = 0; j < arrayName[i].length; j++ )
   {
      for ( int k = 0; k < arrayName[i][j].length; k++ )
      {
         // access and process the element arrayName[i][j][k]
      }
   }
}
```

The following code sequence will print the elements of the three-dimensional array *sales*:

```
for ( int i = 0; i < sales.length; i++ )
{
   for ( int j = 0; j < sales[i].length; j++ )
   {
      for ( int k = 0; k < sales[i][j].length; k++ )
      {
         // access the element at sales[i][j][k]
         System.out.println( sales[i][j][k] + "\t" );
      }
      // skip a line when second dimension index changes
      System.out.println( );
```

```
      }
      // skip a line when first dimension index changes
      System.out.println( );
}
```

If we are interested in keeping track of sales on a state-by-state basis, we can use a four-dimensional array as follows:

1st dimension: state

2nd dimension: year

3rd dimension: week

4th dimension: day of the week

The following code sequence illustrates how to declare, instantiate, and access the elements of such a four-dimensional array:

```
double [ ][ ][ ][ ] stateSales;            // declare a four-dimensional
                                           // array

stateSales = new double [50][10][52][7];   // instantiate the array

stateSales[0][0][0][0] = 58.50;            // access the first element

sales[34][4][22][3] = 98.30;               // access another element

sales[49][9][51][6] = 137.70;              // access the last element
```

To process elements of a four-dimensional array, we use a quadruple *for* loop. That quadruple *for* loop pattern parallels the ones for the two-dimensional and three-dimensional arrays. For a four-dimensional array called *arrayName*, it is:

```
for ( int i = 0; i < arrayName.length; i++ )
{
   for ( int j = 0; j < arrayName[i].length; j++ )
   {
      for ( int k = 0; k < arrayName[i][j].length; k++ )
      {
         for ( int l = 0; l < arrayName[i][j][k].length; l++ )
         {
            // process element arrayName[i][j][k][l]
         }
      }
   }
}
```

9.7 The *ArrayList* Class

As we have seen, single-dimensional and multidimensional arrays are useful in many situations. However, they have limitations.

Let's say you are designing a search engine for a large website, for example, an online bookstore. The user will type a word in a text field box, your code will access a database, retrieve all the books with titles that contain this word, and return them to the user.

We could store the book information in an array of books. One problem, however, is that we don't know how many books we will have. There could be 3, 32, 500, or 5,000 books, or maybe even more. Without knowing the number of books, we do not know what size to make the array. The safest bet would be to create the array with the maximum possible number of elements, that is, the maximum number of books that we anticipate. If we actually have fewer books than we anticipated, however, we will waste space.

If we end up with more books than we anticipated, we would need to increase the size of an array. As we demonstrated in Chapter 8, changing the size of an array is a tedious process. We will have to instantiate a new array and copy the elements of the original array to the new array.

The *ArrayList* class, in the *java.util* package, solves these problems. An *ArrayList* object automatically expands its capacity as needed. The *ArrayList* class uses **generics**. Generics are **parameterized types**, meaning that the data type will be defined at the time a client class declares and instantiates an object of the class. Generics allow programmers to design and code classes that use objects without specifying the class—or data type—of the object.

Thus, for example, we could have an *ArrayList* of *Book* objects, an *ArrayList* of *Auto* objects, or an *ArrayList* of *Strings*. The specified type must be a class, not a primitive type. If we want to store primitive data types in an *ArrayList*, then we need to use one of the wrapper classes such as *Integer*, *Double*, or *Character*.

The *ArrayList* class, and more generally a class using generics, can be used for many purposes. This is another facet of object-oriented programming that allows programmers to reuse code.

 REFERENCE POINT

Wrapper classes are explained in Chapter 3, along with the concepts of autoboxing and unboxing.

Because the *ArrayList* class is in the *java.util* package, programs using an *ArrayList* object will need to provide the following *import* statement:

```
import java.util.ArrayList;
```

9.7.1   Declaring and Instantiating *ArrayList* Objects

Here is the syntax for declaring an *ArrayList* of objects:

```
ArrayList<ClassName> arrayListName;
```

Inside the brackets, we declare the class type of the objects that will be stored in the *ArrayList*. A space is optional between the *ArrayList* class name and the opening bracket.

For example, these two statements declare an *ArrayList* of *Strings* and an *ArrayList* of *Auto* objects:

```
ArrayList<String> listOfStrings;
ArrayList<Auto> listOfCars;
```

If you try to declare an *ArrayList* object reference using a primitive data type instead of a class type, as in

```
ArrayList<int> listOfInts;
```

you will get this compiler error:

```
Test.java:7: unexpected type
  ArrayList<int> listOfInts;
           ^
required: reference
found    : int
1 error
```

Two constructors of the *ArrayList* class are shown in Table 9.4.

If you know how many elements you will store in the *ArrayList* object, you can use the overloaded constructor to specify the initial capacity; other-

TABLE 9.4   *ArrayList* Constructors

ArrayList Constructor Summary
Constructor name and argument list
`ArrayList<ClassName>( )`
constructs an *ArrayList* object of *ClassName* type with an initial capacity of 10
`ArrayList<ClassName>( int initialCapacity )`
constructs an *ArrayList* object of *ClassName* type with the specified initial capacity

wise, simply use the default constructor. As you add elements to the *ArrayList* object, its capacity will increase automatically, as needed.

Here is the syntax for instantiating an *ArrayList* using the default constructor:

```
arrayListName = new ArrayList<ClassName>( );
```

   where *ClassName* is the class type of the objects that will be stored in
   the *ArrayList* and *arrayListName* has been declared previously as an
   ArrayList reference for that class.

These statements will instantiate the *ArrayList* objects declared earlier, with an initial capacity of 10:

```
listOfStrings = new ArrayList<String>( );
listOfCars = new ArrayList<Auto>( );
```

If you try to instantiate an *ArrayList* object without specifying the object type, as in

```
listOfCars = new ArrayList( );
```

you will get the following warnings from the compiler (using Xlint):

```
Test.java:11: warning: [rawtypes] found raw type: ArrayList
    listOfCars = new ArrayList( );
                     ^
  missing type parameters for generic class ArrayList<E>
  where E is a type-variable:
    E extends Object declared in class ArrayList

Test.java:11: warning: [unchecked] unchecked conversion
    listOfCars = new ArrayList( );
                     ^
  required: ArrayList<Auto>
  found:    ArrayList
2 warnings
```

In *ArrayLists*, there is a distinction between capacity and size. The **capacity** of an *ArrayList* is the number of elements allocated to the list. The **size** is the number of those elements that are filled with objects. Thus, when you instantiate an *ArrayList* using the default constructor, its capacity is 10, but its size is 0. In other words, the *ArrayList* has room for 10 objects, but no objects are currently stored in the list.

These statements will declare, then instantiate, an *ArrayList* of *Astronaut* objects with an initial capacity of 5, using the overloaded constructor:

```
ArrayList<Astronaut> listOfAstronauts1;
listOfAstronauts1 = new ArrayList<Astronaut>( 5 );
```

In this case, the capacity of *listOfAstronauts1* is 5 and its size is 0.

We can also combine the declaration and instantiation of an *ArrayList* object into one statement. Here is the syntax using the default constructor:

```
ArrayList<ClassName> arrayListName = new ArrayList<ClassName>( );
```

These statements will declare and instantiate two *ArrayList* objects, *Integers* and *Astronauts*, respectively:

```
ArrayList<Integer> listOfInts = new ArrayList<Integer>( );
ArrayList<Astronaut> listOfAstronauts2 = new ArrayList<Astronaut>( );
```

9.7.2   Methods of the *ArrayList* Class

Like arrays, the *ArrayList* class uses indexes to refer to elements. Among others, it provides methods that provide the following functions:

- add an item at the end of the list

- replace an item at a given index

- remove an item at a given index

- remove all the items in the list

- search the list for a specific item

- retrieve an item at a given index

- retrieve the index of a given item

- check to see if the list is empty

- return the number of items in the list, that is, its size

- optimize the capacity of the list by setting its capacity to the number of items in the list

Some of the most useful methods are shown in Table 9.5. Note that some of the method headers include *E* as their return type or parameter data type (as opposed to a class name or simply the *Object* class). *E* represents the data type of the *ArrayList*. Thus, for an *ArrayList* of *Integer* objects, *E* is an *Integer*, and the *get* method, for example, returns an *Integer* object. Similarly, for an *ArrayList* of *Auto* objects, *E* is an *Auto* object. In this case, the *get* method returns an *Auto* object.

TABLE 9.5   *ArrayList* Methods

Useful Methods of the *ArrayList* Class	
Return value	**Method name and argument list**
boolean	add(E element)
	appends the specified *element* to the end of the list
void	clear( )
	removes all the elements from this list
int	size( )
	returns the number of elements in this list
E	remove(int index)
	removes and returns the element at the specified *index* position in the list
E	get(int index)
	returns the element at the specified *index* position in the list; the element is not removed from the list
E	set(int index, E element)
	replaces the element at the specified *index* position in this list with the specified *element*
void	trimToSize( )
	sets the capacity to the list's current size

9.7.3   Looping Through an *ArrayList* Using an Enhanced *for* Loop

The general pattern for processing elements of an *ArrayList* of *ClassName* objects called *arrayListName* using a *for* loop is

```
ClassName currentObject;
for ( int i = 0; i < arrayListName.size( ); i++ )
{
    currentObject = arrayListName.get( i );
    // process currentObject
}
```

For instance, to process elements of an *ArrayList* of *Auto* object references called *listOfAutos* using a standard *for* loop, the general pattern is:

```
Auto currentAuto;
for ( int i = 0; i < listOfAutos.size( ); i++ )
{
     currentAuto = listOfAutos.get( i );
     // process currentAuto
}
```

Java provides a simplified way to process the elements of an *ArrayList*, called the **enhanced *for* loop**. The general pattern for processing elements of an *ArrayList* of *ClassName* objects called *arrayListName* using the enhanced *for* loop is:

```
for ( ClassName currentObject : arrayListName )
{
     // process currentObject
}
```

A variable of the class type of the objects stored in the *ArrayList* is declared in the enhanced *for* loop header, followed by a colon and name of the *ArrayList*. The enhanced *for* loop enables looping through the *ArrayList* objects automatically. Your code does not call the *get* method; inside the body of the loop, *currentObject* is directly available for processing.

For example, to process elements of an *ArrayList* of *Autos* called *cars* using the enhanced *for* loop, the general pattern is:

```
for ( Auto currentAuto : cars )
{
     // process currentAuto
}
```

Example 9.12 shows how to create and use an *ArrayList* of *Integers*. Line 11 declares and instantiates the *ArrayList* object reference *list* using the default constructor. Three elements are added to *list* using the *add* method at lines 12–14. As the argument to the *add* method, we use *Integer* object references at lines 12 and 13, and an *int* at line 14. As we explained in Chapter 3, the autoboxing feature of Java eliminates the need to convert an *int* to an *Inte-*

ger object. This is done automatically when an *int* variable is used where an *Integer* object is expected.

After an *ArrayList* object has been declared and instantiated as being of a certain class type, you cannot add an object of a different class type. For example, the statement

```
list.add ( new Double ( 6.7 ) );
```

would produce the following compiler error:

```
ArrayListOfIntegers.java:15: cannot find symbol
list.add( new Double( 6.7 ) );
        ^
  symbol  : method add(Double)
  location: class ArrayList<Integer>
1 error
```

At lines 17–18, we print the elements of *list* using a traditional *for* loop, using the *get* method to retrieve the element at the current index. At lines 22–23, we use the enhanced *for* loop to print the elements. At lines 27–28, we also use the enhanced *for* loop to print the elements; but this time, we use an *int* as the looping variable, using the unboxing feature of Java, which converts *Integer* objects to *int* values, as needed. At line 31, we use the *set* method to change the value of the element at index 1 to 100, also using autoboxing. At line 37, we use the *remove* method to delete the element at index 0 and assign it to the variable *removed*, using unboxing again.

The output of this example is shown in Figure 9.15.

```
1 /* A Simple ArrayList of Integers
2    Anderson, Franceschi
3 */
4
5 import java.util.ArrayList;
6
7 public class ArrayListOfIntegers
8 {
```

```
 9  public static void main( String [ ] args )
10  {
11    ArrayList<Integer> list = new ArrayList<Integer>( );
12    list.add( new Integer( 34 ) );
13    list.add( new Integer( 89 ) );
14    list.add( 65 ); // autoboxing
15
16    System.out.println( "Using the traditional for loop:" );
17    for ( int i = 0; i < list.size( ); i++ )
18       System.out.print( list.get( i ) + "\t" );
19    System.out.println( );
20
21    System.out.println( "\nUsing the enhanced for loop:" );
22    for ( Integer currentInteger : list )
23       System.out.print( currentInteger + "\t" );
24    System.out.println( );
25
26    System.out.println( "\nUsing unboxing and enhanced for loop:" );
27    for ( int currentInt : list ) // unboxing
28       System.out.print( currentInt + "\t" );
29    System.out.println( );
30
31    list.set( 1, 100 );
32    System.out.println( "\nAfter calling set( 1, 100 ):" );
33    for ( int currentInt : list ) // unboxing
34       System.out.print( currentInt + "\t" );
35    System.out.println( );
36
37    int removed = list.remove( 0 );
38    System.out.println( "\nAt index 0, " + removed + " was removed" );
39    System.out.println( "\nAfter removing the element at index 0:" );
40    for ( int currentInt : list ) // unboxing
41       System.out.print( currentInt + "\t" );
42    System.out.println( );
43  }
44 }
```

EXAMPLE 9.12   Using *ArrayList* Methods

```
Using the traditional for loop:
34     89     65

Using the enhanced for loop:
34     89     65

Using unboxing and enhanced for loop:
34     89     65

After calling set( 1, 100 ):
34     100     65

At index 0, 34 was removed

After removing the element at index 0:
100     65
```

Figure 9.15
Output of Example 9.12

9.7.4 Using the *ArrayList* Class in a Program

Now let's see how we can use the *ArrayList* class in a Java program. Going back to our example of a bookstore and a search engine, we want to design and code a simple program that enables users to search for books.

We will have three classes in this program:

- a *Book* class, encapsulating the concept of a book
- a *BookStore* class, encapsulating the concept of a bookstore
- a *BookSearchEngine* class, including the *main* method, which provides the user interface

In the interest of keeping things simple, our *Book* class will contain only three instance variables: the book title, which is a *String*; the book's author, which is also a *String*; and the book price, which is a *double*.

Example 9.13 shows a simplified *Book* class with constructors, accessor methods, and a *toString* method.

```
1 /* Book class
2    Anderson, Franceschi
3 */
4
5 public class Book
6 {
7  private String title;
8  private String author;
9  private double price;
10
11  /** default constructor
12  */
13  public Book( )
14  {
15    title = "";
16    author = "";
17    price  = 0.0;
18  }
19
20  /** overloaded constructor
21  *  @param newTitle   the value to assign to title
22  *  @param newAuthor  the value to assign to author
23  *  @param newPrice   the value to assign to price
24  */
25  public Book( String newTitle, String newAuthor, double newPrice )
26  {
27    title = newTitle;
28    author = newAuthor;
29    price  = newPrice;
30  }
31
32  /** getTitle method
33  *   @return the title
34  */
35  public String getTitle( )
36  {
37    return title;
38  }
39
40  /** getAuthor method
41  *   @return the author
42  */
43  public String getAuthor( )
44  {
```

```
45   return author;
46 }
47
48 /** getPrice method
49 *    @return the price
50 */
51 public double getPrice( )
52 {
53   return price;
54 }
55
56 /** toString
57 * @return title, author, and price
58 */
59 public String toString( )
60 {
61   return ( "title: " + title + "\t"
62             + "author: " + author + "\t"
63             + "price: " + price );
64 }
65 }
```

EXAMPLE 9.13   The *Book* Class

Our *BookStore* class, shown in Example 9.14, will simply have one instance variable: an *ArrayList* of *Book* objects, representing the collection of books in the bookstore, which we name *library*.

In most cases, when an *ArrayList* is filled with data, that data will come from a database or a file. In the interest of focusing on the *ArrayList* class and its methods, we have hard-coded the objects for the *ArrayList library* in the *BookStore* class, rather than reading them from a database or a file.

In the default constructor (lines 11 to 24), we instantiate the *library* instance variable, then add six *Book* objects to *library* using the *add* method from the *ArrayList* class. At line 23, we call the *trimToSize* method to set the capacity of *library* to its current size, which is 6, in order to minimize the memory resources used.

The *toString* method is coded from lines 26 to 37. It generates and returns a *String* representing all the books in *library*, one book per line. In order to do that, we use an enhanced *for* loop from lines 32 to 35. The header of that loop, at line 32, follows the general pattern of the enhanced *for* loop header by declaring a *Book* variable named *tempBook*, followed by a colon, followed by *library*, the *ArrayList* object to loop through.

The *searchForTitle* method, coded from lines 39 to 53, performs the task of searching for a keyword within the title of each *Book* object stored in *library*. The keyword, a *String*, is the parameter of the method and is named *searchString*. This method returns an *ArrayList* of *Book* objects. We create another *ArrayList* of *Books*, which we name *searchResult* at line 45 and loop through *library* using an enhanced *for* loop from lines 46 to 50. Inside the body of the loop, we use the *indexOf* method of the *String* class to test if the current *Book* object contains the keyword *searchString* in its *title* instance variable. If it does, we add that *Book* object to *searchResult*. Finally, we call the method *trimToSize* to set the capacity of *searchResult* to the current number of elements, then return the *ArrayList* to the caller.

```
 1 /*  BookStore class
 2      Anderson, Franceschi
 3 */
 4
 5 import java.util.ArrayList;
 6
 7 public class BookStore
 8 {
 9   private ArrayList<Book> library;
10
11   /** default constructor
12    *    instantiates ArrayList of Books
13    */
14   public BookStore( )
15   {
16     library = new ArrayList<Book>( );
17     library.add( new Book( "Intro to Java", "James", 56.99 ) );
18     library.add( new Book( "Advanced Java", "Green", 65.99 ) );
19     library.add( new Book( "Java Servlets", "Brown", 75.99 ) );
20     library.add( new Book( "Intro to HTML", "James", 29.49 ) );
21     library.add( new Book( "Intro to Flash", "James", 34.99 ) );
22     library.add( new Book( "Advanced HTML", "Green", 56.99 ) );
23     library.trimToSize( );
24   }
25
26   /** toString
27    * @return  each book in library, one per line
28    */
29   public String toString( )
30   {
31     String result = "";
```

```
32   for( Book tempBook : library )
33   {
34     result += tempBook.toString( ) + "\n";
35   }
36   return result;
37 }
38
39 /** Generates list of books containing searchString
40  * @param searchString    the keyword to search for
41  * @return           the ArrayList of books containing the keyword
42  */
43 public ArrayList<Book> searchForTitle( String searchString )
44 {
45   ArrayList<Book> searchResult = new ArrayList<Book>( );
46   for ( Book currentBook : library )
47   {
48    if ( ( currentBook.getTitle( ) ).indexOf( searchString ) != -1 )
49        searchResult.add( currentBook );
50   }
51   searchResult.trimToSize( );
52   return searchResult;
53 }
54 }
```

EXAMPLE 9.14   The *BookStore* Class

Our *BookSearchEngine* class, shown in Example 9.15, contains the *main* method: it creates a *BookStore* object, asks the user for a keyword, and searches for partial matches in our *BookStore* object.

A *BookStore* object, *bs*, is declared and instantiated at line 12. At lines 14–15, the user is then prompted for a keyword that will be used to search for books whose title contains that keyword. Lines 16 and 17 simply output the collection of *Books* in the *BookStore* object *bs*; later, when the search results are output, we can compare that output to the original list of *Books* to check our results. At line 19, we call the *searchForTitle* method with *keyword* as its argument; the *ArrayList* of *Book* objects returned is assigned to the variable *results*. At lines 23–24, we loop through *results* and output its contents, again using the enhanced *for* loop. Figure 9.16 shows a run of the program with the user searching for books containing the word "Java."

```
1 /* BookSearchEngine class
2    Anderson, Franceschi
3 */
4
5 import java.util.ArrayList;
```

```
Our book collection is:
title: Intro to Java      author: James    price: 56.99
title: Advanced Java      author: Green    price: 65.99
title: Java Servlets      author: Brown    price: 75.99
title: Intro to HTML      author: James    price: 29.49
title: Intro to Flash     author: James    price: 34.99
title: Advanced HTML      author: Green    price: 56.99

The search results for Java are:
title: Intro to Java      author: James    price: 56.99
title: Advanced Java      author: Green    price: 65.99
title: Java Servlets      author: Brown    price: 75.99
```

Figure 9.16

Results of a Search for the Keyword "Java"

```
 6 import javax.swing.JOptionPane;
 7
 8 public class BookSearchEngine
 9 {
10  public static void main( String [ ] args )
11  {
12    BookStore bs = new BookStore( );
13
14    String keyword = JOptionPane.showInputDialog( null,
15                    "Enter a keyword" );
16    System.out.println( "Our book collection is:" );
17    System.out.println( bs.toString( ) );
18
19    ArrayList<Book> results = bs.searchForTitle( keyword );
20
21    System.out.println( "The search results for " + keyword
22                    + " are:" );
23    for( Book tempBook : results )
24        System.out.println( tempBook.toString( ) );
25  }
26 }
```

EXAMPLE 9.15   A Search Engine for Books

CODE IN ACTION

To see a step-by-step illustration showing how to use the *ArrayList* class, look for the Flash movie on the CD-ROM included with this book. Click on the link for Chapter 9 to start the movie.

9.8   Programming Activity 2:   Working with the *ArrayList* Class

In this activity, you will work with an *ArrayList* object. Specifically, you will write the code to perform the following operations:

1. Fill the *ArrayList* object with *Auto* elements.

2. Print the *Auto* elements contained in the *ArrayList* object.

3. Set the *model* instance variable of every *Auto* element in the *ArrayList* object to a specified model.

4. Find the maximum number of miles of all *Auto* elements contained in the *ArrayList* object.

5. Count the number of *Auto* elements in the *ArrayList* objects with a specified model.

The framework for this Programming Activity will animate your algorithm so that you can check the accuracy of your code. For example, Figure 9.17 shows the application counting the number of *Auto* elements in the *ArrayList* object having a model value equal to "Ferrari." The application accesses each element in the *ArrayList* in order, checking the *model* for the desired value, "Ferrari." At this point, the current element being accessed is a *BMW* and the application has found two *Auto* elements with the *model* value, "Ferrari."

Instructions

In the Chapter 9 Programming Activity 2 directory on the CD-ROM accompanying this book, you will find the source files needed to complete this activity. Copy all the files to a directory on your computer. Note that all files should be in the same directory.

Figure 9.17

Animation of the Programming Activity

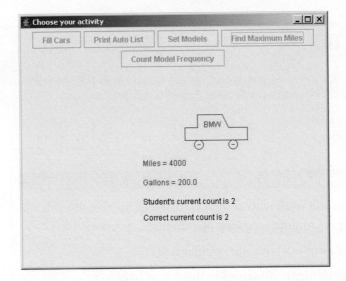

Open the *ArrayListPractice.java* source file. Searching for five asterisks (*****) in the source code will position you to the sample method and the four other locations where you will add your code. We have provided the sample code for task number 1. In every task, you will fill in the code for a method that will manipulate an existing *ArrayList* of *Auto* elements. You should not instantiate the *ArrayList* object; we have done that for you. Example 9.16 shows the section of the *ArrayListPractice* source code where you will add your code.

Note that for the *countFound* and *findMaximumMilesDriven* methods, we provide a dummy *return* statement (*return 0;*). We do this so that the source code will compile. In this way, you can write and test each method separately, using step-wise refinement. When you are ready to write the *countFound* and *findMaximumMilesDriven* methods, just replace the dummy *return* statements with the appropriate *return* statement for that method.

```
// ***** 1.  This method has been coded as an example
/** Fills the carList with hard-coded Auto objects
 *     The instance variable carList is the ArrayList
 *        to be filled with Auto objects
 */
public void fillWithCars( )
{
  // clear carList before adding cars
  carList.clear( );
  // Reset the number of Autos to 0
```

```
    // This is needed so that the animation feedback works correctly
    Auto.clearNumberAutos( );

    Auto car1 = new Auto( "BMW", 0, 0.0 );
    Auto car2 = new Auto( "Ferrari", 100, 500.0 );
    Auto car3 = new Auto( "Jeep", 1000, 90.0 );
    Auto car4 = new Auto( "Ferrari", 10, 3.0 );
    Auto car5 = new Auto( "BMW", 4000, 200.0 );
    Auto car6 = new Auto( "Ferrari", 1000, 50.0 );

    carList.add( car1 );
    carList.add( car2 );
    carList.add( car3 );
    carList.add( car4 );
    carList.add( car5 );
    carList.add( car6 );
    animate( );
  }
  // end of fillWithCars method


  // ***** 2.  Student writes this method
  /**  Prints carList to console, elements are separated by a space
  *     The instance variable carList is the ArrayList to be printed
  */
  public void printAutoList( )
  {
   // Note:  To animate the algorithm, put this method call as the
   // last statement in your for loop
   //                animate( car );
   // where car is the variable name for the current Auto object
   //  as you loop through the ArrayList object
   // Write your code here:

  }
  // end of printAutoList method


  // ***** 3.  Student writes this method
  /** Sets the model of all the elements in carList to parameter value
  * The instance variable carList is the ArrayList to be modified
  * @param model the model to assign to all Auto objects in carList
  */
  public void setModelValues( String model )
  {
   // Note:  To animate the algorithm, put this method call as the
   // last statement in your for loop
   //                animate( car );
   // where car is the variable name for the current Auto object
   //  as you loop through the ArrayList object
```

```
   // Write your code here:

}
// end of setModelValues method

// ***** 4.  Student writes this method
/** Finds maximum number of miles driven
*    Instance variable carList is the ArrayList to search
*   @return     the maximum miles driven by all the Auto objects
*/
public int findMaximumMilesDriven( )
{
  // Note:  To animate the algorithm, put this method call as the
  // last statement in your for loop
  //             animate( car, maximum );
  //   where car is the variable name for the current Auto object
  //   and maximum is the int variable storing the current maximum
  //   number of miles for all Auto elements you have already tested
  //   as you loop through the ArrayList object
  // Write your code here:

    return 0; // replace this statement with your return statement

}
// end of findMaximumMilesDriven method

// ***** 5.  Student writes this method
/** Finds number of times parameter model is found in the carList
*    Instance variable carList is the ArrayList in which we search
*   @param model       the model to count
*   @return            the number of times model was found
*/
public int countFound( String model )
{
  // Note:  To animate the algorithm, put this method call as the
  // last statement in your for loop
  //             animate( car, num );
  //   where car is the variable name for the current Auto object
  //   and num is the int variable storing the current number of
  //   Auto elements whose model is equal to the method's parameter
  //   as you loop through the ArrayList object
  // Write your code here:

    return 0; // replace this statement with your return statement

}
// end of countFound method
```

EXAMPLE 9.16   **Location of Student Code in *ArrayListPractice***

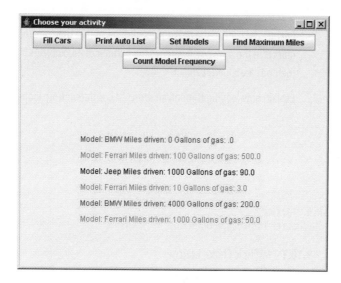

Figure 9.18
The Graphics Window When the Application Begins

The framework will animate your code so that you can watch it work. For this to happen, be sure that your *for* loops call the *animate* method. The arguments that you send to *animate* are not always the same, but the location of the call to *animate* is always the same, that is, the last statement of your *for* loop. Detailed instructions for each task are included in the code.

To test your code, compile and run the *ArrayPractice* source code. Figure 9.18 shows the graphics window when the program begins. Because the *Auto* elements of the *ArrayList* object are hard coded, the values will be the same each time the program runs. To test any method, click on the appropriate button.

Troubleshooting

If your method implementation does not animate, check these tips:

- Verify that the last statement in your single *for* loop or inner *for* loop is a call to the *animate* method and that you passed the loop variable(s) as the argument(s), as in the following:

```
animate( car );              // or
animate( car, maximum );     // or
animate( car, num );
```

- Verify that the headers of your *for* loops are correct. It should always be the same.

- Verify that you update the variables *maximum* and *num* correctly.

1. Change the code in the *fillWithCars* method so that there are more or fewer *Auto* objects in the *ArrayList*. How does the number of *Auto* objects impact how the other methods are coded? Explain.

2. Explain how looping through an *ArrayList* is different from looping through an array.

Skill Practice
with these end-of-chapter questions

9.10.1 Multiple Choice Exercises

Questions 9,10,11,12,13

9.10.2 Reading and Understanding Code

Questions 29,30,31,32

9.10.3 Fill In the Code

Questions 46,47,48,49

9.10.4 Identifying Errors in Code

Questions 55,56,57,58

9.10.5 Debugging Area

Questions 63,64

9.10.6 Write a Short Program

Questions 80,81,82

9.10.8 Technical Writing

Question 98

9.9 Chapter Summary

- Arrays can be single-dimensional, two-dimensional, three-dimensional, or more generally *n*-dimensional.

- In a two-dimensional array, each row is an array.

- Each element in a two-dimensional array is accessed using the array name, a row index, and a column index that refer to the element's position in the array.

- Concepts such as declaration, instantiation, initial values, indexing, and aggregate operations from single-dimensional arrays also apply to two-dimensional arrays.

- Two-dimensional arrays can be instantiated by assigning initial values in a comma-separated list of comma-separated lists at the declaration.

- Each row in a two-dimensional array can have a different number of columns.

- A two-dimensional array has an instance variable, *length*, which holds the number of rows in the array.

- Each row of a two-dimensional array has an instance variable, *length*, which holds the number of elements in that row.

- The *ArrayList* class implements generics and is part of the *java.util* package.

- An *ArrayList* can be thought of as an expandable single-dimensional array of objects.

- To define an *ArrayList* to hold elements of primitive data types, use the wrapper classes.

- An *ArrayList* object expands automatically as needed as objects are added.

- We access an element of an *ArrayList* via its index.

- We can process each element in an *ArrayList* using the enhanced *for* loop.

9.10   Exercises, Problems, and Projects

9.10.1   Multiple Choice Exercises

1. What is/are the valid way(s) to declare a two-dimensional integer array named *a*? (Check all that apply.)

   ❑ `int [ ][ ] a;`

   ❑ `int a [ ][ ];`

   ❑ `array [ ] int a;`

   ❑ `int array [ ] a;`

2. A two-dimensional array is an array of arrays.

   ❑ true

   ❑ false

3. In a two-dimensional array, every row must have the same number of columns.

   ❑ true

   ❑ false

4. What is the default value of the elements of a two-dimensional array of *booleans* after declaration and instantiation of the array?

   ❑ *true*

   ❑ *false*

   ❑ undefined

5. How do you access the element of array *a* located at row 2 and column 4?

   ❑ `a{2}{4}`

   ❑ `a( 2,4 )`

   ❑ `a[2][4]`

   ❑ `a[4][2]`

6. How do you retrieve the number of rows in a two-dimensional array *a*?

   ❑ `a.rows`

   ❑ `a.length`

   ❑ `a.rows( )`

   ❑ `a.size`

7. How do you retrieve the number of columns in row 2 in a two-dimensional array *a*?

   ❑ `a.length`

   ❑ `a[2].length`

   ❑ `a.size`

   ❑ `a[2].size`

8. All the elements of a two-dimensional array must be of the same type.

   ❑ true

   ❑ false

9. An *ArrayList* can be returned by a method.

   ❑ true

   ❑ false

10. It is possible to declare and instantiate an *ArrayList* of a user-defined class type.

    ❑ true

    ❑ false

11. As we add objects to an *ArrayList*, how can we be sure it has enough capacity?

    ❑ Use the *setCapacity* method.

    ❑ Use the *trimToSize* method.

    ❑ We don't need to do anything; capacity expands automatically as needed.

12. Where does the *add* method of the *ArrayList* class add an object?

    ❑ at the beginning of the list

    ❑ at the end of the list

13. To what package does the class *ArrayList* belong?

    ❑ *java.io*

    ❑ *java.util*

❑ *java.array*

❑ *java.list*

9.10.2 Reading and Understanding Code

For Questions 14 to 24, consider the following two-dimensional array declaration and initialization:

```
String [ ][ ] cities = { { "New York", "LA", "San Francisco", "Chicago" },
                         { "Munich", "Stuttgart", "Berlin", "Bonn" },
                         { "Paris", "Ajaccio", "Lyon" },
                         { "Montreal", "Ottawa", "Vancouver" } };
```

14. How many rows are in the array *cities*?

15. What is the value of the expression *cities[2][1]*?

16. What is the index of the last row in the array *cities*?

17. What are the row and column indexes of *Chicago* in the array *cities*?

18. What is the output of this code sequence?

```
System.out.println( cities[3][2] );
```

19. What is the output of this code sequence?

```
for ( int j = 0; j < cities[1].length; j++ )
    System.out.println( cities[1][j] );
```

20. What is the output of this code sequence?

```
for ( int i = 0; i < cities.length; i++ )
    System.out.println( cities[i][1] );
```

21. What is the output of this code sequence?

```
for ( int i = 0; i < cities.length; i++ )
{
    for ( int j = 0; j < cities[i].length; j++ )
        System.out.print( cities[i][j] + "\t" );
    System.out.println( );
}
```

22. What is the output of this code sequence?

```
for ( int i = 0; i < cities.length; i++ )
{
    for ( int j = 0; j < cities[i].length; j++ )
    {
        if ( cities[i][j].length( ) == 6 )
```

```
        System.out.println( cities[i][j] );
    }
}
```

23. What is the output of this code sequence?

```
int count  = 0;
for ( int i = 0; i < cities.length; i++ )
{
    for ( int j = 0; j < cities[i].length; j++ )
    {
        if ( cities[i][j].length( ) == 7 )
            count++;
    }
}
System.out.println( "count is " + count );
```

24. What is the output of this code sequence?

```
for ( int i = 0; i < cities.length; i++ )
{
    for ( int j = 0; j < cities[i].length; j++ )
    {
        if ( cities[i][j].charAt( 0 ) == 'S' )
            System.out.println( cities[i][j] );
    }
}
```

25. What does this method do?

```
public static int foo( double [ ][ ] a )
{
    int b = 0;
    for ( int i = 0; i < a.length; i++ )
    {
        for ( int j = 0; j < a[i].length; j++ )
            b++;
    }
    return b;
}
```

26. What does this method do?

```
public static boolean foo( char [ ][ ] a )
{
    int b = a[0].length;
    for ( int i = 1; i < a.length; i++ )
    {
        if ( a[i].length != b )
```

```
            return false;
      }
    return true;
  }
```

27. What does this method do?

```
public static int foo( String [ ][ ] a )
{
      int b = 0;
      for ( int i = 0; i < a.length; i++ )
      {
            b++;
      }
      return b;
}
```

28. What does this method do?

```
public static int [ ] foo( float [ ][ ] a )
{
      int [ ] temp = new int [a.length];
      for ( int i = 0; i < a.length; i++ )
            temp[i] = a[i].length;
      return temp;
}
```

29. What does this method do?

```
public static int foo( ArrayList<Integer> a )
{
      int b = 0;
      for ( Integer i : a )
      {
          b++;
      }
       return b;
}
```

30. After the following code sequence is executed, what are the contents and index of each element of *a*?

```
ArrayList<Integer> a = new ArrayList<Integer>( );
a.add( 7 );
a.add( 4 );
a.add( 21 );
```

31. After the following code sequence is executed, what are the contents and index of each element of *a*?

```
ArrayList<Integer> a = new ArrayList<Integer>( );
a.add( 7 );
a.add( 4 );
a.add( 21 );
a.set( 1, 45 );
```

32. After the following code sequence is executed, what are the contents and index of each element of *a*?

```
ArrayList<Integer> a = new ArrayList<Integer>( );
a.add( 7 );
a.add( 4 );
a.add( 21 );
a.add( 1, 45 );
```

9.10.3   Fill In the Code

For Questions 33 to 37, consider the following statement:

```
String [ ][ ] geo = { { "MD", "NY", "NJ", "MA", "ME", "CA", "MI", "OR" },
                      { "Detroit", "Newark", "Boston", "Seattle" } };
```

33. This code prints the element at row index 1 and column index 2 of the two-dimensional array *geo*.

```
// your code goes here
```

34. This code prints the element of the array *geo* whose value is "CA."

```
// your code goes here
```

35. This code prints all the states (i.e., the first row) that start with an *M* in the array *geo*.

```
for ( int j = 0; j < geo[0].length; j++ )
{

    // your code goes here

}
```

36. This code prints all the cities (i.e., the second row) in the array *geo*.

```
for ( int j = 0; j < geo[1].length; j++ )
{

    // your code goes here

}
```

37. This code prints all the elements of the array *geo*.

```
for ( int i = 0; i < geo.length; i++ )
{
      // your code goes here


}
```

For Questions 38 to 41, consider the following statement:

```
int [ ][ ] a = { { 9, 6, 8, 10, 5 },
                 { 7, 6, 8, 9, 6 },
                 { 4, 8, 10, 6, 6 } };
```

38. This code calculates and prints the sum of all the elements in the array *a*.

```
int sum = 0;
for ( int i = 0; i < a.length; i++ )
{
      // your code goes here


}
System.out.println( "sum is " + sum );
```

39. This code counts and prints the number of times the value 8 appears in the array *a*.

```
int count = 0;
for ( int i = 0; i < a.length; i++ )
{
      // your code goes here


}
System.out.println( "# of 8s in a: " + count );
```

40. This code counts and prints the number of times the value 6 appears in the second row (i.e., the row whose index is 1) of array *a*.

```
int count = 0;

// your code for the for loop header goes here
{
      if ( a[1][j] == 6 )
            count++;
}
System.out.println( "# of 6s in the 2nd row: " + count );
```

41. This code calculates the sum of the elements in the second column (i.e, the column with index 1) of array *a*.

```
int sum  = 0;
for ( int i = 0; i < a.length; i++ )
{

    // your code goes here


}
System.out.println( "sum is " + sum );
```

42. This method returns *true* if an element in an array of *Strings* is equal to "Java"; otherwise, it returns *false*.

```
public static boolean foo( String [ ][ ] a )
{

    // your code goes here

}
```

43. This method returns the product of all the elements in an array.

```
public static int foo( int [ ][ ] a )
{

    // your code goes here

}
```

44. This method returns *true* if there is at least one row in the array that has exactly five columns; otherwise, it returns *false*.

```
public static boolean foo( char [ ][ ] a )
{

    // your code goes here

}
```

45. This method takes an array of *ints* as a parameter and returns a single-dimensional array of *booleans*. The length of the array returned should be equal to the number of rows in the two-dimensional array parameter. The element at index *i* of the returned array will be *true* if there is a 0 in the corresponding row of the parameter array; otherwise, it will be *false*. Assume that every row in *a* has the same number of columns.

```
public static boolean [ ] foo( int [ ][ ] a )
{

    // your code goes here
    // every row has the same number of columns


}
```

For Questions 46 to 49, consider the following statements:

```
ArrayList<String> languages = new ArrayList<String>( );
languages.add( "SQL" );
languages.add( "Java" );
languages.add( "HTML" );
languages.add( "PHP" );
languages.add( "Perl" );
```

46. This code prints the number of elements in *languages*.

    ```
    // your code goes here
    ```

47. This code retrieves the *String* "HTML" from *languages* (without deleting it) and assigns it to the *String* variable *webLanguage*.

    ```
    // your code goes here
    ```

48. This code replaces "HTML" *with* "C++" in *languages*.

    ```
    // your code goes here
    ```

49. This code prints all the elements of *languages* that start with the letter *P*.

    ```
    for ( String s : languages )
    {
      // your code goes here

    }
    ```

9.10.4   Identifying Errors in Code

50. Where is the error in this code sequence?

    ```
    double [ ][ ] a = { 3.3, 26.0, 48.4 };
    ```

51. Where is the error in this code sequence?

    ```
    int [ ][ ] a = { { 3, 26, 4 }, { 14, 87 } };
    System.out.println( a[1][2] );
    ```

52. Where is the error in this code sequence?

    ```
    double [ ][ ] a = new double [ ][10];
    ```

53. Where is the error in this code sequence?

    ```
    int [ ][ ] a = { { 1, 2 },
                     { 10.1, 10.2 } };
    ```

54. Where is the error in this code sequence? (This code compiles and runs, but outputs garbage.)

    ```
    int [ ][ ] a = { { 3, 26, 48 }, { 5, 2, 9 } };
    System.out.println( "The array elements are " + a );
    ```

55. Where is the error in this code sequence?

```
ArrayList<double> al;
```

56. Where is the error in this code sequence?

```
ArrayList<Float> al = new ArrayList( )<Float>;
```

57. Where is the error in this code sequence? (The compiler may ask you to recompile.)

```
ArrayList<Double> a;
a = new ArrayList<Float>( );
```

58. Where is the error in this code sequence?

```
// a is an ArrayList of Strings
// a has already been declared and instantiated
a.size( ) = 10;
```

9.10.5 Debugging Area—Using Messages from the Java Compiler and Java JVM

59. You coded the following on line 14 of the *Test.java* class:

```
int a[2][ ] = { { 2, 7 }, { 9, 2 } };     // line 14
```

When you compile, you get the following message:

```
Test.java:14: ']' expected
    int a[2][ ] = { { 2, 7 }, { 9, 2 } }; // line 14
          ^
Test.java:14: illegal start of expression
    int a[2][ ] = { { 2, 7 }, { 9, 2 } }; // line 14
        ^
Test.java:14: ';' expected
    int a[2][ ] = { { 2, 7 }, { 9, 2 } }; // line 14
         ^
Test.java:14: illegal start of expression
    int a[2][ ] = { { 2, 7 }, { 9, 2 } }; // line 14
      ^
Test.java:14: illegal start of expression
    int a[2][ ] = { { 2, 7 }, { 9, 2 } }; // line 14
           ^
Test.java:14: not a statement
    int a[2][ ] = { { 2, 7 }, { 9, 2 } }; // line 14
       ^
Test.java:14: ';' expected
    int a[2][ ] = { { 2, 7 }, { 9, 2 } }; // line 14
       ^
```

```
Test.java:14: illegal start of expression
    int a[2][ ] = { { 2, 7 }, { 9, 2 } }; // line 14
             ^

Test.java:14: not a statement
    int a[2][ ] = { { 2, 7 }, { 9, 2 } }; // line 14
                 ^

Test.java:14: ';' expected
    int a[2][ ] = { { 2, 7 }, { 9, 2 } }; // line 14
                      ^

Test.java:16: class, interface, or enum expected
}
^
11 errors
```

Explain what the problem is and how to fix it.

60. You coded the following in the *Test.java* class:

```
int [ ][ ] a = { { 1, 2, 3, 4 },
                 { 10, 20, 30 } };

for ( int i = 0; i < a.length; i++ )
{
    for ( int j = 0; j < a[0].length; j++ )
    {
        System.out.println( a[i][j] );    // line 14
    }
}
```

The code compiles properly but when you run, you get the following output:

```
1
2
3
4
10
20
30
Exception in thread "main" java.lang.ArrayIndexOutOfBoundsException: 3
        at Test.main(Test.java: 14)
```

Explain what the problem is and how to fix it.

61. You coded the following in the *Test.java* class in order to output the smallest element in the array *a*:

```
int [ ][ ] a = { { 9, 8, 7, 6 },
                 { 10, 20, 30, 40 } };
```

```
int min = a[0][0];
for ( int i = 1; i < a.length; i++ )
{
      for ( int j = 0; j < a[i].length; j++ )
      {
            if ( a[i][j] < min )
                  min = a[i][j];
      }
}
System.out.println( "The minimum is " + min );
```

The code compiles properly, but when you run, you get the following output:

```
The minimum is 9
```

You expected the value of *min* to be 6. Explain what the problem is and how to fix it.

62. You coded the following in file *Test.java*:

```
int [ ][ ] a = { { 9, 8, 7, 6 },
                 { 10, 20, 30, 40 } };

for ( int j = 0; j <= a[1].length; j++ )
{
  if ( a[1][j] == 20 )         // line 14
  {
      System.out.println( "Found 20 at column index " + j
                            + " of second row" );
  }
}
```

The code compiles properly, but when you run, you get the following output:

```
Found 20 at column index 1 of second row
Exception in thread "main" java.lang.ArrayIndexOutOfBoundsException: 4
        at Test.main(Test.java:14)
```

Explain what the problem is and how to fix it.

63. You coded the following in the *Test.java* class:

```
public static void main( String [ ] args )
{
  // cars is an ArrayList of Auto objects
  // cars has already been declared and instantiated
  for ( Auto a ; cars )      // line 12
```

```
    {
        System.out.println( a.toString( ) );
    }   // line 15
}       // line 16
```

When you compile, you get the following message :

```
Test.java:12: ';' expected
  for ( Auto a ; cars ) // line 12
                ^
```

```
1 error
```

Explain what the problems are and how to fix them.

64. You coded the following in the *Test.java* class:

```
ArrayList<String> a = new ArrayList<String>( );
a.add( "Cloudy" );
a.add( "Snowy" );
a.add( "Cloudy" );
System.out.println( "Weather is " + a.get( 3 ) ); // line 14
```

The code compiles properly, but when you run, you get the following output:

```
   Exception in thread "main" java.lang.IndexOutOfBoundsException:
Index: 3, Size: 3
           at java.util.ArrayList.RangeCheck(ArrayList.java:599)
           at java.util.ArrayList.get(ArrayList.java:377)
           at Test.main(Test.java:14)
```

Explain what the problem is and how to fix it.

65. You coded the following in the file *Test.java*:

```
ArrayList<Integer> a = new ArrayList ( );
```

When you compile (using Xlint), you get the following warning message:

```
Test.java:10: warning: [rawtypes] found raw type: ArrayList
    ArrayList<Integer> a = new ArrayList( );
                               ^
  missing type parameters for generic class ArrayList<E>
  where E is a type-variable:
    E extends Object declared in class ArrayList

Test.java:10: warning: [unchecked] unchecked conversion
    ArrayList<Integer> a = new ArrayList( );
                               ^
```

```
required: ArrayList<Integer>
found:    ArrayList
2 warnings
```

Explain what the problem is and how to fix it.

66. You coded the following in the file *Test.java*:

```
ArrayList<Double> a = new ArrayList<Double>( );
a.add( new Double ( 2.3 ) );
a.add( 8.4 );
a.add( new Integer( 5 ) ); // line 11
```

When you compile, you get the following message:

```
Test.java:11: cannot find symbol
    a.add( new Integer( 5 ) ); // line 11
         ^
  symbol:   method add(Integer)
  location: class ArrayList<Double>
1 error
```

Explain what the problem is and how to fix it.

67. You coded the following in the file *Test.java*:

```
ArrayList<Character> a = new ArrayList<Character>( );
a.add( 'X' );
a.add( 'A' );
a.add( 'V' );
a.add( 'A' );
a.set( 1, 'J' );
for( Character c : a )
  System.out.print( c + " " );
```

The code compiles properly, but when you run, you get the following output:

```
X J V A
```

when you expected:

```
J A V A
```

Explain what the problem is and how to fix it.

9.10.6 Write a Short Program

68. Write a value-returning method that returns the number of rows in a two-dimensional array of *doubles*. Include code to test your method.

69. Write a value-returning method that returns the number of elements in a two-dimensional array of *floats*. Include code to test your method.

70. Write a value-returning method that returns the number of columns that have two elements in a two-dimensional array of *booleans*. Include code to test your method.

71. Write a value-returning method that returns the number of columns with *n* elements in a two-dimensional array of *chars*, where *n* is a parameter of the method. Include code to test your method.

72. Write a value-returning method that returns the sum of all the elements in a two-dimensional array of *floats*. Include code to test your method.

73. Write a method with a *void* return value that sets to 0 all the elements of the even-numbered rows and sets to 1 all the elements of odd-numbered rows of a two-dimensional array of *ints*. Include code to test your method.

74. Write a value-returning method that returns the sum of the elements in the last column of each row in a two-dimensional array of *ints*. Include code to test your method.

75. Write a method with a *void* return value that inverts all the elements of a two-dimensional array of *booleans* (*true* becomes *false* and *false* becomes *true*). Include code to test your method.

76. Write a method that returns the number of elements having the value *true* in a two-dimensional array of *booleans*. Include code to test your method.

77. Write a method that returns the percentage of elements having the value *false* in a two-dimensional array of *booleans*. Include code to test your method.

78. Write a method that returns the average of all elements in a two-dimensional array of *ints*. Include code to test your method.

79. Write a method that returns the *String* "regular" if all the rows of a two-dimensional array of *floats* have the same number of columns; otherwise, it returns "irregular." Include code to test your method.

80. Write a method that returns the concatenation of all elements in a two-dimensional array of *Strings*. Include code to test your method.

81. Write an array-returning method that takes a two-dimensional array of *chars* as a parameter and returns a single-dimensional array of *Strings* as follows: The array returned should have a number of elements equal to the number of rows in the parameter array; every element of the array returned should be the concatenation of all the column elements of the corresponding row in the parameter array. Include code to test your method.

82. Write an array-returning method that takes a two-dimensional array of *ints* as a parameter and returns a two-dimensional array of *chars*, assigning a letter grade corresponding to the integer grade (A if 90 or above, ..., F if less than 60). Include code to test your method.

83. Write a method that returns the sum of all the elements of an *ArrayList* of *Integer* objects. Include code to test your method.

84. Write a method that returns the *String* "odd" or "even" if the number of elements of an *ArrayList* of *Strings* is odd or even. Include code to test your method.

85. Write a method that takes an *ArrayList* of *Integer* objects and returns an *ArrayList* of *Character* objects of the same size. The returned elements of the *ArrayList* are assigned a letter grade corresponding to the integer grade of the same index element of the *ArrayList* parameter (A if 90 or above, ..., F if less than 60). Include code to test your method.

9.10.7 Programming Projects

86. Write a class (and a client class to test it) that encapsulates statistics for summer job salaries for a group of people over several years. Your only instance variable should be a two-dimensional array of values representing salaries. Dimension 1 represents the people and dimension 2 represents the year of the summer job. Your constructor can simply take two integers representing the number of people and the number of years, then randomly generate the salaries and fill the array. You should include the following methods:

   ❑ a method returning the index of the person having made the most money over the years

   ❑ a method returning the year when the highest salary was earned

   ❑ a method returning the total amount of money made by all the people over the years

87. Write a class (and a client class to test it) that encapsulates the evolution of the passwords of three students over four months. Your only instance variable should be a two-dimensional array of values representing the passwords. Dimension 1 represents the student and dimension 2 represents the month. (Since we are concerned about security, we are assuming that people change their password once a month; we only care about the value of the password at the end of a given month.) Your constructor can simply take a single-dimensional array of words representing the 12 passwords; they can be assigned to the two-dimensional array elements one at a time, starting with the first row. You should include the following methods:

❑ a method returning the index of the person who changed his or her password the most times

❑ a method returning the longest password

❑ a method changing all the passwords to "unlock"

❑ a method returning *true* if at least one person had a given word—the method's parameter—as his/her password in at least one month; *false* otherwise

88. Write a class (and a client class to test it) that encapsulates the evolution of the sales tax rates in the 50 U.S. states over the last 10 years. Your only instance variable should be a two-dimensional array of values representing the sales tax rates. Dimension 1 represents the state and dimension 2 represents the year. Your constructor can simply be a default constructor, randomly generating the sales tax rates, which should be between 0 and 0.06. You should include the following methods:

❑ a method returning the index of the state that has the biggest average tax rate over the years

❑ a method returning an array of indexes of the states that have had at least one year with a tax rate less than 0.001

❑ a method returning the highest sales tax rate over the years for a given state (which will be a parameter)

89. Write a class (and a client class to test it) that encapsulates the evolution of the quality ratings of various hotels over the years. Hotel ratings

are represented by a number of stars, which can vary from one star (lowest quality) to five stars (highest quality). Your only instance variable should be a two-dimensional array of values representing the quality ratings. Dimension 1 represents the hotel and dimension 2 represents the year. Your constructor can take two parameters representing the number of hotels and the number of years. The ratings can simply be generated randomly. You should include the following methods:

❏ a method returning an array of indexes of the hotels that have earned five stars at least once over the years

❏ a method returning the average rating of all the hotels over the years

❏ a method printing the indexes of the hotels that have earned five stars every year

❏ a method returning *true* if at least one hotel earned five stars for at least one year; *false* otherwise

90. Write a class (and a client class to test it) that encapsulates the value of the 26 letters of the English alphabet in the game of Scrabble in 10 countries. You should have three instance variables:

❏ a two-dimensional array of integers representing the point values of the letters in the various countries

❏ a single-dimensional array representing the alphabet from a to z

❏ another single-dimensional array representing 10 countries

For the two-dimensional array, dimension 1 represents the letter and dimension 2 represents the country. Your constructor can simply be a default constructor, randomly generating the values between 1 and 10. You should include the following methods:

❏ a method returning an array of letters with their highest point value in any country

❏ a method printing the names of the countries that have at least one letter with a point value of 10

❏ a method taking a *String* as a parameter and printing the score of the word represented by that *String* in every country

91. Write a class (and a client class to test it) that encapsulates the numbers of the various chessboard pieces in a chess game. You should have two instance variables:

    ❏ a two-dimensional array of integers; each array element represents how many of a particular chess piece of a particular color are on the board. In order to set it up, consider the following:

      ▪ The first dimension represents the color of the pieces. On a chessboard, there are white and black pieces.

      ▪ The second dimension represents the pieces themselves. On a chessboard, we have on each side: one king, one queen, two bishops, two knights, two rooks, and eight pawns.

    ❏ a single-dimensional array describing the pieces (king, queen, etc.)

    Your constructor can simply be a default constructor, declaring and instantiating the two arrays to match the preceding information. You should include the following methods:

    ❏ a method with a *void* return value, called *playerATakesPlayerB*, updating the array based on a piece being taken by the opponent. It takes two parameters:

      ▪ a *boolean* parameter representing whether "white takes black" or "black takes white"

      ▪ an *int* parameter representing which piece gets taken

    ❏ a method returning how many of a particular piece are on the board (this method takes a parameter representing the piece)

    ❏ a method taking a *boolean* as a parameter, representing a color and returning the value of the board for that particular color. You can consider that a king is worth 0 points, a queen is worth 6 points, a rook is worth 4 points, a knight and a bishop are each worth 3 points, and a pawn is worth 1 point

92. Write a class (and a client class to test it) that encapsulates a deck of cards. A deck of cards is made up of 52 cards. You should have three instance variables:

    ❏ a two-dimensional array of values representing the cards

❏ a single-dimensional array describing the suit: spades, hearts, diamonds, and clubs

❏ an instance variable representing the trump suit

For the two-dimensional array, dimension 1 represents the suit and dimension 2 represents the type of card (ace, two, three, ..., jack, queen, king). Your constructor should take one parameter, which will represent the suit of the trump. Based on that, the cards should be given the following values:

❏ Non-trump from 2 to 10: 1 point

❏ Non-trump jack = 2

❏ Non-trump queen = 3

❏ Non-trump king = 4

❏ Non-trump ace = 5

❏ Any trump card = Non-trump value + 1

You should include the following methods:

❏ a method returning the trump suit, by name

❏ a method printing the whole deck of cards, suit by suit, with the value for each card

❏ a method taking a *String* as a parameter representing a suit, and returning the total value of the cards of that suit

93. Write a class (and a client class to test it) that encapsulates a tic-tac-toe board. A tic-tac-toe board looks like a table of three rows and three columns partially or completely filled with the characters X and O. At any point, a cell of that table could be empty or could contain an X or an O. You should have one instance variable, a two-dimensional array of values representing the tic-tac-toe board.

Your default constructor should instantiate the array so that it represents an empty board.

You should include the following methods:

❏ a method, returning a *boolean*, simulating a play with three parameters as follows: If the first parameter is *true*, then X is playing; otherwise, O is playing. The other two parameters represent what cell on the board is being played. If the play is legal, that is, the cell is a legal cell on the board and is empty, then the method should update the array and return *true*; otherwise, the array should not be updated and the method should return *false*

❏ a method returning how many valid plays have been made so far

❏ a method checking if a player has won based on the contents of the board; this method takes no parameter. It returns X if the "X player" has won, O if the "O player" has won, T if the game was a tie. A player wins if he or she has placed an X (or an O) in all cells in a row, all cells in a column, or all cells in one of the two diagonals

94. Modify the *BookStore* and *BookSearchEngine* classes from the chapter.

   You should include the following additional methods and test them:

   ❏ a method returning the book with the lowest price in the library

   ❏ a method searching the library for *Books* of a given author and returning an *ArrayList* of such *Books*

   ❏ a method returning an *ArrayList* of *Books* whose price is less than a given number

95. Write a *Garage* class (and a client class to test it) with one instance variable: an *ArrayList* of *Autos* (you can use the *Auto* class from Chapter 7).

   You should include the following methods:

   ❏ a method returning the average number of miles of all cars in the garage

   ❏ a method returning "full" if the garage has 100 cars or more, "below minimum" if the garage has fewer than 25 cars, and "normal load" if the garage has between 25 and 100 cars in it

   ❏ a method returning the total number of gallons of gas used by all cars in the garage

96. Write a *ComputerPart* class and a *ComputerKit* class (and a client class to test them).

   The *ComputerPart* class has two instance variables: a *String* representing an item (for instance, "cpu" or "disk drive"), and a *double* representing the price of that item. The *ComputerKit* class has just one instance variable: an *ArrayList* of *ComputerPart* objects (they make up a computer) representing the list of parts for the computer kit.

You should include the following methods:

❏ a method returning "expensive" if the total of the prices of the *ComputerPart* objects is greater than 1,000, "cheap" if it is less than 250, "normal" if it is between 250 and 1,000

❏ a method returning *true* if a certain item is included in the list of parts; *false* otherwise

❏ a method returning how many times a particular item (for instance, "cpu," or "memory") is found in the list of parts

9.10.8 Technical Writing

97. A two-dimensional array can have a different number of columns in every row. Do you see that as an advantage or a disadvantage? Discuss.

98. Discuss the pros and cons of using an array vs. using an *ArrayList*.

9.10.9 Group Project (for a group of 1, 2, or 3 students)

99. Design and code a program including the following classes, as well as a client class to test all the methods coded:

A *Passenger* class, encapsulating a passenger. A passenger has two attributes: a name, and a class of service, which will be 1 or 2.

A *Train* class, encapsulating a train of passengers. A train of passengers has one attribute: a list of passengers, which must be represented with an *ArrayList*. Your constructor will build the list of passengers by reading data from a file called *passengers.txt*. You can assume that *passengers.txt* has the following format:

```
<name1>   <class1>
<name2>   <class2>
...
```

For instance, the file could contain:

```
James      1
Ben        2
Suri       1
Sarah      1
Jane       2

...
```

You should include the following methods in your *Train* class:

❑ a method returning the percentage of passengers traveling in first class

❑ a method taking two parameters representing the price of traveling in first and second class and returning the total revenue for the train

❑ a method checking if a certain person is on the train; if he/she is, the method returns *true*; otherwise, it returns *false*

Java Reserved Words and Keywords

These words have contextual meaning for the Java language and cannot be used as identifiers.

abstract	default	goto	package	synchronized
assert	do	if	private	this
boolean	double	implements	protected	throw
break	else	import	public	throws
byte	enum	instanceof	return	transient
case	extends	int	short	true
catch	false	interface	static	try
char	final	long	strictfp	void
class	finally	native	super	volatile
const	float	new	switch	while
continue	for	null		

The words *true*, *false*, and *null* are literals. The remainder of the words are Java keywords, although *const* and *goto* are not currently used in the Java language.

APPENDIX B

Operator Precedence

These rules of operator precedence are followed when expressions are evaluated. Operators in a higher level in the hierarchy—defined by their row position in the table—are evaluated before operators in a lower level. Thus, an expression in parentheses is evaluated before a shortcut postincrement is performed, and so on with the operators in each level. When two or more operators on the same level appear in an expression, the evaluation of the expression follows the corresponding rule for same-statement evaluation shown in the second column.

Operators	Order of Same-Statement Evaluation	Operation
( )	left to right	parentheses for explicit grouping
++ −−	right to left	shortcut postincrement and postdecrement
++ −− !	right to left	shortcut preincrement and predecrement, logical unary NOT
* / %	left to right	multiplication, division, modulus
+ -	left to right	addition or *String* concatenation, subtraction
< <= > >= instanceof	left to right	relational operators: less than, less than or equal to, greater than, greater than or equal to; instanceof
== !=	left to right	equality operators: equal to and not equal to
&&	left to right	logical AND
||	left to right	logical OR
?:	left to right	conditional operator
= += -= *= /= %=	right to left	assignment operator and shortcut assignment operators

APPENDIX C

The Unicode Character Set

Java characters are encoded using the Unicode Character Set, which is designed to support international alphabets, punctuation, and mathematical and technical symbols. Each character is stored as 16 bits, so as many as 65,536 characters are supported.

The American Standard Code for Information Interchange (ASCII) character set is supported by the first 128 Unicode characters from 0000 to 007F, which are called the controls and Basic Latin characters, as shown on the next page.

Any character from the Unicode set can be specified as a *char* literal in a Java program by using the following syntax: '\uNNNN' where NNNN are the four hexadecimal digits that specify the Unicode encoding for the character.

For more information on the Unicode character set, visit the Unicode Consortium's website: *www.unicode.org*.

Controls and Basic Latin Characters

	000	001	002	003	004	005	006	007
0	NUL 0000	DLE 0010	SP 0020	0 0030	@ 0040	P 0050	` 0060	p 0070
1	SOH 0001	DC1 0011	! 0021	1 0031	A 0041	Q 0051	a 0061	q 0071
2	STX 0002	DC2 0012	" 0022	2 0032	B 0042	R 0052	b 0062	r 0072
3	ETX 0003	DC3 0013	# 0023	3 0033	C 0043	S 0053	c 0063	s 0073
4	EOT 0004	DC4 0014	$ 0024	4 0034	D 0044	T 0054	d 0064	t 0074
5	ENQ 0005	NAK 0015	% 0025	5 0035	E 0045	U 0055	e 0065	u 0075
6	ACK 0006	SYN 0016	& 0026	6 0036	F 0046	V 0056	f 0066	v 0076
7	BEL 0007	ETB 0017	' 0027	7 0037	G 0047	W 0057	g 0067	w 0077
8	BS 0008	CAN 0018	(0028	8 0038	H 0048	X 0058	h 0068	x 0078
9	HT 0009	EM 0019	) 0029	9 0039	I 0049	Y 0059	i 0069	y 0079
A	LF 000A	SUB 001A	* 002A	: 003A	J 004A	Z 005A	j 006A	z 007A
B	VT 000B	ESC 001B	+ 002B	; 003B	K 004B	[005B	k 006B	{ 007B
C	FF 000C	FS 001C	, 002C	< 003C	L 004C	\ 005C	l 006C	| 007C
D	CR 000D	GS 001D	- 002D	= 003D	M 004D	] 005D	m 006D	} 007D
E	SO 000E	RS 001E	. 002E	> 003E	N 004E	^ 005E	n 006E	~ 007E
F	SI 000F	US 001F	/ 002F	? 003F	O 004F	_ 005F	o 006F	DEL 007F

APPENDIX D

Representing Negative Integers

The industry standard method for representing negative integers is called **two's complement**. Here is how it works:

For an integer represented using 16 bits, the leftmost bit is reserved for the sign bit. If the sign bit is 0, then the integer is positive; if the sign bit is 1, then the integer is negative.

For example, let's consider two numbers, one positive and one negative.

0000 0101 0111 1001 is a positive integer, which we call a.

1111 1111 1101 1010 is a negative integer, which we will call b.

Using the methodology presented in Chapter 1 for converting a binary number to a decimal number, we can convert the binary number, a, to its decimal equivalent. Hence, the value of a is calculated as follows:

$$a = 2^{10} + 2^8 + 2^6 + 2^5 + 2^4 + 2^3 + 2^0$$
$$= 1{,}024 + 256 + 64 + 32 + 16 + 8 + 1$$
$$= 1{,}401$$

In contrast, b, the negative number, is represented in binary using the two's complement method. The leftmost bit, which is the sign bit, is a 1, indicating that b is negative. To calculate the value of a negative number, we first calculate its two's complement. The two's complement of any binary number is another binary number, which, when added to the original number, will yield a sum consisting of all 0s and a carry bit of 1 at the end.

To calculate the two's complement of a binary number, *n*, subtract *n* from 2^d, where *d* is the number of binary digits in *n*. The following formula summarizes that rule:

```
Two's complement of n = 2ᵈ - n
```

Knowing that $2^d - 1$ is always a binary number containing all 1s, we can simplify our calculations by first subtracting 1 from 2^d, then adding a 1 at the end.

```
Two's complement of n = 2ᵈ - 1 - n + 1
```

So to calculate the two's complement of *b*, which has 16 digits, we subtract *b* from a binary number consisting of 16 1s, then add 1, as shown here.

```
              2ᵈ - 1   1111 1111 1111 1111
                - b    1111 1111 1101 1010
                       0000 0000 0010 0101
                + 1  _____1
two's complement of b  0000 0000 0010 0110
```

Thus, the two's complement of *b*, which we will call *c*, is 0000 0000 0010 0110.

Another, simpler, way to calculate a two's complement is to invert each bit, then add 1. Inverting bits means to change all 0s to 1s and to change all 1s to 0s. Using this method, we get

```
        b    1111 1111 1101 1010

b inverted   0000 0000 0010 0101
      + 1  _____1
        c    0000 0000 0010 0110
```

We can verify that the two's complement of *b* is correct by calculating the sum of *b* and *c*.

```
    b    1111 1111 1101 1010
    c    0000 0000 0010 0110
b + c  1 0000 0000 0000 0000
```

Converting *c* to decimal will give us the value of our original number *b*, which, as we remember, is negative. We have

```
b =  - (  2⁵ + 2² + 2¹  )
  =  - ( 32  +  4  + 2  )
  =   -38
```

Because a leftmost bit of 0 indicates that the number is positive, using 16 bits, the largest positive number (we will call it *max*) that we can represent is

0111 1111 1111 1111

$$max = (2^{14} + 2^{13} + 2^{12} + 2^{11} + 2^{10} + 2^9 + 2^8 + 2^7 + 2^6 + 2^5 + 2^4 + 2^3 + 2^2 + 2^1 + 2^0)$$

This is equivalent to $2^{15} - 1$, which is $32,768 - 1$, or $32,767$.

Using 16 bits, then, the smallest negative number (we will call it *min*) that we can represent is

1000 0000 0000 0000

The two's complement of *min* is *min* itself. If we invert the bits and add 1, we get the same value we started with:

```
        min          1000 0000 0000 0000

  min inverted       0111 1111 1111 1111
          + 1        _____   1
two's complement     1000 0000 0000 0000
```

and therefore *min* is -2^{15} or $-32,768$.

Thus, using 16 bits, we can represent integers between $-32,768$ and $32,767$.

APPENDIX E

Representing Floating-Point Numbers

IEEE 754, a specification accepted worldwide and used by the Java language, defines how to represent floating-point numbers in binary numbers. Single-precision floating-point numbers use 32 bits of memory, and double-precision floating-point numbers use 64 bits.

Here is how single- and double-precision floating-point numbers are represented:

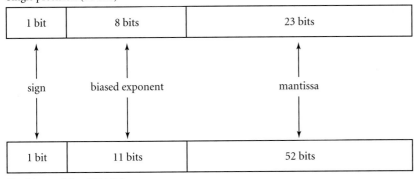

Single precision (32 bits)

1 bit	8 bits	23 bits
sign	biased exponent	mantissa

| 1 bit | 11 bits | 52 bits |

Double precision (64 bits)

The leftmost bit stores the sign of the floating-point number; a 0 indicates a positive number, while a 1 indicates a negative number.

To represent the exponent of the number, which can be positive or negative, each representation stores a positive, biased exponent, calculated by adding a fixed bias, or scaling factor, to the real exponent of the number.

The purpose of the bias is to be able to represent both extremely large and extremely small numbers. The bias is equal to

$$2^{(\text{\# of bits of the biased exponent} - 1)} - 1$$

Thus, for single precision, the bias is

$$2^{(8-1)} - 1 = 2^7 - 1 = 127$$

In single-precision, the 8-bit biased exponent can store 256 positive values (0 to 255). Thus, with a bias of 127, we can represent floating-point numbers with real exponents from -127 to 128, as shown here:

```
Real exponent     −127   −126   ...    0    ...   127    128
     + Bias         127    127   ...   127   ...   127    127
Biased exponent      0      1    ...   127   ...   254    255
```

Conversely, to find the real exponent from the biased exponent, we subtract the bias. For example, if the biased exponent is 150, then the real exponent is $150 - 127$, which is 23. Similarly, if the biased exponent is 3, the actual exponent is $3 - 127$, which is -124.

For double precision, the bias is

$$2^{(11-1)} - 1 = 2^{10} - 1 = 1023$$

A floating-point number is considered to be in the form

$$(-1)^{\text{sign}} * (1 + \text{significand}) * 2^{(\text{biased exponent} - \text{bias})}$$

By definition, the significand is of the form 0 followed by a dot followed by a string of 0s and 1s, for example, 0.1101. That string of 0s and 1s is known as the mantissa.

For example, if the significand is 0.1101, then the mantissa is 110100...0

As an example, let's convert a single-precision binary number to a decimal floating-point number. We will convert the following single-precision IEEE 754 floating-point number:

0	10000111	11010000...0

The leftmost digit, 0, tells us that the number is positive. The biased exponent is 10000111, which converted to decimal, is

$$= 2^7 + 2^2 + 2^1 + 2^0$$
$$= 128 + 4 + 2 + 1$$
$$= 135$$

The bias for single-precision floating-point numbers is 127, so the number is

$$= (-1)^0 * (1 + .1101) * 2^{(135 - 127)}$$
$$= 1.1101 * 2^8$$
$$= 1\ 1101\ 0000$$

In decimal, the number is

$$= 2^8 + 2^7 + 2^6 + 2^4$$
$$= 256 + 128 + 64 + 16$$
$$= 464$$

Given that .1 is $\frac{1}{2}^1$ or $\frac{1}{2}$ in decimal, and .01 is $\frac{1}{2}^2$ or $\frac{1}{4}$, and .0001 is $\frac{1}{2}^4$ or $\frac{1}{16}$ in decimal, we also could have calculated the number using this method:

$$= 1.1101 * 2^8$$
$$= (1 + 1 * \frac{1}{2}^1 + 1 * \frac{1}{2}^2 + 0 * \frac{1}{2}^3 + 1 * \frac{1}{2}^4) * 2^8$$
$$= (1 + \frac{1}{2} + \frac{1}{4} + \frac{1}{16}) * 2^8$$
$$= (1 + \frac{1}{2} + \frac{1}{4} + \frac{1}{16}) * 256$$
$$= 464$$

Now, let's convert a decimal floating-point number into single-precision, binary format. Here, we will convert the number -5.375, which we'll call y. First we convert the whole number portion (5) to binary, getting 101:

$$5 = 101$$

Then we convert the fractional part to binary:

$$.375 = .25 + .125$$
$$= \frac{1}{4} + \frac{1}{8}$$
$$= \frac{1}{2}^2 + \frac{1}{2}^3$$
$$= 0 * \frac{1}{2}^1 + 1 * \frac{1}{2}^2 + 1 * \frac{1}{2}^3$$

Thus, .375 as represented in binary is .011.

Therefore, y can be represented in binary as

$$y = -101.011$$
$$= -1.01011 * 2^2$$

We now can deduce the sign, the biased exponent, and the mantissa. The sign is 1 because the number is negative. The significand is 1.01011, and therefore the mantissa is 01011000...00. The exponent is 2, so the biased exponent is 129 (2 plus the bias for single-precision numbers, which is 127):

$$\text{Biased exponent} = 2 + 127$$
$$= 129$$

Converting 129 to binary, we get

129 = 1000 0001

Therefore, the IEEE 754 single-precision value of the number y is

1	10000001	010110000...0

APPENDIX F

Java Classes APIs

In this appendix, we have compiled the APIs for the Java classes and interfaces used in this book. There are more methods and constructors for the classes presented here, and there are many more classes in the Java class library. We invite you to explore the Java APIs at *www.oracle.com/technetwork/java*.

ArrayList

Package: java.util

Description: implements a dynamically resizable array of object references

Constructors

```
ArrayList<E>( )
```
        constructs an *ArrayList* object of data type *E* with an initial capacity of 10

```
ArrayList<E>( int initialCapacity )
```
        constructs an *ArrayList* object of data type *E* with the specified initial capacity. Throws an *IllegalArgumentException*

Useful Methods of the *ArrayList* Class (*E* represents the data type of the *ArrayList*.)	
Return value	**Method name and argument list**
boolean	add(E element)
	appends the specified *element* to the end of the list. Returns *true*.
void	clear( )
	removes all the elements from the list
E	get(int index)
	returns the element at the specified *index* position; the element is not removed from the list.
E	remove(int index)
	returns and removes the element at the specified *index* position
E	set(int index, E newElement)
	returns the element at the specified *index* position and replaces that element with *newElement*.
int	size( )
	returns the number of elements in the list
void	trimToSize( )
	sets the capacity to the list's current size

BigDecimal

Package: java.math

Description: provides methods that perform addition, subtraction, multiplication, and division so that the results are exact, without the rounding errors caused by floating-point operations.

Constructor

BigDecimal(String num)

creates a *BigDecimal* object equivalent to the decimal number *num* expressed as a *String*. Throws a *NumberFormatException*.

Useful Methods of the *BigDecimal* Class

Return value	Method name and argument list
BigDecimal	add(BigDecimal num)
	returns a *BigDecimal* object equal to the current *BigDecimal* object plus *num*
BigDecimal	subtract(BigDecimal num)
	returns a *BigDecimal* object equal to the current *BigDecimal* object minus *num*
BigDecimal	multiply(BigDecimal num)
	returns a *BigDecimal* object equal to the current *BigDecimal* object times *num*
BigDecimal	divide(BigDecimal num)
	returns a *BigDecimal* object equal to the current *BigDecimal* object divided by *num*. Throws an *ArithmeticException*.
int	compareTo(BigDecimal num)
	returns 0 if the current *BigDecimal* object is equal to *num*; -1 if the current *BigDecimal* object is less than *num*; and 1 if the current *BigDecimal* object is greater than *num*.

Color

Package: java.awt

Description: creates colors to be used in producing graphical output

Constructor

Color(int red, int green, int blue)

instantiates a *Color* object with the combined color intensities of *red*, *green*, and *blue*. Each color intensity can range from 0 to 255.

Predefined *Color* Constants			
Color Constant	Red	Green	Blue
Color.BLACK	0	0	0
Color.BLUE	0	0	255
Color.CYAN	0	255	255
Color.DARK_GRAY	64	64	64
Color.GRAY	128	128	128
Color.GREEN	0	255	0
Color.LIGHT_GRAY	192	192	192
Color.MAGENTA	255	0	255
Color.ORANGE	255	200	0
Color.PINK	255	175	175
Color.RED	255	0	0
Color.WHITE	255	255	255
Color.YELLOW	255	255	0

DecimalFormat

Package: java.text

Description: provides methods for formatting numbers for output

Constructor
DecimalFormat(String pattern)

instantiates a *DecimalFormat* object with the output *pattern* specified in the argument

A Useful Method of the *DecimalFormat* Class

Return value	Method name and argument list
String	format(double number)

returns a *String* representation of *number* formatted according to the *DecimalFormat* pattern used to instantiate the object. This method is inherited from the *NumberFormat* class.

Commonly Used Pattern Symbols for a *DecimalFormat* Object	
Symbol	**Meaning**
0	Required digit. If the value for the digit in this position is 0, insert a zero.
#	Digit. Don't insert a character if the digit is 0.
.	Decimal point
,	Comma separator
%	Multiply by 100 and display a percentage sign

Double

Package: java.lang

Description: wrapper class that creates an equivalent object from a *double* variable and provides methods for converting a *String* to a *double* primitive type and a *Double* object.

Constructor

```
Double( double d )
```

instantiates a *Double* object with a *double* instance variable having the same value as *d*.

Useful Methods of the *Double* Wrapper Class	
Return value	**Method name and argument list**
double	parseDouble(String s)
	static method that converts the *String s* to a *double* and returns that value. Throws a *NumberFormatException*.
Double	valueOf(String s)
	static method that converts the *String s* to a *Double* object and returns that object. Throws a *NumberFormatException*.

Enum

Package: java.lang

Description: provides for creation of enumerated types

Useful Methods for *enum* Objects

Return value	Method name and argument list
int	compareTo(Enum eObj)
	compares two *enum* objects and returns a negative number if *this* object is less than the argument, a positive number if *this* object is greater than the argument, and 0 if the two objects are equal.
boolean	equals(Object eObj)
	returns *true* if *this* object is equal to the argument *eObj*; returns *false* otherwise.
int	ordinal( )
	returns the numeric value of the *enum* object. By default, the value of the first object in the list is 0, the value of the second object is 1, and so on.
String	toString( )
	returns the name of the *enum* constant
Enum	valueOf(String enumName)
	static method that returns the *enum* object whose name is the same as the *String* argument *enumName*.

File

Package: java.io

Description: represents platform-independent file names

Constructor

File(String pathname)

constructs a *File* object with the *pathname* file name so that the file name is platform-independent.

Graphics

Package: java.awt

Description: represents the current graphical context, including the component on which drawing will take place and the current color.

Useful Methods of the *Graphics* Class

Return value	Method name and argument list
void	`clearRect( int x, int y, int width, int height )`
	draws a solid rectangle in the current background color with its top left corner at (x, y), with the specified *width* and *height* in pixels.
void	`drawLine( int xStart, int yStart, int xEnd, int yEnd )`
	draws a line starting at (*xStart, yStart*) and ending at (*xEnd, yEnd*)
void	`drawOval( int x, int y, int width, int height )`
	draws the outline of an oval inside an invisible rectangle with the specified *width* and *height* in pixels. The top left corner of the rectangle is (x, y).
void	`drawRect( int x, int y, int width, int height )`
	draws the outline of a rectangle with its top left corner at (x, y), with the specified *width* and *height* in pixels.
void	`drawPolygon( Polygon p )`
	draws the outline of *Polygon p*.
void	`drawString( String s, int x, int y )`
	displays the *String s*. If you were to draw an invisible rectangle around the first letter of the *String*, (x, y) would be the lower left corner of that rectangle.
void	`fillOval( int x, int y, int width, int height )`
	draws a solid oval inside an invisible rectangle with the specified *width* and *height* in pixels. The top left corner of the rectangle is (x, y).
void	`fillRect( int x, int y, int width, int height )`
	draws a solid rectangle with its top left corner at (x, y), with the specified *width* and *height* in pixels.

void	`fillPolygon( Polygon p )`

draws the *Polygon p* and fills its area with the current color.

void	`setColor( Color c )`

sets the current foreground color to the *Color* specified by *c*.

Integer

Package: java.lang

Description: wrapper class that creates an equivalent object for an *int* variable and provides methods for converting a *String* to an *int* primitive type and an *Integer* object

Constructor

`Integer( int i )`

instantiates an *Integer* object with an *int* instance variable having the same value as *i*.

Useful Methods of the *Integer* Wrapper Class

Return value	Method name and argument list
int	`parseInt( String s )`

static method that converts the *String s* to an *int* and returns that value. Throws a *NumberFormatException*.

Integer	`valueOf( String s )`

static method that converts the *String s* to an *Integer* object and returns that object. Throws a *NumberFormatException*.

JOptionPane

Package: javax.swing

Description: pops up an input or output dialog box

Useful Methods of the *JOptionPane* Class

Return value	Method name and argument list
String	`showInputDialog( Component parent, Object prompt )`

static method that pops up an input dialog box, where *prompt* asks the user for input. Returns the characters typed by the user as a *String*.

void	showMessageDialog(Component parent, Object message)

static method that pops up an output dialog box with *message* displayed. The *message* argument is usually a *String*.

Math

Package: java.lang

Description: provides methods for performing common mathematical computations. All methods are *static*.

Predefined *static* Constants

	Data type	Description
E	double	the base of the natural logarithm. Approximate value is 2.78
PI	double	pi, the ratio of the circumference of a circle to its diameter. Approximate value is 3.14.

Math Class Method Summary
Note: All methods are *static*.

Return value	Method name and argument list
dataTypeOfArg	abs(arg)
	returns the absolute value of the argument *arg*, which can be a *double, float, int,* or *long.*
double	log(double a)
	returns the natural logarithm (in base e) of its argument. For example, log(1) returns 0 and log(*Math.E*) returns 1.
dataTypeOfArgs	max(argA, argB)
	returns the larger of the two arguments. The arguments can be *doubles, floats, ints,* or *longs.*
dataTypeOfArgs	min(argA, argB)
	returns the smaller of the two arguments. The arguments can be *doubles, floats, ints,* or *longs.*
double	pow(double base, double exp)
	returns the value of *base* raised to the *exp* power

int	`round( float a )`
	returns the closest integer to its argument, *a*.
double	`sqrt( double a )`
	returns the positive square root of *a*.

NumberFormat

Package: java.text

Description: provides methods for formatting numbers in currency, percent, and other formats. There are no constructors for this class.

Useful Methods of the *NumberFormat* Class	
Return value	**Method name and argument list**
String	`format( double number )`
	returns a *String* representation of *number* formatted according to the *NumberFormat* object reference used to call the method.
NumberFormat	`getCurrencyInstance( )`
	static method that creates a format for printing money.
NumberFormat	`getPercentInstance( )`
	static method that creates a format for printing a percentage.

Polygon

Package: java.awt

Description: encapsulates a polygon represented by a set of (*x*, *y*) coordinates that are the vertices of a polygon.

Constructor
`Polygon( )`
creates an empty *Polygon*.

A Useful Method of the *Polygon* Class	
Return value	**Method name and argument list**
void	`addPoint( int x, int y )`
	appends the coordinate to the polygon.

Random

Package: java.util

Description: Generates random numbers

Constructor

```
Random( )
```
creates a random number generator.

A Useful Method of the *Random* Class

Return value   **Method name and argument list**

```
int                    nextInt ( int number )
```
returns a random number ranging from 0 up to, but not including, *number* in uniform distribution.

Scanner

Package: java.util

Description: provides support for reading from an input stream or file

Constructors

```
Scanner( InputStream source )
```
creates a *Scanner* object for reading from *source*. If *source* is *System.in*, this instantiates a *Scanner* object for reading from the Java console.

```
Scanner( File source )
```
creates a *Scanner* object for reading from a file. (See the *File* class.) Throws a *FileNotFoundException*.

Selected Methods of the *Scanner* Class

Return value   **Method name and argument list**

```
void                   close( )
```
releases resources associated with an open input stream.

```
boolean                hasNext( )
```
returns *true* if there is another token in the input stream; *false*, otherwise.

boolean	hasNextBoolean( )

returns *true* if the next token in the input stream can be read as a *boolean*; *false*, otherwise.

boolean	hasNextByte( )

returns *true* if the next token in the input stream can be read as a *byte*; *false*, otherwise.

boolean	hasNextDouble( )

returns *true* if the next token in the input stream can be read as a *double*; *false*, otherwise.

boolean	hasNextFloat( )

returns *true* if the next token in the input stream can be read as a *float*; *false*, otherwise.

boolean	hasNextInt( )

returns *true* if the next token in the input stream can be read as an *int*; *false*, otherwise.

boolean	hasNextLong( )

returns *true* if the next token in the input stream can be read as a *long*; *false*, otherwise.

boolean	hasNextShort( )

returns *true* if the next token can be read as a *short*; *false*, otherwise.

String	next( )

returns the next token in the input stream as a *String*.

boolean	nextBoolean( )

returns the next input token as a *boolean*. Throws an *Input-MismatchException*.

byte	nextByte( )

returns the next input token as a *byte*. Throws an *InputMismatchException*.

double	nextDouble( )

returns the next input token as a *double*. Throws an *Input-MismatchException*.

float	nextFloat( )
	returns the next input token as a *float*. Throws an *Input-MismatchException*.
int	nextInt( )
	returns the next input token as an *int*. Throws an *Input-MismatchException*.
String	nextLine( )
	returns the remainder of the input line as a *String*.
long	nextLong( )
	returns the next input token as a *long*. Throws an *Input-MismatchException*.
short	nextShort( )
	returns the next input token as a *short*. Throws an *Input-MismatchException*.

String

Package: java.lang

Description: provides support for storing, searching, and manipulating sequences of characters

Constructors

String(String str)

creates a *String* object with the value of *str*, which can be a *String* object or a *String* literal.

String( )

creates an empty *String* object.

String(char [ ] charArray)

creates a *String* object containing the characters in the *char* array *charArray.*

Methods	
Return value	**Method name and argument list**
char	`charAt( int index )`
	returns the character at the position specified by *index*. The first index is 0.
int	`compareTo( String str )`
	compares the value of the two *Strings*. If the *String* object is less than the argument, a negative integer is returned. If the *String* object is greater than the *String* argument, a positive number is returned; if the two *Strings* are equal, a 0 is returned.
boolean	`equals( Object str )`
	compares the value of two *Strings*. Returns *true* if *str* is a *String,* is not *null,* and is equal to the *String* object; *false* otherwise.
boolean	`equalsIgnoreCase( String str )`
	compares the value of two *Strings,* treating upper- and lowercase characters as equal. Returns *true* if the *Strings* are equal; *false* otherwise.
int	`indexOf( char searchChar )`
	returns the index of the first occurrence of *searchChar* in the *String.* Returns −1 if not found.
int	`indexOf( String substring )`
	returns the index of the first occurrence of *substring* in the *String.* Returns −1 if not found.
int	`length( )`
	returns the number of characters in the *String*.
String	`substring( int startIndex, int endIndex )`
	returns a substring of the *String* object beginning at the character at index *startIndex* and ending at the character at index (*endIndex* − *1*)
String	`toLowerCase( )`
	converts all letters in the *String* to lowercase
String	`toUpperCase( )`
	converts all letters in the *String* to uppercase

System

Package: java.lang

System.out

The *out* class constant of the *System* class is a *PrintStream* object, which represents the standard system output device. The following *PrintStream* methods can be called using the object reference **System.out** in order to print to the Java console.

Methods	
Return value	**Method name and argument list**
void	print(argument)
	prints *argument* to the standard output device. The argument is usually any primitive data type or a *String* object.
void	println(argument)
	prints *argument* to the standard output device, then prints a new-line character. The argument is usually any primitive data type or a *String* object.

APPENDIX G

Solutions to Selected Exercises

1.7 Exercises, Problems, and Projects

1.7.1 Multiple Choice Exercises:

1. Java

4. servers.

7. is a multiple of 4.

10. C

13. *javac Hello.java*

1.7.2 Converting Numbers

16. 11000011100

19. 0x15

1.7.3 General Questions

22. 1.5 billion

25. red = 51; green = 171; blue = 18

28. *javac*

2.7   Exercises, Problems, and Projects

2.7.1   Multiple Choice Exercises

1. ```
int a;
```

### 2.7.2     Reading and Understanding Code

4. 12.5

7. 2.0

10. 4

13. 5

16. 2.4

19. 5

22. 0

### 2.7.3     Fill In the Code

25. ```
boolean a;
a = false;
```

28. ```
float avg = (float) (a + b) / 2;
System.out.println("The average is " + avg);
```

31. ```
a *= 3;
```

2.7.4   Identifying Errors in Code

34. Cannot assign a *double* to a *float* variable (possible loss of precision).

37. There should not be a space between – and =.

2.7.5   Debugging Area—Using Messages from the Java Compiler and Java JVM

40. Cannot assign a *double* to an *int* variable (possible loss of precision). Change to:

    ```
    int a = 26;
    ```

43. =+ is different from += (shortcut operator). Here, *a* is assigned the value + 3. To add 3 to *a*, change the second statement to:

    ```
    a += 3;
    ```

3.19 Exercises, Problems, and Projects

3.19.1 Multiple Choice Exercises

1. `import`

4. `new`

7. It is a class method.

10. `double`

13. `Math.E;`

3.19.2 Reading and Understanding Code

16. hello

19. 3.141592653589793

22. 8

3.19.3 Fill In the Code

25.
```
System.out.println( s.length( ) );
```

28.
```
System.out.print( "Welcome" );
System.out.print( "to" );
System.out.print( "Java" );
System.out.print( "Illuminated\n" );
```

31.
```
// code below assumes we have imported Scanner
Scanner scan = new Scanner( System.in );
System.out.print( "Enter two integers > " );
int i = scan.nextInt( );
int j = scan.nextInt( );
int min = Math.min( i, j );
System.out.println( "min of " + i + " and " + j + " is " + min );
```

34.
```
// code below assumes we have imported Scanner
Scanner scan = new Scanner( System.in );
System.out.print( "Enter a double > " );
double number = scan.nextDouble( );
double square = Math.pow( number, 2 );
System.out.println( number + " square = " + square );
```

3.19.4   Identifying Errors in Code

37. The Java compiler does not recognize system. It should be *System*, not system.

40. The *round* method of the *Math* class returns a *long*; a *long* cannot be assigned to a *short* variable due to a potential loss of precision.

43. The *char* 'H' cannot be assigned to the *String s*. The two data types are not compatible.

3.19.5   Debugging Area—Using Messages from the Java Compiler and Java JVM

46. Java is case sensitive. The *Math* class needs to be spelled with an upper-case M.

49. In the output statement, we are just printing the value of *grade* without any formatting. To format *grade* as a percentage, the output statement should be:

```
System.out.println( "Your grade is " + percent.format( grade ) );
```

4.7   Exercises, Problems, and Projects

4.7.1   Multiple Choice Exercises

1. *java.awt*

4. true

7. the (x, y) coordinate of the upper-left corner of the rectangle we are drawing

10. 256

4.7.2   Reading and Understanding Code

13. 250 pixels

4.7.3   Fill In the Code

16. `g.setColor( Color.RED );`

19. `g.fillRect( 50, 30, 50, 270 );`

4.7.4   Identifying Errors in Code

22. There should be double quotes around the literal *Find a bug*, not single quotes. Single quotes are used for a *char*, not a *String*.

25. There is no *public color* instance variable in the *Graphics* class. The *set-Color* mutator method should be used to set the color of the *Graphics* object.

4.7.5   Debugging Area—Using Messages from the Java Compiler and Java JVM

28. We are trying to override the *paint* method, which is an instance method. The header of *paint* should therefore not include the keyword *static*.

5.14   Exercises, Problems, and Projects

5.14.1   Multiple Choice Exercises

1.

❏	`a < b`	true
❏	`a != b`	true
❏	`a == 4`	false
❏	`( b - a ) <= 1`	false
❏	`Math.abs( a - b ) >= 2`	true
❏	`( b % 2 == 1 )`	true
❏	`b <= 5`	true

4. yes

7.

❏	`a < b || b < 10`	no
❏	`a != b && b < 10`	yes
❏	`a == 4 || b < 10`	yes
❏	`a > b && b < 10`	no

5.14.2   Reading and Understanding Code

10. *true*

13. 27 is divisible by 3
    End of sequence

16. Hello 3
    Hello 4
    Done

19. Number 3
    Number 4
    Other number

5.14.3   Fill In the Code

22. ```
    if ( a )
        a = false;
    else
        a = true;
    ```

25. ```
    if ( b % c == 0 )
        a = true;
    else
        a = false;
    ```

28. ```
    if ( a && b > 10 )
        c++;
    ```

5.14.4   Identifying Errors in Code

31. The *&&* operator cannot be applied to two *int* operands (*a1* and *a2*).

34. We need a set of parentheses around *b1*.

37. There is no error.

5.14.5   Debugging Area—Using Messages from the Java Compiler and Java JVM

40. The expression `a = 31` evaluates to an *int*, 31. The *if* condition requires a *boolean* expression. To fix the problem, replace `a = 31` with `a == 31`.

6.14   Exercises, Problems, and Projects

6.14.1   Multiple Choice Exercises

1. The code runs forever.

4. true
    ```

6.14.2   Reading and Understanding Code

7. Enter an int > 3
    Enter an int > 5
    Hello
    Enter an int > –1
    Hello

10. 8 and 42

13. 3

16. 40 and 60

19. 3
    3
    3
    3
    4

6.14.3   Fill In the Code

22.
```java
System.out.print( "Enter an integer > " );
int value = scan.nextInt( );
while ( value != 20 )
{
  if ( value >= start )
    System.out.println( value );
  System.out.print( "Enter an integer > " );
  value = scan.nextInt( );
}
```

25.
```java
Scanner scan = new Scanner( System.in );
word = scan.next( );
while ( ! word.equals( "end" ) )
{
  // and your code goes here
  sentence += word;
  word = scan.next( );
}
```

28.
```java
Scanner scan = new Scanner( System.in );
int sum = 0;
System.out.println( "Enter an integer > " );
int value = scan.nextInt( );
while ( value != 0 && value != 100 )
```

```
{
    sum += value;
    System.out.println( "Enter an integer > " );
    value = scan.nextInt( );
}
System.out.println( "sum is " + sum );
```

6.14.4   Identifying Errors in Code

31. The variable *num* needs to be initialized after it is declared, and a priming read is needed.

34. The loop is infinite. *Number* is always different from 5 or different from 7. The logical OR (||) should be changed to a logical AND (&&).

6.14.5   Debugging Area—Using Messages from the Java Compiler and Java JVM

37. It is an infinite loop; *i* should be incremented, not decremented, inside the body of the *while* loop so that the loop eventually terminates.

40. In the *for* loop header, the loop initialization statement, the loop condition, and the loop update statement should be separated by semicolons (;), not commas(,).

7.18   Exercises, Problems, and Projects

7.18.1   Multiple Choice Exercises

1. The convention is to start with an uppercase letter.

4. true

7. can be basic data types, existing Java types, or user-defined types (from user-defined classes).

10. one parameter, of the same type as the corresponding field.

13. these fields do not need to be passed as parameters to the methods because the class methods have direct access to them.

16. All of the above.

7.18.2   Reading and Understanding Code

19. *double*

22. an instance method (keyword *static* not used)

25. `public static void foo3( double d );`

7.18.3   Fill In the Code

28. ```
private int grade;
private char letterGrade;
```

31. ```
public TelevisionChannel( String newName, int newNumber,
                            boolean newCable )
{
  name = newName;
  number  = newNumber;
  cable = newCable;
}
```

34. ```
public String toString( )
{
    return ("name: " + name + "\tnumber: "
            + number + "\tcable: " + cable);
}
```

37. ```
public String typeOfChannel( )
{
  if ( cable )
    return "cable";
  else
    return "network";
}
```

7.18.4   Identifying Errors in Code

40. The *toString* method needs to return a *String*, not output data.

43. The method header is incorrect; it should be

    `public double calcTax( )`

46. There are two errors: The assignment operator = should not be used when declaring an *enum* set. And the *enum* constant objects should not be *String* literals but identifiers.

7.18.5   Debugging Area—Using Messages from the Java Compiler and Java JVM

49. The compiler understands that *Grade* is a method since its header says it returns a *char*. It looks as if it is intended to be a constructor so the keyword *char* should be deleted from the constructor header.

52. The constructor assigns the parameter *letterGrade* to itself, therefore not changing the value of the instance variable *letterGrade*, which by default is the space character. The constructor could be recoded as follows:

```
public Grade( char newLetterGrade )
{
    letterGrade = newLetterGrade;
}
```

8.10   Exercises, Problems, and Projects

8.10.1   Multiple Choice Exercises:

1. `int [ ] a;` and `int a[ ];`

4. 0

7. `a.length`

10. false

8.10.2   Reading and Understanding Code

13. 48.3

16. 12

    48

    65

19. 14

22. It counts how many elements in the argument array have the value 5.

25. It returns an array of *Strings* identical to the argument array except that the *Strings* are all in lowercase.

8.10.3   Fill In the Code

28.
```
if ( a[i] > 20 )
    System.out.println( a[i] );
```

31.
```
System.out.println( "a[" + i + "] = " + a[i] );
```

34.
```
if ( a.length < 2 )
    return false;
else if ( a[0].equals( a[1] ) )
    return true;
else
    return false;
```

8.10.4   Identifying Errors in Code

37. Index −1 is out of bounds; the statement `System.out.println( a[-1] );` will generate a run-time exception.

40. When declaring an array, the square brackets should be empty. Replace `a[3]` by `a[ ]`.

43. Although the code compiles, it outputs the hash code of the array *a*. To output the elements of the array, we need to loop through the array elements and output them one by one.

8.10.5   Debugging Area—Using Messages from the Java Compiler and Java JVM

46. Index `a.length` is out of bounds; when *i* is equal to `a.length`, the expression `a[i]` will generate a run-time exception. Replace `<=` with `<` in the loop condition.

9.10   Exercises, Problems, and Projects

9.10.1   Multiple Choice Exercises

1. `int[ ][ ] a;` and `int a[ ][ ];`

4. *false*

7. `a[2].length`

10. true

13. *java.util*

9.10.2   Reading and Understanding Code

16. 3

19. Munich
    Stuttgart
    Berlin
    Bonn

22. Munich
    Berlin
    Ottawa

25. It counts and returns the number of elements in the argument array *a*.

28. It returns an *int* array of the same length as the length of the array argument *a*. Each element of the returned array stores the number of columns of the corresponding row in the array argument *a*.

31. 7 (at index 0) 45 (at index 1) 21 (at index 2)

9.10.3   Fill In the Code

34.
```java
System.out.println( geo[0][5] );
```

37.
```java
for ( int i = 0; i < geo.length; i++ )
{
    for ( int j = 0; j < geo[i].length; j++ )
        System.out.println( geo[i][j] );
}
```

40.
```java
int count = 0;
for ( int j = 0; j < a[1].length; j++ )
{
    if ( a[1][j] == 6 )
        count++;
}
System.out.println( "# of 6s in the 2nd row: " + count );
```

43. This method returns the product of all the elements in an array.
```java
public static int foo( int [ ][ ] a )
{
    int product = 1;
    for ( int i = 0; i < a.length; i++ )
    {
        for ( int j = 0; j < a[i].length; j++ )
        {
            product *= a[i][j];
        }
    }
    return product;
}
```

46.
```java
System.out.println( languages.size( ) );
```

49.
```java
for ( String s : languages )
{
    if ( s.charAt( 0 ) == 'P' )
        System.out.println( s );
}
```

9.10.4   Identifying Errors in Code

52. array dimension missing in `new double [ ][10]`

    Example of correct code: `double [ ][ ] a = new double [4][10];`

55. Cannot declare an *ArrayList* of a basic data type; the type needs to be a class (for example: *Double*)

58. Correct syntax is `variable = expression`. Because `a.size( )` is not a variable, we cannot assign a value to it.

9.10.5   Debugging Area—Using Messages from the Java Compiler and Java JVM

61. Other than `a[0][0]`, the first row is not taken into account because *i* is initialized to 1 in the outer loop. It should be `int i = 0;` not `int i = 1`.

64. Index 3 is out of bounds. There are only 3 elements in *a*; the last index is 2.

67. Because *ArrayList* elements begin at index 0, the statement

    `a.set( 1, 'J' );`

    sets the value of the second element of the *ArrayList*. To set the value of the first element, use this statement:

    `a.set( 0, 'J' );`

Index